*The Editor*

ELIZABETH AMMONS is Harriet H. Fay Professor of Literature at Tufts University. She is the author of *Conflicting Stories: American Women Writers at the Turn into the Twentieth Century*, *Edith Wharton's Argument with America*, and *Brave New Words: How Literature Will Save the Planet*. She is editor or co-editor of many volumes, including *Tricksterism in Turn-of-the-Century American Literature: A Multicultural Perspective*, *Uncle Tom's Cabin: A Casebook*, *American Local Color Writing, 1880–1920*, *Short Fiction by Black Women, 1900–1920*, and the Norton Critical Edition of Edith Wharton's *The House of Mirth*.

A NORTON CRITICAL EDITION

Harriet Beecher Stowe

# UNCLE TOM'S CABIN

**SECOND EDITION**

AUTHORITATIVE TEXT
BACKGROUNDS AND CONTEXTS
CRITICISM

*Edited by*

ELIZABETH AMMONS
TUFTS UNIVERSITY

W • W • NORTON & COMPANY • *New York* • *London*

W. W. Norton & Company has been independent since its founding in 1923, when William Warder Norton and Mary D. Herter Norton first published lectures delivered at the People's Institute, the adult education division of New York City's Cooper Union. The firm soon expanded its program beyond the Institute, publishing books by celebrated academics from America and abroad. By mid-century, the two major pillars of Norton's publishing program—trade books and college text—were firmly established. In the 1950s, the Norton family transferred control of the company to its employees, and today—with a staff of four hundred and a comparable number of trade, college, and professional titles published each year—W. W. Norton & Company stands as the largest and oldest publishing house owned wholly by its employees.

This title is printed on permanent paper containing 30 percent post-consumer waste recycled fiber.


Printed in the United States of America

Manufacturing by the Maple-Vail Book Group.
Book design by Antonina Krass
Production manager: Eric Pier-Hocking

Library of Congress Cataloging-in-Publication Data

Stowe, Harriet Beecher, 1811–1896.
Uncle Tom's cabin : authoritative text, backgrounds and contexts, criticism / Harriet Beecher Stowe; edited by Elizabeth Ammons.—2nd ed.
p. cm.—(A Norton critical edition)
Includes bibliographical references.
**ISBN 978-0-393-93399-4 (pbk.)**
1. Uncle Tom (Fictitious character)—Fiction. 2. Master and servant—Fiction. 3. Fugitive slaves—Fiction. 4. Plantation life—Fiction. 5. Southern States—Fiction. 6. Slavery—Fiction. 7. Slaves—Fiction. 8. Stowe, Harriet Beecher, 1811–1896. Uncle Tom's cabin. I. Ammons, Elizabeth. II. Title.
PS2954.U5 2009a
813'.3—dc22

2009049381

W. W. Norton & Company. Inc., 500 Fifth Avenue, New York, N.Y. 10110
wwnorton.com
W. W. Norton & Company Ltd., Castle House, 75/76 Wells Street, London W1T 3QT

6 7 8 9 0

# Contents

Preface vii
A Note on the Text x
Acknowledgments x

## The Text of *Uncle Tom's Cabin*

First-Edition Title Page xii
Preface xiii
Table of Contents xv
List of Illustrations xix
*Uncle Tom's Cabin* 1

## Backgrounds and Contexts

*Map*: The Eastern United States in the Antebellum Period 411
Slave Sale Announcements 412
Escaped Slave Advertisements 416
Abolition Posters 418
Visual Records of Torture 420
J. Hector St. John de Crèvecoeur • [A Visitor's Description of Slavery's Atrocity] 422
David Walker • *From* Appeal, In Four Articles 423
Josiah Henson • Life of Josiah Henson 426
Solomon Northup • A Slave Auction Described by a Slave, 1841 435
Henrietta King • [A Freeperson's Memory of Slavery's Horror] 437
Harriet Jacobs • The Trials of Girlhood 439
William Wells Brown • Another Kidnapping, 1844 442
• The Flight of Ellen and William Craft, 1849 443
Harriet Beecher Stowe • Letter to the Abolitionist Eliza Cabot Follen 444
• *From* A Key To "Uncle Tom's Cabin" 446
Uncle Tom 446
The Execution of Justice 453
• Appeal to the Women of the Free States 459

Martin Delany • *From* Blake; or, The Huts of America 462
George M. Frederickson • Uncle Tom and the Anglo-Saxons: Romantic Racialism in the North 464
George Cruikshank • Illustrations for *Uncle Tom's Cabin*
• Tom reading his Bible. 474
• The poor bleeding heart. 475
• Emmeline about to be sold to the highest bidder. 476
Thomas F. Gossett • Anti–Uncle Tom Literature 477
Mary C. Henderson • [Tom-Shows] 490
Tom-Show Poster 492

## Criticism

NINETEENTH-CENTURY REVIEWS AND RECEPTION
George Sand • Review of *Uncle Tom's Cabin* 495
William G. Allen • [About *Uncle Tom's Cabin*] 499
Ethiop • Review of *Uncle Tom's Cabin* 502
George F. Holmes • Review of *Uncle Tom's Cabin* 504
Anonymous • Review of *Uncle Tom's Cabin* 515
Charles Dudley Warner • [*Uncle Tom's Cabin* a Half Century Later] 520
Frances Ellen Watkins [Harper] • Eliza Harris 525
Helen Gray Cone • [Harriet Beecher Stowe and American Women Writers] 527
Paul Laurence Dunbar • Harriet Beecher Stowe 528
G. Grant Williams • Reminiscences of the Life of Harriet Beecher Stowe and Her Family 528
MODERN CRITICAL VIEWS
James Baldwin • Everybody's Protest Novel 532
Jane P. Tompkins • Sentimental Power: *Uncle Tom's Cabin* and the Politics of Literary History 539
Robert S. Levine • *Uncle Tom's Cabin* in *Frederick Douglass' Paper*: An Analysis of Reception 562
Sophia Cantave • Who Gets to Create the Lasting Images? The Problem of Black Representation in *Uncle Tom's Cabin* 582
Susan M. Ryan • Charity Begins at Home: Stowe's Antislavery Novels and the Forms of Benevolent Citizenship 595

Harriet Beecher Stowe: A Chronology 611
A Brief Time Line of Slavery in America 613
Selected Bibliography 615

# Preface

Harriet Beecher Stowe had to write *Uncle Tom's Cabin*. Her political convictions and religious faith, she believed, gave her no choice. She did not write to make money or attract fame, although the book generated both, but to use her words as an activist to try to help end slavery in the United States.

If and when slavery would end was by no means certain in 1851 when Stowe began the novel as a serial for the small antislavery newspaper *The National Era*. We look back today and abolition may seem inevitable. Economic, political, regional, and global factors combined to make it happen, we argue. But in the early 1850s no abolitionist, white or black, knew if, when, or how slavery would ever end in the United States. It had existed across countless cultures for all of recorded history. What could possibly bring its abolition in the United States in the nineteenth century?

Stowe and thousands of other activists believed that words could bring an end to slavery. When the Fugitive Slave Act of 1850 required every free person under penalty of law, North or South, to turn in fugitive slaves and therefore made it impossible for anyone to deny involvement in the institution, Stowe's sister wrote to her imploring her to use her pen, her ability to write, to speak out. The result was *Uncle Tom's Cabin*. It began, Stowe said, with a vision of Tom's death that came to her as she wept night after night over her sleeping children and thought of the slave mothers whose children were taken from them. So overpowered by the need to protest that she said not she but God wrote the book, Stowe created *Uncle Tom's Cabin* to bear witness as a Christian to the sin of slavery and the hypocrisy of Christian support for it. Also she wrote as a citizen enraged by the crime and social injustice of slavery. She herself could not vote—no woman could until the passage of the Nineteenth Amendment in 1920, twenty-four years after Stowe's death. Yet she insisted on her right to take a stand. She felt called to use her voice to protest against an institution that forced fellow human beings to endure bondage, torture, rape, trauma, mutilation, and unspeakable degradation in a nation that pretended to be a democracy.

Stowe's passion came in part from being a Beecher. Born in Litchfield, Connecticut, in 1811 to Lyman Beecher and his first wife,

Roxana Foote Beecher, she was the seventh of nine children, most of whom, like their father, became well-known public figures. Her sister, Catharine, advocated for women and for educational reform; and her father, brothers, husband, and sons all were Congregational ministers, two of them, her father and her brother, Henry Ward Beecher, quite famous. Clearly, had the pulpit been open to women, Harriet Beecher Stowe would have followed that path herself, as the evangelical zeal of *Uncle Tom's Cabin* shows.

Instead she married a minister, Calvin Stowe, with whom she had six children; and it was motherhood and the death of her beloved baby Charley, she later said, which quickened her empathy with enslaved Africans. "My heart was bursting with the anguish excited by the cruelty and injustice our nation was showing to the slave, and praying God to let me do a little and to cause my cry for them to be heard. I remember many a night weeping over you as you lay sleeping beside me," she wrote to one of her children, "and I thought of the slave mothers whose babies were torn from them." Her own dead baby wracked her mind: "It was at his dying bed and at his grave that I learned what a poor slave mother may feel when her child is torn away from her." Written in tears, the book participates in a sentimental aesthetic scorned by most intellectuals and the academy in the twentieth and twenty-first centuries but highly valued by readers in the nineteenth. It is intended to evoke tears. In 1852, a copy of the book in hand, the congressman Horace Greeley had to interrupt his railway journey from Boston to Washington, D.C., to stop overnight at a hotel in Springfield, Massachusetts, because he had been weeping so copiously on the train as he read.

Stowe gathered much of her knowledge about slavery during the eighteen years she lived in Cincinnati, Ohio, where she moved with her father in 1832 when he became the president of Lane Seminary, which was where the man she would marry, Calvin Stowe, worked as a faculty member. Only a river's width away from the slave-holding state of Kentucky, Cincinnati forced Stowe to confront slavery at close range. Race riots in the city, the presence of fugitive slaves and the underground railroad, the spectacle of bounty hunters forcing escaped slaves back into captivity, the fear and anger of free blacks who could at any time be kidnapped and sold South, and the activism of abolitionists, black and white: all were inescapable realities of life in southern Ohio in the 1830s and 1840s. Also, hardships in Stowe's own experience deepened her insights. In addition to having to watch helplessly as her baby died from cholera, she had little money as a minister's wife so she knew what it meant to work endlessly from dawn till night—cooking, cleaning, tending children, trying to write, worrying about bills. When Calvin Stowe accepted a position at Bowdoin College in Maine in 1850, she eagerly embraced the return to New England. But without the years in Cincinnati she probably never could have written the novel that caused untold numbers of people, finally, to take a stand against slavery.

*Uncle Tom's Cabin* is controversial and always has been. When it first appeared in book form in 1852, both the publisher and the Stowes thought it would sell so modestly that, as Calvin Stowe said, it might buy his wife a new dress. Instead, it became a phenomenon almost overnight. The novel kept printing presses running day and night, outsold every book in the nineteenth century except the Bible, rapidly appeared in translation in many languages, and spurred President Abraham Lincoln to greet Stowe at the White House, so the story goes, with the words, "So you are the little woman who started the great war." It also spawned an unprecedented outpouring of commercial paraphernalia—figurines, candles, cups, wallpaper—and scores of traveling Tom-shows, most of which distorted and sensationalized the book by playing up prurient and overtly racist themes. In the 1850s, Southern whites attacked the novel as a pack of lies and its author as an unfeminine monster. Abolitionists, on the other hand, praised it vigorously, even as some criticized its treatment of race and, especially, its endorsement of African American emigration to Liberia.

Over the past 150 years controversy has continued. Some readers, as selections by Paul Laurence Dunbar, Jane Tompkins, and Susan Ryan in this volume suggest, have always admired the book for its social vision and artistry. Others, as pieces by James Baldwin and Sophia Cantave suggest, argue that the book's racism promotes misperceptions and its continued prominence does damage.

However one reads *Uncle Tom's Cabin*—and for most people no simple or easy verdict on the novel emerges—it remains one of the most important activist texts in the nation's literature. It stands with David Walker's *Appeal,* Frederick Douglass's *Narrative,* Henry David Thoreau's *Walden,* W. E. B. Du Bois's *The Souls of Black Folk,* John Okada's *No-No Boy,* Leonard Peltier's *Prison Writings,* Helena María Viramontes' *Under the Feet of Jesus,* and countless other courageous works as one of the great activist texts in the progressive struggle for social justice in the United States. It is not a perfect book or one that provokes indifference. But precisely for those reasons it remains alive today and continues to do important work, making readers question and debate their own values, the purpose of literature, the meaning of democracy, and the ways in which art counts in the fight for justice.

## A Note on the Text

*Uncle Tom's Cabin* originally appeared in serialized form in the antislavery newspaper *The National Era* in 1851–52 and was then published in book form in two volumes in 1852 by the Boston, Massachusetts, publisher John P. Jewett and Company. This edition of the novel is reprinted from that original 1852 book edition. No editorial changes have been made.

## Acknowledgments

For excellent research assistance, I am grateful to Chiyo Crawford, who created the time line in this volume, and to Valerie Rohy, who prepared the notes. Also, I wish to thank Ronald A. Tyson for providing a number of biblical references. I am indebted to my late colleague in Tufts' History Department, Professor Gerald Gill, for his generous suggestions when I prepared the first edition of this book as well as to the staffs of the Tisch Library at Tufts and the Stowe-Day Foundation in Hartford, Connecticut.

# The Text of UNCLE TOM'S CABIN

## or, Life Among the Lowly

Textual annotations prepared by Valerie Rohy.

# UNCLE TOM'S CABIN;

OR,

# LIFE AMONG THE LOWLY.

BY

HARRIET BEECHER STOWE.

VOL. I.

BOSTON:
JOHN P. JEWETT & COMPANY.
CLEVELAND, OHIO:
JEWETT, PROCTOR & WORTHINGTON.
1852.

# Preface

The scenes of this story, as its title indicates, lie among a race hitherto ignored by the associations of polite and refined society; an exotic race, whose ancestors, born beneath a tropic sun, brought with them, and perpetuated to their descendants, a character so essentially unlike the hard and dominant Anglo-Saxon race, as for many years to have won from it only misunderstanding and contempt.

But, another and better day is dawning; every influence of literature, of poetry and of art, in our times, is becoming more and more in unison with the great master chord of Christianity, "good will to man."[1]

The poet, the painter, and the artist, now seek out and embellish the common and gentler humanities of life, and, under the allurements of fiction, breathe a humanizing and subduing influence, favorable to the development of the great principles of Christian brotherhood.

The hand of benevolence is everywhere stretched out, searching into abuses, righting wrongs, alleviating distresses, and bringing to the knowledge and sympathies of the world the lowly, the oppressed, and the forgotten.

In this general movement, unhappy Africa at last is remembered; Africa, who began the race of civilization and human progress in the dim, gray dawn of early time, but who, for centuries, has lain bound and bleeding at the foot of civilized and Christianized humanity, imploring compassion in vain.

But the heart of the dominant race, who have been her conquerors, her hard masters, has at length been turned towards her in mercy; and it has been seen how far nobler it is in nations to protect the feeble than to oppress them. Thanks be to God, the world has at last outlived the slave-trade!

The object of these sketches is to awaken sympathy and feeling for the African race, as they exist among us; to show their wrongs and sorrows, under a system so necessarily cruel and unjust as to defeat and do away the good effects of all that can be attempted for them, by their best friends, under it.

In doing this, the author can sincerely disclaim any invidious feeling towards those individuals who, often without any fault of their own, are involved in the trials and embarrassments of the legal relations of slavery.

Experience has shown her that some of the noblest of minds and hearts are often thus involved; and no one knows better than they

1. "Glory to God in the highest, and on earth peace, good will toward man" (Luke 2.14).

do, that what may be gathered of the evils of slavery from sketches like these, is not the half that could be told, of the unspeakable whole.

In the northern states, these representations may, perhaps, be thought caricatures; in the southern states are witnesses who know their fidelity. What personal knowledge the author has had, of the truth of incidents such as here are related, will appear in its time.[2]

It is a comfort to hope, as so many of the world's sorrows and wrongs have, from age to age, been lived down, so a time shall come when sketches similar to these shall be valuable only as memorials of what has long ceased to be.

When an enlightened and Christianized community shall have, on the shores of Africa, laws, language and literature, drawn from among us, may then the scenes of the house of bondage be to them like the remembrance of Egypt to the Israelite,[3]—a motive of thankfulness to Him who hath redeemed them!

For, while politicians contend, and men are swerved this way and that by conflicting tides of interest and passion, the great cause of human liberty is in the hands of one, of whom it is said:

> "He shall not fail nor be discouraged
> Till He have set judgment in the earth."
> "He shall deliver the needy when he crieth,
> The poor, and him that hath no helper."
> "He shall redeem their soul from deceit and violence,
> And precious shall their blood be in His sight."[4]

2. In *A Key to "Uncle Tom's Cabin"* (1853), Stowe documents the historical antecedents of characters and situations in the novel; readers have pointed out, however, that much of the evidence in *Key* was gathered after the novel's publication. According to Stowe, for example, the famous scene of Eliza crossing the ice is drawn from an incident in which her husband and brother helped a female fugitive.
3. The Israelites were enslaved in Egypt by Pharaoh until Moses led them to freedom (Exodus 1–14). This biblical story became an important metaphor for American slaves seeking freedom.
4. These quotations can be found in Isaiah 42.4 and Psalm 72.12, 14.

# Table of Contents

## *Vol. I*

CHAPTER I

In Which the Reader Is Introduced to a Man of Humanity . . . . . . . . 1

CHAPTER II

The Mother . . . . . . . . . . . . . . . . . . . . . . . . . . . . . . . . . . . . 10

CHAPTER III

The Husband and Father . . . . . . . . . . . . . . . . . . . . . . . . . . . 13

CHAPTER IV

An Evening in Uncle Tom's Cabin . . . . . . . . . . . . . . . . . . . . . 17

CHAPTER V

Showing the Feelings of Living Property on Changing Owners . . . . 28

CHAPTER VI

Discovery . . . . . . . . . . . . . . . . . . . . . . . . . . . . . . . . . . . . 37

CHAPTER VII

The Mother's Struggle . . . . . . . . . . . . . . . . . . . . . . . . . . . . 45

CHAPTER VIII

Eliza's Escape . . . . . . . . . . . . . . . . . . . . . . . . . . . . . . . . . 56

CHAPTER IX

In Which It Appears That a Senator Is But a Man . . . . . . . . . . . . 70

CHAPTER X

The Property Is Carried Off . . . . . . . . . . . . . . . . . . . . . . . . . 84

CHAPTER XI

In Which Property Gets into an Improper State of Mind . . . . . . . . 93

CHAPTER XII

Select Incident of Lawful Trade ........ 105

CHAPTER XIII

The Quaker Settlement ........ 121

CHAPTER XIV

Evangeline ........ 129

CHAPTER XV

Of Tom's New Master, and Various Other Matters ........ 138

CHAPTER XVI

Tom's Mistress and Her Opinions ........ 153

CHAPTER XVII

The Freeman's Defence ........ 169

CHAPTER XVIII

Miss Ophelia's Experiences and Opinions ........ 185

*Vol. II*

CHAPTER XIX

Miss Ophelia's Experiences and Opinions, Continued ........ 200

CHAPTER XX

Topsy ........ 217

CHAPTER XXI

Kentuck ........ 230

CHAPTER XXII

"The Grass Withereth—the Flower Fadeth" ........ 235

CHAPTER XXIII

Henrique ........ 242

CHAPTER XXIV

Foreshadowings . . . . . . . . . . . . . . . . . . . . . . . . . . . . . . . 249

CHAPTER XXV

The Little Evangelist . . . . . . . . . . . . . . . . . . . . . . . . . . . 255

CHAPTER XXVI

Death . . . . . . . . . . . . . . . . . . . . . . . . . . . . . . . . . . . . . 259

CHAPTER XXVII

"This Is the Last of Earth" . . . . . . . . . . . . . . . . . . . . . . . 271

CHAPTER XXVIII

Reunion . . . . . . . . . . . . . . . . . . . . . . . . . . . . . . . . . . . 278

CHAPTER XXIX

The Unprotected . . . . . . . . . . . . . . . . . . . . . . . . . . . . . 291

CHAPTER XXX

The Slave Warehouse . . . . . . . . . . . . . . . . . . . . . . . . . . 297

CHAPTER XXXI

The Middle Passage . . . . . . . . . . . . . . . . . . . . . . . . . . . 306

CHAPTER XXXII

Dark Places . . . . . . . . . . . . . . . . . . . . . . . . . . . . . . . . 312

CHAPTER XXXIII

Cassy . . . . . . . . . . . . . . . . . . . . . . . . . . . . . . . . . . . . 319

CHAPTER XXXIV

The Quadroon's Story . . . . . . . . . . . . . . . . . . . . . . . . . . 326

CHAPTER XXXV

The Tokens . . . . . . . . . . . . . . . . . . . . . . . . . . . . . . . . . 336

CHAPTER XXXVI

Emmeline and Cassy . . . . . . . . . . . . . . . . . . . . . . . . . . . 342

CHAPTER XXXVII

Liberty .......... 348

CHAPTER XXXVIII

The Victory .......... 353

CHAPTER XXXIX

The Stratagem .......... 363

CHAPTER XL

The Martyr .......... 372

CHAPTER XLI

The Young Master .......... 378

CHAPTER XLII

An Authentic Ghost Story .......... 384

CHAPTER XLIII

Results .......... 389

CHAPTER XLIV

The Liberator .......... 396

CHAPTER XLV

Concluding Remarks .......... 400

# List of Illustrations

Eliza comes to tell Uncle Tom that he is sold, and that she is running away to save her child . . . . . . . . . . . . . . . . . . . . . 35

The auction sale . . . . . . . . . . . . . . . . . . . . . . . . . . . . . . . . . . . . 109

The freeman's defence. . . . . . . . . . . . . . . . . . . . . . . . . . . . . . . . 181

Little Eva reading the Bible to Uncle Tom in the arbor . . . . . . . . . 237

Cassy ministering to Uncle Tom after his whipping. . . . . . . . . . . . 328

The fugitives are safe in a free land . . . . . . . . . . . . . . . . . . . . . . . 355

# Volume I

## Chapter I

### *In Which the Reader Is Introduced to a Man of Humanity*

Late in the afternoon of a chilly day in February, two gentlemen were sitting alone over their wine, in a well-furnished dining parlor, in the town of P——, in Kentucky. There were no servants present, and the gentlemen, with chairs closely approaching, seemed to be discussing some subject with great earnestness.

For convenience sake, we have said, hitherto, two *gentlemen*. One of the parties, however, when critically examined, did not seem, strictly speaking, to come under the species. He was a short, thick-set man, with coarse, commonplace features, and that swaggering air of pretension which marks a low man who is trying to elbow his way upward in the world. He was much over-dressed, in a gaudy vest of many colors, a blue neckerchief, bedropped gayly with yellow spots, and arranged with a flaunting tie, quite in keeping with the general air of the man. His hands, large and coarse, were plentifully bedecked with rings; and he wore a heavy gold watch-chain, with a bundle of seals of portentous size, and a great variety of colors, attached to it,—which, in the ardor of conversation, he was in the habit of flourishing and jingling with evident satisfaction. His conversation was in free and easy defiance of Murray's Grammar,[1] and was garnished at convenient intervals with various profane expressions, which not even the desire to be graphic in our account shall induce us to transcribe.

His companion, Mr. Shelby, had the appearance of a gentleman; and the arrangements of the house, and the general air of the housekeeping, indicated easy, and even opulent circumstances. As we before stated, the two were in the midst of an earnest conversation.

"That is the way I should arrange the matter," said Mr. Shelby.

"I can't make trade that way—I positively can't, Mr. Shelby," said the other, holding up a glass of wine between his eye and the light.

1. The popular *English Grammar* (first ed. pub. 1795), by Lindley Murray (1745–1826), an American grammarian.

"Why, the fact is, Haley, Tom is an uncommon fellow; he is certainly worth that sum anywhere,—steady, honest, capable, manages my whole farm like a clock."

"You mean honest, as niggers go," said Haley, helping himself to a glass of brandy.

"No; I mean, really, Tom is a good, steady, sensible, pious fellow. He got religion at a camp-meeting,[2] four years ago; and I believe he really *did* get it. I've trusted him, since then, with everything I have,—money, house, horses,—and let him come and go round the country; and I always found him true and square in everything."

"Some folks don't believe there is pious niggers,[3] Shelby," said Haley, with a candid flourish of his hand, "but *I do.* I had a fellow, now, in this yer last lot I took to Orleans[4]—'t was as good as a meetin, now, really, to hear that critter pray; and he was quite gentle and quiet like. He fetched me a good sum, too, for I bought him cheap of a man that was 'bliged to sell out; so I realized six hundred on him. Yes, I consider religion a valeyable thing in a nigger, when it's the genuine article, and no mistake."

"Well, Tom's got the real article, if ever a fellow had," rejoined the other. "Why, last fall, I let him go to Cincinnati[5] alone, to do business for me, and bring home five hundred dollars. 'Tom,' says I to him, 'I trust you, because I think you're a Christian—I know you wouldn't cheat.' Tom comes back, sure enough; I knew he would. Some low fellows, they say, said to him—'Tom, why don't you make tracks for Canada?'[6] 'Ah, master trusted me, and I couldn't,'—they told me about it. I am sorry to part with Tom, I must say. You ought to let him cover the whole balance of the debt; and you would, Haley, if you had any conscience."

"Well, I've got just as much conscience as any man in business can afford to keep,—just a little, you know, to swear by, as 't were," said the trader, jocularly; "and, then, I'm ready to do anything in reason to 'blige friends; but this yer, you see, is a leetle too hard on a fellow—a leetle too hard." The trader sighed contemplatively, and poured out some more brandy.

2. A religious gathering held outdoors or in a tent, usually lasting several days; associated with the revivalist movements of the early 1800s and with evangelical Christian sects such as the Methodists, Baptists, or Cumberland Presbyterians.
3. A slang form of *negro*; it is almost always derogatory when used by whites and often but not always so when used by blacks.
4. New Orleans, a port city in southeast Louisiana where the Mississippi River enters the Gulf of Mexico.
5. A city in southwest Ohio, on the Ohio River opposite Covington, Kentucky. Situated on the Mason-Dixon line, the border of slave and free territories, Cincinnati remained loyal to the North despite economic and cultural ties to the South.
6. Fugitives from slavery tried to escape to Canada because in the northern states they were in danger of return under the Fugitive Slave Laws, especially after 1850.

"Well, then, Haley, how will you trade?" said Mr. Shelby, after an uneasy interval of silence.

"Well, haven't you a boy or gal that you could throw in with Tom?"

"Hum!—none that I could well spare; to tell the truth, it's only hard necessity makes me willing to sell at all. I don't like parting with any of my hands, that's a fact."

Here the door opened, and a small quadroon[7] boy, between four and five years of age, entered the room. There was something in his appearance remarkably beautiful and engaging. His black hair, fine as floss silk, hung in glossy curls about his round, dimpled face, while a pair of large dark eyes, full of fire and softness, looked out from beneath the rich, long lashes, as he peered curiously into the apartment. A gay robe of scarlet and yellow plaid, carefully made and neatly fitted, set off to advantage the dark and rich style of his beauty; and a certain comic air of assurance, blended with bashfulness, showed that he had been not unused to being petted and noticed by his master.

"Hulloa, Jim Crow!"[8] said Mr. Shelby, whistling, and snapping a bunch of raisins towards him, "pick that up, now!"

The child scampered, with all his little strength, after the prize, while his master laughed.

"Come here, Jim Crow," said he. The child came up, and the master patted the curly head, and chucked him under the chin.

"Now, Jim, show this gentleman how you can dance and sing." The boy commenced one of those wild, grotesque songs common among the negroes, in a rich, clear voice, accompanying his singing with many comic evolutions of the hands, feet, and whole body, all in perfect time to the music.

"Bravo!" said Haley, throwing him a quarter of an orange.

"Now, Jim, walk like old Uncle Cudjoe, when he has the rheumatism," said his master.

Instantly the flexible limbs of the child assumed the appearance of deformity and distortion, as, with his back humped up, and his master's stick in his hand, he hobbled about the room, his childish face drawn into a doleful pucker, and spitting from right to left, in imitation of an old man.

Both gentlemen laughed uproariously.

"Now, Jim," said his master, "show us how old Elder Robbins leads the psalm." The boy drew his chubby face down to a formidable

7. A person of one-quarter African heritage.
8. Stereotyped name for a black person, especially a singer, clown, or minstrel; from the folk song "Jim Crow." From the 1880s through the 1960s, the name "Jim Crow" was applied to state and local laws in the South that enforced segregation or prevented African Americans from voting.

length, and commenced toning a psalm tune through his nose, with imperturbable gravity.

"Hurrah! bravo! what a young 'un!" said Haley; "that chap's a case, I'll promise. Tell you what," said he, suddenly clapping his hand on Mr. Shelby's shoulder, "fling in that chap, and I'll settle the business—I will. Come, now, if that ain't doing the thing up about the rightest!"

At this moment, the door was pushed gently open, and a young quadroon woman, apparently about twenty-five, entered the room.

There needed only a glance from the child to her, to identify her as its mother. There was the same rich, full, dark eye, with its long lashes; the same ripples of silky black hair. The brown of her complexion gave way on the cheek to a perceptible flush, which deepened as she saw the gaze of the strange man fixed upon her in bold and undisguised admiration. Her dress was of the neatest possible fit, and set off to advantage her finely moulded shape;—a delicately formed hand and a trim foot and ankle were items of appearance that did not escape the quick eye of the trader, well used to run up at a glance the points of a fine female article.

"Well, Eliza?" said her master, as she stopped and looked hesitatingly at him.

"I was looking for Harry, please, sir;" and the boy bounded toward her, showing his spoils, which he had gathered in the skirt of his robe.

"Well, take him away, then," said Mr. Shelby; and hastily she withdrew, carrying the child on her arm.

"By Jupiter," said the trader, turning to him in admiration, "there's an article, now! You might make your fortune on that ar gal in Orleans, any day. I've seen over a thousand, in my day, paid down for gals not a bit handsomer."

"I don't want to make my fortune on her," said Mr. Shelby, dryly; and, seeking to turn the conversation, he uncorked a bottle of fresh wine, and asked his companion's opinion of it.

"Capital, sir,—first chop!" said the trader; then turning, and slapping his hand familiarly on Shelby's shoulder, he added—

"Come, how will you trade about the gal?—what shall I say for her—what'll you take?"

"Mr. Haley, she is not to be sold," said Shelby. "My wife would not part with her for her weight in gold."

"Ay, ay! women always say such things, cause they ha'nt no sort of calculation. Just show 'em how many watches, feathers, and trinkets, one's weight in gold would buy, and that alters the case, *I* reckon."

"I tell you, Haley, this must not be spoken of; I say no, and I mean no," said Shelby, decidedly.

"Well, you'll let me have the boy, though," said the trader; "you must own I've come down pretty handsomely for him."

"What on earth can you want with the child?" said Shelby.

"Why, I've got a friend that's going into this yer branch of the business—wants to buy up handsome boys to raise for the market. Fancy articles entirely—sell for waiters, and so on, to rich 'uns, that can pay for handsome 'uns. It sets off one of yer great places—a real handsome boy to open door, wait, and tend. They fetch a good sum; and this little devil is such a comical, musical concern, he's just the article."

"I would rather not sell him," said Mr. Shelby, thoughtfully; "the fact is, sir, I'm a humane man, and I hate to take the boy from his mother, sir."

"O, you do?—La! yes—something of that ar natur. I understand, perfectly. It is mighty onpleasant getting on with women, sometimes. I al'ays hates these yer screachin', screamin' times. They are *mighty* onpleasant; but, as I manages business, I generally avoids 'em, sir. Now, what if you get the girl off for a day, or a week, or so; then the thing's done quietly,—all over before she comes home. Your wife might get her some ear-rings, or a new gown, or some such truck, to make up with her."

"I'm afraid not."

"Lor bless ye, yes! These critters an't like white folks, you know; they gets over things, only manage right. Now, they say," said Haley, assuming a candid and confidential air, "that this kind o' trade is hardening to the feelings; but I never found it so. Fact is, I never could do things up the way some fellers manage the business. I've seen 'em as would pull a woman's child out of her arms, and set him up to sell, and she screechin' like mad all the time;—very bad policy—damages the article—makes 'em quite unfit for service sometimes. I knew a real handsome gal once, in Orleans, as was entirely ruined by this sort o' handling. The fellow that was trading for her didn't want her baby; and she was one of your real high sort, when her blood was up. I tell you, she squeezed up her child in her arms, and talked, and went on real awful. It kinder makes my blood run cold to think on't; and when they carried off the child, and locked her up, she jest went ravin' mad, and died in a week. Clear waste, sir, of a thousand dollars, just for want of management,—there's where 't is. It's always best to do the humane thing, sir; that's been *my* experience." And the trader leaned back in his chair, and folded his arm, with an air of virtuous decision, apparently considering himself a second Wilberforce.[9]

9. William Wilberforce (1759–1833), an English statesman and active opponent of slavery.

The subject appeared to interest the gentleman deeply; for while Mr. Shelby was thoughtfully peeling an orange, Haley broke out afresh, with becoming diffidence, but as if actually driven by the force of truth to say a few words more.

"It don't look well, now, for a feller to be praisin' himself; but I say it jest because it's the truth. I believe I'm reckoned to bring in about the finest droves of niggers that is brought in,—at least, I've been told so; if I have once, I reckon I have a hundred times,—all in good case,—fat and likely, and I lose as few as any man in the business. And I lays it all to my management, sir; and humanity, sir, I may say, is the great pillar of *my* management."

Mr. Shelby did not know what to say, and so he said, "Indeed!"

"Now, I've been laughed at for my notions, sir, and I've been talked to. They an't pop'lar, and they an't common; but I stuck to 'em, sir; I've stuck to 'em, and realized well on 'em; yes, sir, they have paid their passage, I may say," and the trader laughed at his joke.

There was something so piquant and original in these elucidations of humanity, that Mr. Shelby could not help laughing in company. Perhaps you laugh too, dear reader; but you know humanity comes out in a variety of strange forms now-a-days, and there is no end to the odd things that humane people will say and do.

Mr. Shelby's laugh encouraged the trader to proceed.

"It's strange now, but I never could beat this into people's heads. Now, there was Tom Loker, my old partner, down in Natchez;[1] he was a clever fellow, Tom was, only the very devil with niggers,—on principle 't was, you see, for a better hearted feller never broke bread; 't was his *system*, sir. I used to talk to Tom. 'Why, Tom,' I used to say, 'when your gals takes on and cry, what's the use o' crackin on 'em over the head, and knockin' on 'em round? It's ridiculous,' says I, 'and don't do no sort o' good. Why, I don't see no harm in their cryin',' says I; 'it's natur,' says I, 'and if natur can't blow off one way, it will another. Besides, Tom,' says I, 'it jest spiles your gals; they get sickly, and down in the mouth; and sometimes they gets ugly,—particular yallow gals do,—and it's the devil and all gettin' on 'em broke in. Now,' says I, 'why can't you kinder coax 'em up, and speak 'em fair? Depend on it, Tom, a little humanity, thrown in along, goes a heap further than all your jawin' and crackin'; and it pays better,' says I, 'depend on 't.' But Tom couldn't get the hang on 't; and he spiled so many for me, that I had to break off with him, though he was a good-hearted fellow, and as fair a business hand as is goin'."

"And do you find your ways of managing do the business better than Tom's?" said Mr. Shelby.

1. City in southwest Mississippi, on the Mississippi River.

"Why, yes, sir, I may say so. You see, when I any ways can, I takes a leetle care about the onpleasant parts like selling young uns and that,—get the gals out of the way—out of sight, out of mind, you know,—and when it's clean done, and can't be helped, they naturally gets used to it. 'Tan't, you know, as if it was white folks, that's brought up in the way of 'spectin' to keep their children and wives, and all that. Niggers, you know, that's fetched up properly, ha'n't no kind of 'spectations of no kind; so all these things comes easier."

"I'm afraid mine are not properly brought up, then," said Mr. Shelby.

"S'pose not; you Kentucky folks spile your niggers. You mean well by 'em, but 'tan't no real kindness, arter all. Now, a nigger, you see, what's got to be hacked and tumbled round the world, and sold to Tom, and Dick, and the Lord knows who, 'tan't no kindness to be givin' on him notions and expectations, and bringin' on him up too well, for the rough and tumble comes all the harder on him arter. Now, I venture to say, your niggers would be quite chop-fallen in a place where some of your plantation niggers would be singing and whooping like all possessed. Every man, you know, Mr. Shelby, naturally thinks well of his own ways; and I think I treat niggers just about as well as it's ever worth while to treat 'em."

"It's a happy thing to be satisfied," said Mr. Shelby, with a slight shrug, and some perceptible feelings of a disagreeable nature.

"Well," said Haley, after they had both silently picked their nuts[2] for a season, "what do you say?"

"I'll think the matter over, and talk with my wife," said Mr. Shelby. "Meantime, Haley, if you want the matter carried on in the quiet way you speak of, you'd best not let your business in this neighborhood be known. It will get out among my boys, and it will not be a particularly quiet business getting away any of my fellows, if they know it, I'll promise you."

"O! certainly, by all means, mum! of course. But I'll tell you, I'm in a devil of a hurry, and shall want to know, as soon as possible, what I may depend on," said he, rising and putting on his overcoat.

"Well, call up this evening, between six and seven, and you shall have my answer," said Mr. Shelby, and the trader bowed himself out of the apartment.

"I'd like to have been able to kick the fellow down the steps," said he to himself, as he saw the door fairly closed, "with his impudent assurance; but he knows how much he has me at advantage. If anybody had ever said to me that I should sell Tom down south to one of those rascally traders, I should have said, 'Is thy servant a dog,

2. I.e., pondered. "Nut" is slang for the head, brains, or mind; to "pick one's brains" is to get ideas.

that he should do this thing?' And now it must come, for aught I see. And Eliza's child, too! I know that I shall have some fuss with wife about that; and, for that matter, about Tom, too. So much for being in debt,—heigho! The fellow sees his advantage, and means to push it."

Perhaps the mildest form of the system of slavery is to be seen in the State of Kentucky. The general prevalence of agricultural pursuits of a quiet and gradual nature, not requiring those periodic seasons of hurry and pressure that are called for in the business of more southern districts, makes the task of the negro a more healthful and reasonable one; while the master, content with a more gradual style of acquisition, has not those temptations to hard-heartedness which always overcome frail human nature when the prospect of sudden and rapid gain is weighed in the balance, with no heavier counterpoise than the interests of the helpless and unprotected.

Whoever visits some estates there, and witnesses the goodhumored indulgence of some masters and mistresses, and the affectionate loyalty of some slaves, might be tempted to dream the oft-fabled poetic legend of a patriarchal institution, and all that; but over and above the scene there broods a portentous shadow—the shadow of *law.* So long as the law considers all these human beings, with beating hearts and living affections, only as so many *things* belonging to a master,—so long as the failure, or misfortune, or imprudence, or death of the kindest owner, may cause them any day to exchange a life of kind protection and indulgence for one of hopeless misery and toil,—so long it is impossible to make anything beautiful or desirable in the best regulated administration of slavery.

Mr. Shelby was a fair average kind of man, good-natured and kindly, and disposed to easy indulgence of those around him, and there had never been a lack of anything which might contribute to the physical comfort of the negroes on his estate. He had, however, speculated largely and quite loosely; had involved himself deeply, and his notes to a large amount had come into the hands of Haley; and this small piece of information is the key to the preceding conversation.

Now, it had so happened that, in approaching the door, Eliza had caught enough of the conversation to know that a trader was making offers to her master for somebody.

She would gladly have stopped at the door to listen, as she came out; but her mistress just then calling, she was obliged to hasten away.

Still she thought she heard the trader make an offer for her boy;—could she be mistaken? Her heart swelled and throbbed, and she involuntarily strained him so tight that the little fellow looked up into her face in astonishment.

"Eliza, girl, what ails you to-day?" said her mistress, when Eliza had upset the wash-pitcher, knocked down the work-stand,[3] and finally was abstractedly offering her mistress a long night-gown in place of the silk dress she had ordered her to bring from the wardrobe.

Eliza started. "O, missis!" she said, raising her eyes; then, bursting into tears, she sat down in a chair, and began sobbing.

"Why, Eliza, child! what ails you?" said her mistress.

"O! missis, missis," said Eliza, "there's been a trader talking with master in the parlor! I heard him."

"Well, silly child, suppose there has."

"O, missis, *do* you suppose mas'r would sell my Harry?" And the poor creature threw herself into a chair, and sobbed convulsively.

"Sell him! No, you foolish girl! You know your master never deals with those southern traders, and never means to sell any of his servants, as long as they behave well. Why, you silly child, who do you think would want to buy your Harry? Do you think all the world are set on him as you are, you goosie? Come, cheer up, and hook my dress. There now, put my back hair up in that pretty braid you learnt the other day, and don't go listening at doors any more."

"Well, but, missis, *you* never would give your consent—to—to—"

"Nonsense, child! to be sure, I shouldn't. What do you talk so for? I would as soon have one of my own children sold. But really, Eliza, you are getting altogether too proud of that little fellow. A man can't put his nose into the door, but you think he must be coming to buy him."

Reassured by her mistress' confident tone, Eliza proceeded nimbly and adroitly with her toilet, laughing at her own fears, as she proceeded.

Mrs. Shelby was a woman of a high class, both intellectually and morally. To that natural magnanimity and generosity of mind which one often marks as characteristic of the women of Kentucky, she added high moral and religious sensibility and principle, carried out with great energy and ability into practical results. Her husband, who made no professions to any particular religious character, nevertheless reverenced and respected the consistency of hers, and stood, perhaps, a little in awe of her opinion. Certain it was that he gave her unlimited scope in all her benevolent efforts for the comfort, instruction, and improvement of her servants, though he never took any decided part in them himself. In fact, if not exactly a believer in the doctrine of the efficiency of the extra good works of saints, he really seemed somehow or other to fancy that his wife

3. A small table equipped with drawers or other conveniences for needlework.

had piety and benevolence enough for two—to indulge a shadowy expectation of getting into heaven through her superabundance of qualities to which he made no particular pretension.

The heaviest load on his mind, after his conversation with the trader, lay in the foreseen necessity of breaking to his wife the arrangement contemplated,—meeting the importunities and opposition which he knew he should have reason to encounter.

Mrs. Shelby, being entirely ignorant of her husband's embarrassments, and knowing only the general kindliness of his temper, had been quite sincere in the entire incredulity with which she had met Eliza's suspicions. In fact, she dismissed the matter from her mind, without a second thought; and being occupied in preparations for an evening visit, it passed out of her thoughts entirely.

## Chapter II

### *The Mother*

Eliza had been brought up by her mistress, from girlhood, as a petted and indulged favorite.

The traveller in the south must often have remarked that peculiar air of refinement, that softness of voice and manner, which seems in many cases to be a particular gift to the quadroon and mulatto[1] women. These natural graces in the quadroon are often united with beauty of the most dazzling kind, and in almost every case with a personal appearance prepossessing and agreeable. Eliza, such as we have described her, is not a fancy sketch, but taken from remembrance, as we saw her, years ago, in Kentucky. Safe under the protecting care of her mistress, Eliza had reached maturity without those temptations which make beauty so fatal an inheritance to a slave. She had been married to a bright and talented young mulatto man, who was a slave on a neighboring estate, and bore the name of George Harris.

This young man had been hired out by his master to work in a bagging factory,[2] where his adroitness and ingenuity caused him to be considered the first hand in the place. He had invented a machine for the cleaning of the hemp, which, considering the education and circumstances of the inventor, displayed quite as much mechanical genius as Whitney's cotton-gin.[3]

1. A person of mixed European and African ancestry.
2. A factory that manufactures coarse fabric, like burlap or gunny.
3. A machine of this description was really the invention of a young colored man in Kentucky [*Stowe's note*]. In 1793 the American manufacturer Eli Whitney (1765–1825) patented the cotton gin, a machine that separated cotton from its seeds. There were persistent rumors in Stowe's time that this cotton gin was actually the invention of a

He was possessed of a handsome person and pleasing manners, and was a general favorite in the factory. Nevertheless, as this young man was in the eye of the law not a man, but a thing, all these superior qualifications were subject to the control of a vulgar, narrow-minded, tyrannical master. This same gentleman, having heard of the fame of George's invention, took a ride over to the factory, to see what this intelligent chattel had been about. He was received with great enthusiasm by the employer, who congratulated him on possessing so valuable a slave.

He was waited upon over the factory, shown the machinery by George, who, in high spirits, talked so fluently, held himself so erect, looked so handsome and manly, that his master began to feel an uneasy consciousness of inferiority. What business had his slave to be marching round the country, inventing machines, and holding up his head among gentlemen? He'd soon put a stop to it. He'd take him back, and put him to hoeing and digging, and "see if he'd step about so smart." Accordingly, the manufacturer and all hands concerned were astounded when he suddenly demanded George's wages, and announced his intention of taking him home.

"But, Mr. Harris," remonstrated the manufacturer, "isn't this rather sudden?"

"What if it is?—isn't the man *mine*?"

"We would be willing, sir, to increase the rate of compensation."

"No object at all, sir. I don't need to hire any of my hands out, unless I've a mind to."

"But, sir, he seems peculiarly adapted to this business."

"Dare say he may be; never was much adapted to anything that I set him about, I'll be bound."

"But only think of his inventing this machine," interposed one of the workmen, rather unluckily.

"O yes!—a machine for saving work, is it? He'd invent that, I'll be bound; let a nigger alone for that, any time. They are all labor-saving machines themselves, every one of 'em. No, he shall tramp!"

George had stood like one transfixed, at hearing his doom thus suddenly pronounced by a power that he knew was irresistible. He folded his arms, tightly pressed in his lips, but a whole volcano of bitter feelings burned in his bosom, and sent streams of fire through his veins. He breathed short, and his large dark eyes flashed like live coals; and he might have broken out into some dangerous ebullition, had not the kindly manufacturer touched him on the arm, and said, in a low tone,

slave or was based on a slave's idea. Slaves, however, could not patent their own inventions by law.

"Give way, George; go with him for the present. We'll try to help you, yet."

The tyrant observed the whisper, and conjectured its import though he could not hear what was said; and he inwardly strengthened himself in his determination to keep the power he possessed over his victim.

George was taken home, and put to the meanest drudgery of the farm. He had been able to repress every disrespectful word; but the flashing eye, the gloomy and troubled brow, were part of a natural language that could not be repressed,—indubitable signs, which showed too plainly that the man could not become a thing.

It was during the happy period of his employment in the factory that George had seen and married his wife. During that period,—being much trusted and favored by his employer,—he had free liberty to come and go at discretion. The marriage was highly approved of by Mrs. Shelby, who, with a little womanly complacency in match-making, felt pleased to unite her handsome favorite with one of her own class who seemed in every way suited to her; and so they were married in her mistress' great parlor, and her mistress herself adorned the bride's beautiful hair with orange-blossoms, and threw over it the bridal veil, which certainly could scarce have rested on a fairer head; and there was no lack of white gloves, and cake and wine,—of admiring guests to praise the bride's beauty, and her mistress' indulgence and liberality. For a year or two Eliza saw her husband frequently, and there was nothing to interrupt their happiness, except the loss of two infant children, to whom she was passionately attached, and whom she mourned with a grief so intense as to call for gentle remonstrance from her mistress, who sought, with maternal anxiety, to direct her naturally passionate feelings within the bounds of reason and religion.

After the birth of little Harry, however, she had gradually become tranquillized and settled; and every bleeding tie and throbbing nerve, once more entwined with that little life, seemed to become sound and healthful, and Eliza was a happy woman up to the time that her husband was rudely torn from his kind employer, and brought under the iron sway of his legal owner.

The manufacturer, true to his word, visited Mr. Harris a week or two after George had been taken away, when, as he hoped, the heat of the occasion had passed away, and tried every possible inducement to lead him to restore him to his former employment.

"You needn't trouble yourself to talk any longer," said he, doggedly; "I know my own business, sir."

"I did not presume to interfere with it, sir. I only thought that you might think it for your interest to let your man to us on the terms proposed."

"O, I understand the matter well enough. I saw your winking and whispering, the day I took him out of the factory; but you don't come it over me that way. It's a free country, sir; the man's *mine*, and I do what I please with him,—that's it!"

And so fell George's last hope;—nothing before him but a life of toil and drudgery, rendered more bitter by every little smarting vexation and indignity which tyrannical ingenuity could devise.

A very humane jurist once said, The worst use you can put a man to is to hang him. No; there is another use that a man can be put to that is WORSE!

## Chapter III

### *The Husband and Father*

Mrs. Shelby had gone on her visit, and Eliza stood in the verandah, rather dejectedly looking after the retreating carriage, when a hand was laid on her shoulder. She turned, and a bright smile lighted up her fine eyes.

"George, is it you? How you frightened me! Well; I am so glad you's come! Missis is gone to spend the afternoon; so come into my little room, and we'll have the time all to ourselves."

Saying this, she drew him into a neat little apartment opening on the verandah, where she generally sat at her sewing, within call of her mistress.

"How glad I am!—why don't you smile?—and look at Harry—how he grows." The boy stood shyly regarding his father through his curls, holding close to the skirts of his mother's dress. "Isn't he beautiful?" said Eliza, lifting his long curls and kissing him.

"I wish he'd never been born!" said George, bitterly. "I wish I'd never been born myself!"

Surprised and frightened, Eliza sat down, leaned her head on her husband's shoulder, and burst into tears.

"There now, Eliza, it's too bad for me to make you feel so, poor girl!" said he, fondly; "it's too bad. O, how I wish you never had seen me—you might have been happy!"

"George! George! how can you talk so? What dreadful thing has happened, or is going to happen? I'm sure we've been very happy, till lately."

"So we have, dear," said George. Then drawing his child on his knee, he gazed intently on his glorious dark eyes, and passed his hands through his long curls.

"Just like you, Eliza; and you are the handsomest woman I ever saw, and the best one I ever wish to see; but, oh, I wish I'd never seen you, nor you me!"

"O, George, how can you!"

"Yes, Eliza, it's all misery, misery, misery! My life is bitter as wormwood;[1] the very life is burning out of me. I'm a poor, miserable, forlorn drudge; I shall only drag you down with me, that's all. What's the use of our trying to do anything, trying to know anything, trying to be anything? What's the use of living? I wish I was dead!"

"O, now, dear George, that is really wicked! I know how you feel about losing your place in the factory, and you have a hard master; but pray be patient, and perhaps something—"

"Patient!" said he, interrupting her; "haven't I been patient? Did I say a word when he came and took me away, for no earthly reason, from the place where everybody was kind to me? I'd paid him truly every cent of my earnings,—and they all say I worked well."

"Well, it *is* dreadful," said Eliza; "but, after all, he is your master, you know."

"My master! and who made him my master? That's what I think of—what right has he to me? I'm a man as much as he is. I'm a better man than he is. I know more about business than he does; I am a better manager than he is; I can read better than he can; I can write a better hand,—and I've learned it all myself, and no thanks to him,—I've learned it in spite of him; and now what right has he to make a dray-horse[2] of me?—to take me from things I can do, and do better than he can, and put me to work that any horse can do? He tries to do it; he says he'll bring me down and humble me, and he puts me to just the hardest, meanest and dirtiest work, on purpose!"

"O, George! George! you frighten me! Why, I never heard you talk so; I'm afraid you'll do something dreadful. I don't wonder at your feelings, at all; but oh, do be careful—do, do—for my sake—for Harry's!"

"I have been careful, and I have been patient, but it's growing worse and worse; flesh and blood can't bear it any longer;—every chance he can get to insult and torment me, he takes. I thought I could do my work well, and keep on quiet, and have some time to read and learn out of work hours; but the more he sees I can do, the more he loads on. He says that though I don't say anything, he sees I've got the devil in me, and he means to bring it out; and one of these days it will come out in a way that he won't like, or I'm mistaken!"

"O dear! what shall we do?" said Eliza, mournfully.

"It was only yesterday," said George, "as I was busy loading stones into a cart, that young Mas'r Tom stood there, slashing his whip so

1. "For the lips of a strange woman drop as a honeycomb, and her mouth is smoother than oil. But her end is bitter as wormwood, sharp as a two-edged sword" (Proverbs 5.3–4).
2. A workhorse; a dray is a strong low cart used for carrying loads, often for hire.

near the horse that the creature was frightened. I asked him to stop, as pleasant as I could,—he just kept right on. I begged him again, and then he turned on me, and began striking me. I held his hand, and then he screamed and kicked and ran to his father, and told him that I was fighting him. He came in a rage, and said he'd teach me who was my master; and he tied me to a tree, and cut switches for young master, and told him that he might whip me till he was tired;—and he did do it! If I don't make him remember it, some time!" and the brow of the young man grew dark, and his eyes burned with an expression that made his young wife tremble. "Who made this man my master? That's what I want to know!" he said.

"Well," said Eliza, mournfully, "I always thought that I must obey my master and mistress, or I couldn't be a Christian."

"There is some sense in it, in your case; they have brought you up like a child, fed you, clothed you, indulged you, and taught you, so that you have a good education; that is some reason why they should claim you. But I have been kicked and cuffed and sworn at, and at the best only let alone; and what do I owe? I've paid for all my keeping a hundred times over. I *won't* bear it. No, I *won't!*" he said, clenching his hand with a fierce frown.

Eliza trembled, and was silent. She had never seen her husband in this mood before; and her gentle system of ethics seemed to bend like a reed in the surges of such passions.

"You know poor little Carlo, that you gave me," added George; "the creature has been about all the comfort that I've had. He has slept with me nights, and followed me around days, and kind o' looked at me as if he understood how I felt. Well, the other day I was just feeding him with a few old scraps I picked up by the kitchen door, and Mas'r came along, and said I was feeding him up at his expense, and that he couldn't afford to have every nigger keeping his dog, and ordered me to tie a stone to his neck and throw him in the pond."

"O, George, you didn't do it!"

"Do it? not I!—but he did. Mas'r and Tom pelted the poor drowning creature with stones. Poor thing! he looked at me so mournful, as if he wondered why I didn't save him. I had to take a flogging because I wouldn't do it myself. I don't care. Mas'r will find out that I'm one that whipping won't tame. My day will come yet, if he don't look out."

"What are you going to do? O, George, don't do anything wicked; if you only trust in God, and try to do right, he'll deliver you."

"I an't a Christian like you, Eliza; my heart's full of bitterness; I can't trust in God. Why does he let things be so?"

"O, George, we must have faith. Mistress says that when all things go wrong to us, we must believe that God is doing the very best."

"That's easy to say for people that are sitting on their sofas and riding in their carriages; but let 'em be where I am, I guess it would come some harder. I wish I could be good; but my heart burns, and can't be reconciled, anyhow. You couldn't, in my place,—you can't now, if I tell you all I've got to say. You don't know the whole yet."

"What can be coming now?"

"Well, lately Mas'r has been saying that he was a fool to let me marry off the place; that he hates Mr. Shelby and all his tribe, because they are proud, and hold their heads up above him, and that I've got proud notions from you; and he says he won't let me come here any more, and that I shall take a wife and settle down on his place. At first he only scolded and grumbled these things; but yesterday he told me that I should take Mina for a wife, and settle down in a cabin with her, or he would sell me down river."[3]

"Why—but you were married to *me*, by the minister, as much as if you'd been a white man!" said Eliza, simply.

"Don't you know a slave can't be married? There is no law in this country for that; I can't hold you for my wife, if he chooses to part us. That's why I wish I'd never seen you,—why I wish I'd never been born; it would have been better for us both,—it would have been better for this poor child if he had never been born. All this may happen to him yet!"

"O, but master is so kind!"

"Yes, but who knows?—he may die—and then he may be sold to nobody knows who. What pleasure is it that he is handsome, and smart, and bright? I tell you, Eliza, that a sword will pierce through your soul for every good and pleasant thing your child is or has; it will make him worth too much for you to keep!"

The words smote heavily on Eliza's heart; the vision of the trader came before her eyes, and, as if some one had struck her a deadly blow, she turned pale and gasped for breath. She looked nervously out on the verandah, where the boy, tired of the grave conversation, had retired, and where he was riding triumphantly up and down on Mr. Shelby's walking-stick. She would have spoken to tell her husband her fears, but checked herself.

"No, no,—he has enough to bear, poor fellow!" she thought. "No, I won't tell him; besides, it an't true; Missis never deceives us."

"So, Eliza, my girl," said the husband, mournfully, "bear up, now; and good-by, for I'm going."

"Going, George! Going where?"

"To Canada," said he, straightening himself up; "and when I'm there, I'll buy you; that's all the hope that's left us. You have a kind

3. I.e., the lower Mississippi, where slave conditions were at their worst. For slaves, to be "sold down river" was to be punished by being sold to a plantation farther south.

master, that won't refuse to sell you. I'll buy you and the boy;—God helping me, I will!"

"O, dreadful! if you should be taken?"

"I won't be taken, Eliza; I'll *die* first! I'll be free, or I'll die!"

"You won't kill yourself!"

"No need of that. They will kill me, fast enough; they never will get me down the river alive!"

"O, George, for my sake, do be careful! Don't do anything wicked; don't lay hands on yourself, or anybody else! You are tempted too much—too much; but don't—go you must—but go carefully, prudently; pray God to help you."

"Well, then, Eliza, hear my plan. Mas'r took it into his head to send me right by here, with a note to Mr. Symmes, that lives a mile past. I believe he expected I should come here to tell you what I have. It would please him, if he thought it would aggravate 'Shelby's folks,' as he calls 'em. I'm going home quite resigned, you understand, as if all was over. I've got some preparations made,—and there are those that will help me; and, in the course of a week or so, I shall be among the missing, some day. Pray for me, Eliza; perhaps the good Lord will hear *you*."

"O, pray yourself, George, and go trusting in him; then you won't do anything wicked."

"Well, now, *good-by*," said George, holding Eliza's hands, and gazing into her eyes, without moving. They stood silent; then there were last words, and sobs, and bitter weeping,—such parting as those may make whose hope to meet again is as the spider's web,—and the husband and wife were parted.

# Chapter IV

## *An Evening in Uncle Tom's Cabin*

The cabin of Uncle Tom was a small log building, close adjoining to "the house," as the negro *par excellence* designates his master's dwelling. In front it had a neat garden-patch, where, every summer, strawberries, raspberries, and a variety of fruits and vegetables, flourished under careful tending. The whole front of it was covered by a large scarlet bignonia and a native multiflora rose, which, entwisting and interlacing, left scarce a vestige of the rough logs to be seen. Here, also, in summer, various brilliant annuals, such as marigolds, petunias, four-o'clocks, found an indulgent corner in which to unfold their splendors, and were the delight and pride of Aunt Chloe's heart.[1]

1. *Aunt* and *Uncle* were generic terms of address for older black women and men.

Let us enter the dwelling. The evening meal at the house is over, and Aunt Chloe, who presided over its preparation as head cook, has left to inferior officers in the kitchen the business of clearing away and washing dishes, and come out into her own snug territories, to "get her ole man's supper;" therefore, doubt not that it is her you see by the fire, presiding with anxious interest over certain frizzling items in a stew-pan, and anon with grave consideration lifting the cover of a bake-kettle, from whence steam forth indubitable intimations of "something good." A round, black, shining face is hers, so glossy as to suggest the idea that she might have been washed over with white of eggs, like one of her own tea rusks.[2] Her whole plump countenance beams with satisfaction and contentment from under her well-starched checked turban, bearing on it, however, if we must confess it, a little of that tinge of self-consciousness which becomes the first cook of the neighborhood, as Aunt Chloe was universally held and acknowledged to be.

A cook she certainly was, in the very bone and centre of her soul. Not a chicken or turkey or duck in the barn-yard but looked grave when they saw her approaching, and seemed evidently to be reflecting on their latter end; and certain it was that she was always meditating on trussing, stuffing and roasting, to a degree that was calculated to inspire terror in any reflecting fowl living. Her corncake, in all its varieties of hoe-cake, dodgers, muffins,[3] and other species too numerous to mention, was a sublime mystery to all less practised compounders; and she would shake her fat sides with honest pride and merriment, as she would narrate the fruitless efforts that one and another of her compeers had made to attain to her elevation.

The arrival of company at the house, the arranging of dinners and suppers "in style," awoke all the energies of her soul; and no sight was more welcome to her than a pile of travelling trunks launched on the verandah, for then she foresaw fresh efforts and fresh triumphs.

Just at present, however, Aunt Chloe is looking into the bake-pan; in which congenial operation we shall leave her till we finish our picture of the cottage.

In one corner of it stood a bed, covered neatly with a snowy spread; and by the side of it was a piece of carpeting, of some considerable size. On this piece of carpeting Aunt Chloe took her stand, as being decidedly in the upper walks of life; and it and the bed by which it lay, and the whole corner, in fact, were treated with distinguished consideration, and made, so far as possible, sacred from the marauding inroads and desecrations of little folks. In fact, that corner was

2. Breads baked twice to make them dry and crisp.
3. All are breads or cakes made from cornmeal.

the *drawing-room* of the establishment. In the other corner was a bed of much humbler pretensions, and evidently designed for *use*. The wall over the fireplace was adorned with some very brilliant scriptural prints, and a portrait of General Washington,[4] drawn and colored in a manner which would certainly have astonished that hero, if ever he had happened to meet with its like.

On a rough bench in the corner, a couple of woolly-headed boys, with glistening black eyes and fat shining cheeks, were busy in superintending the first walking operations of the baby, which, as is usually the case, consisted in getting up on its feet, balancing a moment, and then tumbling down,—each successive failure being violently cheered, as something decidedly clever.

A table, somewhat rheumatic in its limbs, was drawn out in front of the fire, and covered with a cloth, displaying cups and saucers of a decidedly brilliant pattern, with other symptoms of an approaching meal. At this table was seated Uncle Tom, Mr. Shelby's best hand, who, as he is to be the hero of our story, we must daguerreotype[5] for our readers. He was a large, broad-chested, powerfully-made man, of a full glossy black, and a face whose truly African features were characterized by an expression of grave and steady good sense, united with much kindliness and benevolence. There was something about his whole air self-respecting and dignified, yet united with a confiding and humble simplicity.

He was very busily intent at this moment on a slate lying before him, on which he was carefully and slowly endeavoring to accomplish a copy of some letters, in which operation he was overlooked by young Mas'r George, a smart, bright boy of thirteen, who appeared fully to realize the dignity of his position as instructor.

"Not that way, Uncle Tom,—not that way," said he, briskly, as Uncle Tom laboriously brought up the tail of his *g* the wrong side out; "that makes a *q*, you see."

"La sakes, now, does it?" said Uncle Tom, looking with a respectful, admiring air, as his young teacher flourishingly scrawled *q*'s and *g*'s innumerable for his edification; and then, taking the pencil in his big, heavy fingers, he patiently re-commenced.

"How easy white folks al'us does things!" said Aunt Chloe, pausing while she was greasing a griddle with a scrap of bacon on her fork, and regarding young Master George with pride. "The way he can write, now! and read, too! and then to come out here evenings and read his lessons to us,—it's mighty interestin'!"

4. George Washington (1732–1799), first president of the United States and commander in chief of the Continental army during the War for Independence, 1775–83.
5. Describe very directly or vividly. A daguerrotype was a photograph produced on a silver plate.

"But, Aunt Chloe, I'm getting mighty hungry," said George. "Isn't that cake in the skillet almost done?"

"Mose done, Mas'r George," said Aunt Chloe, lifting the lid and peeping in,—"browning beautiful—a real lovely brown. Ah! let me alone for dat. Missis let Sally try to make some cake, t'other day, jes to *larn* her, she said. 'O, go way, Missis,' says I; 'it really hurts my feelin's, now, to see good vittles spiled dat ar way! Cake ris all to one side—no shape at all; no more than my shoe;—go way!"

And with this final expression of contempt for Sally's greenness, Aunt Chloe whipped the cover off the bake-kettle, and disclosed to view a neatly-baked pound-cake, of which no city confectioner need to have been ashamed. This being evidently the central point of the entertainment, Aunt Chloe began now to bustle about earnestly in the supper department.

"Here you, Mose and Pete! get out de way, you niggers! Get away, Polly, honey,—mammy'll give her baby somefin, by and by. Now, Mas'r George, you jest take off dem books, and set down now with my old man, and I'll take up de sausages, and have de first griddle full of cakes on your plates in less dan no time."

"They wanted me to come to supper in the house," said George; "but I knew what was what too well for that, Aunt Chloe."

"So you did—so you did, honey," said Aunt Chloe, heaping the smoking batter-cakes on his plate; "you know'd your old aunty'd keep the best for you. O, let you alone for dat! Go way!" And, with that, aunty gave George a nudge with her finger, designed to be immensely facetious, and turned again to her griddle with great briskness.

"Now for the cake," said Mas'r George, when the activity of the griddle department had somewhat subsided; and, with that, the youngster flourished a large knife over the article in question.

"La bless you, Mas'r George!" said Aunt Chloe, with earnestness, catching his arm, "you wouldn't be for cuttin' it wid dat ar great heavy knife! Smash all down—spile all de pretty rise of it. Here, I've got a thin old knife, I keeps sharp a purpose. Dar now, see! comes apart light as a feather! Now eat away—you won't get anything to beat dat ar."

"Tom Lincon says," said George, speaking with his mouth full, "that their Jinny is a better cook than you."

"Dem Lincons an't much count, no way!" said Aunt Chloe, contemptuously; "I mean, set along side *our* folks. They's 'spectable folks enough in a kinder plain way; but, as to gettin' up anything in style, they don't begin to have a notion on't. Set Mas'r Lincon, now, alongside Mas'r Shelby! Good Lor! and Missis Lincon,—can she kinder sweep it into a room like my missis,—so kinder splendid, yer know! O, go way! don't tell me nothin' of dem Lincons!"—and Aunt

Chloe tossed her head as one who hoped she did know something of the world.

"Well, though, I've heard you say," said George, "that Jinny was a pretty fair cook."

"So I did," said Aunt Chloe,—"I may say dat. Good, plain, common cookin', Jinny'll do;—make a good pone o' bread,[6]—bile her taters *far,*—her corn cakes isn't extra, not extra now, Jinny's corn cakes isn't, but then they's far,—but, Lor, come to de higher branches, and what *can* she do? Why, she makes pies—sartin she does; but what kinder crust? Can she make your real flecky paste,[7] as melts in your mouth, and lies all up like a puff? Now, I went over thar when Miss Mary was gwine to be married, and Jinny she jest showed me de weddin' pies. Jinny and I is good friends, ye know. I never said nothin'; but go long, Mas'r George! Why, I shouldn't sleep a wink for a week, if I had a batch of pies like dem ar. Why, dey wan't no 'count 't all."

"I suppose Jinny thought they were ever so nice," said George.

"Thought so!—didn't she? Thar she was, showing 'em, as innocent—ye see, it's jest here, Jinny *don't know.* Lor, the family an't nothing! She can't be spected to know! 'Ta'nt no fault o' hern. Ah, Mas'r George, you doesn't know half your privileges in yer family and bringin' up!" Here Aunt Chloe sighed, and rolled up her eyes with emotion.

"I'm sure, Aunt Chloe, I understand all my pie and pudding privileges," said George. "Ask Tom Lincon if I don't crow over him, every time I meet him."

Aunt Chloe sat back in her chair, and indulged in a hearty guffaw of laughter, at this witticism of young Mas'r's, laughing till the tears rolled down her black, shining cheeks, and varying the exercise with playfully slapping and poking Mas'r Georgey, and telling him to go way, and that he was a case—that he was fit to kill her, and that he sartin would kill her, one of these days; and, between each of these sanguinary predictions, going off into a laugh, each longer and stronger than the other, till George really began to think that he was a very dangerously witty fellow, and that it became him to be careful how he talked "as funny as he could."

"And so ye telled Tom, did ye? O, Lor! what young uns will be up ter! Ye crowed over Tom? O, Lor! Mas'r George, if ye wouldn't make a hornbug[8] laugh!"

"Yes," said George, "I says to him, 'Tom, you ought to see some of Aunt Chloe's pies; they're the right sort,' says I."

6. Cornbread in the form of a small oval loaf.
7. Dough used for making fancy rolls, containing a large proportion of lard.
8. I.e., a horned bug—a stag beetle, June bug, or Betsy bug.

"Pity, now, Tom couldn't," said Aunt Chloe, on whose benevolent heart the idea of Tom's benighted condition seemed to make a strong impression. "Ye oughter just ask him here to dinner, some o' these times, Mas'r George," she added; "it would look quite pretty of ye. Ye know, Mas'r George, ye oughtenter feel 'bove nobody, on 'count yer privileges, 'cause all our privileges is gi'n to us; we ought al'ays to 'member that," said Aunt Chloe, looking quite serious.

"Well, I mean to ask Tom here, some day next week," said George; "and you do your prettiest, Aunt Chloe, and we'll make him stare. Won't we make him eat so he won't get over it for a fortnight?"

"Yes, yes—sartin," said Aunt Chloe, delighted; "you'll see. Lor! to think of some of our dinners! Yer mind dat ar great chicken pie I made when we guv de dinner to General Knox? I and Missis, we come pretty near quarrelling about dat ar crust. What does get into ladies sometimes, I don't know; but, sometimes, when a body has de heaviest kind o' 'sponsibility on 'em, as ye may say, and is all kinder *'seris'* and taken up, dey takes dat ar time to be hangin' round and kinder interferin'! Now, Missis, she wanted me to do dis way, and she wanted me to do dat way; and, finally, I got kinder sarcy, and, says I, 'Now, Missis, do jist look at dem beautiful white hands o' yourn, with long fingers, and all a sparkling with rings, like my white lilies when de dew's on 'em; and look at my great black stumpin hands. Now, don't ye think dat de Lord must have meant *me* to make de pie-crust, and you to stay in de parlor? Dar! I was jist so sarcy, Mas'r George."

"And what did mother say?" said George.

"Say?—why, she kinder larfed in her eyes—dem great handsome eyes o' hern; and, says she, 'Well, Aunt Chloe, I think you are about in the right on 't,' says she; and she went off in de parlor. She oughter cracked me over de head for bein' so sarcy; but dar's whar 't is—I can't do nothin' with ladies in de kitchen!"

"Well, you made out well with that dinner,—I remember everybody said so," said George.

"Didn't I? And wan't I behind de dinin'-room door dat bery day? and didn't I see de General pass his plate three times for some more dat bery pie?—and, says he, 'You must have an uncommon cook, Mrs. Shelby.' Lor! I was fit to split myself.

"And de Gineral, he knows what cookin' is," said Aunt Chloe, drawing herself up with an air. "Bery nice man, de Gineral! He comes of one of de bery *fustest* families in Old Virginny![9] He knows what's what, now, as well as I do—de Gineral. Ye see, there's *pints* in all pies, Mas'r George; but tan't everybody knows what they is, or orter be. But the Gineral, he knows; I knew by his 'marks he made. Yes, he knows what de pints is!"

9. The state of Virginia.

By this time, Master George had arrived at that pass to which even a boy can come (under uncommon circumstances,) when he really could not eat another morsel and, therefore, he was at leisure to notice the pile of woolly heads and glistening eyes which were regarding their operations hungrily from the opposite corner.

"Here, you Mose, Pete," he said, breaking off liberal bits, and throwing it at them; "you want some, don't you? Come, Aunt Chloe, bake them some cakes."

And George and Tom moved to a comfortable seat in the chimney-corner, while Aunt Chloe, after baking a goodly pile of cakes, took her baby on her lap, and began alternately filling its mouth and her own, and distributing to Mose and Pete, who seemed rather to prefer eating theirs as they rolled about on the floor under the table, tickling each other, and occasionally pulling the baby's toes.

"O! go long, will ye?" said the mother, giving now and then a kick, in a kind of general way, under the table, when the movement became too obstreperous. "Can't ye be decent when white folks comes to see ye? Stop dat ar, now, will ye? Better mind yerselves, or I'll take ye down a button-hole lower, when Mas'r George is gone!"

What meaning was couched under this terrible threat, it is difficult to say; but certain it is that its awful indistinctness seemed to produce very little impression on the young sinners addressed.

"La, now!" said Uncle Tom, "they are so full of tickle all the while, they can't behave theirselves."

Here the boys emerged from under the table, and, with hands and faces well plastered with molasses, began a vigorous kissing of the baby.

"Get along wid ye!" said the mother, pushing away their woolly heads. "Ye'll all stick together, and never get clar, if ye do dat fashion. Go long to de spring and wash yerselves!" she said, seconding her exhortations by a slap, which resounded very formidably, but which seemed only to knock out so much more laugh from the young ones, as they tumbled precipitately over each other out of doors, where they fairly screamed with merriment.

"Did ye ever see such aggravating young uns?" said Aunt Chloe, rather complacently, as, producing an old towel, kept for such emergencies, she poured a little water out of the cracked tea-pot on it, and began rubbing off the molasses from the baby's face and hands; and, having polished her till she shone, she set her down in Tom's lap, while she busied herself in clearing away supper. The baby employed the intervals in pulling Tom's nose, scratching his face, and burying her fat hands in his woolly hair, which last operation seemed to afford her special content.

"Aint she a peart young un?" said Tom, holding her from him to take a full-length view; then, getting up, he set her on his broad shoulder, and began capering and dancing with her, while Mas'r George snapped at her with his pocket-handkerchief, and Mose and Pete, now returned again, roared after her like bears, till Aunt Chloe declared that they "fairly took her head off" with their noise. As, according to her own statement, this surgical operation was a matter of daily occurrence in the cabin, the declaration no whit abated the merriment, till every one had roared and tumbled and danced themselves down to a state of composure.

"Well, now, I hopes you're done," said Aunt Chloe, who had been busy in pulling out a rude box of a trundle-bed;[1] and now, you Mose and you Pete, get into thar; for we's goin' to have the meetin'."

"O mother, we don't wanter. We wants to sit up to meetin',—meetin's is so curis. We likes 'em."

"La, Aunt Chloe, shove it under, and let 'em sit up," said Mas'r George, decisively, giving a push to the rude machine.

Aunt Chloe, having thus saved appearances, seemed highly delighted to push the thing under, saying, as she did so, "Well, mebbe 't will do 'em some good."

The house now resolved itself into a committee of the whole, to consider the accommodations and arrangements for the meeting.

"What we's to do for cheers, now, *I* declar I don't know," said Aunt Chloe. As the meeting had been held at Uncle Tom's, weekly, for an indefinite length of time, without any more "cheers," there seemed some encouragement to hope that a way would be discovered at present.

"Old Uncle Peter sung both de legs out of dat oldest cheer, last week," suggested Mose.

"You go long! I'll boun' you pulled 'em out; some o' your shines," said Aunt Chloe.

"Well, it'll stand, if it only keeps jam up agin de wall!" said Mose.

"Den Uncle Peter mus'n't sit in it, cause he al'ays hitches when he gets a singing. He hitched pretty nigh across de room, t' other night," said Pete.

"Good Lor! get him in it, then," said Mose, "and den he'd begin, 'Come saints and sinners, hear me tell,'[2] and den down he'd go,"—and Mose imitated precisely the nasal tones of the old man, tumbling on the floor, to illustrate the supposed catastrophe.

1. A low bed that can be pushed under a higher one.
2. From the Methodist hymn "Come Saints and Sinners" (also called "Heavenly Union"):

> Come saints and sinners, hear me tell
> The wonders of Immanuel
> Who snatch'd me from a burning hell,
> And brought my soul with him to dwell,
> To dwell, in sweetest union.

"Come now, be decent, can't ye?" said Aunt Chloe; "an't yer shamed?"

Mas'r George, however, joined the offender in the laugh, and declared decidedly that Mose was a "buster." So the maternal admonition seemed rather to fail of effect.

"Well, ole man," said Aunt Chloe, "you'll have to tote in them ar bar'ls."

"Mother's bar'ls is like dat ar widder's, Mas'r George was reading 'bout, in de good book,—dey never fails," said Mose, aside to Pete.

"I'm sure one on 'em caved in last week," said Pete, "and let 'em all down in de middle of de singin'; dat ar was failin', warnt it?"

During this aside between Mose and Pete, two empty casks had been rolled into the cabin, and being secured from rolling, by stones on each side, boards were laid across them, which arrangement, together with the turning down of certain tubs and pails, and the disposing of the rickety chairs, at last completed the preparation.

"Mas'r George is such a beautiful reader, now, I know he'll stay to read for us," said Aunt Chloe; "'pears like 't will be so much more interestin'."

George very readily consented, for your boy is always ready for anything that makes him of importance.

The room was soon filled with a motley assemblage, from the old gray-headed patriarch of eighty, to the young girl and lad of fifteen. A little harmless gossip ensued on various themes, such as where old Aunt Sally got her new red headkerchief, and how "Missis was a going to give Lizzy that spotted muslin gown, when she'd got her new berage[3] made up;" and how Mas'r Shelby was thinking of buying a new sorrel colt, that was going to prove an addition to the glories of the place. A few of the worshippers belonged to families hard by, who had got permission to attend, and who brought in various choice scraps of information, about the sayings and doings at the house and on the place, which circulated as freely as the same sort of small change does in higher circles.

After a while the singing commenced, to the evident delight of all present. Not even all the disadvantage of nasal intonation could prevent the effect of the naturally fine voices, in airs at once wild and spirited. The words were sometimes the well-known and common hymns sung in the churches about, and sometimes of a wilder, more indefinite character, picked up at camp-meetings.

The chorus of one of them, which ran as follows, was sung with great energy and unction:

3. Usually *barége*, a light, silky, gauzelike fabric, or a dress made from it.

"Die on the field of battle,
Die on the field of battle,
Glory in my soul."[4]

Another special favorite had oft repeated the words—

"O, I'm going to glory,—won't you come along with me?
Don't you see the angels beck'ning, and a calling me away?
Don't you see the golden city and the everlasting day?"[5]

There were others, which made incessant mention of "Jordan's banks," and "Canaan's fields," and the "New Jerusalem;"[6] for the negro mind, impassioned and imaginative, always attaches itself to hymns and expressions of a vivid and pictorial nature; and, as they sung, some laughed, and some cried, and some clapped hands, or shook hands rejoicingly with each other, as if they had fairly gained the other side of the river.

Various exhortations, or relations of experience, followed, and intermingled with the singing. One old gray-headed woman, long past work, but much revered as a sort of chronicle of the past, rose, and leaning on her staff, said—

"Well, chil'en! Well, I'm mighty glad to hear ye all and see ye all once more, 'cause I don't know when I'll be gone to glory; but I've done got ready, chil'en; 'pears like I'd got my little bundle all tied up, and my bonnet on, jest a waitin' for the stage to come along and take me home; sometimes, in the night, I think I hear the wheels a rattlin', and I'm lookin' out all the time; now, you jest be ready too, for I tell ye all, chil'en," she said, striking her staff hard on the floor, "dat ar *glory* is a mighty thing! It's a mighty thing, chil'en,—you

4. A version of the hymn "Die in the Field" by Samuel Wakefield:

Firmly, brethren, firmly stand
All united heart and hand
One unbroken valiant band
Dauntless, brave and true.

Die in the field of battle (×3)
Glory in your soul.

5. Similar to the spiritual "Bound for the Promised Land":

I am bound for the promised land
I am bound for the promised land
Oh, who will come and go with me,
I am bound for the promised land.

6. New Jerusalem is a name for the holy city that awaits good Christians after Judgment Day (Revelation 3.12 and 21.2). The Jordan River marked the limit of the land promised by God to the Israelites after their escape from Egypt; to American slaves it symbolized a boundary between bondage and freedom. See Deuteronomy 11.31: "For ye shall pass over Jordan to go in to possess the land which the Lord your God giveth you, and ye shall possess it, and dwell therein." Canaan, the Israelites' promised land, meant a land of freedom, either earthly or heavenly, to slaves. See Exodus 6.4: "And I have also established my covenant with them, to give them the land of Canaan, the land of their pilgrimage, wherein they were strangers."

don'no nothing about it,—it's *wonderful.*" And the old creature sat down, with streaming tears, as wholly overcome, while the whole circle struck up—

> "O Canaan, bright Canaan,
> I'm bound for the land of Canaan."[7]

Mas'r George, by request, read the last chapters of Revelation,[8] often interrupted by such exclamations as "The *sakes* now!" "Only hear that!" "Jest think on't!" "Is all that a comin' sure enough?"

George, who was a bright boy, and well trained in religious things by his mother, finding himself an object of general admiration, threw in expositions of his own, from time to time, with a commendable seriousness and gravity, for which he was admired by the young and blessed by the old; and it was agreed, on all hands, that "a minister couldn't lay it off better than he did;" that "'twas reely 'mazin'!"

Uncle Tom was a sort of patriarch in religious matters, in the neighborhood. Having, naturally, an organization in which the *morale*[9] was strongly predominant, together with a greater breadth and cultivation of mind than obtained among his companions, he was looked up to with great respect, as a sort of minister among them; and the simple, hearty, sincere style of his exhortations might have edified even better educated persons. But it was in prayer that he especially excelled. Nothing could exceed the touching simplicity, the child-like earnestness, of his prayer, enriched with the language of Scripture, which seemed so entirely to have wrought itself into his being, as to have become a part of himself, and to drop from his lips unconsciously; in the language of a pious old negro, he "prayed right up." And so much did his prayer always work on the devotional feelings of his audiences, that there seemed often a danger that it would be lost altogether in the abundance of the responses which broke out everywhere around him.

While this scene was passing in the cabin of the man, one quite otherwise passed in the halls of the master.

The trader and Mr. Shelby were seated together in the dining room afore-named, at a table covered with papers and writing utensils.

7. From the hymn "Bound for the Land of Canaan" by John Wesley:

> How happy is the pilgrim's lot
> I am bound for the land of Canaan
> How free from ev'ry anxious thought
> I am bound for the land of Canaan.

8. The last book of the New Testament, describing the punishment of sinners and the reward of the saved on Judgment Day.
9. Mental or moral faculties (French).

Mr. Shelby was busy in counting some bundles of bills, which, as they were counted, he pushed over to the trader, who counted them likewise.

"All fair," said the trader; "and now for signing these yer."

Mr. Shelby hastily drew the bills of sale towards him, and signed them, like a man that hurries over some disagreeable business, and then pushed them over with the money. Haley produced, from a well-worn valise, a parchment, which, after looking over it a moment, he handed to Mr. Shelby, who took it with a gesture of suppressed eagerness.

"Wal, now, the thing's *done!*" said the trader, getting up.

"It's *done!*" said Mr. Shelby, in a musing tone; and, fetching a long breath, he repeated, "*It's done!*"

"Yer don't seem to feel much pleased with it, 'pears to me," said the trader.

"Haley," said Mr. Shelby, "I hope you'll remember that you promised, on your honor, you wouldn't sell Tom, without knowing what sort of hands he's going into."

"Why, you've just done it, sir," said the trader.

"Circumstances, you well know, *obliged* me," said Shelby, haughtily.

"Wal, you know, they may 'blige *me*, too," said the trader. "Howsomever, I'll do the very best I can in gettin' Tom a good berth; as to my treatin' on him bad, you needn't be a grain afeard. If there's anything that I thank the Lord for, it is that I'm never noways cruel."

After the expositions which the trader had previously given of his humane principles, Mr. Shelby did not feel particularly reassured by these declarations; but, as they were the best comfort the case admitted of, he allowed the trader to depart in silence, and betook himself to a solitary cigar.

## Chapter V

### *Showing the Feelings of Living Property on Changing Owners*

Mr. and Mrs. Shelby had retired to their apartment for the night. He was lounging in a large easy-chair, looking over some letters that had come in the afternoon mail, and she was standing before her mirror, brushing out the complicated braids and curls in which Eliza had arranged her hair; for, noticing her pale cheeks and haggard eyes, she had excused her attendance that night, and ordered her to bed. The employment, naturally enough, suggested her conversation with the girl in the morning; and, turning to her husband, she said, carelessly,

"By the by, Arthur, who was that low-bred fellow that you lugged in to our dinner-table to-day?"

"Haley is his name," said Shelby, turning himself rather uneasily in his chair, and continuing with his eyes fixed on a letter.

"Haley! Who is he, and what may be his business here, pray?"

"Well, he's a man that I transacted some business with, last time I was at Natchez," said Mr. Shelby.

"And he presumed on it to make himself quite at home, and call and dine here, ay?"

"Why, I invited him; I had some accounts with him," said Shelby.

"Is he a negro-trader?" said Mrs. Shelby, noticing a certain embarrassment in her husband's manner.

"Why, my dear, what put that into your head?" said Shelby, looking up.

"Nothing,—only Eliza came in here, after dinner, in a great worry, crying and taking on, and said you were talking with a trader, and that she heard him make an offer for her boy—the ridiculous little goose!"

"She did, hey?" said Mr. Shelby, returning to his paper, which he seemed for a few moments quite intent upon, not perceiving that he was holding it bottom upwards.

"It will have to come out," said he, mentally; "as well now as ever."

"I told Eliza," said Mrs. Shelby, as she continued brushing her hair, "that she was a little fool for her pains, and that you never had anything to do with that sort of persons. Of course, I knew you never meant to sell any of our people,—least of all, to such a fellow."

"Well, Emily," said her husband, "so I have always felt and said; but the fact is that my business lies so that I cannot get on without. I shall have to sell some of my hands."

"To that creature? Impossible! Mr. Shelby, you cannot be serious."

"I'm sorry to say that I am," said Mr. Shelby. "I've agreed to sell Tom."

"What! our Tom?—that good, faithful creature—been your faithful servant from a boy! O, Mr. Shelby!—and you have promised him his freedom, too,—you and I have spoken to him a hundred times of it. Well I can believe anything now,—I can believe *now* that you could sell little Harry, poor Eliza's only child!" said Mrs. Shelby, in a tone between grief and indignation.

"Well, since you must know all, it is so. I have agreed to sell Tom and Harry both; and I don't know why I am to be rated, as if I were a monster, for doing what every one does every day."

"But why, of all others, choose these?" said Mrs. Shelby. "Why sell them, of all on the place, if you must sell at all?"

"Because they will bring the highest sum of any,—that's why. I could choose another, if you say so. The fellow made me a high bid on Eliza, if that would suit you any better," said Mr. Shelby.

"The wretch!" said Mrs. Shelby, vehemently.

"Well, I didn't listen to it, a moment,—out of regard to your feelings, I wouldn't;—so give me some credit."

"My dear," said Mrs. Shelby, recollecting herself, "forgive me. I have been hasty. I was surprised, and entirely unprepared for this;—but surely you will allow me to intercede for these poor creatures. Tom is a noble-hearted, faithful fellow, if he is black. I do believe, Mr. Shelby, that if he were put to it, he would lay down his life for you."

"I know it,—I dare say;—but what's the use of all this?—I can't help myself."

"Why not make a pecuniary sacrifice? I'm willing to bear my part of the inconvenience. O, Mr. Shelby, I have tried—tried most faithfully, as a Christian woman should—to do my duty to these poor, simple, dependent creatures. I have cared for them, instructed them, watched over them, and known all their little cares and joys, for years; and how can I ever hold up my head again among them, if, for the sake of a little paltry gain, we sell such a faithful, excellent, confiding creature as poor Tom, and tear from him in a moment all we have taught him to love and value? I have taught them the duties of the family, of parent and child, and husband and wife; and how can I bear to have this open acknowledgment that we care for no tie, no duty, no relation, however sacred, compared with money? I have talked with Eliza about her boy—her duty to him as a Christian mother, to watch over him, pray for him, and bring him up in a Christian way; and now what can I say, if you tear him away, and sell him, soul and body, to a profane, unprincipled man, just to save a little money? I have told her that one soul is worth more than all the money in the world; and how will she believe me when she sees us turn round and sell her child?—sell him, perhaps, to certain ruin of body and soul!"

"I'm sorry you feel so about it, Emily,—indeed I am," said Mr. Shelby; "and I respect your feelings, too, though I don't pretend to share them to their full extent; but I tell you now, solemnly, it's of no use—I can't help myself. I didn't mean to tell you this, Emily; but, in plain words, there is no choice between selling these two and selling everything. Either they must go, or *all* must. Haley has come into possession of a mortgage, which, if I don't clear off with him directly, will take everything before it. I've raked, and scraped, and borrowed, and all but begged,—and the price of these two was needed to make up the balance, and I had to give them up. Haley fancied the child; he agreed to settle the matter that way, and no other. I was in his power, and *had* to do it. If you feel so to have them sold, would it be any better to have *all* sold?"

Mrs. Shelby stood like one stricken. Finally, turning to her toilet, she rested her face in her hands, and gave a sort of groan.

"This is God's curse on slavery!—a bitter, bitter, most accursed thing!—a curse to the master and a curse to the slave! I was a fool to think I could make anything good out of such a deadly evil. It is a sin to hold a slave under laws like ours,—I always felt it was,—I always thought so when I was a girl,—I thought so still more after I joined the church; but I thought I could gild it over,—I thought, by kindness, and care, and instruction, I could make the condition of mine better than freedom—fool that I was!"

"Why, wife, you are getting to be an abolitionist,[1] quite."

"Abolitionist! if they knew all I know about slavery they *might* talk! We don't need them to tell us; you know I never thought that slavery was right—never felt willing to own slaves."

"Well, therein you differ from many wise and pious men," said Mr. Shelby. "You remember Mr. B.'s sermon, the other Sunday?"

"I don't want to hear such sermons; I never wish to hear Mr. B. in our church again. Ministers can't help the evil, perhaps,—can't cure it, any more than we can,—but defend it!—it always went against my common sense. And I think you didn't think much of that sermon, either."

"Well," said Shelby, "I must say these ministers sometimes carry matters further than we poor sinners would exactly dare to do. We men of the world must wink pretty hard at various things, and get used to a deal that isn't the exact thing. But we don't quite fancy, when women and ministers come out broad and square, and go beyond us in matters of either modesty or morals, that's a fact. But now, my dear, I trust you see the necessity of the thing, and you see that I have done the very best that circumstances would allow."

"O yes, yes!" said Mrs. Shelby, hurriedly and abstractedly fingering her gold watch,—"I haven't any jewelry of any amount," she added, thoughtfully; "but would not this watch do something?—it was an expensive one, when it was bought. If I could only at least save Eliza's child, I would sacrifice anything I have."

1. An active opponent of slavery; one who sought the emancipation of all slaves. Though it had existed since the Revolution, the abolitionist movement reached its full force in the 1830s, when antislavery literature achieved wide circulation and evangelical religious revivals involving, among others, Stowe's father, Lyman Beecher, added to abolitionist sentiment. By 1838, there were in the United States over 1,350 antislavery societies with almost 250,000 members, many of them women. One prominent group, the American Anti-Slavery Society, was organized in 1833 by Arthur and Lewis Tappan and William Lloyd Garrison (1805–1879), publisher of the abolitionist journal *The Liberator.* Abolitionism grew further after the passage of the stringent Fugitive Slave Act in 1850.

"I'm sorry, very sorry, Emily," said Mr. Shelby, "I'm sorry this takes hold of you so; but it will do no good. The fact is, Emily, the thing's done; the bills of sale are already signed, and in Haley's hands; and you must be thankful it is no worse. That man has had it in his power to ruin us all,—and now he is fairly off. If you knew the man as I do, you'd think that we had had a narrow escape."

"Is he so hard, then?"

"Why, not a cruel man, exactly, but a man of leather,—a man alive to nothing but trade and profit,—cool, and unhesitating, and unrelenting, as death and the grave. He'd sell his own mother at a good percentage—not wishing the old woman any harm, either."

"And this wretch owns that good, faithful Tom, and Eliza's child!"

"Well, my dear, the fact is that this goes rather hard with me; it's a thing I hate to think of. Haley wants to drive matters, and take possession to-morrow. I'm going to get out my horse bright and early, and be off. I can't see Tom, that's a fact; and you had better arrange a drive somewhere, and carry Eliza off. Let the thing be done when she is out of sight."

"No, no," said Mrs. Shelby; "I'll be in no sense accomplice or help in this cruel business. I'll go and see poor old Tom, God help him, in his distress! They shall see, at any rate, that their mistress can feel for and with them. As to Eliza, I dare not think about it. The Lord forgive us! What have we done, that this cruel necessity should come on us?"

There was one listener to this conversation whom Mr. and Mrs. Shelby little suspected.

Communicating with their apartment was a large closet, opening by a door into the outer passage. When Mrs. Shelby had dismissed Eliza for the night, her feverish and excited mind had suggested the idea of this closet; and she had hidden herself there, and, with her ear pressed close against the crack of the door, had lost not a word of the conversation.

When the voices died into silence, she rose and crept stealthily away. Pale, shivering, with rigid features and compressed lips, she looked an entirely altered being from the soft and timid creature she had been hitherto. She moved cautiously along the entry, paused one moment at her mistress' door, and raised her hands in mute appeal to Heaven, and then turned and glided into her own room. It was a quiet, neat apartment, on the same floor with her mistress. There was the pleasant sunny window, where she had often sat singing at her sewing; there a little case of books, and various little fancy articles, ranged by them, the gifts of Christmas holidays; there was her simple wardrobe in the closet and in the drawers:—here was, in short, her home; and, on the whole, a happy one it had been to her. But there, on the bed, lay her slumbering boy, his long curls falling negligently around his unconscious face, his rosy mouth half open, his little fat hands thrown out over the bedclothes, and a smile spread like a sunbeam over his whole face.

"Poor boy! poor fellow!" said Eliza; "they have sold you! but your mother will save you yet!"

No tear dropped over that pillow; in such straits as these, the heart has no tears to give,—it drops only blood, bleeding itself away in silence. She took a piece of paper and a pencil, and wrote, hastily,

"O, Missis! dear Missis! don't think me ungrateful,—don't think hard of me, any way,—I heard all you and master said to-night. I am going to try to save my boy—you will not blame me! God bless and reward you for all your kindness!"

Hastily folding and directing this, she went to a drawer and made up a little package of clothing for her boy, which she tied with a handkerchief firmly round her waist; and, so fond is a mother's remembrance, that, even in the terrors of that hour, she did not forget to put in the little package one or two of his favorite toys, reserving a gayly painted parrot to amuse him, when she should be called on to awaken him. It was some trouble to arouse the little sleeper; but, after some effort, he sat up, and was playing with his bird, while his mother was putting on her bonnet and shawl.

"Where are you going, mother?" said he, as she drew near the bed, with his little coat and cap.

His mother drew near, and looked so earnestly into his eyes, that he at once divined that something unusual was the matter.

"Hush, Harry," she said; "musn't speak loud, or they will hear us. A wicked man was coming to take little Harry away from his mother, and carry him 'way off in the dark; but mother won't let him—she's going to put on her little boy's cap and coat, and run off with him, so the ugly man can't catch him."

Saying these words, she had tied and buttoned on the child's simple outfit, and, taking him in her arms, she whispered to him to be very still; and, opening a door in her room which led into the outer verandah, she glided noiselessly out.

It was a sparkling, frosty, star-light night, and the mother wrapped the shawl close round her child, as, perfectly quiet with vague terror, he clung round her neck.

Old Bruno, a great Newfoundland,[2] who slept at the end of the porch, rose, with a low growl, as she came near. She gently spoke his name, and the animal, an old pet and playmate of hers, instantly, wagging his tail, prepared to follow her, though apparently revolving much, in his simple dog's head, what such an indiscreet midnight

2. One of a breed of very large, usually black, shaggy dogs bred in Newfoundland, Canada.

promenade might mean. Some dim ideas of imprudence or impropriety in the measure seemed to embarrass him considerably; for he often stopped, as Eliza glided forward, and looked wistfully, first at her and then at the house, and then, as if reassured by reflection, he pattered along after her again. A few minutes brought them to the window of Uncle Tom's cottage, and Eliza, stopping, tapped lightly on the window-pane.

The prayer-meeting at Uncle Tom's had, in the order of hymn-singing, been protracted to a very late hour; and, as Uncle Tom had indulged himself in a few lengthy solos afterwards, the consequence was, that, although it was now between twelve and one o'clock, he and his worthy helpmeet were not yet asleep.

"Good Lord! what's that?" said Aunt Chloe, starting up and hastily drawing the curtain. "My sakes alive, if it an't Lizy! Get on your clothes, old man, quick!—there's old Bruno, too, a pawin' round; what on airth! I'm gwine to open the door."

And, suiting the action to the word, the door flew open, and the light of the tallow candle, which Tom had hastily lighted, fell on the haggard face and dark, wild eyes of the fugitive.

"Lord bless you!—I'm skeered to look at ye, Lizy! Are ye tuck sick, or what's come over ye?"

"I'm running away—Uncle Tom and Aunt Chloe—carrying off my child—Master sold him!"

"Sold him?" echoed both, lifting up their hands in dismay.

"Yes, sold him!" said Eliza, firmly; "I crept into the closet by Mistress' door to-night, and I heard Master tell Missis that he had sold my Harry, and you, Uncle Tom, both, to a trader; and that he was going off this morning on his horse, and that the man was to take possession to-day."

Tom had stood, during this speech, with his hands raised, and his eyes dilated, like a man in a dream. Slowly and gradually, as its meaning came over him, he collapsed, rather than seated himself, on his old chair, and sunk his head down upon his knees.

"The good Lord have pity on us!" said Aunt Chloe. "O! it don't seem as if it was true! What has he done, that Mas'r should sell *him?*"

"He hasn't done anything,—it isn't for that. Master don't want to sell; and Missis—she's always good. I heard her plead and beg for us; but he told her 'twas no use; that he was in this man's debt, and that this man had got the power over him; and that if he didn't pay him off clear, it would end in his having to sell the place and all the people, and move off. Yes, I heard him say there was no choice between selling these two and selling all, the man was driving him so hard. Master said he was sorry; but oh, Missis—you ought to have heard her talk! If she an't a Christian and an angel, there

Eliza comes to tell Uncle Tom that he is sold, and that she is running away to save her child.

never was one. I'm a wicked girl to leave her so; but, then, I can't help it. She said, herself, one soul was worth more than the world; and this boy has a soul, and if I let him be carried off, who knows what'll become of it? It must be right: but, if it an't right, the Lord forgive me, for I can't help doing it!"

"Well, old man!" said Aunt Chloe, "why don't you go, too? Will you wait to be toted down river, where they kill niggers with hard work and starving? I'd a heap rather die than go there, any day! There's time for ye,—be off with Lizy,—you've got a pass to come and go any time. Come, bustle up, and I'll get your things together."

Tom slowly raised his head, and looked sorrowfully but quietly around, and said,

"No, no—I an't going. Let Eliza go—it's her right! I wouldn't be the one to say no—'t an't in *natur* for her to stay; but you heard what she said! If I must be sold, or all the people on the place, and everything go to rack, why, let me be sold. I s'pose I can b'ar it as well as any on 'em," he added, while something like a sob and a sigh shook his broad, rough chest convulsively. "Mas'r always found me on the spot—he always will. I never have broke trust, nor used my pass no ways contrary to my word, and I never will. It's better for me alone to go, than to break up the place and sell all. Mas'r an't to blame, Chloe, and he'll take care of you and the poor—"

Here he turned to the rough trundle-bed full of little woolly heads, and broke fairly down. He leaned over the back of the chair, and covered his face with his large hands. Sobs, heavy, hoarse and loud, shook the chair, and great tears fell through his fingers on the floor: just such tears, sir, as you dropped into the coffin where lay your first-born son; such tears, woman, as you shed when you heard the cries of your dying babe. For, sir, he was a man,—and you are but another man. And, woman, though dressed in silk and jewels, you are but a woman, and, in life's great straits and mighty griefs, ye feel but one sorrow!

"And now," said Eliza, as she stood in the door, "I saw my husband only this afternoon, and I little knew then what was to come. They have pushed him to the very last standing-place, and he told me, to-day, that he was going to run away. Do try, if you can, to get word to him. Tell him how I went, and why I went; and tell him I'm going to try and find Canada. You must give my love to him, and tell him, if I never see him again,"—she turned away, and stood with her back to them for a moment, and then added, in a husky voice, "tell him to be as good as he can, and try and meet me in the kingdom of heaven."

"Call Bruno in there," she added. "Shut the door on him, poor beast! He mustn't go with me!"

A few last words and tears, a few simple adieus and blessings, and, clasping her wondering and affrighted child in her arms, she glided noiselessly away.

## Chapter VI

### *Discovery*

Mr. and Mrs. Shelby, after their protracted discussion of the night before, did not readily sink to repose, and, in consequence, slept somewhat later than usual, the ensuing morning.

"I wonder what keeps Eliza," said Mrs. Shelby, after giving her bell repeated pulls, to no purpose.

Mr. Shelby was standing before his dressing-glass, sharpening his razor; and just then the door opened, and a colored boy entered, with his shaving-water.

"Andy," said his mistress, "step to Eliza's door, and tell her I have rung for her three times. Poor thing!" she added, to herself, with a sigh.

Andy soon returned, with eyes very wide in astonishment.

"Lor, Missis! Lizy's drawers is all open, and her things all lying every which way; and I believe she's just done clared out!"

The truth flashed upon Mr. Shelby and his wife at the same moment. He exclaimed,

"Then she suspected it, and she's off!"

"The Lord be thanked!" said Mrs. Shelby. "I trust she is."

"Wife, you talk like a fool! Really, it will be something pretty awkward for me, if she is. Haley saw that I hesitated about selling this child, and he'll think I connived at it, to get him out of the way. It touches my honor!" And Mr. Shelby left the room hastily.

There was great running and ejaculating, and opening and shutting of doors, and appearances of faces in all shades of color in different places, for about a quarter of an hour. One person only, who might have shed some light on the matter, was entirely silent, and that was the head cook, Aunt Chloe. Silently, and with a heavy cloud settled down over her once joyous face, she proceeded making out her breakfast biscuits, as if she heard and saw nothing of the excitement around her.

Very soon, about a dozen young imps were roosting, like so many crows, on the verandah railings, each one determined to be the first one to apprize the strange Mas'r of his ill luck.

"He'll be rael mad, I'll be bound," said Andy.

"*Won't* he swar!" said little black Jake.

"Yes, for he *does* swar," said woolly-headed Mandy. "I hearn him yesterday, at dinner. I hearn all about it then, 'cause I got into the closet where Missis keeps the great jugs, and I hearn every word." And Mandy, who had never in her life thought of the meaning of a word she had heard, more than a black cat, now took airs of superior wisdom, and strutted about, forgetting to state that, though actually coiled up among the jugs at the time specified, she had been fast asleep all the time.

When, at last, Haley appeared, booted and spurred, he was saluted with the bad tidings on every hand. The young imps on the verandah were not disappointed in their hope of hearing him "swar," which he did with a fluency and fervency which delighted them all amazingly, as they ducked and dodged hither and thither, to be out of the reach of his riding-whip; and, all whooping off together, they tumbled, in a pile of immeasurable giggle, on the withered turf under the verandah, where they kicked up their heels and shouted to their full satisfaction.

"If I had the little devils!" muttered Haley, between his teeth.

"But you ha'nt got 'em, though!" said Andy, with a triumphant flourish, and making a string of indescribable mouths at the unfortunate trader's back, when he was fairly beyond hearing.

"I say now, Shelby, this yer's a most extro'rnary business!" said Haley, as he abruptly entered the parlor. "It seems that gal's off, with her young un."

"Mr. Haley, Mrs. Shelby is present," said Mr. Shelby.

"I beg pardon, ma'am," said Haley, bowing slightly, with a still lowering brow; "but still I say, as I said before, this yer's a sing'lar report. Is it true, sir?"

"Sir," said Mr. Shelby, "if you wish to communicate with me, you must observe something of the decorum of a gentleman. Andy, take Mr. Haley's hat and riding-whip. Take a seat, sir. Yes, sir; I regret to say that the young woman, excited by overhearing, or having reported to her, something of this business, has taken her child in the night, and made off."

"I did expect fair dealing in this matter, I confess," said Haley.

"Well, sir," said Mr. Shelby, turning sharply round upon him, "what am I to understand by that remark? If any man calls my honor in question, I have but one answer for him."

The trader cowered at this, and in a somewhat lower tone said that "it was plaguy hard on a fellow, that had made a fair bargain, to be gulled that way."

"Mr. Haley," said Mr. Shelby, "if I did not think you had some cause for disappointment, I should not have borne from you the rude and unceremonious style of your entrance into my parlor this morning. I say thus much, however, since appearances call for it, that I shall allow of no insinuations cast upon me, as if I were at all partner to any unfairness in this matter. Moreover, I shall feel bound to give you every assistance, in the use of horses, servants, &c., in the recovery of your property. So, in short, Haley," said he, suddenly dropping from the tone of dignified coolness to his ordinary one of easy frankness, "the best way for you is to keep good-natured and eat some breakfast, and we will then see what is to be done."

Mrs. Shelby now rose, and said her engagements would prevent her being at the breakfast-table that morning; and, deputing a very respectable mulatto woman to attend to the gentlemen's coffee at the sideboard, she left the room.

"Old lady don't like your humble servant, over and above," said Haley, with an uneasy effort to be very familiar.

"I am not accustomed to hear my wife spoken of with such freedom," said Mr. Shelby, dryly.

"Beg pardon; of course, only a joke, you know," said Haley, forcing a laugh.

"Some jokes are less agreeable than others," rejoined Shelby.

"Devilish free, now I've signed those papers, cuss him!" muttered Haley to himself; "quite grand, since yesterday!"

Never did fall of any prime minister at court occasion wider surges of sensation than the report of Tom's fate among his compeers on the place. It was the topic in every mouth, everywhere; and nothing was done in the house or in the field, but to discuss its probable results. Eliza's flight—an unprecedented event on the place—was also a great accessory in stimulating the general excitement.

Black Sam, as he was commonly called, from his being about three shades blacker than any other son of ebony on the place, was revolving the matter profoundly in all its phases and bearings, with a comprehensiveness of vision and a strict look-out to his own personal well-being, that would have done credit to any white patriot in Washington.

"It's an ill wind dat blows nowhar,—dat ar a fact," said Sam, sententiously, giving an additional hoist to his pantaloons, and adroitly substituting a long nail in place of a missing suspender-button, with which effort of mechanical genius he seemed highly delighted.

"Yes, it's an ill wind blows nowhar," he repeated. "Now, dar, Tom's down—wal, course der's room for some nigger to be up—and why not dis nigger?—dat's de idee. Tom, a ridin' round de country—boots blacked—pass in his pocket—all grand as Cuffee[1]—who but he? Now, why shouldn't Sam?—dat's what I want to know."

1. Cuffee or Cuffy was a name given to black men in the South, later generalized to any black male. "Grand as Cuffee" is a version of the patronizing phrase "proud as Cuffy," i.e., proud as an African decked out in gaudy splendor.

"Halloo, Sam—O Sam! Mas'r wants you to cotch Bill and Jerry," said Andy, cutting short Sam's soliloquy.

"High! what's afoot now, young un?"

"Why, you don't know, I s'pose, that Lizy's cut stick,[2] and clared out, with her young un?"

"You teach your granny!" said Sam, with infinite contempt; "knowed it a heap sight sooner than you did; this nigger an't so green, now!"

"Well, anyhow, Mas'r wants Bill and Jerry geared right up; and you and I's to go with Mas'r Haley, to look arter her."

"Good, now! dat's de time o' day!" said Sam. "It's Sam dat's called for in dese yer times. He's de nigger. See if I don't cotch her, now; Mas'r'll see what Sam can do!"

"Ah! but, Sam," said Andy, "you'd better think twice; for Missis don't want her cotched, and she'll be in yer wool."

"High!" said Sam, opening his eyes. "How you know dat?"

"Heard her say so, my own self, dis blessed mornin', when I bring in Mas'r's shaving-water. She sent me to see why Lizy didn't come to dress her; and when I telled her she was off, she jest ris up, and ses she, 'The Lord be praised;' and Mas'r, he seemed rael mad, and ses he, 'Wife, you talk like a fool.' But Lor! she'll bring him to! I knows well enough how that'll be,—it's allers best to stand Missis' side the fence, now I tell yer."

Black Sam, upon this, scratched his woolly pate, which, if it did not contain very profound wisdom, still contained a great deal of a particular species much in demand among politicians of all complexions and countries, and vulgarly denominated "knowing which side the bread is buttered;" so, stopping with grave consideration, he again gave a hitch to his pantaloons, which was his regularly organized method of assisting his mental perplexities.

"Der an't no sayin'—never—'bout no kind o' thing in *dis* yer world," he said, at last.

Sam spoke like a philosopher, emphasizing *this*—as if he had had a large experience in different sorts of worlds, and therefore had come to his conclusions advisedly.

"Now, sartin I'd a said that Missis would a scoured the varsal world after Lizy," added Sam, thoughtfully.

"So she would," said Andy; "but can't ye see through a ladder, ye black nigger? Missis don't want dis yer Mas'r Haley to get Lizy's boy; dat's de go!"

"High!" said Sam, with an indescribable intonation, known only to those who have heard it among the negroes.

2. Departed hastily (from "cut quick sticks").

"And I'll tell yer more'n all," said Andy; "I specs you'd better be making tracks for dem hosses,—mighty sudden, too,—for I hearn Missis 'quirin' arter yer,—so you've stood foolin' long enough."

Sam, upon this, began to bestir himself in real earnest, and after a while appeared, bearing down gloriously towards the house, with Bill and Jerry in a full canter, and adroitly throwing himself off before they had any idea of stopping, he brought them up alongside of the horse-post like a tornado. Haley's horse, which was a skittish young colt, winced, and bounced, and pulled hard at his halter.

"Ho, ho!" said Sam, "skeery, ar ye?" and his black visage lighted up with a curious, mischievous gleam. "I'll fix ye now!" said he.

There was a large beech-tree overshadowing the place, and the small, sharp, triangular beech-nuts lay scattered thickly on the ground. With one of these in his fingers, Sam approached the colt, stroked and patted, and seemed apparently busy in soothing his agitation. On pretence of adjusting the saddle, he adroitly slipped under it the sharp little nut, in such a manner that the least weight brought upon the saddle would annoy the nervous sensibilities of the animal, without leaving any perceptible graze or wound.

"Dar!" he said, rolling his eyes with an approving grin; "me fix 'em!"

At this moment Mrs. Shelby appeared on the balcony, beckoning to him. Sam approached with as good a determination to pay court as did ever suitor after a vacant place at St. James' or Washington.[3]

"Why have you been loitering so, Sam? I sent Andy to tell you to hurry."

"Lord bless you, Missis!" said Sam, "horses won't be cotched all in a mimit; they'd done clared out way down to the south pasture, and the Lord knows whar!"

"Sam, how often must I tell you not to say 'Lord bless you, and the Lord knows,' and such things? It's wicked."

"O, Lord bless my soul! I done forgot, Missis! I won't say nothing of de sort no more."

"Why, Sam, you just *have* said it again."

"Did I? O, Lord! I mean—I didn't go fur to say it."

"You must be *careful*, Sam."

"Just let me get my breath, Missis, and I'll start fair. I'll be berry careful."

"Well, Sam, you are to go with Mr. Haley, to show him the road, and help him. Be careful of the horses, Sam; you know Jerry was a little lame last week; *don't ride them too fast.*"

3. I.e., one who is driven by political or careerist ambitions. St. James, a palace in Westminster, England, was the royal residence from 1697 to 1837; Washington refers to the capital of the United States.

Mrs. Shelby spoke the last words with a low voice, and strong emphasis.

"Let dis child alone for dat!" said Sam, rolling up his eyes with a volume of meaning. "Lord knows! High! Didn't say dat!" said he, suddenly catching his breath, with a ludicrous flourish of apprehension, which made his mistress laugh, spite of herself. "Yes, Missis, I'll look out for de hosses!"

"Now, Andy," said Sam, returning to his stand under the beech-trees, "you see I wouldn't be 'tall surprised if dat ar gen'lman's crittur should gib a fling, by and by, when he comes to be a gettin' up. You know, Andy, critturs *will* do such things;" and therewith Sam poked Andy in the side, in a highly suggestive manner.

"High!" said Andy, with an air of instant appreciation.

"Yes, you see, Andy, Missis wants to make time,—dat ar's clar to der most or'nary 'bserver. I jis make a little for her. Now, you see, get all dese yer hosses loose, caperin' permiscus round dis yer lot and down to de wood dar, and I spec Mas'r won't be off in a hurry."

Andy grinned.

"Yer see," said Sam, "yer see, Andy, if any such thing should happen as that Mas'r Haley's horse *should* begin to act contrary, and cut up, you and I jist lets go of our'n to help him, and *we'll help him*—oh yes!" And Sam and Andy laid their heads back on their shoulders, and broke into a low, immoderate laugh, snapping their fingers and flourishing their heels with exquisite delight.

At this instant, Haley appeared on the verandah. Somewhat mollified by certain cups of very good coffee, he came out smiling and talking, in tolerably restored humor. Sam and Andy, clawing for certain fragmentary palm-leaves,[4] which they were in the habit of considering as hats, flew to the horse-posts, to be ready to "help Mas'r."

Sam's palm-leaf had been ingeniously disentangled from all pretensions to braid, as respects its brim; and the slivers starting apart, and standing upright, gave it a blazing air of freedom and defiance, quite equal to that of any Fejee[5] chief; while the whole brim of Andy's being departed bodily, he rapped the crown on his head with a dexterous thump, and looked about well pleased, as if to say, "Who says I haven't got a hat?"

"Well, boys," said Haley, "look alive now; we must lose no time."

"Not a bit of him, Mas'r!" said Sam, putting Haley's rein in his hand, and holding his stirrup, while Andy was untying the other two horses.

4. Hats woven of palm fibers.
5. Usually *Fiji*, a country occupying a group of islands in the southeast Pacific, north of New Zealand.

The instant Haley touched the saddle, the mettlesome creature bounded from the earth with a sudden spring, that threw his master sprawling, some feet off, on the soft, dry turf. Sam, with frantic ejaculations, made a dive at the reins, but only succeeded in brushing the blazing palm-leaf afore-named into the horse's eyes, which by no means tended to allay the confusion of his nerves. So, with great vehemence, he overturned Sam, and, giving two or three contemptuous snorts, flourished his heels vigorously in the air, and was soon prancing away towards the lower end of the lawn, followed by Bill and Jerry, whom Andy had not failed to let loose, according to contract, speeding them off with various direful ejaculations. And now ensued a miscellaneous scene of confusion. Sam and Andy ran and shouted,—dogs barked here and there,—and Mike, Mose, Mandy, Fanny, and all the smaller specimens on the place, both male and female, raced, clapped hands, whooped, and shouted, with outrageous officiousness and untiring zeal.

Haley's horse, which was a white one, and very fleet and spirited, appeared to enter into the spirit of the scene with great gusto; and having for his coursing ground a lawn of nearly half a mile in extent, gently sloping down on every side into indefinite woodland, he appeared to take infinite delight in seeing how near he could allow his pursuers to approach him, and then, when within a hand's breadth, whisk off with a start and a snort, like a mischievous beast as he was, and career far down into some alley of the wood-lot. Nothing was further from Sam's mind than to have any one of the troop taken until such season as should seem to him most befitting,—and the exertions that he made were certainly most heroic. Like the sword of Cœur De Lion,[6] which always blazed in the front and thickest of the battle, Sam's palm-leaf was to be seen everywhere when there was the least danger that a horse could be caught;—there he would bear down full tilt, shouting, "Now for it! cotch him! cotch him!" in a way that would set everything to indiscriminate rout in a moment.

Haley ran up and down, and cursed and swore and stamped miscellaneously. Mr. Shelby in vain tried to shout directions from the balcony, and Mrs. Shelby from her chamber window alternately laughed and wondered,—not without some inkling of what lay at the bottom of all this confusion.

At last, about twelve o'clock, Sam appeared triumphant, mounted on Jerry, with Haley's horse by his side, reeking with sweat, but with flashing eyes and dilated nostrils, showing that the spirit of freedom had not yet entirely subsided.

6. King Richard I of England (1157–1199), called Richard Lion-Heart.

"He's cotched!" he exclaimed, triumphantly. "If't hadn't been for me, they might a bust theirselves, all on 'em; but I cotched him!"

"You!" growled Haley, in no amiable mood. "If it hadn't been for you, this never would have happened."

"Lord bless us, Mas'r," said Sam, in a tone of the deepest concern, "and me that has been racin' and chasin' till the swet jest pours off me!"

"Well, well!" said Haley, "you've lost me near three hours, with your cursed nonsense. Now let's be off, and have no more fooling."

"Why, Mas'r," said Sam, in a deprecating tone, "I believe you mean to kill us all clar, horses and all. Here we are all just ready to drop down, and the critters all in a reek of sweat. Why, Mas'r won't think of startin' on now till arter dinner. Mas'r's hoss wants rubben down; see how he splashed hisself; and Jerry limps too; don't think Missis would be willin' to have us start dis yer way, no how. Lord bless you, Mas'r, we can ketch up, if we do stop. Lizy never was no great of a walker."

Mrs. Shelby, who, greatly to her amusement, had overheard this conversation from the verandah, now resolved to do her part. She came forward, and, courteously expressing her concern for Haley's accident, pressed him to stay to dinner, saying that the cook should bring it on the table immediately.

Thus, all things considered, Haley, with rather an equivocal grace, proceeded to the parlor, while Sam, rolling his eyes after him with unutterable meaning, proceeded gravely with the horses to the stable-yard.

"Did yer see him, Andy? *did* yer see him?" said Sam, when he had got fairly beyond the shelter of the barn, and fastened the horse to a post. "O, Lor, if it warn't as good as a meetin', now, to see him a dancin' and kickin' and swarin' at us. Didn't I hear him? Swar away, ole fellow (says I to myself); will yer have yer hoss now, or wait till you cotch him? (says I). Lor, Andy, I think I can see him now." And Sam and Andy leaned up against the barn, and laughed to their hearts' content.

"Yer oughter seen how mad he looked, when I brought the hoss up. Lord, he'd a killed me, if he durs' to; and there I was a standin' as innercent and as humble."

"Lor, I seed you," said Andy; "an't you an old hoss, Sam?"

"Rather specks I am," said Sam; "did yer see Missis up stars at the winder? I seed her laughin'."

"I'm sure, I was racin' so, I didn't see nothing," said Andy.

"Well, yer see," said Sam, proceeding gravely to wash down Haley's pony, "I'se 'quired what yer may call a habit o' *bobservation*, Andy. It's a very 'portant habit, Andy; and I 'commend yer to be cultivatin' it, now yer young. Hist up that hind foot, Andy. Yer see, Andy, it's *bobservation* makes all de difference in niggers. Didn't I see which way the wind blew dis yer mornin'? Didn't I see what Missis wanted, though she never let on? Dat ar's bobservation, Andy. I 'spects it's what you may call a faculty. Faculties is different in different peoples, but cultivation of 'em goes a great way."

"I guess if I hadn't helped your bobservation dis mornin', yer wouldn't have seen your way so smart," said Andy.

"Andy," said Sam, "you's a promisin' child, der an't no manner o' doubt. I thinks lots of yer, Andy; and I don't feel no ways ashamed to take idees from you. We oughtenter overlook nobody, Andy, cause the smartest on us gets tripped up sometimes. And so, Andy, let's go up to the house now. I'll be boun' Missis'll give us an uncommon good bite, dis yer time."

# Chapter VII

## *The Mother's Struggle*

It is impossible to conceive of a human creature more wholly desolate and forlorn than Eliza, when she turned her footsteps from Uncle Tom's cabin.

Her husband's suffering and dangers, and the danger of her child, all blended in her mind, with a confused and stunning sense of the risk she was running, in leaving the only home she had ever known, and cutting loose from the protection of a friend whom she loved and revered. Then there was the parting from every familiar object,—the place where she had grown up, the trees under which she had played, the groves where she had walked many an evening in happier days, by the side of her young husband,—everything, as it lay in the clear, frosty starlight, seemed to speak reproachfully to her, and ask her whither could she go from a home like that?

But stronger than all was maternal love, wrought into a paroxysm of frenzy by the near approach of a fearful danger. Her boy was old enough to have walked by her side, and, in an indifferent case, she would only have led him by the hand; but now the bare thought of putting him out of her arms made her shudder, and she strained him to her bosom with a convulsive grasp, as she went rapidly forward.

The frosty ground creaked beneath her feet, and she trembled at the sound; every quaking leaf and fluttering shadow sent the blood backward to her heart, and quickened her footsteps. She wondered within herself at the strength that seemed to be come upon her; for she felt the weight of her boy as if it had been a feather, and every flutter of fear seemed to increase the supernatural power that bore her on, while from her pale lips burst forth, in frequent ejaculations, the prayer to a Friend above—"Lord, help! Lord, save me!"

If it were *your* Harry, mother, or your Willie, that were going to be torn from you by a brutal trader, to-morrow morning,—if you had seen the man, and heard that the papers were signed and delivered, and you had only from twelve o'clock till morning to make good your escape,—how fast could *you* walk? How many miles could you make in those few brief hours, with the darling at your bosom,—the little sleepy head on your shoulder,—the small, soft arms trustingly holding on to your neck?

For the child slept. At first, the novelty and alarm kept him waking; but his mother so hurriedly repressed every breath or sound, and so assured him that if he were only still she would certainly save him, that he clung quietly round her neck, only asking, as he found himself sinking to sleep,

"Mother, I don't need to keep awake, do I?"

"No, my darling; sleep, if you want to."

"But, mother, if I do get asleep, you won't let him get me?"

"No! so may God help me!" said his mother, with a paler cheek, and a brighter light in her large dark eyes.

"You're *sure*, an't you, mother?"

"Yes, *sure!*" said the mother, in a voice that startled herself; for it seemed to her to come from a spirit within, that was no part of her; and the boy dropped his little weary head on her shoulder, and was soon asleep. How the touch of those warm arms, the gentle breathings that came in her neck, seemed to add fire and spirit to her movements! It seemed to her as if strength poured into her in electric streams, from every gentle touch and movement of the sleeping, confiding child. Sublime is the dominion of the mind over the body, that, for a time, can make flesh and nerve impregnable, and string the sinews like steel, so that the weak become so mighty.

The boundaries of the farm, the grove, the wood-lot, passed by her dizzily, as she walked on; and still she went, leaving one familiar object after another, slacking not, pausing not, till reddening daylight found her many a long mile from all traces of any familiar objects upon the open highway.

She had often been, with her mistress, to visit some connections, in the little village of T——, not far from the Ohio river, and knew the road well. To go thither, to escape across the Ohio river, were the first hurried outlines of her plan of escape; beyond that, she could only hope in God.

When horses and vehicles began to move along the highway, with that alert perception peculiar to a state of excitement, and which seems to be a sort of inspiration, she became aware that her headlong pace and distracted air might bring on her remark and suspicion. She therefore put the boy on the ground, and, adjusting her dress and bonnet, she walked on at as rapid a pace as she thought consistent with the preservation of appearances. In her little bundle she had provided a store of cakes and apples, which she used as expedients for quickening the speed of the child, rolling the apple some yards before them, when the boy would run with all his might after it; and this ruse, often repeated, carried them over many a half-mile.

After a while, they came to a thick patch of woodland, through which murmured a clear brook. As the child complained of hunger and thirst, she climbed over the fence with him; and, sitting down behind a large rock which concealed them from the road, she gave him a breakfast out of her little package. The boy wondered and grieved that she could not eat; and when, putting his arms round her neck, he tried to wedge some of his cake into her mouth, it seemed to her that the rising in her throat would choke her.

"No, no, Harry darling! mother can't eat till you are safe! We must go on—on—till we come to the river!" And she hurried again into the road, and again constrained herself to walk regularly and composedly forward.

She was many miles past any neighborhood where she was personally known. If she should chance to meet any who knew her, she reflected that the well-known kindness of the family would be of itself a blind to suspicion, as making it an unlikely supposition that she could be a fugitive. As she was also so white as not to be known as of colored lineage, without a critical survey, and her child was white also, it was much easier for her to pass on unsuspected.

On this presumption, she stopped at noon at a neat farmhouse, to rest herself, and buy some dinner for her child and self;[1] for, as the danger decreased with the distance, the supernatural tension of the nervous system lessened, and she found herself both weary and hungry.

The good woman, kindly and gossipping, seemed rather pleased than otherwise with having somebody come in to talk with; and accepted, without examination, Eliza's statement, that she "was going on a little piece, to spend a week with her friends,"—all which she hoped in her heart might prove strictly true.

An hour before sunset, she entered the village of T——, by the Ohio river, weary and foot-sore, but still strong in heart. Her first glance was at the river, which lay, like Jordan, between her and the Canaan of liberty on the other side.

It was now early spring, and the river was swollen and turbulent; great cakes of floating ice were swinging heavily to and fro in the turbid waters. Owing to the peculiar form of the shore on the

1. Slaves on occasion were able to earn money from being "hired out" by their masters to a private employer; in such cases, master and slave sometimes divided the slave's wages.

Kentucky side, the land bending far out into the water, the ice had been lodged and detained in great quantities, and the narrow channel which swept round the bend was full of ice, piled one cake over another, thus forming a temporary barrier to the descending ice, which lodged, and formed a great, undulating raft, filling up the whole river, and extending almost to the Kentucky shore.

Eliza stood, for a moment, contemplating this unfavorable aspect of things, which she saw at once must prevent the usual ferry-boat from running, and then turned into a small public house on the bank, to make a few inquiries.

The hostess, who was busy in various fizzing and stewing operations over the fire, preparatory to the evening meal, stopped, with a fork in her hand, as Eliza's sweet and plaintive voice arrested her.

"What is it?" she said.

"Isn't there any ferry or boat, that takes people over to B——, now?" she said.

"No, indeed!" said the woman; "the boats has stopped running."

Eliza's look of dismay and disappointment struck the woman, and she said, inquiringly,

"May be you're wanting to get over?—anybody sick? Ye seem mighty anxious?"

"I've got a child that's very dangerous," said Eliza. "I never heard of it till last night, and I've walked quite a piece to-day, in hopes to get to the ferry."

"Well, now, that's onlucky," said the woman, whose motherly sympathies were much aroused; "I'm re'lly consarned for ye. Solomon!" she called, from the window, towards a small back building. A man, in leather apron and very dirty hands, appeared at the door.

"I say, Sol," said the woman, "is that ar man going to tote them bar'ls over to-night?"

"He said he should try, if't was any way prudent," said the man.

"There's a man a piece down here, that's going over with some truck this evening, if he durs'to; he'll be in here to supper to-night, so you'd better set down and wait. That's a sweet little fellow," added the woman, offering him a cake.

But the child, wholly exhausted, cried with weariness.

"Poor fellow! he isn't used to walking, and I've hurried him on so," said Eliza.

"Well, take him into this room," said the woman, opening into a small bed-room, where stood a comfortable bed. Eliza laid the weary boy upon it, and held his hands in hers till he was fast asleep. For her there was no rest. As a fire in her bones, the thought of the pursuer urged her on; and she gazed with longing eyes on the sullen, surging waters that lay between her and liberty.

Here we must take our leave of her for the present, to follow the course of her pursuers.

Though Mrs. Shelby had promised that the dinner should be hurried on table, yet it was soon seen, as the thing has often been seen before, that it required more than one to make a bargain. So, although the order was fairly given out in Haley's hearing, and carried to Aunt Chloe by at least half a dozen juvenile messengers, that dignitary only gave certain very gruff snorts, and tosses of her head, and went on with every operation in an unusually leisurely and circumstantial manner.

For some singular reason, an impression seemed to reign among the servants generally that Missis would not be particularly disobliged by delay; and it was wonderful what a number of counter accidents occurred constantly, to retard the course of things. One luckless wight contrived to upset the gravy; and then gravy had to be got up *de novo*,[2] with due care and formality, Aunt Chloe watching and stirring with dogged precision, answering shortly, to all suggestions of haste, that she "warn't a going to have raw gravy on the table, to help nobody's catchings." One tumbled down with the water, and had to go to the spring for more; and another precipitated the butter into the path of events; and there was from time to time giggling news brought into the kitchen that "Mas'r Haley was mighty oneasy, and that he couldn't sit in his cheer no ways, but was a walkin' and stalkin' to the winders and through the porch."

"Sarves him right!" said Aunt Chloe, indignantly. "He'll get wus nor oneasy, one of these days, if he don't mend his ways. *His* master'll be sending for him, and then see how he'll look!"

"He'll go to torment, and no mistake," said little Jake.

"He desarves it!" said Aunt Chloe, grimly; "he's broke a many, many, many hearts,—I tell ye all!" she said, stopping, with a fork uplifted in her hands; "it's like what Mas'r George reads in Ravelations,—souls a callin' under the altar![3] and a callin' on the Lord for vengeance on sich!—and by and by the Lord he'll hear 'em—so he will!"

Aunt Chloe, who was much revered in the kitchen, was listened to with open mouth; and, the dinner being now fairly sent in, the

2. Once more; anew (Latin).
3. In the Book of Revelation, on Judgment Day the Lamb of God (Christ) opens the seven seals of a book one by one: "And when he had opened the fifth seal, I saw under the altar the souls of them that were slain for the word of God, and for the testimony which they held: And they cried with a loud voice, saying, How long, O lord, holy and true, dost thou not judge and avenge our blood on them that dwell on the earth?" (Revelation 6.9–10).

whole kitchen was at leisure to gossip with her, and to listen to her remarks.

"Sich 'll be burnt up forever, and no mistake; won't ther?" said Andy.

"I'd be glad to see it, I'll be boun'," said little Jake.

"Chil'en!" said a voice, that made them all start. It was Uncle Tom, who had come in, and stood listening to the conversation at the door.

"Chil'en!" he said, "I'm afeard you don't know what ye're sayin'. Forever is a *dre'ful* word, chil'en; it's awful to think on 't. You oughtenter wish that ar to any human crittur."

"We wouldn't to anybody but the soul-drivers," said Andy; "nobody can help wishing it to them, they's so awful wicked."

"Don't natur herself kinder cry out on em?" said Aunt Chloe. "Don't dey tear der suckin' baby right off his mother's breast, and sell him, and der little children as is crying and holding on by her clothes,—don't dey pull 'em off and sells em? Don't dey tear wife and husband apart?" said Aunt Chloe, beginning to cry, "when it's jest takin' the very life on 'em?—and all the while does they feel one bit,—don't dey drink and smoke, and take it oncommon easy? Lor, if the devil don't get them, what's he good for?" And Aunt Chloe covered her face with her checked apron, and began to sob in good earnest.

"Pray for them that 'spitefully use you, the good book says,"[4] says Tom.

"Pray for 'em!" said Aunt Chloe; "Lor, it's too tough! I can't pray for 'em."

"It's natur, Chloe, and natur's strong," said Tom, "but the Lord's grace is stronger; besides, you oughter think what an awful state a poor crittur's soul's in that'll do them ar things,—you oughter thank God that you an't *like* him, Chloe. I'm sure I'd rather be sold, ten thousand times over, than to have all that ar poor crittur's got to answer for."

"So'd I, a heap," said Jake. "Lor, *shouldn't* we cotch it, Andy?"

Andy shrugged his shoulders, and gave an acquiescent whistle.

"I'm glad Mas'r didn't go off this morning, as he looked to," said Tom; "that ar hurt me more than sellin', it did. Mebbe it might have been natural for him, but 't would have come desp't hard on me, as has known him from a baby; but I've seen Mas'r, and I begin ter feel sort o' reconciled to the Lord's will now. Mas'r couldn't help hisself; he did right, but I'm feared things will be kinder goin' to rack, when I'm gone. Mas'r can't be spected to be a pryin' round everywhar, as I've done, a keepin' up all the ends. The boys all means well, but they's powerful car'less. That ar troubles me."

4. Matthew 5.44–8.

The bell here rang, and Tom was summoned to the parlor.

"Tom," said his master, kindly, "I want you to notice that I give this gentleman bonds to forfeit a thousand dollars if you are not on the spot when he wants you; he's going to-day to look after his other business, and you can have the day to yourself. Go anywhere you like, boy."

"Thank you, Mas'r," said Tom.

"And mind yerself," said the trader, "and don't come it over your master with any o' yer nigger tricks; for I'll take every cent out of him, if you an't thar. If he'd hear to me, he wouldn't trust any on ye—slippery as eels!"

"Mas'r," said Tom,—and he stood very straight,—"I was jist eight years old when ole Missis put you into my arms, and you wasn't a year old. 'Thar,' says she, 'Tom, that's to be *your* young Mas'r; take good care on him,' says she. And now I jist ask you, Mas'r, have I ever broke word to you, or gone contrary to you, 'specially since I was a Christian?"

Mr. Shelby was fairly overcome, and the tears rose to his eyes.

"My good boy," said he, "the Lord knows you say but the truth; and if I was able to help it, all the world shouldn't buy you."

"And sure as I am a Christian woman," said Mrs. Shelby, "you shall be redeemed as soon as I can any way bring together means. Sir," she said to Haley, "take good account of who you sell him to, and let me know."

"Lor, yes, for that matter," said the trader, "I may bring him up in a year, not much the wuss for wear, and trade him back."

"I'll trade with you then, and make it for your advantage," said Mrs. Shelby.

"Of course," said the trader, "all's equal with me; li'ves trade 'em up as down, so I does a good business. All I want is a livin', you know, ma'am; that's all any on us wants, I s'pose."

Mr. and Mrs. Shelby both felt annoyed and degraded by the familiar impudence of the trader, and yet both saw the absolute necessity of putting a constraint on their feelings. The more hopelessly sordid and insensible he appeared, the greater became Mrs. Shelby's dread of his succeeding in recapturing Eliza and her child, and of course the greater her motive for detaining him by every female artifice. She therefore graciously smiled, assented, chatted familiarly, and did all she could to make time pass imperceptibly.

At two o'clock Sam and Andy brought the horses up to the posts, apparently greatly refreshed and invigorated by the scamper of the morning.

Sam was there new oiled from dinner, with an abundance of zealous and ready officiousness. As Haley approached, he was boasting, in flourishing style, to Andy, of the evident and eminent success of the operation, now that he had "farly come to it."

"Your master, I s'pose, don't keep no dogs," said Haley, thoughtfully, as he prepared to mount.

"Heaps on 'em," said Sam, triumphantly; "thar's Bruno—he's a roarer! and, besides that, 'bout every nigger of us keeps a pup of some natur or uther."

"Poh!" said Haley,—and he said something else, too, with regard to the said dogs, at which Sam muttered,

"I don't see no use cussin' on 'em, no way."

"But your master don't keep no dogs (I pretty much know he don't) for trackin' out niggers."

Sam knew exactly what he meant, but he kept on a look of earnest and desperate simplicity.

"Our dogs all smells round considable sharp. I spect they's the kind, though they han't never had no practice. They's *far* dogs, though, at most anything, if you'd get 'em started. Here, Bruno," he called, whistling to the lumbering Newfoundland, who came pitching tumultuously toward them.

"You go hang!" said Haley, getting up. "Come, tumble up now."

Sam tumbled up accordingly, dexterously contriving to tickle Andy as he did so, which occasioned Andy to split out into a laugh, greatly to Haley's indignation, who made a cut at him with his riding-whip.

"I's 'stonished at yer, Andy," said Sam, with awful gravity. "This yer's a seris bisness, Andy. Yer mustn't be a makin' game. This yer an't no way to help Mas'r."

"I shall take the straight road to the river," said Haley, decidedly, after they had come to the boundaries of the estate. "I know the way of all of 'em,—they makes tracks for the underground."

"Sartin," said Sam, "dat's de idee. Mas'r Haley hits de thing right in de middle. Now, der's two roads to de river,—de dirt road and der pike,—which Mas'r mean to take?"

Andy looked up innocently at Sam, surprised at hearing this new geographical fact, but instantly confirmed what he said, by a vehement reiteration.

"Cause," said Sam, "I'd rather be 'clined to 'magine that Lizy'd take de dirt road, bein' it 's the least travelled."

Haley, notwithstanding that he was a very old bird, and naturally inclined to be suspicious of chaff, was rather brought up by this view of the case.

"If yer warn't both on yer such cussed liars, now!" he said, contemplatively, as he pondered a moment.

The pensive, reflective tone in which this was spoken appeared to amuse Andy prodigiously, and he drew a little behind, and shook so as apparently to run a great risk of falling off his horse, while Sam's face was immovably composed into the most doleful gravity.

"Course," said Sam, "Mas'r can do as he 'd ruther; go de straight road, if Mas'r thinks best,—it's all one to us. Now, when I study 'pon it, I think de straight road do best, *deridedly*."

"She would naturally go a lonesome way," said Haley, thinking aloud, and not minding Sam's remark.

"Dar an't no sayin'," said Sam; "gals is pecular; they never does nothin' ye thinks they will; mose gen'lly the contrar. Gals is nat'lly made contrary; and so, if you thinks they've gone one road, it is sartin you'd better go t' other, and then you'll be sure to find 'em. Now, my private 'pinion is, Lizy took der dirt road; so I think we'd better take de straight one."

This profound generic view of the female sex did not seem to dispose Haley particularly to the straight road; and he announced decidedly that he should go the other, and asked Sam when they should come to it.

"A little piece ahead," said Sam, giving a wink to Andy with the eye which was on Andy's side of the head; and he added, gravely, "but I've studded on de matter, and I'm quite clar we ought not to go dat ar way. I nebber been over it no way. It's despit lonesome, and we might lose our way,—whar we'd come to, de Lord only knows."

"Nevertheless," said Haley, "I shall go that way."

"Now I think on 't, I think I hearn 'em tell that dat ar road was all fenced up and down by der creek, and thar, an't it, Andy?"

Andy wasn't certain; he'd only "hearn tell" about that road, but never been over it. In short, he was strictly noncommittal.

Haley, accustomed to strike the balance of probabilities between lies of greater or lesser magnitude, thought that it lay in favor of the dirt road aforesaid. The mention of the thing he thought he perceived was involuntary on Sam's part at first, and his confused attempts to dissuade him he set down to a desperate lying on second thoughts, as being unwilling to implicate Eliza.

When, therefore, Sam indicated the road, Haley plunged briskly into it, followed by Sam and Andy.

Now, the road, in fact, was an old one, that had formerly been a thoroughfare to the river, but abandoned for many years after the laying of the new pike. It was open for about an hour's ride, and after that it was cut across by various farms and fences. Sam knew this fact perfectly well,—indeed, the road had been so long closed up, that Andy had never heard of it. He therefore rode along with an air of dutiful submission, only groaning and vociferating occasionally that 't was "desp't rough, and bad for Jerry's foot."

"Now, I jest give yer warning," said Haley, "I know yer; yer won't get me to turn off this yer road, with all yer fussin'—so you shet up!"

"Mas'r will go his own way!" said Sam, with rueful submission, at the same time winking most portentously to Andy, whose delight was now very near the explosive point.

Sam was in wonderful spirits,—professed to keep a very brisk look out,—at one time exclaiming that he saw "a gal's bonnet" on the top of some distant eminence, or calling to Andy "if that thar wasn't 'Lizy' down in the hollow;" always making these exclamations in some rough or craggy part of the road, where the sudden quickening of speed was a special inconvenience to all parties concerned, and thus keeping Haley in a state of constant commotion.

After riding about an hour in this way, the whole party made a precipitate and tumultuous descent into a barn-yard belonging to a large farming establishment. Not a soul was in sight, all the hands being employed in the fields; but, as the barn stood conspicuously and plainly square across the road, it was evident that their journey in that direction had reached a decided finale.

"Wan't dat ar what I telled Mas'r?" said Sam, with an air of injured innocence. "How does strange gentleman spect to know more about a country dan de natives born and raised?"

"You rascal!" said Haley, "you knew all about this."

"Didn't I tell yer I *know'd*, and yer wouldn't believe me? I telled Mas'r 't was all shet up, and fenced up, and I didn't spect we could get through,—Andy heard me."

It was all too true to be disputed, and the unlucky man had to pocket his wrath with the best grace he was able, and all three faced to the right about, and took up their line of march for the highway.

In consequence of all the various delays, it was about three-quarters of an hour after Eliza had laid her child to sleep in the village tavern that the party came riding into the same place. Eliza was standing by the window, looking out in another direction, when Sam's quick eye caught a glimpse of her. Haley and Andy were two yards behind. At this crisis, Sam contrived to have his hat blown off, and uttered a loud and characteristic ejaculation, which startled her at once; she drew suddenly back; the whole train swept by the window, round to the front door.

A thousand lives seemed to be concentrated in that one moment to Eliza. Her room opened by a side door to the river. She caught her child, and sprang down the steps towards it. The trader caught a full glimpse of her, just as she was disappearing down the bank; and throwing himself from his horse, and calling loudly on Sam and Andy, he was after her like a hound after a deer. In that dizzy moment her feet to her scarce seemed to touch the ground, and a moment brought her to the water's edge. Right on behind they came; and, nerved with strength such as God gives only to the desperate, with one wild cry and flying leap, she vaulted sheer over the turbid current by the shore, on to the raft of ice beyond. It was a desperate leap—impossible to anything but madness and despair; and Haley, Sam, and Andy, instinctively cried out, and lifted up their hands, as she did it.

The huge green fragment of ice on which she alighted pitched and creaked as her weight came on it, but she staid there not a moment. With wild cries and desperate energy she leaped to another and still another cake;—stumbling—leaping—slipping—springing upwards again! Her shoes are gone—her stockings cut from her feet—while blood marked every step; but she saw nothing, felt nothing, till dimly, as in a dream, she saw the Ohio side, and a man helping her up the bank.

"Yer a brave gal, now, whoever ye ar!" said the man, with an oath.

Eliza recognized the voice and face of a man who owned a farm not far from her old home.

"O, Mr. Symmes!—save me—do save me—do hide me!" said Eliza.

"Why, what's this?" said the man. "Why, if 'tan't Shelby's gal!"

"My child!—this boy!—he'd sold him! There is his Mas'r," said she, pointing to the Kentucky shore. "O, Mr. Symmes, you've got a little boy!"

"So I have," said the man, as he roughly, but kindly, drew her up the steep bank. "Besides, you're a right brave gal. I like grit, wherever I see it."

When they had gained the top of the bank, the man paused.

"I'd be glad to do something for ye," said he; "but then there's nowhar I could take ye. The best I can do is to tell ye to go *thar,*" said he, pointing to a large white house which stood by itself, off the main street of the village. "Go thar; they're kind folks. Thar's no kind o' danger but they'll help you,—they're up to all that sort o' thing."

"The Lord bless you!" said Eliza, earnestly.

"No 'casion, no 'casion in the world," said the man. "What I've done's of no 'count."

"And, oh, surely, sir, you won't tell any one!"

"Go to thunder, gal! What do you take a feller for? In course not," said the man. "Come, now, go along like a likely, sensible gal, as you are. You've arnt your liberty, and you shall have it, for all me."

The woman folded her child to her bosom, and walked firmly and swiftly away. The man stood and looked after her.

"Shelby, now, mebbe won't think this yer the most neighborly thing in the world; but what's a feller to do? If he catches one of my gals in the same fix, he's welcome to pay back. Somehow I never could see no kind o' critter a strivin' and pantin', and trying to clar theirselves, with the dogs arter 'em, and go agin 'em. Besides, I don't see no kind of 'casion for me to be hunter and catcher for other folks, neither."

So spoke this poor, heathenish Kentuckian, who had not been instructed in his constitutional relations,[5] and consequently was betrayed into acting in a sort of Christianized manner, which, if he had been better situated and more enlightened, he would not have been left to do.

Haley had stood a perfectly amazed spectator of the scene, till Eliza had disappeared up the bank, when he turned a blank, inquiring look on Sam and Andy.

"That ar was a tolable fair stroke of business," said Sam.

"The gal's got seven devils in her, I believe!" said Haley. "How like a wildcat she jumped!"

"Wal, now," said Sam, scratching his head, "I hope Mas'r'll 'scuse us tryin' dat ar road. Don't think I feel spry enough for dat ar, no way!" and Sam gave a hoarse chuckle.

"*You* laugh!" said the trader, with a growl.

"Lord bless you, Mas'r, I couldn't help it, now," said Sam, giving way to the long pent-up delight of his soul. "She looked so curi's, a leapin' and springin'—ice a crackin'—and only to hear her,—plump! ker chunk! ker splash! Spring! Lord! how she goes it!" and Sam and Andy laughed till the tears rolled down their cheeks.

"I'll make ye laugh t'other side yer mouths!" said the trader, laying about their heads with his riding-whip.

Both ducked, and ran shouting up the bank, and were on their horses before he was up.

"Good-evening, Mas'r!" said Sam, with much gravity. "I berry much spect Missis be anxious 'bout Jerry. Mas'r Haley won't want us no longer. Missis wouldn't hear of our ridin' the critters over Lizy's bridge to-night;" and, with a facetious poke into Andy's ribs, he started off, followed by the latter, at full speed,—their shouts of laughter coming faintly on the wind.

# Chapter VIII

## *Eliza's Escape*

Eliza made her desperate retreat across the river just in the dusk of twilight. The gray mist of evening, rising slowly from the river, enveloped her as she disappeared up the bank, and the swollen current and floundering masses of ice presented a hopeless barrier between her and her pursuer. Haley therefore slowly and discontentedly returned to the little tavern, to ponder further what was to be done.

5. Probably a reference to fugitive slave policies.

The woman opened to him the door of a little parlor, covered with a rag carpet, where stood a table with a very shining black oil-cloth, sundry lank, high-backed wood chairs, with some plaster images in resplendent colors on the mantel-shelf, above a very dimly-smoking grate; a long hard-wood settle extended its uneasy length by the chimney, and here Haley sat him down to meditate on the instability of human hopes and happiness in general.

"What did I want with the little cuss, now," he said to himself, "that I should have got myself treed like a coon, as I am, this yer way?" and Haley relieved himself by repeating over a not very select litany of imprecations on himself, which, though there was the best possible reason to consider them as true, we shall, as a matter of taste, omit.

He was startled by the loud and dissonant voice of a man who was apparently dismounting at the door. He hurried to the window.

"By the land! if this yer an't the nearest, now, to what I've heard folks call Providence," said Haley. "I do b'lieve that ar's Tom Loker."

Haley hastened out. Standing by the bar, in the corner of the room, was a brawny, muscular man, full six feet in height, and broad in proportion. He was dressed in a coat of buffalo-skin, made with the hair outward, which gave him a shaggy and fierce appearance, perfectly in keeping with the whole air of his physiognomy. In the head and face every organ and lineament expressive of brutal and unhesitating violence was in a state of the highest possible development. Indeed, could our readers fancy a bull-dog come unto man's estate, and walking about in a hat and coat, they would have no unapt idea of the general style and effect of his physique. He was accompanied by a travelling companion, in many respects an exact contrast to himself. He was short and slender, lithe and cat-like in his motions, and had a peering, mousing expression about his keen black eyes, with which every feature of his face seemed sharpened into sympathy; his thin, long nose, ran out as if it was eager to bore into the nature of things in general; his sleek, thin, black hair was stuck eagerly forward, and all his motions and evolutions expressed a dry, cautious acuteness. The great big man poured out a big tumbler half full of raw spirits, and gulped it down without a word. The little man stood tip-toe, and putting his head first to one side and then to the other, and snuffing considerately in the directions of the various bottles, ordered at last a mint julep, in a thin and quivering voice, and with an air of great circumspection. When poured out, he took it and looked at it with a sharp, complacent air, like a man who thinks he has done about the right thing, and hit the nail on the head, and proceeded to dispose of it in short and well-advised sips.

"Wal, now, who'd a thought this yer luck 'ad come to me? Why, Loker, how are ye?" said Haley, coming forward, and extending his hand to the big man.

"The devil!" was the civil reply. "What brought you here, Haley?"

The mousing man, who bore the name of Marks, instantly stopped his sipping, and, poking his head forward, looked shrewdly on the new acquaintance, as a cat sometimes looks at a moving dry leaf, or some other possible object of pursuit.

"I say, Tom, this yer's the luckiest thing in the world. I'm in a devil of a hobble, and you must help me out."

"Ugh? aw! like enough!" grunted his complacent acquaintance. "A body may be pretty sure of that, when *you're* glad to see 'em; something to be made off of 'em. What's the blow now?"

"You've got a friend here?" said Haley, looking doubtfully at Marks; "partner, perhaps?"

"Yes, I have. Here, Marks! here's that ar feller that I was in with in Natchez."

"Shall be pleased with his acquaintance," said Marks, thrusting out a long, thin hand, like a raven's claw. "Mr. Haley, I believe?"

"The same, sir," said Haley. "And now, gentlemen, seein' as we've met so happily, I think I'll stand up to a small matter of a treat in this here parlor. So, now, old coon," said he to the man at the bar, "get us hot water, and sugar, and cigars, and plenty of the *real stuff*, and we'll have a blow-out."

Behold, then, the candles lighted, the fire stimulated to the burning point in the grate, and our three worthies seated round a table, well spread with all the accessories to good fellowship enumerated before.

Haley began a pathetic recital of his peculiar troubles. Loker shut up his mouth, and listened to him with gruff and surly attention. Marks, who was anxiously and with much fidgeting compounding a tumbler of punch to his own peculiar taste, occasionally looked up from his employment, and, poking his sharp nose and chin almost into Haley's face, gave the most earnest heed to the whole narrative. The conclusion of it appeared to amuse him extremely, for he shook his shoulders and sides in silence, and perked up his thin lips with an air of great internal enjoyment.

"So, then, ye'r fairly sewed up, an't ye?" he said; "he! he! he! It's neatly done, too."

"This yer young-un business makes lots of trouble in the trade," said Haley, dolefully.

"If we could get a breed of gals that didn't care, now, for their young uns," said Marks; "tell ye, I think 't would be 'bout the greatest mod'rn improvement I knows on,"—and Marks patronized his joke by a quiet introductory sniggle.

"Jes so," said Haley; "I never couldn't see into it; young uns is heaps of trouble to 'em; one would think, now, they'd be glad to get clar on 'em; but they arn't. And the more trouble a young un is, and the more good for nothing, as a gen'l thing, the tighter they sticks to 'em."

"Wal, Mr. Haley," said Marks, "jest pass the hot water. Yes, sir; you say jest what I feel and all'us have. Now, I bought a gal once, when I was in the trade,—a tight, likely wench she was, too, and quite considerable smart,—and she had a young un that was mis'able sickly; it had a crooked back, or something or other; and I jest gin't away to a man that thought he'd take his chance raising on 't, being it didn't cost nothin';—never thought, yer know, of the gal's takin' on about it,—but, Lord, yer oughter seen how she went on. Why, re'lly, she did seem to me to valley the child more 'cause *'t was* sickly and cross, and plagued her; and she warn't making b'lieve, neither,—cried about it, she did, and lopped round, as if she'd lost every friend she had. It re'lly was droll to think on 't. Lord, there an't no end to women's notions."

"Wal, jest so with me," said Haley. "Last summer, down on Red river, I got a gal traded off on me, with a likely lookin' child enough, and his eyes looked as bright as yourn; but, come to look, I found him stone blind.[1] Fact—he was stone blind. Wal, ye see, I thought there warn't no harm in my jest passing him along, and not sayin' nothin'; and I'd got him nicely swapped off for a keg o' whiskey; but come to get him away from the gal, she was jest like a tiger. So 't was before we started, and I hadn't got my gang chained up; so what should she do but ups on a cotton-bale, like a cat, ketches a knife from one of the deck hands, and, I tell ye, she made all fly for a minit, till she saw 'twan't no use; and she jest turns round, and pitches head first, young un and all, into the river,—went down plump, and never ris."

"Bah!" said Tom Loker, who had listened to these stories with ill-repressed disgust,—"shif'less, both on ye! *my* gals don't cut up no such shines,[2] I tell ye!"

"Indeed! how do you help it?" said Marks, briskly.

"Help it? why, I buys a gal, and if she's got a young un to be sold, I jest walks up and puts my fist to her face, and says, 'Look here, now, if you give me one word out of your head, I'll smash yer face in. I won't hear one word—not the beginning of a word.' I says to 'em, 'This yer young un's mine, and not yourn, and you've no kind o' business with it. I'm going to sell it, first chance; mind, you don't cut up none o' yer shines about it, or I'll make ye wish ye'd never been born.' I tell ye, they sees it an't no play, when I gets hold. I makes 'em

1. Totally blind.
2. Mischief or misbehavior.

as whist as fishes;[3] and if one on 'em begins and gives a yelp, why,—" and Mr. Loker brought down his fist with a thump that fully explained the hiatus.

"That ar's what ye may call *emphasis,*" said Marks poking Haley in the side, and going into another small giggle. "An't Tom peculiar? he! he! he! I say, Tom, I s'pect you make 'em *understand*, for all niggers' heads is woolly. They don't never have no doubt o' your meaning, Tom. If you an't the devil, Tom, you's his twin brother, I'll say that for ye!"

Tom received the compliment with becoming modesty, and began to look as affable as was consistent, as John Bunyan says, "with his doggish nature."[4]

Haley, who had been imbibing very freely of the staple of the evening, began to feel a sensible elevation and enlargement of his moral faculties,—a phenomenon not unusual with gentlemen of a serious and reflective turn, under similar circumstances.

"Wal, now, Tom," he said, "ye re'lly is too bad, as I al'ays have told ye; ye know, Tom, you and I used to talk over these yer matters down in Natchez, and I used to prove to ye that we made full as much, and was as well off for this yer world, by treatin' on 'em well, besides keepin' a better chance for comin' in the kingdom at last, when wust comes to wust, and thar an't nothing else left to get, ye know."

"Boh!" said Tom, "*don't* I know?—don't make me too sick with any yer stuff,—my stomach is a leetle riled now;" and Tom drank half a glass of raw brandy.

"I say," said Haley, and leaning back in his chair and gesturing impressively, "I'll say this now, I al'ays meant to drive my trade so as to make money on 't, *fust and foremost*, as much as any man; but, then, trade an't everything, and money an't everything, 'cause we's all got souls. I don't care, now, who hears me say it,—and I think a cussed sight on it,—so I may as well come out with it. I b'lieve in religion, and one of these days, when I've got matters tight and snug, I calculates to tend to my soul and them ar matters; and so what's the use of doin' any more wickedness than's re'lly necessary?—it don't seem to me it's 't all prudent."

"Tend to yer soul!" repeated Tom, contemptuously; "take a bright look-out to find a soul in you,—save yourself any care on that score. If the devil sifts you through a hair sieve,[5] he won't find one."

3. Absolutely quiet.
4. I.e., with his devilish nature. In part 2 of *Pilgrim's Progress* (1678), Mercy and Christiana knock at a gate guarded by a fierce dog whose barking signifies Satan's attempts to foil prayers. The gatekeeper tells Christiana: "I also give my pilgrims timely help, so they are not delivered up to his power, to do to them what his doggish nature would prompt him to." *Pilgrim's Progress* was an extremely popular Protestant allegory of spiritual quest, by the English preacher John Bunyan (1628–1688).
5. A very fine sieve whose bottom is made of hair.

"Why, Tom, you're cross," said Haley; "why can't ye take it pleasant, now, when a feller's talking for your good?"

"Stop that ar jaw o' yourn, there," said Tom, gruffly. "I can stand most any talk o' yourn, but your pious talk,—that kills me right up. After all, what's the odds between me and you? 'Tan't that you care one bit more, or have a bit more feelin',—it's clean, sheer, dog meanness, wanting to cheat the devil and save your own skin; don't I see through it? And your 'gettin' religion,' as you call it, arter all, is too p'isin mean for any crittur;—run up a bill with the devil all your life, and then sneak out when pay time comes! Boh!"

"Come, come, gentlemen, I say; this isn't business," said Marks. "There's different ways, you know, of looking at all subjects. Mr. Haley is a very nice man, no doubt, and has his own conscience; and, Tom, you have your ways, and very good ones, too, Tom; but quarrelling, you know, won't answer no kind of purpose. Let's go to business. Now, Mr. Haley, what is it?—you want us to undertake to catch this yer gal?"

"The gal's no matter of mine,—she's Shelby's; it's only the boy. I was a fool for buying the monkey!"

"You're generally a fool!" said Tom, gruffly.

"Come, now, Loker, none of your huffs," said Marks, licking his lips; "you see, Mr. Haley's a puttin' us in a way of a good job, I reckon; just hold still,—these yer arrangements is my forte. This yer gal, Mr. Haley, how is she? what is she?"

"Wal! white and handsome—well brought up. I'd a gin Shelby eight hundred or a thousand, and then made well on her."

"White and handsome—well brought up!" said Marks, his sharp eyes, nose and mouth, all alive with enterprise. "Look here, now, Loker, a beautiful opening. We'll do a business here on our own account;—we does the catchin'; the boy, of course, goes to Mr. Haley,—we takes the gal to Orleans to speculate on. An't it beautiful?"

Tom, whose great heavy mouth had stood ajar during this communication, now suddenly snapped it together, as a big dog closes on a piece of meat, and seemed to be digesting the idea at his leisure.

"Ye see," said Marks to Haley, stirring his punch as he did so, "ye see, we has justices convenient at all p'ints along shore, that does up any little jobs in our line quite reasonable.[6] Tom, he does

6. I.e., officials who will falsify bills of sale. Stowe discusses the practice of kidnapping free blacks and selling them into slavery in *A Key to "Uncle Tom's Cabin"* (340–45) and says of this scene from Eliza's pursuit: "What knowledge the author has had of the facilities which some justices of the peace, under the old fugitive law of Ohio, were in the habit of giving to kidnapping, may be inferred by comparing the statement in her book with some in her personal knowledge." Stowe goes on to tell the story of an ex-slave from Kentucky whose escape to Cincinnati the Stowes assisted when they feared she would be kidnapped by the son of the woman who freed her (35–36).

the knockin' down and that ar; and I come in all dressed up—shining boots—everything first chop, when the swearin' 's to be done. You oughter see, now," said Marks, in a glow of professional pride, "how I can tone it off. One day, I'm Mr. Twickem, from New Orleans; 'nother day, I'm just come from my plantation on Pearl river, where I works seven hundred niggers; then, again, I come out a distant relation of Henry Clay, or some old cock in Kentuck. Talents is different, you know. Now, Tom's a roarer when there's any thumping or fighting to be done; but at lying he an't good, Tom an't,—ye see it don't come natural to him; but, Lord, if thar's a feller in the country that can swear to anything and everything, and put in all the circumstances and flourishes with a longer face, and carry't through better'n I can, why, I'd like to see him, that's all! I b'lieve my heart, I could get along and snake through, even if justices were more particular than they is. Sometimes I rather wish they was more particular; 't would be a heap more relishin' if they was,—more fun, yer know."

Tom Loker, who, as we have made it appear, was a man of slow thoughts and movements, here interrupted Marks by bringing his heavy fist down on the table, so as to make all ring again. "*It'll do!*" he said.

"Lord bless ye, Tom, ye needn't break all the glasses!" said Marks; "save your fist for time o' need."

"But, gentlemen, an't I to come in for a share of the profits?" said Haley.

"An't it enough we catch the boy for ye?" said Loker. "What do ye want?"

"Wal," said Haley, "if I gives you the job, it's worth something,—say ten per cent. on the profits, expenses paid."

"Now," said Loker, with a tremendous oath, and striking the table with his heavy fist, "don't I know *you*, Dan Haley? Don't you think to come it over me! Suppose Marks and I have taken up the catchin' trade, jest to 'commodate gentlemen like you, and get nothin' for ourselves?—Not by a long chalk! we'll have the gal out and out, and you keep quiet, or, ye see, we'll have both,—what's to hinder? Han't you show'd us the game? It's as free to us as you, I hope. If you or Shelby wants to chase us, look where the partridges was last year; if you find them or us, you're quite welcome."

"O, wal, certainly, jest let it go at that," said Haley, alarmed; "you catch the boy for the job;—you allers did trade *far* with me, Tom, and was up to yer word."

"Ye know that," said Tom; "I don't pretend none of your snivelling ways, but I won't lie in my 'counts with the devil himself. What I ses I'll do, I will do,—you know *that*, Dan Haley."

"Jes so, jes so,—I said so, Tom," said Haley; "and if you'd only promise to have the boy for me in a week, at any point you'll name, that's all I want."

"But it an't all I want, by a long jump," said Tom. "Ye don't think I did business with you, down in Natchez, for nothing, Haley; I've learned to hold an eel, when I catch him. You've got to fork over fifty dollars, flat down, or this child don't start a peg. I know yer."

"Why, when you have a job in hand that may bring a clean profit of somewhere about a thousand or sixteen hundred, why, Tom, you're onreasonable," said Haley.

"Yes, and hasn't we business booked for five weeks to come,—all we can do? And suppose we leaves all, and goes to bushwhacking round arter yer young un, and finally doesn't catch the gal,—and gals allers is the devil *to* catch,—what's then? would you pay us a cent—would you? I think I see you a doin' it—ugh! No, no; flap down your fifty. If we get the job, and it pays, I'll hand it back; if we don't, it's for our trouble,—that's *far*, an't it, Marks?"

"Certainly, certainly," said Marks, with a conciliatory tone; "it's only a retaining fee, you see,—he! he! he!—we lawyers, you know. Wal, we must all keep good-natured,—keep easy, yer know. Tom'll have the boy for yer, anywhere ye'll name; won't ye, Tom?"

"If I find the young un, I'll bring him on to Cincinnati, and leave him at Granny Belcher's, on the landing," said Loker.

Marks had got from his pocket a greasy pocket-book, and taking a long paper from thence, he sat down, and fixing his keen black eyes on it, began mumbling over its contents: "Barnes—Shelby County[7]—boy Jim, three hundred dollars for him, dead or alive.

"Edwards—Dick and Lucy—man and wife, six hundred dollars; wench Polly and two children—six hundred for her or her head.

"I'm jest a runnin' over our business, to see if we can take up this yer handily. Loker," he said, after a pause, "we must set Adams and Springer on the track of these yer; they've been booked some time."

"They'll charge too much," said Tom.

"I'll manage that ar; they's young in the business, and must spect to work cheap," said Marks, as he continued to read. "Ther's three on 'em easy cases, 'cause all you've got to do is to shoot 'em, or swear they is shot; they couldn't, of course, charge much for that. Them other cases," he said, folding the paper, "will bear puttin' off a spell. So now let's come to the particulars. Now, Mr. Haley, you saw this yer gal when she landed?"

"To be sure,—plain as I see you."

"And a man helpin' on her up the bank?" said Loker.

7. A county in north-central Kentucky, east of Louisville.

"To be sure, I did."

"Most likely," said Marks, "she's took in somewhere but where, 's a question. Tom, what do you say?"

"We must cross the river to-night, no mistake," said Tom.

"But there's no boat about," said Marks. "The ice is running awfully, Tom; an't it dangerous?"

"Don'no nothing 'bout that,—only it's got to be done," said Tom, decidedly.

"Dear me," said Marks, fidgeting, "it'll be—I say," he said, walking to the window, "it's dark as a wolf's mouth, and, Tom—"

"The long and short is, you're scared, Marks; but I can't help that,—you've got to go. Suppose you want to lie by a day or two, till the gal's been carried on the underground line up to Sandusky[8] or so, before you start."

"O, no; I an't a grain afraid," said Marks, "only—"

"Only what?" said Tom.

"Well, about the boat. Yer see there an't any boat."

"I heard the woman say there was one coming along this evening, and that a man was going to cross over in it. Neck or nothin,[9] we must go with him," said Tom.

"I s'pose you've got good dogs," said Haley.

"First rate," said Marks. "But what's the use? you han't got nothin' o' hers to smell on."

"Yes, I have," said Haley, triumphantly. "Here's her shawl she left on the bed in her hurry; she left her bonnet, too."

"That ar's lucky," said Loker; "fork over."

"Though the dogs might damage the gal, if they come on her unawars," said Haley.

"That ar's a consideration," said Marks. "Our dogs tore a feller half to pieces, once, down in Mobile,[1] fore we could get 'em off."

"Well, ye see, for this sort that's to be sold for their looks, that ar won't answer, ye see," said Haley.

"I do see," said Marks. "Besides, if she's got took in, 'tan't no go, neither. Dogs is no 'count in these yer up states where these critters gets carried; of course, ye can't get on their track. They only does down in plantations, where niggers, when they runs, has to do their own running, and don't get no help."

"Well," said Loker, who had just stepped out to the bar to make some inquiries, "they say the man's come with the boat; so, Marks—"

8. A city in north-central Ohio, on Lake Erie, a center for shipping and a point of departure to Canada for escaping slaves. *Underground line*: also called "underground railroad," a system organized by both white and black abolitionists to help escaped slaves make their way to Canada or to the northern free states.
9. Desperately.
1. A seaport in southwest Alabama.

That worthy cast a rueful look at the comfortable quarters he was leaving, but slowly rose to obey. After exchanging a few words of further arrangement, Haley, with visible reluctance, handed over the fifty dollars to Tom, and the worthy trio separated for the night.

If any of our refined and Christian readers object to the society into which this scene introduces them, let us beg them to begin and conquer their prejudices in time. The catching business, we beg to remind them, is rising to the dignity of a lawful and patriotic profession. If all the broad land between the Mississippi and the Pacific becomes one great market for bodies and souls, and human property retains the locomotive tendencies of this nineteenth century, the trader and catcher may yet be among our aristocracy.

While this scene was going on at the tavern, Sam and Andy, in a state of high felicitation, pursued their way home.

Sam was in the highest possible feather, and expressed his exultation by all sorts of supernatural howls and ejaculations, by divers odd motions and contortions of his whole system. Sometimes he would sit backward, with his face to the horse's tail and sides, and then, with a whoop and a somerset,[2] come right side up in his place again, and, drawing on a grave face, begin to lecture Andy in high-sounding tones for laughing and playing the fool. Anon, slapping his sides with his arms, he would burst forth in peals of laughter, that made the old woods ring as they passed. With all these evolutions, he contrived to keep the horses up to the top of their speed, until, between ten and eleven, their heels resounded on the gravel at the end of the balcony. Mrs. Shelby flew to the railings.

"Is that you, Sam? Where are they?"

"Mas'r Haley's a-restin' at the tavern; he's drefful fatigued, Missis."

"And Eliza, Sam?"

"Wal, she's clar 'cross Jordan. As a body may say, in the land o' Canaan."

"Why, Sam, what *do* you mean?" said Mrs. Shelby, breathless, and almost faint, as the possible meaning of these words came over her.

"Wal, Missis, de Lord he persarves his own. Lizy's done gone over the river into 'Hio, as 'markably as if de Lord took her over in a charrit of fire and two hosses."

Sam's vein of piety was always uncommonly fervent in his mistress' presence; and he made great capital of scriptural figures and images.

2. Somersault.

"Come up here, Sam," said Mr. Shelby, who had followed on to the verandah, "and tell your mistress what she wants. Come, come, Emily," said he, passing his arm round her, "you are cold and all in a shiver; you allow yourself to feel too much."

"Feel too much! Am not I a woman,—a mother? Are we not both responsible to God for this poor girl? My God! lay not this sin to our charge."

"What sin, Emily? You see yourself that we have only done what we were obliged to."

"There's an awful feeling of guilt about it, though," said Mrs. Shelby. "I can't reason it away."

"Here, Andy, you nigger, be alive!" called Sam, under the verandah; "take these yer hosses to der barn; don't ye hear Mas'r a callin'?" and Sam soon appeared, palm-leaf in hand, at the parlor door.

"Now, Sam, tell us distinctly how the matter was," said Mr. Shelby. "Where is Eliza, if you know?"

"Wal, Mas'r, I saw her, with my own eyes, a crossin' on the floatin' ice. She crossed most 'markably; it wasn't no less nor a miracle; and I saw a man help her up the 'Hio side, and then she was lost in the dusk."

"Sam, I think this rather apocryphal,—this miracle. Crossing on floating ice isn't so easily done," said Mr. Shelby.

"Easy! couldn't nobody a done it, without de Lord. Why, now," said Sam, " 't was jist dis yer way. Mas'r Haley, and me, and Andy, we comes up to de little tavern by the river, and I rides a leetle ahead,—(I's so zealous to be a cotchin' Lizy, that I couldn't hold in, no way),—and when I comes by the tavern winder, sure enough there she was, right in plain sight, and dey diggin' on behind. Wal, I loses off my hat, and sings out nuff to raise the dead. Course Lizy she hars, and she dodges back, when Mas'r Haley he goes past the door; and then, I tell ye, she clared out de side door; she went down de river bank;—Mas'r Haley he seed her, and yelled out, and him, and me, and Andy, we took arter. Down she come to the river, and thar was the current running ten feet wide by the shore, and over t' other side ice a sawin' and a jiggling up and down, kinder as 't were a great island. We come right behind her, and I thought my soul he'd got her sure enough,—when she gin sich a screech as I never hearn, and thar she was, clar over t' other side the current, on the ice, and then on she went, a screeching and a jumpin',—the ice went crack! c'wallop! cracking! chunk! and she a boundin' like a buck! Lord, the spring that ar gal's got in her an't common, I'm o' 'pinion."

Mrs. Shelby sat perfectly silent, pale with excitement, while Sam told his story.

"God be praised, she isn't dead!" she said; "but where is the poor child now?"

"De Lord will pervide," said Sam, rolling up his eyes piously. "As I've been a sayin', dis yer's a providence and no mistake, as Missis has allers been a instructin' on us. Thar's allers instruments ris up to do de Lord's will. Now, if't hadn't been for me to-day, she'd a been took a dozen times. Warn't it I started off de hosses, dis yer mornin', and kept 'em chasin' till nigh dinner time? And didn't I car Mas'r Haley nigh five miles out of de road, dis evening, or else he'd a come up with Lizy as easy as a dog arter a coon. These yer's all providences."

"They are a kind of providences that you'll have to be pretty sparing of, Master Sam. I allow no such practices with gentlemen on my place," said Mr. Shelby, with as much sternness as he could command, under the circumstances.

Now, there is no more use in making believe be angry with a negro than with a child; both instinctively see the true state of the case, through all attempts to affect the contrary; and Sam was in no wise disheartened by this rebuke, though he assumed an air of doleful gravity, and stood with the corners of his mouth lowered in most penitential style.

"Mas'r's quite right,—quite; it was ugly on me,—there's no disputin' that ar; and of course Mas'r and Missis wouldn't encourage no such works. I'm sensible of dat ar; but a poor nigger like me's 'mazin' tempted to act ugly sometimes, when fellers will cut up such shines as dat ar Mas'r Haley; he an't no gen'l'man no way; anybody's been raised as I've been can't help a seein' dat ar."

"Well, Sam," said Mrs. Shelby, "as you appear to have a proper sense of your errors, you may go now and tell Aunt Chloe she may get you some of that cold ham that was left of dinner to-day. You and Andy must be hungry."

"Missis is a heap too good for us," said Sam, making his bow with alacrity, and departing.

It will be perceived, as has been before intimated, that Master Sam had a native talent that might, undoubtedly, have raised him to eminence in political life,—a talent of making capital out of everything that turned up, to be invested for his own especial praise and glory; and having done up his piety and humility, as he trusted, to the satisfaction of the parlor, he clapped his palm-leaf on his head, with a sort of rakish, free-and-easy air, and proceeded to the dominions of Aunt Chloe, with the intention of flourishing largely in the kitchen.

"I'll speechify these yer niggers," said Sam to himself, "now I've got a chance. Lord, I'll reel it off to make 'em stare!"

It must be observed that one of Sam's especial delights had been to ride in attendance on his master to all kinds of political gatherings, where, roosted on some rail fence, or perched aloft in some tree, he would sit watching the orators, with the greatest apparent gusto, and then, descending among the various brethren of his own color, assembled on the same errand, he would edify and delight them with the most ludicrous burlesques and imitations, all delivered with the most imperturbable earnestness and solemnity; and though the auditors immediately about him were generally of his own color, it not unfrequently happened that they were fringed pretty deeply with those of a fairer complexion, who listened, laughing and winking, to Sam's great self-congratulation. In fact, Sam considered oratory as his vocation, and never let slip an opportunity of magnifying his office.

Now, between Sam and Aunt Chloe there had existed, from ancient times, a sort of chronic feud, or rather a decided coolness; but, as Sam was meditating something in the provision department, as the necessary and obvious foundation of his operations, he determined, on the present occasion, to be eminently conciliatory; for he well knew that although "Missis' orders" would undoubtedly be followed to the letter, yet he should gain a considerable deal by enlisting the spirit also. He therefore appeared before Aunt Chloe with a touchingly subdued, resigned expression, like one who has suffered immeasurable hardships in behalf of a persecuted fellow-creature,—enlarged upon the fact that Missis had directed him to come to Aunt Chloe for whatever might be wanting to make up the balance in his solids and fluids,—and thus unequivocally acknowledged her right and supremacy in the cooking department, and all thereto pertaining.

The thing took accordingly. No poor, simple, virtuous body was ever cajoled by the attentions of an electioneering politician with more ease than Aunt Chloe was won over by Master Sam's suavities; and if he had been the prodigal son himself, he could not have been overwhelmed with more maternal bountifulness; and he soon found himself seated, happy and glorious, over a large tin pan, containing a sort of *olla podrida*[3] of all that had appeared on the table for two or three days past. Savory morsels of ham, golden blocks of corn-cake, fragments of pie of every conceivable mathematical figure, chicken wings, gizzards, and drum-sticks, all appeared in picturesque confusion; and Sam, as monarch of all he surveyed, sat with his palm-leaf cocked rejoicingly to one side, and patronizing Andy at his right hand.

The kitchen was full of all his compeers, who had hurried and crowded in, from the various cabins, to hear the termination of the day's exploits. Now was Sam's hour of glory. The story of the day was rehearsed, with all kinds of ornament and varnishing which

3. A stew with a variety of ingredients (Spanish).

might be necessary to heighten its effect; for Sam, like some of our fashionable dilettanti, never allowed a story to lose any of its gilding by passing through his hands. Roars of laughter attended the narration, and were taken up and prolonged by all the smaller fry, who were lying, in any quantity, about on the floor, or perched in every corner. In the height of the uproar and laughter, Sam, however, preserved an immovable gravity, only from time to time rolling his eyes up, and giving his auditors divers inexpressibly droll glances, without departing from the sententious elevation of his oratory.

"Yer see, fellow-countrymen," said Sam, elevating a turkey's leg, with energy, "yer see, now, what dis yer chile's up ter, for fendin' yer all,—yes, all on yer. For him as tries to get one o' our people, is as good as tryin' to get all; yer see the principle's de same,—dat ar's clar. And any one o' these yer drivers that comes smelling round arter any our people, why, he's got *me* in his way; *I'm* the feller he's got to set in with,—I'm the feller for yer all to come to, bredren,—I'll stand up for yer rights,—I'll fend 'em to the last breath!"

"Why, but Sam, yer telled me, only this mornin', that you'd help this yer Mas'r to cotch Lizy; seems to me yer talk don't hang together," said Andy.

"I tell you now, Andy," said Sam, with awful superiority, "don't yer be a talkin' 'bout what yer don't know nothin' on; boys like you, Andy, means well, but they can't be spected to collusitate the great principles of action."

Andy looked rebuked, particularly by the hard word collusitate, which most of the youngerly members of the company seemed to consider as a settler in the case, while Sam proceeded.

"Dat ar was *conscience*, Andy; when I thought of gwine arter Lizy, I railly spected Mas'r was sot dat way. When I found Missis was sot the contrar, dat ar was conscience *more yet*,—cause fellers allers gets more by stickin' to Missis' side,—so yer see I's persistent either way, and sticks up to conscience, and holds on to principles. Yes, *principles*," said Sam, giving an enthusiastic toss to a chicken's neck,—"what's principles good for, if we isn't persistent, I wanter know? Thar, Andy, you may have dat ar bone,—'tan't picked quite clean."

Sam's audience hanging on his words with open mouth, he could not but proceed.

"Dis yer matter 'bout persistence, feller-niggers," said Sam, with the air of one entering into an abstruse subject, "dis yer 'sistency 's a thing what an't seed into very clar, by most anybody. Now, yer see, when a feller stands up for a thing one day and night, de contrar de next, folks ses (and nat'rally enough dey ses), why he an't persistent,—hand me dat ar bit o' corn-cake, Andy. But let's look inter it. I hope the gen'lmen and der fair sex will scuse my usin' an or'nary sort o' 'parison. Here! I'm a tryin' to get top o' der hay. Wal, I puts up my larder dis yer side; 'tan't no go;—den, cause I don't try dere no more, but puts my larder right de contrar side, an't I persistent? I'm persistent in wantin' to get up which ary side my larder is; don't you see, all on yer?"

"It's the only thing ye ever was persistent in, Lord knows!" muttered Aunt Chloe, who was getting rather restive; the merriment of the evening being to her somewhat after the Scripture comparison,—like "vinegar upon nitre."[4]

"Yes, indeed!" said Sam, rising, full of supper and glory, for a closing effort. "Yes, my feller-citizens and ladies of de other sex in general, I has principles,—I'm proud to 'oon 'em,—they's perquisite to dese yer times, and ter *all* times. I has principles, and I sticks to 'em like forty,—jest anything that I thinks is principle, I goes in to 't;—I wouldn't mind if dey burnt me 'live,—I'd walk right up to de stake, I would, and say, here I comes to shed my last blood fur my principles, fur my country, fur der gen'l interests of s'ciety."

"Well," said Aunt Chloe, "one o' yer principles will have to be to get to bed some time to-night, and not be a keepin' everybody up till mornin'; now, every one of you young uns that don't want to be cracked, had better be scase, mighty sudden."

"Niggers! all on yer," said Sam, waving his palm-leaf with benignity, "I give yer my blessin'; go to bed now, and be good boys."

And, with this pathetic benediction, the assembly dispersed.

# Chapter IX

## *In Which It Appears That a Senator Is But a Man*

The light of the cheerful fire shone on the rug and carpet of a cosey parlor, and glittered on the sides of the tea-cups and well-brightened tea-pot, as Senator Bird was drawing off his boots, preparatory to inserting his feet in a pair of new handsome slippers, which his wife had been working for him while away on his senatorial tour. Mrs. Bird, looking the very picture of delight, was superintending the arrangements of the table, ever and anon mingling admonitory remarks to a number of frolicsome juveniles, who were effervescing in all those modes of untold gambol and mischief that have astonished mothers ever since the flood.

"Tom, let the door-knob alone,—there's a man! Mary! Mary! don't pull the cat's tail,—poor pussy! Jim, you mustn't climb on that table,—no, no!—You don't know, my dear, what a surprise it is to us

4. See Proverbs 25.20: "As he that taketh away a garment in cold weather, and as vinegar upon nitre, so is he who singeth songs to an heavy heart."

all, to see you here to-night!" said she, at last, when she found a space to say something to her husband.

"Yes, yes, I thought I'd just make a run down, spend the night, and have a little comfort at home. I'm tired to death, and my head aches!"

Mrs. Bird cast a glance at a camphor-bottle,[1] which stood in the half-open closet, and appeared to meditate an approach to it, but her husband interposed.

"No, no, Mary, no doctoring! a cup of your good hot tea, and some of our good home living, is what I want. It's a tiresome business, this legislating!"

And the senator smiled, as if he rather liked the idea of considering himself a sacrifice to his country.

"Well," said his wife, after the business of the tea-table was getting rather slack, "and what have they been doing in the Senate?"

Now, it was a very unusual thing for gentle little Mrs. Bird ever to trouble her head with what was going on in the house of the state, very wisely considering that she had enough to do to mind her own. Mr. Bird, therefore, opened his eyes in surprise, and said,

"Not very much of importance."

"Well; but is it true that they have been passing a law forbidding people to give meat and drink to those poor colored folks that come along? I heard they were talking of some such law, but I didn't think any Christian legislature would pass it!"

"Why, Mary, you are getting to be a politician, all at once."

"No, nonsense! I wouldn't give a fip for all your politics, generally, but I think this is something downright cruel and unchristian. I hope, my dear, no such law has been passed."

"There has been a law passed forbidding people to help off the slaves that come over from Kentucky, my dear; so much of that thing has been done by these reckless Abolitionists, that our brethren in Kentucky are very strongly excited, and it seems necessary, and no more than Christian and kind, that something should be done by our state to quiet the excitement."

"And what is the law? It don't forbid us to shelter these poor creatures a night, does it, and to give 'em something comfortable to eat, and a few old clothes, and send them quietly about their business?"

"Why, yes, my dear; that would be aiding and abetting, you know."

Mrs. Bird was a timid, blushing little woman, of about four feet in height, and with mild blue eyes, and a peach-blow complexion, and the gentlest, sweetest voice in the world;—as for courage, a moderate-sized cock-turkey had been known to put her to rout at the very first gobble, and a stout house-dog, of moderate capacity,

1. Camphor was used medicinally to relieve colic or intestinal pain or as a stimulant.

would bring her into subjection merely by a show of his teeth. Her husband and children were her entire world, and in these she ruled more by entreaty and persuasion than by command or argument. There was only one thing that was capable of arousing her, and that provocation came in on the side of her unusually gentle and sympathetic nature;—anything in the shape of cruelty would throw her into a passion, which was the more alarming and inexplicable in proportion to the general softness of her nature. Generally the most indulgent and easy to be entreated of all mothers, still her boys had a very reverent remembrance of a most vehement chastisement she once bestowed on them, because she found them leagued with several graceless boys of the neighborhood, stoning a defenceless kitten.

"I'll tell you what," Master Bill used to say, "I was scared that time. Mother came at me so that I thought she was crazy, and I was whipped and tumbled off to bed, without any supper, before I could get over wondering what had come about; and, after that, I heard mother crying outside the door, which made me feel worse than all the rest. I'll tell you what," he'd say, "we boys never stoned another kitten!"

On the present occasion, Mrs. Bird rose quickly, with very red cheeks, which quite improved her general appearance, and walked up to her husband, with quite a resolute air, and said, in a determined tone,

"Now, John, I want to know if you think such a law as that is right and Christian?"

"You won't shoot me, now, Mary, if I say I do!"

"I never could have thought it of you, John; you didn't vote for it?"

"Even so, my fair politician."

"You ought to be ashamed, John! Poor, homeless, houseless creatures! It's a shameful, wicked, abominable law, and I'll break it, for one, the first time I get a chance; and I hope I *shall* have a chance, I do! Things have got to a pretty pass, if a woman can't give a warm supper and a bed to poor, starving creatures, just because they are slaves, and have been abused and oppressed all their lives, poor things!"

"But, Mary, just listen to me. Your feelings are all quite right, dear, and interesting, and I love you for them; but, then, dear, we mustn't suffer our feelings to run away with our judgment; you must consider it's not a matter of private feeling,—there are great public interests involved,—there is such a state of public agitation rising, that we must put aside our private feelings."

"Now, John, I don't know anything about politics, but I can read my Bible; and there I see that I must feed the hungry, clothe the naked, and comfort the desolate; and that Bible I mean to follow."

"But in cases where your doing so would involve a great public evil—"

"Obeying God never brings on public evils. I know it can't. It's always safest, all round, to *do as He* bids us."

"Now, listen to me, Mary, and I can state to you a very clear argument, to show—"

"O, nonsense, John! you can talk all night, but you wouldn't do it. I put it to you, John,—would *you* now turn away a poor, shivering, hungry creature from your door, because he was a runaway? *Would* you, now?"

Now, if the truth must be told, our senator had the misfortune to be a man who had a particularly humane and accessible nature, and turning away anybody that was in trouble never had been his forte; and what was worse for him in this particular pinch of the argument was, that his wife knew it, and, of course, was making an assault on rather an indefensible point. So he had recourse to the usual means of gaining time for such cases made and provided; he said "ahem," and coughed several times, took out his pocket-handkerchief, and began to wipe his glasses. Mrs. Bird, seeing the defenceless condition of the enemy's territory, had no more conscience than to push her advantage.

"I should like to see you doing that, John—I really should! Turning a woman out of doors in a snow-storm, for instance; or, may be you'd take her up and put her in jail, wouldn't you? You would make a great hand at that!"

"Of course, it would be a very painful duty," began Mr. Bird, in a moderate tone.

"Duty, John! don't use that word! You know it isn't a duty—it can't be a duty! If folks want to keep their slaves from running away, let 'em treat 'em well,—that's my doctrine. If I had slaves (as I hope I never shall have), I'd risk their wanting to run away from me, or you either, John. I tell you folks don't run away when they are happy; and when they do run, poor creatures! they suffer enough with cold and hunger and fear, without everybody's turning against them; and, law or no law, I never will, so help me God!"

"Mary! Mary! My dear, let me reason with you."

"I hate reasoning, John,—especially reasoning on such subjects. There's a way you political folks have of coming round and round a plain right thing; and you don't believe in it yourselves, when it comes to practice. I know *you* well enough, John. You don't believe it's right any more than I do; and you wouldn't do it any sooner than I."

At this critical juncture, old Cudjoe, the black man-of-all-work, put his head in at the door, and wished "Missis would come into the kitchen;" and our senator, tolerably relieved, looked after his little wife with a whimsical mixture of amusement and vexation, and, seating himself in the arm-chair, began to read the papers.

After a moment, his wife's voice was heard at the door, in a quick, earnest tone,—"John! John! I do wish you'd come here, a moment."

He laid down his paper, and went into the kitchen, and started, quite amazed at the sight that presented itself:—A young and slender woman, with garments torn and frozen, with one shoe gone, and the stocking torn away from the cut and bleeding foot, was laid back in a deadly swoon upon two chairs. There was the impress of the despised race on her face, yet none could help feeling its mournful and pathetic beauty, while its stony sharpness, its cold, fixed, deathly aspect, struck a solemn chill over him. He drew his breath short, and stood in silence. His wife, and their only colored domestic, old Aunt Dinah, were busily engaged in restorative measures; while old Cudjoe had got the boy on his knee, and was busy pulling off his shoes and stockings, and chafing his little cold feet.

"Sure, now, if she an't a sight to behold!" said old Dinah, compassionately; "'pears like 'twas the heat that made her faint. She was tol'able peart when she cum in, and asked if she couldn't warm herself here a spell; and I was just a askin' her where she cum from, and she fainted right down. Never done much hard work, guess, by the looks of her hands."

"Poor creature!" said Mrs. Bird, compassionately, as the woman slowly unclosed her large, dark eyes, and looked vacantly at her. Suddenly an expression of agony crossed her face, and she sprang up, saying, "O, my Harry! Have they got him?"

The boy, at this, jumped from Cudjoe's knee, and, running to her side, put up his arms. "O, he's here! he's here!" she exclaimed.

"O, ma'am!" said she, wildly, to Mrs. Bird, "do protect us! don't let them get him!"

"Nobody shall hurt you here, poor woman," said Mrs. Bird, encouragingly. "You are safe; don't be afraid."

"God bless you!" said the woman, covering her face and sobbing; while the little boy, seeing her crying, tried to get into her lap.

With many gentle and womanly offices, which none knew better how to render than Mrs. Bird, the poor woman was, in time, rendered more calm. A temporary bed was provided for her on the settle, near the fire; and, after a short time, she fell into a heavy slumber, with the child, who seemed no less weary, soundly sleeping on her arm; for the mother resisted, with nervous anxiety, the kindest attempts to take him from her; and, even in sleep, her arm encircled him with an unrelaxing clasp, as if she could not even then be beguiled of her vigilant hold.

Mr. and Mrs. Bird had gone back to the parlor, where, strange as it may appear, no reference was made, on either side, to the preceding conversation; but Mrs. Bird busied herself with her knitting-work, and Mr. Bird pretended to be reading the paper.

"I wonder who and what she is!" said Mr. Bird, at last, as he laid it down.

"When she wakes up and feels a little rested, we will see," said Mrs. Bird.

"I say, wife!" said Mr. Bird, after musing in silence over his newspaper.

"Well, dear!"

"She couldn't wear one of your gowns, could she, by any letting down, or such matter? She seems to be rather larger than you are."

A quite perceptible smile glimmered on Mrs. Bird's face, as she answered, "We'll see."

Another pause, and Mr. Bird again broke out,

"I say, wife!"

"Well! What now?"

"Why, there's that old bombazin[2] cloak, that you keep on purpose to put over me when I take my afternoon's nap; you might as well give her that,—she needs clothes."

At this instant, Dinah looked in to say that the woman was awake, and wanted to see Missis.

Mr. and Mrs. Bird went into the kitchen, followed by the two eldest boys, the smaller fry having, by this time, been safely disposed of in bed.

The woman was now sitting up on the settle, by the fire. She was looking steadily into the blaze, with a calm, heartbroken expression, very different from her former agitated wildness.

"Did you want me?" said Mrs. Bird, in gentle tones. "I hope you feel better now, poor woman!"

A long-drawn, shivering sigh was the only answer; but she lifted her dark eyes, and fixed them on her with such a forlorn and imploring expression, that the tears came into the little woman's eyes.

"You needn't be afraid of anything; we are friends here, poor woman! Tell me where you came from, and what you want," said she.

"I came from Kentucky," said the woman.

"When?" said Mr. Bird, taking up the interrogatory.

"To-night."

"How did you come?"

"I crossed on the ice."

"Crossed on the ice!" said every one present.

"Yes," said the woman, slowly, "I did. God helping me, I crossed on the ice; for they were behind me—right behind—and there was no other way!"

2. A fabric with a twill weave.

"Law, Missis," said Cudjoe, "the ice is all in broken-up blocks, a swinging and a tetering up and down in the water!"

"I know it was—I know it!" said she, wildly; "but I did it! I wouldn't have thought I could,—I didn't think I should get over, but I didn't care! I could but die, if I didn't. The Lord helped me; nobody knows how much the Lord can help 'em, till they try," said the woman, with a flashing eye.

"Were you a slave?" said Mr. Bird.

"Yes, sir; I belonged to a man in Kentucky."

"Was he unkind to you?"

"No, sir; he was a good master."

"And was your mistress unkind to you?"

"No, sir—no! my mistress was always good to me."

"What could induce you to leave a good home, then, and run away, and go through such dangers?"

The woman looked up at Mrs. Bird, with a keen, scrutinizing glance, and it did not escape her that she was dressed in deep mourning.

"Ma'am," she said, suddenly, "have you ever lost a child?"

The question was unexpected, and it was a thrust on a new wound; for it was only a month since a darling child of the family had been laid in the grave.

Mr. Bird turned around and walked to the window, and Mrs. Bird burst into tears; but, recovering her voice, she said,

"Why do you ask that? I have lost a little one."

"Then you will feel for me. I have lost two, one after another,—left 'em buried there when I came away; and I had only this one left. I never slept a night without him; he was all I had. He was my comfort and pride, day and night; and, ma'am, they were going to take him away from me,—to *sell* him,—sell him down south, ma'am, to go all alone,—a baby that had never been away from his mother in his life! I couldn't stand it, ma'am. I knew I never should be good for anything, if they did; and when I knew the papers were signed, and he was sold, I took him and came off in the night; and they chased me,—the man that bought him, and some of Mas'r's folks,—and they were coming down right behind me, and I heard 'em. I jumped right on to the ice; and how I got across, I don't know,—but, first I knew, a man was helping me up the bank."

The woman did not sob nor weep. She had gone to a place where tears are dry; but every one around her was, in some way characteristic of themselves, showing signs of hearty sympathy.

The two little boys, after a desperate rummaging in their pockets, in search of those pocket-handkerchiefs which mothers know are never to be found there, had thrown themselves disconsolately into the skirts of their mother's gown, where they were sobbing, and wiping their eyes and noses, to their hearts' content;—Mrs. Bird had her face fairly hidden in her pocket-handkerchief; and old Dinah, with tears streaming down her black, honest face, was ejaculating, "Lord have mercy on us!" with all the fervor of a camp-meeting;—while old Cudjoe, rubbing his eyes very hard with his cuffs, and making a most uncommon variety of wry faces, occasionally responded in the same key, with great fervor. Our senator was a statesman, and of course could not be expected to cry, like other mortals; and so he turned his back to the company, and looked out of the window, and seemed particularly busy in clearing his throat and wiping his spectacle-glasses, occasionally blowing his nose in a manner that was calculated to excite suspicion, had any one been in a state to observe critically.

"How came you to tell me you had a kind master?" he suddenly exclaimed, gulping down very resolutely some kind of rising in his throat, and turning suddenly round upon the woman.

"Because he *was* a kind master; I'll say that of him, any way;—and my mistress was kind; but they couldn't help themselves. They were owing money; and there was some way, I can't tell how, that a man had a hold on them, and they were obliged to give him his will. I listened, and heard him telling mistress that, and she begging and pleading for me,—and he told her he couldn't help himself, and that the papers were all drawn;—and then it was I took him and left my home, and came away. I knew 'twas no use of my trying to live, if they did it; for 't 'pears like this child is all I have."

"Have you no husband?"

"Yes, but he belongs to another man. His master is real hard to him, and won't let him come to see me, hardly ever; and he's grown harder and harder upon us, and he threatens to sell him down south;—it's like I'll never see *him* again!"

The quiet tone in which the woman pronounced these words might have led a superficial observer to think that she was entirely apathetic; but there was a calm, settled depth of anguish in her large, dark eye, that spoke of something far otherwise.

"And where do you mean to go, my poor woman?" said Mrs. Bird.

"To Canada, if I only knew where that was. Is it very far off, is Canada?" said she, looking up, with a simple, confiding air, to Mrs. Bird's face.

"Poor thing!" said Mrs. Bird, involuntarily.

"Is't a very great way off, think?" said the woman, earnestly.

"Much further than you think, poor child!" said Mrs. Bird; "but we will try to think what can be done for you. Here, Dinah, make her up a bed in your own room, close by the kitchen, and I'll think what to do for her in the morning. Meanwhile, never fear, poor woman; put your trust in God; he will protect you."

Mrs. Bird and her husband reëntered the parlor. She sat down in her little rocking-chair before the fire, swaying thoughtfully to and fro. Mr. Bird strode up and down the room, grumbling to himself, "Pish! pshaw! confounded awkward business!" At length, striding up to his wife, he said,

"I say, wife, she'll have to get away from here, this very night. That fellow will be down on the scent bright and early to-morrow morning; if 'twas only the woman, she could lie quiet till it was over; but that little chap can't be kept still by a troop of horse and foot, I'll warrant me; he'll bring it all out, popping his head out of some window or door. A pretty kettle of fish it would be for me, too, to be caught with them both here, just now! No; they'll have to be got off to-night."

"To-night! How is it possible?—where to?"

"Well, I know pretty well where to," said the senator, beginning to put on his boots, with a reflective air; and, stopping when his leg was half in, he embraced his knee with both hands, and seemed to go off in deep meditation.

"It's a confounded awkward, ugly business," said he, at last, beginning to tug at his boot-straps again, "and that's a fact!" After one boot was fairly on, the senator sat with the other in his hand, profoundly studying the figure of the carpet. "It will have to be done, though, for aught I see,—hang it all!" and he drew the other boot anxiously on, and looked out of the window.

Now, little Mrs. Bird was a discreet woman,—a woman who never in her life said, "I told you so!" and, on the present occasion, though pretty well aware of the shape her husband's meditations were taking, she very prudently forbore to meddle with them, only sat very quietly in her chair, and looked quite ready to hear her liege lord's intentions, when he should think proper to utter them.

"You see," he said, "there's my old client, Van Trompe, has come over from Kentucky, and set all his slaves free; and he has bought a place seven miles up the creek, here, back in the woods, where nobody goes, unless they go on purpose; and it's a place that isn't found in a hurry. There she'd be safe enough; but the plague of the thing is, nobody could drive a carriage there to-night, but *me*."

"Why not? Cudjoe is an excellent driver."

"Ay, ay, but here it is. The creek has to be crossed twice; and the second crossing is quite dangerous, unless one knows it as I do. I have crossed it a hundred times on horseback, and know exactly the turns to take. And so, you see, there's no help for it. Cudjoe must put in the horses, as quietly as may be, about twelve o'clock, and I'll take her over; and then, to give color to the matter, he must carry me on to the next tavern, to take the stage for Columbus,[3] that

3. The capital of Ohio, in the central part of the state.

comes by about three or four, and so it will look as if I had had the carriage only for that. I shall get into business bright and early in the morning. But I'm thinking I shall feel rather cheap there, after all that's been said and done; but, hang it, I can't help it!"

"Your heart is better than your head, in this case, John," said the wife, laying her little white hand on his. "Could I ever have loved you, had I not known you better than you know yourself?" And the little woman looked so handsome, with the tears sparkling in her eyes, that the senator thought he must be a decidedly clever fellow, to get such a pretty creature into such a passionate admiration of him; and so, what could he do but walk off soberly, to see about the carriage. At the door, however, he stopped a moment, and then coming back, he said, with some hesitation,

"Mary, I don't know how you'd feel about it, but there's that drawer full of things—of—of—poor little Henry's." So saying, he turned quickly on his heel, and shut the door after him.

His wife opened the little bed-room door adjoining her room, and, taking the candle, set it down on the top of a bureau there; then from a small recess she took a key, and put it thoughtfully in the lock of a drawer, and made a sudden pause, while two boys, who, boy like, had followed close on her heels, stood looking, with silent, significant glances, at their mother. And oh! mother that reads this, has there never been in your house a drawer, or a closet, the opening of which has been to you like the opening again of a little grave? Ah! happy mother that you are, if it has not been so.

Mrs. Bird slowly opened the drawer. There were little coats of many a form and pattern, piles of aprons, and rows of small stockings; and even a pair of little shoes, worn and rubbed at the toes, were peeping from the folds of a paper. There was a toy horse and wagon, a top, a ball,—memorials gathered with many a tear and many a heart-break! She sat down by the drawer, and, leaning her head on her hands over it, wept till the tears fell through her fingers into the drawer; then suddenly raising her head, she began, with nervous haste, selecting the plainest and most substantial articles, and gathering them into a bundle.

"Mamma," said one of the boys, gently touching her arm, "are you going to give away *those* things?"

"My dear boys," she said, softly and earnestly, "if our dear, loving little Henry looks down from heaven, he would be glad to have us do this. I could not find it in my heart to give them away to any common person—to anybody that was happy; but I give them to a mother more heart-broken and sorrowful than I am; and I hope God will send his blessings with them!"

There are in this world blessed souls, whose sorrows all spring up into joys for others; whose earthly hopes, laid in the grave with many tears, are the seed from which spring healing flowers and balm for the desolate and the distressed. Among such was the delicate woman who sits there by the lamp, dropping slow tears, while she prepares the memorials of her own lost one for the outcast wanderer.

After a while, Mrs. Bird opened a wardrobe, and, taking from thence a plain, serviceable dress or two, she sat down busily to her work-table, and, with needle, scissors, and thimble, at hand, quietly commenced the "letting down" process which her husband had recommended, and continued busily at it till the old clock in the corner struck twelve, and she heard the low rattling of wheels at the door.

"Mary," said her husband, coming in, with his overcoat in his hand, "you must wake her up now; we must be off."

Mrs. Bird hastily deposited the various articles she had collected in a small plain trunk, and locking it, desired her husband to see it in the carriage, and then proceeded to call the woman. Soon, arrayed in a cloak, bonnet, and shawl, that had belonged to her benefactress, she appeared at the door with her child in her arms. Mr. Bird hurried her into the carriage, and Mrs. Bird pressed on after her to the carriage steps. Eliza leaned out of the carriage, and put out her hand,—a hand as soft and beautiful as was given in return. She fixed her large, dark eyes, full of earnest meaning, on Mrs. Bird's face, and seemed going to speak. Her lips moved,—she tried once or twice, but there was no sound,—and pointing upward, with a look never to be forgotten, she fell back in the seat, and covered her face. The door was shut, and the carriage drove on.

What a situation, now, for a patriotic senator, that had been all the week before spurring up the legislature of his native state to pass more stringent resolutions against escaping fugitives, their harborers and abettors!

Our good senator in his native state had not been exceeded by any of his brethren at Washington, in the sort of eloquence which has won for them immortal renown! How sublimely he had sat with his hands in his pockets, and scouted all sentimental weakness of those who would put the welfare of a few miserable fugitives before great state interests!

He was as bold as a lion about it, and "mightily convinced" not only himself, but everybody that heard him;—but then his idea of a fugitive was only an idea of the letters that spell the word,—or, at the most, the image of a little newspaper picture of a man with a stick and bundle, with "Ran away from the subscriber" under it.[4] The magic of the real presence of distress,—the imploring human

4. Advertisements were sometimes placed in newspapers in attempts to find escaped slaves. See below, pp. 416–17.

eye, the frail, trembling human hand, the despairing appeal of helpless agony,—these he had never tried. He had never thought that a fugitive might be a hapless mother, a defenceless child,—like that one which was now wearing his lost boy's little well-known cap; and so, as our poor senator was not stone or steel,—as he was a man, and a downright noblehearted one, too,—he was, as everybody must see, in a sad case for his patriotism. And you need not exult over him, good brother of the Southern States; for we have some inklings that many of you, under similar circumstances, would not do much better. We have reason to know, in Kentucky, as in Mississippi, are noble and generous hearts, to whom never was tale of suffering told in vain. Ah, good brother! is it fair for you to expect of us services which your own brave, honorable heart would not allow you to render, were you in our place?

Be that as it may, if our good senator was a political sinner, he was in a fair way to expiate it by his night's penance. There had been a long continuous period of rainy weather, and the soft, rich earth of Ohio, as every one knows, is admirably suited to the manufacture of mud,—and the road was an Ohio railroad of the good old times.

"And pray, what sort of a road may that be?" says some eastern traveller, who has been accustomed to connect no ideas with a railroad, but those of smoothness or speed.

Know, then, innocent eastern friend, that in benighted regions of the west, where the mud is of unfathomable and sublime depth, roads are made of round rough logs, arranged transversely side by side, and coated over in their pristine freshness with earth, turf, and whatsoever may come to hand, and then the rejoicing native calleth it a road, and straightway essayeth to ride thereupon. In process of time, the rains wash off all the turf and grass aforesaid, move the logs hither and thither, in picturesque positions, up, down and crosswise, with divers chasms and ruts of black mud intervening.

Over such a road as this our senator went stumbling along, making moral reflections as continuously as under the circumstances could be expected,—the carriage proceeding along much as follows,—bump! bump! bump! slush! down in the mud!—the senator, woman and child, reversing their positions so suddenly as to come, without any very accurate adjustment, against the windows of the downhill side. Carriage sticks fast, while Cudjoe on the outside is heard making a great muster among the horses. After various ineffectual pullings and twitchings, just as the senator is losing all patience, the carriage suddenly rights itself with a bounce,—two front wheels go down into another abyss, and senator, woman, and child, all tumble promiscuously on to the front seat,—senator's hat is jammed over his eyes and nose quite unceremoniously, and he considers himself fairly extinguished;—child cries, and Cudjoe on the outside delivers animated addresses to the horses, who are kicking, and floundering, and straining, under repeated cracks of the whip. Carriage springs up, with another bounce,—down go the hind wheels,—senator, woman, and child, fly over on to the back seat, his elbows encountering her bonnet, and both her feet being jammed into his hat, which flies off in the concussion. After a few moments the "slough" is passed, and the horses stop, panting;—the senator finds his hat, the woman straightens her bonnet and hushes her child, and they brace themselves firmly for what is yet to come.

For a while only the continuous bump! bump! intermingled, just by way of variety, with divers side plunges and compound shakes; and they begin to flatter themselves that they are not so badly off, after all. At last, with a square plunge, which puts all on to their feet and then down into their seats with incredible quickness, the carriage stops,—and, after much outside commotion, Cudjoe appears at the door.

"Please, sir, it's powerful bad spot, this yer. I don't know how we's to get clar out. I'm a thinkin' we'll have to be a gettin' rails."

The senator despairingly steps out, picking gingerly for some firm foothold; down goes one foot an immeasurable depth,—he tries to pull it up, loses his balance, and tumbles over into the mud, and is fished out, in a very despairing condition, by Cudjoe.

But we forbear, out of sympathy to our readers' bones. Western travellers, who have beguiled the midnight hour in the interesting process of pulling down rail fences, to pry their carriages out of mud holes, will have a respectful and mournful sympathy with our unfortunate hero. We beg them to drop a silent tear, and pass on.

It was full late in the night when the carriage emerged, dripping and bespattered, out of the creek, and stood at the door of a large farmhouse.

It took no inconsiderable perseverance to arouse the inmates; but at last the respectable proprietor appeared, and undid the door. He was a great, tall, bristling Orson of a fellow,[5] full six feet and some inches in his stockings, and arrayed in a red flannel hunting-shirt. A very heavy *mat* of sandy hair, in a decidedly tousled condition, and a beard of some days' growth, gave the worthy man an appearance, to say the least, not particularly prepossessing. He stood for a few minutes holding the candle aloft, and blinking on our travellers with a dismal and mystified expression that was truly ludicrous. It cost some effort of our senator to induce him to comprehend the case fully; and while he is doing his best at that, we shall give him a little introduction to our readers.

5. An allusion to a then well-known character from a medieval romance called "Valentine and Orson," where Orson is a man raised by a bear. A strong, wild man is the intention here.

Honest old John Van Trompe was once quite a considerable land-holder and slave-owner in the State of Kentucky. Having "nothing of the bear about him but the skin," and being gifted by nature with a great, honest, just heart, quite equal to his gigantic frame, he had been for some years witnessing with repressed uneasiness the workings of a system equally bad for oppressor and oppressed. At last, one day, John's great heart had swelled altogether too big to wear his bonds any longer; so he just took his pocket-book out of his desk, and went over into Ohio, and bought a quarter of a township of good, rich land, made out free papers for all his people,—men, women, and children,—packed them up in wagons, and sent them off to settle down; and then honest John turned his face up the creek, and sat quietly down on a snug, retired farm, to enjoy his conscience and his reflections.

"Are you the man that will shelter a poor woman and child from slave-catchers?" said the senator, explicitly.

"I rather think I am," said honest John, with some considerable emphasis.

"I thought so," said the senator.

"If there's anybody comes," said the good man, stretching his tall, muscular form upward, "why here I'm ready for him: and I've got seven sons, each six foot high, and they'll be ready for 'em. Give our respects to 'em," said John; "tell 'em it's no matter how soon they call,—make no kinder difference to us," said John, running his fingers through the shock of hair that thatched his head, and bursting out into a great laugh.

Weary, jaded, and spiritless, Eliza dragged herself up to the door, with her child lying in a heavy sleep on her arm. The rough man held the candle to her face, and uttering a kind of compassionate grunt, opened the door of a small bedroom adjoining to the large kitchen where they were standing, and motioned her to go in. He took down a candle, and lighting it, set it upon the table, and then addressed himself to Eliza.

"Now, I say, gal, you needn't be a bit afeard, let who will come here. I'm up to all that sort o' thing," said he, pointing to two or three goodly rifles over the mantel-piece; "and most people that know me know that 't wouldn't be healthy to try to get anybody out o' my house when I'm agin it. So *now* you jist go to sleep now, as quiet as if yer mother was a rockin' ye," said he, as he shut the door.

"Why, this is an uncommon handsome un," he said to the senator. "Ah, well; handsome uns has the greatest cause to run, sometimes, if they has any kind o' feelin, such as decent women should. I know all about that."

The senator, in a few words, briefly explained Eliza's history.

"O! ou! aw! now, I want to know?" said the good man, pitifully; "sho! now sho! That's natur now, poor crittur! hunted down now like a deer,—hunted down, jest for havin' natural feelin's, and doin' what no kind o' mother could help a doin'! I tell ye what, these yer things make me come the nighest to swearin', now, o' most anything," said honest John, as he wiped his eyes with the back of a great, freckled, yellow hand. "I tell yer what, stranger, it was years and years before I'd jine the church, 'cause the ministers round in our parts used to preach that the Bible went in for these ere cuttings up,—and I couldn't be up to 'em with their Greek and Hebrew, and so I took up agin 'em, Bible and all. I never jined the church till I found a minister that was up to 'em all in Greek and all that, and he said right the contrary; and then I took right hold, and jined the church,—I did now, fact," said John, who had been all this time uncorking some very frisky bottled cider, which at this juncture he presented.

"Ye'd better jest put up here, now, till daylight," said he, heartily, "and I'll call up the old woman, and have a bed got ready for you in no time."

"Thank you, my good friend," said the senator, "I must be along, to take the night stage for Columbus."

"Ah! well, then, if you must, I'll go a piece with you, and show you a cross road that will take you there better than the road you came on. That road's mighty bad."

John equipped himself, and, with a lantern in hand, was soon seen guiding the senator's carriage towards a road that ran down in a hollow, back of his dwelling. When they parted, the senator put into his hand a ten-dollar bill.

"It's for her," he said, briefly.

"Ay, ay," said John, with equal conciseness.

They shook hands, and parted.

## Chapter X

### *The Property Is Carried Off*

The February morning looked gray and drizzling through the window of Uncle Tom's cabin. It looked on downcast faces, the images of mournful hearts. The little table stood out before the fire, covered with an ironing-cloth; a coarse but clean shirt or two, fresh from the iron, hung on the back of a chair by the fire, and Aunt Chloe had another spread out before her on the table. Carefully she rubbed and ironed every fold and every hem, with the most scrupulous exactness, every now and then raising her hand to her face to wipe off the tears that were coursing down her cheeks.

Tom sat by, with his Testament[1] open on his knee, and his head leaning upon his hand;—but neither spoke. It was yet early, and the children lay all asleep together in their little rude trundle-bed.

Tom, who had, to the full, the gentle, domestic heart, which, woe for them! has been a peculiar characteristic of his unhappy race, got up and walked silently to look at his children.

"It's the last time," he said.

Aunt Chloe did not answer, only rubbed away over and over on the coarse shirt, already as smooth as hands could make it; and finally setting her iron suddenly down with a despairing plunge, she sat down to the table, and "lifted up her voice and wept."[2]

"S'pose we must be resigned; but oh Lord! how ken I? If I know'd anything whar you 's goin', or how they'd sarve you! Missis says she'll try and 'deem ye, in a year or two; but Lor! nobody never comes up that goes down thar! They kills 'em! I've hearn 'em tell how dey works 'em up on dem ar plantations."

"There'll be the same God there, Chloe, that there is here."

"Well," said Aunt Chloe, "s'pose dere will; but de Lord lets dreful things happen, sometimes. I don't seem to get no comfort dat way."

"I'm in the Lord's hands," said Tom; "nothin' can go no furder than he lets it;—and thar's *one* thing I can thank him for. It's *me* that's sold and going down, and not you nur the chil'en. Here you're safe;—what comes will come only on me; and the Lord, he'll help me,—I know he will."

Ah, brave, manly heart,—smothering thine own sorrow, to comfort thy beloved ones! Tom spoke with a thick utterance, and with a bitter choking in his throat,—but he spoke brave and strong.

"Let's think on our marcies!" he added, tremulously, as if he was quite sure he needed to think on them very hard indeed.

"Marcies!" said Aunt Chloe; "don't see no marcy in 't! 'tan't right! tan't right it should be so! Mas'r never ought ter left it so that ye *could* be took for his debts. Ye've arnt him all he gets for ye, twice over. He owed ye yer freedom, and ought ter gin 't to yer years ago. Mebbe he can't help himself now, but I feel it's wrong. Nothing can't beat that ar out o' me. Sich a faithful crittur as ye've been,—and allers sot his business 'fore yer own every way,—and reckoned on him more than yer own wife and chil'en! Them as sells heart's love and heart's blood, to get out thar scrapes, de Lord'll be up to 'em!"

"Chloe! now, if ye love me, ye won't talk so, when perhaps jest the last time we'll ever have together! And I'll tell ye, Chloe, it goes agin me to hear one word agin Mas'r. Wan't he put in my arms a

1. Bible.
2. A common biblical phrase; see Genesis 21.16, 27.38, 29.11, et al.

baby?—it's natur I should think a heap of him. And he couldn't be spected to think so much of poor Tom. Mas'rs is used to havin' all these yer things done for 'em, and nat'lly they don't think so much on 't. They can't be spected to, no way. Set him 'longside of other Mas'rs—who's had the treatment and the livin' I've had? And he never would have let this yer come on me, if he could have seed it aforehand. I know he wouldn't."

"Wal, any way, thar's wrong about it *somewhar*," said Aunt Chloe, in whom a stubborn sense of justice was a predominant trait; "I can't jest make out whar 't is, but thar's wrong somewhar, I'm *clar* o' that."

"Yer ought ter look up to the Lord above—he's above all—thar don't a sparrow fall without him."

"It don't seem to comfort me, but I spect it orter," said Aunt Chloe. "But dar's no use talkin'; I'll jes wet up de corn-cake, and get ye one good breakfast, 'cause nobody knows when you'll get another."

In order to appreciate the sufferings of the negroes sold south, it must be remembered that all the instinctive affections of that race are peculiarly strong. Their local attachments are very abiding. They are not naturally daring and enterprising, but home-loving and affectionate. Add to this all the terrors with which ignorance invests the unknown, and add to this, again, that selling to the south is set before the negro from childhood as the last severity of punishment. The threat that terrifies more than whipping or torture of any kind is the threat of being sent down river. We have ourselves heard this feeling expressed by them, and seen the unaffected horror with which they will sit in their gossipping hours, and tell frightful stories of that "down river," which to them is

> "That undiscovered country, from whose bourn
> No traveller returns."[3]

A missionary among the fugitives in Canada told us that many of the fugitives confessed themselves to have escaped from comparatively kind masters, and that they were induced to brave the perils of escape, in almost every case, by the desperate horror with which they regarded being sold south,—a doom which was hanging either over themselves or their husbands, their wives or children. This nerves the African, naturally patient, timid and unenterprising, with heroic courage, and leads him to suffer hunger, cold, pain, the perils of the wilderness, and the more dread penalties of re-capture.

The simple morning meal now smoked on the table, for Mrs. Shelby had excused Aunt Chloe's attendance at the great house that morning. The poor soul had expended all her little energies on this fare-

3. I.e., death. The quotation is from Shakespeare, *Hamlet* 3.1.56–57.

well feast,—had killed and dressed her choicest chicken, and prepared her corn-cake with scrupulous exactness, just to her husband's taste, and brought out certain mysterious jars on the mantel-piece, some preserves that were never produced except on extreme occasions.

"Lor, Pete," said Mose, triumphantly, "han't we got a buster of a breakfast!" at the same time catching at a fragment of the chicken.

Aunt Chloe gave him a sudden box on the ear. "Thar now! crowing over the last breakfast yer poor daddy's gwine to have to home!"

"O, Chloe!" said Tom, gently.

"Wal, I can't help it," said Aunt Chloe, hiding her face in her apron; "I's so tossed about, it makes me act ugly."

The boys stood quite still, looking first at their father and then at their mother, while the baby, climbing up her clothes, began an imperious, commanding cry.

"Thar!" said Aunt Chloe, wiping her eyes and taking up the baby; "now I's done, I hope,—now do eat something. This yer's my nicest chicken. Thar, boys, ye shall have some, poor critturs! Yer mammy's been cross to yer."

The boys needed no second invitation, and went in with great zeal for the eatables; and it was well they did so, as otherwise there would have been very little performed to any purpose by the party.

"Now," said Aunt Chloe, bustling about after breakfast, "I must put up yer clothes. Jest like as not, he'll take 'em all away. I know thar ways—mean as dirt, they is! Wal, now, yer flannels for rhumatis is in this corner; so be carful, 'cause there won't nobody make ye no more. Then here's yer old shirts, and these yer is new ones. I toed off these yer stockings last night, and put de ball[4] in 'em to mend with. But Lor! who'll ever mend for ye?" and Aunt Chloe, again overcome, laid her head on the box side, and sobbed. "To think on 't! no crittur to do for ye, sick or well! I don't railly think I ought ter be good now!"

The boys, having eaten everything there was on the breakfast-table, began now to take some thought of the case; and, seeing their mother crying, and their father looking very sad, began to whimper and put their hands to their eyes. Uncle Tom had the baby on his knee, and was letting her enjoy herself to the utmost extent, scratching his face and pulling his hair, and occasionally breaking out into clamorous explosions of delight, evidently arising out of her own internal reflections.

"Ay, crow away, poor crittur!" said Aunt Chloe; "ye'll have to come to it, too! ye'll live to see yer husband sold, or mebbe be sold yerself; and these yer boys, they's to be sold, I s'pose, too, jest like as not, when dey gets good for somethin'; an't no use in niggers havin' nothin'!"

4. An object used to hold fabric taut for mending, especially for darning socks.

Here one of the boys called out, "Thar's Missis a-comin' in!"

"She can't do no good; what's she coming for?" said Aunt Chloe.

Mrs. Shelby entered. Aunt Chloe set a chair for her in a manner decidedly gruff and crusty. She did not seem to notice either the action or the manner. She looked pale and anxious.

"Tom," she said, "I come to—" and stopping suddenly, and regarding the silent group, she sat down in the chair, and, covering her face with her handkerchief, began to sob.

"Lor, now, Missis, don't—don't!" said Aunt Chloe, bursting out in her turn; and for a few moments they all wept in company. And in those tears they all shed together, the high and the lowly, melted away all the heart-burnings and anger of the oppressed. O, ye who visit the distressed, do ye know that everything your money can buy, given with a cold, averted face, is not worth one honest tear shed in real sympathy?

"My good fellow," said Mrs. Shelby, "I can't give you anything to do you any good. If I give you money, it will only be taken from you. But I tell you solemnly, and before God, that I will keep trace of you, and bring you back as soon as I can command the money;—and, till then, trust in God!"

Here the boys called out that Mas'r Haley was coming, and then an unceremonious kick pushed open the door. Haley stood there in very ill humor, having ridden hard the night before, and being not at all pacified by his ill success in re-capturing his prey.

"Come," said he, "ye nigger, ye'r ready? Servant, ma'am!" said he, taking off his hat, as he saw Mrs. Shelby.

Aunt Chloe shut and corded the box, and, getting up, looked gruffly on the trader, her tears seeming suddenly turned to sparks of fire.

Tom rose up meekly, to follow his new master, and raised up his heavy box on his shoulder. His wife took the baby in her arms to go with him to the wagon, and the children, still crying, trailed on behind.

Mrs. Shelby, walking up to the trader, detained him for a few moments, talking with him in an earnest manner; and while she was thus talking, the whole family party proceeded to a wagon, that stood ready harnessed at the door. A crowd of all the old and young hands on the place stood gathered around it, to bid farewell to their old associate. Tom had been looked up to, both as a head servant and a Christian teacher, by all the place, and there was much honest sympathy and grief about him, particularly among the women.

"Why, Chloe, you bar it better 'n we do!" said one of the women, who had been weeping freely, noticing the gloomy calmness with which Aunt Chloe stood by the wagon.

"I's done *my* tears!" she said, looking grimly at the trader, who was coming up. "I does not feel to cry 'fore dat ar old limb,[5] no how!"

"Get in!" said Haley to Tom, as he strode through the crowd of servants, who looked at him with lowering brows.

Tom got in, and Haley, drawing out from under the wagon seat a heavy pair of shackles, made them fast around each ankle.

A smothered groan of indignation ran through the whole circle, and Mrs. Shelby spoke from the verandah,—

"Mr. Haley, I assure you that precaution is entirely unnecessary."

"Do'n know, ma'am; I've lost one five hundred dollars from this yer place, and I can't afford to run no more risks."

"What else could she spect on him?" said Aunt Chloe, indignantly, while the two boys, who now seemed to comprehend at once their father's destiny, clung to her gown, sobbing and groaning vehemently.

"I'm sorry," said Tom, "that Mas'r George happened to be away."

George had gone to spend two or three days with a companion on a neighboring estate, and having departed early in the morning, before Tom's misfortune had been made public, had left without hearing of it.

"Give my love to Mas'r George," he said, earnestly.

Haley whipped up the horse, and, with a steady, mournful look, fixed to the last on the old place, Tom was whirled away.

Mr. Shelby at this time was not at home. He had sold Tom under the spur of a driving necessity, to get out of the power of a man whom he dreaded,—and his first feeling, after the consummation of the bargain, had been that of relief. But his wife's expostulations awoke his half-slumbering regrets; and Tom's manly disinterestedness increased the unpleasantness of his feelings. It was in vain that he said to himself that he had a *right* to do it,—that everybody did it,—and that some did it without even the excuse of necessity;—he could not satisfy his own feelings; and that he might not witness the unpleasant scenes of the consummation, he had gone on a short business tour up the country, hoping that all would be over before he returned.

Tom and Haley rattled on along the dusty road, whirling past every old familiar spot, until the bounds of the estate were fairly passed, and they found themselves out on the open pike. After they had ridden about a mile, Haley suddenly drew up at the door of a blacksmith's shop, when, taking out with him a pair of handcuffs, he stepped into the shop, to have a little alteration in them.

"These yer's a little too small for his build," said Haley, showing the fetters, and pointing out to Tom.

5. A mischievous child.

"Lor! now, if thar an't Shelby's Tom. He han't sold him, now?" said the smith.

"Yes, he has," said Haley.

"Now, ye don't! well, reely," said the smith, "who'd a thought it! Why, ye needn't go to fetterin' him up this yer way. He's the faithfullest, best crittur—"

"Yes, yes," said Haley; "but your good fellers are just the critturs to want ter run off. Them stupid ones, as doesn't care whar they go, and shifless, drunken ones, as don't care for nothin', they'll stick by, and like as not be rather pleased to be toted round; but these yer prime fellers, they hates it like sin. No way but to fetter 'em; got legs,—they'll use 'em,—no mistake."

"Well," said the smith, feeling among his tools, "them plantations down thar, stranger, an't jest the place a Kentuck nigger wants to go to; they dies thar tol'able fast, don't they?"

"Wal, yes, tol'able fast, ther dying is; what with the 'climating and one thing and another, they dies so as to keep the market up pretty brisk," said Haley.

"Wal, now, a feller can't help thinkin' it's a mighty pity to have a nice, quiet, likely feller, as good un as Tom is, go down to be fairly ground up on one of them ar sugar plantations."

"Wal, he's got a fa'r chance. I promised to do well by him. I'll get him in house-servant in some good old family, and then, if he stands the fever and 'climating, he'll have a berth good as any nigger ought ter ask for."

"He leaves his wife and chil'en up here, s'pose?"

"Yes; but he'll get another thar. Lord, thar's women enough everywhar," said Haley.

Tom was sitting very mournfully on the outside of the shop while this conversation was going on. Suddenly he heard the quick, short click of a horse's hoof behind him; and, before he could fairly awake from his surprise, young Master George sprang into the wagon, threw his arms tumultuously round his neck, and was sobbing and scolding with energy.

"I declare, it's real mean! I don't care what they say, any of 'em! It's a nasty, mean shame! If I was a man, they shouldn't do it,—they should not, *so!*" said George, with a kind of subdued howl.

"O! Mas'r George! this does me good!" said Tom. "I couldn't bar to go off without seein' ye! It does me real good, ye can't tell!" Here Tom made some movement of his feet, and George's eye fell on the fetters.

"What a shame!" he exclaimed, lifting his hands. "I'll knock that old fellow down—I will!"

"No you won't, Mas'r George; and you must not talk so loud. It won't help me any, to anger him."

"Well, I won't, then, for your sake; but only to think of it—isn't it a shame? They never sent for me, nor sent me any word, and, if it hadn't been for Tom Lincon, I shouldn't have heard it. I tell you, I blew 'em up well, all of 'em, at home!"

"That ar wasn't right, I'm 'feard, Mas'r George."

"Can't help it! I say it's a shame! Look here, Uncle Tom," said he, turning his back to the shop, and speaking in a mysterious tone, "*I've brought you my dollar!*"[6]

"O! I couldn't think o' takin' on 't, Mas'r George, no ways in the world!" said Tom, quite moved.

"But you *shall* take it!" said George; "look here—I told Aunt Chloe I'd do it, and she advised me just to make a hole in it, and put a string through, so you could hang it round your neck, and keep it out of sight; else this mean scamp would take it away. I tell ye, Tom, I want to blow him up! it would do me good!"

"No, don't, Mas'r George, for it won't do *me* any good."

"Well, I won't, for your sake," said George, busily tying his dollar round Tom's neck; "but there, now, button your coat tight over it, and keep it, and remember, every time you see it, that I'll come down after you, and bring you back. Aunt Chloe and I have been talking about it. I told her not to fear; I'll see to it, and I'll tease father's life out, if he don't do it."

"O! Mas'r George, ye mustn't talk so 'bout yer father!"

"Lor, Uncle Tom, I don't mean anything bad."

"And now, Mas'r George," said Tom, "ye must be a good boy; 'member how many hearts is sot on ye. Al'ays keep close to yer mother. Don't be gettin' into any of them foolish ways boys has of gettin' too big to mind their mothers. Tell ye what, Mas'r George, the Lord gives good many things twice over; but he don't give ye a mother but once. Ye'll never see sich another woman, Mas'r George, if ye live to be a hundred years old. So, now, you hold on to her, and grow up, and be a comfort to her, thar's my own good boy,—you will now, won't ye?"

"Yes, I will, Uncle Tom," said George, seriously.

"And be careful of yer speaking, Mas'r George. Young boys, when they comes to your age, is wilful, sometimes—it's natur they should be. But real gentlemen, such as I hopes you'll be, never lets fall no words that isn't 'spectful to thar parents. Ye an't 'fended, Mas'r George?"

"No, indeed, Uncle Tom; you always did give me good advice."

"I's older, ye know," said Tom, stroking the boy's fine, curly head with his large, strong hand, but speaking in a voice as tender as a woman's, "and I sees all that's bound up in you. O, Mas'r George, you has everything,—l'arnin', privileges, readin', writin',—and you'll

6. I.e., a dollar coin, probably silver.

grow up to be a great, learned, good man, and all the people on the place and your mother and father'll be so proud on ye! Be a good Mas'r, like yer father; and be a Christian, like yer mother. 'Member yer Creator in the days o' yer youth, Mas'r George."

"I'll be *real* good, Uncle Tom, I tell you," said George. "I'm going to be a *first-rater*; and don't you be discouraged. I'll have you back to the place, yet. As I told Aunt Chloe this morning, I'll build your house all over, and you shall have a room for a parlor with a carpet on it, when I'm a man. O, you'll have good times yet!"

Haley now came to the door, with the handcuffs in his hands.

"Look here, now, Mister," said George, with an air of great superiority, as he got out, "I shall let father and mother know how you treat Uncle Tom!"

"You're welcome," said the trader.

"I should think you'd be ashamed to spend all your life buying men and women, and chaining them, like cattle! I should think you'd feel mean!" said George.

"So long as your grand folks wants to buy men and women, I'm as good as they is," said Haley; " 'tan't any meaner sellin' on 'em, than 't is buyin'!"

"I'll never do either, when I'm a man," said George; "I'm ashamed, this day, that I'm a Kentuckian. I always was proud of it before;" and George sat very straight on his horse, and looked round with an air, as if he expected the state would be impressed with his opinion.

"Well, good-by, Uncle Tom; keep a stiff upper lip," said George.

"Good-by, Mas'r George," said Tom, looking fondly and admiringly at him. "God Almighty bless you! Ah! Kentucky han't got many like you!" he said, in the fulness of his heart, as the frank, boyish face was lost to his view. Away he went, and Tom looked, till the clatter of his horse's heels died away, the last sound or sight of his home. But over his heart there seemed to be a warm spot, where those young hands had placed that precious dollar. Tom put up his hand, and held it close to his heart.

"Now, I tell ye what, Tom," said Haley, as he came up to the wagon, and threw in the hand-cuffs, "I mean to start fa'r with ye, as I gen'ally do with my niggers; and I'll tell ye now, to begin with, you treat me fa'r, and I'll treat you fa'r; I an't never hard on my niggers. Calculates to do the best for 'em I can. Now, ye see, you'd better jest settle down comfortable, and not be tryin' no tricks; because nigger's tricks of all sorts I'm up to, and it's no use. If niggers is quiet, and don't try to get off, they has good times with me; and if they don't, why, it's thar fault, and not mine."

Tom assured Haley that he had no present intentions of running off. In fact, the exhortation seemed rather a superfluous one to a man with a great pair of iron fetters on his feet. But Mr. Haley had got in the habit of commencing his relations with his stock with little exhortations of this nature, calculated, as he deemed, to inspire cheerfulness and confidence, and prevent the necessity of any unpleasant scenes.

And here, for the present, we take our leave of Tom, to pursue the fortunes of other characters in our story.

## Chapter XI

### *In Which Property Gets into an Improper State of Mind*

It was late in a drizzly afternoon that a traveller alighted at the door of a small country hotel, in the village of N——, in Kentucky. In the bar-room he found assembled quite a miscellaneous company, whom stress of weather had driven to harbor, and the place presented the usual scenery of such reunions. Great, tall, raw-boned Kentuckians, attired in hunting-shirts, and trailing their loose joints over a vast extent of territory, with the easy lounge peculiar to the race,—rifles stacked away in the corner, shot-pouches, game-bags, hunting-dogs, and little negroes, all rolled together in the corners,—were the characteristic features in the picture. At each end of the fireplace sat a long-legged gentleman, with his chair tipped back, his hat on his head, and the heels of his muddy boots reposing sublimely on the mantel-piece,—a position, we will inform our readers, decidedly favorable to the turn of reflection incident to western taverns, where travellers exhibit a decided preference for this particular mode of elevating their understandings.

Mine host, who stood behind the bar, like most of his countrymen, was great of stature, good-natured, and loose-jointed, with an enormous shock of hair on his head, and a great tall hat on the top of that.

In fact, everybody in the room bore on his head this characteristic emblem of man's sovereignty; whether it were felt hat, palm-leaf, greasy beaver, or fine new chapeau,[1] there it reposed with true republican independence. In truth, it appeared to be the characteristic mark of every individual. Some wore them tipped rakishly to one side—these were your men of humor, jolly, free-and-easy dogs; some had them jammed independently down over their noses—these were your hard characters, thorough men, who, when they wore their hats, *wanted* to wear them, and to wear them just as they had a mind to; there were those who had them set far over back—wide-awake

1. Hat (French). "Beaver": a hat made of beaver pelt with a tall cylindrical crown, or a fabric imitation.

men, who wanted a clear prospect; while careless men, who did not know, or care, how their hats sat, had them shaking about in all directions. The various hats, in fact, were quite a Shakespearean study.

Divers negroes, in very free-and-easy pantaloons, and with no redundancy in the shirt line, were scuttling about, hither and thither, without bringing to pass any very particular results, except expressing a generic willingness to turn over everything in creation generally for the benefit of Mas'r and his guests. Add to this picture a jolly, crackling, rollicking fire, going rejoicingly up a great wide chimney,—the outer door and every window being set wide open, and the calico window-curtain flopping and snapping in a good stiff breeze of damp raw air,—and you have an idea of the jollities of a Kentucky tavern.

Your Kentuckian of the present day is a good illustration of the doctrine of transmitted instincts and peculiarities. His fathers were mighty hunters,—men who lived in the woods, and slept under the free, open heavens, with the stars to hold their candles; and their descendant to this day always acts as if the house were his camp,—wears his hat at all hours, tumbles himself about, and puts his heels on the tops of chairs or mantel-pieces, just as his father rolled on the green sward, and put his upon trees and logs,—keeps all the windows and doors open, winter and summer, that he may get air enough for his great lungs,—calls everybody "stranger," with nonchalant bonhommie,[2] and is altogether the frankest, easiest, most jovial creature living.

Into such an assembly of the free and easy our traveller entered. He was a short, thick-set man, carefully dressed, with a round, good-natured countenance, and something rather fussy and particular in his appearance. He was very careful of his valise and umbrella, bringing them in with his own hands, and resisting, pertinaciously, all offers from the various servants to relieve him of them. He looked round the bar-room with rather an anxious air, and, retreating with his valuables to the warmest corner, disposed them under his chair, sat down, and looked rather apprehensively up at the worthy whose heels illustrated the end of the mantel-piece, who was spitting from right to left, with a courage and energy rather alarming to gentlemen of weak nerves and particular habits.

"I say, stranger, how are ye?" said the aforesaid gentleman, firing an honorary salute of tobacco-juice in the direction of the new arrival.

"Well, I reckon," was the reply of the other, as he dodged, with some alarm, the threatening honor.

"Any news?" said the respondent, taking out a strip of tobacco and a large hunting-knife from his pocket.

2. Good-natured friendliness.

"Not that I know of," said the man.

"Chaw?" said the first speaker, handing the old gentleman a bit of his tobacco, with a decidedly brotherly air.

"No, thank ye—it don't agree with me," said the little man, edging off.

"Don't, eh?" said the other, easily, and stowing away the morsel in his own mouth, in order to keep up the supply of tobacco-juice, for the general benefit of society.

The old gentleman uniformly gave a little start whenever his long-sided brother fired in his direction; and this being observed by his companion, he very good-naturedly turned his artillery to another quarter, and proceeded to storm one of the fire-irons[3] with a degree of military talent fully sufficient to take a city.

"What's that?" said the old gentleman, observing some of the company formed in a group around a large handbill.

"Nigger advertised!" said one of the company, briefly.

Mr. Wilson, for that was the old gentleman's name, rose up, and, after carefully adjusting his valise and umbrella, proceeded deliberately to take out his spectacles and fix them on his nose; and, this operation being performed, read as follows:

> "Ran away from the subscriber, my mulatto boy, George. Said George six feet in height, a very light mulatto, brown curly hair; is very intelligent, speaks handsomely, can read and write; will probably try to pass for a white man; is deeply scarred on his back and shoulders; has been branded in his right hand with the letter H.
>
> "I will give four hundred dollars for him alive, and the same sum for satisfactory proof that he has been killed."

The old gentleman read this advertisement from end to end, in a low voice, as if he were studying it.

The long-legged veteran, who had been besieging the fire-iron, as before related, now took down his cumbrous length, and rearing aloft his tall form, walked up to the advertisement, and very deliberately spit a full discharge of tobacco-juice on it.

"There's my mind upon that!" said he, briefly, and sat down again.

"Why, now, stranger, what's that for?" said mine host.

"I'd do it all the same to the writer of that ar paper, if he was here," said the long man, coolly resuming his old employment of cutting tobacco. "Any man that owns a boy like that, and can't find any better way o' treating on him, *deserves* to lose him. Such papers as these is a shame to Kentucky; that's my mind right out, if anybody wants to know!"

3. Utensils for a fireplace: tongs, poker, and shovel.

"Well, now, that's a fact," said mine host, as he made an entry in his book.

"I've got a gang of boys, sir," said the long man, resuming his attack on the fire-irons, "and I jest tells 'em—'Boys,' says I,—'*run* now! dig! put! jest when ye want to! I never shall come to look after you!' That's the way I keep mine. Let 'em know they are free to run any time, and it jest breaks up their wanting to. More 'n all, I've got free papers[4] for 'em all recorded, in case I gets keeled up any o' these times, and they knows it; and I tell ye, stranger, there an't a fellow in our parts gets more out of his niggers than I do. Why, my boys have been to Cincinnati, with five hundred dollars' worth of colts, and brought me back the money, all straight, time and agin. It stands to reason they should. Treat 'em like dogs, and you'll have dogs' works and dogs' actions. Treat 'em like men, and you'll have men's works." And the honest drover, in his warmth, endorsed this moral sentiment by firing a perfect *feu de joie*[5] at the fireplace.

"I think you're altogether right, friend," said Mr. Wilson; "and this boy described here *is* a fine fellow—no mistake about that. He worked for me some half-dozen years in my bagging factory, and he was my best hand, sir. He is an ingenious fellow, too: he invented a machine for the cleaning of hemp—a really valuable affair; it's gone into use in several factories. His master holds the patent of it."

"I'll warrant ye," said the drover, "holds it and makes money out of it, and then turns round and brands the boy in his right hand. If I had a fair chance, I'd mark him, I reckon, so that he'd carry it *one* while."

"These yer knowin' boys is allers aggravatin' and sarcy," said a coarse-looking fellow, from the other side of the room; "that's why they gets cut up and marked so. If they behaved themselves, they wouldn't."

"That is to say, the Lord made 'em men, and it's a hard squeeze getting 'em down into beasts," said the drover, dryly.

"Bright niggers isn't no kind of 'vantage to their masters," continued the other, well intrenched, in a coarse, unconscious obtuseness, from the contempt of his opponent; "what's the use o' talents and them things, if you can't get the use of 'em yourself? Why, all the use they make on 't is to get round you. I've had one or two of these fellers, and I jest sold 'em down river. I knew I'd got to lose 'em, first or last, if I didn't."

"Better send orders up to the Lord, to make you a set, and leave out their souls entirely," said the drover.

4. Certificates given to freed slaves as proof of their manumission.
5. A salute fired by rifles to celebrate a victory.

Here the conversation was interrupted by the approach of a small one-horse buggy to the inn. It had a genteel appearance, and a well-dressed, gentlemanly man sat on the seat, with a colored servant driving.

The whole party examined the new comer with the interest with which a set of loafers in a rainy day usually examine every new comer. He was very tall, with a dark, Spanish complexion, fine, expressive black eyes, and close-curling hair, also of a glossy blackness. His well-formed aquiline nose, straight thin lips, and the admirable contour of his finely-formed limbs, impressed the whole company instantly with the idea of something uncommon. He walked easily in among the company, and with a nod indicated to his waiter where to place his trunk, bowed to the company, and, with his hat in his hand, walked up leisurely to the bar, and gave in his name as Henry Butler, Oaklands, Shelby County. Turning, with an indifferent air, he sauntered up to the advertisement, and read it over.

"Jim," he said to his man, "seems to me we met a boy something like this, up at Bernan's, didn't we?"

"Yes, Mas'r," said Jim, "only I an't sure about the hand."

"Well, I didn't look, of course," said the stranger, with a careless yawn. Then, walking up to the landlord, he desired him to furnish him with a private apartment, as he had some writing to do immediately.

The landlord was all obsequious, and a relay of about seven negroes, old and young, male and female, little and big, were soon whizzing about, like a covey of partridges, bustling, hurrying, treading on each other's toes, and tumbling over each other, in their zeal to get Mas'r's room ready, while he seated himself easily on a chair in the middle of the room, and entered into conversation with the man who sat next to him.

The manufacturer, Mr. Wilson, from the time of the entrance of the stranger, had regarded him with an air of disturbed and uneasy curiosity. He seemed to himself to have met and been acquainted with him somewhere, but he could not recollect. Every few moments, when the man spoke, or moved, or smiled, he would start and fix his eyes on him, and then suddenly withdraw them, as the bright, dark eyes met his with such unconcerned coolness. At last, a sudden recollection seemed to flash upon him, for he stared at the stranger with such an air of blank amazement and alarm, that he walked up to him.

"Mr. Wilson, I think," said he, in a tone of recognition, and extending his hand. "I beg your pardon, I didn't recollect you before. I see you remember me,—Mr. Butler, of Oaklands, Shelby County."

"Ye—yes—yes, sir," said Mr. Wilson, like one speaking in a dream.

Just then a negro boy entered, and announced that Mas'r's room was ready.

"Jim, see to the trunks," said the gentleman, negligently; then addressing himself to Mr. Wilson, he added—"I should like to have a few moments' conversation with you on business, in my room, if you please."

Mr. Wilson followed him, as one who walks in his sleep; and they proceeded to a large upper chamber, where a new-made fire was crackling, and various servants flying about, putting finishing touches to the arrangements.

When all was done, and the servants departed, the young man deliberately locked the door, and putting the key in his pocket, faced about, and folding his arms on his bosom, looked Mr. Wilson full in the face.

"George!" said Mr. Wilson.

"Yes, George," said the young man.

"I couldn't have thought it!"

"I am pretty well disguised, I fancy," said the young man, with a smile. "A little walnut bark has made my yellow skin a genteel brown, and I've dyed my hair black; so you see I don't answer to the advertisement at all."

"O, George! but this is a dangerous game you are playing. I could not have advised you to it."

"I can do it on my own responsibility," said George, with the same proud smile.

We remark, *en passant*,[6] that George was, by his father's side, of white descent. His mother was one of those unfortunates of her race, marked out by personal beauty to be the slave of the passions of her possessor, and the mother of children who may never know a father. From one of the proudest families in Kentucky he had inherited a set of fine European features, and a high, indomitable spirit. From his mother he had received only a slight mulatto tinge, amply compensated by its accompanying rich, dark eye. A slight change in the tint of the skin and the color of his hair had metamorphosed him into the Spanish-looking fellow he then appeared; and as gracefulness of movement and gentlemanly manners had always been perfectly natural to him, he found no difficulty in playing the bold part he had adopted—that of a gentleman travelling with his domestic.

Mr. Wilson, a good-natured but extremely fidgety and cautious old gentleman, ambled up and down the room, appearing, as John Bunyan hath it, "much tumbled up and down in his mind,"[7] and divided

6. In passing; incidentally (French).
7. In part 2 of *Pilgrim's Progress* (see above, p. 60, n. 4), Christiana and Mercy find a fierce dog guarding the gate they must enter: "Now, therefore, they were greatly tumbled up and down in their minds, and knew not what to do; knock they durst not, for fear of the dog; go back they durst not, for fear the Keeper of that gate should espy them as they so went, and should be offended with them."

between his wish to help George, and a certain confused notion of maintaining law and order: so, as he shambled about, he delivered himself as follows:

"Well, George, I s'pose you're running away—leaving your lawful master, George—(I don't wonder at it)—at the same time, I'm sorry, George,—yes, decidedly—I think I must say that, George—it's my duty to tell you so."

"Why are you sorry, sir?" said George, calmly.

"Why, to see you, as it were, setting yourself in opposition to the laws of your country."

"*My* country!" said George, with a strong and bitter emphasis; "what country have I, but the grave,—and I wish to God that I was laid there!"

"Why, George, no—no—it won't do; this way of talking is wicked—unscriptural. George, you've got a hard master—in fact, he is—well he conducts himself reprehensibly—I can't pretend to defend him. But you know how the angel commanded Hagar to return to her mistress, and submit herself under her hand; and the apostle sent back Onesimus to his master."[8]

"Don't quote Bible at me that way, Mr. Wilson," said George, with a flashing eye, "don't! for my wife is a Christian, and I mean to be, if ever I get to where I can; but to quote Bible to a fellow in my circumstances, is enough to make him give it up altogether. I appeal to God Almighty;—I'm willing to go with the case to Him, and ask Him if I do wrong to seek my freedom."

"These feelings are quite natural, George," said the good-natured man, blowing his nose. "Yes they're natural, but it is my duty not to encourage 'em in you. Yes, my boy, I'm sorry for you, now; it's a bad case—very bad; but the apostle says, 'Let every one abide in the condition in which he is called.'[9] We must all submit to the indications of Providence, George,—don't you see?"

George stood with his head drawn back, his arms folded tightly over his broad breast, and a bitter smile curling his lips.

"I wonder, Mr. Wilson, if the Indians should come and take you a prisoner away from your wife and children, and want to keep you all your life hoeing corn for them, if you'd think it your duty to abide in the condition in which you were called. I rather think that you'd think the first stray horse you could find an indication of Providence—shouldn't you?"

8. Onesimus is named in Paul's letter to Philemon (10–16). Treated harshly by Sarah, her mistress, Hagar ran away into the wilderness, but an angel commanded her to go back: "And the angel of the lord said unto her, Return to thy mistress, and submit thyself under her hands" (Genesis 16.9).

9. Paul writes of freedom and servitude: "Let every man abide in the same calling wherein he was called" (1 Corinthians 7.20).

The little old gentleman stared with both eyes at this illustration of the case; but, though not much of a reasoner, he had the sense in which some logicians on this particular subject do not excel,—that of saying nothing, where nothing could be said. So, as he stood carefully stroking his umbrella, and folding and patting down all the creases in it, he proceeded on with his exhortations in a general way.

"You see, George, you know, now, I always have stood your friend; and whatever I've said, I've said for your good. Now, here, it seems to me, you're running an awful risk. You can't hope to carry it out. If you're taken, it will be worse with you than ever; they'll only abuse you, and half kill you, and sell you down river."

"Mr. Wilson, I know all this," said George. "I *do* run a risk, but—" he threw open his overcoat, and showed two pistols and a bowie-knife. "There!" he said, "I'm ready for 'em! Down south I never *will* go. No! if it comes to that, I can earn myself at least six feet of free soil,—the first and last I shall ever own in Kentucky!"

"Why, George, this state of mind is awful; it's getting really desperate, George. I'm concerned. Going to break the laws of your country!"

"My country again! Mr. Wilson, *you* have a country; but what country have *I*, or any one like me, born of slave mothers? What laws are there for us? We don't make them,—we don't consent to them,—we have nothing to do with them; all they do for us is to crush us, and keep us down. Haven't I heard your Fourth-of-July speeches? Don't you tell us all, once a year, that governments derive their just power from the consent of the governed?[1] Can't a fellow *think*, that hears such things? Can't he put this and that together, and see what it comes to?"

Mr. Wilson's mind was one of those that may not unaptly be represented by a bale of cotton,—downy, soft, benevolently fuzzy and confused. He really pitied George with all his heart, and had a sort of dim and cloudy perception of the style of feeling that agitated him; but he deemed it his duty to go on talking *good* to him, with infinite pertinacity.

"George, this is bad. I must tell you, you know, as a friend, you'd better not be meddling with such notions; they are bad, George, very bad, for boys in your condition,—very;" and Mr. Wilson sat down to a table, and began nervously chewing the handle of his umbrella.

"See here, now, Mr. Wilson," said George, coming up and sitting himself determinately down in front of him; "look at me, now. Don't

1. From the Declaration of Independence of the United States (1776): "We hold these truths to be self-evident, that all men are created equal, that they are endowed by their Creator with certain unalienable Rights, that among these are Life, Liberty, and the pursuit of Happiness—That to secure these rights, Governments are instituted among Men, deriving their just powers from the consent of the governed . . ."

I sit before you, every way, just as much a man as you are? Look at my face,—look at my hands,—look at my body," and the young man drew himself up proudly; "why am I *not* a man, as much as anybody? Well, Mr. Wilson, hear what I can tell you. I had a father—one of your Kentucky gentlemen—who didn't think enough of me to keep me from being sold with his dogs and horses, to satisfy the estate, when he died. I saw my mother put up at sheriff's sale,[2] with her seven children. They were sold before her eyes, one by one, all to different masters; and I was the youngest. She came and kneeled down before old Mas'r, and begged him to buy her with me, that she might have at least one child with her; and he kicked her away with his heavy boot. I saw him do it; and the last that I heard was her moans and screams, when I was tied to his horse's neck, to be carried off to his place."

"Well, then?"

"My master traded with one of the men, and bought my oldest sister. She was a pious, good girl,—a member of the Baptist church,—and as handsome as my poor mother had been. She was well brought up, and had good manners. At first, I was glad she was bought, for I had one friend near me. I was soon sorry for it. Sir, I have stood at the door and heard her whipped, when it seemed as if every blow cut into my naked heart, and I couldn't do anything to help her; and she was whipped, sir, for wanting to live a decent Christian life, such as your laws give no slave girl a right to live; and at last I saw her chained with a trader's gang, to be sent to market in Orleans,—sent there for nothing else but that,—and that's the last I know of her. Well, I grew up,—long years and years,—no father, no mother, no sister, not a living soul that cared for me more than a dog; nothing but whipping, scolding, starving. Why, sir, I've been so hungry that I have been glad to take the bones they threw to their dogs; and yet, when I was a little fellow, and laid awake whole nights and cried, it wasn't the hunger, it wasn't the whipping, I cried for. No, sir; it was for *my mother* and *my sisters,*—it was because I hadn't a friend to love me on earth. I never knew what peace or comfort was. I never had a kind word spoken to me till I came to work in your factory. Mr. Wilson, you treated me well; you encouraged me to do well, and to learn to read and write, and to try to make something of myself; and God knows how grateful I am for it. Then, sir, I found my wife; you've seen her,—you know how beautiful she is. When I found she loved me, when I married her, I scarcely could believe I was alive, I was so happy; and, sir, she is as good as she is beautiful. But now what? Why, now comes my master, takes me right away from my work, and my friends, and all I like, and grinds me

2. A public sale of property conducted by a sheriff in compliance with a writ of execution.

down into the very dirt! And why? Because, he says, I forgot who I was; he says, to teach me that I am only a nigger! After all, and last of all, he comes between me and my wife, and says I shall give her up, and live with another woman. And all this your laws give him power to do, in spite of God or man. Mr. Wilson, look at it! There isn't *one* of all these things, that have broken the hearts of my mother and my sister, and my wife and myself, but your laws allow, and give every man power to do, in Kentucky, and none can say to him nay! Do you call these the laws of *my* country? Sir, I haven't any country, any more than I have any father. But I'm going to have one. I don't want anything of *your* country, except to be let alone,—to go peacably out of it; and when I get to Canada, where the laws will own me and protect me, *that* shall be my country, and its laws I will obey. But if any man tries to stop me, let him take care, for I am desperate. I'll fight for my liberty to the last breath I breathe. You say your fathers did it; if it was right for them, it is right for me!"

This speech, delivered partly while sitting at the table, and partly walking up and down the room,—delivered with tears, and flashing eyes, and despairing gestures,—was altogether too much for the good-natured old body to whom it was addressed, who had pulled out a great yellow silk pocket-handkerchief, and was mopping up his face with great energy.

"Blast 'em all!" he suddenly broke out. "Haven't I always said so—the infernal old cusses! I hope I an't swearing, now. Well! go ahead, George, go ahead; but be careful, my boy; don't shoot anybody, George, unless—well—you'd *better* not shoot, I reckon; at least, I wouldn't *hit* anybody, you know. Where is your wife, George?" he added, as he nervously rose, and began walking the room.

"Gone, sir, gone, with her child in her arms, the Lord only knows where;—gone after the north star; and when we ever meet, or whether we meet at all in this world, no creature can tell."

"Is it possible! astonishing! from such a kind family?"

"Kind families get in debt, and the laws of *our* country allow them to sell the child out of its mother's bosom to pay its master's debts," said George, bitterly.

"Well, well," said the honest old man, fumbling in his pocket. "I s'pose, perhaps, I an't following my judgment,—hang it, I *won't* follow my judgment!" he added, suddenly; "so here, George," and, taking out a roll of bills from his pocket-book, he offered them to George.

"No, my kind, good sir!" said George, "you've done a great deal for me, and this might get you into trouble. I have money enough, I hope, to take me as far as I need it."

"No; but you must, George. Money is a great help everywhere;—can't have too much, if you get it honestly. Take it,—*do* take it, *now*,—do, my boy!"

"On condition, sir, that I may repay it at some future time, I will," said George, taking up the money.

"And now, George, how long are you going to travel in this way?—not long or far, I hope. It's well carried on, but too bold. And this black fellow,—who is he?"

"A true fellow, who went to Canada more than a year ago. He heard, after he got there, that his master was so angry at him for going off that he had whipped his poor old mother; and he has come all the way back to comfort her, and get a chance to get her away."

"Has he got her?"

"Not yet; he has been hanging about the place, and found no chance yet. Meanwhile, he is going with me as far as Ohio, to put me among friends that helped him, and then he will come back after her."

"Dangerous, very dangerous!" said the old man.

George drew himself up, and smiled disdainfully.

The old gentleman eyed him from head to foot, with a sort of innocent wonder.

"George, something has brought you out wonderfully. You hold up your head, and speak and move like another man," said Mr. Wilson.

"Because I'm a *freeman!*" said George, proudly. "Yes, sir; I've said Mas'r for the last time to any man. *I'm free!*"

"Take care! You are not sure,—you may be taken."

"All men are free and equal *in the grave*, if it comes to that, Mr. Wilson," said George.

"I'm perfectly dumb-foundered with your boldness!" said Mr. Wilson,—"to come right here to the nearest tavern!"

"Mr. Wilson, it is *so* bold, and this tavern is so near, that they will never think of it; they will look for me on ahead, and you yourself wouldn't know me. Jim's master don't live in this county; he isn't known in these parts. Besides, he is given up; nobody is looking after him, and nobody will take me up from the advertisement, I think."

"But the mark in your hand?"

George drew off his glove, and showed a newly-healed scar in his hand.

"That is a parting proof of Mr. Harris' regard," he said, scornfully. "A fortnight ago, he took it into his head to give it to me, because he said he believed I should try to get away one of these days. Looks interesting, doesn't it?" he said, drawing his glove on again.

"I declare, my very blood runs cold when I think of it,—your condition and your risks!" said Mr. Wilson.

"Mine has run cold a good many years, Mr. Wilson; at present, it's about up to the boiling point," said George.

"Well, my good sir," continued George, after a few moments' silence, "I saw you knew me; I thought I'd just have this talk with you, lest your surprised looks should bring me out. I leave early to-morrow morning, before daylight, by to-morrow night I hope to sleep safe in Ohio. I shall travel by daylight, stop at the best hotels, go to the dinner-tables with the lords of the land. So, good-by, sir; if you hear that I'm taken, you may know that I'm dead!"

George stood up like a rock, and put out his hand with the air of a prince. The friendly little old man shook it heartily, and after a little shower of caution, he took his umbrella, and fumbled his way out of the room.

George stood thoughtfully looking at the door, as the old man closed it. A thought seemed to flash across his mind. He hastily stepped to it, and opening it, said,

"Mr. Wilson, one word more."

The old gentleman entered again, and George, as before, locked the door, and then stood for a few moments looking on the floor, irresolutely. At last, raising his head with a sudden effort—

"Mr. Wilson, you have shown yourself a Christian in your treatment of me,—I want to ask one last deed of Christian kindness of you."

"Well, George."

"Well, sir,—what you said was true. I *am* running a dreadful risk. There isn't, on earth, a living soul to care if I die," he added, drawing his breath hard, and speaking with a great effort,—"I shall be kicked out and buried like a dog, and nobody'll think of it a day after,—*only my poor wife!* Poor soul! she'll mourn and grieve; and if you'd only contrive, Mr. Wilson, to send this little pin to her. She gave it to me for a Christmas present, poor child! Give it to her, and tell her I loved her to the last. Will you? *Will* you?" he added, earnestly.

"Yes, certainly—poor fellow!" said the old gentleman, taking the pin, with watery eyes, and a melancholy quiver in his voice.

"Tell her one thing," said George; "it's my last wish, if she *can* get to Canada, to go there. No matter how kind her mistress is,—no matter how much she loves her home; beg her not to go back,—for slavery always ends in misery. Tell her to bring up our boy a free man, and then he won't suffer as I have. Tell her this, Mr. Wilson, will you?"

"Yes, George, I'll tell her; but I trust you won't die; take heart,—you're a brave fellow. Trust in the Lord, George. I wish in my heart you were safe through, though,—that's what I do."

"*Is* there a God to trust in?" said George, in such a tone of bitter despair as arrested the old gentleman's words. "O, I've seen things all my life that have made me feel that there can't be a God. You

Christians don't know how these things look to us. There's a God for you, but is there any for us?"

"O, now, don't—don't, my boy!" said the old man, almost sobbing as he spoke; "don't feel so! There is—there is; clouds and darkness are around about him, but righteousness and judgment are the habitation of his throne.[3] There's a *God*, George,—believe it; trust in Him, and I'm sure He'll help you. Everything will be set right,—if not in this life, in another."

The real piety and benevolence of the simple old man invested him with a temporary dignity and authority, as he spoke. George stopped his distracted walk up and down the room, stood thoughtfully a moment, and then said, quietly,

"Thank you for saying that, my good friend; I'll *think of that.*"

## Chapter XII

### *Select Incident of Lawful Trade*

> "In Ramah there was a voice heard,—weeping, and lamentation, and great mourning; Rachel weeping for her children, and would not be comforted."[1]

Mr. Haley and Tom jogged onward in their wagon, each, for a time, absorbed in his own reflections. Now, the reflections of two men sitting side by side are a curious thing,—seated on the same seat, having the same eyes, ears, hands and organs of all sorts, and having pass before their eyes the same objects,—it is wonderful what a variety we shall find in these same reflections!

As, for example, Mr. Haley: he thought first of Tom's length, and breadth, and height, and what he would sell for, if he was kept fat and in good case till he got him into market. He thought of how he should make out his gang; he thought of the respective market value of certain supposititious men and women and children who were to compose it, and other kindred topics of the business; then he thought of himself, and how humane he was, that whereas other men chained their "niggers" hand and foot both, he only put fetters on the feet, and left Tom the use of his hands, as long as he behaved well; and he sighed to think how ungrateful human nature was, so that there was even room to doubt whether Tom appreciated his mercies. He had been taken in so by "niggers" whom he had favored; but still he was astonished to consider how good-natured he yet remained!

3. Psalm 97.1–2.
1. Adapted from Jeremiah 31.15–16.

As to Tom, he was thinking over some words of an unfashionable old book, which kept running through his head again and again, as follows: "We have here no continuing city, but we seek one to come; wherefore God himself is not ashamed to be called our God; for he hath prepared for us a city."[2] These words of an ancient volume, got up principally by "ignorant and unlearned men," have, through all time, kept up, somehow, a strange sort of power over the minds of poor, simple fellows, like Tom. They stir up the soul from its depths, and rouse, as with trumpet call, courage, energy, and enthusiasm, where before was only the blackness of despair.

Mr. Haley pulled out of his pocket sundry newspapers, and began looking over their advertisements, with absorbed interest. He was not a remarkably fluent reader, and was in the habit of reading in a sort of recitative half-aloud, by way of calling in his ears to verify the deductions of his eyes. In this tone he slowly recited the following paragraph:

> "EXECUTOR'S SALE,—NEGROES!—Agreeably to order of court, will be sold, on Tuesday, February 20, before the Court-house door, in the town of Washington, Kentucky, the following negroes: Hagar, aged 60; John, aged 30; Ben, aged 21; Saul, aged 25; Albert, aged 14. Sold for the benefit of the creditors and heirs of the estate of Jesse Blutchford, Esq.
>
> SAMUEL MORRIS,
> THOMAS FLINT,
> *Executors*."

"This yer I must look at," said he to Tom, for want of somebody else to talk to.

"Ye see, I'm going to get up a prime gang to take down with ye, Tom; it'll make it sociable and pleasant like,—good company will, ye know. We must drive right to Washington first and foremost, and then I'll clap you into jail, while I does the business."

Tom received this agreeable intelligence quite meekly; simply wondering, in his own heart, how many of these doomed men had wives and children, and whether they would feel as he did about leaving them. It is to be confessed, too, that the naïve, off-hand information that he was to be thrown into jail by no means produced an agreeable impression on a poor fellow who had always prided himself on a strictly honest and upright course of life. Yes, Tom, we must confess it, was rather proud of his honesty, poor fellow,—not having very much else to be proud of;—if he had belonged to some of the higher walks of society, he, perhaps, would never have been reduced to such straits. However, the day wore on, and the evening

2. In Hebrews 13.14–16, Paul advises the Hebrews to preach Christianity outside the borders of their own towns.

saw Haley and Tom comfortably accommodated in Washington,—the one in a tavern, and the other in a jail.

About eleven o'clock the next day, a mixed throng was gathered around the court-house steps,—smoking, chewing, spitting, swearing, and conversing, according to their respective tastes and turns,—waiting for the auction to commence. The men and women to be sold sat in a group apart, talking in a low tone to each other. The woman who had been advertised by the name of Hagar was a regular African in feature and figure. She might have been sixty, but was older than that by hard work and disease, was partially blind, and somewhat crippled with rheumatism. By her side stood her only remaining son, Albert, a bright-looking little fellow of fourteen years. The boy was the only survivor of a large family, who had been successively sold away from her to a southern market. The mother held on to him with both her shaking hands, and eyed with intense trepidation every one who walked up to examine him.

"Don't be feard, Aunt Hagar," said the oldest of the men, "I spoke to Mas'r Thomas 'bout it, and he thought he might manage to sell you in a lot both together."

"Dey needn't call me worn out yet," said she, lifting her shaking hands. "I can cook yet, and scrub, and scour,—I'm wuth a buying, if I do come cheap;—tell em dat ar,—you *tell* em," she added, earnestly.

Haley here forced his way into the group, walked up to the old man, pulled his mouth open and looked in, felt of his teeth, made him stand and straighten himself, bend his back, and perform various evolutions to show his muscles; and then passed on to the next, and put him through the same trial. Walking up last to the boy, he felt of his arms, straightened his hands, and looked at his fingers, and made him jump, to show his agility.

"He an't gwine to be sold widout me!" said the old woman, with passionate eagerness; "he and I goes in a lot together; I's rail strong yet, Mas'r, and can do heaps o' work,—heaps on it, Mas'r."

"On plantation?" said Haley, with a contemptuous glance. "Likely story!" and, as if satisfied with his examination, he walked out and looked, and stood with his hands in his pocket, his cigar in his mouth, and his hat cocked on one side, ready for action.

"What think of 'em?" said a man who had been following Haley's examination, as if to make up his own mind from it.

"Wal," said Haley, spitting, "I shall put in, I think, for the youngerly ones and the boy."

"They want to sell the boy and the old woman together," said the man.

"Find it a tight pull;—why, she's an old rack o' bones,—not worth her salt."

"You wouldn't, then?" said the man.

"Anybody'd be a fool 't would. She's half blind, crooked with rheumatism, and foolish to boot."

"Some buys up these yer old critturs, and ses there's a sight more wear in 'em than a body'd think," said the man, reflectively.

"No go, 't all," said Haley; "wouldn't take her for a present,—fact,—I've *seen*, now."

"Wal, 'tis kinder pity, now, not to buy her with her son,—her heart seems so sot on him,—s'pose they fling her in cheap."

"Them that's got money to spend that ar way, it's all well enough. I shall bid off on that ar boy for a plantation-hand;—wouldn't be bothered with her, no way,—not if they'd give her to me," said Haley.

"She'll take on desp't," said the man.

"Nat'lly, she will," said the trader, coolly.

The conversation was here interrupted by a busy hum in the audience; and the auctioneer, a short, bustling, important fellow, elbowed his way into the crowd. The old woman drew in her breath, and caught instinctively at her son.

"Keep close to yer mammy, Albert,—close,—dey'll put us up togedder," she said.

"O, mammy, I'm feared they won't," said the boy.

"Dey must, child; I can't live, no ways, if they don't," said the old creature, vehemently.

The stentorian tones of the auctioneer, calling out to clear the way, now announced that the sale was about to commence. A place was cleared, and the bidding began. The different men on the list were soon knocked off at prices which showed a pretty brisk demand in the market; two of them fell to Haley.

"Come, now, young un," said the auctioneer, giving the boy a touch with his hammer, "be up and show your springs, now."

"Put us two up togedder, togedder,—do please, Mas'r," said the old woman, holding fast to her boy.

"Be off," said the man, gruffly, pushing her hands away; "you come last. Now, darkey, spring;" and, with the word, he pushed the boy toward the block, while a deep, heavy groan rose behind him. The boy paused, and looked back; but there was no time to stay, and, dashing the tears from his large, bright eyes, he was up in a moment.

His fine figure, alert limbs, and bright face, raised an instant competition, and half a dozen bids simultaneously met the ear of the auctioneer. Anxious, half-frightened, he looked from side to side, as he heard the clatter of contending bids,—now here, now there,—till the hammer fell. Haley had got him. He was pushed from the block toward his new master, but stopped one moment, and looked back, when his poor old mother, trembling in every limb, held out her shaking hands toward him.

The auction sale.

"Buy me too, Mas'r, for de dear Lord's sake!—buy me,—I shall die if you don't!"

"You'll die if I do, that's the kink of it," said Haley,—"no!" And he turned on his heel.

The bidding for the poor old creature was summary. The man who had addressed Haley, and who seemed not destitute of compassion, bought her for a trifle, and the spectators began to disperse.

The poor victims of the sale, who had been brought up in one place together for years, gathered round the despairing old mother, whose agony was pitiful to see.

"Couldn't dey leave me one? Mas'r allers said I should have one,—he did," she repeated over and over, in heartbroken tones.

"Trust in the Lord, Aunt Hagar," said the oldest of the men, sorrowfully.

"What good will it do?" said she, sobbing passionately.

"Mother, mother,—don't! don't!" said the boy. "They say you's got a good master."

"I don't care,—I don't care. O, Albert! oh, my boy! you's my last baby. Lord, how ken I?"

"Come, take her off, can't some of ye?" said Haley, dryly; "don't do no good for her to go on that ar way."

The old men of the company, partly by persuasion and partly by force, loosed the poor creature's last despairing hold, and, as they led her off to her new master's wagon, strove to comfort her.

"Now!" said Haley, pushing his three purchases together, and producing a bundle of handcuffs, which he proceeded to put on their wrists; and fastening each handcuff to a long chain, he drove them before him to the jail.

A few days saw Haley, with his possessions, safely deposited on one of the Ohio boats. It was the commencement of his gang, to be augmented, as the boat moved on, by various other merchandise of the same kind, which he, or his agent, had stored for him in various points along shore.

The La Belle Rivière,[3] as brave and beautiful a boat as ever walked the waters of her namesake river, was floating gayly down the stream, under a brilliant sky, the stripes and stars of free America waving and fluttering over head; the guards crowded with well-dressed ladies and gentlemen walking and enjoying the delightful day. All was full of life, buoyant and rejoicing;—all but Haley's gang, who were stored, with other freight, on the lower deck, and who, somehow, did not seem to appreciate their various privileges, as they sat in a knot, talking to each other in low tones.

3. The Beautiful River (French).

"Boys," said Haley, coming up, briskly, "I hope you keep up good heart, and are cheerful. Now, no sulks, ye see; keep stiff upper lip, boys; do well by me, and I'll do well by you."

The boys addressed responded the invariable "Yes, Mas'r," for ages the watchword of poor Africa; but it's to be owned they did not look particularly cheerful; they had their various little prejudices in favor of wives, mothers, sisters, and children, seen for the last time,—and though "they that wasted them required of them mirth,"[4] it was not instantly forthcoming.

"I've got a wife," spoke out the article enumerated as "John, aged thirty," and he laid his chained hand on Tom's knee,—"and she don't know a word about this, poor girl!"

"Where does she live?" said Tom.

"In a tavern a piece down here," said John; "I wish, now, I *could* see her once more in this world," he added.

Poor John! It *was* rather natural; and the tears that fell, as he spoke, came as naturally as if he had been a white man. Tom drew a long breath from a sore heart, and tried, in his poor way, to comfort him.

And over head, in the cabin, sat fathers and mothers, husbands and wives; and merry, dancing children moved round among them, like so many little butterflies, and everything was going on quite easy and comfortable.

"O, mamma," said a boy, who had just come up from below, "there's a negro trader on board, and he's brought four or five slaves down there."

"Poor creatures!" said the mother, in a tone between grief and indignation.

"What's that?" said another lady.

"Some poor slaves below," said the mother.

"And they've got chains on," said the boy.

"What a shame to our country that such sights are to be seen!" said another lady.

"O, there's a great deal to be said on both sides of the subject," said a genteel woman, who sat at her state-room door sewing, while her little girl and boy were playing round her. "I've been south, and I must say I think the negroes are better off than they would be to be free."

"In some respects, some of them are well off, I grant," said the lady to whose remark she had answered. "The most dreadful part of slavery, to my mind, is its outrages on the feelings and affections,—the separating of families, for example."

4. "For there they that carried us away captive required of us a song; and they that wasted us required of us mirth, saying, Sing us one of the songs of Zion" (Psalm 137.3).

"That *is* a bad thing, certainly," said the other lady, holding up a baby's dress she had just completed, and looking intently on its trimmings; "but then, I fancy, it don't occur often."

"O, it does," said the first lady, eagerly; "I've lived many years in Kentucky and Virginia both, and I've seen enough to make any one's heart sick. Suppose, ma'am, your two children, there, should be taken from you, and sold?"

"We can't reason from our feelings to those of this class of persons," said the other lady, sorting out some worsteds on her lap.

"Indeed, ma'am, you can know nothing of them, if you say so," answered the first lady, warmly. "I was born and brought up among them. I know they *do* feel, just as keenly,—even more so, perhaps,—as we do."

The lady said "Indeed!" yawned, and looked out the cabin window, and finally repeated, for a finale, the remark with which she had begun,—"After all, I think they are better off than they would be to be free."

"It's undoubtedly the intention of Providence that the African race should be servants,—kept in a low condition," said a grave-looking gentleman in black, a clergyman, seated by the cabin door. "'Cursed be Canaan; a servant of servants shall he be,' the scripture says."[5]

"I say, stranger, is that ar what that text means?" said a tall man, standing by.

"Undoubtedly. It pleased Providence, for some inscrutable reason, to doom the race to bondage, ages ago; and we must not set up our opinion against that."

"Well, then, we'll all go ahead and buy up niggers," said the man, "if that's the way of Providence,—won't we, Squire?" said he, turning to Haley, who had been standing, with his hands in his pockets, by the stove, and intently listening to the conversation.

"Yes," continued the tall man, "we must all be resigned to the decrees of Providence. Niggers must be sold, and trucked round, and kept under; it's what they's made for. 'Pears like this yer view's quite refreshing, an't it, stranger?" said he to Haley.

"I never thought on 't," said Haley. "I couldn't have said as much, myself; I ha'nt no larning. I took up the trade just to make a living; if 't an't right, I calculated to 'pent on 't in time, *ye* know."

5. According to Genesis, Noah's son Ham, the father of Canaan, accidentally saw his father drunk and naked and told his two brothers; the brothers walked backward into their father's tent to cover him without looking at him. When Noah awoke and found out what had happened, he cursed the children of Ham: "And he said, cursed be Canaan, a servant of servants shall he be unto his brethren" (Genesis 9.25). This passage was frequently adduced as justification of slavery by whites who considered Africans Ham's descendants.

"And now you'll save yerself the trouble, won't ye?" said the tall man. "See what 't is, now, to know scripture. If ye'd only studied yer Bible, like this yer good man, ye might have know'd it before, and saved ye a heap o' trouble. Ye could jist have said, 'Cussed be'—what's his name?—'and 't would all have come right.'" And the stranger, who was no other than the honest drover whom we introduced to our readers in the Kentucky tavern, sat down, and began smoking, with a curious smile on his long, dry face.

A tall, slender young man, with a face expressive of great feeling and intelligence, here broke in, and repeated the words, "'All things whatsoever ye would that men should do unto you, do ye even so unto them.'[6] I suppose," he added, "*that* is scripture, as much as 'Cursed be Canaan.'"

"Wal, it seems quite *as* plain a text, stranger," said John the drover, "to poor fellows like us, now;" and John smoked on like a volcano.

The young man paused, looked as if he was going to say more, when suddenly the boat stopped, and the company made the usual steamboat rush, to see where they were landing.

"Both them ar chaps parsons?" said John to one of the men, as they were going out.

The man nodded.

As the boat stopped, a black woman came running wildly up the plank, darted into the crowd, flew up to where the slave gang sat, and threw her arms round that unfortunate piece of merchandise before enumerated—'John, aged thirty,' and with sobs and tears bemoaned him as her husband.

But what needs tell the story, told too oft,—every day told,—of heart-strings rent and broken,—the weak broken and torn for the profit and convenience of the strong! It needs not to be told;—every day is telling it,—telling it, too, in the ear of One who is not deaf, though he be long silent.

The young man who had spoken for the cause of humanity and God before stood with folded arms, looking on this scene. He turned, and Haley was standing at his side. "My friend," he said, speaking with thick utterance, "how can you, how dare you, carry on a trade like this? Look at those poor creatures! Here I am, rejoicing in my heart that I am going home to my wife and child; and the same bell which is a signal to carry me onward towards them will part this poor man and his wife forever. Depend upon it, God will bring you into judgment for this."

6. From Christ's Sermon on the Mount: "Therefore all things whatsoever ye would that men should do unto you, do ye even so to them: for this is the law and the prophets" (Matthew 7.12).

The trader turned away in silence.

"I say, now," said the drover, touching his elbow, "there's differences in parsons, an't there? 'Cussed be Canaan' don't seem to go down with this 'un, does it?"

Haley gave an uneasy growl.

"And that ar an't the worse on 't," said John; "mabbe it won't go down with the Lord, neither, when ye come to settle with Him, one o' these days, as all on us must, I reckon."

Haley walked reflectively to the other end of the boat.

"If I make pretty handsomely on one or two next gangs," he thought, "I reckon I'll stop off this yer; it's really getting dangerous." And he took out his pocket-book, and began adding over his accounts,—a process which many gentlemen besides Mr. Haley have found a specific[7] for an uneasy conscience.

The boat swept proudly away from the shore, and all went on merrily, as before. Men talked, and loafed, and read, and smoked. Women sewed, and children played, and the boat passed on her way.

One day, when she lay to for a while at a small town in Kentucky, Haley went up into the place on a little matter of business.

Tom, whose fetters did not prevent his taking a moderate circuit, had drawn near the side of the boat, and stood listlessly gazing over the railings. After a time, he saw the trader returning, with an alert step, in company with a colored woman, bearing in her arms a young child. She was dressed quite respectably, and a colored man followed her, bringing along a small trunk. The woman came cheerfully onward, talking, as she came, with the man who bore her trunk, and so passed up the plank into the boat. The bell rung, the steamer whizzed, the engine groaned and coughed, and away swept the boat down the river.

The woman walked forward among the boxes and bales of the lower deck, and, sitting down, busied herself with chirruping to her baby.

Haley made a turn or two about the boat, and then, coming up, seated himself near her, and began saying something to her in an indifferent undertone.

Tom soon noticed a heavy cloud passing over the woman's brow; and that she answered rapidly, and with great vehemence.

"I don't believe it,—I won't believe it!" he heard her say. "You're jist a foolin with me."

"If you won't believe it, look here!" said the man, drawing out a paper; "this yer's the bill of sale, and there's your master's name to it; and I paid down good solid cash for it, too, I can tell you,—so, now!"

7. A drug that has a particular mitigating effect on a disease.

"I don't believe Mas'r would cheat me so; it can't be true!" said the woman, with increasing agitation.

"You can ask any of these men here, that can read writing. Here!" he said, to a man that was passing by, "jist read this yer, won't you! This yer gal won't believe me, when I tell her what 't is."

"Why, it's a bill of sale, signed by John Fosdick," said the man, "making over to you the girl Lucy and her child. It's all straight enough, for aught I see."

The woman's passionate exclamations collected a crowd around her, and the trader briefly explained to them the cause of the agitation.

"He told me that I was going down to Louisville,[8] to hire out as cook to the same tavern where my husband works,—that's what Mas'r told me, his own self; and I can't believe he'd lie to me," said the woman.

"But he has sold you, my poor woman, there's no doubt about it," said a good-natured looking man, who had been examining the papers; "he has done it, and no mistake."

"Then it's no account talking," said the woman, suddenly growing quite calm; and, clasping her child tighter in her arms, she sat down on her box, turned her back round, and gazed listlessly into the river.

"Going to take it easy, after all!" said the trader. "Gal's got grit, I see."

The woman looked calm, as the boat went on; and a beautiful soft summer breeze passed like a compassionate spirit over her head,—the gentle breeze, that never inquires whether the brow is dusky or fair that it fans. And she saw sunshine sparkling on the water, in golden ripples, and heard gay voices, full of ease and pleasure, talking around her everywhere; but her heart lay as if a great stone had fallen on it. Her baby raised himself up against her, and stroked her cheeks with his little hands; and, springing up and down, crowing and chatting, seemed determined to arouse her. She strained him suddenly and tightly in her arms, and slowly one tear after another fell on his wondering, unconscious face; and gradually she seemed, and little by little, to grow calmer, and busied herself with tending and nursing him.

The child, a boy of ten months, was uncommonly large and strong of his age, and very vigorous in his limbs. Never, for a moment, still, he kept his mother constantly busy in holding him, and guarding his springing activity.

"That's a fine chap!" said a man, suddenly stopping opposite to him, with his hands in his pockets. "How old is he?"

"Ten months and a half," said the mother.

8. A city in northern Kentucky on the Ohio River.

The man whistled to the boy, and offered him part of a stick of candy, which he eagerly grabbed at, and very soon had it in a baby's general depository, to wit, his mouth.

"Rum fellow!" said the man. "Knows what's what!" and he whistled, and walked on. When he had got to the other side of the boat, he came across Haley, who was smoking on top of a pile of boxes.

The stranger produced a match, and lighted a cigar, saying, as he did so,

"Decentish kind o' wench you've got round there, stranger."

"Why, I reckon she *is* tol'able fair," said Haley, blowing the smoke out of his mouth.

"Taking her down south?" said the man.

Haley nodded, and smoked on.

"Plantation hand?" said the man.

"Wal," said Haley, "I'm fillin' out an order for a plantation, and I think I shall put her in. They telled me she was a good cook; and they can use her for that, or set her at the cotton-picking. She's got the right fingers for that; I looked at 'em. Sell well, either way;" and Haley resumed his cigar.

"They won't want the young 'un on a plantation," said the man.

"I shall sell him, first chance I find," said Haley, lighting another cigar.

"S'pose you'd be selling him tol'able cheap," said the stranger, mounting the pile of boxes, and sitting down comfortably.

"Don't know 'bout that," said Haley; "he's a pretty smart young 'un,—straight, fat, strong; flesh as hard as a brick!"

"Very true, but then there's all the bother and expense of raisin'."

"Nonsense!" said Haley; "they is raised as easy as any kind of critter there is going; they an't a bit more trouble than pups. This yer chap will be running all round, in a month."

"I've got a good place for raisin', and I thought of takin' in a little more stock," said the man. "One cook lost a young 'un last week,—got drownded in a wash-tub, while she was a hangin' out clothes,—and I reckon it would be well enough to set her to raisin' this yer."

Haley and the stranger smoked a while in silence, neither seeming willing to broach the test question of the interview. At last the man resumed:

"You wouldn't think of wantin' more than ten dollars for that ar chap, seeing you *must* get him off yer hand, any how?"

Haley shook his head, and spit impressively.

"That won't do, no ways," he said, and began his smoking again.

"Well, stranger, what will you take?"

"Well, now," said Haley, "I *could* raise that ar chap myself, or get him raised; he's oncommon likely and healthy, and he'd fetch a hundred dollars, six months hence; and, in a year or two, he'd bring two hundred, if I had him in the right spot;—so I shan't take a cent less nor fifty for him now."

"O, stranger! that's rediculous, altogether," said the man.

"Fact!" said Haley, with a decisive nod of his head.

"I'll give thirty for him," said the stranger, "but not a cent more."

"Now, I'll tell ye what I will do," said Haley, spitting again, with renewed decision. "I'll split the difference, and say forty-five; and that's the most I will do."

"Well, agreed!" said the man, after an interval.

"Done!" said Haley. "Where do you land?"

"At Louisville," said the man.

"Louisville," said Haley. "Very fair, we get there about dusk. Chap will be asleep,—all fair,—get him off quietly, and no screaming,—happens beautiful,—I like to do everything quietly,—I hates all kind of agitation and fluster." And so, after a transfer of certain bills had passed from the man's pocket-book to the trader's, he resumed his cigar.

It was a bright, tranquil evening when the boat stopped at the wharf at Louisville. The woman had been sitting with her baby in her arms, now wrapped in a heavy sleep. When she heard the name of the place called out, she hastily laid the child down in a little cradle formed by the hollow among the boxes, first carefully spreading under it her cloak; and then she sprung to the side of the boat, in hopes that, among the various hotel-waiters who thronged the wharf, she might see her husband. In this hope, she pressed forward to the front rails, and, stretching far over them, strained her eyes intently on the moving heads on the shore, and the crowd pressed in between her and the child.

"Now's your time," said Haley, taking the sleeping child up, and handing him to the stranger. "Don't wake him up, and set him to crying, now; it would make a devil of a fuss with the gal." The man took the bundle carefully, and was soon lost in the crowd that went up the wharf.

When the boat, creaking, and groaning, and puffing, had loosed from the wharf, and was beginning slowly to strain herself along, the woman returned to her old seat. The trader was sitting there,—the child was gone!

"Why, why,—where?" she began, in bewildered surprise.

"Lucy," said the trader, "your child's gone; you may as well know it first as last. You see, I know'd you couldn't take him down south; and I got a chance to sell him to a first-rate family, that'll raise him better than you can."

The trader had arrived at that stage of Christian and political perfection which has been recommended by some preachers and politicians of the north, lately, in which he had completely overcome every humane weakness and prejudice. His heart was exactly where yours, sir, and mine could be brought, with proper effort and cultivation. The wild look of anguish and utter despair that the woman cast on him might have disturbed one less practised; but he was used to it. He had seen that same look hundreds of times. You can get used to such things, too, my friend; and it is the great object of recent efforts to make our whole northern community used to them, for the glory of the Union. So the trader only regarded the mortal anguish which he saw working in those dark features, those clenched hands, and suffocating breathings, as necessary incidents of the trade, and merely calculated whether she was going to scream, and get up a commotion on the boat; for, like other supporters of our peculiar institution, he decidedly disliked agitation.

But the woman did not scream. The shot had passed too straight and direct through the heart, for cry or tear.

Dizzily she sat down. Her slack hands fell lifeless by her side. Her eyes looked straight forward, but she saw nothing. All the noise and hum of the boat, the groaning of the machinery, mingled dreamily to her bewildered ear; and the poor, dumb-stricken heart had neither cry nor tear to show for its utter misery. She was quite calm.

The trader, who, considering his advantages, was almost as humane as some of our politicians, seemed to feel called on to administer such consolation as the case admitted of.

"I know this yer comes kinder hard, at first, Lucy," said he; "but such a smart, sensible gal as you are, won't give way to it. You see it's *necessary*, and can't be helped!"

"O! don't, Mas'r, don't!" said the woman, with a voice like one that is smothering.

"You're a smart wench, Lucy," he persisted; "I mean to do well by ye, and get ye a nice place down river; and you'll soon get another husband,—such a likely gal as you—"

"O! Mas'r, if you *only* won't talk to me now," said the woman, in a voice of such quick and living anguish that the trader felt that there was something at present in the case beyond his style of operation. He got up, and the woman turned away, and buried her head in her cloak.

The trader walked up and down for a time, and occasionally stopped and looked at her.

"Takes it hard, rather," he soliloquized, "but quiet, tho';—let her sweat a while; she'll come right, by and by!"

Tom had watched the whole transaction from first to last, and had a perfect understanding of its results. To him, it looked like something unutterably horrible and cruel, because, poor, ignorant black soul! he had not learned to generalize, and to take enlarged views. If he had only been instructed by certain ministers of Christianity,[9] he might have thought better of it, and seen in it an every-day incident of a lawful trade; a trade which is the vital support of an institution which some American divines tell us has no evils but such as are inseparable from any other relations in social and domestic life. But Tom, as we see, being a poor, ignorant fellow, whose reading had been confined entirely to the New Testament, could not comfort and solace himself with views like these. His very soul bled within him for what seemed to him the *wrongs* of the poor suffering thing that lay like a crushed reed on the boxes; the feeling, living, bleeding, yet immortal *thing*, which American state law coolly classes with the bundles, and bales, and boxes, among which she is lying.

Tom drew near, and tried to say something; but she only groaned. Honestly, and with tears running down his own cheeks, he spoke of a heart of love in the skies, of a pitying Jesus, and an eternal home; but the ear was deaf with anguish, and the palsied heart could not feel.

Night came on,—night calm, unmoved, and glorious, shining down with her innumerable and solemn angel eyes, twinkling, beautiful, but silent. There was no speech nor language, no pitying voice nor helping hand, from that distant sky. One after another, the voices of business or pleasure died away; all on the boat were sleeping, and the ripples at the prow were plainly heard. Tom stretched himself out on a box, and there, as he lay, he heard, ever and anon, a smothered sob or cry from the prostrate creature,—"O! what shall I do? O Lord! O good Lord, do help me!" and so, ever and anon, until the murmur died away in silence.

At midnight, Tom waked, with a sudden start. Something black passed quickly by him to the side of the boat, and he heard a splash in the water. No one else saw or heard anything. He raised his head,—the woman's place was vacant! He got up, and sought about him in vain. The poor bleeding heart was still, at last, and the river rippled and dimpled just as brightly as if it had not closed above it.

Patience! patience! ye whose hearts swell indignant at wrongs like these. Not one throb of anguish, not one tear of the oppressed, is forgotten by the Man of Sorrows, the Lord of Glory. In his patient, generous bosom he bears the anguish of a world. Bear thou, like

9. In some first editions, Stowe named the minister Joel Parker here. He sued, however, so she removed the specific name in subsequent editions.

him, in patience, and labor in love; for sure as he is God, "the year of his redeemed *shall* come."[1]

The trader waked up bright and early, and came out to see to his live stock. It was now his turn to look about in perplexity.

"Where alive is that gal?" he said to Tom.

Tom, who had learned the wisdom of keeping counsel, did not feel called on to state his observations and suspicions, but said he did not know.

"She surely couldn't have got off in the night at any of the landings, for I was awake, and on the look-out, whenever the boat stopped. I never trust these yer things to other folks."

This speech was addressed to Tom quite confidentially, as if it was something that would be specially interesting to him. Tom made no answer.

The trader searched the boat from stem to stern, among boxes, bales and barrels, around the machinery, by the chimneys, in vain.

"Now, I say, Tom, be fair about this yer," he said, when, after a fruitless search, he came where Tom was standing. "You know something about it, now. Don't tell me,—I know you do. I saw the gal stretched out here about ten o'clock, and ag'in at twelve, and ag'in between one and two; and then at four she was gone, and you was sleeping right there all the time. Now, you know something,—you can't help it."

"Well, Mas'r," said Tom, "towards morning something brushed by me, and I kinder half woke; and then I hearn a great splash, and then I clare woke up, and the gal was gone. That's all I know on 't."

The trader was not shocked nor amazed; because, as we said before, he was used to a great many things that you are not used to. Even the awful presence of Death struck no solemn chill upon him. He had seen Death many times,—met him in the way of trade, and got acquainted with him,—and he only thought of him as a hard customer, that embarrassed his property operations very unfairly; and so he only swore that the gal was a baggage, and that he was devilish unlucky, and that, if things went on in this way, he should not make a cent on the trip. In short, he seemed to consider himself an ill-used man, decidedly; but there was no help for it, as the woman had escaped into a state which *never will* give up a fugitive,—not even at the demand of the whole glorious Union. The trader, therefore, sat discontentedly down, with his little account-book, and put down the missing body and soul under the head of *losses!*

"He's a shocking creature, isn't he,—this trader? so unfeeling! It's dreadful, really!"

1. Isaiah 63.4.

"O, but nobody thinks anything of these traders! They are universally despised,—never received into any decent society."

But who, sir, makes the trader? Who is most to blame? The enlightened, cultivated, intelligent man, who supports the system of which the trader is the inevitable result, or the poor trader himself? You make the public sentiment that calls for his trade, that debauches and depraves him, till he feels no shame in it; and in what are you better than he?

Are you educated and he ignorant, you high and he low, you refined and he coarse, you talented and he simple?

In the day of a future Judgment, these very considerations may make it more tolerable for him than for you.

In concluding these little incidents of lawful trade, we must beg the world not to think that American legislators are entirely destitute of humanity, as might, perhaps, be unfairly inferred from the great efforts made in our national body to protect and perpetuate this species of traffic.

Who does not know how our great men are outdoing themselves, in declaiming against the *foreign* slave-trade. There are a perfect host of Clarksons and Wilberforces[2] risen up among us on that subject, most edifying to hear and behold. Trading negroes from Africa, dear reader, is so horrid! It is not to be thought of! But trading them from Kentucky,—that's quite another thing!

## Chapter XIII

### *The Quaker Settlement*[1]

A quiet scene now rises before us. A large, roomy, neatly-painted kitchen, its yellow floor glossy and smooth, and without a particle of dust; a neat, well-blacked cooking-stove; rows of shining tin, suggestive of unmentionable good things to the appetite; glossy green wood chairs, old and firm; a small flag-bottomed rocking-chair, with a patch-work cushion in it, neatly contrived out of small pieces of different colored woollen goods, and a larger sized one, motherly and old, whose wide arms breathed hospitable invitation, seconded by the solicitation of its feather cushions,—a real comfortable, persuasive old chair, and worth, in the way of honest, homely enjoy-

2. I.e., abolitionists. Thomas Clarkson (1760–1846) was an English abolitionist associated with Granville Sharp and William Wilberforce. England outlawed the slave trade in 1807 and officially freed all slaves in its Caribbean colonies in 1834. In 1807 Thomas Jefferson signed an Act of Congress banning the importation of slaves from Africa into the United States.
1. The Quakers, or Religious Society of Friends, are a Christian sect known for involvement in American and English abolitionist causes during the nineteenth century.

ment, a dozen of your plush or brochetelle[2] drawing-room gentry; and in the chair, gently swaying back and forward, her eyes bent on some fine sewing, sat our old friend Eliza. Yes, there she is, paler and thinner than in her Kentucky home, with a world of quiet sorrow lying under the shadow of her long eyelashes, and marking the outline of her gentle mouth! It was plain to see how old and firm the girlish heart was grown under the discipline of heavy sorrow; and when, anon, her large dark eye was raised to follow the gambols of her little Harry, who was sporting, like some tropical butterfly, hither and thither over the floor, she showed a depth of firmness and steady resolve that was never there in her earlier and happier days.

By her side sat a woman with a bright tin pan in her lap, into which she was carefully sorting some dried peaches. She might be fifty-five or sixty; but hers was one of those faces that time seems to touch only to brighten and adorn. The snowy lisse crape[3] cap, made after the strait Quaker pattern,—the plain white muslin handkerchief, lying in placid folds across her bosom,—the drab shawl and dress,—showed at once the community to which she belonged. Her face was round and rosy, with a healthful downy softness, suggestive of a ripe peach. Her hair, partially silvered by age, was parted smoothly back from a high placid forehead, on which time had written no inscription, except peace on earth, good will to men, and beneath shone a large pair of clear, honest, loving brown eyes; you only needed to look straight into them, to feel that you saw to the bottom of a heart as good and true as ever throbbed in woman's bosom. So much has been said and sung of beautiful young girls, why don't somebody wake up to the beauty of old women? If any want to get up an inspiration under this head, we refer them to our good friend Rachel Halliday, just as she sits there in her little rocking-chair. It had a turn for quacking and squeaking,—that chair had,—either from having taken cold in early life, or from some asthmatic affection, or perhaps from nervous derangement; but, as she gently swung backward and forward, the chair kept up a kind of subdued "creechy crawchy," that would have been intolerable in any other chair. But old Simeon Halliday often declared it was as good as any music to him, and the children all avowed that they wouldn't miss of hearing mother's chair for anything in the world. For why? for twenty years or more, nothing but loving words and gentle moralities, and motherly loving kindness, had come from that chair;—head-aches and heart-aches innumerable had been cured there,—difficulties spiritual and temporal solved there,—all by one good, loving woman, God bless her!

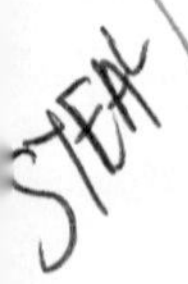


2. Usually *brocatelle*, a fabric similar to brocade, used for tapestry and upholstery.
3. A light silk gauze used for dresses and trimmings.

"And so thee still thinks of going to Canada, Eliza?" she said, as she was quietly looking over her peaches.

"Yes, ma'am," said Eliza, firmly. "I must go onward. I dare not stop."

"And what'll thee do, when thee gets there? Thee must think about that, my daughter."

"My daughter" came naturally from the lips of Rachel Halliday; for hers was just the face and form that made "mother" seem the most natural word in the world.

Eliza's hands trembled, and some tears fell on her fine work; but she answered, firmly,

"I shall do—anything I can find. I hope I can find something."

"Thee knows thee can stay here, as long as thee pleases," said Rachel.

"O, thank you," said Eliza, "but"—she pointed to Harry—"I can't sleep nights; I can't rest. Last night I dreamed I saw that man coming into the yard," she said, shuddering.

"Poor child!" said Rachel, wiping her eyes; "but thee mustn't feel so. The Lord hath ordered it so that never hath a fugitive been stolen from our village. I trust thine will not be the first."

The door here opened, and a little short, round, pincushiony woman stood at the door, with a cheery, blooming face, like a ripe apple. She was dressed, like Rachel, in sober gray, with the muslin folded neatly across her round, plump little chest.

"Ruth Stedman," said Rachel, coming joyfully forward; "how is thee, Ruth?" she said, heartily taking both her hands.

"Nicely," said Ruth, taking off her little drab bonnet, and dusting it with her handkerchief, displaying, as she did so, a round little head, on which the Quaker cap sat with a sort of jaunty air, despite all the stroking and patting of the small fat hands, which were busily applied to arranging it. Certain stray locks of decidedly curly hair, too, had escaped here and there, and had to be coaxed and cajoled into their place again; and then the new comer, who might have been five-and-twenty, turned from the small looking-glass, before which she had been making these arrangements, and looked well pleased,—as most people who looked at her might have been,—for she was decidedly a wholesome, whole-hearted, chirruping little woman, as ever gladdened man's heart withal.

"Ruth, this friend is Eliza Harris; and this is the little boy I told thee of."

"I am glad to see thee, Eliza,—very," said Ruth, shaking hands, as if Eliza were an old friend she had long been expecting; "and this is thy dear boy,—I brought a cake for him," she said, holding out a little heart to the boy, who came up, gazing through his curls, and accepted it shyly.

"Where's thy baby, Ruth?" said Rachel.

"O, he's coming; but thy Mary caught him as I came in, and ran off with him to the barn, to show him to the children."

At this moment, the door opened, and Mary, an honest, rosy-looking girl, with large brown eyes, like her mother's, came in with the baby.

"Ah! ha!" said Rachel, coming up, and taking the great, white, fat fellow in her arms; "how good he looks, and how he does grow!"

"To be sure, he does," said little bustling Ruth as she took the child, and began taking off a little blue silk hood, and various layers and wrappers of outer garments; and having given a twitch here, and a pull there, and variously adjusted and arranged him, and kissed him heartily, she set him on the floor to collect his thoughts. Baby seemed quite used to this mode of proceeding, for he put his thumb in his mouth (as if it were quite a thing of course), and seemed soon absorbed in his own reflections, while the mother seated herself, and taking out a long stocking of mixed blue and white yarn, began to knit with briskness.

"Mary, thee'd better fill the kettle, hadn't thee?" gently suggested the mother.

Mary took the kettle to the well, and soon reappearing, placed it over the stove, where it was soon purring and steaming, a sort of censer of hospitality and good cheer. The peaches, moreover, in obedience to a few gentle whispers from Rachel, were soon deposited, by the same hand, in a stew-pan over the fire.

Rachel now took down a snowy moulding-board, and, tying on an apron, proceeded quietly to making up some biscuits, first saying to Mary,—"Mary, hadn't thee better tell John to get a chicken ready?" and Mary disappeared accordingly.

"And how is Abigail Peters?" said Rachel, as she went on with her biscuits.

"O, she's better," said Ruth; "I was in, this morning; made the bed, tidied up the house. Leah Hills went in, this afternoon, and baked bread and pies enough to last some days and I engaged to go back to get her up, this evening."

"I will go in to-morrow, and do any cleaning there may be, and look over the mending," said Rachel.

"Ah! that is well," said Ruth. "I've heard," she added, "that Hannah Stanwood is sick. John was up there, last night,—I must go there tomorrow."

"John can come in here to his meals, if thee needs to stay all day," suggested Rachel.

"Thank thee, Rachel; will see, to-morrow; but, here comes Simeon."

Simeon Halliday, a tall, straight, muscular man, in drab coat and pantaloons, and broad-brimmed hat, now entered.

"How is thee, Ruth?" he said, warmly, as he spread his broad open hand for her little fat palm; "and how is John?"

"O! John is well, and all the rest of our folks," said Ruth, cheerily.

"Any news, father?" said Rachel, as she was putting her biscuits into the oven.

"Peter Stebbins told me that they should be along to-night, with *friends*," said Simeon, significantly, as he was washing his hands at a neat sink, in a little back porch.

"Indeed!" said Rachel, looking thoughtfully, and glancing at Eliza.

"Did thee say thy name was Harris?" said Simeon to Eliza, as he reentered.

Rachel glanced quickly at her husband, as Eliza tremulously answered "yes;" her fears, ever uppermost, suggesting that possibly there might be advertisements out for her.

"Mother!" said Simeon, standing in the porch, and calling Rachel out.

"What does thee want, father?" said Rachel, rubbing her floury hands, as she went into the porch.

"This child's husband is in the settlement, and will be here to-night," said Simeon.

"Now, thee doesn't say that, father?" said Rachel, all her face radiant with joy.

"It's really true. Peter was down yesterday, with the wagon, to the other stand, and there he found an old woman and two men; and one said his name was George Harris; and, from what he told of his history, I am certain who he is. He is a bright, likely fellow, too."

"Shall we tell her now?" said Simeon.

"Let's tell Ruth," said Rachel. "Here, Ruth,—come here."

Ruth laid down her knitting-work, and was in the back porch in a moment.

"Ruth, what does thee think?" said Rachel. "Father says Eliza's husband is in the last company, and will be here to-night."

A burst of joy from the little Quakeress interrupted the speech. She gave such a bound from the floor, as she clapped her little hands, that two stray curls fell from under her Quaker cap, and lay brightly on her white neckerchief.

"Hush thee, dear!" said Rachel, gently; "hush, Ruth! Tell us, shall we tell her now?"

"Now! to be sure,—this very minute. Why, now, suppose 'twas my John, how should I feel? Do tell her, right off."

"Thee uses thyself only to learn how to love thy neighbor, Ruth," said Simeon, looking, with a beaming face, on Ruth.

"To be sure. Isn't it what we are made for? If I didn't love John and the baby, I should not know how to feel for her. Come, now, do tell her,—do!" and she laid her hands persuasively on Rachel's arm. "Take her into thy bed-room, there, and let me fry the chicken while thee does it."

Rachel came out into the kitchen, where Eliza was sewing, and opening the door of a small bed-room, said, gently, "Come in here with me, my daughter; I have news to tell thee."

The blood flushed in Eliza's pale face; she rose, trembling with nervous anxiety, and looked towards her boy.

"No, no," said little Ruth, darting up, and seizing her hands. "Never thee fear; it's good news, Eliza,—go in, go in!" And she gently pushed her to the door, which closed after her; and then, turning round, she caught little Harry in her arms, and began kissing him.

"Thee'll see thy father, little one. Does thee know it? Thy father is coming," she said, over and over again, as the boy looked wonderingly at her.

Meanwhile, within the door, another scene was going on. Rachel Halliday drew Eliza toward her, and said, "The Lord hath had mercy on thee, daughter; thy husband hath escaped from the house of bondage."

The blood flushed to Eliza's cheek in a sudden glow, and went back to her heart with as sudden a rush. She sat down, pale and faint.

"Have courage, child," said Rachel, laying her hand on her head. "He is among friends, who will bring him here to-night."

"To-night!" Eliza repeated, "to-night!" The words lost all meaning to her; her head was dreamy and confused; all was mist for a moment.

When she awoke, she found herself snugly tucked up on the bed, with a blanket over her, and little Ruth rubbing her hands with camphor. She opened her eyes in a state of dreamy, delicious languor, such as one has who has long been bearing a heavy load, and now feels it gone, and would rest. The tension of the nerves, which had never ceased a moment since the first hour of her flight, had given way, and a strange feeling of security and rest came over her; and, as she lay, with her large, dark eyes open, she followed, as in a quiet dream, the motions of those about her. She saw the door open into the other room; saw the supper-table, with its snowy cloth; heard the dreamy murmur of the singing tea-kettle, saw Ruth tripping backward and forward, with plates of cake and saucers of preserves, and ever and anon stopping to put a cake into Harry's hand, or pat his head, or twine his long curls round her snowy fingers. She saw the ample, motherly form of Rachel, as she ever and anon came to the bed-side, and smoothed and arranged something about the bedclothes, and gave a tuck here and there, by way of expressing her good-will; and was conscious of a kind of sunshine beaming down upon her from her large, clear, brown eyes. She saw Ruth's husband come in,—saw her fly up to him, and commence whispering very earnestly, ever and anon, with impressive gesture, pointing her little finger toward the room. She saw her, with the baby in her arms, sitting down to tea; she saw them all at table, and little Harry in a high chair, under the shadow of Rachel's ample wing; there were low murmurs of talk, gentle tinkling of tea-spoons, and musical clatter of cups and saucers, and all mingled in a delightful dream of rest; and Eliza slept, as she had not slept before, since the fearful midnight hour when she had taken her child and fled through the frosty star-light.

She dreamed of a beautiful country,—a land, it seemed to her, of rest,—green shores, pleasant islands, and beautifully glittering water; and there, in a house which kind voices told her was a home, she saw her boy playing, a free and happy child. She heard her husband's footsteps; she felt him coming nearer; his arms were around her, his tears falling on her face, and she awoke! It was no dream. The daylight had long faded; her child lay calmly sleeping by her side; a candle was burning dimly on the stand, and her husband was sobbing by her pillow.

The next morning was a cheerful one at the Quaker house. "Mother" was up betimes, and surrounded by busy girls and boys, whom we had scarce time to introduce to our readers yesterday, and who all moved obediently to Rachel's gentle "Thee had better," or more gentle "Hadn't thee better?" in the work of getting breakfast; for a breakfast in the luxurious valleys of Indiana is a thing complicated and multiform, and, like picking up the rose-leaves and trimming the bushes in Paradise, asking other hands than those of the original mother. While, therefore, John ran to the spring for fresh water, and Simeon the second sifted meal for corn-cakes, and Mary ground coffee, Rachel moved gently and quietly about, making biscuits, cutting up chicken, and diffusing a sort of sunny radiance over the whole proceeding generally. If there was any danger of friction or collision from the ill-regulated zeal of so many young operators, her gentle "Come! come!" or "I wouldn't, now," was quite sufficient to allay the difficulty. Bards have written of the cestus of Venus,[4] that turned the heads of all the world in successive generations. We had rather, for our part, have the cestus of Rachel Halliday,

4. The Roman goddess of love and beauty. "Cestus": a woman's belt, especially a symbolic belt worn by a bride.

that kept heads from being turned, and made everything go on harmoniously. We think it is more suited to our modern days, decidedly.

While all other preparations were going on, Simeon the elder stood in his shirt-sleeves before a little looking-glass in the corner, engaged in the anti-patriarchal operation of shaving. Everything went on so sociably, so quietly, so harmoniously, in the great kitchen,—it seemed so pleasant to every one to do just what they were doing, there was such an atmosphere of mutual confidence and good fellowship everywhere,—even the knives and forks had a social clatter as they went on to the table; and the chicken and ham had a cheerful and joyous fizzle in the pan, as if they rather enjoyed being cooked than otherwise;—and when George and Eliza and little Harry came out, they met such a hearty, rejoicing welcome, no wonder it seemed to them like a dream.

At last, they were all seated at breakfast, while Mary stood at the stove, baking griddle-cakes, which, as they gained the true exact golden-brown tint of perfection, were transferred quite handily to the table.

Rachel never looked so truly and benignly happy as at the head of her table. There was so much motherliness and full-heartedness even in the way she passed a plate of cakes or poured a cup of coffee, that it seemed to put a spirit into the food and drink she offered.

It was the first time that ever George had sat down on equal terms at any white man's table; and he sat down, at first, with some constraint and awkwardness; but they all exhaled and went off like fog, in the genial morning rays of this simple, overflowing kindness.

This, indeed, was a home,—*home,*—a word that George had never yet known a meaning for; and a belief in God, and trust in his providence, began to encircle his heart, as, with a golden cloud of protection and confidence, dark, misanthropic, pining, atheistic doubts, and fierce despair, melted away before the light of a living Gospel, breathed in living faces, preached by a thousand unconscious acts of love and good will, which, like the cup of cold water given in the name of a disciple, shall never lose their reward.

"Father, what if thee should get found out again?" said Simeon second, as he buttered his cake.

"I should pay my fine," said Simeon, quietly.

"But what if they put thee in prison?"

"Couldn't thee and mother manage the farm?" said Simeon, smiling.

"Mother can do almost everything," said the boy. "But isn't it a shame to make such laws?"

"Thee mustn't speak evil of thy rulers, Simeon," said his father, gravely. "The Lord only gives us our worldly goods that we may do justice and mercy; if our rulers require a price of us for it, we must deliver it up."

"Well, I hate those old slaveholders!" said the boy, who felt as unchristian as became any modern reformer.

"I am surprised at thee, son," said Simeon; "thy mother never taught thee so. I would do even the same for the slaveholder as for the slave, if the Lord brought him to my door in affliction."

Simeon second blushed scarlet; but his mother only smiled, and said, "Simeon is my good boy; he will grow older, by and by, and then he will be like his father."

"I hope, my good sir, that you are not exposed to any difficulty on our account," said George, anxiously.

"Fear nothing, George, for therefore are we sent into the world. If we would not meet trouble for a good cause, we were not worthy of our name."

"But, for *me*," said George, "I could not bear it."

"Fear not, then, friend George; it is not for thee, but for God and man, we do it," said Simeon. "And now thou must lie by quietly this day, and to-night, at ten o'clock, Phineas Fletcher will carry thee onward to the next stand,—thee and the rest of thy company. The pursuers are hard after thee; we must not delay."

"If that is the case, why wait till evening?" said George.

"Thou art safe here by daylight, for every one in the settlement is a Friend, and all are watching. It has been found safer to travel by night."

# Chapter XIV

## *Evangeline*

> "A young star! which shone
> O'er life—too sweet an image for such glass!
> A lovely being, scarcely formed or moulded;
> A rose with all its sweetest leaves yet folded."[1]

The Mississippi! How, as by an enchanted wand, have its scenes been changed, since Chateaubriand[2] wrote his prose-poetic

1. From *Don Juan* 14.43 (1818–24), by George Gordon, Lord Byron (1788–1824), English poet.
2. Vicomte François René de Chateaubriand (1768–1848), a French statesman and writer, in 1826 published "Les Natchez," a description of life on the Mississippi, which is the second-longest river in the United States, flowing south from northern Minnesota to the Gulf of Mexico through the states of Missouri, Kentucky, Tennessee, Arkansas, Mississippi, and Louisiana.

description of it, as a river of mighty, unbroken solitudes, rolling amid undreamed wonders of vegetable and animal existence.

But, as in an hour, this river of dreams and wild romance has emerged to a reality scarcely less visionary and splendid. What other river of the world bears on its bosom to the ocean the wealth and enterprise of such another country?—a country whose products embrace all between the tropics and the poles! Those turbid waters, hurrying, foaming, tearing along, an apt resemblance of that headlong tide of business which is poured along its wave by a race more vehement and energetic than any the old world ever saw. Ah! would that they did not also bear along a more fearful freight,—the tears of the oppressed, the sighs of the helpless, the bitter prayers of poor, ignorant hearts to an unknown God—unknown, unseen and silent, but who will yet "come out of his place to save all the poor of the earth!"[3]

The slanting light of the setting sun quivers on the sea-like expanse of the river; the shivery canes, and the tall, dark cypress, hung with wreaths of dark, funereal moss, glow in the golden ray, as the heavily-laden steamboat marches onward.

Piled with cotton-bales, from many a plantation, up over deck and sides, till she seems in the distance a square, massive block of gray, she moves heavily onward to the nearing mart. We must look some time among its crowded decks before we shall find again our humble friend Tom. High on the upper deck, in a little nook among the everywhere predominant cotton-bales, at last we may find him.

Partly from confidence inspired by Mr. Shelby's representations, and partly from the remarkably inoffensive and quiet character of the man, Tom had insensibly won his way far into the confidence even of such a man as Haley.

At first he had watched him narrowly through the day, and never allowed him to sleep at night unfettered; but the uncomplaining patience and apparent contentment of Tom's manner led him gradually to discontinue these restraints, and for some time Tom had enjoyed a sort of parole of honor, being permitted to come and go freely where he pleased on the boat.

Ever quiet and obliging, and more than ready to lend a hand in every emergency which occurred among the workmen below, he had won the good opinion of all the hands, and spent many hours in helping them with as hearty a good will as ever he worked on a Kentucky farm.

When there seemed to be nothing for him to do, he would climb to a nook among the cotton-bales of the upper deck, and busy himself in studying over his Bible,—and it is there we see him now.

3. Reference unknown.

For a hundred or more miles above New Orleans, the river is higher than the surrounding country, and rolls its tremendous volume between massive levees twenty feet in height. The traveller from the deck of the steamer, as from some floating castle top, overlooks the whole country for miles and miles around. Tom, therefore, had spread out full before him, in plantation after plantation, a map of the life to which he was approaching.

He saw the distant slaves at their toil; he saw afar their villages of huts gleaming out in long rows on many a plantation, distant from the stately mansions and pleasure-grounds of the master;—and as the moving picture passed on, his poor, foolish heart would be turning backward to the Kentucky farm, with its old shadowy beeches,—to the master's house, with its wide, cool halls, and, near by, the little cabin, overgrown with the multiflora and bignonia. There he seemed to see familiar faces of comrades, who had grown up with him from infancy; he saw his busy wife, bustling in her preparations for his evening meals; he heard the merry laugh of his boys at their play, and the chirrup of the baby at his knee; and then, with a start, all faded, and he saw again the cane-brakes[4] and cypresses and gliding plantations, and heard again the creaking and groaning of the machinery, all telling him too plainly that all that phase of life had gone by forever.

In such a case, you write to your wife, and send messages to your children; but Tom could not write,—the mail for him had no existence, and the gulf of separation was unbridged by even a friendly word or signal.

Is it strange, then, that some tears fall on the pages of his Bible, as he lays it on the cotton-bale, and, with patient finger, threading his slow way from word to word, traces out its promises? Having learned late in life, Tom was but a slow reader, and passed on laboriously from verse to verse. Fortunate for him was it that the book he was intent on was one which slow reading cannot injure,—nay, one whose words, like ingots of gold, seem often to need to be weighed separately, that the mind may take in their priceless value. Let us follow him a moment, as, pointing to each word, and pronouncing each half aloud, he reads,

"Let—not—your—heart—be—troubled. In—my—Father's—house—are—many—mansions. I—go—to—prepare—a—place—for—you."[5]

Cicero,[6] when he buried his darling and only daughter, had a heart as full of honest grief as poor Tom's,—perhaps no fuller, for

4. Thickets of sugarcane or another bamboolike grass.
5. Christ comforted his disciples after foretelling his own death: "Let not your heart be troubled: ye believe in God, Believe also in me. In my Father's house are many mansions: if it were not so, I would have told you. I go to prepare a place for you" (John 14.1–2).
6. Marcus Tullius Cicero (106–43 B.C.E.), Roman statesman, orator, and philosopher.

both were only men;—but Cicero could pause over no such sublime words of hope, and look to no such future reunion; and if he *had* seen them, ten to one he would not have believed,—he must fill his head first with a thousand questions of authenticity of manuscript, and correctness of translation. But, to poor Tom, there it lay, just what he needed, so evidently true and divine that the possibility of a question never entered his simple head. It must be true; for, if not true, how could he live?

As for Tom's Bible, though it had no annotations and helps in margin from learned commentators, still it had been embellished with certain way-marks and guide-boards of Tom's own invention, and which helped him more than the most learned expositions could have done. It had been his custom to get the Bible read to him by his master's children, in particular by young Master George; and, as they read, he would designate, by bold, strong marks and dashes, with pen and ink, the passages which more particularly gratified his ear or affected his heart. His Bible was thus marked through, from one end to the other, with a variety of styles and designations; so he could in a moment seize upon his favorite passages, without the labor of spelling out what lay between them;—and while it lay there before him, every passage breathing of some old home scene, and recalling some past enjoyment, his Bible seemed to him all of this life that remained, as well as the promise of a future one.

Among the passengers on the boat was a young gentleman of fortune and family, resident in New Orleans, who bore the name of St. Clare. He had with him a daughter between five and six years of age, together with a lady who seemed to claim relationship to both, and to have the little one especially under her charge.

Tom had often caught glimpses of this little girl,—for she was one of those busy, tripping creatures, that can be no more contained in one place than a sunbeam or a summer breeze,—nor was she one that, once seen, could be easily forgotten.

Her form was the perfection of childish beauty, without its usual chubbiness and squareness of outline. There was about it an undulating and aerial grace, such as one might dream of for some mythic and allegorical being. Her face was remarkable less for its perfect beauty of feature than for a singular and dreamy earnestness of expression, which made the ideal start when they looked at her, and by which the dullest and most literal were impressed, without exactly knowing why. The shape of her head and the turn of her neck and bust was peculiarly noble, and the long golden-brown hair that floated like a cloud around it, the deep spiritual gravity of her violet blue eyes, shaded by heavy fringes of golden brown,—all marked her out from other children, and made every one turn and look after her, as she glided hither and thither on the boat. Nevertheless, the little one was not what you would have called either a grave child or a sad one. On the contrary, an airy and innocent playfulness seemed to flicker like the shadow of summer leaves over her childish face, and around her buoyant figure. She was always in motion, always with a half smile on her rosy mouth, flying hither and thither, with an undulating and cloud-like tread, singing to herself as she moved as in a happy dream. Her father and female guardian were incessantly busy in pursuit of her,—but, when caught, she melted from them again like a summer cloud; and as no word of chiding or reproof ever fell on her ear for whatever she chose to do, she pursued her own way all over the boat. Always dressed in white, she seemed to move like a shadow through all sorts of places, without contracting spot or stain; and there was not a corner or nook, above or below, where those fairy footsteps had not glided, and that visionary golden head, with its deep blue eyes, fleeted along.

The fireman, as he looked up from his sweaty toil, sometimes found those eyes looking wonderingly into the raging depths of the furnace, and fearfully and pityingly at him, as if she thought him in some dreadful danger. Anon the steersman at the wheel paused and smiled, as the picture-like head gleamed through the window of the round house, and in a moment was gone again. A thousand times a day rough voices blessed her, and smiles of unwonted softness stole over hard faces, as she passed; and when she tripped fearlessly over dangerous places, rough, sooty hands were stretched involuntarily out to save her, and smooth her path.

Tom, who had the soft, impressible nature of his kindly race, ever yearning toward the simple and childlike, watched the little creature with daily increasing interest. To him she seemed something almost divine; and whenever her golden head and deep blue eyes peered out upon him from behind some dusky cotton-bale, or looked down upon him over some ridge of packages, he half believed that he saw one of the angels stepped out of his New Testament.

Often and often she walked mournfully round the place where Haley's gang of men and women sat in their chains. She would glide in among them, and look at them with an air of perplexed and sorrowful earnestness; and sometimes she would lift their chains with her slender hands, and then sigh wofully, as she glided away. Several times she appeared suddenly among them, with her hands full of candy, nuts, and oranges, which she would distribute joyfully to them, and then be gone again.

Tom watched the little lady a great deal, before he ventured on any overtures towards acquaintanceship. He knew an abundance of simple acts to propitiate and invite the approaches of the little people, and he resolved to play his part right skilfully. He could cut cunning little baskets out of cherry-stones, could make grotesque faces on hickory-nuts, or odd-jumping figures out of elder-pith, and he was a very Pan[7] in the manufacture of whistles of all sizes and sorts. His pockets were full of miscellaneous articles of attraction, which he had hoarded in days of old for his master's children, and which he now produced, with commendable prudence and economy, one by one, as overtures for acquaintance and friendship.

The little one was shy, for all her busy interest in everything going on, and it was not easy to tame her. For a while, she would perch like a canary-bird on some box or package near Tom, while busy in the little arts afore-named, and take from him, with a kind of grave bashfulness, the little articles he offered. But at last they got on quite confidential terms.

"What's little missy's name?" said Tom, at last, when he thought matters were ripe to push such an inquiry.

"Evangeline St. Clare," said the little one, "though papa and everybody else call me Eva. Now, what's your name?"

"My name's Tom; the little chil'en used to call me Uncle Tom, way back thar in Kentuck."

"Then I mean to call you Uncle Tom, because, you see, I like you," said Eva. "So, Uncle Tom, where are you going?"

"I don't know, Miss Eva."

"Don't know?" said Eva.

"No. I am going to be sold to somebody. I don't know who."

"My papa can buy you," said Eva, quickly; "and if he buys you, you will have good times. I mean to ask him to, this very day."

"Thank you, my little lady," said Tom.

The boat here stopped at a small landing to take in wood, and Eva, hearing her father's voice, bounded nimbly away. Tom rose up, and went forward to offer his service in wooding, and soon was busy among the hands.

Eva and her father were standing together by the railings to see the boat start from the landing-place, the wheel had made two or three revolutions in the water, when, by some sudden movement, the little one suddenly lost her balance, and fell sheer over the side of the boat into the water. Her father, scarce knowing what he did, was plunging in after her, but was held back by some behind him, who saw that more efficient aid had followed his child.

Tom was standing just under her on the lower deck, as she fell. He saw her strike the water, and sink, and was after her in a moment.

7. Greek god of fields, forests, wild animals, flocks, and shepherds, represented as having the legs of a goat and playing a flute.

A broad-chested, strong-armed fellow, it was nothing for him to keep afloat in the water, till, in a moment or two, the child rose to the surface, and he caught her in his arms, and, swimming with her to the boat-side, handed her up, all dripping, to the grasp of hundreds of hands, which, as if they had all belonged to one man, were stretched eagerly out to receive her. A few moments more, and her father bore her, dripping and senseless, to the ladies' cabin, where, as is usual in cases of the kind, there ensued a very well-meaning and kind-hearted strife among the female occupants generally, as to who should do the most things to make a disturbance, and to hinder her recovery in every way possible.

It was a sultry, close day, the next day, as the steamer drew near to New Orleans. A general bustle of expectation and preparation was spread through the boat; in the cabin, one and another were gathering their things together, and arranging them, preparatory to going ashore. The steward and chambermaid, and all, were busily engaged in cleaning, furbishing, and arranging the splendid boat, preparatory to a grand entree.

On the lower deck sat our friend Tom, with his arms folded, and anxiously, from time to time, turning his eyes towards a group on the other side of the boat.

There stood the fair Evangeline, a little paler than the day before, but otherwise exhibiting no traces of the accident which had befallen her. A graceful, elegantly-formed young man stood by her, carelessly leaning one elbow on a bale of cotton, while a large pocket-book lay open before him. It was quite evident, at a glance, that the gentleman was Eva's father. There was the same noble cast of head, the same large blue eyes, the same golden-brown hair; yet the expression was wholly different. In the large, clear blue eyes, though in form and color exactly similar, there was wanting that misty, dreamy depth of expression; all was clear, bold, and bright, but with a light wholly of this world: the beautifully cut mouth had a proud and somewhat sarcastic expression, while an air of free-and-easy superiority sat not ungracefully in every turn and movement of his fine form. He was listening, with a good-humored, negligent air, half comic, half contemptuous, to Haley, who was very volubly expatiating on the quality of the article for which they were bargaining.

"All the moral and Christian virtues bound in black morocco,[8] complete!" he said, when Haley had finished. "Well, now, my good fellow, what's the damage, as they say in Kentucky; in short, what's to be paid out for this business? How much are you going to cheat me, now? Out with it!"

8. A fine leather made from goatskin.

"Wal," said Haley, "if I should say thirteen hundred dollars for that ar fellow, I shouldn't but just save myself; I shouldn't, now, re'ly."

"Poor fellow!" said the young man, fixing his keen, mocking blue eye on him; "but I suppose you'd let me have him for that, out of a particular regard for me."

"Well, the young lady here seems to be sot on him, and nat'lly enough."

"O! certainly, there's a call on your benevolence, my friend. Now, as a matter of Christian charity, how cheap could you afford to let him go, to oblige a young lady that's particular sot on him?"

"Wal, now, just think on 't," said the trader; "just look at them limbs,—broad-chested, strong as a horse. Look at his head; them high forrads allays shows calculatin niggers, that'll do any kind o' thing. I've marked that ar. Now, a nigger of that ar heft and build is worth considerable, just, as you may say, for his body, supposin he's stupid; but come to put in his calculatin faculties, and them which I can show he has oncommon, why, of course, it makes him come higher. Why, that ar fellow managed his master's whole farm. He has a strornary talent for business."

"Bad, bad, very bad; knows altogether too much!" said the young man, with the same mocking smile playing about his mouth. "Never will do, in the world. Your smart fellows are always running off, stealing horses, and raising the devil generally. I think you'll have to take off a couple of hundred for his smartness."

"Wal, there might be something in that ar, if it warnt for his character; but I can show recommends from his master and others, to prove he is one of your real pious,—the most humble, prayin, pious crittur ye ever did see. Why, he's been called a preacher in them parts he came from."

"And I might use him for a family chaplain, possibly," added the young man, dryly. "That's quite an idea. Religion is a remarkably scarce article at our house."

"You're joking, now."

"How do you know I am? Didn't you just warrant him for a preacher? Has he been examined by any synod or council? Come, hand over your papers."

If the trader had not been sure, by a certain good-humored twinkle in the large blue eye, that all this banter was sure, in the long run, to turn out a cash concern, he might have been somewhat out of patience; as it was, he laid down a greasy pocket-book on the cotton-bales, and began anxiously studying over certain papers in it, the young man standing by, the while, looking down on him with an air of careless, easy drollery.

"Papa, do buy him! it's no matter what you pay," whispered Eva, softly, getting up on a package, and putting her arm around her father's neck. "You have money enough, I know. I want him."

"What for, pussy? Are you going to use him for a rattle-box, or a rocking-horse, or what?"

"I want to make him happy."

"An original reason, certainly."

Here the trader handed up a certificate, signed by Mr. Shelby, which the young man took with the tips of his long fingers, and glanced over carelessly.

"A gentlemanly hand," he said, "and well spelt, too. Well, now, but I'm not sure, after all, about this religion," said he, the old wicked expression returning to his eye; "the country is almost ruined with pious white people: such pious politicians as we have just before elections,—such pious goings on in all departments of church and state, that a fellow does not know who'll cheat him next. I don't know, either, about religion's being up in the market, just now. I have not looked in the papers lately, to see how it sells. How many hundred dollars, now, do you put on for this religion?"

"You like to be a jokin, now," said the trader; "but, then, there's *sense* under all that ar. I know there's differences in religion. Some kinds is mis'rable: there's your meetin pious; there's your singin, roarin pious; them ar an't no account, in black or white;—but these rayly is; and I've seen it in niggers as often as any, your rail softly, quiet, stiddy, honest, pious, that the hull world couldn't tempt 'em to do nothing that they thinks is wrong; and ye see in this letter what Tom's old master says about him."

"Now," said the young man, stooping gravely over his book of bills, "if you can assure me that I really can buy *this* kind of pious, and that it will be set down to my account in the book up above, as something belonging to me, I wouldn't care if I did go a little extra for it. How d' ye say?"

"Wal, raily, I can't do that," said the trader. "I'm a thinkin that every man'll have to hang on his own hook, in them ar quarters."

"Rather hard on a fellow that pays extra on religion, and can't trade with it in the state where he wants it most, an't it, now?" said the young man, who had been making out a roll of bills while he was speaking. "There, count your money, old boy!" he added, as he handed the roll to the trader.

"All right," said Haley, his face beaming with delight; and pulling out an old inkhorn, he proceeded to fill out a bill of sale, which, in a few moments, he handed to the young man.

"I wonder, now, if I was divided up and inventoried," said the latter, as he ran over the paper, "how much I might bring. Say so much for the shape of my head, so much for a high forehead, so much for arms, and hands, and legs, and then so much for education, learning, talent, honesty, religion! Bless me! there would be small charge on that last, I'm thinking. But come, Eva," he said; and taking the hand of his daughter, he stepped across the boat, and carelessly putting the tip of his finger under Tom's chin, said good-humoredly, "Look up, Tom, and see how you like your new master."

Tom looked up. It was not in nature to look into that gay, young, handsome face, without a feeling of pleasure; and Tom felt the tears start in his eyes as he said, heartily, "God bless you, Mas'r!"

"Well, I hope he will. What's your name? Tom? Quite as likely to do it for your asking as mine, from all accounts. Can you drive horses, Tom?"

"I've been allays used to horses," said Tom. "Mas'r Shelby raised heaps on 'em."

"Well, I think I shall put you in coachy, on condition that you won't be drunk more than once a week, unless in cases of emergency, Tom."

Tom looked surprised, and rather hurt, and said, "I never drink, Mas'r."

"I've heard that story before, Tom; but then we'll see. It will be a special accommodation to all concerned, if you don't. Never mind, my boy," he added, good-humoredly, seeing Tom still looked grave; "I don't doubt you mean to do well."

"I sartin do, Mas'r," said Tom.

"And you shall have good times," said Eva. "Papa is very good to everybody, only he always will laugh at them."

"Papa is much obliged to you for his recommendation," said St. Clare, laughing, as he turned on his heel and walked away.

## Chapter XV

### *Of Tom's New Master, and Various Other Matters*

Since the thread of our humble hero's life has now become interwoven with that of higher ones, it is necessary to give some brief introduction to them.

Augustine St. Clare was the son of a wealthy planter of Louisiana. The family had its origin in Canada. Of two brothers, very similar in temperament and character, one had settled on a flourishing farm in Vermont, and the other became an opulent planter in Louisiana. The mother of Augustine was a Huguenot[1] French lady, whose family had emigrated to Louisiana during the days of

1. French Protestant.

its early settlement. Augustine and another brother were the only children of their parents. Having inherited from his mother an exceeding delicacy of constitution, he was, at the instance of physicians, during many years of his boyhood, sent to the care of his uncle in Vermont, in order that his constitution might be strengthened by the cold of a more bracing climate.

In childhood, he was remarkable for an extreme and marked sensitiveness of character, more akin to the softness of woman than the ordinary hardness of his own sex. Time, however, overgrew this softness with the rough bark of manhood, and but few knew how living and fresh it still lay at the core. His talents were of the very first order, although his mind showed a preference always for the ideal and the aesthetic, and there was about him that repugnance to the actual business of life which is the common result of this balance of the faculties. Soon after the completion of his college course, his whole nature was kindled into one intense and passionate effervescence of romantic passion. His hour came,—the hour that comes only once; his star rose in the horizon,—that star that rises so often in vain, to be remembered only as a thing of dreams; and it rose for him in vain. To drop the figure,—he saw and won the love of a high-minded and beautiful woman, in one of the northern states, and they were affianced. He returned south to make arrangements for their marriage, when, most unexpectedly, his letters were returned to him by mail, with a short note from her guardian, stating to him that ere this reached him the lady would be the wife of another. Stung to madness, he vainly hoped, as many another has done, to fling the whole thing from his heart by one desperate effort. Too proud to supplicate or seek explanation, he threw himself at once into a whirl of fashionable society, and in a fortnight from the time of the fatal letter was the accepted lover of the reigning belle of the season; and as soon as arrangements could be made, he became the husband of a fine figure, a pair of bright dark eyes, and a hundred thousand dollars; and, of course, everybody thought him a happy fellow.

The married couple were enjoying their honeymoon, and entertaining a brilliant circle of friends in their splendid villa, near Lake Pontchartrain,[2] when, one day, a letter was brought to him in *that* well-remembered writing. It was handed to him while he was in full tide of gay and successful conversation, in a whole room-full of company. He turned deadly pale when he saw the writing, but still preserved his composure, and finished the playful warfare of badinage which he was at the moment carrying on with a lady opposite; and, a short time after, was missed from the circle. In his room, alone,

2. A shallow saltwater lake in southeast Louisiana, north of New Orleans.

he opened and read the letter, now worse than idle and useless to be read. It was from her, giving a long account of a persecution to which she had been exposed by her guardian's family, to lead her to unite herself with their son: and she related how, for a long time, his letters had ceased to arrive; how she had written time and again, till she became weary and doubtful; how her health had failed under her anxieties, and how, at last, she had discovered the whole fraud which had been practised on them both. The letter ended with expressions of hope and thankfulness, and professions of undying affection, which were more bitter than death to the unhappy young man. He wrote to her immediately:

"I have received yours,—but too late. I believed all I heard. I was desperate. *I am married*, and all is over. Only forget,—it is all that remains for either of us."

And thus ended the whole romance and ideal of life for Augustine St. Clare. But the *real* remained,—the *real*, like the flat, bare, oozy tide-mud, when the blue sparkling wave, with all its company of gliding boats and white-winged ships, its music of oars and chiming waters, has gone down, and there it lies, flat, slimy, bare,—exceedingly real.

Of course, in a novel, people's hearts break, and they die, and that is the end of it; and in a story this is very convenient. But in real life we do not die when all that makes life bright dies to us. There is a most busy and important round of eating, drinking, dressing, walking, visiting, buying, selling, talking, reading, and all that makes up what is commonly called *living*, yet to be gone through; and this yet remained to Augustine. Had his wife been a whole woman, she might yet have done something—as woman can—to mend the broken threads of life, and weave again into a tissue of brightness. But Marie St. Clare could not even see that they had been broken. As before stated, she consisted of a fine figure, a pair of splendid eyes, and a hundred thousand dollars; and none of these items were precisely the ones to minister to a mind diseased.

When Augustine, pale as death, was found lying on the sofa, and pleaded sudden sick-headache as the cause of his distress, she recommended to him to smell of hartshorn;[3] and when the paleness and headache came on week after week, she only said that she never thought Mr. St. Clare was sickly; but it seems he was very liable to sick-headaches, and that it was a very unfortunate thing for her, because he didn't enjoy going into company with her, and it seemed odd to go so much alone, when they were just married. Augustine was glad in his heart that he had married so undiscerning a woman;

3. Also called smelling salts; an ammonia preparation used by women to relieve fainting or headaches.

but as the glosses and civilities of the honeymoon wore away, he discovered that a beautiful young woman, who has lived all her life to be caressed and waited on, might prove quite a hard mistress in domestic life. Marie never had possessed much capability of affection, or much sensibility, and the little that she had, had been merged into a most intense and unconscious selfishness; a selfishness the more hopeless, from its quiet obtuseness, its utter ignorance of any claims but her own. From her infancy, she had been surrounded with servants, who lived only to study her caprices; the idea that they had either feelings or rights had never dawned upon her, even in distant perspective. Her father, whose only child she had been, had never denied her anything that lay within the compass of human possibility; and when she entered life, beautiful, accomplished, and an heiress, she had, of course, all the eligibles and non-eligibles of the other sex sighing at her feet, and she had no doubt that Augustine was a most fortunate man in having obtained her. It is a great mistake to suppose that a woman with no heart will be an easy creditor in the exchange of affection. There is not on earth a more merciless exactor of love from others than a thoroughly selfish woman; and the more unlovely she grows, the more jealously and scrupulously she exacts love, to the uttermost farthing. When, therefore, St. Clare began to drop off those gallantries and small attentions which flowed at first through the habitude of courtship, he found his sultana no way ready to resign her slave; there were abundance of tears, poutings, and small tempests, there were discontents, pinings, upbraidings. St. Clare was good-natured and self-indulgent, and sought to buy off with presents and flatteries; and when Marie became mother to a beautiful daughter, he really felt awakened, for a time, to something like tenderness.

St. Clare's mother had been a woman of uncommon elevation and purity of character, and he gave to this child his mother's name, fondly fancying that she would prove a reproduction of her image. The thing had been remarked with petulant jealousy by his wife, and she regarded her husband's absorbing devotion to the child with suspicion and dislike; all that was given to her seemed so much taken from herself. From the time of the birth of this child, her health gradually sunk. A life of constant inaction, bodily and mental,—the friction of ceaseless ennui and discontent, united to the ordinary weakness which attended the period of maternity,—in course of a few years changed the blooming young belle into a yellow, faded, sickly woman, whose time was divided among a variety of fanciful diseases, and who considered herself, in every sense, the most ill-used and suffering person in existence.

There was no end of her various complaints; but her principal forte appeared to lie in sick-headache, which sometimes would confine her to her room three days out of six. As, of course, all family arrangements fell into the hands of servants, St. Clare found his menage[4] anything but comfortable. His only daughter was exceedingly delicate, and he feared that, with no one to look after her and attend to her, her health and life might yet fall a sacrifice to her mother's inefficiency. He had taken her with him on a tour to Vermont, and had persuaded his cousin, Miss Ophelia St. Clare, to return with him to his southern residence; and they are now returning on this boat, where we have introduced them to our readers.

And now, while the distant domes and spires of New Orleans rise to our view, there is yet time for an introduction to Miss Ophelia.

Whoever has travelled in the New England States will remember, in some cool village, the large farm-house, with its clean-swept grassy yard, shaded by the dense and massive foliage of the sugar maple; and remember the air of order and stillness, of perpetuity and unchanging repose, that seemed to breathe over the whole place. Nothing lost, or out of order; not a picket loose in the fence, not a particle of litter in the turfy yard, with its clumps of lilac-bushes growing up under the windows. Within, he will remember wide, clean rooms, where nothing ever seems to be doing or going to be done, where everything is once and forever rigidly in place, and where all household arrangements move with the punctual exactness of the old clock in the corner. In the family "keeping-room," as it is termed, he will remember the staid respectable old book-case, with its glass doors, where Rollin's History, Milton's Paradise Lost, Bunyan's Pilgrim's Progress, and Scott's Family Bible,[5] stand side by side in decorous order, with multitudes of other books, equally solemn and respectable. There are no servants in the house, but the lady in the snowy cap, with the spectacles, who sits sewing every afternoon among her daughters, as if nothing ever had been done, or were to be done,—she and her girls, in some long-forgotten fore part of the day, "*did up the work,*" and for the rest of the time, probably, at all hours when you would see them, it is "*done up.*" The old kitchen floor never seems stained or spotted; the tables, the chairs, and the various cooking utensils, never seem deranged or disordered; though three and sometimes four meals a day are got there, though the family washing and ironing is there performed, and though pounds of butter and cheese are in some silent and mysterious manner there brought into existence.

4. A domestic establishment or household.
5. The popular *Commentary on the Bible* (1788–92), by Thomas Scott (1747–1821), English clergyman and scholar. "Rollin's History": *Histoire Ancienne des Egyptians* (1825), by Charles Rollin (1661–1741). "Milton's Paradise Lost": a long epic poem (1667) about Satan's rebellion against God and Adam and Eve's expulsion from Eden, by the English poet John Milton (1608–1674). "Bunyan's Pilgrim's Progress": see above, p. 60, n. 4.

On such a farm, in such a house and family, Miss Ophelia had spent a quiet existence of some forty-five years, when her cousin invited her to visit his southern mansion. The eldest of a large family, she was still considered by her father and mother as one of "the children," and the proposal that she should go to *Orleans* was a most momentous one to the family circle. The old gray-headed father took down Morse's Atlas out of the book-case, and looked out the exact latitude and longitude; and read Flint's Travels in the South and West,[6] to make up his own mind as to the nature of the country.

The good mother inquired, anxiously, "if Orleans wasn't an awful wicked place," saying, "that it seemed to her most equal to going to the Sandwich Islands,[7] or anywhere among the heathen."

It was known at the minister's, and at the doctor's, and at Miss Peabody's milliner shop, that Ophelia St. Clare was "talking about" going away down to Orleans with her cousin; and of course the whole village could do no less than help this very important process of *talking about* the matter. The minister, who inclined strongly to abolitionist views, was quite doubtful whether such a step might not tend somewhat to encourage the southerners in holding on to their slaves; while the doctor, who was a staunch colonizationist, inclined to the opinion that Miss Ophelia ought to go, to show the Orleans people that we don't think hardly of them, after all. He was of opinion, in fact, that southern people needed encouraging. When, however, the fact that she had resolved to go was fully before the public mind, she was solemnly invited out to tea by all her friends and neighbors for the space of a fortnight, and her prospects and plans duly canvassed and inquired into. Miss Moseley, who came into the house to help to do the dress-making, acquired daily accessions of importance from the developments with regard to Miss Ophelia's wardrobe which she had been enabled to make. It was credibly ascertained that Squire Sinclare, as his name was commonly contracted in the neighborhood, had counted out fifty dollars, and given them to Miss Ophelia, and told her to buy any clothes she thought best; and that two new silk dresses, and a bonnet, had been sent for from Boston. As to the propriety of this extraordinary outlay, the public mind was divided,—some affirming that it was well enough, all things considered, for once in one's life, and others stoutly affirming that the money had better have

6. *Recollections of the Last Ten Years in the Valley of the Mississippi* (1826), by Timothy Flint (1780–1840), an American author and missionary. "Morse's Atlas": Jedidiah Morse (1761–1826), an American clergyman and geographer, wrote the first textbook on American geography published in the United States, *Geography Made Easy* (1784), as well as *The American Geography* (1789) and others.
7. Former name of the Hawaiian islands.

been sent to the missionaries; but all parties agreed that there had been no such parasol seen in those parts as had been sent on from New York, and that she had one silk dress that might fairly be trusted to stand alone, whatever might be said of its mistress. There were credible rumors, also, of a hemstitched pocket-handkerchief; and report even went so far as to state that Miss Ophelia had one pocket-handkerchief with lace all around it,—it was even added that it was worked in the corners; but this latter point was never satisfactorily ascertained, and remains, in fact, unsettled to this day.

Miss Ophelia, as you now behold her, stands before you, in a very shining brown linen travelling-dress, tall, square-formed, and angular. Her face was thin, and rather sharp in its outlines; the lips compressed, like those of a person who is in the habit of making up her mind definitely on all subjects; while the keen, dark eyes had a peculiarly searching, advised movement, and travelled over everything, as if they were looking for something to take care of.

All her movements were sharp, decided, and energetic; and, though she was never much of a talker, her words were remarkably direct, and to the purpose, when she did speak.

In her habits, she was a living impersonation of order, method, and exactness. In punctuality, she was as inevitable as a clock, and as inexorable as a railroad engine; and she held in most decided contempt and abomination anything of a contrary character.

The great sin of sins, in her eyes,—the sum of all evils,—was expressed by one very common and important word in her vocabulary—"shiftlessness." Her finale and ultimatum of contempt consisted in a very emphatic pronunciation of the word "shiftless;" and by this she characterized all modes of procedure which had not a direct and inevitable relation to accomplishment of some purpose then definitely had in mind. People who did nothing, or who did not know exactly what they were going to do, or who did not take the most direct way to accomplish what they set their hands to, were objects of her entire contempt,—a contempt shown less frequently by anything she said, than by a kind of stony grimness, as if she scorned to say anything about the matter.

As to mental cultivation,—she had a clear, strong, active mind, was well and thoroughly read in history and the older English classics, and thought with great strength within certain narrow limits. Her theological tenets were all made up, labelled in most positive and distinct forms, and put by, like the bundles in her patch trunk; there were just so many of them, and there were never to be any more. So, also, were her ideas with regard to most matters of practical life,—such as housekeeping in all its branches, and the various political relations of her native village. And, underlaying all, deeper than anything else, higher and broader, lay the strongest principle of her being—conscientiousness. Nowhere is conscience so dominant and all-absorbing as with New England women. It is the granite formation, which lies deepest, and rises out, even to the tops of the highest mountains.

Miss Ophelia was the absolute bond-slave of the *"ought."* Once make her certain that the "path of duty," as she commonly phrased it, lay in any given direction, and fire and water could not keep her from it. She would walk straight down into a well, or up to a loaded cannon's mouth, if she were only quite sure that there the path lay. Her standard of right was so high, so all-embracing, so minute, and making so few concessions to human frailty, that, though she strove with heroic ardor to reach it, she never actually did so, and of course was burdened with a constant and often harassing sense of deficiency;—this gave a severe and somewhat gloomy cast to her religious character.

But, how in the world can Miss Ophelia get along with Augustine St. Clare,—gay, easy, unpunctual, unpractical, sceptical,—in short, walking with impudent and nonchalant freedom over every one of her most cherished habits and opinions?

To tell the truth, then, Miss Ophelia loved him. When a boy, it had been hers to teach him his catechism, mend his clothes, comb his hair, and bring him up generally in the way he should go; and her heart having a warm side to it, Augustine had, as he usually did with most people, monopolized a large share of it for himself, and therefore it was that he succeeded very easily in persuading her that the "path of duty" lay in the direction of New Orleans, and that she must go with him to take care of Eva, and keep everything from going to wreck and ruin during the frequent illnesses of his wife. The idea of a house without anybody to take care of it went to her heart; then she loved the lovely little girl, as few could help doing; and though she regarded Augustine as very much of a heathen, yet she loved him, laughed at his jokes, and forbore with his failings, to an extent which those who knew him thought perfectly incredible. But what more or other is to be known of Miss Ophelia our reader must discover by a personal acquaintance.

There she is, sitting now in her state-room, surrounded by a mixed multitude of little and big carpet-bags,[8] boxes, baskets, each containing some separate responsibility which she is tying, binding up, packing, or fastening, with a face of great earnestness.

"Now, Eva, have you kept count of your things? Of course you haven't,—children never do: there's the spotted carpet-bag and the little blue band-box with your best bonnet,—that's two; then the

8. A popular style of traveling bag.

India rubber satchel is three; and my tape and needle box is four; and my band-box, five; and my collar-box, six; and that little hair trunk,[9] seven. What have you done with your sunshade? Give it to me, and let me put a paper round it, and tie it to my umbrella with my shade;—there, now."

"Why, aunty, we are only going up home;—what is the use?"

"To keep it nice, child; people must take care of their things, if they ever mean to have anything; and now, Eva, is your thimble put up?"

"Really, aunty, I don't know."

"Well, never mind; I'll look your box over,—thimble, wax, two spools, scissors, knife, tape-needle;[1] all right,—put it in here. What did you ever do, child, when you were coming on with only your papa. I should have thought you'd a lost everything you had."

"Well, aunty, I did lose a great many; and then, when we stopped anywhere, papa would buy some more of whatever it was."

"Mercy on us, child,—what a way!"

"It was a very easy way, aunty," said Eva.

"It's a dreadful shiftless one," said aunty.

"Why, aunty, what'll you do now?" said Eva; "that trunk is too full to be shut down."

"It *must* shut down," said aunty, with the air of a general, as she squeezed the things in, and sprung upon the lid;—still a little gap remained about the mouth of the trunk.

"Get up here, Eva!" said Miss Ophelia, courageously; "what has been done can be done again. This trunk has *got to be* shut and locked—there are no two ways about it."

And the trunk, intimidated, doubtless, by this resolute statement, gave in. The hasp snapped sharply in its hole, and Miss Ophelia turned the key, and pocketed it in triumph.

"Now we're ready. Where's your papa? I think it time this baggage was set out. Do look out, Eva, and see if you see your papa."

"O, yes, he's down the other end of the gentlemen's cabin, eating an orange."

"He can't know how near we are coming," said aunty; "hadn't you better run and speak to him?"

"Papa never is in a hurry about anything," said Eva, "and we haven't come to the landing. Do step on the guards, aunty. Look! there's our house, up that street!"

The boat now began, with heavy groans, like some vast, tired monster, to prepare to push up among the multiplied steamers at the

9. A trunk covered with hide from which the hair has not been removed. "Band-box": a cylindrical box used to hold ruffs, collars, or hats.

1. A needle or bodkin used for inserting strips of fabric that serve as fastenings for garments.

levee. Eva joyously pointed out the various spires, domes, and waymarks, by which she recognized her native city.

"Yes, yes, dear; very fine," said Miss Ophelia. "But mercy on us! the boat has stopped! where is your father?"

And now ensued the usual turmoil of landing—waiters running twenty ways at once—men tugging trunks, carpet-bags, boxes—women anxiously calling to their children, and everybody crowding in a dense mass to the plank towards the landing.

Miss Ophelia seated herself resolutely on the lately vanquished trunk, and marshalling all her goods and chattels in fine military order, seemed resolved to defend them to the last.

"Shall I take your trunk, ma'am?" "Shall I take your baggage?" "Let me 'tend to your baggage, Missis?" "Shan't I carry out these yer, Missis?" rained down upon her unheeded. She sat with grim determination, upright as a darning-needle stuck in a board, holding on her bundle of umbrella and parasols, and replying with a determination that was enough to strike dismay even into a hackman,[2] wondering to Eva, in each interval, "what upon earth her papa could be thinking of; he couldn't have fallen over, now,—but something must have happened;"—and just as she had begun to work herself into a real distress, he came up, with his usually careless motion, and giving Eva a quarter of the orange he was eating, said,

"Well, Cousin Vermont, I suppose you are all ready."

"I've been ready, waiting, nearly an hour," said Miss Ophelia; "I began to be really concerned about you."

"That's a clever fellow, now," said he. "Well, the carriage is waiting, and the crowd are now off, so that one can walk out in a decent and Christian manner, and not be pushed and shoved. Here," he added to a driver who stood behind him, "take these things."

"I'll go and see to his putting them in," said Miss Ophelia.

"O, pshaw, cousin, what's the use?" said St. Clare.

"Well, at any rate, I'll carry this, and this, and this," said Miss Ophelia, singling out three boxes and a small carpet-bag.

"My dear Miss Vermont, positively, you mustn't come the Green Mountains over us that way.[3] You must adopt at least a piece of a southern principle, and not walk out under all that load. They'll take you for a waiting-maid; give them to this fellow; he'll put them down as if they were eggs, now."

Miss Ophelia looked despairingly, as her cousin took all her treasures from her, and rejoiced to find herself once more in the carriage with them, in a state of preservation.

2. A cabdriver.
3. I.e., try to impose a northern way of doing things. The Green Mountains are a range of the Appalachian Mountains in Vermont.

"Where's Tom?" said Eva.

"O, he's on the outside, Pussy. I'm going to take Tom up to mother for a peace-offering, to make up for that drunken fellow that upset the carriage."

"O, Tom will make a splendid driver, I know," said Eva; "he'll never get drunk."

The carriage stopped in front of an ancient mansion, built in that odd mixture of Spanish and French style, of which there are specimens in some parts of New Orleans. It was built in the Moorish fashion,[4]—a square building enclosing a court-yard, into which the carriage drove through an arched gateway. The court, in the inside, had evidently been arranged to gratify a picturesque and voluptuous ideality. Wide galleries ran all around the four sides, whose Moorish arches, slender pillars, and arabesque ornaments, carried the mind back, as in a dream, to the reign of oriental romance in Spain. In the middle of the court, a fountain threw high its silvery water, falling in a never-ceasing spray into a marble basin, fringed with a deep border of fragrant violets. The water in the fountain, pellucid as crystal, was alive with myriads of gold and silver fishes, twinkling and darting through it like so many living jewels. Around the fountain ran a walk, paved with a mosaic of pebbles, laid in various fanciful patterns; and this, again, was surrounded by turf, smooth as green velvet, while a carriage-drive enclosed the whole. Two large orange-trees, now fragrant with blossoms, threw a delicious shade; and, ranged in a circle round upon the turf, were marble vases of arabesque sculpture, containing the choicest flowering plants of the tropics. Huge pomegranate trees, with their glossy leaves and flame-colored flowers, dark-leaved Arabian jessamines, with their silvery stars, geraniums, luxuriant roses bending beneath their heavy abundance of flowers, golden jessamines, lemon-scented verbenum, all united their bloom and fragrance, while here and there a mystic old aloe,[5] with its strange, massive leaves, sat looking like some hoary old enchanter, sitting in weird grandeur among the more perishable bloom and fragrance around it.

The galleries that surrounded the court were festooned with a curtain of some kind of Moorish stuff, and could be drawn down at pleasure, to exclude the beams of the sun. On the whole, the appearance of the place was luxurious and romantic.

As the carriage drove in, Eva seemed like a bird ready to burst from a cage, with the wild eagerness of her delight.

4. The Moorish, or Islamic, architecture of North Africa and Spain features arches, tile decorations, and intricate wooden carving.
5. A flowering plant of the lily family. "Jessamines": tropical plants with fragrant flowers, also called *jasmine*. "Verbenum": an American herb or flowering shrub.

"O, isn't it beautiful, lovely! my own dear, darling home!" she said to Miss Ophelia. "Isn't it beautiful?"

"'Tis a pretty place," said Miss Ophelia, as she alighted; "though it looks rather old and heathenish to me."

Tom got down from the carriage, and looked about with an air of calm, still enjoyment. The negro, it must be remembered, is an exotic of the most gorgeous and superb countries of the world, and he has, deep in his heart, a passion for all that is splendid, rich, and fanciful; a passion which, rudely indulged by an untrained taste, draws on them the ridicule of the colder and more correct white race.

St. Clare, who was in his heart a poetical voluptuary, smiled as Miss Ophelia made her remark on his premises, and, turning to Tom, who was standing looking round, his beaming black face perfectly radiant with admiration, he said,

"Tom, my boy, this seems to suit you."

"Yes, Mas'r, it looks about the right thing," said Tom.

All this passed in a moment, while trunks were being hustled off, hackman paid, and while a crowd, of all ages and sizes,—men, women, and children,—came running through the galleries, both above and below, to see Mas'r come in. Foremost among them was a highly-dressed young mulatto man, evidently a very *distingue*[6] personage, attired in the ultra extreme of the mode, and gracefully waving a scented cambric handkerchief in his hand.

This personage had been exerting himself, with great alacrity, in driving all the flock of domestics to the other end of the verandah.

"Back! all of you. I am ashamed of you," he said, in a tone of authority. "Would you intrude on Master's domestic relations, in the first hour of his return?"

All looked abashed at this elegant speech, delivered with quite an air, and stood huddled together at a respectful distance, except two stout porters, who came up and began conveying away the baggage.

Owing to Mr. Adolph's systematic arrangements, when St. Clare turned round from paying the hackman, there was nobody in view but Mr. Adolph himself, conspicuous in satin vest, gold guard-chain, and white pants, and bowing with inexpressible grace and suavity.

"Ah, Adolph, is it you?" said his master, offering his hand to him; "how are you, boy?" while Adolph poured forth, with great fluency, an extemporary speech, which he had been preparing, with great care, for a fortnight before.

"Well, well," said St. Clare, passing on, with his usual air of negligent drollery, "that's very well got up, Adolph. See that the baggage is well bestowed. I'll come to the people in a minute;" and, so saying, he led Miss Ophelia to a large parlor that opened on to the verandah.

6. Distinguished in manner or bearing; superior in fashion or culture.

While this had been passing, Eva had flown like a bird, through the porch and parlor, to a little boudoir[7] opening likewise on the verandah.

A tall, dark-eyed, sallow woman, half rose from a couch on which she was reclining.

"Mamma!" said Eva, in a sort of a rapture, throwing herself on her neck, and embracing her over and over again.

"That'll do,—take care, child,—don't, you make my head ache," said the mother, after she had languidly kissed her.

St. Clare came in, embraced his wife in true, orthodox, husbandly fashion, and then presented to her his cousin. Marie lifted her large eyes on her cousin with an air of some curiosity, and received her with languid politeness. A crowd of servants now pressed to the entry door, and among them a middle-aged mulatto woman, of very respectable appearance, stood foremost, in a tremor of expectation and joy, at the door.

"O, there's Mammy!" said Eva, as she flew across the room; and, throwing herself into her arms, she kissed her repeatedly.

This woman did not tell her that she made her head ache, but, on the contrary, she hugged her, and laughed, and cried, till her sanity was a thing to be doubted of; and when released from her, Eva flew from one to another, shaking hands and kissing, in a way that Miss Ophelia afterwards declared fairly turned her stomach.

"Well!" said Miss Ophelia, "you southern children can do something that *I* couldn't."

"What, now, pray?" said St. Clare.

"Well, I want to be kind to everybody, and I wouldn't have anything hurt; but as to kissing—"

"Niggers," said St. Clare, "that you're not up to,—hey?"

"Yes, that's it. How can she?"

St. Clare laughed, as he went into the passage. "Halloa, here, what's to pay out here? Here, you all—Mammy, Jimmy, Polly, Sukey—glad to see Mas'r?" he said, as he went shaking hands from one to another. "Look out for the babies!" he added, as he stumbled over a sooty little urchin, who was crawling upon all fours. "If I step upon anybody, let 'em mention it."

There was an abundance of laughing and blessing Mas'r, as St. Clare distributed small pieces of change among them.

"Come, now, take yourselves off, like good boys and girls," he said; and the whole assemblage, dark and light, disappeared through a door into a large verandah, followed by Eva, who carried a large satchel, which she had been filling with apples, nuts, candy, ribbons, laces, and toys of every description, during her whole homeward journey.

7. A woman's bedroom, dressing room, or private sitting room.

As St. Clare turned to go back, his eye fell upon Tom, who was standing uneasily, shifting from one foot to the other, while Adolph stood negligently leaning against the banisters, examining Tom through an opera-glass, with an air that would have done credit to any dandy living.

"Puh! you puppy," said his master, striking down the opera glass; "is that the way you treat your company? Seems to me, Dolph," he added, laying his finger on the elegant figured satin vest that Adolph was sporting, "seems to me that's *my* vest."

"O! Master, this vest all stained with wine; of course, a gentleman in Master's standing never wears a vest like this. I understood I was to take it. It does for a poor nigger-fellow, like me."

And Adolph tossed his head, and passed his fingers through his scented hair, with a grace.

"So, that's it, is it?" said St. Clare, carelessly. "Well, here, I'm going to show this Tom to his mistress, and then you take him to the kitchen; and mind you don't put on any of your airs to him. He's worth two such puppies as you."

"Master always will have his joke," said Adolph, laughing. "I'm delighted to see Master in such spirits."

"Here, Tom," said St. Clare, beckoning.

Tom entered the room. He looked wistfully on the velvet carpets, and the before unimagined splendors of mirrors, pictures, statues, and curtains, and, like the Queen of Sheba before Solomon,[8] there was no more spirit in him. He looked afraid even to set his feet down.

"See here, Marie," said St. Clare to his wife, "I've bought you a coachman, at last, to order. I tell you, he's a regular hearse for blackness and sobriety, and will drive you like a funeral, if you want. Open your eyes, now, and look at him. Now, don't say I never think about you when I'm gone."

Marie opened her eyes, and fixed them on Tom, without rising.

"I know he'll get drunk," she said.

"No, he's warranted a pious and sober article."

"Well, I hope he may turn out well," said the lady; "it's more than I expect, though."

"Dolph," said St. Clare, "show Tom down stairs; and, mind yourself," he added; "remember what I told you."

Adolph tripped gracefully forward, and Tom, with lumbering tread, went after.

"He's a perfect behemoth!" said Marie.

8. Solomon, the king of Israel, was visited by the queen of Sheba, who, having heard of his wisdom, "came to prove him with hard questions"; after hearing his answers, "there was no more spirit in her." See 1 Kings 10.1–13 and 2 Chronicles 9.1–12.

"Come, now, Marie," said St. Clare, seating himself on a stool beside her sofa, "be gracious, and say something pretty to a fellow."

"You've been gone a fortnight beyond the time," said the lady, pouting.

"Well, you know I wrote you the reason."

"Such a short, cold letter!" said the lady.

"Dear Me! the mail was just going, and it had to be that or nothing."

"That's just the way, always," said the lady; "always something to make your journeys long, and letters short."

"See here, now," he added, drawing an elegant velvet case out of his pocket, and opening it, "here's a present I got for you in New York."

It was a daguerreotype, clear and soft as an engraving, representing Eva and her father sitting hand in hand.

Marie looked at it with a dissatisfied air.

"What made you sit in such an awkward position?" she said.

"Well, the position may be a matter of opinion; but what do you think of the likeness?"

"If you don't think anything of my opinion in one case, I suppose you wouldn't in another," said the lady, shutting the daguerreotype.

"Hang the woman!" said St. Clare, mentally; but aloud he added, "Come, now, Marie, what do you think of the likeness? Don't be nonsensical, now."

"It's very inconsiderate of you, St. Clare," said the lady, "to insist on my talking and looking at things. You know I've been lying all day with the sick-headache; and there's been such a tumult made ever since you came, I'm half dead."

"You're subject to the sick-headache, ma'am?" said Miss Ophelia, suddenly rising from the depths of the large armchair, where she had sat quietly, taking an inventory of the furniture, and calculating its expense.

"Yes, I'm a perfect martyr to it," said the lady.

"Juniper-berry tea is good for sick-headache," said Miss Ophelia; "at least, Auguste, Deacon Abraham Perry's wife, used to say so; and she was a great nurse."

"I'll have the first juniper-berries that get ripe in our garden by the lake brought in for that especial purpose," said St. Clare, gravely pulling the bell as he did so; "meanwhile, cousin, you must be wanting to retire to your apartment, and refresh yourself a little, after your journey. Dolph," he added, "tell Mammy to come here." The decent mulatto woman whom Eva had caressed so rapturously soon entered; she was dressed neatly, with a high red and yellow turban on her head, the recent gift of Eva, and which the child had been arranging on her head. "Mammy," said St. Clare, "I put this lady under your care; she is tired, and wants rest; take her to her chamber, and be sure she is made comfortable;" and Miss Ophelia disappeared in the rear of Mammy.

## Chapter XVI

### *Tom's Mistress and Her Opinions*

"And now, Marie," said St. Clare, "your golden days are dawning. Here is our practical, business-like New England cousin, who will take the whole budget of cares off your shoulders, and give you time to refresh yourself, and grow young and handsome. The ceremony of delivering the keys had better come off forthwith."

This remark was made at the breakfast-table, a few mornings after Miss Ophelia had arrived.

"I'm sure she's welcome," said Marie, leaning her head languidly on her hand. "I think she'll find one thing, if she does, and that is, that it's we mistresses that are the slaves, down here."

"O, certainly, she will discover that, and a world of wholesome truths besides, no doubt," said St. Clare.

"Talk about our keeping slaves, as if we did it for our *convenience*," said Marie. "I'm sure, if we consulted *that*, we might let them all go at once."

Evangeline fixed her large, serious eyes on her mother's face, with an earnest and perplexed expression, and said, simply, "What do you keep them for, mamma?"

"I don't know, I'm sure, except for a plague; they are the plague of my life. I believe that more of my ill health is caused by them than by any one thing; and ours, I know, are the very worst that ever anybody was plagued with."

"O, come, Marie, you've got the blues, this morning," said St. Clare. "You know't isn't so. There's Mammy, the best creature living,—what could you do without her?"

"Mammy is the best I ever knew," said Marie; "and yet Mammy, now, is selfish—dreadfully selfish; it's the fault of the whole race."

"Selfishness *is* a dreadful fault," said St. Clare, gravely.

"Well, now, there's Mammy," said Marie, "I think it's selfish of her to sleep so sound nights; she knows I need little attentions almost every hour, when my worst turns are on, and yet she's so hard to wake. I absolutely am worse, this very morning, for the efforts I had to make to wake her last night."

"Hasn't she sat up with you a good many nights, lately, mamma?" said Eva.

"How should you know that?" said Marie, sharply; "she's been complaining, I suppose."

"She didn't complain; she only told me what bad nights you'd had,—so many in succession."

"Why don't you let Jane or Rosa take her place, a night or two," said St. Clare, "and let her rest?"

"How can you propose it?" said Marie. "St. Clare, you really are inconsiderate. So nervous as I am, the least breath disturbs me; and a strange hand about me would drive me absolutely frantic. If Mammy felt the interest in me she ought to, she'd wake easier,—of course, she would. I've heard of people who had such devoted servants, but it never was *my* luck;" and Marie sighed.

Miss Ophelia had listened to this conversation with an air of shrewd, observant gravity; and she still kept her lips tightly compressed, as if determined fully to ascertain her longitude and position, before she committed herself.

"Now Mammy has a *sort* of goodness," said Marie; "she's smooth and respectful, but she's selfish at heart. Now, she never will be done fidgeting and worrying about that husband of hers. You see, when I was married and came to live here, of course, I had to bring her with me, and her husband my father couldn't spare. He was a blacksmith, and, of course, very necessary; and I thought and said, at the time, that Mammy and he had better give each other up, as it wasn't likely to be convenient for them ever to live together again. I wish, now, I'd insisted on it, and married Mammy to somebody else; but I was foolish and indulgent, and didn't want to insist. I told Mammy, at the time, that she mustn't ever expect to see him more than once or twice in her life again, for the air of father's place doesn't agree with my health, and I can't go there; and I advised her to take up with somebody else; but no—she wouldn't. Mammy has a kind of obstinacy about her, in spots, that everybody don't see as I do."

"Has she children?" said Miss Ophelia.

"Yes; she has two."

"I suppose she feels the separation from them?"

"Well, of course, I couldn't bring them. They were little dirty things—I couldn't have them about; and, besides, they took up too much of her time; but I believe that Mammy has always kept up a sort of sulkiness about this. She won't marry anybody else; and I do believe, now, though she knows how necessary she is to me, and how feeble my health is, she would go back to her husband to-morrow, if she only could. I *do*, indeed," said Marie; "they are just so selfish, now, the best of them."

"It's distressing to reflect upon," said St. Clare, dryly.

Miss Ophelia looked keenly at him, and saw the flush of mortification and repressed vexation, and the sarcastic curl of the lip, as he spoke.

"Now, Mammy has always been a pet with me," said Marie. "I wish some of your northern servants could look at her closets of dresses,—silks and muslins, and one real linen cambric, she has hanging there. I've worked sometimes whole afternoons, trimming her caps, and getting her ready to go to a party. As to abuse, she don't know what it is. She never was whipped more than once or twice in her whole life. She has her strong coffee or her tea every day, with white sugar in it. It's abominable, to be sure; but St. Clare will have high life below-stairs, and they every one of them live just as they please. The fact is, our servants are over-indulged. I suppose it is partly our fault that they are selfish, and act like spoiled children; but I've talked to St. Clare till I am tired."

"And I, too," said St. Clare, taking up the morning paper.

Eva, the beautiful Eva, had stood listening to her mother, with that expression of deep and mystic earnestness which was peculiar to her. She walked softly round to her mother's chair, and put her arms round her neck.

"Well, Eva, what now?" said Marie.

"Mamma, couldn't I take care of you one night—just one? I know I shouldn't make you nervous, and I shouldn't sleep. I often lie awake nights, thinking—"

"O, nonsense, child—nonsense!" said Marie; "you are such a strange child!"

"But may I, mamma? I think," she said, timidly, "that Mammy isn't well. She told me her head ached all the time, lately."

"O, that's just one of Mammy's fidgets! Mammy is just like all the rest of them—makes such a fuss about every little head-ache or finger-ache; it'll never do to encourage it—never! I'm principled about this matter," said she, turning to Miss Ophelia; "you'll find the necessity of it. If you encourage servants in giving way to every little disagreeable feeling, and complaining of every little ailment, you'll have your hands full. I never complain myself—nobody knows what I endure. I feel it a duty to bear it quietly, and I do."

Miss Ophelia's round eyes expressed an undisguised amazement at this peroration, which struck St. Clare as so supremely ludicrous, that he burst into a loud laugh.

"St. Clare always laughs when I make the least allusion to my ill health," said Marie, with the voice of a suffering martyr. "I only hope the day won't come when he'll remember it!" and Marie put her handkerchief to her eyes.

Of course, there was rather a foolish silence. Finally, St. Clare got up, looked at his watch, and said he had an engagement down street. Eva tripped away after him, and Miss Ophelia and Marie remained at the table alone.

"Now, that's just like St. Clare!" said the latter, withdrawing her handkerchief with somewhat of a spirited flourish when the criminal to be affected by it was no longer in sight. "He never realizes, never can, never will, what I suffer, and have, for years. If I was one of the complaining sort, or ever made any fuss about my ailments, there would be some reason for it. Men do get tired, naturally, of a complaining wife. But I've kept things to myself, and borne, and borne, till St. Clare has got in the way of thinking I can bear anything."

Miss Ophelia did not exactly know what she was expected to answer to this.

While she was thinking what to say, Marie gradually wiped away her tears, and smoothed her plumage in a general sort of way, as a dove might be supposed to make toilet after a shower, and began a housewifely chat with Miss Ophelia, concerning cupboards, closets, linen-presses,[1] store-rooms, and other matters, of which the latter was, by common understanding, to assume the direction,—giving her so many cautious directions and charges, that a head less systematic and business-like than Miss Ophelia's would have been utterly dizzied and confounded.

"And now," said Marie, "I believe I've told you everything; so that, when my next sick turn comes on, you'll be able to go forward entirely, without consulting me;—only about Eva,—she requires watching."

"She seems to be a good child, very," said Miss Ophelia; "I never saw a better child."

"Eva's peculiar," said her mother, "very. There are things about her so singular; she isn't like me, now, a particle;" and Marie sighed, as if this was a truly melancholy consideration.

Miss Ophelia in her own heart said, "I hope she isn't," but had prudence enough to keep it down.

"Eva always was disposed to be with servants; and I think that well enough with some children. Now, I always played with father's little negroes—it never did me any harm. But Eva somehow always seems to put herself on an equality with every creature that comes near her. It's a strange thing about the child. I never have been able to break her of it. St. Clare, I believe, encourages her in it. The fact is, St. Clare indulges every creature under this roof but his own wife."

Again Miss Ophelia sat in blank silence.

1. Upright closets in which clothes or household linens are kept.

"Now, there's no way with servants," said Marie, "but to *put them down*, and keep them down. It was always natural to me, from a child. Eva is enough to spoil a whole house-full. What she will do when she comes to keep house herself, I'm sure I don't know. I hold to being *kind* to servants—I always am; but you must make 'em *know their place*. Eva never does; there's no getting into the child's head the first beginning of an idea what a servant's place is! You heard her offering to take care of me nights, to let Mammy sleep! That's just a specimen of the way the child would be doing all the time, if she was left to herself."

"Why," said Miss Ophelia, bluntly, "I suppose you think your servants are human creatures, and ought to have some rest when they are tired."

"Certainly, of course. I'm very particular in letting them have everything that comes convenient,—anything that doesn't put one at all out of the way, you know. Mammy can make up her sleep, some time or other; there's no difficulty about that. She's the sleepiest concern that ever I saw; sewing, standing, or sitting, that creature will go to sleep, and sleep anywhere and everywhere. No danger but Mammy gets sleep enough. But this treating servants as if they were exotic flowers, or china vases, is really ridiculous," said Marie, as she plunged languidly into the depths of a voluminous and pillowy lounge, and drew towards her an elegant cut-glass vinaigrette.[2]

"You see," she continued, in a faint and lady-like voice, like the last dying breath of an Arabian jessamine, or something equally ethereal, "you see, Cousin Ophelia, I don't often speak of myself. It isn't my *habit;* 'tisn't agreeable to me. In fact, I haven't strength to do it. But there are points where St. Clare and I differ. St. Clare never understood me, never appreciated me. I think it lies at the root of all my ill health. St. Clare means well, I am bound to believe; but men are constitutionally selfish and inconsiderate to woman. That, at least, is my impression."

Miss Ophelia, who had not a small share of the genuine New England caution, and a very particular horror of being drawn into family difficulties, now began to foresee something of this kind impending; so, composing her face into a grim neutrality, and drawing out of her pocket about a yard and a quarter of stocking, which she kept as a specific against what Dr. Watts[3] asserts to be a personal habit of Satan when people have idle hands, she proceeded to knit most energetically, shutting her lips together in a way that said, as plain as words could, "You needn't try to make me speak. I don't

2. A small box or bottle with a perforated top, filled with smelling salts.
3. Isaac Watts (1674–1748), an English clergyman and writer of hymns.

want anything to do with your affairs,"—in fact, she looked about as sympathizing as a stone lion. But Marie didn't care for that. She had got somebody to talk to, and she felt it her duty to talk, and that was enough; and reinforcing herself by smelling again at her vinaigrette, she went on.

"You see, I brought my own property and servants into the connection, when I married St. Clare, and I am legally entitled to manage them my own way. St. Clare had his fortune and his servants, and I'm well enough content he should manage them his way; but St. Clare will be interfering. He has wild, extravagant notions about things, particularly about the treatment of servants. He really does act as if he set his servants before me, and before himself, too; for he lets them make him all sorts of trouble, and never lifts a finger. Now, about some things, St. Clare is really frightful—he frightens me—good-natured as he looks, in general. Now, he has set down his foot that, come what will, there shall not be a blow struck in this house, except what he or I strike; and he does it in a way that I really dare not cross him. Well, you may see what that leads to; for St. Clare wouldn't raise his hand, if every one of them walked over him, and I—you see how cruel it would be to require me to make the exertion. Now, you know these servants are nothing but grown-up children."

"I don't know anything about it, and I thank the Lord that I don't!" said Miss Ophelia, shortly.

"Well, but you will have to know something, and know it to your cost, if you stay here. You don't know what a provoking, stupid, careless, unreasonable childish, ungrateful set of wretches they are."

Marie seemed wonderfully supported, always, when she got upon this topic; and she now opened her eyes, and seemed quite to forget her languor.

"You don't know, and you can't, the daily, hourly trials that beset a housekeeper from them, everywhere and every way. But it's no use to complain to St. Clare. He talks the strangest stuff. He says we have made them what they are, and ought to bear with them. He says their faults are all owing to us, and that it would be cruel to make the fault and punish it too. He says we shouldn't do any better, in their place; just as if one could reason from them to us, you know."

"Don't you believe that the Lord made them of one blood with us?" said Miss Ophelia, shortly.

"No, indeed, not I! A pretty story, truly! They are a degraded race."

"Don't you think they've got immortal souls?" said Miss Ophelia, with increasing indignation.

"O, well," said Marie, yawning, "that, of course—nobody doubts that. But as to putting them on any sort of equality with us, you know, as if we could be compared, why, it's impossible! Now, St. Clare really has talked to me as if keeping Mammy from her husband was like keeping me from mine. There's no comparing in this way. Mammy couldn't have the feelings that I should. It's a different thing altogether,—of course, it is,—and yet St. Clare pretends not to see it. And just as if Mammy could love her little dirty babies as I love Eva! Yet St. Clare once really and soberly tried to persuade me that it was my duty, with my weak health, and all I suffer, to let Mammy go back, and take somebody else in her place. That was a little too much even for *me* to bear. I don't often show my feelings. I make it a principle to endure everything in silence; it's a wife's hard lot, and I bear it. But I did break out, that time; so that he has never alluded to the subject since. But I know by his looks, and little things that he says, that he thinks so as much as ever, and it's so trying, so provoking!"

Miss Ophelia looked very much as if she was afraid she should say something; but she rattled away with her needles in a way that had volumes of meaning in it, if Marie could only have understood it.

"So, you just see," she continued, "what you've got to manage. A household without any rule; where servants have it all their own way, do what they please, and have what they please, except so far as I, with my feeble health, have kept up government. I keep my cowhide[4] about, and sometimes I do lay it on; but the exertion is always too much for me. If St. Clare would only have this thing done as others do—"

"And how's that?"

"Why, send them to the calaboose,[5] or some of the other places to be flogged. That's the only way. If I wasn't such a poor, feeble piece, I believe I should manage with twice the energy that St. Clare does."

"And how does St. Clare contrive to manage?" said Miss Ophelia. "You say he never strikes a blow."

"Well, men have a more commanding way, you know; it is easier for them; besides, if you ever looked full in his eye, it's peculiar,—that eye,—and if he speaks decidedly, there's a kind of flash. I'm afraid of it, myself; and the servants know they must mind. I couldn't do as much by a regular storm and scolding as St. Clare can by one turn of his eye, if once he is in earnest. O, there's no trouble about St. Clare; that's the reason he's no more feeling for me. But you'll find, when you come to manage, that there's no getting along without severity,—they are so bad, so deceitful, so lazy."

4. A coarse whip made of rawhide or braided leather.
5. The local jail (slang).

"The old tune," said St. Clare, sauntering in. "What an awful account these wicked creatures will have to settle, at last, especially for being lazy! You see, cousin," said he, as he stretched himself at full length on a lounge opposite to Marie, "it's wholly inexcusable in them, in the light of the example that Marie and I set them,—this laziness."

"Come, now, St. Clare, you are too bad!" said Marie.

"Am I, now? Why, I thought I was talking good, quite remarkably for me. I try to enforce your remarks, Marie, always."

"You know you meant no such thing, St. Clare," said Marie.

"O, I must have been mistaken, then. Thank you, my dear, for setting me right."

"You do really try to be provoking," said Marie.

"O, come, Marie, the day is growing warm, and I have just had a long quarrel with Dolph, which has fatigued me excessively; so, pray be agreeable, now, and let a fellow repose in the light of your smile."

"What's the matter about Dolph?" said Marie. "That fellow's impudence has been growing to a point that is perfectly intolerable to me. I only wish I had the undisputed management of him a while. I'd bring him down!"

"What you say, my dear, is marked with your usual acuteness and good sense," said St. Clare. "As to Dolph, the case is this: that he has so long been engaged in imitating my graces and perfections, that he has, at last, really mistaken himself for his master; and I have been obliged to give him a little insight into his mistake."

"How?" said Marie.

"Why, I was obliged to let him understand explicitly that I preferred to keep *some* of my clothes for my own personal wearing; also, I put his magnificence upon an allowance of cologne-water, and actually was so cruel as to restrict him to one dozen of my cambric handkerchiefs. Dolph was particularly huffy about it, and I had to talk to him like a father, to bring him round."

"O! St. Clare, when will you learn how to treat your servants? It's abominable, the way you indulge them!" said Marie.

"Why, after all, what's the harm of the poor dog's wanting to be like his master; and if I haven't brought him up any better than to find his chief good in cologne and cambric handkerchiefs, why shouldn't I give them to him?"

"And why haven't you brought him up better?" said Miss Ophelia, with blunt determination.

"Too much trouble,—laziness, cousin, laziness,—which ruins more souls than you can shake a stick at. If it weren't for laziness, I should have been a perfect angel, myself. I'm inclined to think that laziness is what your old Dr. Botherem, up in Vermont, used to call the 'essence of moral evil.' It's an awful consideration, certainly."

"I think you slaveholders have an awful responsibility upon you," said Miss Ophelia. "I wouldn't have it, for a thousand worlds. You ought to educate your slaves, and treat them like reasonable creatures,—like immortal creatures, that you've got to stand before the bar of God with. That's my mind," said the good lady, breaking suddenly out with a tide of zeal that had been gaining strength in her mind all the morning.

"O! come, come," said St. Clare, getting up quickly; "what do you know about us?" And he sat down to the piano, and rattled a lively piece of music. St. Clare had a decided genius for music. His touch was brilliant and firm, and his fingers flew over the keys with a rapid and bird-like motion, airy, and yet decided. He played piece after piece, like a man who is trying to play himself into a good humor. After pushing the music aside, he rose up, and said, gayly, "Well, now, cousin, you've given us a good talk, and done your duty; on the whole, I think the better of you for it. I make no manner of doubt that you threw a very diamond of truth at me, though you see it hit me so directly in the face that it wasn't exactly appreciated, at first."

"For my part, I don't see any use in such sort of talk," said Marie. "I'm sure, if anybody does more for servants than we do, I'd like to know who; and it don't do 'em a bit good,—not a particle,—they get worse and worse. Aş to talking to them, or anything like that, I'm sure I have talked till I was tired and hoarse, telling them their duty, and all that; and I'm sure they can go to church when they like, though they don't understand a word of the sermon, more than so many pigs,—so it isn't of any great use for them to go, as I see; but they do go, and so they have every chance; but, as I said before, they are a degraded race, and always will be, and there isn't any help for them; you can't make anything of them, if you try. You see, Cousin Ophelia, I've tried, and you haven't; I was born and bred among them, and I know."

Miss Ophelia thought she had said enough, and therefore sat silent. St. Clare whistled a tune.

"St. Clare, I wish you wouldn't whistle," said Marie; "it makes my head worse."

"I won't," said St. Clare. "Is there anything else you wouldn't wish me to do?"

"I wish you *would* have some kind of sympathy for my trials; you never have any feeling for me."

"My dear accusing angel!" said St. Clare.

"It's provoking to be talked to in that way."

"Then, how will you be talked to? I'll talk to order,—any way you'll mention,—only to give satisfaction."

A gay laugh from the court rang through the silken curtains of the verandah. St. Clare stepped out, and lifting up the curtain, laughed too.

"What is it?" said Miss Ophelia, coming to the railing.

There sat Tom, on a little mossy seat in the court, every one of his button-holes stuck full of cape jessamines, and Eva, gayly laughing, was hanging a wreath of roses round his neck; and then she sat down on his knee, like a chip-sparrow, still laughing.

"O, Tom, you look so funny!"

Tom had a sober, benevolent smile, and seemed, in his quiet way, to be enjoying the fun quite as much as his little mistress. He lifted his eyes, when he saw his master, with a half-deprecating, apologetic air.

"How can you let her?" said Miss Ophelia.

"Why not?" said St. Clare.

"Why, I don't know, it seems so dreadful!"

"You would think no harm in a child's caressing a large dog, even if he was black; but a creature that can think, and reason, and feel, and is immortal, you shudder at; confess it, cousin. I know the feeling among some of you northerners well enough. Not that there is a particle of virtue in our not having it; but custom with us does what Christianity ought to do,—obliterates the feeling of personal prejudice. I have often noticed, in my travels north, how much stronger this was with you than with us. You loathe them as you would a snake or a toad, yet you are indignant at their wrongs. You would not have them abused; but you don't want to have anything to do with them yourselves. You would send them to Africa, out of your sight and smell, and then send a missionary or two to do up all the self-denial of elevating them compendiously. Isn't that it?"

"Well, cousin," said Miss Ophelia, thoughtfully, "there may be some truth in this."

"What would the poor and lowly do, without children?" said St. Clare, leaning on the railing, and watching Eva, as she tripped off, leading Tom with her. "Your little child is your only true democrat. Tom, now, is a hero to Eva; his stories are wonders in her eyes, his songs and Methodist hymns are better than an opera, and the traps and little bits of trash in his pocket a mine of jewels, and he the most wonderful Tom that ever wore a black skin. This is one of the roses of Eden that the Lord has dropped down expressly for the poor and lowly, who get few enough of any other kind."

"It's strange, cousin," said Miss Ophelia; "one might almost think you were a *professor*, to hear you talk."

"A professor?" said St. Clare.

"Yes; a professor of religion."

"Not at all; not a professor, as your town-folks have it; and, what is worse, I'm afraid, not a *practiser*, either."

"What makes you talk so, then?"

"Nothing is easier than talking," said St. Clare. "I believe Shakspeare makes somebody say, 'I could sooner show twenty what were good to be done, than be one of the twenty to follow my own showing.'[6] Nothing like division of labor. My forte lies in talking, and yours, cousin, lies in doing."

In Tom's external situation, at this time, there was, as the world says, nothing to complain of. Little Eva's fancy for him—the instinctive gratitude and loveliness of a noble nature—had led her to petition her father that he might be her especial attendant, whenever she needed the escort of a servant, in her walks or rides; and Tom had general orders to let everything else go, and attend to Miss Eva whenever she wanted him,—orders which our readers may fancy were far from disagreeable to him. He was kept well dressed, for St. Clare was fastidiously particular on this point. His stable services were merely a sinecure, and consisted simply in a daily care and inspection, and directing an under-servant in his duties; for Marie St. Clare declared that she could not have any smell of the horses about him when he came near her, and that he must positively not be put to any service that would make him unpleasant to her, as her nervous system was entirely inadequate to any trial of that nature; one snuff of anything disagreeable being, according to her account, quite sufficient to close the scene, and put an end to all her earthly trials at once. Tom, therefore, in his well-brushed broadcloth suit, smooth beaver, glossy boots, faultless wristbands and collar, with his grave, good-natured black face, looked respectable enough to be a Bishop of Carthage,[7] as men of his color were, in other ages.

Then, too, he was in a beautiful place, a consideration to which his sensitive race are never indifferent; and he did enjoy with a quiet joy the birds, the flowers, the fountains, the perfume, and light and beauty of the court, the silken hangings, and pictures, and lustres, and statuettes, and gilding, that made the parlors within a kind of Aladdin's palace[8] to him.

If ever Africa shall show an elevated and cultivated race,—and come it must, some time, her turn to figure in the great drama of human improvement,—life will awake there with a gorgeousness

6. Adapted from Shakespeare, *The Merchant of Venice* 1.2.15.
7. Ancient city in North Africa near Tunis.
8. I.e., a fabulously rich or magical place. The reference is to "Aladdin's Magic Lamp," a story in *A Thousand and One Nights*, the collection of traditional Arabic tales.

and splendor of which our cold western tribes faintly have conceived. In that far-off mystic land of gold, and gems, and spices, and waving palms, and wondrous flowers, and miraculous fertility, will awake new forms of art, new styles of splendor; and the negro race, no longer despised and trodden down, will, perhaps, show forth some of the latest and most magnificent revelations of human life. Certainly they will, in their gentleness, their lowly docility of heart, their aptitude to repose on a superior mind and rest on a higher power, their childlike simplicity of affection, and facility of forgiveness. In all these they will exhibit the highest form of the peculiarly *Christian life*, and, perhaps, as God chasteneth whom he loveth, he hath chosen poor Africa in the furnace of affliction, to make her the highest and noblest in that kingdom which he will set up, when every other kingdom has been tried, and failed; for the first shall be last, and the last first.[9]

Was this what Marie St. Clare was thinking of, as she stood, gorgeously dressed, on the verandah, on Sunday morning, clasping a diamond bracelet on her slender wrist? Most likely it was. Or, if it wasn't that, it was something else; for Marie patronized good things, and she was going now, in full force,—diamonds, silk, and lace, and jewels, and all,—to a fashionable church, to be very religious. Marie always made a point to be very pious on Sundays. There she stood, so slender, so elegant, so airy and undulating in all her motions, her lace scarf enveloping her like a mist. She looked a graceful creature, and she felt very good and very elegant indeed. Miss Ophelia stood at her side, a perfect contrast. It was not that she had not as handsome a silk dress and shawl, and as fine a pocket-handkerchief; but stiffness and squareness, and bolt-uprightness, enveloped her with as indefinite yet appreciable a presence as did grace her elegant neighbor; not the grace of God, however,—that is quite another thing!

"Where's Eva?" said Marie.

"The child stopped on the stairs, to say something to Mammy."

And what was Eva saying to Mammy on the stairs? Listen, reader, and you will hear, though Marie does not.

"Dear Mammy, I know your head is aching dreadfully."

"Lord bless you, Miss Eva! my head allers aches lately. You don't need to worry."

"Well, I'm glad you're going out; and here,"—and the little girl threw her arms around her,—"Mammy, you shall take my vinaigrette."

"What! your beautiful gold thing, thar, with them diamonds! Lor, Miss, 't wouldn't be proper, no ways."

9. Matthew 20.16.

"Why not? You need it, and I don't. Mamma always uses it for headache, and it'll make you feel better. No, you shall take it, to please me, now."

"Do hear the darlin talk!" said Mammy, as Eva thrust it into her bosom, and, kissing her, ran down stairs to her mother.

"What were you stopping for?"

"I was just stopping to give Mammy my vinaigrette, to take to church with her."

"Eva!" said Marie, stamping impatiently,—"your gold vinaigrette to *Mammy!* When will you learn what's *proper?* Go right and take it back, this moment!"

Eva looked downcast and aggrieved, and turned slowly.

"I say, Marie, let the child alone; she shall do as she pleases," said St. Clare.

"St. Clare, how will she ever get along in the world?" said Marie.

"The Lord knows," said St. Clare; "but she'll get along in heaven better than you or I."

"O, papa, don't," said Eva, softly touching his elbow; "it troubles mother."

"Well, cousin, are you ready to go to meeting?" said Miss Ophelia, turning square about on St. Clare.

"I'm not going, thank you."

"I do wish St. Clare ever would go to church," said Marie; "but he hasn't a particle of religion about him. It really isn't respectable."

"I know it," said St. Clare. "You ladies go to church to learn how to get along in the world, I suppose, and your piety sheds respectability on us. If I did go at all, I would go where Mammy goes; there's something to keep a fellow awake there, at least."

"What! those shouting Methodists? Horrible!" said Marie.

"Anything but the dead sea of your respectable churches, Marie. Positively, it's too much to ask of a man. Eva, do you like to go? Come, stay at home and play with me."

"Thank you, papa; but I'd rather go to church."

"Isn't it dreadful tiresome?" said St. Clare.

"I think it is tiresome, some," said Eva; "and I am sleepy, too, but I try to keep awake."

"What do you go for, then?"

"Why, you know, papa," she said, in a whisper, "cousin told me that God wants to have us; and he gives us everything, you know; and it isn't much to do it, if he wants us to. It isn't so very tiresome, after all."

"You sweet, little obliging soul!" said St. Clare, kissing her; "go along, that's a good girl, and pray for me."

"Certainly, I always do," said the child, as she sprang after her mother into the carriage.

St. Clare stood on the steps and kissed his hand to her, as the carriage drove away; large tears were in his eyes.

"O, Evangeline! rightly named," he said; "hath not God made thee an evangel to me?"

So he felt a moment; and then he smoked a cigar, and read the Picayune,[1] and forgot his little gospel. Was he much unlike other folks?

"You see, Evangeline," said her mother, "it's always right and proper to be kind to servants, but it isn't proper to treat them *just* as we would our relations, or people in our own class of life. Now, if Mammy was sick, you wouldn't want to put her in your own bed."

"I should feel just like it, mamma," said Eva, "because then it would be handier to take care of her, and because, you know, my bed is better than hers."

Marie was in utter despair at the entire want of moral perception evinced in this reply.

"What can I do to make this child understand me?" she said.

"Nothing," said Miss Ophelia, significantly.

Eva looked sorry and disconcerted for a moment; but children, luckily, do not keep to one impression long, and in a few moments she was merrily laughing at various things which she saw from the coach-windows, as it rattled along.

"Well, ladies," said St. Clare, as they were comfortably seated at the dinner-table, "and what was the bill of fare at church to-day?"

"O, Dr. C——preached a splendid sermon," said Marie. "It was just such a sermon as you ought to hear; it expressed all my views exactly."

"It must have been very improving," said St. Clare. "The subject must have been an extensive one."

"Well, I mean all my views about society, and such things," said Marie. "The text was, 'He hath made everything beautiful in its season;' and he showed how all the orders and distinctions in society came from God; and that it was so appropriate, you know, and beautiful, that some should be high and some low, and that some were born to rule and some to serve, and all that, you know; and he applied it so well to all this ridiculous fuss that is made about slavery, and he proved distinctly that the Bible was on our side, and supported all our institutions so convincingly. I only wish you'd heard him."

1. The first New Orleans newspaper, founded in 1837; the picayune is a local coin of small value.

"O, I didn't need it," said St. Clare. "I can learn what does me as much good as that from the Picayune, any time, and smoke a cigar besides; which I can't do, you know, in a church."

"Why," said Miss Ophelia, "don't you believe in these views?"

"Who,—I? You know I'm such a graceless dog that these religious aspects of such subjects don't edify me much. If I was to say anything on this slavery matter, I would say out fair and square, 'We're in for it; we've got 'em, and mean to keep 'em,—it's for our convenience and our interest;' for that's the long and short of it,—that's just the whole of what all this sanctified stuff amounts to, after all; and I think that will be intelligible to everybody, everywhere."

"I do think, Augustine, you are so irreverent!" said Marie. "I think it's shocking to hear you talk."

"Shocking! it's the truth. This religious talk on such matters,—why don't they carry it a little further, and show the beauty, in its season, of a fellow's taking a glass too much, and sitting a little too late over his cards, and various providential arrangements of that sort, which are pretty frequent among us young men;—we'd like to hear that those are right and godly, too."

"Well," said Miss Ophelia, "do you think slavery right or wrong?"

"I'm not going to have any of your horrid New England directness, cousin," said St. Clare, gayly. "If I answer that question, I know you'll be at me with half a dozen others, each one harder than the last; and I'm not a going to define my position. I am one of the sort that lives by throwing stones at other people's glass houses, but I never mean to put up one for them to stone."

"That's just the way he's always talking," said Marie; "you can't get any satisfaction out of him. I believe it's just because he don't like religion, that he's always running out in this way he's been doing."

"Religion!" said St. Clare, in a tone that made both ladies look at him. "Religion! Is what you hear at church religion? Is that which can bend and turn, and descend and ascend, to fit every crooked phase of selfish, worldly society, religion? Is that religion which is less scrupulous, less generous, less just, less considerate for man, than even my own ungodly, worldly, blinded nature? No! When I look for a religion, I must look for something above me, and not something beneath."

"Then you don't believe that the Bible justifies slavery," said Miss Ophelia.

"The Bible was my *mother's* book," said St. Clare. "By it she lived and died, and I would be very sorry to think it did. I'd as soon desire to have it proved that my mother could drink brandy, chew tobacco, and swear, by way of satisfying me that I did right in doing the same. It wouldn't make me at all more satisfied with these things in myself, and it would take from me the comfort of respecting her; and it really is a comfort, in this world, to have anything one can respect. In short, you see," said he, suddenly resuming his gay tone, "all I want is that different things be kept in different boxes. The whole frame-work of society, both in Europe and America, is made up of various things which will not stand the scrutiny of any very ideal standard of morality. It's pretty generally understood that men don't aspire after the absolute right, but only to do about as well as the rest of the world. Now, when any one speaks up, like a man, and says slavery is necessary to us, we can't get along without it, we should be beggared if we give it up, and, of course, we mean to hold on to it,—this is strong, clear, well-defined language; it has the respectability of truth to it; and if we may judge by their practice, the majority of the world will bear us out in it. But when he begins to put on a long face, and snuffle, and quote Scripture, I incline to think he isn't much better than he should be."

"You are very uncharitable," said Marie.

"Well," said St. Clare, "suppose that something should bring down the price of cotton once and forever, and make the whole slave property a drug in the market, don't you think we should soon have another version of the Scripture doctrine? What a flood of light would pour into the church, all at once, and how immediately it would be discovered that everything in the Bible and reason went the other way!"

"Well, at any rate," said Marie, as she reclined herself on a lounge, "I'm thankful I'm born where slavery exists; and I believe it's right,—indeed, I feel it must be; and, at any rate, I'm sure I couldn't get along without it."

"I say, what do you think, Pussy?" said her father to Eva, who came in at this moment, with a flower in her hand.

"What about, papa?"

"Why, which do you like the best,—to live as they do at your uncle's, up in Vermont, or to have a house-full of servants, as we do?"

"O, of course, our way is the pleasantest," said Eva.

"Why so?" said St. Clare, stroking her head.

"Why, it makes so many more round you to love, you know," said Eva, looking up earnestly.

"Now, that's just like Eva," said Marie; "just one of her odd speeches."

"Is it an odd speech, papa?" said Eva, whisperingly, as she got upon his knee.

"Rather, as this world goes, Pussy," said St. Clare. "But where has my little Eva been, all dinner-time?"

"O, I've been up in Tom's room, hearing him sing, and Aunt Dinah gave me my dinner."

"Hearing Tom sing, hey?"

"O, yes! he sings such beautiful things about the New Jerusalem, and bright angels, and the land of Canaan."

"I dare say; it's better than the opera, isn't it?"

"Yes, and he's going to teach them to me."

"Singing lessons, hey?—you *are* coming on."

"Yes, he sings for me, and I read to him in my Bible; and he explains what it means, you know."

"On my word," said Marie, laughing, "that is the latest joke of the season."

"Tom isn't a bad hand, now, at explaining Scripture, I'll dare swear," said St. Clare. "Tom has a natural genius for religion. I wanted the horses out early, this morning, and I stole up to Tom's cubiculum[2] there, over the stables, and there I heard him holding a meeting by himself; and, in fact, I haven't heard anything quite so savory as Tom's prayer, this some time. He put in for me, with a zeal that was quite apostolic."

"Perhaps he guessed you were listening. I've heard of that trick before."

"If he did, he wasn't very politic; for he gave the Lord his opinion of me, pretty freely. Tom seemed to think there was decidedly room for improvement in me, and seemed very earnest that I should be converted."

"I hope you'll lay it to heart," said Miss Ophelia.

"I suppose you are much of the same opinion," said St. Clare. "Well, we shall see,—shan't we, Eva?"

# Chapter XVII

## *The Freeman's Defence*

There was a gentle bustle at the Quaker house, as the afternoon drew to a close. Rachel Halliday moved quietly to and fro, collecting from her household stores such needments as could be arranged in the smallest compass, for the wanderers who were to go forth that night. The afternoon shadows stretched eastward, and the round red sun stood thoughtfully on the horizon, and his beams shone yellow and calm into the little bed-room where George and his wife were sitting. He was sitting with his child on his knee, and his

2. A small room in a catacomb.

wife's hand in his. Both looked thoughtful and serious, and traces of tears were on their cheeks.

"Yes, Eliza," said George, "I know all you say is true. You are a good child,—a great deal better than I am; and I will try to do as you say. I'll try to act worthy of a free man. I'll try to feel like a Christian. God Almighty knows that I've meant to do well,—tried hard to do well,—when everything has been against me; and now I'll forget all the past, and put away every hard and bitter feeling, and read my Bible, and learn to be a good man."

"And when we get to Canada," said Eliza, "I can help you. I can do dress-making very well; and I understand fine washing and ironing; and between us we can find something to live on."

"Yes, Eliza, so long as we have each other and our boy. O! Eliza, if these people only knew what a blessing it is for a man to feel that his wife and child belong to *him!* I've often wondered to see men that could call their wives and children *their own* fretting and worrying about anything else. Why, I feel rich and strong, though we have nothing but our bare hands. I feel as if I could scarcely ask God for any more. Yes, though I've worked hard every day, till I am twenty-five years old, and have not a cent of money, nor a roof to cover me, nor a spot of land to call my own, yet, if they will only let me alone now, I will be satisfied—thankful; I will work, and send back the money for you and my boy. As to my old master, he has been paid five times over for all he ever spent for me. I don't owe him anything."

"But yet we are not quite out of danger," said Eliza; "we are not yet in Canada."

"True," said George, "but it seems as if I smelt the free air, and it makes me strong."

At this moment, voices were heard in the outer apartment, in earnest conversation, and very soon a rap was heard on the door. Eliza started and opened it.

Simeon Halliday was there, and with him a Quaker brother, whom he introduced as Phineas Fletcher. Phineas was tall and lathy, red-haired, with an expression of great acuteness and shrewdness in his face. He had not the placid, quiet, unworldly air of Simeon Halliday; on the contrary, a particularly wide-awake and *au fait*[1] appearance, like a man who rather prides himself on knowing what he is about, and keeping a bright look-out ahead; peculiarities which sorted rather oddly with his broad brim and formal phraseology.

"Our friend Phineas hath discovered something of importance to the interests of thee and thy party, George," said Simeon; "it were well for thee to hear it."

1. Fully competent or fully informed (French).

"That I have," said Phineas, "and it shows the use of a man's always sleeping with one ear open, in certain places, as I've always said. Last night I stopped at a little lone tavern, back on the road. Thee remembers the place, Simeon, where we sold some apples, last year, to that fat woman, with the great ear-rings. Well, I was tired with hard driving; and, after my supper, I stretched myself down on a pile of bags in the corner, and pulled a buffalo[2] over me, to wait till my bed was ready; and what does I do, but get fast asleep."

"With one ear open, Phineas?" said Simeon, quietly.

"No; I slept, ears and all, for an hour or two, for I was pretty well tired; but when I came to myself a little, I found that there were some men in the room, sitting round a table, drinking and talking; and I thought, before I made much muster, I'd just see what they were up to, especially as I heard them say something about the Quakers. 'So,' says one, 'they are up in the Quaker settlement, no doubt,' says he. Then I listened with both ears, and I found that they were talking about this very party. So I lay and heard them lay off all their plans. This young man, they said, was to be sent back to Kentucky, to his master, who was going to make an example of him, to keep all niggers from running away; and his wife two of them were going to run down to New Orleans to sell, on their own account, and they calculated to get sixteen or eighteen hundred dollars for her; and the child, they said, was going to a trader, who had bought him; and then there was the boy, Jim, and his mother, they were to go back to their masters in Kentucky. They said that there were two constables, in a town a little piece ahead, who would go in with 'em to get 'em taken up, and the young woman was to be taken before a judge; and one of the fellows, who is small and smooth-spoken, was to swear to her for his property, and get her delivered over to him to take south. They've got a right notion of the track we are going tonight; and they'll be down after us, six or eight strong. So, now, what's to be done?"

The group that stood in various attitudes, after this communication, were worthy of a painter. Rachel Halliday, who had taken her hands out of a batch of biscuit, to hear the news, stood with them upraised and floury, and with a face of the deepest concern. Simeon looked profoundly thoughtful; Eliza had thrown her arms around her husband, and was looking up to him. George stood with clenched hands and glowing eyes, and looking as any other man might look, whose wife was to be sold at auction, and son sent to a trader, all under the shelter of a Christian nation's laws.

"What *shall* we do, George?" said Eliza, faintly.

2. A coverlet or rug of buffalo hide.

"I know what *I* shall do," said George, as he stepped into the little room, and began examining his pistols.

"Ay, ay," said Phineas, nodding his head to Simeon; "thou seest, Simeon, how it will work."

"I see," said Simeon, sighing; "I pray it come not to that."

"I don't want to involve any one with or for me," said George. "If you will lend me your vehicle and direct me, I will drive alone to the next stand. Jim is a giant in strength, and brave as death and despair, and so am I."

"Ah, well, friend," said Phineas, "but thee'll need a driver, for all that. Thee's quite welcome to do all the fighting, thee knows; but I know a thing or two about the road, that thee doesn't."

"But I don't want to involve you," said George.

"Involve," said Phineas, with a curious and keen expression of face. "When thee does involve me, please to let me know."

"Phineas is a wise and skilful man," said Simeon. "Thee does well, George, to abide by his judgment; and," he added, laying his hand kindly on George's shoulder, and pointing to the pistols, "be not over hasty with these,—young blood is hot."

"I will attack no man," said George. "All I ask of this country is to be let alone, and I will go out peaceably; but,"—he paused, and his brow darkened and his face worked,—"I've had a sister sold in that New Orleans market. I know what they are sold for; and am I going to stand by and see them take my wife and sell her, when God has given me a pair of strong arms to defend her? No; God help me! I'll fight to the last breath, before they shall take my wife and son. Can you blame me?"

"Mortal man cannot blame thee, George. Flesh and blood could not do otherwise," said Simeon. "Woe unto the world because of offences, but woe unto them through whom the offence cometh."[3]

"Would not even you, sir, do the same, in my place?"

"I pray that I be not tried," said Simeon; "the flesh is weak."

"I think my flesh would be pretty tolerable strong, in such a case," said Phineas, stretching out a pair of arms like the sails of a windmill. "I an't sure, friend George, that I shouldn't hold a fellow for thee, if thee had any accounts to settle with him."

"If man should *ever* resist evil," said Simeon, "then George should feel free to do it now: but the leaders of our people taught a more excellent way; for the wrath of man worketh not the righteousness of God; but it goes sorely against the corrupt will of man, and none can receive it save they to whom it is given. Let us pray the Lord that we be not tempted."

3. Matthew 18.7.

"And so *I* do," said Phineas; "but if we are tempted too much—why, let them look out, that's all."

"It's quite plain thee wasn't born a Friend,"[4] said Simeon, smiling. "The old nature hath its way in thee pretty strong as yet."

To tell the truth, Phineas had been a hearty, two-listed backwoodsman, a vigorous hunter, and a dead shot at a buck; but, having wooed a pretty Quakeress, had been moved by the power of her charms to join the society in his neighborhood; and though he was an honest, sober, and efficient member, and nothing particular could be alleged against him, yet the more spiritual among them could not but discern an exceeding lack of savor in his developments.

"Friend Phineas will ever have ways of his own," said Rachel Halliday, smiling; "but we all think that his heart is in the right place, after all."

"Well," said George, "isn't it best that we hasten our flight?"

"I got up at four o'clock, and came on with all speed, full two or three hours ahead of them, if they start at the time they planned. It isn't safe to start till dark, at any rate; for there are some evil persons in the villages ahead, that might be disposed to meddle with us, if they saw our wagon, and that would delay us more than the waiting; but in two hours I think we may venture. I will go over to Michael Cross, and engage him to come behind on his swift nag, and keep a bright look-out on the road, and warn us if any company of men come on. Michael keeps a horse that can soon get ahead of most other horses; and he could shoot ahead and let us know, if there were any danger. I am going out now to warn Jim and the old woman to be in readiness, and to see about the horse. We have a pretty fair start, and stand a good chance to get to the stand before they can come up with us. So, have good courage, friend George; this isn't the first ugly scrape that I've been in with thy people," said Phineas, as he closed the door.

"Phineas is pretty shrewd," said Simeon. "He will do the best that can be done for thee, George."

"All I am sorry for," said George, "is the risk to you."

"Thee'll much oblige us, friend George, to say no more about that. What we do we are conscience bound to do; we can do no other way. And now, mother," said he, turning to Rachel, "hurry thy preparations for these friends, for we must not send them away fasting."

And while Rachel and her children were busy making corncake, and cooking ham and chicken, and hurrying on the *et ceteras* of the evening meal, George and his wife sat in their little room, with

4. A Quaker.

their arms folded about each other, in such talk as husband and wife have when they know that a few hours may part them forever.

"Eliza," said George, "people that have friends, and houses, and lands, and money, and all those things, *can't* love as we do, who have nothing but each other. Till I knew you, Eliza, no creature ever had loved me, but my poor, heartbroken mother and sister. I saw poor Emily that morning the trader carried her off. She came to the corner where I was lying asleep, and said, 'Poor George, your last friend is going. What will become of you, poor boy?' And I got up and threw my arms round her, and cried and sobbed, and she cried too; and those were the last kind words I got for ten long years; and my heart all withered up, and felt as dry as ashes, till I met you. And your loving me,—why, it was almost like raising one from the dead! I've been a new man ever since! And now, Eliza, I'll give my last drop of blood, but they *shall not* take you from me. Whoever gets you must walk over my dead body."

"O Lord, have mercy!" said Eliza, sobbing. "If he will only let us get out of this country together, that is all we ask."

"Is God on their side?" said George, speaking less to his wife than pouring out his own bitter thoughts. "Does he see all they do? Why does he let such things happen? And they tell us that the Bible is on their side; certainly all the power is. They are rich, and healthy, and happy; they are members of churches, expecting to go to heaven; and they get along so easy in the world, and have it all their own way; and poor, honest, faithful Christians,—Christians as good or better than they,—are lying in the very dust under their feet. They buy 'em and sell 'em, and make trade of their heart's blood, and groans and tears,—and God *lets* them."

"Friend George," said Simeon, from the kitchen, "listen to this Psalm; it may do thee good."

George drew his seat near the door, and Eliza, wiping her tears, came forward also to listen, while Simeon read as follows:

"But as for me, my feet were almost gone; my steps had well-nigh slipped. For I was envious of the foolish, when I saw the prosperity of the wicked. They are not in trouble like other men, neither are they plagued like other men. Therefore, pride compasseth them as a chain; violence covereth them as a garment. Their eyes stand out with fatness; they have more than heart could wish. They are corrupt, and speak wickedly concerning oppression; they speak loftily. Therefore his people return, and the waters of a full cup are wrung out to them, and they say, How doth God know? and is there knowledge in the Most High?"

"Is not that the way thee feels, George?"

"It is so, indeed," said George,—"as well as I could have written it myself."

"Then, hear," said Simeon: "When I thought to know this, it was too painful for me until I went unto the sanctuary of God. Then understood I their end. Surely thou didst set them in slippery places, thou castedst them down to destruction. As a dream when one awaketh, so, oh Lord, when thou awakest, thou shalt despise their image. Nevertheless, I am continually with thee; thou hast holden me by my right hand. Thou shalt guide me by thy counsel, and afterwards receive me to glory. It is good for me to draw near unto God. I have put my trust in the Lord God."[5]

The words of holy trust, breathed by the friendly old man, stole like sacred music over the harassed and chafed spirit of George; and after he ceased, he sat with a gentle and subdued expression on his fine features.

"If this world were all, George," said Simeon, "thee might, indeed, ask, where is the Lord? But it is often those who have least of all in this life whom he chooseth for the kingdom. Put thy trust in him, and, no matter what befalls thee here, he will make all right hereafter."

If these words had been spoken by some easy, self-indulgent exhorter, from whose mouth they might have come merely as pious and rhetorical flourish, proper to be used to people in distress, perhaps they might not have had much effect; but coming from one who daily and calmly risked fine and imprisonment for the cause of God and man, they had a weight that could not but be felt, and both the poor, desolate fugitives found calmness and strength breathing into them from it.

And now Rachel took Eliza's hand kindly, and led the way to the supper-table. As they were sitting down, a light tap sounded at the door, and Ruth entered.

"I just ran in," she said, "with these little stockings for the boy,—three pair, nice, warm woollen ones. It will be so cold, thee knows, in Canada. Does thee keep up good courage, Eliza?" she added, tripping round to Eliza's side of the table, and shaking her warmly by the hand, and slipping a seed-cake into Harry's hand. "I brought a little parcel of these for him," she said, tugging at her pocket to get out the package. "Children, thee knows, will always be eating."

"O, thank you; you are too kind," said Eliza.

"Come, Ruth, sit down to supper," said Rachel.

"I couldn't, any way. I left John with the baby, and some biscuits in the oven; and I can't stay a moment, else John will burn up all the biscuits, and give the baby all the sugar in the bowl. That's the way he does," said the little Quakeress, laughing. "So, good-by, Eliza;

5. Abbreviated from Psalm 73.2–28.

good-by, George; the Lord grant thee a safe journey;" and, with a few tripping steps, Ruth was out of the apartment.

A little while after supper, a large covered-wagon drew up before the door; the night was clear starlight; and Phineas jumped briskly down from his seat to arrange his passengers. George walked out of the door, with his child on one arm and his wife on the other. His step was firm, his face settled and resolute. Rachel and Simeon came out after them.

"You get out, a moment," said Phineas to those inside, "and let me fix the back of the wagon, there, for the womenfolks and the boy."

"Here are the two buffaloes," said Rachel. "Make the seats as comfortable as may be; it's hard riding all night."

Jim came out first, and carefully assisted out his old mother, who clung to his arm, and looked anxiously about, as if she expected the pursuer every moment.

"Jim, are your pistols all in order?" said George, in a low, firm voice.

"Yes, indeed," said Jim.

"And you've no doubt what you shall do, if they come?"

"I rather think I haven't," said Jim, throwing open his broad chest, and taking a deep breath. "Do you think I'll let them get mother again?"

During this brief colloquy, Eliza had been taking her leave of her kind friend, Rachel, and was handed into the carriage by Simeon, and, creeping into the back part with her boy, sat down among the buffalo-skins. The old woman was next handed in and seated, and George and Jim placed on a rough board seat front of them, and Phineas mounted in front.

"Farewell, my friends," said Simeon, from without.

"God bless you!" answered all from within.

And the wagon drove off, rattling and jolting over the frozen road.

There was no opportunity for conversation, on account of the roughness of the way and the noise of the wheels. The vehicle, therefore, rumbled on, through long, dark stretches of woodland,—over wide, dreary plains,—up hills, and down valleys,—and on, on, on they jogged, hour after hour. The child soon fell asleep, and lay heavily in his mother's lap. The poor, frightened old woman at last forgot her fears; and, even Eliza, as the night waned, found all her anxieties insufficient to keep her eyes from closing. Phineas seemed, on the whole, the briskest of the company, and beguiled his long drive with whistling certain very unquaker-like songs, as he went on.

But about three o'clock George's ear caught the hasty and decided click of a horse's hoof coming behind them at some distance, and jogged Phineas by the elbow. Phineas pulled up his horses, and listened.

"That must be Michael," he said; "I think I know the sound of his gallop;" and he rose up and stretched his head anxiously back over the road.

A man riding in hot haste was now dimly descried at the top of a distant hill.

"There he is, I do believe!" said Phineas. George and Jim both sprang out of the wagon, before they knew what they were doing. All stood intensely silent, with their faces turned towards the expected messenger. On he came. Now he went down into a valley, where they could not see him; but they heard the sharp, hasty tramp, rising nearer and nearer; at last they saw him emerge on the top of an eminence, within hail.

"Yes, that's Michael!" said Phineas; and, raising his voice, "Halloa, there, Michael!"

"Phineas! is that thee?"

"Yes; what news—they coming?"

"Right on behind, eight or ten of them, hot with brandy, swearing and foaming like so many wolves."

And, just as he spoke, a breeze brought the faint sound of galloping horsemen towards them.

"In with you,—quick, boys, *in!*" said Phineas. "If you must fight, wait till I get you a piece ahead." And, with the word, both jumped in, and Phineas lashed the horses to a run, the horseman keeping close beside them. The wagon rattled, jumped, almost flew, over the frozen ground; but plainer, and still plainer, came the noise of pursuing horsemen behind. The women heard it, and, looking anxiously out, saw, far in the rear, on the brow of a distant hill, a party of men looming up against the red-streaked sky of early dawn. Another hill, and their pursuers had evidently caught sight of their wagon, whose white cloth-covered top made it conspicuous at some distance, and a loud yell of brutal triumph came forward on the wind. Eliza sickened, and strained her child closer to her bosom; the old woman prayed and groaned, and George and Jim clenched their pistols with the grasp of despair. The pursuers gained on them fast; the carriage made a sudden turn, and brought them near a ledge of a steep overhanging rock, that rose in an isolated ridge or clump in a large lot, which was, all around it, quite clear and smooth. This isolated pile, or range of rocks, rose up black and heavy against the brightening sky, and seemed to promise shelter and concealment. It was a place well known to Phineas, who had been familiar with the spot in his hunting days; and it was to gain this point he had been racing his horses.

"Now for it!" said he, suddenly checking his horses, and springing from his seat to the ground. "Out with you, in a twinkling, every one, and up into these rocks with me. Michael, thee tie thy horse to the wagon, and drive ahead to Amariah's, and get him and his boys to come back and talk to these fellows."

In a twinkling they were all out of the carriage.

"There," said Phineas, catching up Harry, "you, each of you, see to the women; and run, *now*, if you ever *did* run!"

There needed no exhortation. Quicker than we can say it, the whole party were over the fence, making with all speed for the rocks, while Michael, throwing himself from his horse, and fastening the bridle to the wagon, began driving it rapidly away.

"Come ahead," said Phineas, as they reached the rocks, and saw, in the mingled starlight and dawn, the traces of a rude but plainly marked foot-path leading up among them; "this is one of our old hunting-dens. Come up!"

Phineas went before, springing up the rocks like a goat, with the boy in his arms. Jim came second, bearing his trembling old mother over his shoulder, and George and Eliza brought up the rear. The party of horsemen came up to the fence, and, with mingled shouts and oaths, were dismounting, to prepare to follow them. A few moments' scrambling brought them to the top of the ledge; the path then passed between a narrow defile, where only one could walk at a time, till suddenly they came to a rift or chasm more than a yard in breadth, and beyond which lay a pile of rocks, separate from the rest of the ledge, standing full thirty feet high, with its sides steep and perpendicular as those of a castle. Phineas easily leaped the chasm, and sat down the boy on a smooth, flat platform of crisp white moss, that covered the top of the rock.

"Over with you!" he called; "spring, now, once, for your lives!" said he, as one after another sprang across. Several fragments of loose stone formed a kind of breastwork, which sheltered their position from the observation of those below.

"Well, here we all are," said Phineas, peeping over the stone breast-work to watch the assailants, who were coming tumultuously up under the rocks. "Let 'em get us, if they can. Whoever comes here has to walk single file between those two rocks, in fair range of your pistols, boys, d'ye see?"

"I do see," said George; "and now, as this matter is ours, let us take all the risk, and do all the fighting."

"Thee's quite welcome to do the fighting, George," said Phineas, chewing some checkerberry-leaves[6] as he spoke; "but I may have the fun of looking on, I suppose. But see, these fellows are kinder

6. Wintergreen leaves.

debating down there, and looking up, like hens when they are going to fly up on to the roost. Hadn't thee better give 'em a word of advice, before they come up, just to tell 'em handsomely they'll be shot if they do?"

The party beneath, now more apparent in the light of the dawn, consisted of our old acquaintances, Tom Loker and Marks, with two constables, and a posse consisting of such rowdies at the last tavern as could be engaged by a little brandy to go and help the fun of trapping a set of niggers.

"Well, Tom, yer coons are farly treed," said one.

"Yes, I see 'em go up right here," said Tom; "and here's a path. I'm for going right up. They can't jump down in a hurry, and it won't take long to ferret 'em out."

"But, Tom, they might fire at us from behind the rocks," said Marks. "That would be ugly, you know."

"Ugh!" said Tom, with a sneer. "Always for saving your skin, Marks! No danger! niggers are too plaguy scared!"

"I don't know why I *shouldn't* save my skin," said Marks. "It's the best I've got; and niggers *do* fight like the devil, sometimes."

At this moment, George appeared on the top of a rock above them, and, speaking in a calm, clear voice, said,

"Gentlemen, who are you, down there, and what do you want?"

"We want a party of runaway niggers," said Tom Loker. "One George Harris, and Eliza Harris, and their son, and Jim Selden, and an old woman. We've got the officers, here, and a warrant to take 'em; and we're going to have 'em, too. D'ye hear? An't you George Harris, that belongs to Mr. Harris, of Shelby county, Kentucky?"

"I am George Harris. A Mr. Harris, of Kentucky, did call me his property. But now I'm a free man, standing on God's free soil; and my wife and my child I claim as mine. Jim and his mother are here. We have arms to defend ourselves, and we mean to do it. You can come up, if you like; but the first one of you that comes within the range of our bullets is a dead man, and the next, and the next; and so on till the last."

"O, come! come!" said a short, puffy man, stepping forward, and blowing his nose as he did so. "Young man, this an't no kind of talk at all for you. You see, we're officers of justice. We've got the law on our side, and the power, and so forth; so you'd better give up peaceably, you see; for you'll certainly have to give up, at last."

"I know very well that you've got the law on your side, and the power," said George, bitterly. "You mean to take my wife to sell in New Orleans, and put my boy like a calf in a trader's pen, and send Jim's old mother to the brute that whipped and abused her before, because he couldn't abuse her son. You want to send Jim and me back to be whipped and tortured, and ground down under the heels of them that you call masters; and your laws *will* bear you out in it,—more shame for you and them! But you haven't got us. We don't own your laws; we don't own your country; we stand here as free, under God's sky, as you are; and, by the great God that made us, we'll fight for our liberty till we die."

George stood out in fair sight, on the top of the rock, as he made his declaration of independence; the glow of dawn gave a flush to his swarthy cheek, and bitter indignation and despair gave fire to his dark eye; and, as if appealing from man to the justice of God, he raised his hand to heaven as he spoke.

If it had been only a Hungarian youth,[7] now bravely defending in some mountain fastness the retreat of fugitives escaping from Austria into America, this would have been sublime heroism; but as it was a youth of African descent, defending the retreat of fugitives through America into Canada, of course we are too well instructed and patriotic to see any heroism in it; and if any of our readers do, they must do it on their own private responsibility. When despairing Hungarian fugitives make their way, against all the search-warrants and authorities of their lawful government, to America, press and political cabinet ring with applause and welcome. When despairing African fugitives do the same thing,—it is—what *is* it?

Be it as it may, it is certain that the attitude, eye, voice, manner, of the speaker, for a moment struck the party below to silence. There is something in boldness and determination that for a time hushes even the rudest nature. Marks was the only one who remained wholly untouched. He was deliberately cocking his pistol, and, in the momentary silence that followed George's speech, he fired at him.

"Ye see ye get jist as much for him dead as alive in Kentucky," he said, coolly, as he wiped his pistol on his coatsleeve.

George sprang backward,—Eliza uttered a shriek,—the ball had passed close to his hair, had nearly grazed the cheek of his wife, and struck in the tree above.

"It's nothing, Eliza," said George, quickly.

"Thee'd better keep out of sight, with thy speechifying," said Phineas; "they're mean scamps."

"Now, Jim," said George, "look that your pistols are all right, and watch that pass with me. The first man that shows himself I fire at; you take the second, and so on. It won't do, you know, to waste two shots on one."

"But what if you don't hit?"

"I *shall* hit," said George, coolly.

7. Following Hungary's failed bid for independence from Austria in 1848–49, about ten thousand Hungarians came to the United States during the 1850s.

The freeman's defence.

"Good! now, there's stuff in that fellow," muttered Phineas, between his teeth.

The party below, after Marks had fired, stood, for a moment, rather undecided.

"I think you must have hit some on 'em," said one of the men. "I heard a squeal!"

"I'm going right up for one," said Tom. "I never was afraid of niggers, and I an't going to be now. Who goes after?" he said, springing up the rocks.

George heard the words distinctly. He drew up his pistol, examined it, pointed it towards that point in the defile where the first man would appear.

One of the most courageous of the party followed Tom, and, the way being thus made, the whole party began pushing up the rock,—the hindermost pushing the front ones faster than they would have gone of themselves. On they came, and in a moment the burly form of Tom appeared in sight, almost at the verge of the chasm.

George fired,—the shot entered his side,—but, though wounded, he would not retreat, but, with a yell like that of a mad bull, he was leaping right across the chasm into the party.

"Friend," said Phineas, suddenly stepping to the front, and meeting him with a push from his long arms, "thee isn't wanted here."

Down he fell into the chasm, crackling down among trees, bushes, logs, loose stones, till he lay, bruised and groaning, thirty feet below. The fall might have killed him, had it not been broken and moderated by his clothes catching in the branches of a large tree; but he came down with some force, however,—more than was at all agreeable or convenient.

"Lord help us, they are perfect devils!" said Marks, heading the retreat down the rocks with much more of a will than he had joined the ascent, while all the party came tumbling precipitately after him,—the fat constable, in particular, blowing and puffing in a very energetic manner.

"I say, fellers," said Marks, "you jist go round and pick up Tom, there, while I run and get on to my horse, to go back for help,—that's you;" and, without minding the hootings and jeers of his company, Marks was as good as his word, and was soon seen galloping away.

"Was ever such a sneaking varmint?" said one of the men; "to come on his business, and he clear out and leave us this yer way!"

"Well, we must pick up that feller," said another. "Cuss me if I much care whether he is dead or alive."

The men, led by the groans of Tom, scrambled and crackled through stumps, logs and bushes, to where that hero lay groaning and swearing, with alternate vehemence.

"Ye keep it agoing pretty loud, Tom," said one. "Ye much hurt?"

"Don't know. Get me up, can't ye? Blast that infernal Quaker! If it hadn't been for him, I'd a pitched some on 'em down here, to see how they liked it."

With much labor and groaning, the fallen hero was assisted to rise; and, with one holding him up under each shoulder, they got him as far as the horses.

"If you could only get me a mile back to that ar tavern. Give me a handkerchief or something, to stuff into this place, and stop this infernal bleeding."

George looked over the rocks, and saw them trying to lift the burly form of Tom into the saddle. After two or three ineffectual attempts, he reeled, and fell heavily to the ground.

"O, I hope he isn't killed!" said Eliza, who, with all the party, stood watching the proceeding.

"Why not?" said Phineas; "serves him right."

"Because, after death comes the judgment," said Eliza.

"Yes," said the old woman, who had been groaning and praying, in her Methodist fashion, during all the encounter, "it's an awful case for the poor crittur's soul."

"On my word, they're leaving him, I do believe," said Phineas.

It was true; for after some appearance of irresolution and consultation, the whole party got on their horses and rode away. When they were quite out of sight, Phineas began to bestir himself.

"Well, we must go down and walk a piece," he said. "I told Michael to go forward and bring help, and be along back here with the wagon; but we shall have to walk a piece along the road, I reckon, to meet them. The Lord grant he be along soon! It's early in the day; there won't be much travel afoot yet a while; we an't much more than two miles from our stopping-place. If the road hadn't been so rough last night, we could have outrun 'em entirely."

As the party neared the fence, they discovered in the distance, along the road, their own wagon coming back, accompanied by some men on horseback.

"Well, now, there's Michael, and Stephen, and Amariah," exclaimed Phineas, joyfully. "Now we *are* made,—as safe as if we'd got there."

"Well, do stop, then," said Eliza, "and do something for that poor man; he's groaning dreadfully."

"It would be no more than Christian," said George; "let's take him up and carry him on."

"And doctor him up among the Quakers!" said Phineas; "pretty well, that! Well, I don't care if we do. Here, let's have a look at him;" and Phineas, who, in the course of his hunting and backwoods life, had acquired some rude experience of surgery, kneeled down by the wounded man, and began a careful examination of his condition.

"Marks," said Tom, feebly, "is that you, Marks?"

"No; I reckon 'tan't, friend," said Phineas. "Much Marks cares for thee, if his own skin's safe. He's off, long ago."

"I believe I'm done for," said Tom. "The cussed sneaking dog, to leave me to die alone! My poor old mother always told me 'twould be so."

"La sakes! jist hear the poor crittur. He's got a mammy, now," said the old negress. "I can't help kinder pityin' on him."

"Softly, softly; don't thee snap and snarl, friend," said Phineas, as Tom winced and pushed his hand away. "Thee has no chance, unless I stop the bleeding." And Phineas busied himself with making some off-hand surgical arrangements with his own pocket-handkerchief, and such as could be mustered in the company.

"You pushed me down there," said Tom, faintly.

"Well, if I hadn't, thee would have pushed us down, thee sees," said Phineas, as he stooped to apply his bandage. "There, there,—let me fix this bandage. We mean well to thee; we bear no malice. Thee shall be taken to a house where they'll nurse thee first rate,—as well as thy own mother could."

Tom groaned, and shut his eyes. In men of his class, vigor and resolution are entirely a physical matter, and ooze out with the flowing of the blood; and the gigantic fellow really looked piteous in his helplessness.

The other party now came up. The seats were taken out of the wagon. The buffalo-skins, doubled in fours, were spread all along one side, and four men, with great difficulty, lifted the heavy form of Tom into it. Before he was gotten in, he fainted entirely. The old negress, in the abundance of her compassion, sat down on the bottom, and took his head in her lap. Eliza, George and Jim, bestowed themselves, as well as they could, in the remaining space, and the whole party set forward.

"What do you think of him?" said George, who sat by Phineas in front.

"Well, it's only a pretty deep flesh-wound; but, then, tumbling and scratching down that place didn't help him much. It has bled pretty freely,—pretty much dreaned him out, courage and all,—but he'll get over it, and may be learn a thing or two by it."

"I'm glad to hear you say so," said George. "It would always be a heavy thought to me, if I'd caused his death, even in a just cause."

"Yes," said Phineas, "killing is an ugly operation, any way they'll fix it,—man or beast. I've been a great hunter, in my day, and I tell thee I've seen a buck that was shot down, and a dying, look that way on a feller with his eye, that it reely most made a feller feel wicked for killing on him; and human creatures is a more serious consideration yet, bein', as thy wife says, that the judgment comes to 'em after death. So I don't know as our people's notions on these matters is too strict; and, considerin' how I was raised, I fell in with them pretty considerably."

"What shall you do with this poor fellow?" said George.

"O, carry him along to Amariah's. There's old Grandmam Stephens there,—Dorcas, they call her,—she's most an amazin' nurse. She takes to nursing real natural, and an't never better suited than when she gets a sick body to tend. We may reckon on turning him over to her for a fortnight or so."

A ride of about an hour more brought the party to a neat farmhouse, where the weary travellers were received to an abundant breakfast. Tom Loker was soon carefully deposited in a much cleaner and softer bed than he had ever been in the habit of occupying. His wound was carefully dressed and bandaged, and he lay languidly opening and shutting his eyes on the white window-curtains and gently-gliding figures of his sick room, like a weary child. And here, for the present, we shall take our leave of one party.

## Chapter XVIII

### *Miss Ophelia's Experiences and Opinions*

Our friend Tom, in his own simple musings, often compared his more fortunate lot, in the bondage into which he was cast, with that of Joseph in Egypt;[1] and, in fact, as time went on, and he developed more and more under the eye of his master, the strength of the parallel increased.

St. Clare was indolent and careless of money. Hitherto the providing and marketing had been principally done by Adolph, who was, to the full, as careless and extravagant as his master; and, between them both, they had carried on the dispersing process with great alacrity. Accustomed, for many years, to regard his master's property as his own care, Tom saw, with an uneasiness he could scarcely repress, the wasteful expenditure of the establishment; and, in the quiet, indirect way which his class often acquire, would sometimes make his own suggestions.

St. Clare at first employed him occasionally; but, struck with his soundness of mind and good business capacity, he confided in him more and more, till gradually all the marketing and providing for the family were intrusted to him.

1. Joseph's brothers sold him into slavery in Egypt, where God eventually allowed him to prosper and become powerful (Genesis 37–50).

"No, no, Adolph," he said, one day, as Adolph was deprecating the passing of power out of his hands; "let Tom alone. You only understand what you want; Tom understands cost and come to; and there may be some end to money, bye and bye if we don't let somebody do that."

Trusted to an unlimited extent by a careless master, who handed him a bill without looking at it, and pocketed the change without counting it, Tom had every facility and temptation to dishonesty; and nothing but an impregnable simplicity of nature, strengthened by Christian faith, could have kept him from it. But, to that nature, the very unbounded trust reposed in him was bond and seal for the most scrupulous accuracy.

With Adolph the case had been different. Thoughtless and self-indulgent, and unrestrained by a master who found it easier to indulge than to regulate, he had fallen into an absolute confusion as to *meum tuum*[2] with regard to himself and his master, which sometimes troubled even St. Clare. His own good sense taught him that such a training of his servants was unjust and dangerous. A sort of chronic remorse went with him everywhere, although not strong enough to make any decided change in his course; and this very remorse reacted again into indulgence. He passed lightly over the most serious faults, because he told himself that, if he had done his part, his dependents had not fallen into them.

Tom regarded his gay, airy, handsome young master with an odd mixture of fealty, reverence, and fatherly solicitude. That he never read the Bible; never went to church; that he jested and made free with any and every thing that came in the way of his wit; that he spent his Sunday evenings at the opera or theatre; that he went to wine parties, and clubs, and suppers, oftener than was at all expedient,—were all things that Tom could see as plainly as anybody, and on which he based a conviction that "Mas'r wasn't a Christian;"—a conviction, however, which he would have been very slow to express to any one else, but on which he founded many prayers, in his own simple fashion, when he was by himself in his little dormitory. Not that Tom had not his own way of speaking his mind occasionally, with something of the tact often observable in his class; as, for example, the very day after the Sabbath we have described, St. Clare was invited out to a convivial party of choice spirits, and was helped home, between one and two o'clock at night, in a condition when the physical had decidedly attained the upper hand of the intellectual.

2. A reference to Plautus, *Trinummus* 2.2.47: "*Quad tuum'st meum'st; omne est autem tuum*" (What is thine is mine, and all mine is thine).

Tom and Adolph assisted to get him composed for the night, the latter in high spirits, evidently regarding the matter as a good joke, and laughing heartily at the rusticity of Tom's horror, who really was simple enough to lie awake most of the rest of the night, praying for his young master.

"Well, Tom, what are you waiting for?" said St. Clare, the next day, as he sat in his library, in dressing-gown and slippers. St. Clare had just been intrusting Tom with some money, and various commissions. "Isn't all right there, Tom?" he added, as Tom still stood waiting.

"I'm 'fraid not, Mas'r," said Tom, with a grave face.

St. Clare laid down his paper, and set down his coffee-cup, and looked at Tom.

"Why, Tom, what's the case? You look as solemn as a coffin."

"I feel very bad, Mas'r. I allays have thought that Mas'r would be good to everybody."

"Well, Tom, haven't I been? Come, now, what do you want? There's something you haven't got, I suppose, and this is the preface."

"Mas'r allays been good to me. I haven't nothing to complain of, on that head. But there is one that Mas'r isn't good to."

"Why, Tom, what's got into you? Speak out; what do you mean?"

"Last night, between one and two, I thought so. I studied upon the matter then. Mas'r isn't good to *himself*."

Tom said this with his back to his master, and his hand on the door-knob. St. Clare felt his face flush crimson, but he laughed.

"O, that's all, is it?" he said, gayly.

"All!" said Tom, turning suddenly round and falling on his knees. "O, my dear young Mas'r! I'm 'fraid it will be *loss of all—all*—body and soul. The good Book says, 'it biteth like a serpent and stingeth like an adder!'[3] my dear Mas'r!"

Tom's voice choked, and the tears ran down his cheeks.

"You poor, silly fool!" said St. Clare, with tears in his own eyes. "Get up, Tom. I'm not worth crying over."

But Tom wouldn't rise, and looked imploring.

"Well, I won't go to any more of their cursed nonsense, Tom," said St. Clare; "on my honor, I won't. I don't know why I haven't stopped long ago. I've always despised *it*, and myself for it,—so now, Tom, wipe up your eyes, and go about your errands. Come, come," he added, "no blessings. I'm not so wonderfully good, now," he said, as he gently pushed Tom to the door. "There, I'll pledge my honor to

3. "Look not thou upon the wine when it is red, when it giveth his colour in the cup, when it moveth itself aright. At the last it biteth like a serpent, and stingeth like an adder" (Proverbs 23.31–32).

you, Tom, you don't see me so again," he said; and Tom went off, wiping his eyes, with great satisfaction.

"I'll keep my faith with him, too," said St. Clare, as he closed the door.

And St. Clare did so,—for gross sensualism, in any form, was not the peculiar temptation of his nature.

But, all this time, who shall detail the tribulations manifold of our friend Miss Ophelia, who had begun the labors of a Southern housekeeper?

There is all the difference in the world in the servants of Southern establishments, according to the character and capacity of the mistresses who have brought them up.

South as well as north, there are women who have an extraordinary talent for command, and tact in educating. Such are enabled, with apparent ease, and without severity, to subject to their will, and bring into harmonious and systematic order, the various members of their small estate,—to regulate their peculiarities, and so balance and compensate the deficiencies of one by the excess of another, as to produce a harmonious and orderly system.

Such a housekeeper was Mrs. Shelby, whom we have already described; and such our readers may remember to have met with. If they are not common at the South, it is because they are not common in the world. They are to be found there as often as anywhere; and, when existing, find in that peculiar state of society a brilliant opportunity to exhibit their domestic talent.

Such a housekeeper Marie St. Clare was not, nor her mother before her. Indolent and childish, unsystematic and improvident, it was not to be expected that servants trained under her care should not be so likewise; and she had very justly described to Miss Ophelia the state of confusion she would find in the family, though she had not ascribed it to the proper cause.

The first morning of her regency, Miss Ophelia was up at four o'clock; and having attended to all the adjustments of her own chamber, as she had done ever since she came there, to the great amazement of the chamber-maid, she prepared for a vigorous onslaught on the cupboards and closets of the establishment of which she had the keys.

The store-room, the linen-presses, the china-closet, the kitchen and cellar, that day, all went under an awful review. Hidden things of darkness were brought to light to an extent that alarmed all the principalities and powers of kitchen and chamber, and caused many wonderings and murmurings about "dese yer northern ladies" from the domestic cabinet.

Old Dinah, the head cook, and principal of all rule and authority in the kitchen department, was filled with wrath at what she considered an invasion of privilege. No feudal baron in *Magna Charta*[4] times could have more thoroughly resented some incursion of the crown.

Dinah was a character in her own way, and it would be injustice to her memory not to give the reader a little idea of her. She was a native and essential cook, as much as Aunt Chloe,—cooking being an indigenous talent of the African race; but Chloe was a trained and methodical one, who moved in an orderly domestic harness, while Dinah was a self-taught genius, and, like geniuses in general, was positive, opinionated and erratic, to the last degree.

Like a certain class of modern philosophers, Dinah perfectly scorned logic and reason in every shape, and always took refuge in intuitive certainty; and here she was perfectly impregnable. No possible amount of talent, or authority, or explanation, could ever make her believe that any other way was better than her own, or that the course she had pursued in the smallest matter could be in the least modified. This had been a conceded point with her old mistress, Marie's mother; and "Miss Marie," as Dinah always called her young mistress, even after her marriage, found it easier to submit than contend; and so Dinah had ruled supreme. This was the easier, in that she was perfect mistress of that diplomatic art which unites the utmost subservience of manner with the utmost inflexibility as to measure.

Dinah was mistress of the whole art and mystery of excuse-making, in all its branches. Indeed, it was an axiom with her that the cook can do no wrong; and a cook in a Southern kitchen finds abundance of heads and shoulders on which to lay off every sin and frailty, so as to maintain her own immaculateness entire. If any part of the dinner was a failure, there were fifty indisputably good reasons for it; and it was the fault undeniably of fifty other people, whom Dinah berated with unsparing zeal.

But it was very seldom that there was any failure in Dinah's last results. Though her mode of doing everything was peculiarly meandering and circuitous, and without any sort of calculation as to time and place,—though her kitchen generally looked as if it had been arranged by a hurricane blowing through it, and she had about as many places for each cooking utensil as there were days in the year,—yet, if one would have patience to wait her own good time, up would come her dinner in perfect order, and in a style of preparation with which an epicure could find no fault.

It was now the season of incipient preparation for dinner. Dinah, who required large intervals of reflection and repose, and was

4. A famous document issued by King John of England in 1215; a symbol of constitutional power (as opposed to monarchy) because it suggests that people are protected by law against oppression by their king.

studious of ease in all her arrangements, was seated on the kitchen floor, smoking a short, stumpy pipe, to which she was much addicted, and which she always kindled up, as a sort of censer, whenever she felt the need of an inspiration in her arrangements. It was Dinah's mode of invoking the domestic Muses.[5]

Seated around her were various members of that rising race with which a Southern household abounds, engaged in shelling peas, peeling potatoes, picking pin-feathers out of fowls, and other preparatory arrangements,—Dinah every once in a while interrupting her meditations to give a poke, or a rap on the head, to some of the young operators, with the pudding-stick that lay by her side. In fact, Dinah ruled over the woolly heads of the younger members with a rod of iron, and seemed to consider them born for no earthly purpose but to "save her steps," as she phrased it. It was the spirit of the system under which she had grown up, and she carried it out to its full extent.

Miss Ophelia, after passing on her reformatory tour through all the other parts of the establishment, now entered the kitchen. Dinah had heard, from various sources, what was going on, and resolved to stand on defensive and conservative ground,—mentally determined to oppose and ignore every new measure, without any actual and observable contest.

The kitchen was a large brick-floored apartment, with a great old-fashioned fireplace stretching along one side of it,—an arrangement which St. Clare had vainly tried to persuade Dinah to exchange for the convenience of a modern cook-stove. Not she. No Puseyite,[6] or conservative of any school, was ever more inflexibly attached to time-honored inconveniencies than Dinah.

When St. Clare had first returned from the north, impressed with the system and order of his uncle's kitchen arrangements, he had largely provided his own with an array of cupboards, drawers, and various apparatus, to induce systematic regulation, under the sanguine illusion that it would be of any possible assistance to Dinah in her arrangements. He might as well have provided them for a squirrel or a magpie. The more drawers and closets there were, the more hiding-holes could Dinah make for the accommodation of old rags, hair-combs, old shoes, ribbons, cast-off artificial flowers, and other articles of *vertu*,[7] wherein her soul delighted.

When Miss Ophelia entered the kitchen, Dinah did not rise, but smoked on in sublime tranquillity, regarding her movements obliquely

5. In Greek myth, the nine sister goddesses who preside over learning and the creative arts.
6. A High Churchman or Tractarian; a reference to E. B. Pusey (1800–1882), an English theologian who advocated principles set forth in a series of pamphlets issued at Oxford between 1833 and 1841, urging the revival of the sacramental piety and theology of the seventeenth century.
7. Also *virtu*; curious or antique artworks.

out of the corner of her eye, but apparently intent only on the operations around her.

Miss Ophelia commenced opening a set of drawers.

"What is this drawer for, Dinah?" she said.

"It's handy for most anything, Missis," said Dinah. So it appeared to be. From the variety it contained, Miss Ophelia pulled out first a fine damask table-cloth stained with blood, having evidently been used to envelop some raw meat.

"What's this, Dinah? You don't wrap up meat in your mistress' best table-cloths?"

"O Lor, Missis, no; the towels was all a missin',—so I jest did it. I laid out to wash that ar,—that's why I put it thar."

"Shif'less!" said Miss Ophelia to herself, proceeding to tumble over the drawer, where she found a nutmeg-grater and two or three nutmegs, a Methodist hymn-book, a couple of soiled Madras[8] handkerchiefs, some yarn and knitting-work, a paper of tobacco and a pipe, a few crackers, one or two gilded china-saucers with some pomade[9] in them, one or two thin old shoes, a piece of flannel carefully pinned up enclosing some small white onions, several damask table-napkins, some coarse crash[1] towels, some twine and darning-needles, and several broken papers, from which sundry sweet herbs were sifting into the drawer.

"Where do you keep your nutmegs, Dinah?" said Miss Ophelia, with the air of one who prayed for patience.

"Most anywhar, Missis; there's some in that cracked teacup, up there, and there's some over in that ar cupboard."

"Here are some in the grater," said Miss Ophelia, holding them up.

"Laws, yes, I put 'em there this morning,—I likes to keep my things handy," said Dinah. "You, Jake! what are you stopping for! You'll cotch it! Be still, thar!" she added, with a dive of her stick at the criminal.

"What's this?" said Miss Ophelia, holding up the saucer of pomade.

"Laws, it's my har *grease*;—I put it thar to have it handy."

"Do you use your mistress' best saucers for that?"

"Law! it was cause I was driv, and in sich a hurry;—I was gwine to change it this very day."

"Here are two damask table-napkins."

"Them table-napkins I put thar, to get 'em washed out, some day."

"Don't you have some place here on purpose for things to be washed?"

8. Fine cotton shirting fabric, usually striped or plaid, named for the city of Madras, India.
9. Perfumed ointment for the hair or scalp.
1. A coarse fabric used for draperies, toweling, and table linen. "Damask": a patterned satin fabric.

"Well, Mas'r St. Clare got dat ar chest, he said, for dat; but I likes to mix up biscuit and hev my things on it some days, and then it an't handy a liftin' up the lid."

"Why don't you mix your biscuits on the pastry-table, there?"

"Law, Missis, it gets sot so full of dishes, and one thing and another, der an't no room, noways—"

"But you should *wash* your dishes, and clear them away."

"Wash my dishes!" said Dinah, in a high key, as her wrath began to rise over her habitual respect of manner; "what does ladies know 'bout work, I want to know? When'd Mas'r ever get his dinner, if I was to spend all my time a washin' and a puttin' up dishes? Miss Marie never telled me so, nohow."

"Well, here are these onions."

"Laws, yes!" said Dinah; "thar *is* whar I put 'em, now. I couldn't 'member. Them's particular onions I was a savin' for dis yer very stew. I'd forgot they was in dat ar old flannel."

Miss Ophelia lifted out the sifting papers of sweet herbs.

"I wish Missis wouldn't touch dem ar. I likes to keep my things where I knows whar to go to 'em," said Dinah, rather decidedly.

"But you don't want these holes in the papers."

"Them's handy for siftin' on 't out," said Dinah.

"But you see it spills all over the drawer."

"Laws, yes! if Missis will go a tumblin' things all up so, it will. Missis has spilt lots dat ar way," said Dinah, coming uneasily to the drawers. "If Missis only will go up stars till my clarin' up time comes, I'll have everything right; but I can't do nothin' when ladies is round, a henderin'. You, Sam, don't you gib the baby dat ar sugar-bowl! I'll crack ye over, if ye don't mind!"

"I'm going through the kitchen, and going to put everything in order, *once*, Dinah; and then I'll expect you to *keep* it so."

"Lor, now! Miss Phelia; dat ar an't no way for ladies to do. I never did see ladies doin' no sich; my old Missis nor Miss Marie never did, and I don't see no kinder need on 't;" and Dinah stalked indignantly about, while Miss Ophelia piled and sorted dishes, emptied dozens of scattering bowls of sugar into one receptacle, sorted napkins, table-cloths, and towels, for washing; washing, wiping, and arranging with her own hands, and with a speed and alacrity which perfectly amazed Dinah.

"Lor, now! if dat ar de way dem northern ladies do, dey an't ladies, nohow," she said to some of her satellites, when at a safe hearing distance. "I has things as straight as anybody, when my clarin' up time comes; but I don't want ladies round, a henderin', and getting my things all where I can't find 'em."

To do Dinah justice, she had, at irregular periods, paroxysms of reformation and arrangement, which she called "clarin' up times," when she would begin with great zeal, and turn every drawer and closet wrong side outward, on to the floor or tables, and make the ordinary confusion seven-fold more confounded. Then she would light her pipe, and leisurely go over her arrangements, looking things over, and discoursing upon them; making all the young fry scour most vigorously on the tin things, and keeping up for several hours a most energetic state of confusion, which she would explain to the satisfaction of all inquirers, by the remark that she was a "clarin' up." "She couldn't hev things a gwine on so as they had been, and she was gwine to make these yer young ones keep better order;" for Dinah herself, somehow, indulged the illusion that she, herself, was the soul of order, and it was only the *young uns*, and the everybody else in the house, that were the cause of anything that fell short of perfection in this respect. When all the tins were scoured, and the tables scrubbed snowy white, and everything that could offend tucked out of sight in holes and corners, Dinah would dress herself up in a smart dress, clean apron, and high, brilliant Madras turban, and tell all marauding "young uns" to keep out of the kitchen, for she was gwine to have things kept nice. Indeed, these periodic seasons were often an inconvenience to the whole household; for Dinah would contract such an immoderate attachment to her scoured tin, as to insist upon it that it shouldn't be used again for any possible purpose,—at least, till the ardor of the "clarin' up" period abated.

Miss Ophelia, in a few days, thoroughly reformed every department of the house to a systematic pattern; but her labors in all departments that depended on the cooperation of servants were like those of Sisyphus or the Danaides.[2] In despair, she one day appealed to St. Clare.

"There is no such thing as getting anything like system in this family!"

"To be sure, there isn't," said St. Clare.

"Such shiftless management, such waste, such confusion, I never saw!"

"I dare say you didn't."

"You would not take it so coolly, if you were housekeeper."

"My dear cousin, you may as well understand, once for all, that we masters are divided into two classes, oppressors and oppressed. We who are good-natured and hate severity make up our minds to a good deal of inconvenience. If we *will keep* a shambling, loose, untaught set in the community, for our convenience, why, we must

2. In Greek myth, the fifty daughters of King Danaus of Argos, of whom forty-nine murdered their husbands at their father's command and were condemned in Hades to draw water in a sieve forever. "Sisyphus": the greedy king of Corinth who was doomed to roll uphill a heavy stone that forever rolled back down.

take the consequence. Some rare cases I have seen, of persons, who, by a peculiar tact, can produce order and system without severity; but I'm not one of them,—and so I made up my mind, long ago, to let things go just as they do. I will not have the poor devils thrashed and cut to pieces, and they know it,—and, of course, they know the staff is in their own hands."

"But to have no time, no place, no order,—all going on in this shiftless way!"

"My dear Vermont, you natives up by the North Pole set an extravagant value on time! What on earth is the use of time to a fellow who has twice as much of it as he knows what to do with? As to order and system, where there is nothing to be done but to lounge on the sofa and read, an hour sooner or later in breakfast or dinner isn't of much account. Now, there's Dinah gets you a capital dinner,—soup, ragout, roast fowl, dessert, ice-creams and all,—and she creates it all out of chaos and old night down there, in that kitchen. I think it really sublime, the way she manages. But, Heaven bless us! if we are to go down there, and view all the smoking and squatting about, and hurry-scurryation of the preparatory process, we should never eat more! My good cousin, absolve yourself from that! It's more than a Catholic penance, and does no more good. You'll only lose your own temper, and utterly confound Dinah. Let her go her own way."

"But, Augustine, you don't know how I found things."

"Don't I? Don't I know that the rolling-pin is under her bed, and the nutmeg-grater in her pocket with her tobacco,—that there are sixty-five different sugar-bowls, one in every hole in the house,—that she washes dishes with a dinner-napkin one day, and with a fragment of an old petticoat the next? But the upshot is, she gets up glorious dinners, makes superb coffee; and you must judge her as warriors and statesmen are judged, by *her success*."

"But the waste,—the expense!"

"O, well! Lock everything you can, and keep the key. Give out by driblets, and never inquire for odds and ends,—it isn't best."

"That troubles me, Augustine. I can't help feeling as if these servants were not *strictly honest*. Are you sure they can be relied on?"

Augustine laughed immoderately at the grave and anxious face with which Miss Ophelia propounded the question.

"O, cousin, that's too good,—*honest!*—as if that's a thing to be expected! Honest!—why, of course, they arn't. Why should they be? What upon earth is to make them so?"

"Why don't you instruct?"

"Instruct! O, fiddlestick! What instructing do you think I should do? I look like it! As to Marie, she has spirit enough, to be sure, to kill off a whole plantation, if I'd let her manage; but she wouldn't get the cheatery out of them."

"Are there no honest ones?"

"Well, now and then one, whom Nature makes so impracticably simple, truthful and faithful, that the worst possible influence can't destroy it in. But, you see, from the mother's breast the colored child feels and sees that there are none but underhand ways open to it. It can get along no other way with its parents, its mistress, its young master and missie play-fellows. Cunning and deception become necessary, inevitable habits. It isn't fair to expect anything else of him. He ought not to be punished for it. As to honesty, the slave is kept in that dependent, semi-childish state, that there is no making him realize the rights of property, or feel that his master's goods are not his own, if he can get them. For my part, I don't see how they *can* be honest. Such a fellow as Tom, here, is—is a moral miracle!"

"And what becomes of their souls?" said Miss Ophelia.

"That isn't my affair as I know of," said St. Clare; "I am only dealing in facts of the present life. The fact is, that the whole race are pretty generally understood to be turned over to the devil, for our benefit, in this world, however it may turn out in another!"

"This is perfectly horrible!" said Miss Ophelia; "you ought to be ashamed of yourselves!"

"I don't know as I am. We are in pretty good company, for all that," said St. Clare, "as people in the broad road generally are. Look at the high and the low, all the world over, and it's the same story,—the lower class used up, body, soul and spirit, for the good of the upper. It is so in England; it is so everywhere; and yet all Christendom stands aghast, with virtuous indignation, because we do the thing in a little different shape from what they do it."

"It isn't so in Vermont."

"Ah, well, in New England, and in the free States, you have the better of us, I grant. But there's the bell; so, Cousin, let us for a while lay aside our sectional prejudices, and come out to dinner."

As Miss Ophelia was in the kitchen in the latter part of the afternoon, some of the sable children called out, "La, sakes! thar's Prue a coming, grunting along like she allers does."

A tall, bony colored woman now entered the kitchen, bearing on her head a basket of rusks and hot rolls.

"Ho, Prue! you've come," said Dinah.

Prue had a peculiar scowling expression of countenance, and a sullen, grumbling voice. She set down her basket, squatted herself down, and resting her elbows on her knees said,

"O Lord! I wish't I's dead!"

"Why do you wish you were dead?" said Miss Ophelia.

"I'd be out o' my misery," said the woman, gruffly, without taking her eyes from the floor.

"What need you getting drunk, then, and cutting up, Prue?" said a spruce quadroon chambermaid, dangling, as she spoke, a pair of coral ear-drops.

The woman looked at her with a sour, surly glance.

"Maybe you'll come to it, one of these yer days. I'd be glad to see you, I would; then you'll be glad of a drop, like me, to forget your misery."

"Come, Prue," said Dinah, "let's look at your rusks. Here's Missis will pay for them."

Miss Ophelia took out a couple of dozen.

"Thar's some tickets in that ar old cracked jug on the top shelf," said Dinah. "You, Jake, climb up and get it down."

"Tickets,—what are they for?" said Miss Ophelia.

"We buys tickets of her Mas'r, and she gives us bread for 'em."

"And they counts my money and tickets, when I gets home, to see if I's got the change; and if I han't, they half kills me."

"And serves you right," said Jane, the pert chambermaid, "if you will take their money to get drunk on. That's what she does, Missis."

"And that's what I *will* do,—I can't live no other ways,—drink and forget my misery."

"You are very wicked and very foolish," said Miss Ophelia, "to steal your master's money to make yourself a brute with."

"It's mighty likely, Missis; but I will do it,—yes, I will. O Lord! I wish I's dead, I do,—I wish I's dead, and out of my misery!" and slowly and stiffly the old creature rose, and got her basket on her head again; but before she went out, she looked at the quadroon girl, who still stood playing with her ear-drops.

"Ye think ye're mighty fine with them ar, a frolickin' and a tossin' your head, and a lookin' down on everybody. Well, never mind,—you may live to be a poor, old, cut-up crittur, like me. Hope to the Lord ye will, I do; then see if ye won't drink,—drink,—drink,—yerself into torment; and sarve ye right, too—ugh!" and, with a malignant howl, the woman left the room.

"Disgusting old beast!" said Adolph, who was getting his master's shaving-water. "If I was her master, I'd cut her up worse than she is."

"Ye couldn't do that ar, no ways," said Dinah. "Her back's a far sight now,—she can't never get a dress together over it."

"I think such low creatures ought not to be allowed to go round to genteel families," said Miss Jane. "What do you think, Mr. St. Clare?" she said, coquettishly tossing her head at Adolph.

It must be observed that, among other appropriations from his master's stock, Adolph was in the habit of adopting his name and address; and that the style under which he moved, among the colored circles of New Orleans, was that of *Mr. St. Clare*.

"I'm certainly of your opinion, Miss Benoir," said Adolph.

Benoir was the name of Marie St. Clare's family, and Jane was one of her servants.

"Pray, Miss Benoir, may I be allowed to ask if those drops are for the ball, to-morrow night? They are certainly bewitching!"

"I wonder, now, Mr. St. Clare, what the impudence of you men will come to!" said Jane, tossing her pretty head till the ear-drops twinkled again. "I shan't dance with you for a whole evening, if you go to asking me any more questions."

"O, you couldn't be so cruel, now! I was just dying to know whether you would appear in your pink tarletane,"[3] said Adolph.

"What is it?" said Rosa, a bright, piquant little quadroon, who came skipping down stairs at this moment.

"Why, Mr. St. Clare's so impudent!"

"On my honor," said Adolph, "I'll leave it to Miss Rosa, now."

"I know he's always a saucy creature," said Rosa, poising herself on one of her little feet, and looking maliciously at Adolph. "He's always getting me so angry with him."

"O! ladies, ladies, you will certainly break my heart, between you," said Adolph. "I shall be found dead in my bed, some morning, and you'll have it to answer for."

"Do hear the horrid creature talk!" said both ladies, laughing immoderately.

"Come,—clar out, you! I can't have you cluttering up the kitchen," said Dinah; "in my way, foolin' round here."

"Aunt Dinah's glum, because she can't go to the ball," said Rosa.

"Don't want none o' your light-colored balls," said Dinah; "cuttin' round, makin' b'lieve you's white folks. Arter all, you's niggers, much as I am."

"Aunt Dinah greases her wool stiff, every day, to make it lie straight," said Jane.

"And it will be wool, after all," said Rosa, maliciously shaking down her long, silky curls.

"Well, in the Lord's sight, an't wool as good as har, any time?" said Dinah. "I'd like to have Missis say which is worth the most,—a couple such as you, or one like me. Get out wid ye, ye trumpery,—I won't have ye round!"

Here the conversation was interrupted in a two-fold manner. St. Clare's voice was heard at the head of the stairs, asking Adolph if he meant to stay all night with his shaving-water; and Miss Ophelia, coming out of the dining-room, said,

"Jane and Rosa, what are you wasting your time for, here? Go in and attend to your muslins."

3. Dress made of a sheer cotton fabric.

Our friend Tom, who had been in the kitchen during the conversation with the old rusk-woman, had followed her out into the street. He saw her go on, giving every once in a while a suppressed groan. At last she set her basket down on a door-step, and began arranging the old, faded shawl which covered her shoulders.

"I'll carry your basket a piece," said Tom, compassionately.

"Why should ye?" said the woman. "I don't want no help."

"You seem to be sick, or in trouble, or somethin'," said Tom.

"I an't sick," said the woman, shortly.

"I wish," said Tom, looking at her earnestly,—"I wish I could persuade you to leave off drinking. Don't you know it will be the ruin of ye, body and soul?"

"I knows I'm gwine to torment," said the woman, sullenly. "Ye don't need to tell me that ar. I's ugly,—I's wicked,—I's gwine straight to torment. O, Lord! I wish I's thar!"

Tom shuddered at these frightful words, spoken with a sullen, impassioned earnestness.

"O, Lord have mercy on ye! poor crittur. Han't ye never heard of Jesus Christ?"

"Jesus Christ,—who's he?"

"Why, he's *the Lord*," said Tom.

"I think I've hearn tell o' the Lord, and the judgment and torment. I've heard o' that."

"But didn't anybody ever tell you of the Lord Jesus, that loved us poor sinners, and died for us?"

"Don't know nothin' 'bout that," said the woman; "nobody han't never loved me, since my old man died."

"Where was you raised?" said Tom.

"Up in Kentuck. A man kept me to breed chil'en for market, and sold 'em as fast as they got big enough; last of all, he sold me to a speculator, and my Mas'r got me o' him."

"What set you into this bad way of drinkin'?"

"To get shet o' my misery. I had one child after I come here; and I thought then I'd have one to raise, cause Mas'r wasn't a speculator. It was de peartest little thing! and Missis she seemed to think a heap on 't, at first; it never cried,—it was likely and fat. But Missis tuck sick, and I tended her; and I tuck the fever, and my milk all left me, and the child it pined to skin and bone, and Missis wouldn't buy milk for it. She wouldn't hear to me, when I telled her I hadn't milk. She said she knowed I could feed it on what other folks eat; and the child kinder pined, and cried, and cried, and cried, day and night, and got all gone to skin and bones, and Missis got sot agin it, and she said 'twan't nothin' but crossness. She wished it was dead, she said; and she wouldn't let me have it o' nights, cause, she said, it kept me awake, and made me good for nothing. She made me sleep in her room; and I had to put it away off in a little kind o' garret, and thar it cried itself to death, one night. It did; and I tuck to drinkin', to keep its crying out of my ears! I did,—and I will drink! I will, if I do go to torment for it! Mas'r says I shall go to torment, and I tell him I've got thar now!"

"O, ye poor crittur!" said Tom, "han't nobody never telled ye how the Lord Jesus loved ye, and died for ye? Han't they telled ye that he'll help ye, and ye can go to heaven, and have rest, at last?"

"I looks like gwine to heaven," said the woman; "an't thar where white folks is gwine? S'pose they'd have me thar? I'd rather go to torment, and get away from Mas'r and Missis. I had *so*," she said, as, with her usual groan, she got her basket on her head, and walked sullenly away.

Tom turned, and walked sorrowfully back to the house. In the court he met little Eva,—a crown of tuberoses[4] on her head, and her eyes radiant with delight.

"O, Tom! here you are. I'm glad I've found you. Papa says you may get out the ponies, and take me in my little new carriage," she said, catching his hand. "But what's the matter, Tom?—you look sober."

"I feel bad, Miss Eva," said Tom, sorrowfully. "But I'll get the horses for you."

"But do tell me, Tom, what is the matter. I saw you talking to cross old Prue."

Tom, in simple, earnest phrase, told Eva the woman's history. She did not exclaim, or wonder, or weep, as other children do. Her cheeks grew pale, and a deep, earnest shadow passed over her eyes. She laid both hands on her bosom, and sighed heavily.

4. White lilylike flowers.

# Volume II

## Chapter XIX

### *Miss Ophelia's Experiences and Opinions, Continued*

"Tom, you needn't get me the horses. I don't want to go," she said.

"Why not, Miss Eva?"

"These things sink into my heart, Tom," said Eva,—"they sink into my heart," she repeated, earnestly. "I don't want to go;" and she turned from Tom, and went into the house.

A few days after, another woman came; in old Prue's place, to bring the rusks; Miss Ophelia was in the kitchen.

"Lor!" said Dinah, "what's got Prue?"

"Prue isn't coming any more," said the woman, mysteriously.

"Why not?" said Dinah. "She an't dead, is she?"

"We doesn't exactly know. She's down cellar," said the woman, glancing at Miss Ophelia.

After Miss Ophelia had taken the rusks, Dinah followed the woman to the door.

"What *has* got Prue, any how?" she said.

The woman seemed desirous, yet reluctant, to speak, and answered, in a low, mysterious tone.

"Well, you mustn't tell nobody. Prue, she got drunk agin,—and they had her down cellar,—and thar they left her all day,—and I hearn 'em saying that the *flies had got to her*,—and *she's dead!*"

Dinah held up her hands, and, turning, saw close by her side the spirit-like form of Evangeline, her large, mystic eyes dilated with horror, and every drop of blood driven from her lips and cheeks.

"Lor bless us! Miss Eva's gwine to faint away! What got us all, to let her har such talk? Her pa'll be rail mad."

"I shan't faint, Dinah," said the child, firmly; "and why shouldn't I hear it? It an't so much for me to hear it, as for poor Prue to suffer it."

"*Lor sakes!* it isn't for sweet, delicate young ladies, like you,—these yer stories isn't; it's enough to kill 'em!"

Eva sighed again, and walked up stairs with a slow and melancholy step.

Miss Ophelia anxiously inquired the woman's story. Dinah gave a very garrulous version of it, to which Tom added the particulars which he had drawn from her that morning.

"An abominable business,—perfectly horrible!" she exclaimed, as she entered the room where St. Clare lay reading his paper.

"Pray, what iniquity has turned up now?" said he.

"What now? why, those folks have whipped Prue to death!" said Miss Ophelia, going on, with great strength of detail, into the story, and enlarging on its most shocking particulars.

"I thought it would come to that, some time," said St. Clare, going on with his paper.

"Thought so!—an't you going to *do* anything about it?" said Miss Ophelia. "Haven't you got any *selectmen*,[1] or anybody, to interfere and look after such matters?"

"It's commonly supposed that the *property* interest is a sufficient guard in these cases. If people choose to ruin their own possessions, I don't know what's to be done. It seems the poor creature was a thief and a drunkard; and so there won't be much hope to get up sympathy for her."

"It is perfectly outrageous,—it is horrid, Augustine! It will certainly bring down vengeance upon you."

"My dear cousin, I didn't do it, and I can't help it; I would, if I could. If low-minded, brutal people will act like themselves, what am I to do? They have absolute control; they are irresponsible despots. There would be no use in interfering; there is no law that amounts to anything practically, for such a case. The best we can do is to shut our eyes and ears, and let it alone. It's the only resource left us."

"How can you shut your eyes and ears? How can you let such things alone?"

"My dear child, what do you expect? Here is a whole class,—debased, uneducated, indolent, provoking,—put, without any sort of terms or conditions, entirely into the hands of such people as the majority in our world are; people who have neither consideration nor self-control, who haven't even an enlightened regard to their own interest,—for that's the case with the largest half of mankind. Of course, in a community so organized, what can a man of honorable and humane feelings do, but shut his eyes all he can, and harden his heart? I can't buy every poor wretch I see. I can't turn knight-errant, and undertake to redress every individual case of wrong in such a city as this. The most I can do is to try and keep out of the way of it."

St. Clare's fine countenance was for a moment overcast; he looked annoyed, but suddenly calling up a gay smile, he said,

1. Officers who administrate the public business of a town.

"Come, cousin, don't stand there looking like one of the Fates;[2] you've only seen a peep through the curtain,—a specimen of what is going on, the world over, in some shape or other. If we are to be prying and spying into all the dismals of life, we should have no heart to anything. 'Tis like looking too close into the details of Dinah's kitchen;" and St. Clare lay back on the sofa, and busied himself with his paper.

Miss Ophelia sat down, and pulled out her knitting-work, and sat there grim with indignation. She knit and knit, but while she mused the fire burned; at last she broke out—

"I tell you, Augustine, I can't get over things so, if you can. It's a perfect abomination for you to defend such a system,—that's *my* mind!"

"What now?" said St. Clare, looking up. "At it again, hey?"

"I say it's perfectly abominable for you to defend such a system!" said Miss Ophelia, with increasing warmth.

"*I* defend it, my dear lady? Who ever said I did defend it?" said St. Clare.

"Of course, you defend it,—you all do,—all you Southerners. What do you have slaves for, if you don't?"

"Are you such a sweet innocent as to suppose nobody in this world ever does what they don't think is right? Don't you, or didn't you ever, do anything that you did not think quite right?"

"If I do, I repent of it, I hope," said Miss Ophelia, rattling her needles with energy.

"So do I," said St. Clare, peeling his orange; "I'm repenting of it all the time."

"What do you keep on doing it for?"

"Didn't you ever keep on doing wrong, after you'd repented, my good cousin?"

"Well, only when I've been very much tempted," said Miss Ophelia.

"Well, I'm very much tempted," said St. Clare; "that's just my difficulty."

"But I always resolve I won't, and I try to break off."

"Well, I have been resolving I won't, off and on, these ten years," said St. Clare; "but I haven't, some how, got clear. Have you got clear of all your sins, cousin?"

"Cousin Augustine," said Miss Ophelia, seriously, and laying down her knitting-work, "I suppose I deserve that you should reprove my short-comings. I know all you say is true enough; nobody else feels them more than I do; but it does seem to me, after all, there is some

2. In Greek and Roman myth, the three goddesses, represented as crones, who control human life and destiny: Clotho, Lachesis, and Atropos.

difference between me and you. It seems to me I would cut off my right hand sooner than keep on, from day to day, doing what I thought was wrong. But, then, my conduct is so inconsistent with my profession, I don't wonder you reprove me."

"O, now, cousin," said Augustine, sitting down on the floor, and laying his head back in her lap, "don't take on so awfully serious! You know what a good-for-nothing, saucy boy I always was. I love to poke you up,—that's all,—just to see you get earnest. I do think you are desperately, distressingly good; it tires me to death to think of it."

"But this is a serious subject, my boy, Auguste," said Miss Ophelia, laying her hand on his forehead.

"Dismally so," said he; "and I——well, I never want to talk seriously in hot weather. What with mosquitos and all, a fellow can't get himself up to any very sublime moral flights; and I believe," said St. Clare, suddenly rousing himself up, "there's a theory, now! I understand now why northern nations are always more virtuous than southern ones,—I see into that whole subject."

"O, Auguste, you are a sad rattle-brain!"

"Am I? Well, so I am, I suppose; but for once I will be serious, now; but you must hand me that basket of oranges;—you see, you'll have to 'stay me with flagons and comfort me with apples,'[3] if I'm going to make this effort. Now," said Augustine, drawing the basket up, "I'll begin: When, in the course of human events, it becomes necessary for a fellow to hold two or three dozen of his fellow-worms in captivity, a decent regard to the opinions of society requires—"

"I don't see that you are growing more serious," said Miss Ophelia.

"Wait,—I'm coming on,—you'll hear. The short of the matter is, cousin," said he, his handsome face suddenly settling into an earnest and serious expression, "on this abstract question of slavery there can, as I think, be but one opinion. Planters, who have money to make by it,—clergymen, who have planters to please,—politicians, who want to rule by it,—may warp and bend language and ethics to a degree that shall astonish the world at their ingenuity; they can press nature and the Bible, and nobody knows what else, into the service; but, after all, neither they nor the world believe in it one particle the more. It comes from the devil, that's the short of it;—and, to my mind, it's a pretty respectable specimen of what he can do in his own line."

Miss Ophelia stopped her knitting, and looked surprised; and St. Clare, apparently enjoying her astonishment, went on.

3. Song of Solomon 2.5.

"You seem to wonder; but if you will get me fairly at it, I'll make a clean breast of it. This cursed business, accursed of God and man, what is it? Strip it of all its ornament, run it down to the root and nucleus of the whole, and what is it? Why, because my brother Quashy[4] is ignorant and weak, and I am intelligent and strong,—because I know how, and *can* do it,—therefore, I may steal all he has, keep it, and give him only such and so much as suits my fancy. Whatever is too hard, too dirty, too disagreeable, for me, I may set Quashy to doing. Because I don't like work, Quashy shall work. Because the sun burns me, Quashy shall stay in the sun. Quashy shall earn the money, and I will spend it. Quashy shall lie down in every puddle, that I may walk over dry-shod. Quashy shall do my will, and not his, all the days of his mortal life, and have such chance of getting to heaven, at last, as I find convenient. This I take to be about what slavery *is.* I defy anybody on earth to read our slave-code, as it stands in our law-books, and make anything else of it. Talk of the *abuses* of slavery! Humbug! The *thing itself* is the essence of all abuse! And the only reason why the land don't sink under it, like Sodom and Gomorrah,[5] is because it is *used* in a way infinitely better than it is. For pity's sake, for shame's sake, because we are men born of women, and not savage beasts, many of us do not, and dare not,—we would *scorn* to use the full power which our savage laws put into our hands. And he who goes the furthest, and does the worst, only uses within limits the power that the law gives him."

St. Clare had started up, and, as his manner was when excited, was walking, with hurried steps, up and down the floor. His fine face, classic as that of a Greek statue, seemed actually to burn with the fervor of his feelings. His large blue eyes flashed, and he gestured with an unconscious eagerness. Miss Ophelia had never seen him in this mood before, and she sat perfectly silent.

"I declare to you," said he, suddenly stopping before his cousin "(it's no sort of use to talk or to feel on this subject), but I declare to you, there have been times when I have thought, if the whole country would sink, and hide all this injustice and misery from the light, I would willingly sink with it. When I have been travelling up and down on our boats, or about on my collecting tours, and reflected that every brutal, disgusting, mean, low-lived fellow I met, was allowed by our laws to become absolute despot of as many men, women and children, as he could cheat, steal, or gamble money enough to buy,—when I have seen such men in actual ownership of helpless

4. A common name for slaves; derived from *Quassi*, a name from Surinam (Dutch Guiana) on the eastern coast of South America.
5. Two cities destroyed by God in a rain of "brimstone and fire" because of the sinfulness of their people (Genesis 18–19).

children, of young girls and women,—I have been ready to curse my country, to curse the human race!"

"Augustine! Augustine!" said Miss Ophelia, "I'm sure you've said enough. I never, in my life, heard anything like this, even at the North."

"At the North!" said St. Clare, with a sudden change of expression, and resuming something of his habitual careless tone. "Pooh! your northern folks are cold-blooded; you are cool in everything! You can't begin to curse up hill and down as we can, when we get fairly at it."

"Well, but the question is," said Miss Ophelia.

"O, yes, to be sure, the *question is*,—and a deuce of a question it is! How came *you* in this state of sin and misery? Well, I shall answer in the good old words you used to teach me, Sundays. I came so by ordinary generation. My servants were my father's, and, what is more, my mother's; and now they are mine, they and their increase, which bids fair to be a pretty considerable item. My father, you know, came first from New England; and he was just such another man as your father,—a regular old Roman,[6]—upright, energetic, noble-minded, with an iron will. Your father settled down in New England, to rule over rocks and stones, and to force an existence out of Nature; and mine settled in Louisiana, to rule over men and women, and force existence out of them. My mother," said St. Clare, getting up and walking to a picture at the end of the room, and gazing upward with a face fervent with veneration, "*she* was *divine*! Don't look at me so!—you know what I mean! She probably was of mortal birth; but, as far as ever I could observe, there was no trace of any human weakness or error about her; and everybody that lives to remember her, whether bond or free, servant, acquaintance, relation, all say the same. Why, cousin, that mother has been all that has stood between me and utter unbelief for years. She was a direct embodiment and personification of the New Testament,—a living fact, to be accounted for, and to be accounted for in no other way than by its truth. O, mother! mother!" said St. Clare, clasping his hands, in a sort of transport; and then suddenly checking himself, he came back, and seating himself on an ottoman, he went on:

"My brother and I were twins; and they say, you know, that twins ought to resemble each other; but we were in all points a contrast. He had black, fiery eyes, coal-black hair, a strong, fine Roman profile, and a rich brown complexion. I had blue eyes, golden hair, a Greek outline, and fair complexion. He was active and observing, I dreamy and inactive. He was generous to his friends and equals,

6. I.e., one who is honest, strict, courageous, or frugal. A "Roman father" is the dominating head of a family.

but proud, dominant, overbearing, to inferiors, and utterly unmerciful to whatever set itself up against him. Truthful we both were; he from pride and courage, I from a sort of abstract ideality. We loved each other about as boys generally do,—off and on, and in general;—he was my father's pet, and I my mother's.

"There was a morbid sensitiveness and acuteness of feeling in me on all possible subjects, of which he and my father had no kind of understanding, and with which they could have no possible sympathy. But mother did; and so, when I had quarrelled with Alfred, and father looked sternly on me, I used to go off to mother's room, and sit by her. I remember just how she used to look, with her pale cheeks, her deep, soft, serious eyes, her white dress,—she always wore white; and I used to think of her whenever I read in Revelations about the saints that were arrayed in fine linen, clean and white. She had a great deal of genius of one sort and another, particularly in music; and she used to sit at her organ, playing fine old majestic music of the Catholic church, and singing with a voice more like an angel than a mortal woman; and I would lay my head down on her lap, and cry, and dream, and feel,—oh, immeasurably!—things that I had no language to say!

"In those days, this matter of slavery had never been canvassed as it has now; nobody dreamed of any harm in it.

"My father was a born aristocrat. I think, in some preexistent state, he must have been in the higher circles of spirits, and brought all his old court pride along with him; for it was ingrain, bred in the bone, though he was originally of poor and not in any way of noble family. My brother was begotten in his image.

"Now, an aristocrat, you know, the world over, has no human sympathies, beyond a certain line in society. In England the line is in one place, in Burmah in another,[7] and in America in another; but the aristocrat of all these countries never goes over it. What would be hardship and distress and injustice in his own class, is a cool matter of course in another one. My father's dividing line was that of color. *Among his equals*, never was a man more just and generous; but he considered the negro, through all possible gradations of color, as an intermediate link between man and animals, and graded all his ideas of justice or generosity on this hypothesis. I suppose, to be sure, if anybody had asked him, plump and fair, whether they had human immortal souls, he might have hemmed and hawed, and said yes. But my father was not a man much troubled with spiritualism; religious sentiment he had none, beyond a veneration for God, as decidedly the head of the upper classes.

7. Also *Burma*; a country in southeast Asia, on the Indochinese peninsula.

"Well, my father worked some five hundred negroes; he was an inflexible, driving, punctilious business man; everything was to move by system,—to be sustained with unfailing accuracy and precision. Now, if you take into account that all this was to be worked out by a set of lazy, twaddling, shiftless laborers, who had grown up, all their lives, in the absence of every possible motive to learn how to do anything but 'shirk,' as you Vermonters say, and you'll see that there might naturally be, on his plantation, a great many things that looked horrible and distressing to a sensitive child, like me.

"Besides all, he had an overseer,—a great, tall, slab-sided, two-fisted renegade son of Vermont—(begging your pardon),—who had gone through a regular apprenticeship in hardness and brutality, and taken his degree to be admitted to practice. My mother never could endure him, nor I; but he obtained an entire ascendency over my father; and this man was the absolute despot of the estate.

"I was a little fellow then, but I had the same love that I have now for all kinds of human things,—a kind of passion for the study of humanity, come in what shape it would. I was found in the cabins and among the field-hands a great deal, and, of course, was a great favorite; and all sorts of complaints and grievances were breathed in my ear; and I told them to mother, and we, between us, formed a sort of committee for a redress of grievances. We hindered and repressed a great deal of cruelty, and congratulated ourselves on doing a vast deal of good, till, as often happens, my zeal overacted. Stubbs complained to my father that he couldn't manage the hands, and must resign his position. Father was a fond, indulgent husband, but a man that never flinched from anything that he thought necessary; and so he put down his foot, like a rock, between us and the field-hands. He told my mother, in language perfectly respectful and deferential, but quite explicit, that over the house-servants she should be entire mistress, but that with the field-hands he could allow no interference. He revered and respected her above all living beings; but he would have said it all the same to the virgin Mary herself, if she had come in the way of his system.

"I used sometimes to hear my mother reasoning cases with him,—endeavoring to excite his sympathies. He would listen to the most pathetic appeals with the most discouraging politeness and equanimity. 'It all resolves itself into this,' he would say; 'must I part with Stubbs, or keep him? Stubbs is the soul of punctuality, honesty, and efficiency,—a thorough business hand, and as humane as the general run. We can't have perfection; and if I keep him, I must sustain his administration as a *whole*, even if there are, now and then, things that are exceptionable. All government includes some necessary hardness. General rules will bear hard on particular cases.' This last maxim my father seemed to consider a settler in most alleged cases of cruelty. After he had said *that*, he commonly drew up his feet on the sofa, like a man that has disposed of a business, and betook himself to a nap, or the newspaper, as the case might be.

"The fact is, my father showed the exact sort of talent for a statesman. He could have divided Poland as easily as an orange, or trod on Ireland as quietly and systematically as any man living. At last my mother gave up, in despair. It never will be known, till the last account, what noble and sensitive natures like hers have felt, cast, utterly helpless, into what seems to them an abyss of injustice and cruelty, and which seems so to nobody about them. It has been an age of long sorrow of such natures, in such a hell-begotten sort of world as ours. What remained for her, but to train her children in her own views and sentiments? Well, after all you say about training, children will grow up substantially what they *are* by nature, and only that. From the cradle, Alfred was an aristocrat; and as he grew up, instinctively, all his sympathies and all his reasonings were in that line, and all mother's exhortations went to the winds. As to me, they sunk deep into me. She never contradicted, in form, anything that my father said, or seemed directly to differ from him; but she impressed, burnt into my very soul, with all the force of her deep, earnest nature, an idea of the dignity and worth of the meanest human soul. I have looked in her face with solemn awe, when she would point up to the stars in the evening, and say to me, 'See there, Auguste! the poorest, meanest soul on our place will be living, when all these stars are gone forever,—will live as long as God lives!'

"She had some fine old paintings; one, in particular, of Jesus healing a blind man.[8] They were very fine, and used to impress me strongly. 'See there, Auguste,' she would say; 'the blind man was a beggar, poor and loathsome; therefore, he would not heal him *afar off!* He called him to him, and put *his hands on him!* Remember this, my boy.' If I had lived to grow up under her care, she might have stimulated me to I know not what of enthusiasm. I might have been a saint, reformer, martyr,—but, alas! alas! I went from her when I was only thirteen, and I never saw her again!"

St. Clare rested his head on his hands, and did not speak for some minutes. After a while, he looked up, and went on:

"What poor, mean trash this whole business of human virtue is! A mere matter, for the most part, of latitude and longitude, and geographical position, acting with natural temperament. The greater part is nothing but an accident! Your father, for example, settles in Vermont, in a town where all are, in fact, free and equal; becomes a regular church member and deacon, and in due time joins an Abolition society, and thinks us all little better than heathens. Yet

8. See John 9.

he is, for all the world, in constitution and habit, a duplicate of my father. I can see it leaking out in fifty different ways,—just that same strong, overbearing, dominant spirit. You know very well how impossible it is to persuade some of the folks in your village that Squire Sinclair does not feel above them. The fact is, though he has fallen on democratic times, and embraced a democratic theory, he is to the heart an aristocrat, as much as my father, who ruled over five or six hundred slaves."

Miss Ophelia felt rather disposed to cavil at this picture, and was laying down her knitting to begin, but St. Clare stopped her.

"Now, I know every word you are going to say. I do not say they *were* alike, in fact. One fell into a condition where everything acted against the natural tendency, and the other where everything acted for it; and so one turned out a pretty wilful, stout, overbearing old democrat, and the other a wilful, stout old despot. If both had owned plantations in Louisiana, they would have been as like as two old bullets cast in the same mould."

"What an undutiful boy you are!" said Miss Ophelia.

"I don't mean them any disrespect," said St. Clare. "You know reverence is not my forte. But, to go back to my history:

"When father died, he left the whole property to us twin boys, to be divided as we should agree. There does not breathe on God's earth a nobler-souled, more generous fellow, than Alfred, in all that concerns his equals; and we got on admirably with this property question, without a single unbrotherly word or feeling. We undertook to work the plantation together; and Alfred, whose outward life and capabilities had double the strength of mine, became an enthusiastic planter, and a wonderfully successful one.

"But two years' trial satisfied me that I could not be a partner in that matter. To have a great gang of seven hundred, whom I could not know personally, or feel any individual interest in, bought and driven, housed, fed, worked like so many horned cattle, strained up to military precision,—the question of how little of life's commonest enjoyments would keep them in working order being a constantly recurring problem,—the *necessity* of drivers and overseers,—the ever-necessary whip, first, last, and only argument,—the whole thing was insufferably disgusting and loathsome to me; and when I thought of my mother's estimate of one poor human soul, it became even frightful!

"It's all nonsense to talk to me about slaves *enjoying* all this! To this day, I have no patience with the unutterable trash that some of your patronizing Northerners have made up, as in their zeal to apologize for our sins. We all know better. Tell me that any man living wants to work all his days, from day-dawn till dark, under the constant eye of a master, without the power of putting forth one irresponsible volition, on the same dreary, monotonous, unchanging toil, and all for two pairs of pantaloons and a pair of shoes a year, with enough food and shelter to keep him in working order! Any man who thinks that human beings can, as a general thing, be made about as comfortable that way as any other, I wish he might try it. I'd buy the dog, and work him, with a clear conscience!"

"I always have supposed," said Miss Ophelia, "that you, all of you, approved of these things, and thought them *right*,—according to Scripture."

"Humbug! We are not quite reduced to that yet. Alfred, who is as determined a despot as ever walked, does not pretend to this kind of defence;—no, he stands, high and haughty, on that good old respectable ground, *the right of the strongest*; and he says, and I think quite sensibly, that the American planter is 'only doing, in another form, what the English aristocracy and capitalists are doing by the lower classes;' that is, I take it, *appropriating* them, body and bone, soul and spirit, to their use and convenience. He defends both,—and I think, at least, *consistently*. He says that there can be no high civilization without enslavement of the masses, either nominal or real. There must, he says, be a lower class, given up to physical toil and confined to an animal nature; and a higher one thereby acquires leisure and wealth for a more expanded intelligence and improvement, and becomes the directing soul of the lower. So he reasons, because, as I said, he is born an aristocrat;—so I don't believe, because I was born a democrat."

"How in the world can the two things be compared?" said Miss Ophelia. "The English laborer is not sold, traded, parted from his family, whipped."

"He is as much at the will of his employer as if he were sold to him. The slave-owner can whip his refractory slave to death,—the capitalist can starve him to death. As to family security, it is hard to say which is the worst,—to have one's children sold, or see them starve to death at home."

"But it's no kind of apology for slavery, to prove that it isn't worse than some other bad thing."

"I didn't give it for one,—nay, I'll say, besides, that ours is the more bold and palpable infringement of human rights; actually buying a man up, like a horse,—looking at his teeth, cracking his joints, and trying his paces, and then paying down for him,—having speculators, breeders, traders, and brokers in human bodies and souls,—sets the thing before the eyes of the civilized world in a more tangible form, though the thing done be, after all, in its nature, the same; that is, appropriating one set of human beings to the use and improvement of another, without any regard to their own."

"I never thought of the matter in this light," said Miss Ophelia.

"Well, I've travelled in England some, and I've looked over a good many documents as to the state of their lower classes; and I really think there is no denying Alfred, when he says that his slaves are better off than a large class of the population of England. You see, you must not infer, from what I have told you, that Alfred is what is called a hard master; for he isn't. He is despotic, and unmerciful to insubordination; he would shoot a fellow down with as little remorse as he would shoot a buck, if he opposed him. But, in general, he takes a sort of pride in having his slaves comfortably fed and accommodated.

"When I was with him, I insisted that he should do something for their instruction; and, to please me, he did get a chaplain, and used to have them catechized Sunday, though, I believe, in his heart, that he thought it would do about as much good to set a chaplain over his dogs and horses. And the fact is, that a mind stupefied and animalized by every bad influence from the hour of birth, spending the whole of every week-day in unreflecting toil, cannot be done much with by a few hours on Sunday. The teachers of Sunday-schools among the manufacturing population of England, and among plantation-hands in our country, could perhaps testify to the same result, *there and here.* Yet some striking exceptions there are among us, from the fact that the negro is naturally more impressible to religious sentiment than the white."

"Well," said Miss Ophelia, "how came you to give up your plantation life?"

"Well, we jogged on together some time, till Alfred saw plainly that I was no planter. He thought it absurd, after he had reformed, and altered, and improved everywhere, to suit my notions, that I still remained unsatisfied. The fact was, it was, after all, the THING that I hated,—the using these men and women, the perpetuation of all this ignorance, brutality and vice,—just to make money for me!

"Besides, I was always interfering in the details. Being myself one of the laziest of mortals, I had altogether too much fellow-feeling for the lazy; and when poor, shiftless dogs put stones at the bottom of their cotton-baskets to make them weigh heavier, or filled their sacks with dirt, with cotton at the top, it seemed so exactly like what I should do if I were they, I couldn't and wouldn't have them flogged for it. Well, of course, there was an end of plantation discipline; and Alf and I came to about the same point that I and my respected father did, years before. So he told me that I was a womanish sentimentalist, and would never do for business life; and advised me to take the bank-stock and the New Orleans family mansion, and go to writing poetry, and let him manage the plantation. So we parted, and I came here."

"But why didn't you free your slaves?"

"Well, I wasn't up to that. To hold them as tools for money-making, I could not;—have them to help spend money, you know, didn't look quite so ugly to me. Some of them were old house-servants, to whom I was much attached; and the younger ones were children to the old. All were well satisfied to be as they were." He paused, and walked reflectively up and down the room.

"There was," said St. Clare, "a time in my life when I had plans and hopes of doing something in this world, more than to float and drift. I had vague, indistinct yearnings to be a sort of emancipator,—to free my native land from this spot and stain. All young men have had such fever-fits, I suppose, some time,—but then—"

"Why didn't you?" said Miss Ophelia;—"you ought not to put your hand to the plough, and look back."

"O, well, things didn't go with me as I expected, and I got the despair of living that Solomon did. I suppose it was a necessary incident to wisdom in us both; but, some how or other, instead of being actor and regenerator in society, I became a piece of drift-wood, and have been floating and eddying about, ever since. Alfred scolds me, every time we meet; and he has the better of me, I grant,—for he really does something; his life is a logical result of his opinions, and mine is a contemptible *non sequitur*."

"My dear cousin, can you be satisfied with such a way of spending your probation?"

"Satisfied! Was I not just telling you I despised it? But, then, to come back to this point,—we were on this liberation business. I don't think my feelings about slavery are peculiar. I find many men who, in their hearts, think of it just as I do. The land groans under it; and, bad as it is for the slave, it is worse, if anything, for the master. It takes no spectacles to see that a great class of vicious, improvident, degraded people, among us, are an evil to us, as well as to themselves. The capitalist and aristocrat of England cannot feel that as we do, because they do not mingle with the class they degrade as we do. They are in our houses; they are the associates of our children, and they form their minds faster than we can; for they are a race that children always will cling to and assimilate with. If Eva, now, was not more angel than ordinary, she would be ruined. We might as well allow the small-pox to run among them, and think our children would not take it, as to let them be uninstructed and vicious, and think our children will not be affected by that. Yet our laws positively and utterly forbid any efficient general educational system, and they do it wisely, too; for, just begin and thoroughly educate one generation, and the whole thing would be blown sky high. If we did not give them liberty, they would take it."

"And what do you think will be the end of this?" said Miss Ophelia.

"I don't know. One thing is certain,—that there is a mustering among the masses, the world over; and there is a *dies iræ*[9] coming on, sooner or later. The same thing is working in Europe, in England, and in this country. My mother used to tell me of a millennium that was coming, when Christ should reign, and all men should be free and happy. And she taught me, when I was a boy, to pray, 'Thy kingdom come.'[1] Sometimes I think all this sighing, and groaning, and stirring among the dry bones foretells what she used to tell me was coming. But who may abide the day of His appearing?"

"Augustine, sometimes I think you are not far from the kingdom," said Miss Ophelia, laying down her knitting, and looking anxiously at her cousin.

"Thank you for your good opinion; but it's up and down with me,—up to heaven's gate in theory, down in earth's dust in practice. But there's the tea-bell,—do let's go,—and don't say, now, I haven't had one downright serious talk, for once in my life."

At table, Marie alluded to the incident of Prue. "I suppose you'll think, cousin," she said, "that we are all barbarians."

"I think that's a barbarous thing," said Miss Ophelia, "but I don't think you are all barbarians."

"Well, now," said Marie, "I know it's impossible to get along with some of these creatures. They are so bad they ought not to live. I don't feel a particle of sympathy for such cases. If they'd only behave themselves, it would not happen."

"But, mamma," said Eva, "the poor creature was unhappy; that's what made her drink."

"O, fiddlestick! as if that were any excuse! I'm unhappy, very often. I presume," she said, pensively, "that I've had greater trials than ever she had. It's just because they are so bad. There's some of them that you cannot break in by any kind of severity. I remember father had a man that was so lazy he would run away just to get rid of work, and lie round in the swamps, stealing and doing all sorts of horrid things. That man was caught and whipped, time and again, and it never did him any good; and the last time he crawled off, though he couldn't but just go, and died in the swamp. There was no sort of reason for it, for father's hands were always treated kindly."

"I broke a fellow in, once," said St. Clare, "that all the overseers and masters had tried their hands on in vain."

"You!" said Marie; "well, I'd be glad to know when *you* ever did anything of the sort."

9. Literally, "day of wrath" (Latin).
1. From the Lord's Prayer (Matthew 6.9–13).

"Well, he was a powerful, gigantic fellow,—a native-born African; and he appeared to have the rude instinct of freedom in him to an uncommon degree. He was a regular African lion. They called him Scipio. Nobody could do anything with him; and he was sold round from overseer to overseer, till at last Alfred bought him, because he thought he could manage him. Well, one day he knocked down the overseer, and was fairly off into the swamps. I was on a visit to Alf's plantation, for it was after we had dissolved partnership. Alfred was greatly exasperated; but I told him that it was his own fault, and laid him any wager that I could break the man; and finally it was agreed that, if I caught him, I should have him to experiment on. So they mustered out a party of some six or seven, with guns and dogs, for the hunt. People, you know, can get up just as much enthusiasm in hunting a man as a deer, if it is only customary; in fact, I got a little excited myself, though I had only put in as a sort of mediator, in case he was caught.

"Well, the dogs bayed and howled, and we rode and scampered, and finally we started him. He ran and bounded like a buck, and kept us well in the rear for some time; but at last he got caught in an impenetrable thicket of cane; then he turned to bay, and I tell you he fought the dogs right gallantly. He dashed them to right and left, and actually killed three of them with only his naked fists, when a shot from a gun brought him down, and he fell, wounded and bleeding, almost at my feet. The poor fellow looked up at me with manhood and despair both in his eye. I kept back the dogs and the party, as they came pressing up, and claimed him as my prisoner. It was all I could do to keep them from shooting him, in the flush of success; but I persisted in my bargain, and Alfred sold him to me. Well, I took him in hand, and in one fortnight I had him tamed down as submissive and tractable as heart could desire."

"What in the world did you do to him?" said Marie.

"Well, it was quite a simple process. I took him to my own room, had a good bed made for him, dressed his wounds, and tended him myself, until he got fairly on his feet again. And, in process of time, I had free papers made out for him, and told him he might go where he liked."

"And did he go?" said Miss Ophelia.

"No. The foolish fellow tore the paper in two, and absolutely refused to leave me. I never had a braver, better fellow,—trusty and true as steel. He embraced Christianity afterwards, and became as gentle as a child. He used to oversee my place on the lake, and did it capitally, too. I lost him the first cholera[2] season. In fact, he laid

2. An acute bacterial disease caused by infected water or food, occurring in epidemics and usually fatal if untreated.

down his life for me. For I was sick, almost to death; and when, through the panic, everybody else fled, Scipio worked for me like a giant, and actually brought me back into life again. But, poor fellow! he was taken, right after, and there was no saving him. I never felt anybody's loss more."

Eva had come gradually nearer and nearer to her father, as he told the story,—her small lips apart, her eyes wide and earnest with absorbing interest.

As he finished, she suddenly threw her arms around his neck, burst into tears, and sobbed convulsively.

"Eva, dear child! what is the matter?" said St. Clare, as the child's small frame trembled and shook with the violence of her feelings. "This child," he added, "ought not to hear any of this kind of thing,—she's nervous."

"No, papa, I'm not nervous," said Eva, controlling herself, suddenly, with a strength of resolution singular in such a child. "I'm not nervous, but these things *sink into my heart*."

"What do you mean, Eva?"

"I can't tell you, papa. I think a great many thoughts. Perhaps some day I shall tell you."

"Well, think away, dear,—only don't cry and worry your papa," said St. Clare. "Look here,—see what a beautiful peach I have got for you!"

Eva took it, and smiled, though there was still a nervous twitching about the corners of her mouth.

"Come, look at the gold-fish," said St. Clare, taking her hand and stepping on to the verandah. A few moments, and merry laughs were heard through the silken curtains, as Eva and St. Clare were pelting each other with roses, and chasing each other among the alleys of the court.

There is danger that our humble friend Tom be neglected amid the adventures of the higher born; but, if our readers will accompany us up to a little loft over the stable, they may, perhaps, learn a little of his affairs. It was a decent room, containing a bed, a chair, and a small, rough stand, where lay Tom's Bible and hymnbook; and where he sits, at present, with his slate before him, intent on something that seems to cost him a great deal of anxious thought.

The fact was, that Tom's home-yearnings had become so strong, that he had begged a sheet of writing-paper of Eva, and, mustering up all his small stock of literary attainment acquired by Mas'r George's instructions, he conceived the bold idea of writing a letter; and he was busy now, on his slate, getting out his first draft. Tom was in a good deal of trouble, for the forms of some of the letters he had forgotten entirely; and of what he did remember, he did not know exactly which to use. And while he was working, and breathing very hard, in his earnestness, Eva alighted, like a bird, on the round of his chair behind him, and peeped over his shoulder.

"O, Uncle Tom! what funny things you *are* making, there!"

"I'm trying to write to my poor old woman, Miss Eva, and my little chil'en," said Tom, drawing the back of his hand over his eyes; "but, some how, I'm feard I shan't make it out."

"I wish I could help you, Tom! I've learnt to write some. Last year I could make all the letters, but I'm afraid I've forgotten."

So Eva put her little golden head close to his, and the two commenced a grave and anxious discussion, each one equally earnest, and about equally ignorant; and, with a deal of consulting and advising over every word, the composition began, as they both felt very sanguine, to look quite like writing.

"Yes, Uncle Tom, it really begins to look beautiful," said Eva, gazing delightedly on it. "How pleased your wife'll be, and the poor little children! O, it's a shame you ever had to go away from them! I mean to ask papa to let you go back, some time."

"Missis said that she would send down money for me, as soon as they could get it together," said Tom. "I'm 'spectin' she will. Young Mas'r George, he said he'd come for me; and he gave me this yer dollar as a sign;" and Tom drew from under his clothes the precious dollar.

"O, he'll certainly come, then!" said Eva. "I'm so glad!"

"And I wanted to send a letter, you know, to let 'em know whar I was, and tell poor Chloe that I was well off,—cause she felt so dreful, poor soul!"

"I say, Tom!" said St. Clare's voice, coming in the door at this moment.

Tom and Eva both started.

"What's here?" said St. Clare, coming up and looking at the slate.

"O, it's Tom's letter. I'm helping him to write it," said Eva; "isn't it nice?"

"I wouldn't discourage either of you," said St. Clare, "but I rather think, Tom, you'd better get me to write your letter for you. I'll do it, when I come home from my ride."

"It's very important he should write," said Eva, "because his mistress is going to send down money to redeem him, you know, papa; he told me they told him so."

St. Clare thought, in his heart, that this was probably only one of those things which good-natured owners say to their servants, to alleviate their horror of being sold, without any intention of fulfilling the expectation thus excited. But he did not make any audible comment upon it,—only ordered Tom to get the horses out for a ride.

Tom's letter was written in due form for him that evening, and safely lodged in the post-office.

Miss Ophelia still persevered in her labors in the house-keeping line. It was universally agreed, among all the household, from Dinah down to the youngest urchin, that Miss Ophelia was decidedly "curis,"—a term by which a southern servant implies that his or her betters don't exactly suit them.

The higher circle in the family—to wit, Adolph, Jane and Rosa—agreed that she was no lady; ladies never kept working about as she did;—that she had no *air* at all; and they were surprised that she should be any relation of the St. Clares. Even Marie declared that it was absolutely fatiguing to see Cousin Ophelia always so busy. And, in fact, Miss Ophelia's industry was so incessant as to lay some foundation for the complaint. She sewed and stitched away, from daylight till dark, with the energy of one who is pressed on by some immediate urgency; and then, when the light faded, and the work was folded away, with one turn out came the ever-ready knitting-work, and there she was again, going on as briskly as ever. It really was a labor to see her.

# Chapter XX

## *Topsy*

One morning, while Miss Ophelia was busy in some of her domestic cares, St. Clare's voice was heard, calling her at the foot of the stairs.

"Come down here, Cousin; I've something to show you."

"What is it?" said Miss Ophelia, coming down, with her sewing in her hand.

"I've made a purchase for your department,—see here," said St. Clare; and, with the word, he pulled along a little negro girl, about eight or nine years of age.

She was one of the blackest of her race; and her round, shining eyes, glittering as glass beads, moved with quick and restless glances over everything in the room. Her mouth, half open with astonishment at the wonders of the new Mas'r's parlor, displayed a white and brilliant set of teeth. Her woolly hair was braided in sundry little tails, which stuck out in every direction. The expression of her face was an odd mixture of shrewdness and cunning, over which was oddly drawn, like a kind of veil, an expression of the most doleful gravity and solemnity. She was dressed in a single filthy, ragged garment, made of bagging; and stood with her hands demurely folded before her. Altogether, there was something odd and goblin-like about her appearance,—something, as Miss Ophelia afterwards said, "so heathenish," as to inspire that good lady with utter dismay; and, turning to St. Clare, she said,

"Augustine, what in the world have you brought that thing here for?"

"For you to educate, to be sure, and train in the way she should go.[1] I thought she was rather a funny specimen in the Jim Crow line. Here, Topsy," he added, giving a whistle, as a man would to call the attention of a dog, "give us a song, now, and show us some of your dancing."

The black, glassy eyes glittered with a kind of wicked drollery, and the thing struck up, in a clear shrill voice, an odd negro melody, to which she kept time with her hands and feet, spinning round, clapping her hands, knocking her knees together, in a wild, fantastic sort of time, and producing in her throat all those odd guttural sounds which distinguish the native music of her race; and finally, turning a summerset or two, and giving a prolonged closing note, as odd and unearthly as that of a steam-whistle, she came suddenly down on the carpet, and stood with her hands folded, and a most sanctimonious expression of meekness and solemnity over her face, only broken by the cunning glances which she shot askance from the corners of her eyes.

Miss Ophelia stood silent, perfectly paralyzed with amazement.

St. Clare, like a mischievous fellow as he was, appeared to enjoy her astonishment; and, addressing the child again, said,

"Topsy, this is your new mistress. I'm going to give you up to her; see now that you behave yourself."

"Yes, Mas'r," said Topsy, with sanctimonious gravity, her wicked eyes twinkling as she spoke.

"You're going to be good, Topsy, you understand," said St. Clare.

"O yes, Mas'r," said Topsy, with another twinkle, her hands still devoutly folded.

"Now, Augustine, what upon earth is this for?" said Miss Ophelia. "Your house is so full of these little plagues, now, that a body can't set down their foot without treading on 'em. I get up in the morning, and find one asleep behind the door, and see one black head poking out from under the table, one lying on the door-mat,—and they are mopping and mowing and grinning between all the railings, and tumbling over the kitchen floor! What on earth did you want to bring this one for?"

"For you to educate—didn't I tell you? You're always preaching about educating. I thought I would make you a present of a fresh-

1. "Train up a child in the way he should go: and when he is old, he will not depart from it" (Proverbs 23.6).

caught specimen, and let you try your hand on her, and bring her up in the way she should go."

"*I* don't want her, I am sure;—I have more to do with 'em now than I want to."

"That's you Christians, all over!—you'll get up a society, and get some poor missionary to spend all his days among just such heathen. But let me see one of you that would take one into your house with you, and take the labor of their conversion on yourselves! No; when it comes to that, they are dirty and disagreeable, and it's too much care, and so on."

"Augustine, you know I didn't think of it in that light," said Miss Ophelia, evidently softening. "Well, it might be a real missionary work," said she, looking rather more favorably on the child.

St. Clare had touched the right string. Miss Ophelia's conscientiousness was ever on the alert. "But," she added, "I really didn't see the need of buying this one;—there are enough now, in your house, to take all my time and skill."

"Well, then, Cousin," said St. Clare, drawing her aside; "I ought to beg your pardon for my good-for-nothing speeches. You are so good, after all, that there's no sense in them. Why, the fact is, this concern belonged to a couple of drunken creatures that keep a low restaurant that I have to pass by every day, and I was tired of hearing her screaming, and them beating and swearing at her. She looked bright and funny, too, as if something might be made of her;—so I bought her, and I'll give her to you. Try, now, and give her a good orthodox New England bringing up, and see what it'll make of her. You know I haven't any gift that way; but I'd like you to try."

"Well, I'll do what I can," said Miss Ophelia; and she approached her new subject very much as a person might be supposed to approach a black spider, supposing them to have benevolent designs toward it.

"She's dreadfully dirty, and half naked," she said.

"Well, take her down stairs, and make some of them clean and clothe her up."

Miss Ophelia carried her to the kitchen regions.

"Don't see what Mas'r St. Clare wants of 'nother nigger!" said Dinah, surveying the new arrival with no friendly air. "Won't have her round under *my* feet, *I* know!"

"Pah!" said Rosa and Jane, with supreme disgust; "let her keep out of our way! What in the world Mas'r wanted another of these low niggers for, I can't see!"

"You go long! No more nigger dan you be, Miss Rosa," said Dinah, who felt this last remark a reflection on herself. "You seem to tink yourself white folks. You an't nerry one, black *nor* white. I'd like to be one or turrer."

Miss Ophelia saw that there was nobody in the camp that would undertake to oversee the cleansing and dressing of the new arrival; and so she was forced to do it herself, with some very ungracious and reluctant assistance from Jane.

It is not for ears polite to hear the particulars of the first toilet of a neglected, abused child. In fact, in this world, multitudes must live and die in a state that it would be too great a shock to the nerves of their fellow-mortals even to hear described. Miss Ophelia had a good, strong, practical deal of resolution; and she went through all the disgusting details with heroic thoroughness, though, it must be confessed, with no very gracious air,—for endurance was the utmost to which her principles could bring her. When she saw, on the back and shoulders of the child, great welts and calloused spots, ineffaceable marks of the system under which she had grown up thus far, her heart became pitiful within her.

"See there!" said Jane, pointing to the marks, "don't that show she's a limb? We'll have fine works with her, I reckon. I hate these nigger young uns! so disgusting! I wonder that Mas'r would buy her!"

The "young un" alluded to heard all these comments with the subdued and doleful air which seemed habitual to her, only scanning, with a keen and furtive glance of her flickering eyes, the ornaments which Jane wore in her ears. When arrayed at last in a suit of decent and whole clothing, her hair cropped short to her head, Miss Ophelia, with some satisfaction, said she looked more Christian-like than she did, and in her own mind began to mature some plans for her instruction.

Sitting down before her, she began to question her.

"How old are you, Topsy?"

"Dun no, Missis," said the image, with a grin that showed all her teeth.

"Don't know how old you are? Didn't anybody ever tell you? Who was your mother?"

"Never had none!" said the child, with another grin.

"Never had any mother? What do you mean? Where were you born?"

"Never was born!" persisted Topsy, with another grin, that looked so goblin-like, that, if Miss Ophelia had been at all nervous, she might have fancied that she had got hold of some sooty gnome from the land of Diablerie;[2] but Miss Ophelia was not nervous, but plain and business-like, and she said, with some sternness,

"You mustn't answer me in that way, child; I'm not playing with you. Tell me where you were born, and who your father and mother were."

2. I.e., Hell. Diablerie is witchcraft, devilry, or wickedness.

"Never was born," reiterated the creature, more emphatically; "never had no father nor mother, nor nothin'. I was raised by a speculator, with lots of others. Old Aunt Sue used to take car on us."

The child was evidently sincere; and Jane, breaking into a short laugh, said,

"Laws, Missis, there's heaps of 'em. Speculators buys 'em up cheap, when they's little, and gets 'em raised for market."

"How long have you lived with your master and mistress?"

"Dun no, Missis."

"Is it a year, or more, or less?"

"Dun no, Missis."

"Laws, Missis, those low negroes,—they can't tell; they don't know anything about time," said Jane; "they don't know what a year is; they don't know their own ages."

"Have you ever heard anything about God, Topsy?"

The child looked bewildered, but grinned as usual.

"Do you know who made you?"

"Nobody, as I knows on," said the child, with a short laugh.

The idea appeared to amuse her considerably; for her eyes twinkled, and she added,

"I spect I grow'd. Don't think nobody never made me."

"Do you know how to sew?" said Miss Ophelia, who thought she would turn her inquiries to something more tangible.

"No, Missis."

"What can you do?—what did you do for your master and mistress?"

"Fetch water, and wash dishes, and rub knives, and wait on folks."

"Were they good to you?"

"Spect they was," said the child, scanning Miss Ophelia cunningly.

Miss Ophelia rose from this encouraging colloquy; St. Clare was leaning over the back of her chair.

"You find virgin soil there, Cousin; put in your own ideas,—you won't find many to pull up."

Miss Ophelia's ideas of education, like all her other ideas, were very set and definite; and of the kind that prevailed in New England a century ago, and which are still preserved in some very retired and unsophisticated parts, where there are no railroads. As nearly as could be expressed, they could be comprised in very few words: to teach them to mind when they were spoken to; to teach them the catechism, sewing, and reading; and to whip them if they told lies. And though, of course, in the flood of light that is now poured on education, these are left far away in the rear, yet it is an undisputed fact that our grandmothers raised some tolerably fair men and women under this régime, as many of us can remember and testify.

At all events, Miss Ophelia knew of nothing else to do; and, therefore, applied her mind to her heathen with the best diligence she could command.

The child was announced and considered in the family as Miss Ophelia's girl; and, as she was looked upon with no gracious eye in the kitchen, Miss Ophelia resolved to confine her sphere of operation and instruction chiefly to her own chamber. With a self-sacrifice which some of our readers will appreciate, she resolved, instead of comfortably making her own bed, sweeping and dusting her own chamber,—which she had hitherto done, in utter scorn of all offers of help from the chambermaid of the establishment,—to condemn herself to the martyrdom of instructing Topsy to perform these operations,—ah, woe the day! Did any of our readers ever do the same, they will appreciate the amount of her self-sacrifice.

Miss Ophelia began with Topsy by taking her into her chamber, the first morning, and solemnly commencing a course of instruction in the art and mystery of bed-making.

Behold, then, Topsy, washed and shorn of all the little braided tails wherein her heart had delighted, arrayed in a clean gown, with well-starched apron, standing reverently before Miss Ophelia, with an expression of solemnity well befitting a funeral.

"Now, Topsy, I'm going to show you just how my bed is to be made. I am very particular about my bed. You must learn exactly how to do it."

"Yes, ma'am," says Topsy, with a deep sigh, and a face of woful earnestness.

"Now, Topsy, look here;—this is the hem of the sheet,—this is the right side of the sheet, and this is the wrong;—will you remember?"

"Yes, ma'am," says Topsy, with another sigh.

"Well, now, the under sheet you must bring over the bolster,—so,—and tuck it clear down under the mattress nice and smooth,—so,—do you see?"

"Yes, ma'am," said Topsy, with profound attention.

"But the upper sheet," said Miss Ophelia, "must be brought down in this way, and tucked under firm and smooth at the foot,—so,—the narrow hem at the foot."

"Yes, ma'am," said Topsy, as before;—but we will add, what Miss Ophelia did not see, that, during the time when the good lady's back was turned, in the zeal of her manipulations, the young disciple had contrived to snatch a pair of gloves and a ribbon, which she had adroitly slipped into her sleeves, and stood with her hands dutifully folded, as before.

"Now, Topsy, let's see *you* do this," said Miss Ophelia, pulling off the clothes, and seating herself.

Topsy, with great gravity and adroitness, went through the exercise completely to Miss Ophelia's satisfaction; smoothing the sheets, patting out every wrinkle, and exhibiting, through the whole process, a gravity and seriousness with which her instructress was greatly edified. By an unlucky slip, however, a fluttering fragment of the ribbon hung out of one of her sleeves, just as she was finishing, and caught Miss Ophelia's attention. Instantly she pounced upon it. "What's this? You naughty, wicked child,—you've been stealing this!"

The ribbon was pulled out of Topsy's own sleeve, yet was she not in the least disconcerted; she only looked at it with an air of the most surprised and unconscious innocence.

"Laws! why, that ar's Miss Feely's ribbon, an't it? How could it a got caught in my sleeve?"

"Topsy, you naughty girl, don't you tell me a lie,—you stole that ribbon!"

"Missis, I declar for 't, I didn't;—never seed it till dis yer blessed minnit."

"Topsy," said Miss Ophelia, "don't you know it's wicked to tell lies?"

"I never tells no lies, Miss Feely," said Topsy, with virtuous gravity; "it's jist the truth I've been a tellin now, and an't nothin else."

"Topsy, I shall have to whip you, if you tell lies so."

"Laws, Missis, if you's to whip all day, couldn't say no other way," said Topsy, beginning to blubber. "I never seed dat ar,—it must a got caught in my sleeve. Miss Feely must have left it on the bed, and it got caught in the clothes, and so got in my sleeve."

Miss Ophelia was so indignant at the barefaced lie, that she caught the child and shook her.

"Don't you tell me that again!"

The shake brought the gloves on to the floor, from the other sleeve.

"There, you!" said Miss Ophelia, "will you tell me now, you didn't steal the ribbon?"

Topsy now confessed to the gloves, but still persisted in denying the ribbon.

"Now, Topsy," said Miss Ophelia, "if you'll confess all about it, I won't whip you this time." Thus adjured, Topsy confessed to the ribbon and gloves, with woful protestations of penitence.

"Well, now, tell me. I know you must have taken other things since you have been in the house, for I let you run about all day yesterday. Now, tell me if you took anything, and I shan't whip you."

"Laws, Missis! I took Miss Eva's red thing she wars on her neck."

"You did, you naughty child!—Well, what else?"

"I took Rosa's yer-rings,—them red ones."

"Go bring them to me this minute, both of 'em."

"Laws, Missis! I can't,—they's burnt up!"

"Burnt up!—what a story! Go get 'em, or I'll whip you."

Topsy, with loud protestations, and tears, and groans, declared that she *could* not. "They's burnt up,—they was."

"What did you burn 'em up for?" said Miss Ophelia.

"Cause I's wicked,—I is. I's mighty wicked, any how. I can't help it."

Just at this moment, Eva came innocently into the room, with the identical coral necklace on her neck.

"Why, Eva, where did you get your necklace?" said Miss Ophelia.

"Get it? Why, I've had it on all day," said Eva.

"Did you have it on yesterday?"

"Yes; and what is funny, Aunty, I had it on all night. I forgot to take it off when I went to bed."

Miss Ophelia looked perfectly bewildered; the more so, as Rosa, at that instant, came into the room, with a basket of newly-ironed linen poised on her head, and the coral ear-drops shaking in her ears!

"I'm sure I can't tell anything what to do with such a child!" she said, in despair. "What in the world did you tell me you took those things for, Topsy?"

"Why, Missis said I must 'fess; and I couldn't think of nothin' else to 'fess," said Topsy, rubbing her eyes.

"But, of course, I didn't want you to confess things you didn't do," said Miss Ophelia; "that's telling a lie, just as much as the other."

"Laws, now, is it?" said Topsy, with an air of innocent wonder.

"La, there an't any such thing as truth in that limb," said Rosa, looking indignantly at Topsy. "If I was Mas'r St. Clare, I'd whip her till the blood run. I would,—I'd let her catch it!"

"No, no, Rosa," said Eva, with an air of command, which the child could assume at times; "you mustn't talk so, Rosa. I can't bear to hear it."

"La sakes! Miss Eva, you's so good, you don't know nothing how to get along with niggers. There's no way but to cut 'em well up, I tell ye."

"Rosa!" said Eva, "hush! Don't you say another word of that sort!" and the eye of the child flashed, and her cheek deepened its color.

Rosa was cowed in a moment.

"Miss Eva has got the St. Clare blood in her, that's plain. She can speak, for all the world, just like her papa," she said, as she passed out of the room.

Eva stood looking at Topsy.

There stood the two children, representatives of the two extremes of society. The fair, high-bred child, with her golden head, her deep eyes, her spiritual, noble brow, and prince-like movements; and her black, keen, subtle, cringing, yet acute neighbor. They stood the representatives of their races. The Saxon, born of ages of cultivation, command, education, physical and moral eminence; the Afric, born of ages of oppression, submission, ignorance, toil, and vice!

Something, perhaps, of such thoughts struggled through Eva's mind. But a child's thoughts are rather dim, undefined instincts; and in Eva's noble nature many such were yearning and working, for which she had no power of utterance. When Miss Ophelia expatiated on Topsy's naughty, wicked conduct, the child looked perplexed and sorrowful, but said, sweetly,

"Poor Topsy, why need you steal? You're going to be taken good care of, now. I'm sure I'd rather give you anything of mine, than have you steal it."

It was the first word of kindness the child had ever heard in her life; and the sweet tone and manner struck strangely on the wild, rude heart, and a sparkle of something like a tear shone in the keen, round, glittering eye; but it was followed by the short laugh and habitual grin. No! the ear that has never heard anything but abuse is strangely incredulous of anything so heavenly as kindness; and Topsy only thought Eva's speech something funny and inexplicable,—she did not believe it.

But what was to be done with Topsy? Miss Ophelia found the case a puzzler; her rules for bringing up didn't seem to apply. She thought she would take time to think of it; and, by the way of gaining time, and in hopes of some indefinite moral virtues supposed to be inherent in dark closets, Miss Ophelia shut Topsy up in one till she had arranged her ideas further on the subject.

"I don't see," said Miss Ophelia to St. Clare, "how I'm going to manage that child, without whipping her."

"Well, whip her, then, to your heart's content; I'll give you full power to do what you like."

"Children always have to be whipped," said Miss Ophelia; "I never heard of bringing them up without."

"O, well, certainly," said St. Clare: "do as you think best. Only I'll make one suggestion: I've seen this child whipped with a poker, knocked down with the shovel or tongs, whichever came handiest, & c.; and, seeing that she is used to that style of operation, I think your whippings will have to be pretty energetic, to make much impression."

"What is to be done with her, then?" said Miss Ophelia.

"You have started a serious question," said St. Clare; "I wish you'd answer it. What is to be done with a human being that can be governed only by the lash,—*that* fails,—it's a very common state of things down here!"

"I'm sure I don't know; I never saw such a child as this."

"Such children are very common among us, and such men and women, too. How are they to be governed?" said St. Clare.

"I'm sure it's more than I can say," said Miss Ophelia.

"Or I either," said St. Clare. "The horrid cruelties and outrages that once and a while find their way into the papers,—such cases as Prue's, for example,—what do they come from? In many cases, it is a gradual hardening process on both sides,—the owner growing more and more cruel, as the servant more and more callous. Whipping and abuse are like laudanum[3] you have to double the dose as the sensibilities decline. I saw this very early when I became an owner; and I resolved never to begin, because I did not know when I should stop,—and I resolved, at least, to protect my own moral nature. The consequence is, that my servants act like spoiled children; but I think that better than for us both to be brutalized together. You have talked a great deal about our responsibilities in educating, Cousin. I really wanted you to *try* with one child, who is a specimen of thousands among us."

"It is your system makes such children," said Miss Ophelia.

"I know it; but they are *made*,—they exist,—and what *is* to be done with them?"

"Well, I can't say I thank you for the experiment. But, then, as it appears to be a duty, I shall persevere and try, and do the best I can," said Miss Ophelia; and Miss Ophelia, after this, did labor, with a commendable degree of zeal and energy, on her new subject. She instituted regular hours and employments for her, and undertook to teach her to read and to sew.

In the former art, the child was quick enough. She learned her letters as if by magic, and was very soon able to read plain reading; but the sewing was a more difficult matter. The creature was as lithe as a cat, and as active as a monkey, and the confinement of sewing was her abomination; so she broke her needles, threw them slyly out of windows, or down in chinks of the walls; she tangled, broke, and dirtied her thread, or, with a sly movement, would throw a spool away altogether. Her motions were almost as quick as those of a practised conjurer, and her command of her face quite as great; and though Miss Ophelia could not help feeling that so many accidents could not possibly happen in succession, yet she could not, without a watchfulness which would leave her no time for anything else, detect her.

Topsy was soon a noted character in the establishment. Her talent for every species of drollery, grimace, and mimicry,—for dancing, tumbling, climbing, singing, whistling, imitating every sound that hit her fancy,—seemed inexhaustible. In her play-hours, she invariably had every child in the establishment at her heels, openmouthed with admiration and wonder,—not excepting Miss Eva,

3. An opium preparation formerly used medicinally to relieve pain; it is addictive.

who appeared to be fascinated by her wild diablerie, as a dove is sometimes charmed by a glittering serpent. Miss Ophelia was uneasy that Eva should fancy Topsy's society so much, and implored St. Clare to forbid it.

"Poh! let the child alone," said St. Clare. "Topsy will do her good."

"But so depraved a child,—are you not afraid she will teach her some mischief?"

"She can't teach her mischief; she might teach it to some children, but evil rolls off Eva's mind like dew off a cabbage-leaf,—not a drop sinks in."

"Don't be too sure," said Miss Ophelia. "I know I'd never let a child of mine play with Topsy."

"Well, your children needn't," said St. Clare, "but mine may; if Eva could have been spoiled, it would have been done years ago."

Topsy was at first despised and contemned by the upper servants. They soon found reason to alter their opinion. It was very soon discovered that whoever cast an indignity on Topsy was sure to meet with some inconvenient accident shortly after;—either a pair of earrings or some cherished trinket would be missing, or an article of dress would be suddenly found utterly ruined, or the person would stumble accidentally into a pail of hot water, or a libation of dirty slop would unaccountably deluge them from above when in full gala dress;—and on all these occasions, when investigation was made, there was nobody found to stand sponsor for the indignity. Topsy was cited, and had up before all the domestic judicatories, time and again; but always sustained her examinations with most edifying innocence and gravity of appearance. Nobody in the world ever doubted who did the things; but not a scrap of any direct evidence could be found to establish the suppositions, and Miss Ophelia was too just to feel at liberty to proceed to any lengths without it.

The mischiefs done were always so nicely timed, also, as further to shelter the aggressor. Thus, the times for revenge on Rosa and Jane, the two chamber-maids, were always chosen in those seasons when (as not unfrequently happened) they were in disgrace with their mistress, when any complaint from them would of course meet with no sympathy. In short, Topsy soon made the household understand the propriety of letting her alone; and she was let alone accordingly.

Topsy was smart and energetic in all manual operations, learning everything that was taught her with surprising quickness. With a few lessons, she had learned to do the proprieties of Miss Ophelia's chamber in a way with which even that particular lady could find no fault. Mortal hands could not lay spread smoother, adjust pillows more accurately, sweep and dust and arrange more perfectly, than Topsy, when she chose,—but she didn't very often choose. If

Miss Ophelia, after three or four days of careful and patient supervision, was so sanguine as to suppose that Topsy had at last fallen into her way, could do without over-looking, and so go off and busy herself about something else, Topsy would hold a perfect carnival of confusion, for some one or two hours. Instead of making the bed, she would amuse herself with pulling off the pillow-cases, butting her woolly head among the pillows, till it would sometimes be grotesquely ornamented with feathers sticking out in various directions; she would climb the posts, and hang head downward from the tops; flourish the sheets and spreads all over the apartment; dress the bolster up in Miss Ophelia's night-clothes, and enact various scenic performances with that,—singing and whistling, and making grimaces at herself in the looking-glass; in short, as Miss Ophelia phrased it, "raising Cain"[4] generally.

On one occasion, Miss Ophelia found Topsy with her very best scarlet India Canton crape[5] shawl wound round her head for a turban, going on with her rehearsals before the glass in great style,—Miss Ophelia having, with carelessness most unheard-of in her, left the key for once in her drawer.

"Topsy!" she would say, when at the end of all patience, "what does make you act so?"

"Dunno, Missis,—I spects cause I's so wicked!"

"I don't know anything what I shall do with you, Topsy."

"Law, Missis, you must whip me; my old Missis allers whipped me. I an't used to workin' unless I gets whipped."

"Why, Topsy, I don't want to whip you. You can do well, if you've a mind to; what is the reason you won't?"

"Laws, Missis, I's used to whippin'; I spects it's good for me."

Miss Ophelia tried the recipe, and Topsy invariably made a terrible commotion, screaming, groaning and imploring, though half an hour afterwards, when roosted on some projection of the balcony, and surrounded by a flock of admiring "young uns," she would express the utmost contempt of the whole affair.

"Law, Miss Feely whip!—wouldn't kill a skeeter, her whippins. Oughter see how old Mas'r made the flesh fly; old Mas'r know'd how!"

Topsy always made great capital of her own sins and enormities, evidently considering them as something peculiarly distinguishing.

"Law, you niggers," she would say to some of her auditors, "does you know you's all sinners? Well, you is—everybody is. White folks is sinners too,—Miss Feely says so; but I spects niggers is the biggest

4. Creating a commotion or causing trouble; from the biblical story of Cain, who killed his brother Abel (Genesis 4.1–16).
5. Lightweight fabric with a crinkled surface, perhaps imported from Canton, China, or from India.

ones; but lor! ye an't any on ye up to me. I's so awful wicked there can't nobody do nothin' with me. I used to keep old Missis a swarin' at me half de time. I spects I's the wickedest critter in the world;" and Topsy would cut a summerset, and come up brisk and shining on to a higher perch, and evidently plume herself on the distinction.

Miss Ophelia busied herself very earnestly on Sundays, teaching Topsy the catechism. Topsy had an uncommon verbal memory, and committed with a fluency that greatly encouraged her instructress.

"What good do you expect it is going to do her?" said St. Clare.

"Why, it always has done children good. It's what children always have to learn, you know," said Miss Ophelia.

"Understand it or not," said St. Clare.

"O, children never understand it at the time; but, after they are grown up, it'll come to them."

"Mine hasn't come to me yet," said St. Clare, "though I'll bear testimony that you put it into me pretty thoroughly when I was a boy."

"Ah, you were always good at learning, Augustine. I used to have great hopes of you," said Miss Ophelia.

"Well, haven't you now?" said St. Clare.

"I wish you were as good as you were when you were a boy, Augustine."

"So do I, that's a fact, Cousin," said St. Clare. "Well, go ahead and catechize Topsy; may be you'll make out something yet."

Topsy, who had stood like a black statue during this discussion, with hands decently folded, now, at a signal from Miss Ophelia, went on:

"Our first parents, being left to the freedom of their own will, fell from the state wherein they were created."[6]

Topsy's eyes twinkled, and she looked inquiringly.

"What is it, Topsy?" said Miss Ophelia.

"Please, Missis, was dat ar state Kintuck?"

"What state, Topsy?"

"Dat state dey fell out of. I used to hear Mas'r tell how we came down from Kintuck."

St. Clare laughed.

"You'll have to give her a meaning, or she'll make one," said he. "There seems to be a theory of emigration suggested there."

"O! Augustine, be still," said Miss Ophelia; "how can I do anything, if you will be laughing?"

6. This discussion of Adam and Eve is taken from the catechism printed in the *New England Primer* (first edition c. 1690): "Q: Did our first parents continue in the estate wherein they were created? A: Our first parents being left to the freedom of their own Will, fell from the state wherein they were created, by sinning against God."

"Well, I won't disturb the exercises again, on my honor;" and St. Clare took his paper into the parlor, and sat down, till Topsy had finished her recitations. They were all very well, only that now and then she would oddly transpose some important words, and persist in the mistake, in spite of every effort to the contrary; and St. Clare, after all his promises of goodness, took a wicked pleasure in these mistakes, calling Topsy to him whenever he had a mind to amuse himself, and getting her to repeat the offending passages, in spite of Miss Ophelia's remonstrances.

"How do you think I can do anything with the child, if you will go on so, Augustine?" she would say.

"Well, it is too bad,—I won't again; but I do like to hear the droll little image stumble over those big words!"

"But you confirm her in the wrong way."

"What's the odds? One word is as good as another to her."

"You wanted me to bring her up right; and you ought to remember she is a reasonable creature, and be careful of your influence over her."

"O, dismal! so I ought; but, as Topsy herself says, 'I's so wicked!'"

In very much this way Topsy's training proceeded, for a year or two,—Miss Ophelia worrying herself, from day to day, with her, as a kind of chronic plague, to whose inflictions she became, in time, as accustomed, as persons sometimes do to the neuralgia[7] or sick head-ache.

St. Clare took the same kind of amusement in the child that a man might in the tricks of a parrot or a pointer. Topsy, whenever her sins brought her into disgrace in other quarters, always took refuge behind his chair; and St. Clare, in one way or other, would make peace for her. From him she got many a stray picayune, which she laid out in nuts and candies, and distributed, with careless generosity, to all the children in the family; for Topsy, to do her justice, was good-natured and liberal, and only spiteful in self-defence. She is fairly introduced into our *corps de ballet*,[8] and will figure, from time to time, in her turn, with other performers.

## Chapter XXI

### *Kentuck*

Our readers may not be unwilling to glance back, for a brief interval, at Uncle Tom's Cabin, on the Kentucky farm, and see what has been transpiring among those whom he had left behind.

7. Acute pain along the length of a nerve.
8. The ensemble of a ballet company, as distinguished from the soloists.

It was late in the summer afternoon, and the doors and windows of the large parlor all stood open, to invite any stray breeze, that might feel in a good humor, to enter. Mr. Shelby sat in a large hall opening into the room, and running through the whole length of the house, to a balcony on either end. Leisurely tipped back in one chair, with his heels in another, he was enjoying his after-dinner cigar. Mrs. Shelby sat in the door, busy about some fine sewing; she seemed like one who had something on her mind, which she was seeking an opportunity to introduce.

"Do you know," she said, "that Chloe has had a letter from Tom?"

"Ah! has she? Tom's got some friend there, it seems. How is the old boy?"

"He has been bought by a very fine family, I should think," said Mrs. Shelby,—"is kindly treated, and has not much to do."

"Ah! well, I'm glad of it,—very glad," said Mr. Shelby, heartily. "Tom, I suppose, will get reconciled to a Southern residence;—hardly want to come up here again."

"On the contrary, he inquires very anxiously," said Mrs. Shelby, "when the money for his redemption is to be raised."

"I'm sure *I* don't know," said Mr. Shelby. "Once get business running wrong, there does seem to be no end to it. It's like jumping from one bog to another, all through a swamp; borrow of one to pay another, and then borrow of another to pay one,—and these confounded notes falling due before a man has time to smoke a cigar and turn round,—dunning letters and dunning messages,—all scamper and hurry-scurry."

"It does seem to me, my dear, that something might be done to straighten matters. Suppose we sell off all the horses, and sell one of your farms, and pay up square?"

"O, ridiculous, Emily! You are the finest woman in Kentucky; but still you haven't sense to know that you don't understand business;—women never do, and never can."

"But, at least," said Mrs. Shelby, "could not you give me some little insight into yours; a list of all your debts, at least, and of all that is owed to you, and let me try and see if I can't help you to economize."

"O, bother! don't plague me, Emily!—I can't tell exactly. I know somewhere about what things are likely to be; but there's no trimming and squaring my affairs, as Chloe trims crust off her pies. You don't know anything about business, I tell you."

And Mr. Shelby, not knowing any other way of enforcing his ideas, raised his voice,—a mode of arguing very convenient and convincing, when a gentleman is discussing matters of business with his wife.

Mrs. Shelby ceased talking, with something of a sigh. The fact was, that though her husband had stated she was a woman, she had a clear, energetic, practical mind, and a force of character every way superior to that of her husband; so that it would not have been so very absurd a supposition, to have allowed her capable of managing, as Mr. Shelby supposed. Her heart was set on performing her promise to Tom and Aunt Chloe, and she sighed as discouragements thickened around her.

"Don't you think we might in some way contrive to raise that money? Poor Aunt Chloe! her heart is so set on it!"

"I'm sorry, if it is. I think I was premature in promising. I'm not sure, now, but it's the best way to tell Chloe, and let her make up her mind to it. Tom'll have another wife, in a year or two; and she had better take up with somebody else."

"Mr. Shelby, I have taught my people that their marriages are as sacred as ours. I never could think of giving Chloe such advice."

"It's a pity, wife, that you have burdened them with a morality above their condition and prospects. I always thought so."

"It's only the morality of the Bible, Mr. Shelby."

"Well, well, Emily, I don't pretend to interfere with your religious notions; only they seem extremely unfitted for people in that condition."

"They are, indeed," said Mrs. Shelby, "and that is why, from my soul, I hate the whole thing. I tell you, my dear, *I* cannot absolve myself from the promises I make to these helpless creatures. If I can get the money no other way, I will take music-scholars;—I could get enough, I know, and earn the money myself."

"You wouldn't degrade yourself that way, Emily? I never could consent to it."

"Degrade! would it degrade me as much as to break my faith with the helpless? No, indeed!"

"Well, you are always heroic and transcendental," said Mr. Shelby, "but I think you had better think before you undertake such a piece of Quixotism."[1]

Here the conversation was interrupted by the appearance of Aunt Chloe, at the end of the verandah.

"If you please, Missis," said she.

"Well, Chloe, what is it?" said her mistress, rising, and going to the end of the balcony.

"If Missis would come and look at dis yer lot o' poetry."

Chloe had a particular fancy for calling poultry poetry,—an application of language in which she always persisted, notwithstanding frequent corrections and advisings from the young members of the family.

1. Extraordinary chivalry or impractical idealism; from the title character in Cervantes' *Don Quixote* (1605–15).

"La sakes!" she would say, "I can't see; one jis good as turry,—poetry suthin good, any how;" and so poetry Chloe continued to call it.

Mrs. Shelby smiled as she saw a prostrate lot of chickens and ducks, over which Chloe stood, with a very grave face of consideration.

"I'm a thinkin whether Missis would be a havin a chicken pie o' dese yer."

"Really, Aunt Chloe, I don't much care;—serve them any way you like."

Chloe stood handling them over abstractedly; it was quite evident that the chickens were not what she was thinking of. At last, with the short laugh with which her tribe often introduce a doubtful proposal, she said,

"Laws me, Missis! what should Mas'r and Missis be a troublin theirselves 'bout de money, and not a usin what's right in der hands?" and Chloe laughed again.

"I don't understand you, Chloe," said Mrs. Shelby, nothing doubting, from her knowledge of Chloe's manner, that she had heard every word of the conversation that had passed between her and her husband.

"Why, laws me, Missis!" said Chloe, laughing again, "other folks hires out der niggers and makes money on 'em! Don't keep sich a tribe eatin 'em out of house and home."

"Well, Chloe, who do you propose that we should hire out?"

"Laws! I an't a proposin nothin; only Sam he said der was one of dese yer *perfectioners*, dey calls 'em, in Louisville, said he wanted a good hand at cake and pastry; and said he'd give four dollars a week to one, he did."

"Well, Chloe."

"Well, laws, I's a thinkin, Missis, it's time Sally was put along to be doin' something. Sally's been under my care, now, dis some time, and she does most as well as me, considerin; and if Missis would only let me go, I would help fetch up de money. I an't afraid to put my cake, nor pies nother, 'long side no *perfectioner's*."

"Confectioner's, Chloe."

"Law sakes, Missis! 'tan't no odds;—words is so curis, can't never get 'em right!"

"But, Chloe, do you want to leave your children?"

"Laws, Missis! de boys is big enough to do day's works; dey does well enough; and Sally, she'll take de baby,—she's such a peart young un, she won't take no lookin arter."

"Louisville is a good way off."

"Law sakes! who's afeard?—it's down river, somer near my old man, perhaps?" said Chloe, speaking the last in the tone of a question, and looking at Mrs. Shelby.

"No, Chloe; it's many a hundred miles off," said Mrs. Shelby.

Chloe's countenance fell.

"Never mind; your going there shall bring you nearer, Chloe. Yes, you may go; and your wages shall every cent of them be laid aside for your husband's redemption."

As when a bright sunbeam turns a dark cloud to silver, so Chloe's dark face brightened immediately,—it really shone.

"Laws! if Missis isn't too good! I was thinking of dat ar very thing; cause I shouldn't need no clothes, nor shoes, nor nothin,—I could save every cent. How many weeks is der in a year, Missis?"

"Fifty-two," said Mrs. Shelby.

"Laws! now, dere is? and four dollars for each on 'em. Why, how much'd dat ar be?"

"Two hundred and eight dollars," said Mrs. Shelby.

"Why-e!" said Chloe, with an accent of surprise and delight; "and how long would it take me to work it out, Missis?"

"Some four or five years, Chloe; but, then, you needn't do it all,—I shall add something to it."

"I wouldn't hear to Missis' givin lessons nor nothin. Mas'r's quite right in dat ar;—'t wouldn't do, no ways. I hope none our family ever be brought to dat ar, while I's got hands."

"Don't fear, Chloe; I'll take care of the honor of the family," said Mrs. Shelby, smiling. "But when do you expect to go?"

"Well, I want spectin nothin; only Sam, he's a gwine to de river with some colts, and he said I could go long with him; so I jes put my things together. If Missis was willin, I'd go with Sam to-morrow morning, if Missis would write my pass, and write me a commendation."

"Well, Chloe, I'll attend to it, if Mr. Shelby has no objections. I must speak to him."

Mrs. Shelby went up stairs, and Aunt Chloe, delighted, went out to her cabin, to make her preparation.

"Law sakes, Mas'r George! ye didn't know I's a gwine to Louisville tomorrow!" she said to George, as, entering her cabin, he found her busy in sorting over her baby's clothes. "I thought I'd jis look over sis's things, and get 'em straightened up. But I'm gwine, Mas'r George,—gwine to have four dollars a week; and Missis is gwine to lay it all up, to buy back my old man agin!"

"Whew!" said George, "here's a stroke of business, to be sure! How are you going?"

"To-morrow, wid Sam. And now, Mas'r George, I knows you'll jis sit down and write to my old man, and tell him all about it,—won't ye?"

"To be sure," said George; "Uncle Tom'll be right glad to hear from us. I'll go right in the house, for paper and ink; and then, you know, Aunt Chloe, I can tell about the new colts and all."

"Sartin, sartin, Mas'r George; you go 'long, and I'll get ye up a bit o'chicken, or some sich; ye won't have many more suppers wid yer poor old aunty."

## Chapter XXII

### *"The Grass Withereth—the Flower Fadeth"*[1]

Life passes, with us all, a day at a time; so it passed with our friend Tom, till two years were gone. Though parted from all his soul held dear, and though often yearning for what lay beyond, still was he never positively and consciously miserable; for, so well is the harp of human feeling strung, that nothing but a crash that breaks every string can wholly mar its harmony; and, on looking back to seasons which in review appear to us as those of deprivation and trial, we can remember that each hour, as it glided, brought its diversions and alleviations, so that, though not happy wholly, we were not, either, wholly miserable.

Tom read, in his only literary cabinet, of one who had "learned in whatsoever state he was, therewith to be content."[2] It seemed to him good and reasonable doctrine, and accorded well with the settled and thoughtful habit which he had acquired from the reading of that same book.

His letter homeward, as we related in the last chapter, was in due time answered by Master George, in a good, round, school-boy hand, that Tom said might be read "most acrost the room." It contained various refreshing items of home intelligence, with which our reader is fully acquainted: stated how Aunt Chloe had been hired out to a confectioner in Louisville, where her skill in the pastry line was gaining wonderful sums of money, all of which, Tom was informed, was to be laid up to go to make up the sum of his redemption money; Mose and Pete were thriving, and the baby was trotting all about the house, under the care of Sally and the family generally.

Tom's cabin was shut up for the present; but George expatiated brilliantly on ornaments and additions to be made to it when Tom came back.

The rest of this letter gave a list of George's school studies, each one headed by a flourishing capital; and also told the names of four new colts that appeared on the premises since Tom left; and stated, in the same connection, that father and mother were well. The style

1. See Isaiah 40.6 and 1 Peter 1.24.
2. "Not that I speak in respect of want: for I have learned, in whatsoever state I am, therewith to be content" (Philippians 4.11).

of the letter was decidedly concise and terse; but Tom thought it the most wonderful specimen of composition that had appeared in modern times. He was never tired of looking at it, and even held a council with Eva on the expediency of getting it framed, to hang up in his room. Nothing but the difficulty of arranging it so that both sides of the page would show at once stood in the way of this undertaking.

The friendship between Tom and Eva had grown with the child's growth. It would be hard to say what place she held in the soft, impressible heart of her faithful attendant. He loved her as something frail and earthly, yet almost worshipped her as something heavenly and divine. He gazed on her as the Italian sailor gazes on his image of the child Jesus,—with a mixture of reverence and tenderness; and to humor her graceful fancies, and meet those thousand simple wants which invest childhood like a many-colored rainbow, was Tom's chief delight. In the market, at morning, his eyes were always on the flower-stalls for rare bouquets for her, and the choicest peach or orange was slipped into his pocket to give to her when he came back; and the sight that pleased him most was her sunny head looking out the gate for his distant approach, and her childish question,—"Well, Uncle Tom, what have you got for me to-day?"

Nor was Eva less zealous in kind offices, in return. Though a child, she was a beautiful reader;—a fine musical ear, a quick poetic fancy, and an instinctive sympathy with what is grand and noble, made her such a reader of the Bible as Tom had never before heard. At first, she read to please her humble friend; but soon her own earnest nature threw out its tendrils, and wound itself around the majestic book; and Eva loved it, because it woke in her strange yearnings, and strong, dim emotions, such as impassioned, imaginative children love to feel.

The parts that pleased her most were the Revelations and the Prophecies,[3]—parts whose dim and wondrous imagery, and fervent language, impressed her the more, that she questioned vainly of their meaning;—and she and her simple friend, the old child and the young one, felt just alike about it. All that they knew was, that they spoke of a glory to be revealed,—a wondrous something yet to come, wherein their soul rejoiced, yet knew not why; and though it be not so in the physical, yet in moral science that which cannot be understood is not always profitless. For the soul awakes, a trembling stranger, between two dim eternities,—the eternal past, the eternal future. The light shines only on a small space around her; there-

3. The Old Testament books of Joshua, Judges, 1 and 2 Samuel, 1 and 2 Kings, Isaiah, Jeremiah, Ezekiel, Hosea, Joel, Amos, Obadiah, Jonah, Micah, Nahum, Habakkuk, Zephaniah, Haggai, Zechariah, and Malachi.

Little Eva reading the Bible to Uncle Tom in the arbor.

fore, she needs must yearn towards the unknown; and the voices and shadowy movings which come to her from out the cloudy pillar of inspiration have each one echoes and answers in her own expecting nature. Its mystic imagery are so many talismans and gems inscribed with unknown hieroglyphics; she folds them in her bosom, and expects to read them when she passes beyond the veil.

At this time in our story, the whole St. Clare establishment is, for the time being, removed to their villa on Lake Pontchartrain. The heats of summer had driven all who were able to leave the sultry and unhealthy city, to seek the shores of the lake, and its cool sea-breezes.

St. Clare's villa was an East Indian cottage,[4] surrounded by light verandahs of bamboo-work, and opening on all sides into gardens and pleasure-grounds. The common sitting-room opened on to a large garden, fragrant with every picturesque plant and flower of the tropics, where winding paths ran down to the very shores of the lake, whose silvery sheet of water lay there, rising and falling in the sunbeams,—a picture never for an hour the same, yet every hour more beautiful.

It is now one of those intensely golden sunsets which kindles the whole horizon into one blaze of glory, and makes the water another sky. The lake lay in rosy or golden streaks, save where white-winged vessels glided hither and thither, like so many spirits, and little golden stars twinkled through the glow, and looked down at themselves as they trembled in the water.

Tom and Eva were seated on a little mossy seat, in an arbor, at the foot of the garden. It was Sunday evening, and Eva's Bible lay open on her knee. She read,—"And I saw a sea of glass, mingled with fire."[5]

"Tom," said Eva, suddenly stopping, and pointing to the lake, "there 'tis."

"What, Miss Eva?"

"Don't you see,—there?" said the child, pointing to the glassy water, which, as it rose and fell, reflected the golden glow of the sky. "There's a 'sea of glass, mingled with fire.'"

"True enough, Miss Eva," said Tom; and Tom sang—

> "O, had I the wings of the morning,
> I'd fly away to Canaan's shore;
> Bright angels should convey me home,
> To the new Jerusalem."[6]

4. I.e., influenced by the architecture of the East Indies (India, Indonesia, Malaysia); most likely a one-story bungalow with wide porches, designed for hot weather.
5. "And I saw as it were a sea of glass mingled with fire: and them that had gotten the victory over the beast, and over his image, and over his mark, and over the number of his name, stand on the sea of glass, having the harps of God" (Revelation 15.2).
6. From the spiritual "Wings of the Morning" or "Western Melody."

"Where do you suppose new Jerusalem is, Uncle Tom?" said Eva.

"O, up in the clouds, Miss Eva."

"Then I think I see it," said Eva. "Look in those clouds!—they look like great gates of pearl;[7] and you can see beyond them—far, far off—it's all gold. Tom, sing about 'spirits bright.'"

Tom sung the words of a well-known Methodist hymn,

> "I see a band of spirits bright,
> That taste the glories there;
> They all are robed in spotless white,
> And conquering palms they bear."[8]

"Uncle Tom, I've seen *them*," said Eva.

Tom had no doubt of it at all; it did not surprise him in the least. If Eva had told him she had been to heaven, he would have thought it entirely probable.

"They come to me sometimes in my sleep, those spirits;" and Eva's eyes grew dreamy, and she hummed, in a low voice,

> "They are all robed in spotless white,
> And conquering palms they bear."

"Uncle Tom," said Eva, "I'm going there."

"Where, Miss Eva?"

The child rose, and pointed her little hand to the sky; the glow of evening lit her golden hair and flushed cheek with a kind of unearthly radiance, and her eyes were bent earnestly on the skies.

"I'm going *there,*" she said, "to the spirits bright, Tom; *I'm going, before long.*"

The faithful old heart felt a sudden thrust; and Tom thought how often he had noticed, within six months, that Eva's little hands had grown thinner, and her skin more transparent, and her breath shorter; and how, when she ran or played in the garden, as she once could for hours, she became soon so tired and languid. He had heard Miss Ophelia speak often of a cough, that all her medicaments could not cure; and even now that fervent cheek and little hand were burning with hectic fever; and yet the thought that Eva's words suggested had never come to him till now.

Has there ever been a child like Eva? Yes, there have been; but their names are always on grave-stones, and their sweet smiles, their heavenly eyes, their singular words and ways, are among the buried treasures of yearning hearts. In how many families do you hear the legend that all the goodness and graces of the living are nothing to the peculiar charms of one who *is not*. It is as if heaven had an

7. See Revelation 21.10–12, 21.
8. This hymn is based on Revelation 7.9.

especial band of angels, whose office it was to sojourn for a season here, and endear to them the wayward human heart, that they might bear it upward with them in their homeward flight. When you see that deep, spiritual light in the eye,—when the little soul reveals itself in words sweeter and wiser than the ordinary words of children,—hope not to retain that child; for the seal of heaven is on it, and the light of immortality looks out from its eyes.

Even so, beloved Eva! fair star of thy dwelling! Thou art passing away; but they that love thee dearest know it not.

The colloquy between Tom and Eva was interrupted by a hasty call from Miss Ophelia.

"Eva—Eva!—why, child, the dew is falling; you mustn't be out there!"

Eva and Tom hastened in.

Miss Ophelia was old, and skilled in the tactics of nursing. She was from New England, and knew well the first guileful footsteps of that soft, insidious disease,[9] which sweeps away so many of the fairest and loveliest, and before one fibre of life seems broken, seals them irrevocably for death.

She had noted the slight, dry cough, the daily brightening cheek; nor could the lustre of the eye, and the airy buoyancy born of fever, deceive her.

She tried to communicate her fears to St. Clare; but he threw back her suggestions with a restless petulance, unlike his usual careless good-humor.

"Don't be croaking, Cousin,—I hate it!" he would say; "don't you see that the child is only growing. Children always lose strength when they grow fast."

"But she has that cough!"

"O! nonsense of that cough!—it is not anything. She has taken a little cold, perhaps."

"Well, that was just the way Eliza Jane was taken, and Ellen and Maria Sanders."

"O! stop these hobgoblin' nurse legends. You old hands got so wise, that a child cannot cough, or sneeze, but you see desperation and ruin at hand. Only take care of the child, keep her from the night air, and don't let her play too hard, and she'll do well enough."

So St. Clare said; but he grew nervous and restless. He watched Eva feverishly day by day, as might be told by the frequency with which he repeated over that "the child was quite well"—that there wasn't anything in that cough,—it was only some little stomach affection, such as children often had. But he kept by her more than before, took her oftener to ride with him, brought home every few

9. Tuberculosis, also called consumption.

days some receipt or strengthening mixture,—"not," he said, "that the child *needed* it, but then it would not do her any harm."

If it must be told, the thing that struck a deeper pang to his heart than anything else was the daily increasing maturity of the child's mind and feelings. While still retaining all a child's fanciful graces, yet she often dropped, unconsciously, words of such a reach of thought, and strange unworldly wisdom, that they seemed to be an inspiration. At such times, St. Clare would feel a sudden thrill, and clasp her in his arms, as if that fond clasp could save her; and his heart rose up with wild determination to keep her, never to let her go.

The child's whole heart and soul seemed absorbed in works of love and kindness. Impulsively generous she had always been; but there was a touching and womanly thoughtfulness about her now, that every one noticed. She still loved to play with Topsy, and the various colored children; but she now seemed rather a spectator than an actor of their plays, and she would sit for half an hour at a time, laughing at the odd tricks of Topsy,—and then a shadow would seem to pass across her face, her eyes grew misty, and her thoughts were afar.

"Mamma," she said, suddenly, to her mother, one day, "why don't we teach our servants to read?"

"What a question, child! People never do."

"Why don't they?" said Eva.

"Because it is no use for them to read. It don't help them to work any better, and they are not made for anything else."

"But they ought to read the Bible, mamma, to learn God's will."

"O! they can get that read to them all *they* need."

"It seems to me, mamma, the Bible is for every one to read themselves. They need it a great many times when there is nobody to read it."

"Eva, you are an odd child," said her mother.

"Miss Ophelia has taught Topsy to read," continued Eva.

"Yes, and you see how much good it does. Topsy is the worst creature I ever saw!"

"Here's poor Mammy!" said Eva. "She does love the Bible so much, and wishes so she could read! And what will she do when I can't read to her?"

Marie was busy, turning over the contents of a drawer, as she answered,

"Well, of course, by and by, Eva, you will have other things to think of, besides reading the Bible round to servants. Not but that is very proper; I've done it myself, when I had health. But when you come to be dressing and going into company, you won't have time. See here!" she added, "these jewels I'm going to give you when you come out. I wore them to my first ball. I can tell you, Eva, I made a sensation."

Eva took the jewel-case, and lifted from it a diamond necklace. Her large, thoughtful eyes rested on them, but it was plain her thoughts were elsewhere.

"How sober you look, child!" said Marie.

"Are these worth a great deal of money, mamma?"

"To be sure, they are. Father sent to France for them. They are worth a small fortune."

"I wish I had them," said Eva, "to do what I pleased with!"

"What would you do with them?"

"I'd sell them, and buy a place in the free states, and take all our people there, and hire teachers, to teach them to read and write."

Eva was cut short by her mother's laughing.

"Set up a boarding-school! Wouldn't you teach them to play on the piano, and paint on velvet?"

"I'd teach them to read their own Bible, and write their own letters, and read letters that are written to them," said Eva, steadily. "I know, mamma, it does come very hard on them, that they can't do these things. Tom feels it,—Mammy does,—a great many of them do. I think it's wrong."

"Come, come, Eva; you are only a child! You don't know anything about these things," said Marie; "besides, your talking makes my head ache."

Marie always had a head-ache on hand for any conversation that did not exactly suit her.

Eva stole away; but after that, she assiduously gave Mammy reading lessons.

## Chapter XXIII

### *Henrique*

About this time, St. Clare's brother Alfred, with his eldest son, a boy of twelve, spent a day or two with the family at the lake.

No sight could be more singular and beautiful than that of these twin brothers. Nature, instead of instituting resemblances between them, had made them opposites on every point; yet a mysterious tie seemed to unite them in a closer friendship than ordinary.

They used to saunter, arm in arm, up and down the alleys and walks of the garden. Augustine, with his blue eyes and golden hair, his ethereally flexible form and vivacious features; and Alfred, dark-eyed, with haughty Roman profile, firmly-knit limbs, and decided bearing. They were always abusing each other's opinions and practices, and yet never a whit the less absorbed in each other's society; in fact, the very contrariety seemed to unite them, like the attraction between opposite poles of the magnet.

Henrique, the eldest son of Alfred, was a noble, dark-eyed, princely boy, full of vivacity and spirit; and, from the first moment of introduction, seemed to be perfectly fascinated by the spirituelle graces of his cousin Evangeline.

Eva had a little pet pony, of a snowy whiteness. It was easy as a cradle, and as gentle as its little mistress; and this pony was now brought up to the back verandah by Tom, while a little mulatto boy of about thirteen led along a small black Arabian,[1] which had just been imported, at a great expense, for Henrique.

Henrique had a boy's pride in his new possession; and, as he advanced and took the reins out of the hands of his little groom, he looked carefully over him, and his brow darkened.

"What's this, Dodo, you little lazy dog! you haven't rubbed my horse down, this morning."

"Yes, Mas'r," said Dodo, submissively; "he got that dust on his own self."

"You rascal, shut your mouth!" said Henrique, violently raising his riding-whip. "How dare you speak?"

The boy was a handsome, bright-eyed mulatto, of just Henrique's size, and his curling hair hung round a high, bold forehead. He had white blood in his veins, as could be seen by the quick flush in his cheek, and the sparkle of his eye, as he eagerly tried to speak.

"Mas'r Henrique!—" he began.

Henrique struck him across the face with his riding-whip, and, seizing one of his arms, forced him on to his knees, and beat him till he was out of breath.

"There, you impudent dog! Now will you learn not to answer back when I speak to you? Take the horse back, and clean him properly. I'll teach you your place!"

"Young Mas'r," said Tom, "I specs what he was gwine to say was, that the horse would roll when he was bringing him up from the stable; he's so full of spirits,—that's the way he got that dirt on him; I looked to his cleaning."

"You hold your tongue till you're asked to speak!" said Henrique, turning on his heel, and walking up the steps to speak to Eva, who stood in her riding-dress.

"Dear Cousin, I'm sorry this stupid fellow has kept you waiting," he said. "Let's sit down here, on this seat, till they come. What's the matter, Cousin?—you look sober."

"How could you be so cruel and wicked to poor Dodo?" said Eva.

1. A horse of a breed originating in North Africa.

"Cruel,—wicked!" said the boy, with unaffected surprise. "What do you mean, dear Eva?"

"I don't want you to call me dear Eva, when you do so," said Eva.

"Dear Cousin, you don't know Dodo; it's the only way to manage him, he's so full of lies and excuses. The only way is to put him down at once,—not let him open his mouth; that's the way papa manages."

"But Uncle Tom said it was an accident, and he never tells what isn't true."

"He's an uncommon old nigger, then!" said Henrique. "Dodo will lie as fast as he can speak."

"You frighten him into deceiving, if you treat him so."

"Why, Eva, you've really taken such a fancy to Dodo, that I shall be jealous."

"But you beat him,—and he didn't deserve it."

"O, well, it may go for some time when he does, and don't get it. A few cuts never come amiss with Dodo,—he's a regular spirit, I can tell you; but I won't beat him again before you, if it troubles you."

Eva was not satisfied, but found it in vain to try to make her handsome cousin understand her feelings.

Dodo soon appeared, with the horses.

"Well, Dodo, you've done pretty well, this time," said his young master, with a more gracious air. "Come, now, and hold Miss Eva's horse, while I put her on to the saddle."

Dodo came and stood by Eva's pony. His face was troubled; his eyes looked as if he had been crying.

Henrique, who valued himself on his gentlemanly adroitness in all matters of gallantry, soon had his fair cousin in the saddle, and, gathering the reins, placed them in her hands.

But Eva bent to the other side of the horse, where Dodo was standing, and said, as he relinquished the reins,—"That's a good boy, Dodo;—thank you!"

Dodo looked up in amazement into the sweet young face; the blood rushed to his cheeks, and the tears to his eyes.

"Here, Dodo," said his master, imperiously.

Dodo sprang and held the horse, while his master mounted.

"There's a picayune for you to buy candy with, Dodo," said Henrique; "go get some."

And Henrique cantered down the walk after Eva. Dodo stood looking after the two children. One had given him money; and one had given him what he wanted far more,—a kind word, kindly spoken. Dodo had been only a few months away from his mother. His master had bought him at a slave warehouse, for his handsome face, to be a match to the handsome pony; and he was now getting his breaking in, at the hands of his young master.

The scene of the beating had been witnessed by the two brothers St. Clare, from another part of the garden.

Augustine's cheek flushed; but he only observed, with his usual sarcastic carelessness,

"I suppose that's what we may call republican education, Alfred?"

"Henrique is a devil of a fellow, when his blood's up," said Alfred, carelessly.

"I suppose you consider this an instructive practice for him," said Augustine, drily.

"I couldn't help it, if I didn't. Henrique is a regular little tempest;—his mother and I have given him up, long ago. But, then, that Dodo is a perfect sprite,—no amount of whipping can hurt him."

"And this by way of teaching Henrique the first verse of a republican's catechism, 'All men are born free and equal!'"[2]

"Poh!" said Alfred; "one of Tom Jefferson's pieces of French sentiment and humbug. It's perfectly ridiculous to have that going the rounds among us, to this day."

"I think it is," said St. Clare, significantly.

"Because," said Alfred, "we can see plainly enough that all men are *not* born free, nor born equal; they are born anything else. For my part, I think half this republican talk sheer humbug. It is the educated, the intelligent, the wealthy, the refined, who ought to have equal rights, and not the canaille."[3]

"If you can keep the canaille of that opinion," said Augustine. "They took *their* turn once, in France."

"Of course, they must be *kept* down, consistently, steadily, as I *should*," said Alfred, setting his foot hard down, as if he were standing on somebody.

"It makes a terrible slip when they get up," said Augustine,—"in St. Domingo, for instance."[4]

"Poh!" said Alfred, "we'll take care of that, in this country. We must set our face against all this educating, elevating talk, that is getting about now; the lower class must not be educated."

"That is past praying for," said Augustine; "educated they will be, and we have only to say how. Our system is educating them in barbarism and brutality. We are breaking all humanizing ties, and making them brute beasts; and, if they get the upper hand, such we shall find them."

2. Stowe seems to combine Thomas Jefferson's Declaration of Independence ("All men are created equal . . .") with a line from the Constitution of Massachusetts (1779) by John Adams: "All men are born free and equal and have certain natural, essential, unalienable rights."
3. Mob, rabble, riffraff.
4. The former French name of Haiti. This island country in the Caribbean was a French colony from the mid-seventeenth century until 1804, when the slaves rebelled and declared their independence.

"They never shall get the upper hand!" said Alfred.

"That's right," said St. Clare; "put on the steam, fasten down the escape-valve, and sit on it, and see where you'll land."

"Well," said Alfred, "we *will* see. I'm not afraid to sit on the escape-valve, as long as the boilers are strong, and the machinery works well."

"The nobles in Louis XVI.'s time thought just so; and Austria and Pius IX. think so now;[5] and, some pleasant morning, you may all be caught up to meet each other in the air, *when the boilers burst.*"

"*Dies declarabit*,"[6] said Alfred, laughing.

"I tell you," said Augustine, "if there is anything that is revealed with the strength of a divine law in our times, it is that the masses are to rise, and the under class become the upper one."

"That's one of your red republican humbugs, Augustine! Why didn't you ever take to the stump;—you'd make a famous stump orator![7] Well, I hope I shall be dead before this millennium of your greasy masses comes on."

"Greasy or not greasy, they will govern *you*, when their time comes," said Augustine; "and they will be just such rulers as you make them. The French noblesse chose to have the people '*sans culottes*,'[8] and they had '*sans culotte*' governors to their hearts' content. The people of Hayti[9]—"

"O, come, Augustine! as if we hadn't had enough of that abominable, contemptible Hayti! The Haytiens were not Anglo Saxons; if they had been, there would have been another story. The Anglo Saxon is the dominant race of the world, and *is to be so.*"

"Well, there is a pretty fair infusion of Anglo Saxon blood among our slaves, now," said Augustine. "There are plenty among them who have only enough of the African to give a sort of tropical warmth and fervor to our calculating firmness and foresight. If ever the San Domingo hour comes, Anglo Saxon blood will lead on the day. Sons of white fathers, with all our haughty feelings burning in their veins, will not always be bought and sold and traded. They will rise, and raise with them their mother's race."

"Stuff!—nonsense!"

5. Pius IX (1792–1878) was pope from 1846 to 1878. Driven out of Rome in 1848 during rioting by Italian nationalists, he returned in 1850 but in 1870 was forced to retreat to the Vatican after refusing to recognize the new Italian state. Louis XVI (1754–93), king of France from 1774 to 1792, was guillotined during the French Revolution. The empire of Austria was shaken in 1848 by rebellions in Vienna, Italy, Bohemia, and Hungary.
6. Literally, "the day will declare" (Latin); i.e., time will tell.
7. One who speaks to the general public as part of a political campaign or in support of a cause.
8. The *sans culottes* were members of the Republican party in France during the Revolution (1789); the term can also refer to any political extremists.
9. Also *Haiti*; see above, p. 245, n. 4.

"Well," said Augustine, "there goes an old saying to this effect 'As it was in the days of Noah, so shall it be;—they ate, they drank, they planted, they builded, and knew not till the flood came and took them.' "[1]

"On the whole, Augustine, I think your talents might do for a circuit rider,"[2] said Alfred, laughing. "Never you fear for us; possession is our nine points. We've got the power. This subject race," said he, stamping firmly, "is down, and shall *stay* down! We have energy enough to manage our own powder."

"Sons trained like your Henrique will be grand guardians of your powder-magazines,"[3] said Augustine,—"so cool and self-possessed! The proverb says, 'They that cannot govern themselves cannot govern others.' "[4]

"There is a trouble there," said Alfred, thoughtfully; "there's no doubt that our system is a difficult one to train children under. It gives too free scope to the passions, altogether, which, in our climate, are hot enough. I find trouble with Henrique. The boy is generous and warm-hearted, but a perfect fire-cracker when excited. I believe I shall send him North for his education, where obedience is more fashionable, and where he will associate more with equals, and less with dependants."

"Since training children is the staple work of the human race," said Augustine, "I should think it something of a consideration that our system does not work well there."

"It does not for some things," said Alfred; "for others, again, it does. It makes boys manly and courageous; and the very vices of an abject race tend to strengthen in them the opposite virtues. I think Henrique, now, has a keener sense of the beauty of truth, from seeing lying and deception the universal badge of slavery."

"A Christian-like view of the subject, certainly!" said Augustine.

"It's true, Christian-like or not; and is about as Christian-like as most other things in the world," said Alfred.

"That may be," said St. Clare.

"Well, there's no use in talking, Augustine. I believe we've been round and round this old track five hundred times, more or less. What do you say to a game of backgammon?"

1. Noah was a patriarch commanded by God to build an ark in which his family and two of every kind of animal survived a global flood sent by God to punish the world (see Genesis 5.28–10.32). In Matthew 24.37–39, Christ makes a lesson of the people who refused to believe the prophecies of the Flood: "they were eating and drinking, marrying and giving in marriage, until the day that Noah entered into the ark, And knew not until the flood came, and took them all away; so shall also the coming of the Son of man be."
2. An itinerant Methodist preacher.
3. Storage rooms for explosives.
4. Perhaps an adaptation of "He that would govern others, first should be master of himself," from *The Bondsman* (1.3) by Philip Massinger (1583–1640).

The two brothers ran up the verandah steps, and were soon seated at a light bamboo stand, with the backgammon-board between them. As they were setting their men, Alfred said,

"I tell you, Augustine, if I thought as you do, I should do something."

"I dare say you would,—you are one of the doing sort,—but what?"

"Why, elevate your own servants, for a specimen," said Alfred, with a half-scornful smile.

"You might as well set Mount Ætna[5] on them flat, and tell them to stand up under it, as tell me to elevate my servants under all the superincumbent mass of society upon them. One man can do nothing, against the whole action of a community. Education, to do anything, must be a state education; or there must be enough agreed in it to make a current."

"You take the first throw," said Alfred; and the brothers were soon lost in the game, and heard no more till the scraping of horses' feet was heard under the verandah.

"There come the children," said Augustine, rising. "Look here, Alf! Did you ever see anything so beautiful?" And, in truth, it *was* a beautiful sight. Henrique, with his bold brow, and dark, glossy curls, and glowing cheek, was laughing gayly, as he bent towards his fair cousin, as they came on. She was dressed in a blue riding-dress, with a cap of the same color. Exercise had given a brilliant hue to her cheeks, and heightened the effect of her singularly transparent skin, and golden hair.

"Good heavens! what perfectly dazzling beauty!" said Alfred. "I tell you, Auguste, won't she make some hearts ache, one of these days?"

"She will, too truly,—God knows I'm afraid so!" said St. Clare, in a tone of sudden bitterness, as he hurried down to take her off her horse.

"Eva, darling! you're not much tired?" he said, as he clasped her in his arms.

"No, papa," said the child; but her short, hard breathing alarmed her father.

"How could you ride so fast, dear?—you know it's bad for you."

"I felt so well, papa, and liked it so much, I forgot."

St. Clare carried her in his arms into the parlor, and laid her on the sofa.

"Henrique, you must be careful of Eva," said he; "you mustn't ride fast with her."

"I'll take her under my care," said Henrique, seating himself by the sofa, and taking Eva's hand.

5. Volcanic mountain on the east coast of Sicily.

Eva soon found herself much better. Her father and uncle resumed their game, and the children were left together.

"Do you know, Eva, I'm so sorry papa is only going to stay two days here, and then I shan't see you again for ever so long! If I stay with you, I'd try to be good, and not be cross to Dodo, and so on. I don't mean to treat Dodo ill; but, you know, I've got such a quick temper. I'm not really bad to him, though. I give him a picayune, now and then; and you see he dresses well. I think, on the whole, Dodo's pretty well off."

"Would you think you were well off, if there were not one creature in the world near you to love you?"

"I?—Well, of course not."

"And you have taken Dodo away from all the friends he ever had, and now he has not a creature to love him;—nobody can be good that way."

"Well, I can't help it, as I know of. I can't get his mother, and I can't love him myself, nor anybody else, as I know of."

"Why can't you?" said Eva.

"*Love* Dodo! Why, Eva, you wouldn't have me! I may *like* him well enough; but you don't *love* your servants."

"I do, indeed."

"How odd!"

"Don't the Bible say we must love everybody?"[6]

"O, the Bible! To be sure, it says a great many such things; but, then, nobody ever thinks of doing them,—you know, Eva, nobody does."

Eva did not speak; her eyes were fixed and thoughtful, for a few moments.

"At any rate," she said, "dear Cousin, do love poor Dodo, and be kind to him, for my sake!"

"I could love anything, for your sake, dear Cousin; for I really think you are the loveliest creature that I ever saw!" And Henrique spoke with an earnestness that flushed his handsome face. Eva received it with perfect simplicity, without even a change of feature; merely saying, "I'm glad you feel so, dear Henrique! I hope you will remember."

The dinner-bell put an end to the interview.

# Chapter XXIV

## *Foreshadowings*

Two days after this, Alfred St. Clare and Augustine parted; and Eva, who had been stimulated, by the society of her young cousin, to

6. See, e.g., Leviticus 19.18; Matthew 5.43, 19.19, and 22.39; Mark 12.31; Luke 10.27; and Romans 13.9.

exertions beyond her strength, began to fail rapidly. St. Clare was at last willing to call in medical advice,—a thing from which he had always shrunk, because it was the admission of an unwelcome truth.

But, for a day or two, Eva was so unwell as to be confined to the house; and the doctor was called.

Marie St. Clare had taken no notice of the child's gradually decaying health and strength, because she was completely absorbed in studying out two or three new forms of disease to which she believed she herself was a victim. It was the first principle of Marie's belief that nobody ever was or could be so great a sufferer as *herself*; and, therefore, she always repelled quite indignantly any suggestion that any one around her could be sick. She was always sure, in such a case, that it was nothing but laziness, or want of energy; and that, if they had had the suffering *she* had, they would soon know the difference.

Miss Ophelia had several times tried to awaken her maternal fears about Eva; but to no avail.

"I don't see as anything ails the child," she would say; "she runs about, and plays."

"But she has a cough."

"Cough! you don't need to tell *me* about a cough. I've always been subject to a cough, all my days. When I was of Eva's age, they thought I was in a consumption. Night after night, Mammy used to sit up with me. O! Eva's cough is not anything."

"But she gets weak, and is short-breathed."

"Law! I've had that, years and years; it's only a nervous affection."

"But she sweats so, nights!"

"Well, I have, these ten years. Very often, night after night, my clothes will be wringing wet. There won't be a dry thread in my night-clothes, and the sheets will be so that Mammy has to hang them up to dry! Eva doesn't sweat anything like that!"

Miss Ophelia shut her mouth for a season. But, now that Eva was fairly and visibly prostrated, and a doctor called, Marie, all on a sudden, took a new turn.

"She knew it," she said; "she always felt it, that she was destined to be the most miserable of mothers. Here she was, with her wretched health, and her only darling child going down to the grave before her eyes;"—and Marie routed up Mammy nights, and rumpussed and scolded, with more energy than ever, all day, on the strength of this new misery.

"My dear Marie, don't talk so!" said St. Clare. "You ought not to give up the case so, at once."

"You have not a mother's feelings, St. Clare! You never could understand me!—you don't now."

"But don't talk so, as if it were a gone case!"

"I can't take it as indifferently as you can, St. Clare. If *you* don't feel when your only child is in this alarming state, *I* do. It's a blow too much for me, with all I was bearing before."

"It's true," said St. Clare, "that Eva is very delicate, *that* I always knew; and that she has grown so rapidly as to exhaust her strength; and that her situation is critical. But just now she is only prostrated by the heat of the weather, and by the excitement of her cousin's visit, and the exertions she made. The physician says there is room for hope."

"Well, of course, if you can look on the bright side, pray do; it's a mercy if people haven't sensitive feelings, in this world. I am sure I wish I didn't feel as I do; it only makes me completely wretched! I wish I *could* be as easy as the rest of you!"

And the "rest of them" had good reason to breathe the same prayer, for Marie paraded her new misery as the reason and apology for all sorts of inflictions on every one about her. Every word that was spoken by anybody, everything that was done or was not done everywhere, was only a new proof that she was surrounded by hard-hearted, insensible beings, who were unmindful of her peculiar sorrows. Poor Eva heard some of these speeches; and nearly cried her little eyes out, in pity for her mamma, and in sorrow that she should make her so much distress.

In a week or two, there was a great improvement of symptoms,—one of those deceitful lulls, by which her inexorable disease so often beguiles the anxious heart, even on the verge of the grave. Eva's step was again in the garden,—in the balconies; she played and laughed again,—and her father, in a transport, declared that they should soon have her as hearty as anybody. Miss Ophelia and the physician alone felt no encouragement from this illusive truce. There was one other heart, too, that felt the same certainty, and that was the little heart of Eva. What is it that sometimes speaks in the soul so calmly, so clearly, that its earthly time is short? Is it the secret instinct of decaying nature, or the soul's impulsive throb, as immortality draws on? Be it what it may, it rested in the heart of Eva, a calm, sweet, prophetic certainty that Heaven was near; calm as the light of sunset, sweet as the bright stillness of autumn, there her little heart reposed, only troubled by sorrow for those who loved her so dearly.

For the child, though nursed so tenderly, and though life was unfolding before her with every brightness that love and wealth could give, had no regret for herself in dying.

In that book which she and her simple old friend had read so much together, she had seen and taken to her young heart the image of one who loved the little child; and, as she gazed and mused, He had ceased to be an image and a picture of the distant past, and come to be a living, all-surrounding reality. His love enfolded her childish heart with more than mortal tenderness; and it was to Him, she said, she was going, and to his home.

But her heart yearned with sad tenderness for all that she was to leave behind. Her father most,—for Eva, though she never distinctly thought so, had an instinctive perception that she was more in his heart than any other. She loved her mother because she was so loving a creature, and all the selfishness that she had seen in her only saddened and perplexed her; for she had a child's implicit trust that her mother could not do wrong. There was something about her that Eva never could make out; and she always smoothed it over with thinking that, after all, it was mamma, and she loved her very dearly indeed.

She felt, too, for those fond, faithful servants, to whom she was as daylight and sunshine. Children do not usually generalize; but Eva was an uncommonly mature child, and the things that she had witnessed of the evils of the system under which they were living had fallen, one by one, into the depths of her thoughtful, pondering heart. She had vague longings to do something for them,—to bless and save not only them, but all in their condition,—longings that contrasted sadly with the feebleness of her little frame.

"Uncle Tom," she said, one day, when she was reading to her friend, "I can understand why Jesus *wanted* to die for us."

"Why, Miss Eva?"

"Because I've felt so, too."

"What is it, Miss Eva?—I don't understand."

"I can't tell you; but, when I saw those poor creatures on the boat, you know, when you came up and I,—some had lost their mothers, and some their husbands, and some mothers cried for their little children,—and when I heard about poor Prue,—oh, wasn't that dreadful!—and a great many other times, I've felt that I would be glad to die, if my dying could stop all this misery. I *would die* for them, Tom, if I could," said the child, earnestly, laying her little thin hand on his.

Tom looked at the child with awe; and when she, hearing her father's voice, glided away, he wiped his eyes many times, as he looked after her.

"It's jest no use tryin' to keep Miss Eva here," he said to Mammy, whom he met a moment after. "She's got the Lord's mark in her forehead."

"Ah, yes, yes," said Mammy, raising her hands; "I've allers said so. She wasn't never like a child that's to live—there was allers something deep in her eyes. I've told Missis so, many the time; it's a comin' true,—we all sees it,—dear, little, blessed lamb!"

Eva came tripping up the verandah steps to her father. It was late in the afternoon, and the rays of the sun formed a kind of glory behind her, as she came forward in her white dress, with her golden hair and glowing cheeks, her eyes unnaturally bright with the slow fever that burned in her veins.

St. Clare had called her to show a statuette that he had been buying for her; but her appearance, as she came on, impressed him suddenly and painfully. There is a kind of beauty so intense, yet so fragile, that we cannot bear to look at it. Her father folded her suddenly in his arms, and almost forgot what he was going to tell her.

"Eva, dear, you are better now-a-days,—are you not?"

"Papa," said Eva, with sudden firmness, "I've had things I wanted to say to you, a great while. I want to say them now, before I get weaker."

St. Clare trembled as Eva seated herself in his lap. She laid her head on his bosom, and said,

"It's all no use, papa, to keep it to myself any longer. The time is coming that I am going to leave you. I am going, and never to come back!" and Eva sobbed.

"O, now, my dear little Eva!" said St. Clare, trembling as he spoke, but speaking cheerfully, "you've got nervous and low-spirited; you mustn't indulge such gloomy thoughts. See here, I've bought a statuette for you!"

"No, papa," said Eva, putting it gently away, "don't deceive yourself!—I am *not* any better, I know it perfectly well,—and I am going, before long. I am not nervous,—I am not low-spirited. If it were not for you, papa, and my friends, I should be perfectly happy. I want to go,—I long to go!"

"Why, dear child, what has made your poor little heart so sad? You have had everything, to make you happy, that could be given you."

"I had rather be in heaven; though, only for my friends' sake, I would be willing to live. There are a great many things here that make me sad, that seem dreadful to me; I had rather be there; but I don't want to leave you,—it almost breaks my heart!"

"What makes you sad, and seems dreadful, Eva?"

"O, things that are done, and done all the time. I feel sad for our poor people; they love me dearly, and they are all good and kind to me. I wish, papa, they were all *free*."

"Why, Eva, child, don't you think they are well enough off now?"

"O, but, papa, if anything should happen to you, what would become of them? There are very few men like you, papa. Uncle Alfred isn't like you, and mamma isn't; and then, think of poor old Prue's owners! What horrid things people do, and can do!" and Eva shuddered.

"My dear child, you are too sensitive. I'm sorry I ever let you hear such stories."

"O, that's what troubles me, papa. You want me to live so happy, and never to have any pain,—never suffer anything,—not even hear a sad story, when other poor creatures have nothing but pain and sorrow, all their lives;—it seems selfish. I ought to know such things, I ought to feel about them! Such things always sunk into my heart; they went down deep; I've thought and thought about them. Papa, isn't there any way to have all slaves made free?"

"That's a difficult question, dearest. There's no doubt that this way is a very bad one; a great many people think so; I do myself. I heartily wish that there were not a slave in the land; but, then, I don't know what is to be done about it!"

"Papa, you are such a good man, and so noble, and kind, and you always have a way of saying things that is so pleasant, couldn't you go all round and try to persuade people to do right about this? When I am dead, papa, then you will think of me, and do it for my sake. I would do it, if I could."

"When you are dead, Eva," said St. Clare, passionately. "O, child, don't talk to me so! You are all I have on earth."

"Poor old Prue's child was all that she had,—and yet she had to hear it crying, and she couldn't help it! Papa, these poor creatures love their children as much as you do me. O! do something for them! There's poor Mammy loves her children; I've seen her cry when she talked about them. And Tom loves his children; and it's dreadful, papa, that such things are happening, all the time!"

"There, there, darling," said St. Clare, soothingly; "only don't distress yourself, and don't talk of dying, and I will do anything you wish."

"And promise me, dear father, that Tom shall have his freedom as soon as"—she stopped, and said, in a hesitating tone—"I am gone!"

"Yes, dear, I will do anything in the world,—anything you could ask me to."

"Dear papa," said the child, laying her burning cheek against his, "how I wish we could go together!"

"Where, dearest?" said St. Clare.

"To our Saviour's home; it's so sweet and peaceful there—it is all so loving there!" The child spoke unconsciously, as of a place where she had often been. "Don't you want to go, papa?" she said.

St. Clare drew her closer to him, but was silent.

"You will come to me," said the child, speaking in a voice of calm certainty which she often used unconsciously.

"I shall come after you. I shall not forget you."

The shadows of the solemn evening closed round them deeper and deeper, as St. Clare sat silently holding the little frail form to his bosom. He saw no more the deep eyes, but the voice came over him as a spirit voice, and, as in a sort of judgment vision, his whole past life rose in a moment before his eyes: his mother's prayers and hymns; his own early yearnings and aspirings for good; and, between them and this hour, years of worldliness and scepticism, and what man calls respectable living. We can think *much*, very much, in a moment. St. Clare saw and felt many things, but spoke nothing; and, as it grew darker, he took his child to her bedroom; and, when she was prepared for rest, he sent away the attendants, and rocked her in his arms, and sung to her till she was asleep.

## Chapter XXV

### *The Little Evangelist*

It was Sunday afternoon. St. Clare was stretched on a bamboo lounge in the verandah, solacing himself with a cigar. Marie lay reclined on a sofa, opposite the window opening on the verandah, closely secluded, under an awning of transparent gauze, from the outrages of the mosquitos, and languidly holding in her hand an elegantly bound prayer-book. She was holding it because it was Sunday, and she imagined she had been reading it,—though, in fact, she had been only taking a succession of short naps, with it open in her hand.

Miss Ophelia, who, after some rummaging, had hunted up a small Methodist meeting within riding distance, had gone out, with Tom as driver, to attend it; and Eva had accompanied them.

"I say, Augustine," said Marie after dozing a while, "I must send to the city after my old Doctor Posey; I'm sure I've got the complaint of the heart."

"Well; why need you send for him? This doctor that attends Eva seems skilful."

"I would not trust him in a critical case," said Marie; "and I think I may say mine is becoming so! I've been thinking of it, these two or three nights past; I have such distressing pains, and such strange feelings."

"O, Marie, you are blue; I don't believe it's heart complaint."

"I dare say *you* don't," said Marie; "I was prepared to expect *that*. You can be alarmed enough, if Eva coughs, or has the least thing the matter with her; but you never think of me."

"If it's particularly agreeable to you to have heart disease, why, I'll try and maintain you have it," said St. Clare; "I didn't know it was."

"Well, I only hope you won't be sorry for this, when it's too late!" said Marie; "but, believe it or not, my distress about Eva, and the exertions I have made with that dear child, have developed what I have long suspected."

What the *exertions* were which Marie referred to, it would have been difficult to state. St. Clare quietly made this commentary to himself, and went on smoking, like a hard-hearted wretch of a man as he was, till a carriage drove up before the verandah, and Eva and Miss Ophelia alighted.

Miss Ophelia marched straight to her own chamber, to put away her bonnet and shawl, as was always her manner, before she spoke a word on any subject; while Eva came, at St. Clare's call, and was sitting on his knee, giving him an account of the services they had heard.

They soon heard loud exclamations from Miss Ophelia's room, which, like the one in which they were sitting, opened on to the verandah, and violent reproof addressed to somebody.

"What new witchcraft has Tops been brewing?" asked St Clare. "That commotion is of her raising, I'll be bound!"

And, in a moment after, Miss Ophelia, in high indignation, came dragging the culprit along.

"Come out here, now!" she said. "I *will* tell your master!"

"What's the case now?" asked Augustine.

"The case is, that I cannot be plagued with this child, any longer! It's past all bearing; flesh and blood cannot endure it! Here, I locked her up, and gave her a hymn to study; and what does she do, but spy out where I put my key, and has gone to my bureau, and got a bonnet-trimming, and cut it all to pieces, to make dolls' jackets! I never saw anything like it, in my life!"

"I told you, Cousin," said Marie, "that you'd find out that these creatures can't be brought up, without severity. If I had *my* way, now," she said, looking reproachfully at St. Clare, "I'd send that child out, and have her thoroughly whipped; I'd have her whipped till she couldn't stand!"

"I don't doubt it," said St. Clare. "Tell me of the lovely rule of woman! I never saw above a dozen women that wouldn't half kill a horse, or a servant, either, if they had their own way with them!—let alone a man."

"There is no use in this shilly-shally way of yours, St. Clare!" said Marie. "Cousin is a woman of sense, and she sees it now, as plain as I do."

Miss Ophelia had just the capability of indignation that belongs to the thorough-paced housekeeper, and this had been pretty actively roused by the artifice and wastefulness of the child; in fact, many of my lady readers must own that they should have felt just so in her circumstances; but Marie's words went beyond her, and she felt less heat.

"I wouldn't have the child treated so, for the world," she said; "but, I am sure, Augustine, I don't know what to do. I've taught and taught; I've talked till I'm tired; I've whipped her; I've punished her in every way I can think of, and still she's just what she was at first."

"Come here, Tops, you monkey!" said St. Clare, calling the child up to him.

Topsy came up; her round, hard eyes glittering and blinking with a mixture of apprehensiveness and their usual odd drollery.

"What makes you behave so?" said St. Clare, who could not help being amused with the child's expression.

"Spects it's my wicked heart," said Topsy, demurely; "Miss Feely says so."

"Don't you see how much Miss Ophelia has done for you? She says she has done everything she can think of."

"Lor, yes, Mas'r! old Missis used to say so, too. She whipped me a heap harder, and used to pull my har, and knock my head agin the door; but it didn't do me no good! I spects, if they's to pull every spear o' har out of my head, it wouldn't do no good, neither,—I's so wicked! Laws! I's nothin but a nigger, no ways!"

"Well, I shall have to give her up," said Miss Ophelia; "I can't have that trouble any longer."

"Well, I'd just like to ask one question," said St. Clare.

"What is it?"

"Why, if your Gospel is not strong enough to save one heathen child, that you can have at home here, all to yourself, what's the use of sending one or two poor missionaries off with it among thousands of just such? I suppose this child is about a fair sample of what thousands of your heathen are."

Miss Ophelia did not make an immediate answer; and Eva, who had stood a silent spectator of the scene thus far, made a silent sign to Topsy to follow her. There was a little glass-room at the corner of the verandah, which St. Clare used as a sort of reading-room; and Eva and Topsy disappeared into this place.

"What's Eva going about, now?" said St. Clare; "I mean to see."

And, advancing on tiptoe, he lifted up a curtain that covered the glass-door, and looked in. In a moment, laying his finger on his lips, he made a silent gesture to Miss Ophelia to come and look. There sat the two children on the floor, with their side faces towards them. Topsy, with her usual air of careless drollery and unconcern; but, opposite to her, Eva, her whole face fervent with feeling, and tears in her large eyes.

"What does make you so bad, Topsy? Why won't you try and be good? Don't you love *anybody*, Topsy?"

"Donno nothing 'bout love; I loves candy and sich, that's all," said Topsy.

"But you love your father and mother?"

"Never had none, ye know. I telled ye that, Miss Eva."

"O, I know," said Eva, sadly; "but hadn't you any brother, or sister, or aunt, or—"

"No, none on 'em,—never had nothing nor nobody."

"But, Topsy, if you'd only try to be good, you might—"

"Couldn't never be nothin' but a nigger, if I was ever so good," said Topsy. "If I could be skinned, and come white, I'd try then."

"But people can love you, if you are black, Topsy. Miss Ophelia would love you, if you were good."

Topsy gave the short, blunt laugh that was her common mode of expressing incredulity.

"Don't you think so?" said Eva.

"No; she can't bar me, 'cause I'm a nigger!—she'd 's soon have a toad touch her! There can't nobody love niggers, and niggers can't do nothin'! *I* don't care," said Topsy, beginning to whistle.

"O, Topsy, poor child, *I* love you!" said Eva, with a sudden burst of feeling, and laying her little thin, white hand on Topsy's shoulder; "I love you, because you haven't had any father, or mother, or friends;—because you've been a poor, abused child! I love you, and I want you to be good. I am very unwell, Topsy, and I think I shan't live a great while; and it really grieves me, to have you be so naughty. I wish you would try to be good, for my sake;—it's only a little while I shall be with you."

The round, keen eyes of the black child were overcast with tears;—large, bright drops rolled heavily down, one by one, and fell on the little white hand. Yes, in that moment, a ray of real belief, a ray of heavenly love, had penetrated the darkness of her heathen soul! She laid her head down between her knees, and wept and sobbed,—while the beautiful child, bending over her, looked like the picture of some bright angel stooping to reclaim a sinner.

"Poor Topsy!" said Eva, "don't you know that Jesus loves all alike? He is just as willing to love you, as me. He loves you just as I do,—only more, because he is better. He will help you to be good; and you can go to Heaven at last, and be an angel forever, just as much as if you were white. Only think of it, Topsy!—*you* can be one of those spirits bright, Uncle Tom sings about."

"O, dear Miss Eva, dear Miss Eva!" said the child; "I will try, I will try; I never did care nothin' about it before."

St. Clare, at this instant, dropped the curtain. "It puts me in mind of mother," he said to Miss Ophelia. "It is true what she told me; if we want to give sight to the blind, we must be willing to do as Christ did,—call them to us, and *put our hands on them*."

"I've always had a prejudice against negroes," said Miss Ophelia, "and it's a fact, I never could bear to have that child touch me; but, I didn't think she knew it."

"Trust any child to find that out," said St. Clare; "there's no keeping it from them. But I believe that all the trying in the world to benefit a child, and all the substantial favors you can do them, will never excite one emotion of gratitude, while that feeling of repugnance remains in the heart;—it's a queer kind of a fact,—but so it is."

"I don't know how I can help it," said Miss Ophelia; "they *are* disagreeable to me,—this child in particular,—how can I help feeling so?"

"Eva does, it seems."

"Well, she's so loving! After all, though, she's no more than Christ-like," said Miss Ophelia; "I wish I were like her. She might teach me a lesson."

"It wouldn't be the first time a little child had been used to instruct an old disciple, if it *were* so," said St. Clare.

## Chapter XXVI

### *Death*

Weep not for those whom the veil of the tomb,
In life's early morning, hath hid from our eyes.[1]

Eva's bed-room was a spacious apartment, which, like all the other rooms in the house, opened on to the broad verandah. The room communicated, on one side, with her father and mother's apartment; on the other, with that appropriated to Miss Ophelia. St. Clare had gratified his own eye and taste, in furnishing this room in a style that had a peculiar keeping with the character of her for whom it was intended. The windows were hung with curtains of rose-colored and white muslin, the floor was spread with a matting which had been ordered in Paris, to a pattern of his own device, having round it a border of rose-buds and leaves, and a centre-piece with full-blown roses. The bedstead, chairs, and lounges, were of bamboo, wrought in peculiarly graceful and fanciful patterns. Over the head of the bed was an alabaster bracket, on which a beautiful sculptured angel stood, with drooping wings, holding out a crown of myrtle-leaves. From this depended, over the bed, light curtains of

1. The first lines of the poem "Weep Not for Those," from the Irish poet Thomas Moore's *Sacred Songs* (1816):

   Weep not for those whom the veil of the tomb
   In life's happy morning hath hid from our eyes,
   Ere sin threw a blight o'er the spirit's young bloom
   Or earth had profaned what was born for the skies.

   Moore (1779–1852) is best known for *Lalla Rookh* (1817).

rose-colored gauze, striped with silver, supplying that protection from mosquitos which is an indispensable addition to all sleeping accommodation in that climate. The graceful bamboo lounges were amply supplied with cushions of rose-colored damask, while over them, depending from the hands of sculptured figures, were gauze curtains similar to those of the bed. A light, fanciful bamboo table stood in the middle of the room, where a Parian vase,[2] wrought in the shape of a white lily, with its buds, stood, ever filled with flowers. On this table lay Eva's books and little trinkets, with an elegantly wrought alabaster writing-stand, which her father had supplied to her when he saw her trying to improve herself in writing. There was a fireplace in the room, and on the marble mantle above stood a beautifully wrought statuette of Jesus receiving little children, and on either side marble vases, for which it was Tom's pride and delight to offer bouquets every morning. Two or three exquisite paintings of children, in various attitudes, embellished the wall. In short, the eye could turn nowhere without meeting images of childhood, of beauty, and of peace. Those little eyes never opened, in the morning light, without falling on something which suggested to the heart soothing and beautiful thoughts.

The deceitful strength which had buoyed Eva up for a little while was fast passing away; seldom and more seldom her light footstep was heard in the verandah, and oftener and oftener she was found reclined on a little lounge by the open window, her large, deep eyes fixed on the rising and falling waters of the lake.

It was towards the middle of the afternoon, as she was so reclining,—her Bible half open, her little transparent fingers lying listlessly between the leaves,—suddenly she heard her mother's voice, in sharp tones, in the verandah.

"What now, you baggage!—what new piece of mischief! You've been picking the flowers, hey?" and Eva heard the sound of a smart slap.

"Law, Missis!—they's for Miss Eva," she heard a voice say, which she knew belonged to Topsy.

"Miss Eva! A pretty excuse!—you suppose she wants *your* flowers, you good-for-nothing nigger! Get along off with you!"

In a moment, Eva was off from her lounge, and in the verandah.

"O, don't, mother! I should like the flowers; do give them to me; I want them!"

"Why, Eva, your room is full now."

"I can't have too many," said Eva. "Topsy, do bring them here."

Topsy, who had stood sullenly, holding down her head, now came up and offered her flowers. She did it with a look of hesitation and

2. A vase made from white porcelain resembling marble from Paros.

bashfulness, quite unlike the eldrich[3] boldness and brightness which was usual with her.

"It's a beautiful bouquet!" said Eva, looking at it.

It was rather a singular one,—a brilliant scarlet geranium, and one single white japonica, with its glossy leaves. It was tied up with an evident eye to the contrast of color, and the arrangement of every leaf had carefully been studied.

Topsy looked pleased, as Eva said,—"Topsy, you arrange flowers very prettily. Here," she said, "is this vase I haven't any flowers for. I wish you'd arrange something every day for it."

"Well, that's odd!" said Marie. "What in the world do you want that for?"

"Never mind, mamma; you'd as lief as not Topsy should do it,—had you not?"

"Of course, anything you please, dear! Topsy, you hear your young mistress;—see that you mind."

Topsy made a short courtesy, and looked down; and, as she turned away, Eva saw a tear roll down her dark cheek.

"You see, mamma, I knew poor Topsy wanted to do something for me," said Eva to her mother.

"O, nonsense! it's only because she likes to do mischief. She knows she mustn't pick flowers,—so she does it; that's all there is to it. But, if you fancy to have her pluck them, so be it."

"Mamma, I think Topsy is different from what she used to be; she's trying to be a good girl."

"She'll have to try a good while before *she* gets to be good," said Marie, with a careless laugh.

"Well, you know, mamma, poor Topsy! everything has always been against her."

"Not since she's been here, I'm sure. If she hasn't been talked to, and preached to, and every earthly thing done that anybody could do;—and she's just so ugly, and always will be; you can't make anything of the creature!"

"But, mamma, it's so different to be brought up as I've been, with so many friends, so many things to make me good and happy; and to be brought up as she's been, all the time, till she came here!"

"Most likely," said Marie, yawning,—"dear me, how hot it is!"

"Mamma, you believe, don't you, that Topsy could become an angel, as well as any of us, if she were a Christian?"

"Topsy! what a ridiculous idea! Nobody but you would ever think of it. I suppose she could, though."

"But, mamma, isn't God her father, as much as ours? Isn't Jesus her Saviour?"

3. Weird, eerie, or uncanny.

"Well, that may be. I suppose God made everybody," said Marie. "Where is my smelling-bottle?"

"It's such a pity,—oh! *such* a pity!" said Eva, looking out on the distant lake, and speaking half to herself.

"What's a pity?" said Marie.

"Why, that any one, who could be a bright angel, and live with angels, should go all down, down, down, and nobody help them!—oh, dear!"

"Well, we can't help it; it's no use worrying, Eva! I don't know what's to be done; we ought to be thankful for our own advantages."

"I hardly can be," said Eva, "I'm so sorry to think of poor folks that haven't any."

"That's odd enough," said Marie;—"I'm sure my religion makes me thankful for my advantages."

"Mamma," said Eva, "I want to have some of my hair cut off,—a good deal of it."

"What for?" said Marie.

"Mamma, I want to give some away to my friends, while I am able to give it to them myself. Won't you ask aunty to come and cut it for me?"

Marie raised her voice, and called Miss Ophelia, from the other room.

The child half rose from her pillow as she came in, and, shaking down her long golden-brown curls, said, rather playfully, "Come, aunty, shear the sheep!"

"What's that?" said St. Clare, who just then entered with some fruit he had been out to get for her.

"Papa, I just want aunty to cut off some of my hair;—there's too much of it, and it makes my head hot. Besides, I want to give some of it away."

Miss Ophelia came, with her scissors.

"Take care,—don't spoil the looks of it!" said her father; "cut underneath, where it won't show. Eva's curls are my pride."

"O, papa!" said Eva, sadly.

"Yes, and I want them kept handsome against the time I take you up to your uncle's plantation, to see Cousin Henrique," said St. Clare, in a gay tone.

"I shall never go there, papa;—I am going to a better country. O, do believe me! Don't you see, papa, that I get weaker, every day?"

"Why do you insist that I shall believe such a cruel thing, Eva?" said her father.

"Only because it is *true*, papa: and, if you will believe it now, perhaps you will get to feel about it as I do."

St. Clare closed his lips, and stood gloomily eying the long, beautiful curls, which, as they were separated from the child's head, were laid, one by one, in her lap. She raised them up, looked earnestly at them, twined them around her thin fingers, and looked, from time to time, anxiously at her father.

"It's just what I've been foreboding!" said Marie; "it's just what has been preying on my health, from day to day, bringing me downward to the grave, though nobody regards it. I have seen this, long. St. Clare, you will see, after a while, that I was right."

"Which will afford you great consolation, no doubt!" said St. Clare, in a dry, bitter tone.

Marie lay back on a lounge, and covered her face with her cambric handkerchief.

Eva's clear blue eye looked earnestly from one to the other. It was the calm, comprehending gaze of a soul half loosed from its earthly bonds; it was evident she saw, felt, and appreciated, the difference between the two.

She beckoned with her hand to her father. He came, and sat down by her.

"Papa, my strength fades away every day, and I know I must go. There are some things I want to say and do,—that I ought to do; and you are so unwilling to have me speak a word on this subject. But it must come; there's no putting it off. Do be willing I should speak now!"

"My child, I *am* willing!" said St. Clare, covering his eyes with one hand, and holding up Eva's hand with the other.

"Then, I want to see all our people together. I have some things I *must* say to them," said Eva.

"*Well*," said St. Clare, in a tone of dry endurance.

Miss Ophelia despatched a messenger, and soon the whole of the servants were convened in the room.

Eva lay back on her pillows; her hair hanging loosely about her face, her crimson cheeks contrasting painfully with the intense whiteness of her complexion and the thin contour of her limbs and features, and her large, soul-like eyes fixed earnestly on every one.

The servants were struck with a sudden emotion. The spiritual face, the long locks of hair cut off and lying by her, her father's averted face, and Marie's sobs, struck at once upon the feelings of a sensitive and impressible race; and, as they came in, they looked one on another, sighed, and shook their heads. There was a deep silence, like that of a funeral.

Eva raised herself, and looked long and earnestly round at every one. All looked sad and apprehensive. Many of the women hid their faces in their aprons.

"I sent for you all, my dear friends," said Eva, "because I love you. I love you all; and I have something to say to you, which I want you always to remember. . . . . . I am going to leave you. In a few more weeks, you will see me no more—"

Here the child was interrupted by bursts of groans, sobs, and lamentations, which broke from all present, and in which her slender voice was lost entirely. She waited a moment, and then, speaking in a tone that checked the sobs of all, she said,

"If you love me, you must not interrupt me so. Listen to what I say. I want to speak to you about your souls. . . . . . Many of you, I am afraid, are very careless. You are thinking only about this world. I want you to remember that there is a beautiful world, where Jesus is. I am going there, and you can go there. It is for you, as much as me. But, if you want to go there, you must not live idle, careless, thoughtless lives. You must be Christians. You must remember that each one of you can become angels, and be angels forever. . . . . . If you want to be Christians, Jesus will help you. You must pray to him; you must read—"

The child checked herself, looked piteously at them, and said, sorrowfully,

"O, dear! you *can't* read,—poor souls!" and she hid her face in the pillow and sobbed, while many a smothered sob from those she was addressing, who were kneeling on the floor, aroused her.

"Never mind," she said, raising her face and smiling brightly through her tears, "I have prayed for you; and I know Jesus will help you, even if you can't read. Try all to do the best you can; pray every day; ask Him to help you, and get the Bible read to you whenever you can; and I think I shall see you all in heaven."

"Amen," was the murmured response from the lips of Tom and Mammy, and some of the elder ones, who belonged to the Methodist church. The younger and more thoughtless ones, for the time completely overcome, were sobbing, with their heads bowed upon their knees.

"I know," said Eva, "you all love me."

"Yes; oh, yes! indeed we do! Lord bless her!" was the involuntary answer of all.

"Yes, I know you do! There isn't one of you that hasn't always been very kind to me; and I want to give you something that, when you look at, you shall always remember me. I'm going to give all of you a curl of my hair; and, when you look at it, think that I loved you and am gone to heaven, and that I want to see you all there."

It is impossible to describe the scene, as, with tears and sobs, they gathered round the little creature, and took from her hands what seemed to them a last mark of her love. They fell on their knees; they sobbed, and prayed, and kissed the hem of her garment; and the elder ones poured forth words of endearment, mingled in prayers and blessings, after the manner of their susceptible race.

As each one took their gift, Miss Ophelia, who was apprehensive for the effect of all this excitement on her little patient, signed to each one to pass out of the apartment.

At last, all were gone but Tom and Mammy.

"Here, Uncle Tom," said Eva, "is a beautiful one for you. O, I am so happy, Uncle Tom, to think I shall see you in heaven,—for I'm sure I shall; and Mammy,—dear, good, kind Mammy!" she said, fondly throwing her arms round her old nurse,—"I know you'll be there, too."

"O, Miss Eva, don't see how I can live without ye, no how!" said the faithful creature. "'Pears like it's just taking everything off the place to oncet!" and Mammy gave way to a passion of grief.

Miss Ophelia pushed her and Tom gently from the apartment, and thought they were all gone; but, as she turned, Topsy was standing there.

"Where did you start up from?" she said, suddenly.

"I was here," said Topsy, wiping the tears from her eyes. "O, Miss Eva, I've been a bad girl; but won't you give *me* one, too?"

"Yes, poor Topsy! to be sure, I will. There—every time you look at that, think that I love you, and wanted you to be a good girl!"

"O, Miss Eva, I *is* tryin!" said Topsy, earnestly; "but, Lor, it's so hard to be good! 'Pears like I an't used to it, no ways!"

"Jesus knows it, Topsy; he is sorry for you; he will help you."

Topsy, with her eyes hid in her apron, was silently passed from the apartment by Miss Ophelia; but, as she went, she hid the precious curl in her bosom.

All being gone, Miss Ophelia shut the door. That worthy lady had wiped away many tears of her own, during the scene; but concern for the consequence of such an excitement to her young charge was upper-most in her mind.

St. Clare had been sitting, during the whole time, with his hand shading his eyes, in the same attitude. When they were all gone, he sat so still.

"Papa!" said Eva, gently, laying her hand on his.

He gave a sudden start and shiver; but made no answer.

"Dear papa!" said Eva.

"I *cannot*," said St. Clare, rising, "I *cannot* have it so! The Almighty hath dealt *very bitterly* with me!" and St. Clare pronounced these words with a bitter emphasis, indeed.

"Augustine! has not God a right to do what he will with his own?" said Miss Ophelia.

"Perhaps so; but that doesn't make it any easier to bear," said he, with a dry, hard, tearless manner, as he turned away.

"Papa, you break my heart!" said Eva, rising and throwing herself into his arms; "you must not feel so!" and the child sobbed and wept with a violence which alarmed them all, and turned her father's thoughts at once to another channel.

"There, Eva,—there, dearest! Hush! hush! I was wrong; I was wicked. I will feel any way, do any way,—only don't distress yourself; don't sob so. I will be resigned; I was wicked to speak as I did."

Eva soon lay like a wearied dove in her father's arms; and he, bending over her, soothed her by every tender word he could think of.

Marie rose and threw herself out of the apartment into her own, when she fell into violent hysterics.

"You didn't give me a curl, Eva," said her father, smiling sadly.

"They are all yours, papa," said she, smiling,—"yours and mamma's; and you must give dear aunty as many as she wants. I only gave them to our poor people myself, because you know, papa, they might be forgotten when I am gone, and because I hoped it might help them remember. . . . . . You are a Christian, are you not, papa?" said Eva, doubtfully.

"Why do you ask me?"

"I don't know. You are so good, I don't see how you can help it."

"What is being a Christian, Eva?"

"Loving Christ most of all," said Eva.

"Do you, Eva?"

"Certainly I do."

"You never saw him," said St. Clare.

"That makes no difference," said Eva. "I believe him, and in a few days I shall *see* him;" and the young face grew fervent, radiant with joy.

St. Clare said no more. It was a feeling which he had seen before in his mother; but no chord within vibrated to it.

Eva, after this, declined rapidly; there was no more any doubt of the event; the fondest hope could not be blinded. Her beautiful room was avowedly a sick room; and Miss Ophelia day and night performed the duties of a nurse,—and never did her friends appreciate her value more than in that capacity. With so well-trained a hand and eye, such perfect adroitness and practice in every art which could promote neatness and comfort, and keep out of sight every disagreeable incident of sickness,—with such a perfect sense of time, such a clear, untroubled head, such exact accuracy in remembering every prescription and direction of the doctors,—she was everything to him. They who had shrugged their shoulders at her little peculiarities and setnesses, so unlike the careless freedom of southern manners, acknowledged that now she was the exact person that was wanted.

Uncle Tom was much in Eva's room. The child suffered much from nervous restlessness, and it was a relief to her to be carried;

and it was Tom's greatest delight to carry her little frail form in his arms, resting on a pillow, now up and down her room, now out into the verandah; and when the fresh sea-breezes blew from the lake,—and the child felt freshest in the morning,—he would sometimes walk with her under the orange-trees in the garden, or, sitting down in some of their old seats, sing to her their favorite old hymns.

Her father often did the same thing; but his frame was slighter, and when he was weary, Eva would say to him,

"O, papa, let Tom take me. Poor fellow! it pleases him; and you know it's all he can do now, and he wants to do something!"

"So do I, Eva!" said her father.

"Well, papa, you can do everything, and are everything to me. You read to me,—you sit up nights,—and Tom has only this one thing, and his singing; and I know, too, he does it easier than you can. He carries me so strong!"

The desire to do something was not confined to Tom. Every servant in the establishment showed the same feeling, and in their way did what they could.

Poor Mammy's heart yearned towards her darling; but she found no opportunity, night or day, as Marie declared that the state of her mind was such, it was impossible for her to rest; and, of course, it was against her principles to let any one else rest. Twenty times in a night, Mammy would be roused to rub her feet, to bathe her head, to find her pocket-handkerchief, to see what the noise was in Eva's room, to let down a curtain because it was too light, or to put it up because it was too dark; and, in the day-time, when she longed to have some share in the nursing of her pet, Marie seemed unusually ingenious in keeping her busy anywhere and everywhere all over the house, or about her own person; so that stolen interviews and momentary glimpses were all she could obtain.

"I feel it my duty to be particularly careful of myself, now," she would say, "feeble as I am, and with the whole care and nursing of that dear child upon me."

"Indeed, my dear," said St. Clare, "I thought our cousin relieved you of that."

"You talk like a man, St. Clare,—just as if a mother *could* be relieved of the care of a child in that state; but, then, it's all alike,—no one ever knows what I feel! I can't throw things off, as you do."

St. Clare smiled. You must excuse him, he couldn't help it,—for St. Clare could smile yet. For so bright and placid was the farewell voyage of the little spirit,—by such sweet and fragrant breezes was the small bark borne towards the heavenly shores,—that it was impossible to realize that it was death that was approaching. The child felt no pain,—only a tranquil, soft weakness, daily and almost insensibly increasing; and she was so beautiful, so loving, so trustful, so happy, that one could not resist the soothing influence of that air of innocence and peace which seemed to breathe around her. St. Clare found a strange calm coming over him. It was not hope,—that was impossible; it was not resignation; it was only a calm resting in the present, which seemed so beautiful that he wished to think of no future. It was like that hush of spirit which we feel amid the bright, mild woods of autumn, when the bright hectic flush is on the trees, and the last lingering flowers by the brook; and we joy in it all the more, because we know that soon it will all pass away.

The friend who knew most of Eva's own imaginings and foreshadowings was her faithful bearer, Tom. To him she said what she would not disturb her father by saying. To him she imparted those mysterious intimations which the soul feels, as the cords begin to unbind, ere it leaves its clay forever.

Tom, at last, would not sleep in his room, but lay all night in the outer verandah, ready to rouse at every call.

"Uncle Tom, what alive have you taken to sleeping anywhere and everywhere, like a dog, for?" said Miss Ophelia. "I thought you was one of the orderly sort, that liked to lie in bed in a Christian way."

"I do, Miss Feely," said Tom, mysteriously. "I do, but now—"

"Well, what now?"

"We mustn't speak loud; Mas'r St. Clare won't hear on't; but Miss Feely, you know there must be somebody watchin' for the bridegroom."

"What do you mean, Tom?"

"You know it says in Scripture, 'At midnight there was a great cry made. Behold, the bridegroom cometh.'[4] That's what I'm spectin now, every night, Miss Feely,—and I couldn't sleep out o' hearin, no ways."

"Why, Uncle Tom, what makes you think so?"

"Miss Eva, she talks to me. The Lord, he sends his messenger in the soul. I must be thar, Miss Feely; for when that ar blessed child goes into the kingdom, they'll open the door so wide, we'll all get a look in at the glory, Miss Feely."

"Uncle Tom, did Miss Eva say she felt more unwell than usual to-night?"

"No; but she telled me, this morning, she was coming nearer,—thar's them that tells it to the child, Miss Feely. It's the angels,—'it's the trumpet sound afore the break o' day,'"[5] said Tom, quoting from a favorite hymn.

4. See Christ's parable of the wise and foolish virgins (Matthew 25.1–12).
5. Reference unknown.

This dialogue passed between Miss Ophelia and Tom, between ten and eleven, one evening, after her arrangements had all been made for the night, when, on going to bolt her outer door, she found Tom stretched along by it, in the outer verandah.

She was not nervous or impressible; but the solemn, heartfelt manner struck her. Eva had been unusually bright and cheerful, that afternoon, and had sat raised in her bed, and looked over all her little trinkets and precious things, and designated the friends to whom she would have them given; and her manner was more animated, and her voice more natural, than they had known it for weeks. Her father had been in, in the evening, and had said that Eva appeared more like her former self than ever she had done since her sickness; and when he kissed her for the night, he said to Miss Ophelia,—"Cousin, we may keep her with us, after all; she is certainly better;" and he had retired with a lighter heart in his bosom than he had had there for weeks.

But at midnight,—strange, mystic hour!—when the veil between the frail present and the eternal future grows thin,—then came the messenger!

There was a sound in that chamber, first of one who stepped quickly. It was Miss Ophelia, who had resolved to sit up all night with her little charge, and who, at the turn of the night, had discerned what experienced nurses significantly call "a change." The outer door was quickly opened, and Tom, who was watching outside, was on the alert, in a moment.

"Go for the doctor, Tom! lose not a moment," said Miss Ophelia, and, stepping across the room, she rapped at St. Clare's door.

"Cousin," she said, "I wish you would come."

Those words fell on his heart like clods upon a coffin. Why did they? He was up and in the room in an instant, and bending over Eva, who still slept.

What was it he saw that made his heart stand still? Why was no word spoken between the two? Thou canst say, who hast seen that same expression on the face dearest to thee;—that look indescribable, hopeless, unmistakable, that says to thee that thy beloved is no longer thine.

On the face of the child, however, there was no ghastly imprint,—only a high and almost sublime expression,—the overshadowing presence of spiritual natures, the dawning of immortal life in that childish soul.

They stood there so still, gazing upon her, that even the ticking of the watch seemed too loud. In a few moments, Tom returned, with the doctor. He entered, gave one look, and stood silent as the rest.

"When did this change take place?" said he, in a low whisper, to Miss Ophelia.

"About the turn of the night," was the reply.

Marie, roused by the entrance of the doctor, appeared, hurriedly, from the next room.

"Augustine! Cousin!—O!—what!" she hurriedly began.

"Hush!" said St. Clare, hoarsely; "*she is dying!*"

Mammy heard the words, and flew to awaken the servants. The house was soon roused,—lights were seen, footsteps heard, anxious faces thronged the verandah, and looked tearfully through the glass doors; but St. Clare heard and said nothing,—he saw only *that look* on the face of the little sleeper.

"O, if she would only wake, and speak once more!" he said; and, stooping over her, he spoke in her ear,—"Eva, darling!"

The large blue eyes unclosed,—a smile passed over her face;—she tried to raise her head, and to speak.

"Do you know me, Eva?"

"Dear papa," said the child, with a last effort, throwing her arms about his neck. In a moment they dropped again; and, as St. Clare raised his head, he saw a spasm of mortal agony pass over the face,—she struggled for breath, and threw up her little hands.

"O, God, this is dreadful!" he said, turning away in agony, and wringing Tom's hand, scarce conscious what he was doing. "O, Tom, my boy, it is killing me!"

Tom had his master's hands between his own; and, with tears streaming down his dark cheeks, looked up for help where he had always been used to look.

"Pray that this may be cut short!" said St. Clare,—"this wrings my heart."

"O, bless the Lord! it's over,—it's over, dear Master!" said Tom; "look at her."

The child lay panting on her pillows, as one exhausted,—the large clear eyes rolled up and fixed. Ah, what said those eyes, that spoke so much of heaven? Earth was past, and earthly pain; but so solemn, so mysterious, was the triumphant brightness of that face, that it checked even the sobs of sorrow. They pressed around her, in breathless stillness.

"Eva," said St. Clare, gently.

She did not hear.

"O, Eva, tell us what you see! What is it?" said her father.

A bright, a glorious smile passed over her face, and she said, brokenly,—"O! love,—joy,—peace!" gave one sigh, and passed from death unto life!

"Farewell, beloved child! the bright, eternal doors have closed after thee; we shall see thy sweet face no more. O, woe for them who watched thy entrance into heaven, when they shall wake and find only the cold gray sky of daily life, and thou gone forever!"

# Chapter XXVII

## *"This Is the Last of Earth."—John Q. Adams*[1]

The statuettes and pictures in Eva's room were shrouded in white napkins, and only hushed breathings and muffled foot-falls were heard there, and the light stole in solemnly through windows partially darkened by closed blinds.

The bed was draped in white; and there, beneath the drooping angel-figure, lay a little sleeping form,—sleeping never to waken!

There she lay, robed in one of the simple white dresses she had been wont to wear when living; the rose-colored light through the curtains cast over the icy coldness of death a warm glow. The heavy eyelashes drooped softly on the pure cheek; the head was turned a little to one side, as if in natural sleep, but there was diffused over every lineament of the face that high celestial expression, that mingling of rapture and repose, which showed it was no earthly or temporary sleep, but the long, sacred rest which "He giveth to his beloved."[2]

There is no death to such as thou, dear Eva! neither darkness nor shadow of death; only such a bright fading as when the morning star fades in the golden dawn. Thine is the victory without the battle,—the crown without the conflict.

So did St. Clare think, as, with folded arms, he stood there gazing. Ah! who shall say what he did think? for, from the hour that voices had said, in the dying chamber, "she is gone," it had been all a dreary mist, a heavy "dimness of anguish."[3] He had heard voices around him; he had had questions asked, and answered them; they had asked him when he would have the funeral, and where they should lay her; and he had answered, impatiently, that he cared not.

Adolph and Rosa had arranged the chamber; volatile, fickle and childish, as they generally were, they were soft-hearted and full of feeling; and, while Miss Ophelia presided over the general details of order and neatness, it was their hands that added those soft, poetic touches to the arrangements, that took from the death-room the grim and ghastly air which too often marks a New England funeral.

There were still flowers on the shelves,—all white, delicate and fragrant, with graceful, drooping leaves. Eva's little table, covered

1. "This is the last of earth! I am content"—last words of John Quincy Adams, February 21, 1848.
2. "It is vain for you to rise up early, to sit up late, to eat the bread of sorrows: for so he giveth to his beloved sleep" (Psalm 127.2).
3. From Isaiah's prophecy of God's judgment of the earth: "And they shall look unto the earth; and behold trouble and darkness, dimness of anguish; and they shall be driven to darkness" (Isaiah 8.22).

with white, bore on it her favorite vase, with a single white moss rose-bud in it. The folds of the drapery, the fall of the curtains, had been arranged and rearranged, by Adolph and Rosa, with that nicety of eye which characterizes their race. Even now, while St. Clare stood there thinking, little Rosa tripped softly into the chamber with a basket of white flowers. She stepped back when she saw St. Clare, and stopped respectfully; but, seeing that he did not observe her, she came forward to place them around the dead. St. Clare saw her as in a dream, while she placed in the small hands a fair cape jessamine, and, with admirable taste, disposed other flowers around the couch.

The door opened again, and Topsy, her eyes swelled with crying, appeared, holding something under her apron. Rosa made a quick, forbidding gesture; but she took a step into the room.

"You must go out," said Rosa, in a sharp, positive whisper; "*you* haven't any business here!"

"O, do let me! I brought a flower,—such a pretty one!" said Topsy, holding up a half-blown tea rose-bud. "Do let me put just one there."

"Get along!" said Rosa, more decidedly.

"Let her stay!" said St. Clare, suddenly stamping his foot. "She shall come."

Rosa suddenly retreated, and Topsy came forward and laid her offering at the feet of the corpse; then suddenly, with a wild and bitter cry, she threw herself on the floor alongside the bed, and wept, and moaned aloud.

Miss Ophelia hastened into the room, and tried to raise and silence her; but in vain.

"O, Miss Eva! oh, Miss Eva! I wish I's dead, too,—I do!"

There was a piercing wildness in the cry; the blood flushed into St. Clare's white, marble-like face, and the first tears he had shed since Eva died stood in his eyes.

"Get up, child," said Miss Ophelia, in a softened voice; "don't cry so. Miss Eva is gone to heaven; she is an angel."

"But I can't see her!" said Topsy. "I never shall see her!" and she sobbed again.

They all stood a moment in silence.

"*She* said she *loved* me," said Topsy,—"she did! O, dear! oh, dear! there an't *nobody* left now,—there an't!"

"That's true enough," said St. Clare; "but do," he said to Miss Ophelia, "see if you can't comfort the poor creature."

"I jist wish I hadn't never been born," said Topsy. "I didn't want to be born, no ways; and I don't see no use on't."

Miss Ophelia raised her gently, but firmly, and took her from the room; but, as she did so, some tears fell from her eyes.

"Topsy, you poor child," she said, as she led her into her room, "don't give up! *I* can love you, though I am not like that dear little child. I hope I've learnt something of the love of Christ from her. I can love you; I do, and I'll try to help you to grow up a good Christian girl."

Miss Ophelia's voice was more than her words, and more than that were the honest tears that fell down her face. From that hour, she acquired an influence over the mind of the destitute child that she never lost.

"O, my Eva, whose little hour on earth did so much of good," thought St. Clare, "what account have I to give for my long years?"

There were, for a while, soft whisperings and foot-falls in the chamber, as one after another stole in, to look at the dead; and then came the little coffin; and then there was a funeral, and carriages drove to the door, and strangers came and were seated; and there were white scarfs and ribbons, and crape bands, and mourners dressed in black crape; and there were words read from the Bible, and prayers offered; and St. Clare lived, and walked, and moved, as one who has shed every tear;—to the last he saw only one thing, that golden head in the coffin; but then he saw the cloth spread over it, the lid of the coffin closed; and he walked, when he was put beside the others, down to a little place at the bottom of the garden, and there, by the mossy seat where she and Tom had talked, and sung, and read so often, was the little grave. St. Clare stood beside it,—looked vacantly down; he saw them lower the little coffin; he heard, dimly, the solemn words, "I am the resurrection and the Life; he that believeth in me, though he were dead, yet shall he live;"[4] and, as the earth was cast in and filled up the little grave, he could not realize that it was his Eva that they were hiding from his sight.

Nor was it!—not Eva, but only the frail seed of that bright, immortal form with which she shall yet come forth, in the day of the Lord Jesus!

And then all were gone, and the mourners went back to the place which should know her no more; and Marie's room was darkened, and she lay on the bed, sobbing and moaning in uncontrollable grief, and calling every moment for the attentions of all her servants. Of course, they had no time to cry,—why should they? the grief was *her* grief, and she was fully convinced that nobody on earth did, could, or would feel it as she did.

"St. Clare did not shed a tear," she said; "he didn't sympathize with her; it was perfectly wonderful to think how hard-hearted and unfeeling he was, when he must know how she suffered."

4. Christ's words in John 11.25–26.

So much are people the slave of their eye and ear, that many of the servants really thought that Missis was the principal sufferer in the case, especially as Marie began to have hysterical spasms, and sent for the doctor, and at last declared herself dying; and, in the running and scampering, and bringing up hot bottles, and heating of flannels, and chafing, and fussing, that ensued, there was quite a diversion.

Tom, however, had a feeling at his own heart, that drew him to his master. He followed him wherever he walked, wistfully and sadly; and when he saw him sitting, so pale and quiet, in Eva's room, holding before his eyes her little open Bible, though seeing no letter or word of what was in it, there was more sorrow to Tom in that still, fixed, tearless eye, than in all Marie's moans and lamentations.

In a few days the St. Clare family were back again in the city; Augustine, with the restlessness of grief, longing for another scene, to change the current of his thoughts. So they left the house and garden, with its little grave, and came back to New Orleans; and St. Clare walked the streets busily, and strove to fill up the chasm in his heart with hurry and bustle, and change of place; and people who saw him in the street, or met him at the café, knew of his loss only by the weed[5] on his hat; for there he was, smiling and talking, and reading the newspaper, and speculating on politics, and attending to business matters; and who could see that all this smiling outside was but a hollow shell over a heart that was a dark and silent sepulchre?

"Mr. St. Clare is a singular man," said Marie to Miss Ophelia, in a complaining tone. "I used to think, if there was anything in the world he did love, it was our dear little Eva; but he seems to be forgetting her very easily. I cannot ever get him to talk about her. I really did think he would show more feeling!"

"Still waters run deepest, they used to tell me," said Miss Ophelia, oracularly.

"O, I don't believe in such things; it's all talk. If people have feeling, they will show it,—they can't help it; but, then, it's a great misfortune to have feeling. I'd rather have been made like St. Clare. My feelings prey upon me so!"

"Sure, Missis, Mas'r St. Clare is gettin' thin as a shader. They say, he don't never eat nothin'," said Mammy. "I know he don't forget Miss Eva; I know there couldn't nobody,—dear, little, blessed cretur!" she added, wiping her eyes.

"Well, at all events, he has no consideration for me," said Marie; "he hasn't spoken one word of sympathy, and he must know how much more a mother feels than any man can."

5. Heavy black crape worn around a man's hat to show mourning.

"The heart knoweth its own bitterness,"[6] said Miss Ophelia, gravely.

"That's just what I think. I know just what I feel,—nobody else seems to. Eva used to, but she is gone!" and Marie lay back on her lounge, and began to sob disconsolately.

Marie was one of those unfortunately constituted mortals, in whose eyes whatever is lost and gone assumes a value which it never had in possession. Whatever she had, she seemed to survey only to pick flaws in it; but, once fairly away, there was no end to her valuation of it.

While this conversation was taking place in the parlor, another was going on in St. Clare's library.

Tom, who was always uneasily following his master about, had seen him go to his library, some hours before; and, after vainly waiting for him to come out, determined, at last, to make an errand in. He entered softly. St. Clare lay on his lounge, at the further end of the room. He was lying on his face, with Eva's Bible open before him, at a little distance. Tom walked up, and stood by the sofa. He hesitated; and, while he was hesitating, St. Clare suddenly raised himself up. The honest face, so full of grief, and with such an imploring expression of affection and sympathy, struck his master. He laid his hand on Tom's, and bowed down his forehead on it.

"O, Tom, my boy, the whole world is as empty as an eggshell."

"I know it, Mas'r,—I know it," said Tom; "but, oh, if Mas'r could only look up,—up where our dear Miss Eva is,—up to the dear Lord Jesus!"

"Ah, Tom! I do look up; but the trouble is, I don't see anything, when I do. I wish I could."

Tom sighed heavily.

"It seems to be given to children, and poor, honest fellows, like you, to see what we can't," said St. Clare. "How comes it?"

"Thou hast 'hid from the wise and prudent, and revealed unto babes,'" murmured Tom; "'even so, Father, for so it seemed good in thy sight.'"[7]

"Tom, I don't believe,—I can't believe,—I've got the habit of doubting," said St. Clare. "I want to believe this Bible,—and I can't."

"Dear Mas'r, pray to the good Lord,—'Lord, I believe; help thou my unbelief.'"[8]

6. "The heart knoweth its own bitterness; and a stranger doth not intermeddle with his joy" (Proverbs 14.10).
7. Christ's words in Matthew 11.25.
8. Stowe alludes to the father who asks Jesus to heal his son, who has a "dumb spirit." "Jesus said unto him, If thou canst believe, all things are possible unto him that

"Who knows anything about anything?" said St. Clare, his eyes wandering dreamily, and speaking to himself. "Was all that beautiful love and faith only one of the ever-shifting phases of human feeling, having nothing real to rest on, passing away with the little breath? And is there no more Eva,—no heaven,—no Christ,—nothing?"

"O, dear Mas'r, there is! I know it; I'm sure of it," said Tom, falling on his knees. "Do, do, dear Mas'r, believe it!"

"How do you know there's any Christ, Tom? You never saw the Lord."

"Felt Him in my soul, Mas'r,—feel Him now! O, Mas'r, when I was sold away from my old woman and the children, I was jest a most broke up. I felt as if there warn't nothin' left; and then the good Lord, he stood by me, and he says, 'Fear not, Tom;' and he brings light and joy into a poor feller's soul,—makes all peace; and I's so happy, and loves everybody, and feels willin' jest to be the Lord's, and have the Lord's will done, and be put jest where the Lord wants to put me. I know it couldn't come from me, cause I's a poor, complainin' cretur; it comes from the Lord; and I know He's willin' to do for Mas'r."

Tom spoke with fast-running tears and choking voice. St. Clare leaned his head on his shoulder, and wrung the hard, faithful, black hand.

"Tom, you love me," he said.

"I's willin' to lay down my life, this blessed day, to see Mas'r a Christian."

"Poor, foolish boy!" said St. Clare, half-raising himself. "I'm not worth the love of one good, honest heart, like yours."

"O, Mas'r, dere's more than me loves you,—the blessed Lord Jesus loves you."

"How do you know that, Tom?" said St. Clare.

"Feels it in my soul. O, Mas'r! 'the love of Christ, that passeth knowledge.'"[9]

"Singular!" said St. Clare, turning away, "that the story of a man that lived and died eighteen hundred years ago can affect people so yet. But he was no man," he added, suddenly. "No man ever had such long and living power! O, that I could believe what my mother taught me, and pray as I did when I was a boy!"

"If Mas'r pleases," said Tom, "Miss Eva used to read this so beautifully. I wish Mas'r'd be so good as read it. Don't get no readin', hardly, now Miss Eva's gone."

---

believeth. And straight-away the father of the child cried out, and said with tears, Lord, I believe, help thou mine unbelief" (Mark 9.23–24).

9. "And to know the love of Christ, which passeth knowledge, that ye might be filled with all the fulness of God" (Ephesians 3.19).

The chapter was the eleventh of John,—the touching account of the raising of Lazarus.[1] St. Clare read it aloud, often pausing to wrestle down feelings which were roused by the pathos of the story. Tom knelt before him, with clasped hands, and with an absorbed expression of love, trust, adoration, on his quiet face.

"Tom," said his Master, "this is all *real* to you!"

"I can jest fairly *see* it, Mas'r," said Tom.

"I wish I had your eyes, Tom."

"I wish, to the dear Lord, Mas'r had!"

"But, Tom, you know that I have a great deal more knowledge than you; what if I should tell you that I don't believe this Bible?"

"O, Mas'r!" said Tom, holding up his hands, with a deprecating gesture.

"Wouldn't it shake your faith some, Tom?"

"Not a grain," said Tom.

"Why, Tom, you must know I know the most."

"O, Mas'r, haven't you jest read how he hides from the wise and prudent, and reveals unto babes?[2] But Mas'r wasn't in earnest, for sartin, now?" said Tom, anxiously.

"No, Tom, I was not. I don't disbelieve, and I think there is reason to believe; and still I don't. It's a troublesome bad habit I've got, Tom."

"If Mas'r would only pray!"

"How do you know I don't, Tom?"

"Does Mas'r?"

"I would, Tom, if there was anybody there when I pray; but it's all speaking unto nothing, when I do. But come, Tom, you pray, now, and show me how."

Tom's heart was full; he poured it out in prayer, like waters that have been long suppressed. One thing was plain enough; Tom thought there was somebody to hear, whether there were or not. In fact, St. Clare felt himself borne, on the tide of his faith and feeling, almost to the gates of that heaven he seemed so vividly to conceive. It seemed to bring him nearer to Eva.

"Thank you, my boy," said St. Clare, when Tom rose. "I like to hear you, Tom; but go, now, and leave me alone; some other time, I'll talk more."

Tom silently left the room.

1. In John 11.1–44, Christ brings back to life a man, Lazarus, who has been dead for four days.
2. Matthew 11.25 and Luke 10.21.

# Chapter XXVIII

## *Reunion*

Week after week glided away in the St. Clare mansion, and the waves of life settled back to their usual flow, where that little bark had gone down. For how imperiously, how coolly, in disregard of all one's feeling, does the hard, cold, uninteresting course of daily realities move on! Still must we eat, and drink, and sleep, and wake again,—still bargain, buy, sell, ask and answer questions,—pursue, in short, a thousand shadows, though all interest in them be over; the cold mechanical habit of living remaining, after all vital interest in it has fled.

All the interests and hopes of St. Clare's life had unconsciously wound themselves around this child. It was for Eva that he had managed his property; it was for Eva that he had planned the disposal of his time; and, to do this and that for Eva,—to buy, improve, alter, and arrange, or dispose something for her,—had been so long his habit, that now she was gone, there seemed nothing to be thought of, and nothing to be done.

True, there was another life,—a life which, once believed in, stands as a solemn, significant figure before the otherwise unmeaning ciphers of time, changing them to orders of mysterious, untold value. St. Clare knew this well; and often, in many a weary hour, he heard that slender, childish voice calling him to the skies, and saw that little hand pointing to him the way of life; but a heavy lethargy of sorrow lay on him,—he could not arise. He had one of those natures which could better and more clearly conceive of religious things from its own perceptions and instincts, than many a matter-of-fact and practical Christian. The gift to appreciate and the sense to feel the finer shades and relations of moral things, often seems an attribute of those whose whole life shows a careless disregard of them. Hence Moore, Byron, Goethe,[1] often speak words more wisely descriptive of the true religious sentiment, than another man, whose whole life is governed by it. In such minds, disregard of religion is a more fearful treason,—a more deadly sin.

St. Clare had never pretended to govern himself by any religious obligation; and a certain fineness of nature gave him such an instinctive view of the extent of the requirements of Christianity, that he shrank, by anticipation, from what he felt would be the exactions of his own conscience, if he once did resolve to assume them. For, so inconsistent is human nature, especially in the ideal,

1. Johann Wolfgang von Goethe (1749–1832), German poet and playwright known for *Faust* (1808–32). For Moore, see above, p. 259, n. 1. For Byron, see above, p. 129, n. 1.

that not to undertake a thing at all seems better than to undertake and come short.

Still St. Clare was, in many respects, another man. He read his little Eva's Bible seriously and honestly; he thought more soberly and practically of his relations to his servants,—enough to make him extremely dissatisfied with both his past and present course; and one thing he did, soon after his return to New Orleans, and that was to commence the legal steps necessary to Tom's emancipation, which was to be perfected as soon as he could get through the necessary formalities. Meantime, he attached himself to Tom more and more, every day. In all the wide world, there was nothing that seemed to remind him so much of Eva; and he would insist on keeping him constantly about him, and, fastidious and unapproachable as he was with regard to his deeper feelings, he almost thought aloud to Tom. Nor would any one have wondered at it, who had seen the expression of affection and devotion with which Tom continually followed his young master.

"Well, Tom," said St. Clare, the day after he had commenced the legal formalities for his enfranchisement, "I'm going to make a free man of you;—so, have your trunk packed, and get ready to set out for Kentuck."

The sudden light of joy that shone in Tom's face as he raised his hands to heaven, his emphatic "Bless the Lord!" rather discomposed St. Clare; he did not like it that Tom should be so ready to leave him.

"You haven't had such very bad times here, that you need be in such a rapture, Tom," he said, drily.

"No, no, Mas'r! 'tan't that,—it's bein' a *free man!* That's what I'm joyin' for."

"Why, Tom, don't you think, for your own part, you've been better off than to be free?"

"*No, indeed,* Mas'r St. Clare," said Tom, with a flash of energy. "No, indeed!"

"Why, Tom, you couldn't possibly have earned, by your work, such clothes and such living as I have given you."

"Knows all that, Mas'r St. Clare; Mas'r's been too good; but, Mas'r, I'd rather have poor clothes, poor house, poor everything, and have 'em *mine*, than have the best, and have 'em any man's else,—I had *so*, Mas'r; I think it's natur Mas'r."

"I suppose so, Tom, and you'll be going off and leaving me, in a month or so," he added, rather discontentedly. "Though why you shouldn't, no mortal knows," he said, in a gayer tone; and, getting up, he began to walk the floor.

"Not while Mas'r is in trouble," said Tom. "I'll stay with Mas'r as long as he wants me,—so as I can be any use."

"Not while I'm in trouble, Tom?" said St. Clare, looking sadly out of the window. . . . . "And when will *my* trouble be over?"

"When Mas'r St. Clare's a Christian," said Tom.

"And you really mean to stay by till that day comes?" said St. Clare, half smiling, as he turned from the window, and laid his hand on Tom's shoulder. "Ah, Tom, you soft, silly boy! I won't keep you till that day. Go home to your wife and children, and give my love to all."

"I's faith to believe that day will come," said Tom, earnestly, and with tears in his eyes; "the Lord has a work for Mas'r."

"A work, hey?" said St. Clare; "well, now, Tom, give me your views on what sort of a work it is;—let's hear."

"Why, even a poor fellow like me has a work from the Lord; and Mas'r St. Clare, that has larnin, and riches, and friends,—how much he might do for the Lord!"

"Tom, you seem to think the Lord needs a great deal done for him," said St. Clare, smiling.

"We does for the Lord when we does for his critturs," said Tom.

"Good theology, Tom; better than Dr. B. preaches, I dare swear," said St. Clare.

The conversation was here interrupted by the announcement of some visiters.

Marie St. Clare felt the loss of Eva as deeply as she could feel anything; and, as she was a woman that had a great faculty of making everybody unhappy when she was, her immediate attendants had still stronger reason to regret the loss of their young mistress, whose winning ways and gentle intercessions had so often been a shield to them from the tyrannical and selfish exactions of her mother. Poor old Mammy, in particular, whose heart, severed from all natural domestic ties, had consoled itself with this one beautiful being, was almost heart-broken. She cried day and night, and was, from excess of sorrow, less skilful and alert in her ministrations on her mistress than usual, which drew down a constant storm of invectives on her defenceless head.

Miss Ophelia felt the loss; but, in her good and honest heart, it bore fruit unto everlasting life. She was more softened, more gentle; and, though equally assiduous in every duty, it was with a chastened and quiet air, as one who communed with her own heart not in vain. She was more diligent in teaching Topsy,—taught her mainly from the Bible,—did not any longer shrink from her touch, or manifest an ill-repressed disgust, because she felt none. She viewed her now through the softened medium that Eva's hand had first held before her eyes, and saw in her only an immortal creature, whom God had sent to be led by her to glory and virtue. Topsy did not become at once a saint; but the life and death of Eva did work a marked change in her. The callous indifference was gone; there was now sensibility, hope, desire, and the striving for good,—a strife irregular, interrupted, suspended oft, but yet renewed again.

One day, when Topsy had been sent for by Miss Ophelia, she came, hastily thrusting something into her bosom.

"What are you doing there, you limb? You've been stealing something, I'll be bound," said the imperious little Rosa, who had been sent to call her, seizing her, at the same time, roughly by the arm.

"You go 'long, Miss Rosa!" said Topsy, pulling from her; "'tan't none o' your business!"

"None o' your sa'ce!" said Rosa. "I saw you hiding something,—I know yer tricks," and Rosa seized her arm, and tried to force her hand into her bosom, while Topsy, enraged, kicked and fought valiantly for what she considered her rights. The clamor and confusion of the battle drew Miss Ophelia and St. Clare both to the spot.

"She's been stealing!" said Rosa.

"I han't, neither!" vociferated Topsy, sobbing with passion.

"Give me that, whatever it is!" said Miss Ophelia, firmly.

Topsy hesitated; but, on a second order, pulled out of her bosom a little parcel done up in the foot of one of her own old stockings.

Miss Ophelia turned it out. There was a small book, which had been given to Topsy by Eva, containing a single verse of Scripture, arranged for every day in the year, and in a paper the curl of hair that she had given her on that memorable day when she had taken her last farewell.

St. Clare was a good deal affected at the sight of it; the little book had been rolled in a long strip of black crape, torn from the funeral weeds.

"What did you wrap *this* round the book for?" said St. Clare, holding up the crape.

"Cause,—cause,—cause 'twas Miss Eva. O, don't take 'em away, please!" she said; and, sitting flat down on the floor, and putting her apron over her head, she began to sob vehemently.

It was a curious mixture of the pathetic and the ludicrous,—the little old stocking,—black crape,—text-book,—fair soft curl,—and Topsy's utter distress.

St. Clare smiled; but there were tears in his eyes, as he said,

"Come, come,—don't cry; you shall have them!" and, putting them together, he threw them into her lap, and drew Miss Ophelia with him into the parlor.

"I really think you can make something of that concern," he said, pointing with his thumb backward over his shoulder. "Any mind that is capable of a *real sorrow* is capable of good. You must try and do something with her."

The child has improved greatly," said Miss Ophelia. "I have great opes of her; but, Augustine," she said, laying her hand on his arm, one thing I want to ask; whose is this child to be?—yours or mine?"

"Why, I gave her to *you*," said Augustine.

"But not legally;—I want her to be mine legally," said Miss Ophelia.

"Whew! cousin, said Augustine. "What will the Abolition Society think? They'll have a day of fasting appointed for this backsliding, if you become a slave-holder!"

"O, nonsense! I want her mine, that I may have a right to take her to the free States, and give her her liberty, that all I am trying to do be not undone."

"O, cousin, what an awful 'doing evil that good may come'![2] I can't encourage it."

"I don't want you to joke, but to reason," said Miss Ophelia. "There is no use in my trying to make this child a Christian child, unless I save her from all the chances and reverses of slavery; and, if you really are willing I should have her, I want you to give me a deed of gift, or some legal paper."

"Well, well," said St. Clare, "I will;" and he sat down, and unfolded a newspaper to read.

"But I want it done now," said Miss Ophelia.

"What's your hurry?"

"Because now is the only time there ever is to do a thing in," said Miss Ophelia. "Come, now, here's paper, pen, and ink; just write a paper."

St. Clare, like most men of his class of mind, cordially hated the present tense of action, generally; and, therefore, he was considerably annoyed by Miss Ophelia's downrightness.

"Why, what's the matter?" said he. "Can't you take my word? One would think you had taken lessons of the Jews, coming at a fellow so!"

"I want to make sure of it," said Miss Ophelia. "You may die, or fail, and then Topsy be hustled off to auction, spite of all I can do."

"Really, you are quite provident. Well, seeing I'm in the hands of a Yankee, there is nothing for it but to concede;" and St. Clare rapidly wrote off a deed of gift, which, as he was well versed in the forms of law, he could easily do, and signed his name to it in sprawling capitals, concluding by a tremendous flourish.

"There, isn't that black and white, now, Miss Vermont?" he said, as he handed it to her.

"Good boy," said Miss Ophelia, smiling. "But must it not be witnessed?"

2. Romans 3.8.

"O, bother!—yes. Here," he said, opening the door into Marie's apartment, "Marie, Cousin wants your autograph; just put your name down here."

"What's this?" said Marie, as she ran over the paper. "Ridiculous! I thought Cousin was too pious for such horrid things," she added, as she carelessly wrote her name, "but, if she has a fancy for that article, I am sure she's welcome."

"There, now, she's yours, body and soul," said St. Clare, handing the paper.

"No more mine now than she was before," said Miss Ophelia. "Nobody but God has a right to give her to me; but I can protect her now."

"Well, she's yours by a fiction of law, then," said St. Clare, as he turned back into the parlor, and sat down to his paper.

Miss Ophelia, who seldom sat much in Marie's company, followed him into the parlor, having first carefully laid away the paper.

"Augustine," she said, suddenly, as she sat knitting, "have you ever made any provision for your servants, in case of your death?"

"No," said St. Clare, as he read on.

"Then all your indulgence to them may prove a great cruelty, by and by."

St. Clare had often thought the same thing himself; but he answered, negligently,

"Well, I mean to make a provision, by and by."

"When?" said Miss Ophelia.

"O, one of these days."

"What if you should die first?"

"Cousin, what's the matter?" said St. Clare, laying down his paper and looking at her. "Do you think I show symptoms of yellow fever or cholera, that you are making post mortem arrangements with such zeal?"

"'In the midst of life we are in death,'"[3] said Miss Ophelia.

St. Clare rose up, and laying the paper down, carelessly, walked to the door that stood open on the verandah, to put an end to a conversation that was not agreeable to him. Mechanically, he repeated the last word again,—*"Death!"*—and, as he leaned against the railings, and watched the sparkling water as it rose and fell in the fountain; and, as in a dim and dizzy haze, saw flowers and trees and vases of the courts, he repeated again the mystic word so common in every mouth, yet of such fearful power,—"DEATH!" "Strange that there should be such a word," he said, "and such a thing, and we ever forget it; that one should be living, warm and beautiful, full of

3. From the *Book of Common Prayer*, the Burial of the Dead (American edition, 1789).

hopes, desires and wants, one day, and the next be gone, utterly gone, and forever!"

It was a warm, golden evening; and, as he walked to the other end of the verandah, he saw Tom busily intent on his Bible, pointing, as he did so, with his finger to each successive word, and whispering them to himself with an earnest air.

"Want me to read to you, Tom?" said St. Clare, seating himself carelessly by him.

"If Mas'r pleases," said Tom, gratefully, "Mas'r makes it so much plainer."

St. Clare took the book and glanced at the place, and began reading one of the passages which Tom had designated by the heavy marks around it. It ran as follows:

"When the Son of man shall come in his glory, and all his holy angels with him, then shall he sit upon the throne of his glory: and before him shall be gathered all nations; and he shall separate them one from another, as a shepherd divideth his sheep from the goats." St. Clare read on in an animated voice, till he came to the last of the verses.

"Then shall the king say unto them on his left hand, Depart from me, ye cursed, into everlasting fire: for I was an hungered, and ye gave me no meat: I was thirsty, and ye gave me no drink: I was a stranger, and ye took me not in: naked, and ye clothed me not: I was sick, and in prison, and ye visited me not. Then shall they answer unto Him, Lord when saw we thee an hungered, or athirst, or a stranger, or naked, or sick, or in prison, and did not minister unto thee? Then shall he say unto them, Inasmuch as ye did it not to one of the least of these my brethren, ye did it not to me."[4]

St. Clare seemed struck with this last passage, for he read it twice,—the second time slowly, and as if he were revolving the words in his mind.

"Tom," he said, "these folks that get such hard measure seem to have been doing just what I have,—living good, easy, respectable lives; and not troubling themselves to inquire how many of their brethren were hungry or athirst, or sick, or in prison."

Tom did not answer.

St. Clare rose up and walked thoughtfully up and down the verandah, seeming to forget everything in his own thoughts; so absorbed was he, that Tom had to remind him twice that the tea-bell had rung, before he could get his attention.

St. Clare was absent and thoughtful, all tea-time. After tea, he and Marie and Miss Ophelia took possession of the parlor, almost in silence.

4. Matthew 25.31–45.

Marie disposed herself on a lounge, under a silken mosquito curtain, and was soon sound asleep. Miss Ophelia silently busied herself with her knitting. St. Clare sat down to the piano, and began playing a soft and melancholy movement with the Æolian[5] accompaniment. He seemed in a deep reverie, and to be soliloquizing to himself by music. After a little, he opened one of the drawers, took out an old music-book whose leaves were yellow with age, and began turning it over.

"There," he said to Miss Ophelia, "this was one of my mother's books,—and here is her handwriting,—come and look at it. She copied and arranged this from Mozart's Requiem." Miss Ophelia came accordingly.

"It was something she used to sing often," said St. Clare. "I think I can hear her now."

He struck a few majestic chords, and began singing that grand old Latin piece, the "Dies Iræ."[6]

Tom, who was listening in the outer verandah, was drawn by the sound to the very door, where he stood earnestly. He did not understand the words, of course; but the music and manner of singing appeared to affect him strongly, especially when St. Clare sang the more pathetic parts. Tom would have sympathized more heartily, if he had known the meaning of the beautiful words:

Recordare Jesu pie
Quod sum causa tuæ viæ
Ne me perdas, illa die
Quærens me sedisti lassus
Redemisti crucem passus
Tantus labor non sit cassus.[7]

St. Clare threw a deep and pathetic expression into the words; for the shadowy veil of years seemed drawn away, and he seemed to hear his mother's voice leading his. Voice and instrument seemed both living, and threw out with vivid sympathy those strains which the ethereal Mozart first conceived as his own dying requiem.

When St. Clare had done singing, he sat leaning his head upon his hand a few moments, and then began walking up and down the floor.

5. An ecclesiastical mode in music that uses chords extending from A to A on the piano.
6. A medieval Latin hymn about Judgment Day; part of the Requiem Mass.
7. These lines have been thus rather inadequately translated:

Think, O Jesus, for what reason
Thou endured'st earth's spite and treason,
Nor me lose, in that dread season;
Seeking me, thy worn feet hasted,
On the cross thy soul death tasted,
Let not all these toils be wasted.

[*Stowe's note*]

"What a sublime conception is that of a last judgment!" said he,—"a righting of all the wrongs of ages!—a solving of all moral problems, by an unanswerable wisdom! It is, indeed, a wonderful image."

"It is a fearful one to us," said Miss Ophelia.

"It ought to be to me, I suppose," said St Clare, stopping, thoughtfully. "I was reading to Tom, this afternoon, that chapter in Matthew that gives an account of it, and I have been quite struck with it. One should have expected some terrible enormities charged to those who are excluded from Heaven, as the reason; but no,—they are condemned for *not* doing positive good, as if that included every possible harm."

"Perhaps," said Miss Ophelia, "it is impossible for a person who does no good not to do harm."

"And what," said St. Clare, speaking abstractedly, but with deep feeling, "what shall be said of one whose own heart, whose education, and the wants of society, have called in vain to some noble purpose; who has floated on, a dreamy, neutral spectator of the struggles, agonies, and wrongs of man, when he should have been a worker?"

"I should say," said Miss Ophelia, "that he ought to repent, and begin now."

"Always practical and to the point!" said St. Clare, his face breaking out into a smile. "You never leave me any time for general reflections, Cousin; you always bring me short up against the actual present; you have a kind of eternal *now*, always in your mind."

"*Now* is all the time I have anything to do with," said Miss Ophelia.

"Dear little Eva,—poor child!" said St. Clare, "she had set her little simple soul on a good work for me."

It was the first time since Eva's death that he had ever said as many words as these of her, and he spoke now evidently repressing very strong feeling.

"My view of Christianity is such," he added, "that I think no man can consistently profess it without throwing the whole weight of his being against this monstrous system of injustice that lies at the foundation of all our society; and, if need be, sacrificing himself in the battle. That is, I mean that *I* could not be a Christian otherwise, though I have certainly had intercourse with a great many enlightened and Christian people who did no such thing; and I confess that the apathy of religious people on this subject, their want of perception of wrongs that filled me with horror, have engendered in me more scepticism than any other thing."

"If you knew all this," said Miss Ophelia, "why didn't you do it?"

"O, because I have had only that kind of benevolence which consists in lying on a sofa, and cursing the church and clergy for not being martyrs and confessors. One can see, you know, very easily, how others ought to be martyrs."

"Well, are you going to do differently now?" said Miss Ophelia.

"God only knows the future," said St. Clare. "I am braver than I was, because I have lost all; and he who has nothing to lose can afford all risks."

"And what are you going to do?"

"My duty, I hope, to the poor and lowly, as fast as I find it out," said St. Clare, "beginning with my own servants, for whom I have yet done nothing; and, perhaps, at some future day, it may appear that I can do something for a whole class; something to save my country from the disgrace of that false position in which she now stands before all civilized nations."

"Do you suppose it possible that a nation ever will voluntarily emancipate?" said Miss Ophelia.

"I don't know," said St. Clare. "This is a day of great deeds. Heroism and disinterestedness are rising up, here and there, in the earth. The Hungarian nobles set free millions of serfs, at an immense pecuniary loss;[8] and, perhaps, among us may be found generous spirits, who do not estimate honor and justice by dollars and cents."

"I hardly think so," said Miss Ophelia.

"But, suppose we should rise up to-morrow and emancipate, who would educate these millions, and teach them how to use their freedom? They never would rise to do much among us. The fact is, we are too lazy and unpractical, ourselves, ever to give them much of an idea of that industry and energy which is necessary to form them into men. They will have to go north, where labor is the fashion,—the universal custom; and tell me, now, is there enough Christian philanthropy, among your northern states, to bear with the process of their education and elevation? You send thousands of dollars to foreign missions; but could you endure to have the heathen sent into your towns and villages, and give your time, and thoughts, and money, to raise them to the Christian standard? That's what I want to know. If we emancipate, are you willing to educate? How many families, in your town, would take in a negro man and woman, teach them, bear with them, and seek to make them Christians? How many merchants would take Adolph, if I wanted to make him a clerk; or mechanics, if I wanted him taught a trade? If I wanted to put Jane and Rosa to a school, how many schools are there in the northern states that would take them in? how many families that would board them? and yet they are as white as many a woman, north or south. You see, Cousin, I want

8. Hungarian peasants were effectively freed by the abolition of feudal dues in Austria-Hungary in 1848.

justice done us. We are in a bad position. We are the more *obvious* oppressors of the negro; but the unchristian prejudice of the north is an oppressor almost equally severe."

"Well, Cousin, I know it is so," said Miss Ophelia,—"I know it was so with me, till I saw that it was my duty to overcome it; but, I trust I have overcome it; and I know there are many good people at the north, who in this matter need only to be *taught* what their duty is, to do it. It would certainly be a greater self-denial to receive heathen among us, than to send missionaries to them; but I think we would do it."

"*You* would, I know," said St. Clare. "I'd like to see anything you wouldn't do, if you thought it your duty!"

"Well, I'm not uncommonly good," said Miss Ophelia. "Others would, if they saw things as I do. I intend to take Topsy home, when I go. I suppose our folks will wonder, at first; but I think they will be brought to see as I do. Besides, I know there are many people at the north who do exactly what you said."

"Yes, but they are a minority; and, if we should begin to emancipate to any extent, we should soon hear from you."

Miss Ophelia did not reply. There was a pause of some moments; and St. Clare's countenance was overcast by a sad, dreamy expression.

"I don't know what makes me think of my mother so much, to-night," he said. "I have a strange kind of feeling, as if she were near me. I keep thinking of things she used to say. Strange, what brings these past things so vividly back to us, sometimes!"

St. Clare walked up and down the room for some minutes more, and then said,

"I believe I'll go down street, a few moments, and hear the news, to-night."

He took his hat, and passed out.

Tom followed him to the passage, out of the court, and asked if he should attend him.

"No, my boy," said St. Clare. "I shall be back in an hour."

Tom sat down in the verandah. It was a beautiful moonlight evening, and he sat watching the rising and falling spray of the fountain, and listening to its murmur. Tom thought of his home, and that he should soon be a free man, and able to return to it at will. He thought how he should work to buy his wife and boys. He felt the muscles of his brawny arms with a sort of joy, as he thought they would soon belong to himself, and how much they could do to work out the freedom of his family. Then he thought of his noble young master, and, ever second to that, came the habitual prayer that he had always offered for him; and then his thoughts passed on to the beautiful Eva, whom he now thought of among the angels; and he thought till he almost fancied that that bright face and golden hair were looking upon him, out of the spray of the fountain. And, so musing, he fell asleep, and dreamed he saw her coming bounding towards him, just as she used to come, with a wreath of jessamine in her hair, her cheeks bright, and her eyes radiant with delight; but, as he looked, she seemed to rise from the ground; her cheeks wore a paler hue,—her eyes had a deep, divine radiance, a golden halo seemed around her head,—and she vanished from his sight; and Tom was awakened by a loud knocking, and a sound of many voices at the gate.

He hastened to undo it; and, with smothered voices and heavy tread, came several men, bringing a body, wrapped in a cloak, and lying on a shutter. The light of the lamp fell full on the face; and Tom gave a wild cry of amazement and despair, that rung through all the galleries, as the men advanced, with their burden, to the open parlor door, where Miss Ophelia still sat knitting.

St. Clare had turned into a café, to look over an evening paper. As he was reading, an affray arose between two gentlemen in the room, who were both partially intoxicated. St. Clare and one or two others made an effort to separate them, and St. Clare received a fatal stab in the side with a bowie-knife, which he was attempting to wrest from one of them.

The house was full of cries and lamentations, shrieks and screams; servants frantically tearing their hair, throwing themselves on the ground, or running distractedly about, lamenting. Tom and Miss Ophelia alone seemed to have any presence of mind; for Marie was in strong hysteric convulsions. At Miss Ophelia's direction, one of the lounges in the parlor was hastily prepared, and the bleeding form laid upon it. St. Clare had fainted, through pain and loss of blood; but, as Miss Ophelia applied restoratives, he revived, opened his eyes, looked fixedly on them, looked earnestly around the room, his eyes travelling wistfully over every object, and finally they rested on his mother's picture.

The physician now arrived, and made his examination. It was evident, from the expression of his face, that there was no hope; but he applied himself to dressing the wound, and he and Miss Ophelia and Tom proceeded composedly with this work, amid the lamentations and sobs and cries of the affrighted servants, who had clustered about the doors and windows of the verandah.

"Now," said the physician, "we must turn all these creatures out; all depends on his being kept quiet."

St. Clare opened his eyes, and looked fixedly on the distressed beings, whom Miss Ophelia and the doctor were trying to urge from the apartment. "Poor creatures!" he said, and an expression of bitter self-reproach passed over his face. Adolph absolutely refused to go. Terror had deprived him of all presence of mind; he threw himself along on the floor, and nothing could persuade him to rise. The rest yielded to Miss Ophelia's urgent representations, that their master's safety depended on their stillness and obedience.

St. Clare could say but little; he lay with his eyes shut, but it was evident that he wrestled with bitter thoughts. After a while, he laid his hand on Tom's, who was kneeling beside him, and said, "Tom! poor fellow!"

"What, Mas'r?" said Tom, earnestly.

"I am dying!" said St. Clare, pressing his hand; "pray!"

"If you would like a clergyman—" said the physician.

St. Clare hastily shook his head, and said again to Tom, more earnestly, "Pray!"

And Tom did pray, with all his mind and strength, for the soul that was passing,—the soul that seemed looking so steadily and mournfully from those large, melancholy blue eyes. It was literally prayer offered with strong crying and tears.[9]

When Tom ceased to speak, St. Clare reached out and took his hand, looking earnestly at him, but saying nothing. He closed his eyes, but still retained his hold; for, in the gates of eternity, the black hand and the white hold each other with an equal clasp. He murmured softly to himself, at broken intervals,

> "Recordare Jesu pie—
> . . . .
> Ne me perdas—ille die
> Quærens me—sedisti lassus."

It was evident that the words he had been singing that evening were passing through his mind,—words of entreaty addressed to Infinite Pity. His lips moved at intervals, as parts of the hymn fell brokenly from them.

"His mind is wandering," said the doctor.

"No! it is coming HOME, at last!" said St. Clare, energetically; "at last! at last!"

The effort of speaking exhausted him. The sinking paleness of death fell on him; but with it there fell, as if shed from the wings of some pitying spirit, a beautiful expression of peace, like that of a wearied child who sleeps.

9. In Hebrews 5.7. Paul compares the ideal Christian to Melchisedec, the priest-king of Salem (Genesis 14.18–20): "Who in the days of his flesh, when he had offered up prayers and supplications with strong crying and tears unto him that was able to save him from death, and was heard in that he feared."

So he lay for a few moments. They saw that the mighty hand was on him. Just before the spirit parted, he opened his eyes, with a sudden light, as of joy and recognition, and said *"Mother!"* and then he was gone!

## Chapter XXIX

### *The Unprotected*

We hear often of the distress of the negro servants, on the loss of a kind master; and with good reason, for no creature on God's earth is left more utterly unprotected and desolate than the slave in these circumstances.

The child who has lost a father has still the protection of friends, and of the law; he is something, and can do something,—has acknowledged rights and position; the slave has none. The law regards him, in every respect, as devoid of rights as a bale of merchandise. The only possible acknowledgment of any of the longings and wants of a human and immortal creature, which are given to him, comes to him through the sovereign and irresponsible will of his master; and when that master is stricken down, nothing remains.

The number of those men who know how to use wholly irresponsible power humanely and generously is small. Everybody knows this, and the slave knows it best of all; so that he feels that there are ten chances of his finding an abusive and tyrannical master, to one of his finding a considerate and kind one. Therefore is it that the wail over a kind master is loud and long, as well it may be.

When St. Clare breathed his last, terror and consternation took hold of all his household. He had been stricken down so in a moment, in the flower and strength of his youth! Every room and gallery of the house resounded with sobs and shrieks of despair.

Marie, whose nervous system had been enervated by a constant course of self-indulgence, had nothing to support the terror of the shock, and, at the time her husband breathed his last, was passing from one fainting fit to another; and he to whom she had been joined in the mysterious tie of marriage passed from her forever, without the possibility of even a parting word.

Miss Ophelia, with characteristic strength and self-control, had remained with her kinsman to the last,—all eye, all ear, all attention; doing everything of the little that could be done, and joining with her whole soul in the tender and impassioned prayers which the poor slave had poured forth for the soul of his dying master.

When they were arranging him for his last rest, they found upon his bosom a small, plain miniature case, opening with a spring. It was the miniature of a noble and beautiful female face; and on the reverse, under a crystal, a lock of dark hair. They laid them back on the lifeless breast,—dust to dust,—poor mournful relics of early dreams, which once made that cold heart beat so warmly!

Tom's whole soul was filled with thoughts of eternity; and while he ministered around the lifeless clay, he did not once think that the sudden stroke had left him in hopeless slavery. He felt at peace about his master; for in that hour, when he had poured forth his prayer into the bosom of his Father, he had found an answer of quietness and assurance springing up within himself. In the depths of his own affectionate nature, he felt able to perceive something of the fulness of Divine love; for an old oracle hath thus written,—"He that dwelleth in love dwelleth in God, and God in him."[1] Tom hoped and trusted, and was at peace.

But the funeral passed, with all its pageant of black crape, and prayers, and solemn faces; and back rolled the cool, muddy waves of every-day life; and up came the everlasting hard inquiry of "What is to be done next?"

It rose to the mind of Marie, as, dressed in loose morning-robes, and surrounded by anxious servants, she sat up in a great easy-chair, and inspected samples of crape and bombazine. It rose to Miss Ophelia, who began to turn her thoughts towards her northern home. It rose, in silent terrors, to the minds of the servants, who well knew the unfeeling, tyrannical character of the mistress in whose hands they were left. All knew, very well, that the indulgences which had been accorded to them were not from their mistress, but from their master; and that, now he was gone, there would be no screen between them and every tyrannous infliction which a temper soured by affliction might devise.

It was about a fortnight after the funeral, that Miss Ophelia, busied one day in her apartment, heard a gentle tap at the door. She opened it, and there stood Rosa, the pretty young quadroon, whom we have before often noticed, her hair in disorder, and her eyes swelled with crying.

"O, Miss Feely," she said, falling on her knees, and catching the skirt of her dress, "*do, do go* to Miss Marie for me! do plead for me! She's goin' to send me out to be whipped,—look there!" And she handed to Miss Ophelia a paper.

It was an order, written in Marie's delicate Italian hand, to the master of a whipping-establishment, to give the bearer fifteen lashes.

"What have you been doing?" said Miss Ophelia.

"You know, Miss Feely, I've got such a bad temper; it's very bad of me. I was trying on Miss Marie's dress, and she slapped my face;

1. 1 John 4.16.

and I spoke out before I thought, and was saucy; and she said that she'd bring me down, and have me know, once for all, that I wasn't going to be so topping as I had been; and she wrote this, and says I shall carry it. I'd rather she'd kill me, right out."

Miss Ophelia stood considering, with the paper in her hand.

"You see, Miss Feely," said Rosa, "I don't mind the whipping so much, if Miss Marie or you was to do it; but, to be sent to a *man!* and such a horrid man,—the shame of it, Miss Feely!"

Miss Ophelia well knew that it was the universal custom to send women and young girls to whipping-houses, to the hands of the lowest of men,—men vile enough to make this their profession,—there to be subjected to brutal exposure and shameful correction. She had *known* it before; but hitherto she had never realized it, till she saw the slender form of Rosa almost convulsed with distress. All the honest blood of womanhood, the strong New England blood of liberty, flushed to her cheeks, and throbbed bitterly in her indignant heart; but, with habitual prudence and self-control, she mastered herself, and, crushing the paper firmly in her hand, she merely said to Rosa,

"Sit down, child, while I go to your mistress."

"Shameful! monstrous! outrageous!" she said to herself, as she was crossing the parlor.

She found Marie sitting up in her easy-chair, with Mammy standing by her, combing her hair; Jane sat on the ground before her, busy in chafing her feet.

"How do you find yourself, to-day?" said Miss Ophelia.

A deep sigh, and a closing of the eyes, was the only reply, for a moment; and then Marie answered, "O, I don't know, Cousin; I suppose I'm as well as I ever shall be!" and Marie wiped her eyes with a cambric handkerchief, bordered with an inch deep of black.

"I came," said Miss Ophelia, with a short, dry cough, such as commonly introduces a difficult subject,—"I came to speak with you about poor Rosa."

Marie's eyes were open wide enough now, and a flush rose to her sallow cheeks, as she answered, sharply,

"Well, what about her?"

"She is very sorry for her fault."

"She is, is she? She'll be sorrier, before I've done with her! I've endured that child's impudence long enough; and now I'll bring her down,—I'll make her lie in the dust!"

"But could not you punish her some other way,—some way that would be less shameful?"

"I mean to shame her; that's just what I want. She has all her life presumed on her delicacy, and her good looks, and her lady-like airs, till she forgets who she is;—and I'll give her one lesson that will bring her down, I fancy!"

"But, Cousin, consider that, if you destroy delicacy and a sense of shame in a young girl, you deprave her very fast."

"Delicacy!" said Marie, with a scornful laugh,—"a fine word for such as she! I'll teach her, with all her airs, that she's no better than the raggedest black wench that walks the streets! She'll take no more airs with me!"

"You will answer to God for such cruelty!" said Miss Ophelia, with energy.

"Cruelty,—I'd like to know what the cruelty is! I wrote orders for only fifteen lashes, and told him to put them on lightly. I'm sure there's no cruelty there!"

"No cruelty!" said Miss Ophelia. "I'm sure any girl might rather be killed outright!"

"It might seem so to anybody with your feeling; but all these creatures get used to it; it's the only way they can be kept in order. Once let them feel that they are to take any airs about delicacy, and all that, and they'll run all over you, just as my servants always have. I've begun now to bring them under; and I'll have them all to know that I'll send one out to be whipped, as soon as another, if they don't mind themselves!" said Marie, looking around her decidedly.

Jane hung her head and cowered at this, for she felt as if it was particularly directed to her. Miss Ophelia sat for a moment, as if she had swallowed some explosive mixture, and were ready to burst. Then, recollecting the utter uselessness of contention with such a nature, she shut her lips resolutely, gathered herself up, and walked out of the room.

It was hard to go back and tell Rosa that she could do nothing for her; and, shortly after, one of the man-servants came to say that her mistress had ordered him to take Rosa with him to the whipping-house, whither she was hurried, in spite of her tears and entreaties.

A few days after, Tom was standing musing by the balconies, when he was joined by Adolph, who, since the death of his master, had been entirely crest-fallen and disconsolate. Adolph knew that he had always been an object of dislike to Marie; but while his master lived he had paid but little attention to it. Now that he was gone, he had moved about in daily dread and trembling, not knowing what might befall him next. Marie had held several consultations with her lawyer; after communicating with St. Clare's brother, it was determined to sell the place, and all the servants, except her own personal property, and these she intended to take with her, and go back to her father's plantation.

"Do ye know, Tom, that we've all got to be sold?" said Adolph.

"How did you hear that?" said Tom.

"I hid myself behind the curtains when Missis was talking with the lawyer. In a few days we shall all be sent off to auction, Tom."

"The Lord's will be done!" said Tom, folding his arms and sighing heavily.

"We'll never get another such a master," said Adolph, apprehensively; "but I'd rather be sold than take my chance under Missis."

Tom turned away; his heart was full. The hope of liberty, the thought of distant wife and children, rose up before his patient soul, as to the mariner shipwrecked almost in port rises the vision of the church-spire and loving roofs of his native village, seen over the top of some black wave only for one last farewell. He drew his arms tightly over his bosom, and choked back the bitter tears, and tried to pray. The poor old soul had such a singular, unaccountable prejudice in favor of liberty, that it was a hard wrench for him; and the more he said, "Thy will be done," the worse he felt.

He sought Miss Ophelia, who, ever since Eva's death, had treated him with marked and respectful kindness.

"Miss Feely," he said, "Mas'r St. Clare promised me my freedom. He told me that he had begun to take it out for me; and now, perhaps, if Miss Feely would be good enough to speak about it to Missis, she would feel like goin' on with it, as it was Mas'r St. Clare's wish."

"I'll speak for you, Tom, and do my best," said Miss Ophelia; "but, if it depends on Mrs. St. Clare, I can't hope much for you;—nevertheless, I will try."

This incident occurred a few days after that of Rosa, while Miss Ophelia was busied in preparations to return north.

Seriously reflecting within herself, she considered that perhaps she had shown too hasty a warmth of language in her former interview with Marie; and she resolved that she would now endeavor to moderate her zeal, and to be as conciliatory as possible. So the good soul gathered herself up, and, taking her knitting, resolved to go into Marie's room, be as agreeable as possible, and negotiate Tom's case with all the diplomatic skill of which she was mistress.

She found Marie reclining at length upon a lounge, supporting herself on one elbow by pillows, while Jane, who had been out shopping, was displaying before her certain samples of thin black stuffs.

"That will do," said Marie, selecting one; "only I'm not sure about its being properly mourning."

"Laws, Missis," said Jane, volubly, "Mrs. General Derbennon wore just this very thing, after the General died, last summer; it makes up lovely!"

"What do you think?" said Marie to Miss Ophelia.

"It's a matter of custom, I suppose," said Miss Ophelia. "You can judge about it better than I."

"The fact is," said Marie, "that I haven't a dress in the world that I can wear; and, as I am going to break up the establishment, and go off, next week, I must decide upon something."

"Are you going so soon?"

"Yes. St. Clare's brother has written, and he and the lawyer think that the servants and furniture had better be put up at auction, and the place left with our lawyer."

"There's one thing I wanted to speak with you about," said Miss Ophelia. "Augustine promised Tom his liberty, and began the legal forms necessary to it. I hope you will use your influence to have it perfected."

"Indeed, I shall do no such thing!" said Marie, sharply. "Tom is one of the most valuable servants on the place,—it couldn't be afforded, any way. Besides, what does he want of liberty? He's a great deal better off as he is."

"But he does desire it, very earnestly, and his master promised it," said Miss Ophelia.

"I dare say he does want it," said Marie; "they all want it, just because they are a discontented set,—always wanting what they haven't got. Now, I'm principled against emancipating, in any case. Keep a negro under the care of a master, and he does well enough, and is respectable; but set them free, and they get lazy, and won't work, and take to drinking, and go all down to be mean, worthless fellows. I've seen it tried, hundreds of times. It's no favor to set them free."

"But Tom is so steady, industrious, and pious."

"O, you needn't tell me! I've seen a hundred like him. He'll do very well, as long as he's taken care of,—that's all."

"But, then, consider," said Miss Ophelia, "when you set him up for sale, the chances of his getting a bad master."

"O, that's all humbug!" said Marie; "it isn't one time in a hundred that a good fellow gets a bad master; most masters are good, for all the talk that is made. I've lived and grown up here, in the South, and I never yet was acquainted with a master that didn't treat his servants well,—quite as well as is worth while. I don't feel any fears on that head."

"Well," said Miss Ophelia, energetically, "I know it was one of the last wishes of your husband that Tom should have his liberty; it was one of the promises that he made to dear little Eva on her death-bed, and I should not think you would feel at liberty to disregard it."

Marie had her face covered with her handkerchief at this appeal, and began sobbing and using her smelling-bottle, with great vehemence.

"Everybody goes against me!" she said. "Everybody is so inconsiderate! I shouldn't have expected that *you* would bring up all these remembrances of my troubles to me,—it's so inconsiderate! But nobody ever does consider,—my trials are so peculiar! It's so hard, that when I had only one daughter, she should have been taken!—and when I had a husband that just exactly suited me,—and I'm so hard to be suited!—he should be taken! And you seem to have so little feeling for me, and keep bringing it up to me so carelessly,—when you know how it overcomes me! I suppose you mean well; but it is very inconsiderate,—very!" And Marie sobbed, and gasped for breath, and called Mammy to open the window, and to bring her the camphor-bottle, and to bathe her head, and unhook her dress. And, in the general confusion that ensued, Miss Ophelia made her escape to her apartment.

She saw, at once, that it would do no good to say anything more; for Marie had an indefinite capacity for hysteric fits; and, after this, whenever her husband's or Eva's wishes with regard to the servants were alluded to, she always found it convenient to set one in operation. Miss Ophelia, therefore, did the next best thing she could for Tom,—she wrote a letter to Mrs. Shelby for him, stating his troubles, and urging them to send to his relief.

The next day, Tom and Adolph, and some half a dozen other servants, were marched down to a slave-warehouse, to await the convenience of the trader, who was going to make up a lot for auction.

# Chapter XXX

## *The Slave Warehouse*

A slave warehouse! Perhaps some of my readers conjure up horrible visions of such a place. They fancy some foul, obscure den, some horrible *Tartarus "informis, ingens, cui lumen ademptum."*[1] But no, innocent friend; in these days men have learned the art of sinning expertly and genteelly, so as not to shock the eyes and senses of respectable society. Human property is high in the market; and is, therefore, well fed, well cleaned, tended, and looked after, that it may come to sale sleek, and strong, and shining. A slave-warehouse in New Orleans is a house externally not much unlike many others, kept with neatness; and where every day you may see arranged, under a sort of shed along the outside, rows of men and women, who stand there as a sign of the property sold within.

Then you shall be courteously entreated to call and examine, and shall find an abundance of husbands, wives, brothers, sisters, fathers, mothers, and young children, to be "sold separately, or in lots to suit the convenience of the purchaser;" and that soul immortal,

1. In Greek mythology, Tartarus is a dark abyss in which Zeus imprisoned the Titans and in which the wicked are punished. The quotation is from Virgil's *Aeneid* 3.658: "frightful, formless, immense, with sight removed."

once bought with blood and anguish by the Son of God, when the earth shook, and the rocks rent, and the graves were opened, can be sold, leased, mortgaged, exchanged for groceries or dry goods, to suit the phases of trade, or the fancy of the purchaser.

It was a day or two after the conversation between Marie and Miss Ophelia, that Tom, Adolph, and about half a dozen others of the St. Clare estate, were turned over to the loving kindness of Mr. Skeggs, the keeper of a depot on———street, to await the auction, next day.

Tom had with him quite a sizable trunk full of clothing, as had most others of them. They were ushered, for the night, into a long room, where many other men, of all ages, sizes and shades of complexion, were assembled, and from which roars of laughter and unthinking merriment were proceeding.

"Ah, ha! that's right. Go it, boys,—go it!" said Mr. Skeggs, the keeper. "My people are always so merry! Sambo, I see!" he said, speaking approvingly to a burly negro who was performing tricks of low buffoonery, which occasioned the shouts which Tom had heard.

As might be imagined, Tom was in no humor to join these proceedings; and, therefore, setting his trunk as far as possible from the noisy group, he sat down on it, and leaned his face against the wall.

The dealers in the human article make scrupulous and systematic efforts to promote noisy mirth among them, as a means of drowning reflection, and rendering them insensible to their condition. The whole object of the training to which the negro is put, from the time he is sold in the northern market till he arrives south, is systematically directed towards making him callous, unthinking, and brutal. The slave-dealer collects his gang in Virginia or Kentucky, and drives them to some convenient, healthy place,—often a watering place,—to be fattened. Here they are fed full daily; and, because some incline to pine, a fiddle is kept commonly going among them, and they are made to dance daily; and he who refuses to be merry—in whose soul thoughts of wife, or child, or home, are too strong for him to be gay—is marked as sullen and dangerous, and subjected to all the evils which the ill will of an utterly irresponsible and hardened man can inflict upon him. Briskness, alertness, and cheerfulness of appearance, especially before observers, are constantly enforced upon them, both by the hope of thereby getting a good master, and the fear of all that the driver may bring upon them, if they prove unsalable.

"What dat ar nigger doin here?" said Sambo, coming up to Tom, after Mr. Skeggs had left the room. Sambo was a full black, of great size, very lively, voluble, and full of trick and grimace.

"What you doin here?" said Sambo, coming up to Tom, and poking him facetiously in the side. "Meditatin', eh?"

"I am to be sold at the auction, to-morrow!" said Tom, quietly.

"Sold at auction,—haw! haw! boys, an't this yer fun? I wish't I was gwine that ar way!—tell ye, wouldn't I make em laugh? But how is it,—dis yer whole lot gwine to-morrow?" said Sambo, laying his hand freely on Adolph's shoulder.

"Please to let me alone!" said Adolph, fiercely, straightening himself up, with extreme disgust.

"Law, now, boys! dis yer's one o' yer white niggers,—kind o' cream color, ye know, scented!" said he, coming up to Adolph and snuffing. "O, Lor! he'd do for a tobaccer-shop; they could keep him to scent snuff! Lor, he'd keep a whole shope agwine,—he would!"

"I say, keep off, can't you?" said Adolph, enraged.

"Lor, now, how touchy we is,—we white niggers! Look at us, now!" and Sambo gave a ludicrous imitation of Adolph's manner; "here's de airs and graces. We's been in a good family, I specs."

"Yes," said Adolph; "I had a master that could have bought you all for old truck!"

"Laws, now, only think," said Sambo, "the gentlemens that we is!"

"I belonged to the St. Clare family," said Adolph, proudly.

"Lor, you did! Be hanged if they ar'n't lucky to get shet of ye. Spects they's gwine to trade ye off with a lot o' cracked tea-pots and sich like!" said Sambo, with a provoking grin.

Adolph, enraged at this taunt, flew furiously at his adversary, swearing and striking on every side of him. The rest laughed and shouted, and the uproar brought the keeper to the door.

"What now, boys? Order,—order!" he said, coming in and flourishing a large whip.

All fled in different directions, except Sambo, who, presuming on the favor which the keeper had to him as a licensed wag, stood his ground, ducking his head with a facetious grin, whenever the master made a dive at him.

"Lor, Mas'r, 'tan't us,—we's reglar stiddy,—it's these yer new hands; they's real aggravatin',—kinder pickin' at us, all time!"

The keeper, at this, turned upon Tom and Adolph, and distributing a few kicks and cuffs without much inquiry, and leaving general orders for all to be good boys and go to sleep, left the apartment.

While this scene was going on in the men's sleeping-room, the reader may be curious to take a peep at the corresponding apartment allotted to the women. Stretched out in various attitudes over the floor, he may see numberless sleeping forms of every shade of complexion, from the purest ebony to white, and of all years, from childhood to old age, lying now asleep. Here is a fine bright girl, of ten years, whose mother was sold out yesterday, and who to-night cried herself to sleep when nobody was looking at her. Here, a worn old negress, whose thin arms and callous fingers tell of hard toil, waiting to be sold to-morrow, as a cast-off article, for what can be got for her; and some forty or fifty others, with heads variously enveloped in blankets or articles of clothing, lie stretched around them. But, in a corner, sitting apart from the rest, are two females of a more interesting appearance than common. One of these is a respectably-dressed mulatto woman between forty and fifty, with soft eyes and a gentle and pleasing physiognomy. She has on her head a high-raised turban, made of a gay red Madras handkerchief, of the first quality, and her dress is neatly fitted, and of good material, showing that she has been provided for with a careful hand. By her side, and nestling closely to her, is a young girl of fifteen,—her daughter. She is a quadroon, as may be seen from her fairer complexion, though her likeness to her mother is quite discernible. She has the same soft, dark eye, with longer lashes, and her curling hair is of a luxuriant brown. She also is dressed with great neatness, and her white, delicate hands betray very little acquaintance with servile toil. These two are to be sold to-morrow, in the same lot with the St. Clare servants; and the gentleman to whom they belong, and to whom the money for their sale is to be transmitted, is a member of a Christian church in New York, who will receive the money, and go thereafter to the sacrament of his Lord and theirs, and think no more of it.

These two, whom we shall call Susan and Emmeline, had been the personal attendants of an amiable and pious lady of New Orleans, by whom they had been carefully and piously instructed and trained. They had been taught to read and write, diligently instructed in the truths of religion, and their lot had been as happy an one as in their condition it was possible to be. But the only son of their protectress had the management of her property; and, by carelessness and extravagance involved it to a large amount, and at last failed. One of the largest creditors was the respectable firm of B. & Co., in New York. B. & Co. wrote to their lawyer in New Orleans, who attached the real estate (these two articles and a lot of plantation hands formed the most valuable part of it), and wrote word to that effect to New York. Brother B., being, as we have said, a Christian man, and a resident in a free State, felt some uneasiness on the subject. He didn't like trading in slaves and souls of men,—of course, he didn't; but, then, there were thirty thousand dollars in the case, and that was rather too much money to be lost for a principle; and so, after much considering, and asking advice from those that he knew would advise to suit him, Brother B. wrote to his lawyer to dispose of the business in the way that seemed to him the most suitable, and remit the proceeds.

The day after the letter arrived in New Orleans, Susan and Emmeline were attached, and sent to the depot to await a general auction on the following morning; and as they glimmer faintly upon us in the moonlight which steals through the grated window, we may listen to their conversation. Both are weeping, but each quietly, that the other may not hear.

"Mother, just lay your head on my lap, and see if you can't sleep a little," says the girl, trying to appear calm.

"I haven't any heart to sleep, Em; I can't; it's the last night we may be together!"

"O, mother, don't say so! perhaps we shall get sold together,—who knows?"

"If't was anybody's else case, I should say so, too, Em," said the woman; "but I'm so feard of losin' you that I don't see anything but the danger."

"Why, mother, the man said we were both likely, and would sell well."

Susan remembered the man's looks and words. With a deadly sickness at her heart, she remembered how he had looked at Emmeline's hands, and lifted up her curly hair, and pronounced her a first-rate article. Susan had been trained as a Christian, brought up in the daily reading of the Bible, and had the same horror of her child's being sold to a life of shame that any other Christian mother might have; but she had no hope,—no protection.

"Mother, I think we might do first rate, if you could get a place as cook, and I as chamber-maid or seamstress, in some family. I dare say we shall. Let's both look as bright and lively as we can, and tell all we can do, and perhaps we shall," said Emmeline.

"I want you to brush your hair all back straight, to-morrow," said Susan.

"What for, mother? I don't look near so well, that way."

"Yes, but you'll sell better so."

"I don't see why!" said the child.

"Respectable families would be more apt to buy you, if they saw you looked plain and decent, as if you wasn't trying to look handsome. I know their ways better 'n you do," said Susan.

"Well, mother, then I will."

"And, Emmeline, if we shouldn't ever see each other again, after to-morrow,—if I'm sold way up on a plantation somewhere, and you somewhere else,—always remember how you've been brought up, and all Missis has told you; take your Bible with you, and your hymn-book; and if you're faithful to the Lord, he'll be faithful to you."

So speaks the poor soul, in sore discouragement; for she knows that to-morrow any man, however vile and brutal, however godless and merciless, if he only has money to pay for her, may become owner of her daughter, body and soul; and then, how is the child to be faithful? She thinks of all this, as she holds her daughter in her arms, and wishes that she were not handsome and attractive. It seems almost an aggravation to her to remember how purely and piously, how much above the ordinary lot, she has been brought up. But she has no resort but to *pray*; and many such prayers to God have gone up from those same trim, neatly-arranged, respectable slave-prisons,—prayers which God has not forgotten, as a coming day shall show; for it is written, "Whoso causeth one of these little ones to offend, it were better for him that a mill-stone were hanged about his neck, and that he were drowned in the depths of the sea."[2]

The soft, earnest, quiet moonbeam looks in fixedly marking the bars of the grated windows on the prostrate, sleeping forms. The mother and daughter are singing together a wild and melancholy dirge, common as a funeral hymn among the slaves:

"O, where is weeping Mary?
O, where is weeping Mary?
'Rived in the goodly land.
She is dead and gone to Heaven;
She is dead and gone to Heaven;
'Rived in the goodly land."[3]

These words, sung by voices of a peculiar and melancholy sweetness, in an air which seemed like the sighing of earthly despair after heavenly hope, floated through the dark prison rooms with a pathetic cadence, as verse after verse was breathed out:

"O, where are Paul and Silas?
O, where are Paul and Silas?
Gone to the goodly land.
They are dead and gone to Heaven;
They are dead and gone to Heaven;
'Rived in the goodly land."

Sing on, poor souls! The night is short, and the morning will part you forever!

But now it is morning, and everybody is astir; and the worthy Mr. Skeggs is busy and bright, for a lot of goods is to be fitted out for

2. Christ's words in Matthew 18.6.
3. This and the following are probably verses of the popular camp-meeting song "Hebrew Children":

Where are the Hebrew children?
Where are the Hebrew children?
Where are the Hebrew children?
Safe in the promised land.

auction. There is a brisk look-out on the toilet; injunctions passed around to every one to put on their best face and be spry; and now all are arranged in a circle for a last review, before they are marched up to the Bourse.[4]

Mr. Skeggs, with his palmetto on and his cigar in his mouth, walks around to put farewell touches on his wares.

"How's this?" he said, stepping in front of Susan and Emmeline. "Where's your curls, gal?"

The girl looked timidly at her mother, who, with the smooth adroitness common among her class, answers,

"I was telling her, last night, to put up her hair smooth and neat, and not havin' it flying about in curls; looks more respectable so."

"Bother!" said the man, peremptorily, turning to the girl; "you go right along, and curl yourself real smart!" He added, giving a crack to a rattan he held in his hand, "And be back in quick time, too!"

"You go and help her," he added, to the mother. "Them curls may make a hundred dollars difference in the sale of her."

Beneath a splendid dome were men of all nations, moving to and fro, over the marble pave. On every side of the circular area were little tribunes, or stations, for the use of speakers and auctioneers. Two of these, on opposite sides of the area, were now occupied by brilliant and talented gentlemen, enthusiastically forcing up, in English and French commingled, the bids of connoisseurs in their various wares. A third one, on the other side, still unoccupied, was surrounded by a group, waiting the moment of sale to begin. And here we may recognize the St. Clare servants,—Tom, Adolph, and others; and there, too, Susan and Emmeline, awaiting their turn with anxious and dejected faces. Various spectators, intending to purchase, or not intending, as the case might be, gathered around the group, handling, examining, and commenting on their various points and faces with the same freedom that a set of jockeys discuss the merits of a horse.

"Hulloa, Alf! what brings you here?" said a young exquisite, slapping the shoulder of a sprucely-dressed young man, who was examining Adolph through an eye-glass.

"Well, I was wanting a valet, and I heard that St. Clare's lot was going. I thought I'd just look at his—"

"Catch me ever buying any of St. Clare's people! Spoilt niggers, every one. Impudent as the devil!" said the other.

"Never fear that!" said the first. "If I get 'em, I'll soon have their airs out of them; they'll soon find that they've another kind of master

4. A place where merchants, bankers, and brokers do business; a market or exchange.

to deal with than Monsieur St. Clare. 'Pon my word, I'll buy that fellow. I like the shape of him."

"You'll find it'll take all you've got to keep him. He's deucedly extravagant!"

"Yes, but my lord will find that he *can't* be extravagant with *me*. Just let him be sent to the calaboose a few times, and thoroughly dressed down! I'll tell you if it don't bring him to a sense of his ways! O, I'll reform him, up hill and down,—you'll see. I buy him, that's flat!"

Tom had been standing wistfully examining the multitude of faces thronging around him, for one whom he would wish to call master. And if you should ever be under the necessity, sir, of selecting, out of two hundred men, one who was to become your absolute owner and disposer, you would, perhaps, realize, just as Tom did, how few there were that you would feel at all comfortable in being made over to. Tom saw abundance of men,—great, burly, gruff men; little, chirping, dried men; long-favored, lank, hard men; and every variety of stubbed-looking, commonplace men, who pick up their fellow-men as one picks up chips, putting them into the fire or a basket with equal unconcern, according to their convenience; but he saw no St. Clare.

A little before the sale commenced, a short, broad, muscular man, in a checked shirt considerably open at the bosom, and pantaloons much the worse for dirt and wear, elbowed his way through the crowd, like one who is going actively into a business; and, coming up to the group, began to examine them systematically. From the moment that Tom saw him approaching, he felt an immediate and revolting horror at him, that increased as he came near. He was evidently, though short, of gigantic strength. His round, bullet head, large, light-gray eyes, with their shaggy, sandy eye-brows, and stiff, wiry, sun-burned hair, were rather unprepossessing items, it is to be confessed; his large, coarse mouth was distended with tobacco, the juice of which, from time to time, he ejected from him with great decision and explosive force; his hands were immensely large, hairy, sunburned, freckled, and very dirty, and garnished with long nails, in a very foul condition. This man proceeded to a very free personal examination of the lot. He seized Tom by the jaw, and pulled open his mouth to inspect his teeth; made him strip up his sleeve, to show his muscle; turned him round, made him jump and spring, to show his paces.

"Where was you raised?" he added, briefly, to these investigations.

"In Kintuck, Mas'r," said Tom, looking about, as if for deliverance.

"What have you done?"

"Had care of Mas'r's farm," said Tom.

"Likely story!" said the other, shortly, as he passed on. He paused a moment before Dolph; then spitting a discharge of tobacco-juice on his well-blacked boots, and giving a contemptuous umph, he walked on. Again he stopped before Susan and Emmeline. He put out his heavy, dirty hand, and drew the girl towards him; passed it over her neck and bust, felt her arms, looked at her teeth, and then pushed her back against her mother, whose patient face showed the suffering she had been going through at every motion of the hideous stranger.

The girl was frightened, and began to cry.

"Stop that, you minx!" said the salesman; "no whimpering here,—the sale is going to begin." And accordingly the sale begun.

Adolph was knocked off, at a good sum, to the young gentleman who had previously stated his intention of buying him; and the other servants of the St. Clare lot went to various bidders.

"Now, up with you, boy! d'ye hear?" said the auctioneer to Tom.

Tom stepped upon the block, gave a few anxious looks round; all seemed mingled in a common, indistinct noise,—the clatter of the salesman crying off his qualifications in French and English, the quick fire of French and English bids; and almost in a moment came the final thump of the hammer, and the clear ring on the last syllable of the word *"dollars,"* as the auctioneer announced his price, and Tom was made over.—He had a master!

He was pushed from the block;—the short, bullet-headed man seizing him roughly by the shoulder, pushed him to one side, saying, in a harsh voice, "Stand there, *you!*"

Tom hardly realized anything; but still the bidding went on,—rattling, clattering, now French, now English. Down goes the hammer again,—Susan is sold! She goes down from the block, stops, looks wistfully back,—her daughter stretches her hands towards her. She looks with agony in the face of the man who has bought her,—a respectable middle-aged man, of benevolent countenance.

"O, Mas'r, please do buy my daughter!"

"I'd like to, but I'm afraid I can't afford it!" said the gentleman, looking, with painful interest, as the young girl mounted the block, and looked around her with a frightened and timid glance.

The blood flushes painfully in her otherwise colorless cheek, her eye has a feverish fire, and her mother groans to see that she looks more beautiful than she ever saw her before. The auctioneer sees his advantage, and expatiates volubly in mingled French and English, and bids rise in rapid succession.

"I'll do anything in reason," said the benevolent-looking gentleman, pressing in and joining with the bids. In a few moments they have run beyond his purse. He is silent; the auctioneer grows warmer; but bids gradually drop off. It lies now between an aristocratic old citizen and our bullet-headed acquaintance. The citizen bids for a few turns, contemptuously measuring his opponent; but the bullet-head has the advantage over him, both in obstinacy and concealed length of purse, and the controversy lasts but a moment; the hammer falls,—he has got the girl, body and soul, unless God help her!

Her master is Mr. Legree, who owns a cotton plantation on the Red river.[5] She is pushed along into the same lot with Tom and two other men, and goes off, weeping as she goes.

The benevolent gentleman is sorry; but, then, the thing happens every day! One sees girls and mothers crying, at these sales, *always!* it can't be helped, &c.; and he walks off, with his acquisition, in another direction.

Two days after, the lawyer of the Christian firm of B. & Co., New York, sent on their money to them. On the reverse of that draft, so obtained, let them write these words of the great Paymaster, to whom they shall make up their account in a future day: *"When he maketh inquisition for blood, he forgetteth not the cry of the humble!"*[6]

## Chapter XXXI

### *The Middle Passage*[1]

> "Thou art of purer eyes than to behold evil, and canst not look upon iniquity: wherefore lookest thou upon them that deal treacherously, and holdest thy tongue when the wicked devoureth the man that is more righteous than he?"—HAB. 1:13.

On the lower part of a small, mean boat, on the Red river, Tom sat,—chains on his wrists, chains on his feet, and a weight heavier than chains lay on his heart. All had faded from his sky,—moon and star; all had passed by him, as the trees and banks were now passing, to return no more. Kentucky home, with wife and children, and indulgent owners; St. Clare home, with all its refinements and splendors; the golden head of Eva, with its saint-like eyes; the proud, gay, handsome, seemingly careless, yet ever-kind St. Clare; hours of ease and indulgent leisure,—all gone! and in place thereof, *what* remains?

It is one of the bitterest apportionments of a lot of slavery, that the negro, sympathetic and assimilative, after acquiring, in a refined family, the tastes and feelings which form the atmosphere of such a place, is not the less liable to become the bond-slave of the coarsest and

5. A tributary of the Mississippi, flowing south along the Texas-Arkansas border to Fulton, Arkansas, then through Louisiana to join the Atchafalaya and Mississippi rivers.
6. Psalm 9.12
1. In the slave trade, the crossing of the Atlantic with a cargo of slaves from Africa.

most brutal,—just as a chair or table, which once decorated the superb saloon, comes, at last, battered and defaced, to the bar-room of some filthy tavern, or some low haunt of vulgar debauchery. The great difference is, that the table and chair cannot feel, and the *man* can; for even a legal enactment that he shall be "taken, reputed, adjudged in law, to be a chattel personal,"[2] cannot blot out his soul, with its own private little world of memories, hopes, loves, fears, and desires.

Mr. Simon Legree, Tom's master, had purchased slaves at one place and another, in New Orleans, to the number of eight, and driven them, handcuffed, in couples of two and two, down to the good steamer Pirate, which lay at the levee, ready for a trip up the Red river.

Having got them fairly on board, and the boat being off, he came round, with that air of efficiency which ever characterized him, to take a review of them. Stopping opposite to Tom, who had been attired for sale in his best broadcloth suit, with well-starched linen and shining boots, he briefly expressed himself as follows:

"Stand up."

Tom stood up.

"Take off that stock!" and, as Tom, encumbered by his fetters, proceeded to do it, he assisted him, by pulling it, with no gentle hand, from his neck, and putting it in his pocket.

Legree now turned to Tom's trunk, which, previous to this, he had been ransacking, and, taking from it a pair of old pantaloons and a dilapidated coat, which Tom had been wont to put on about his stable-work, he said, liberating Tom's hands from the handcuffs, and pointing to a recess in among the boxes,

"You go there, and put these on."

Tom obeyed, and in a few moments returned.

"Take off your boots," said Mr. Legree.

Tom did so.

"There," said the former, throwing him a pair of coarse, stout shoes, such as were common among the slaves, "put these on."

In Tom's hurried exchange, he had not forgotten to transfer his cherished Bible to his pocket. It was well he did so; for Mr. Legree, having refitted Tom's handcuffs, proceeded deliberately to investigate the contents of his pockets. He drew out a silk handkerchief, and put it into his own pocket. Several little trifles, which Tom had treasured, chiefly because they had amused Eva, he looked upon

2. Stowe quotes the South Carolina slave code at greater length in A *Key to "Uncle Tom's Cabin"* (1853): "Slaves shall be deemed, sold, taken, reputed, and adjudged in law to be *chattels personal*, in the hands of their owners and possessors, and their executors, administrators, and assigns, *to all intents, constructions, and purposes whatsoever*" (132). Slave codes in Virginia and elsewhere were similarly worded.

with a contemptuous grunt, and tossed them over his shoulder into the river.

Tom's Methodist hymn-book, which, in his hurry, he had forgotten, he now held up and turned over.

"Humph! pious, to be sure. So, what's yer name,—you belong to the church, eh?"

"Yes, Mas'r," said Tom, firmly.

"Well, I'll soon have *that* out of you. I have none o' yer bawling, praying, singing niggers on my place; so remember. Now, mind yourself," he said, with a stamp and a fierce glance of his gray eye, directed at Tom, "*I'm* your church now! You understand,—you've got to be as I say."

Something within the silent black man answered *No!* and, as if repeated by an invisible voice, came the words of an old prophetic scroll, as Eva had often read them to him,—"Fear not! for I have redeemed thee. I have called thee by my name. Thou art MINE!"[3]

But Simon Legree heard no voice. That voice is one he never shall hear. He only glared for a moment on the downcast face of Tom, and walked off. He took Tom's trunk, which contained a very neat and abundant wardrobe, to the forecastle, where it was soon surrounded by various hands of the boat. With much laughing, at the expense of niggers who tried to be gentlemen, the articles very readily were sold to one and another, and the empty trunk finally put up at auction. It was a good joke, they all thought, especially to see how Tom looked after his things, as they were going this way and that; and then the auction of the trunk, that was funnier than all, and occasioned abundant witticisms.

This little affair being over, Simon sauntered up again to his property.

"Now, Tom, I've relieved you of any extra baggage, you see. Take mighty good care of them clothes. It'll be long enough 'fore you get more. I go in for making niggers careful; one suit has to do for one year, on my place."

Simon next walked up to the place where Emmeline was sitting, chained to another woman.

"Well, my dear," he said, chucking her under the chin, "keep up your spirits."

The involuntary look of horror, fright and aversion, with which the girl regarded him, did not escape his eye. He frowned fiercely.

"None o' your shines, gal! you's got to keep a pleasant face, when I speak to ye,—d'ye hear? And you, you old yellow poco moonshine!"

3. Isaiah 43.1.

he said, giving a shove to the mulatto woman to whom Emmeline was chained, "don't you carry that sort of face! You's got to look chipper, I tell ye!"

"I say, all on ye," he said retreating a pace or two back, "look at me,—look at me,—look me right in the eye,—*straight*, now!" said he, stamping his foot at every pause.

As by a fascination, every eye was now directed to the glaring greenish-gray eye of Simon.

"Now," said he, doubling his great, heavy fist into something resembling a blacksmith's hammer, "d'ye see this fist? Heft it!" he said, bringing it down on Tom's hand. "Look at these yer bones! Well, I tell ye this yer fist has got as hard as iron *knocking down niggers*. I never see the nigger, yet, I couldn't bring down with one crack," said he, bringing his fist down so near to the face of Tom that he winked and drew back. "I don't keep none o' yer cussed overseers; I does my own overseeing; and I tell you things *is* seen to. You's every one on ye got to toe the mark, I tell ye; quick,—straight,—the moment I speak. That's the way to keep in with me. Ye won't find no soft spot in me, nowhere. So, now, mind yerselves; for I don't show no mercy!"

The women involuntarily drew in their breath, and the whole gang sat with downcast, dejected faces. Meanwhile, Simon turned on his heel, and marched up to the bar of the boat for a dram.

"That's the way I begin with my niggers," he said, to a gentlemanly man, who had stood by him during his speech. "It's my system to begin strong,—just let 'em know what to expect."

"Indeed!" said the stranger, looking upon him with the curiosity of a naturalist studying some out-of-the-way specimen.

"Yes, indeed. I'm none o' yer gentlemen planters, with lily fingers, to slop round and be cheated by some old cuss of an overseer! Just feel of my knuckles, now; look at my fist. Tell ye, sir, the flesh on 't has come jest like a stone, practising on niggers,—feel on it."

The stranger applied his fingers to the implement in question, and simply said,

"'T is hard enough; and, I suppose," he added, "practice has made your heart just like it."

"Why, yes, I may say so," said Simon, with a hearty laugh. "I reckon there's as little soft in me as in any one going. Tell you, nobody comes it over me! Niggers never gets round me, neither with squalling nor soft soap,—that's a fact."

"You have a fine lot there."

"Real," said Simon. "There's that Tom, they telled me he was suthin' uncommon. I paid a little high for him, tendin' him for a driver and a managing chap; only get the notions out that he's larnt by bein' treated as niggers never ought to be, he'll do prime! The yellow woman I got took in on. I rayther think she's sickly, but I shall put her through for what she's worth; she may last a year or two. I don't go for savin' niggers. Use up, and buy more, 's my way;—makes you less trouble, and I'm quite sure it comes cheaper in the end;" and Simon sipped his glass.

"And how long do they generally last?" said the stranger.

"Well, donno; 'cordin' as their constitution is. Stout fellers last six or seven years; trashy ones gets worked up in two or three. I used to, when I fust begun, have considerable trouble fussin' with 'em and trying to make 'em hold out,—doctorin' on 'em up when they's sick, and givin' on 'em clothes and blankets, and what not, tryin' to keep 'em all sort o' decent and comfortable. Law, 't wasn't no sort o' use; I lost money on 'em, and 't was heaps o' trouble. Now, you see, I just put 'em straight through, sick or well. When one nigger's dead, I buy another; and I find it comes cheaper and easier, every way."

The stranger turned away, and seated himself beside a gentleman, who had been listening to the conversation with repressed uneasiness.

"You must not take that fellow to be any specimen of Southern planters," said he.

"I should hope not," said the young gentleman, with emphasis.

"He is a mean, low, brutal fellow!" said the other.

"And yet your laws allow him to hold any number of human beings subject to his absolute will, without even a shadow of protection; and, low as he is, you cannot say that there are not many such."

"Well," said the other, "there are also many considerate and humane men among planters."

"Granted," said the young man; "but, in my opinion, it is you considerate, humane men, that are responsible for all the brutality and outrage wrought by these wretches; because, if it were not for your sanction and influence, the whole system could not keep foothold for an hour. If there were no planters except such as that one," said he, pointing with his finger to Legree, who stood with his back to them, "the whole thing would go down like a mill-stone. It is your respectability and humanity that licenses and protects his brutality."

"You certainly have a high opinion of my good nature," said the planter, smiling; "but I advise you not to talk quite so loud, as there are people on board the boat who might not be quite so tolerant to opinion as I am. You had better wait till I get up to my plantation, and there you may abuse us all, quite at your leisure."

The young gentleman colored and smiled, and the two were soon busy in a game of backgammon. Meanwhile, another conversation was going on in the lower part of the boat, between Emmeline and the mulatto woman with whom she was confined. As was natural, they were exchanging with each other some particulars of their history.

"Who did you belong to?" said Emmeline.

"Well, my Mas'r was Mr. Ellis,—lived on Levee-street. P'raps you've seen the house."

"Was he good to you?" said Emmeline.

"Mostly, till he tuk sick. He's lain sick, off and on, more than six months, and been orful oneasy. 'Pears like he warnt willin' to have nobody rest, day nor night; and got so curous, there couldn't nobody suit him. 'Pears like he just grew crosser, every day; kep me up nights till I got farly beat out, and couldn't keep awake no longer; and cause I got to sleep, one night, Lors, he talk so orful to me, and he tell me he'd sell me to just the hardest master he could find; and he'd promised me my freedom, too, when he died."

"Had you any friends?" said Emmeline.

"Yes, my husband,—he's a blacksmith. Mas'r gen'ly hired him out. They took me off so quick, I didn't even have time to see him; and I's got four children, O, dear me!" said the woman, covering her face with her hands.

It is a natural impulse, in every one, when they hear a tale of distress, to think of something to say by way of consolation. Emmeline wanted to say something, but she could not think of anything to say. What was there to be said? As by a common consent, they both avoided, with fear and dread, all mention of the horrible man who was now their master.

True, there is religious trust for even the darkest hour. The mulatto woman was a member of the Methodist church, and had an unenlightened but very sincere spirit of piety. Emmeline had been educated much more intelligently,—taught to read and write, and diligently instructed in the Bible, by the care of a faithful and pious mistress; yet, would it not try the faith of the firmest Christian, to find themselves abandoned, apparently, of God, in the grasp of ruthless violence? How much more must it shake the faith of Christ's poor little ones, weak in knowledge and tender in years!

The boat moved on,—freighted with its weight of sorrow—up the red, muddy, turbid current, through the abrupt, tortuous windings of the Red river; and sad eyes gazed wearily on the steep red-clay banks, as they glided by in dreary sameness. At last the boat stopped at a small town, and Legree, with his party, disembarked.

## Chapter XXXII

### *Dark Places*

"The dark places of the earth are full of the habitations of cruelty."[1]

Trailing wearily behind a rude wagon, and over a ruder road, Tom and his associates faced onward.

In the wagon was seated Simon Legree; and the two women, still fettered together, were stowed away with some baggage in the back part of it, and the whole company were seeking Legree's plantation, which lay a good distance off.

It was a wild, forsaken road, now winding through dreary pine barrens, where the wind whispered mournfully, and now over log causeways, through long cypress swamps, the doleful trees rising out of the slimy, spongy ground, hung with long wreaths of funereal black moss, while ever and anon the loathsome form of the moccasin snake might be seen sliding among broken stumps and shattered branches that lay here and there, rotting in the water.

It is disconsolate enough, this riding, to the stranger, who, with well-filled pocket and well-appointed horse, threads the lonely way on some errand of business; but wilder, drearier, to the man enthralled, whom every weary step bears further from all that man loves and prays for.

So one should have thought, that witnessed the sunken and dejected expression on those dark faces; the wistful, patient weariness with which those sad eyes rested on object after object that passed them in their sad journey.

Simon rode on, however, apparently well pleased, occasionally pulling away at a flask of spirit, which he kept in his pocket.

"I say, *you!*" he said, as he turned back and caught a glance at the dispirited faces behind him! "Strike up a song, boys,—come!"

The men looked at each other, and the *"come"* was repeated, with a smart crack of the whip which the driver carried in his hands. Tom began a Methodist hymn,

"Jerusalem, my happy home,
Name ever dear to me!
When shall my sorrows have an end,
Thy joys when shall—"[2]

1. "Have respect unto the covenant: for the dark places of the earth are full of the habitations of cruelty" (Psalm 74.20; see also Isaiah 45.19).
2. From a hymn titled "Song of Mary" (1601).

"Shut up, you black cuss!" roared Legree; "did ye think I wanted any o' yer infernal old Methodism? I say, tune up, now, something real rowdy,—quick!"

One of the other men struck up one of those unmeaning songs, common among the slaves.

"Mas'r see'd me cotch a coon,
High boys, high!
He laughed to split,—d'ye see the moon,
Ho! ho! ho! boys, ho!
Ho! yo! hi—e! oh!"

The singer appeared to make up the song to his own pleasure, generally hitting on rhyme, without much attempt at reason; and all the party took up the chorus, at intervals,

"Ho! ho! ho! boys, ho!
High—e—oh! high—e—oh!"

It was sung very boisterously, and with a forced attempt at merriment; but no wail of despair, no words of impassioned prayer, could have had such a depth of woe in them as the wild notes of the chorus. As if the poor, dumb heart, threatened,—prisoned,—took refuge in that inarticulate sanctuary of music, and found there a language in which to breathe its prayer to God! There was a prayer in it, which Simon could not hear. He only heard the boys singing noisily, and was well pleased; he was making them "keep up their spirits."

"Well, my little dear," said he, turning to Emmeline, and laying his hand on her shoulder, "we're almost home!"

When Legree scolded and stormed, Emmeline was terrified; but when he laid his hand on her, and spoke as he now did, she felt as if she had rather he would strike her. The expression of his eyes made her soul sick, and her flesh creep. Involuntarily she clung closer to the mulatto woman by her side, as if she were her mother.

"You didn't ever wear ear-rings," he said, taking hold of her small ear with his coarse fingers.

"No, Mas'r!" said Emmeline, trembling and looking down.

"Well, I'll give you a pair, when we get home, if you're a good girl. You needn't be so frightened; I don't mean to make you work very hard. You'll have fine times with me, and live like a lady,—only be a good girl."

Legree had been drinking to that degree that he was inclining to be very gracious; and it was about this time that the enclosures of the plantation rose to view. The estate had formerly belonged to a gentleman of opulence and taste, who had bestowed some considerable attention to the adornment of his grounds. Having died insolvent, it had been purchased, at a bargain, by Legree, who used it, as he did everything else, merely as an implement for money-making. The place had that ragged, forlorn appearance, which is always produced by the evidence that the care of the former owner has been left to go to utter decay.

What was once a smooth-shaven lawn before the house, dotted here and there with ornamental shrubs, was now covered with frowsy tangled grass, with horse-posts set up, here and there, in it, where the turf was stamped away, and the ground littered with broken pails, cobs of corn, and other slovenly remains. Here and there, a mildewed jessamine or honeysuckle hung raggedly from some ornamental support, which had been pushed to one side by being used as a horse-post. What once was a large garden was now all grown over with weeds, through which, here and there, some solitary exotic reared its forsaken head. What had been a conservatory had now no window-sashes, and on the mouldering shelves stood some dry, forsaken flower-pots, with sticks in them, whose dried leaves showed they had once been plants.

The wagon rolled up a weedy gravel walk, under a noble avenue of China trees,[3] whose graceful forms and ever-springing foliage seemed to be the only things there that neglect could not daunt or alter,—like noble spirits, so deeply rooted in goodness, as to flourish and grow stronger amid discouragement and decay.

The house had been large and handsome. It was built in a manner common at the South; a wide verandah of two stories running round every part of the house, into which every outer door opened, the lower tier being supported by brick pillars.

But the place looked desolate and uncomfortable; some windows stopped up with boards, some with shattered panes, and shutters hanging by a single hinge,—all telling of coarse neglect and discomfort.

Bits of board, straw, old decayed barrels and boxes, garnished the ground in all directions; and three or four ferocious-looking dogs, roused by the sound of the wagon-wheels, came tearing out, and were with difficulty restrained from laying hold of Tom and his companions, by the effort of the ragged servants who came after them.

"Ye see what ye'd get!" said Legree, caressing the dogs with grim satisfaction, and turning to Tom and his companions. "Ye see what ye'd get, if ye try to run off. These yer dogs has been raised to track niggers; and they'd jest as soon chaw one on ye up as eat their supper. So, mind yerself! How now, Sambo!" he said, to a ragged fellow,

3. Chinaberry trees, commonly planted as small ornamental or shade trees in the southern United States and in Mexico.

without any brim to his hat, who was officious in his attentions. "How have things been going?"

"Fust rate, Mas'r."

"Quimbo," said Legree to another, who was making zealous demonstrations to attract his attention, "ye minded what I telled ye?"

"Guess I did, didn't I?"

These two colored men were the two principal hands on the plantation. Legree had trained them in savageness and brutality as systematically as he had his bull-dogs; and, by long practice in hardness and cruelty, brought their whole nature to about the same range of capacities. It is a common remark, and one that is thought to militate strongly against the character of the race, that the negro overseer is always more tyrannical and cruel than the white one. This is simply saying that the negro mind has been more crushed and debased than the white. It is no more true of this race than of every oppressed race, the world over. The slave is always a tyrant, if he can get a chance to be one.

Legree, like some potentates we read of in history, governed his plantation by a sort of resolution of forces. Sambo and Quimbo cordially hated each other; the plantation hands, one and all, cordially hated them; and, by playing off one against another, he was pretty sure, through one or the other of the three parties, to get informed of whatever was on foot in the place.

Nobody can live entirely without social intercourse; and Legree encouraged his two black satellites to a kind of coarse familiarity with him,—a familiarity, however, at any moment liable to get one or the other of them into trouble; for, on the slightest provocation, one of them always stood ready, at a nod, to be a minister of his vengeance on the other.

As they stood there now by Legree, they seemed an apt illustration of the fact that brutal men are lower even than animals. Their coarse, dark, heavy features; their great eyes, rolling enviously on each other; their barbarous, guttural, half-brute intonation; their dilapidated garments fluttering in the wind,—were all in admirable keeping with the vile and unwholesome character of everything about the place.

"Here, you Sambo," said Legree, "take these yer boys down to the quarters; and here's a gal I've got for *you*," said he, as he separated the mulatto woman from Emmeline, and pushed her towards him;— "I promised to bring you one, you know."

The woman gave a sudden start, and, drawing back, said, suddenly,

"O, Mas'r! I left my old man in New Orleans."

"What of that, you———; won't you want one here? None o' your words,—go long!" said Legree, raising his whip.

"Come, mistress," he said to Emmeline, "you go in here with me."

A dark, wild face was seen, for a moment, to glance at the window of the house; and, as Legree opened the door, a female voice said something, in a quick, imperative tone. Tom, who was looking, with anxious interest, after Emmeline, as she went in, noticed this, and heard Legree answer, angrily, "You may hold your tongue! I'll do as I please, for all you!"

Tom heard no more; for he was soon following Sambo to the quarters. The quarters was a little sort of street of rude shanties, in a row, in a part of the plantation, far off from the house. They had a forlorn, brutal, forsaken air. Tom's heart sunk when he saw them. He had been comforting himself with the thought of a cottage, rude, indeed, but one which he might make neat and quiet, and where he might have a shelf for his Bible, and a place to be alone out of his laboring hours. He looked into several; they were mere rude shells, destitute of any species of furniture, except a heap of straw, foul with dirt, spread confusedly over the floor, which was merely the bare ground, trodden hard by the tramping of innumerable feet.

"Which of these will be mine?" said he, to Sambo, submissively.

"Dunno; ken turn in here, I spose," said Sambo; "spects thar's room for another thar; thar's a pretty smart heap o' niggers to each on 'em, now; sure, I dunno what I's to do with more."

It was late in the evening when the weary occupants of the shanties came flocking home,—men and women, in soiled and tattered garments, surly and uncomfortable, and in no mood to look pleasantly on new-comers. The small village was alive with no inviting sounds; hoarse, guttural voices contending at the hand-mills where their morsel of hard corn was yet to be ground into meal, to fit it for the cake that was to constitute their only supper. From the earliest dawn of the day, they had been in the fields, pressed to work under the driving lash of the overseers; for it was now in the very heat and hurry of the season, and no means was left untried to press every one up to the top of their capabilities. "True," says the negligent lounger; "picking cotton isn't hard work." Isn't it? And it isn't much inconvenience, either, to have one drop of water fall on your head; yet the worst torture of the inquisition is produced by drop after drop, drop after drop, falling moment after moment, with monotonous succession, on the same spot; and work, in itself not hard, becomes so, by being pressed, hour after hour, with unvarying, unrelenting sameness, with not even the consciousness of free-will to take from its tediousness. Tom looked in vain among the gang, as they poured along, for companionable faces. He saw only sullen, scowling, imbruted men, and feeble, discouraged women, or women that were not women,—the strong pushing away the weak,—the gross, unrestricted animal selfishness of human beings, of whom nothing good was expected and desired; and who, treated in every way like brutes, had sunk as nearly to their level as it was possible for human beings to do. To a late hour in the night the sound of the grinding was protracted; for the mills were few in number compared with the grinders, and the weary and feeble ones were driven back by the strong, and came on last in their turn.

"Ho yo!" said Sambo, coming to the mulatto woman, and throwing down a bag of corn before her; "what a cuss yo name?"

"Lucy," said the woman.

"Wal, Lucy, yo my woman now. Yo grind dis yer corn, and get *my* supper baked, ye har?"

"I an't your woman, and I won't be!" said the woman, with the sharp, sudden courage of despair; "you go long!"

"I'll kick yo, then!" said Sambo, raising his foot threateningly.

"Ye may kill me, if ye choose,—the sooner the better! Wish't I was dead!" said she.

"I say, Sambo, you go to spilin' the hands, I'll tell Mas'r o' you," said Quimbo, who was busy at the mill, from which he had viciously driven two or three tired women, who were waiting to grind their corn.

"And I'll tell him ye won't let the women come to the mills, yo old nigger!" said Sambo. "Yo jes keep to yo own row."

Tom was hungry with his day's journey, and almost faint for want of food.

"Thar, yo!" said Quimbo, throwing down a coarse bag, which contained a peck of corn; "thar, nigger, grab, take car on 't,—yo won't get no more, *dis* yer week."

Tom waited till a late hour, to get a place at the mills; and then, moved by the utter weariness of two women, whom he saw trying to grind their corn there, he ground for them, put together the decaying brands of the fire, where many had baked cakes before them, and then went about getting his own supper. It was a new kind of work there,—a deed of charity, small as it was; but it woke an answering touch in their hearts,—an expression of womanly kindness came over their hard faces; they mixed his cake for him, and tended its baking; and Tom sat down by the light of the fire, and drew out his Bible,—for he had need of comfort.

"What's that?" said one of the women.

"A Bible," said Tom.

"Good Lord! han't seen un since I was in Kentuck."

"Was you raised in Kentuck?" said Tom, with interest.

"Yes, and well raised, too; never 'spected to come to dis yer!" said the woman, sighing.

"What's dat ar book, any way?" said the other woman.

"Why, the Bible."

"Laws a me! what's dat?" said the woman.

"Do tell! you never hearn on 't?" said the other woman. "I used to har Missis a readin' on't, sometimes, in Kentuck; but, laws o' me! we don't har nothin' here but crackin' and swarin'."

"Read a piece, anyways!" said the first woman, curiously, seeing Tom attentively poring over it.

Tom read,—"Come unto ME, all ye that labor and are heavy laden, and I will give you rest."[4]

"Them's good words, enough," said the woman; "who says 'em?"

"The Lord," said Tom.

"I jest wish I know'd whar to find Him," said the woman. "I would go; 'pears like I never should get rested agin. My flesh is fairly sore, and I tremble all over, every day, and Sambo's allers a jawin' at me, 'cause I doesn't pick faster; and nights it's most midnight 'fore I can get my supper; and den 'pears like I don't turn over and shut my eyes, 'fore I hear de horn blow to get up, and at it agin in de mornin'. If I knew whar de Lor was, I'd tell him."

"He's here, he's everywhere," said Tom.

"Lor, you an't gwine to make me believe dat ar! I know de Lord an't here," said the woman; "'t an't no use talking, though. I's jest gwine to camp down, and sleep while I ken."

The women went off to their cabins, and Tom sat alone, by the smouldering fire, that flickered up redly in his face.

The silver, fair-browed moon rose in the purple sky, and looked down, calm and silent, as God looks on the scene of misery and oppression,—looked calmly on the lone black man, as he sat, with his arms folded, and his Bible on his knee.

"Is GOD HERE?" Ah, how is it possible for the untaught heart to keep its faith, unswerving, in the face of dire misrule, and palpable, unrebuked injustice? In that simple heart waged a fierce conflict: the crushing sense of wrong, the foreshadowing of a whole life of future misery, the wreck of all past hopes, mournfully tossing in the soul's sight, like dead corpses of wife, and child, and friend, rising from the dark wave, and surging in the face of the half-drowned mariner! Ah, was it easy *here* to believe and hold fast the great password of Christian faith, that "God IS, and is the REWARDER of them that diligently seek Him"?[5]

4. Matthew 11.28.
5. "But without faith it is impossible to please him: for he that cometh to God must believe that he is, and that he is a rewarder of them that diligently seek him" (Hebrews 11.6).

Tom rose, disconsolate, and stumbled into the cabin that had been allotted to him. The floor was already strewn with weary sleepers, and the foul air of the place almost repelled him; but the heavy night-dews were chill, and his limbs weary, and, wrapping about him a tattered blanket, which formed his only bed-clothing, he stretched himself in the straw and fell asleep.

In dreams, a gentle voice came over his ear; he was sitting on the mossy seat in the garden by Lake Pontchartrain, and Eva, with her serious eyes bent downward, was reading to him from the Bible; and he heard her read,

"When thou passest through the waters, I will be with thee, and the rivers they shall not overflow thee; when thou walkest through the fire, thou shalt not be burned, neither shall the flame kindle upon thee; for I am the Lord thy God, the Holy One of Israel, thy Saviour."[6]

Gradually the words seemed to melt and fade, as in a divine music; the child raised her deep eyes, and fixed them lovingly on him, and rays of warmth and comfort seemed to go from them to his heart; and, as if wafted on the music, she seemed to rise on shining wings, from which flakes and spangles of gold fell off like stars, and she was gone.

Tom woke. Was it a dream? Let it pass for one. But who shall say that that sweet young spirit, which in life so yearned to comfort and console the distressed, was forbidden of God to assume this ministry after death?

> It is a beautiful belief,
> That ever round our head
> Are hovering, on angel wings,
> The spirits of the dead.[7]

## Chapter XXXIII

### *Cassy*

> "And behold, the tears of such as were oppressed, and they had no comforter; and on the side of their oppressors there was *power*, but they had no comforter."—Eccl. 4:1.

It took but a short time to familiarize Tom with all that was to be hoped or feared in his new way of life. He was an expert and efficient workman in whatever he undertook; and was, both from habit and principle, prompt and faithful. Quiet and peaceable in his dis-

6. Isaiah 43.2–3.
7. Reference unknown.

position, he hoped, by unremitting diligence, to avert from himself at least a portion of the evils of his condition. He saw enough of abuse and misery to make him sick and weary; but he determined to toil on, with religious patience, committing himself to Him that judgeth righteously, not without hope that some way of escape might yet be opened to him.

Legree took silent note of Tom's availability. He rated him as a first-class hand; and yet he felt a secret dislike to him,—the native antipathy of bad to good. He saw, plainly, that when, as was often the case, his violence and brutality fell on the helpless, Tom took notice of it; for, so subtle is the atmosphere of opinion, that it will make itself felt, without words; and the opinion even of a slave may annoy a master. Tom in various ways manifested a tenderness of feeling, a commiseration for his fellow-sufferers, strange and new to them, which was watched with a jealous eye by Legree. He had purchased Tom with a view of eventually making him a sort of overseer, with whom he might, at times, intrust his affairs, in short absences; and, in his view, the first, second, and third requisite for that place, was *hardness.* Legree made up his mind, that, as Tom was not hard to his hand, he would harden him forthwith; and some few weeks after Tom had been on the place, he determined to commence the process.

One morning, when the hands were mustered for the field, Tom noticed, with surprise, a new comer among them, whose appearance excited his attention. It was a woman, tall and slenderly formed, with remarkably delicate hands and feet, and dressed in neat and respectable garments. By the appearance of her face, she might have been between thirty-five and forty; and it was a face that, once seen, could never be forgotten,—one of those that, at a glance, seem to convey to us an idea of a wild, painful, and romantic history. Her forehead was high, and her eyebrows marked with beautiful clearness. Her straight, well-formed nose, her finely-cut mouth, and the graceful contour of her head and neck, showed that she must once have been beautiful; but her face was deeply wrinkled with lines of pain, and of proud and bitter endurance. Her complexion was sallow and unhealthy, her cheeks thin, her features sharp, and her whole form emaciated. But her eye was the most remarkable feature,—so large, so heavily black, overshadowed by long lashes of equal darkness, and so wildly, mournfully despairing. There was a fierce pride and defiance in every line of her face, in every curve of the flexible lip, in every motion of her body; but in her eye was a deep, settled night of anguish,—an expression so hopeless and unchanging as to contrast fearfully with the scorn and pride expressed by her whole demeanor.

Where she came from, or who she was, Tom did not know. The first he did know, she was walking by his side, erect and proud, in the dim gray of the dawn. To the gang, however, she was known; for there was much looking and turning of heads, and a smothered yet apparent exultation among the miserable, ragged, half-starved creatures by whom she was surrounded.

"Got to come to it, at last,—glad of it!" said one.

"He! he! he!" said another; "you'll know how good it is, Misse!"

"We'll see her work!"

"Wonder if she'll get a cutting up, at night, like the rest of us!"

"I'd be glad to see her down for a flogging, I'll bound!" said another.

The woman took no notice of these taunts, but walked on, with the same expression of angry scorn, as if she heard nothing. Tom had always lived among refined and cultivated people, and he felt intuitively, from her air and bearing, that she belonged to that class; but how or why she could be fallen to those degrading circumstances, he could not tell. The woman neither looked at him nor spoke to him, though, all the way to the field, she kept close at his side.

Tom was soon busy at his work; but, as the woman was at no great distance from him, he often glanced an eye to her, at her work. He saw, at a glance, that a native adroitness and handiness made the task to her an easier one than it proved to many. She picked very fast and very clean, and with an air of scorn, as if she despised both the work and the disgrace and humiliation of the circumstances in which she was placed.

In the course of the day, Tom was working near the mulatto woman who had been bought in the same lot with himself. She was evidently in a condition of great suffering, and Tom often heard her praying, as she wavered and trembled, and seemed about to fall down. Tom silently, as he came near to her, transferred several handfuls of cotton from his own sack to hers.

"O, don't, don't!" said the woman, looking surprised; "it'll get you into trouble."

Just then Sambo came up. He seemed to have a special spite against this woman; and, flourishing his whip, said, in brutal, guttural tones, "What dis yer, Luce,—foolin' a'?" and, with the word, kicking the woman with his heavy cowhide shoe, he struck Tom across the face with his whip.

Tom silently resumed his task; but the woman, before at the last point of exhaustion, fainted.

"I'll bring her to!" said the driver, with a brutal grin. "I'll give her something better than camphire!" and, taking a pin from his coat-sleeve, he buried it to the head in her flesh. The woman groaned, and half rose. "Get up, you beast, and work, will yer; or I'll show yer a trick more!"

The woman seemed stimulated, for a few moments, to an unnatural strength, and worked with desperate eagerness.

"See that you keep to dat ar," said the man, "or yer'll wish yer's dead to-night, I reckin!"

"That I do now!" Tom heard her say; and again he heard her say, "O, Lord, how long! O, Lord, why don't you help us?"

At the risk of all that he might suffer, Tom came forward again, and put all the cotton in his sack into the woman's.

"O, you mustn't! you donno what they'll do to ye!" said the woman.

"I can bar it!" said Tom, "better'n you;" and he was at his place again. It passed in a moment.

Suddenly, the stranger woman whom we have described, and who had, in the course of her work, come near enough to hear Tom's last words, raised her heavy black eyes, and fixed them, for a second, on him; then, taking a quantity of cotton from her basket, she placed it in his.

"You know nothing about this place," she said, "or you wouldn't have done that. When you've been here a month, you'll be done helping anybody; you'll find it hard enough to take care of your own skin!"

"The Lord forbid, Missis!" said Tom, using instinctively to his field companion the respectful form proper to the high bred with whom he had lived.

"The Lord never visits these parts," said the woman, bitterly, as she went nimbly forward with her work; and again the scornful smile curled her lips.

But the action of the woman had been seen by the driver, across the field; and flourishing his whip, he came up to her.

"What! what!" he said to the woman, with an air of triumph, "YOU a foolin'? Go along! yer under me now,—mind yourself, or yer'll cotch it!"

A glance like sheet-lightning suddenly flashed from those black eyes; and, facing about, with quivering lip and dilated nostrils, she drew herself up, and fixed a glance, blazing with rage and scorn, on the driver.

"Dog!" she said, "touch *me*, if you dare! I've power enough, yet, to have you torn by the dogs, burnt alive, cut to inches! I've only to say the word!"

"What de devil you here for, den?" said the man, evidently cowed, and sullenly retreating a step or two. "Didn't mean no harm, Misse Cassy!"

"Keep your distance, then!" said the woman. And, in truth, the man seemed greatly inclined to attend to something at the other end of the field, and started off in quick time.

The woman suddenly turned to her work, and labored with a despatch that was perfectly astonishing to Tom. She seemed to work by magic. Before the day was through, her basket was filled, crowded down, and piled, and she had several times put largely into Tom's. Long after dusk, the whole weary train, with their baskets on their heads, defiled up to the building appropriated to the storing and weighing the cotton. Legree was there, busily conversing with the two drivers.

"Dat ar Tom's gwine to make a powerful deal o' trouble; kept a puttin' into Lucy's basket.—One o' these yer dat will get all der niggers to feelin' 'bused, if Mas'r don't watch him!" said Sambo.

"Hey-dey! The black cuss!" said Legree. "He'll have to get a breakin' in, won't he, boys?"

Both negroes grinned a horrid grin, at this intimation.

"Ay, ay! let Mas'r Legree alone, for breakin' in! De debil heself couldn't beat Mas'r at dat!" said Quimbo.

"Wal, boys, the best way is to give him the flogging to do, till he gets over his notions. Break him in!"

"Lord, Mas'r 'll have hard work to get dat out o' him!"

"It'll have to come out of him, though!" said Legree, as he rolled his tobacco in his mouth.

"Now, dar's Lucy,—de aggravatinest, ugliest wench on de place!" pursued Sambo.

"Take care, Sam; I shall begin to think what's the reason for your spite agin Lucy."

"Well, Mas'r knows she sot herself up agin Mas'r, and wouldn't have me, when he telled her to."

"I'd a flogged her into 't," said Legree, spitting, "only there's such a press o' work, it don't seem wuth a while to upset her jist now. She's slender; but these yer slender gals will bear half killin' to get their own way!"

"Wal, Lucy was real aggravatin' and lazy, sulkin' round; wouldn't do nothin',—and Tom he tuck up for her."

"He did, eh! Wal, then, Tom shall have the pleasure of flogging her. It'll be a good practice for him, and he won't put it on to the gal like you devils, neither."

"Ho, ho! haw! haw! haw!" laughed both the sooty wretches; and the diabolical sounds seemed, in truth, a not unapt expression of the fiendish character which Legree gave them.

"Wal, but, Mas'r, Tom and Misse Cassy, and dey among 'em, filled Lucy's basket. I ruther guess der weight's in it, Mas'r!"

*"I do the weighing!"* said Legree, emphatically.

Both the drivers again laughed their diabolical laugh.

"So!" he added, "Misse Cassy did her day's work."

"She picks like de debil and all his angels!"

"She's got 'em all in her, I believe!" said Legree; and, growling a brutal oath, he proceeded to the weighing-room.

Slowly the weary, dispirited creatures, wound their way into the room, and, with crouching reluctance, presented their baskets to be weighed.

Legree noted on a slate, on the side of which was pasted a list of names, the amount.

Tom's basket was weighed and approved; and he looked, with an anxious glance, for the success of the woman he had befriended.

Tottering with weakness, she came forward, and delivered her basket. It was of full weight, as Legree well perceived; but, affecting anger, he said,

"What, you lazy beast! short again! stand aside, you'll catch it, pretty soon!"

The woman gave a groan of utter despair, and sat down on a board.

The person who had been called Misse Cassy now came forward, and, with a haughty, negligent air, delivered her basket. As she delivered it, Legree looked in her eyes with a sneering yet inquiring glance.

She fixed her black eyes steadily on him, her lips moved slightly, and she said something in French. What it was, no one knew; but Legree's face became perfectly demoniacal in its expression, as she spoke; he half raised his hand, as if to strike,—a gesture which she regarded with fierce disdain, as she turned and walked away.

"And now," said Legree, "come here, you Tom. You see, I telled ye I didn't buy ye jest for the common work; I mean to promote ye, and make a driver of ye; and to-night ye may jest as well begin to get yer hand in. Now, ye jest take this yer gal and flog her; ye've seen enough on 't to know how."

"I beg Mas'r's pardon," said Tom; "hopes Mas'r won't set me at that. It's what I an't used to,—never did,—and can't do, no way possible."

"Ye'll larn a pretty smart chance of things ye never did know, before I've done with ye!" said Legree, taking up a cow-hide, and striking Tom a heavy blow across the cheek, and following up the infliction by a shower of blows.

"There!" he said, as he stopped to rest; "now, will ye tell me ye can't do it?"

"Yes, Mas'r," said Tom, putting up his hand, to wipe the blood, that trickled down his face. "I'm willin' to work, night and day, and work while there's life and breath in me; but this yer thing I can't feel it right to do;—and, Mas'r, I *never* shall do it,—*never!*"

Tom had a remarkably smooth, soft voice, and a habitually respectful manner, that had given Legree an idea that he would be cowardly, and easily subdued. When he spoke these last words, a thrill of amazement went through every one; the poor woman clasped her hands, and said, "O Lord!" and every one involuntarily looked at each other and drew in their breath, as if to prepare for the storm that was about to burst.

Legree looked stupefied and confounded; but at last burst forth,—

"What! ye blasted black beast! tell *me* ye don't think it *right* to do what I tell ye! What have any of you cussed cattle to do with thinking what's right? I'll put a stop to it! Why, what do ye think ye are? May be ye think ye'r a gentleman, master Tom, to be a telling your master what's right, and what an't! So you pretend it's wrong to flog the gal!"

"I think so, Mas'r," said Tom; "the poor crittur's sick and feeble; 't would be downright cruel, and it's what I never will do, nor begin to. Mas'r, if you mean to kill me, kill me; but, as to my raising my hand agin any one here, I never shall,—I'll die first!"

Tom spoke in a mild voice, but with a decision that could not be mistaken. Legree shook with anger; his greenish eyes glared fiercely, and his very whiskers seemed to curl with passion; but, like some ferocious beast, that plays with its victim before he devours it, he kept back his strong impulse to proceed to immediate violence, and broke out into bitter raillery.

"Well, here's a pious dog, at last, let down among us sinners!—a saint, a gentleman, and no less, to talk to us sinners about our sins! Powerful holy critter, he must be! Here, you rascal, you make believe to be so pious,—didn't you never hear, out of yer Bible, 'Servants, obey yer masters'?[1] An't I yer master? Didn't I pay down twelve hundred dollars, cash, for all there is inside yer old cussed black shell? An't yer mine, now, body and soul?" he said, giving Tom a violent kick with his heavy boot; "tell me!"

In the very depth of physical suffering, bowed by brutal oppression, this question shot a gleam of joy and triumph through Tom's soul. He suddenly stretched himself up, and, looking earnestly to heaven, while the tears and blood that flowed down his face mingled, he exclaimed,

"No! no! no! my soul an't yours, Mas'r! You haven't bought it,—ye can't buy it! It's been bought and paid for, by one that is able to keep it;—no matter, no matter, you can't harm me!"

"I can't!" said Legree, with a sneer; "we'll see,—we'll see! Here, Sambo, Quimbo, give this dog such a breakin' in as he won't get over, this month!"

The two gigantic negroes that now laid hold of Tom, with fiendish exultation in their faces, might have formed no unapt personification

1. "Servants, obey in all things your masters according to the flesh; not with eyeservice, as men-pleasers; but in singleness of heart, fearing God" (Colossians 3.22).

of powers of darkness. The poor woman screamed with apprehension, and all rose, as by a general impulse, while they dragged him unresisting from the place.

## Chapter XXXIV

### *The Quadroon's Story*

> And behold the tears of such as are oppressed; and on the side of their oppressors there was power. Wherefore I praised the dead that are already dead more than the living that are yet alive.
> —ECCL. 4:1.

It was late at night, and Tom lay groaning and bleeding alone, in an old forsaken room of the gin-house, among pieces of broken machinery, piles of damaged cotton, and other rubbish which had there accumulated.

The night was damp and close, and the thick air swarmed with myriads of mosquitos, which increased the restless torture of his wounds; whilst a burning thirst—a torture beyond all others—filled up the uttermost measure of physical anguish.

"O, good Lord! *Do* look down,—give me the victory!—give me the victory over all!" prayed poor Tom, in his anguish.

A footstep entered the room, behind him, and the light of a lantern flashed on his eyes.

"Who's there? O, for the Lord's massy, please give me some water!"

The woman Cassy—for it was she—set down her lantern, and, pouring water from a bottle, raised his head, and gave him drink. Another and another cup were drained, with feverish eagerness.

"Drink all ye want," she said; "I knew how it would be. It isn't the first time I've been out in the night, carrying water to such as you."

"Thank you, Missis," said Tom, when he had done drinking.

"Don't call me Missis! I'm a miserable slave, like yourself,—a lower one than you can ever be!" said she, bitterly; "but now," said she, going to the door, and dragging in a small pallaise,[1] over which she had spread linen cloths wet with cold water, "try, my poor fellow, to roll yourself on to this."

Stiff with wounds and bruises, Tom was a long time in accomplishing this movement; but, when done, he felt a sensible relief from the cooling application to his wounds.

The woman, whom long practice with the victims of brutality had made familiar with many healing arts, went on to make many

1. Usually *palliasse*, a mattress filled with straw or sawdust.

applications to Tom's wounds, by means of which he was soon somewhat relieved.

"Now," said the woman, when she had raised his head on a roll of damaged cotton, which served for a pillow, "there's the best I can do for you."

Tom thanked her; and the woman, sitting down on the floor, drew up her knees, and embracing them with her arms, looked fixedly before her, with a bitter and painful expression of countenance. Her bonnet fell back, and long wavy streams of black hair fell around her singular and melancholy face.

"It's no use, my poor fellow!" she broke out, at last, "it's of no use, this you've been trying to do. You were a brave fellow,—you had the right on your side; but it's all in vain, and out of the question, for you to struggle. You are in the devil's hands;—he is the strongest, and you must give up!"

Give up! and, had not human weakness and physical agony whispered that, before? Tom started; for the bitter woman, with her wild eyes and melancholy voice, seemed to him an embodiment of the temptation with which he had been wrestling.

"O Lord! O Lord!" he groaned, "how can I give up?"

"There's no use calling on the Lord,—he never hears," said the woman, steadily; "there isn't any God, I believe; or, if there is, he's taken sides against us. All goes against us, heaven and earth. Everything is pushing us into hell. Why shouldn't we go?"

Tom closed his eyes, and shuddered at the dark, atheistic words.

"You see," said the woman, "*you* don't know anything about it;—I do. I've been on this place five years, body and soul, under this man's foot; and I hate him as I do the devil! Here you are, on a lone plantation, ten miles from any other, in the swamps; not a white person here, who could testify, if you were burned alive,—if you were scalded, cut into inch-pieces, set up for the dogs to tear, or hung up and whipped to death. There's no law here, of God or man, that can do you, or any one of us, the least good; and, this man! there's no earthly thing that he's too good to do. I could make any one's hair rise, and their teeth chatter, if I should only tell what I've seen and been knowing to, here,—and it's no use resisting! Did I *want* to live with him? Wasn't I a woman delicately bred; and he—God in heaven! what was he, and is he? And yet, I've lived with him, these five years, and cursed every moment of my life,—night and day! And now, he's got a new one,—a young thing, only fifteen, and she brought up, she says, piously. Her good mistress taught her to read the Bible; and she's brought her Bible here—to hell with her!"—and the woman laughed a wild and doleful laugh, that rung, with a strange, supernatural sound, through the old ruined shed.

Tom folded his hands; all was darkness and horror.

Cassy ministering to Uncle Tom after his whipping.

"O Jesus! Lord Jesus! have you quite forgot us poor critturs?" burst forth, at last;—"help, Lord, I perish!"

The woman sternly continued:

"And what are these miserable low dogs you work with, that you should suffer on their account? Every one of them would turn against you, the first time they got a chance. They are all of 'em as low and cruel to each other as they can be; there's no use in your suffering to keep from hurting them."

"Poor critturs!" said Tom,—"what made 'em cruel?—and, if I give out, I shall get used to't, and grow, little by little, just like 'em! No, no, Missis! I've lost everything,—wife, and children, and home, and a kind Mas'r,—and he would have set me free, if he'd only lived a week longer; I've lost everything in *this* world, and it's clean gone, forever,—and now I *can't* lose Heaven, too; no, I can't get to be wicked, besides all!"

"But it can't be that the Lord will lay sin to our account," said the woman; "he won't charge it to us, when we're forced to it; he'll charge it to them that drove us to it."

"Yes," said Tom; "but that won't keep us from growing wicked. If I get to be as hard-hearted as that ar' Sambo, and as wicked, it won't make much odds to me how I come so; it's the *bein' so*,—that ar's what I'm a dreadin'."

The woman fixed a wild and startled look on Tom, as if a new thought had struck her; and then, heavily groaning, said,

"O God a' mercy! you speak the truth! O—O—O!"—and, with groans, she fell on the floor, like one crushed and writhing under the extremity of mental anguish.

There was a silence, a while, in which the breathing of both parties could be heard, when Tom faintly said, "O, please, Missis!"

The woman suddenly rose up, with her face composed to its usual stern, melancholy expression.

"Please, Missis, I saw 'em throw my coat in that ar' corner, and in my coat-pocket is my Bible;—if Missis would please get it for me."

Cassy went and got it. Tom opened, at once, to a heavily marked passage, much worn, of the last scenes in the life of Him by whose stripes we are healed.

"If Missis would only be so good as read that ar',—it's better than water."

Cassy took the book, with a dry, proud air, and looked over the passage. She then read aloud, in a soft voice, and with a beauty of intonation that was peculiar, that touching account of anguish and of glory. Often, as she read, her voice faltered, and sometimes failed her altogether, when she would stop, with an air of frigid composure, till she had mastered herself. When she came to the touching words, "Father forgive them, for they know not what they do,"[2] she threw down the book, and, burying her face in the heavy masses of her hair, she sobbed aloud, with a convulsive violence.

Tom was weeping, also, and occasionally uttering a smothered ejaculation.

"If we only could keep up to that ar'!" said Tom;—"it seemed to come so natural to him, and we have to fight so hard for 't! O Lord, help us! O blessed Lord Jesus, do help us!"

"Missis," said Tom, after a while, "I can see that, some how, you're quite 'bove me in everything; but there's one thing Missis might learn even from poor Tom. Ye said the Lord took sides against us, because he lets us be 'bused and knocked round; but ye see what come on his own Son,—the blessed Lord of Glory,—wan't he allays poor? and have we, any on us, yet come so low as he come? The Lord han't forgot us,—I'm sartin' o' that ar'. If we suffer with him, we shall also reign, Scripture says; but, if we deny Him, he also will deny us. Didn't they all suffer?—the Lord and all his? It tells how they was stoned and sawn asunder, and wandered about in sheep-skins and goat-skins, and was destitute, afflicted, tormented. Sufferin' an't no reason to make us think the Lord's turned agin us; but jest the contrary, if only we hold on to him, and doesn't give up to sin."

"But why does he put us where we can't help but sin?" said the woman.

"I think we *can* help it," said Tom.

"You'll see," said Cassy; "what'll you do? To-morrow they'll be at you again. I know 'em; I've seen all their doings; I can't bear to think of all they'll bring you to;—and they'll make you give out, at last!"

"Lord Jesus!" said Tom, "you *will* take care of my soul? O Lord, do!—don't let me give out!"

"O dear!" said Cassy; "I've heard all this crying and praying before; and yet, they've been broken down, and brought under. There's Emmeline, she's trying to hold on, and you're trying,—but what use? You must give up, or be killed by inches."

"Well, then, I *will* die!" said Tom. "Spin it out as long as they can, they can't help my dying, some time!—and, after that, they can't do no more. I'm clar, I'm set! I *know* the Lord'll help me, and bring me through."

The woman did not answer; she sat with her black eyes intently fixed on the floor.

"May be it's the way," she murmured to herself; "but those that *have* given up, there's no hope for them!—none! We live in filth, and

2. Spoken by Christ on the Cross: "Father, forgive them, for they know not what they do" (Luke 23.34).

grow loathsome, till we loathe ourselves! And we long to die, and we don't dare to kill ourselves!—No hope! no hope! no hope!—this girl now,—just as old as I was!

"You see me now," she said, speaking to Tom very rapidly; "see what I am! Well, I was brought up in luxury; the first I remember is, playing about, when I was a child, in splendid parlors;—when I was kept dressed up like a doll, and company and visiters used to praise me. There was a garden opening from the saloon windows; and there I used to play hide-and-go-seek, under the orange-trees, with my brothers and sisters. I went to a convent, and there I learned music, French and embroidery, and what not; and when I was fourteen, I came out to my father's funeral. He died very suddenly, and when the property came to be settled, they found that there was scarcely enough to cover the debts; and when the creditors took an inventory of the property, I was set down in it. My mother was a slave woman, and my father had always meant to set me free; but he had not done it, and so I was set down in the list. I'd always known who I was, but never thought much about it. Nobody ever expects that a strong, healthy man is a going to die. My father was a well man only four hours before he died;—it was one of the first cholera cases in New Orleans. The day after the funeral, my father's wife took her children, and went up to her father's plantation. I thought they treated me strangely, but didn't know. There was a young lawyer who they left to settle the business; and he came every day, and was about the house, and spoke very politely to me. He brought with him, one day, a young man, whom I thought the handsomest I had ever seen. I shall never forget that evening. I walked with him in the garden. I was lonesome and full of sorrow, and he was so kind and gentle to me; and he told me that he had seen me before I went to the convent, and that he had loved me a great while, and that he would be my friend and protector;—in short, though he didn't tell me, he had paid two thousand dollars for me, and I was his property,—I became his willingly, for I loved him. Loved!" said the woman, stopping. "O, how I *did* love that man! How I love him now,—and always shall, while I breathe! He was so beautiful, so high, so noble! He put me into a beautiful house, with servants, horses, and carriages, and furniture, and dresses. Everything that money could buy, he gave me; but I didn't set any value on all that,—I only cared for him. I loved him better than my God and my own soul; and, if I tried, I couldn't do any other way from what he wanted me to.

"I wanted only one thing—I did want him to *marry* me. I thought, if he loved me as he said he did, and if I was what he seemed to think I was, he would be willing to marry me and set me free. But he convinced me that it would be impossible; and he told me that, if we were only faithful to each other, it was marriage before God.

If that is true, wasn't I that man's wife? Wasn't I faithful? For seven years, didn't I study every look and motion, and only live and breathe to please him? He had the yellow fever,[3] and for twenty days and nights I watched with him. I alone,—and gave him all his medicine, and did everything for him; and then he called me his good angel, and said I'd saved his life. We had two beautiful children. The first was a boy, and we called him Henry. He was the image of his father,—he had such beautiful eyes, such a forehead, and his hair hung all in curls around it; and he had all his father's spirit, and his talent, too. Little Elise, he said, looked like me. He used to tell me that I was the most beautiful woman in Louisiana, he was so proud of me and the children. He used to love to have me dress them up, and take them and me about in an open carriage, and hear the remarks that people would make on us; and he used to fill my ears constantly with the fine things that were said in praise of me and the children. O, those were happy days! I thought I was as happy as any one could be; but then there came evil times. He had a cousin come to New Orleans, who was his particular friend,—he thought all the world of him;—but, from the first time I saw him, I couldn't tell why, I dreaded him; for I felt sure he was going to bring misery on us. He got Henry to going out with him, and often he would not come home nights till two or three o'clock. I did not dare say a word; for Henry was so high-spirited, I was afraid to. He got him to the gaming-houses; and he was one of the sort that, when he once got a going there, there was no holding back. And then he introduced him to another lady, and I saw soon that his heart was gone from me. He never told me, but I saw it,—I knew it, day after day,—I felt my heart breaking, but I could not say a word! At this, the wretch offered to buy me and the children of Henry, to clear off his gambling debts, which stood in the way of his marrying as he wished,—and *he sold us.* He told me, one day, that he had business in the country, and should be gone two or three weeks. He spoke kinder than usual, and said he should come back; but it didn't deceive me. I knew that the time had come; I was just like one turned into stone; I couldn't speak, nor shed a tear. He kissed me and kissed the children, a good many times, and went out. I saw him get on his horse, and I watched him till he was quite out of sight; and then I fell down, and fainted.

"Then *he* came, the cursed wretch! he came to take possession. He told me that he had bought me and my children; and showed me the papers. I cursed him before God, and told him I'd die sooner than live with him.

3. Infectious disease transmitted by mosquitoes and occurring in epidemics in tropical areas of Africa and the Americas, causing fever and often death.

"'Just as you please,' said he; 'but, if you don't behave reasonably, I'll sell both the children, where you shall never see them again.' He told me that he always had meant to have me, from the first time he saw me; and that he had drawn Henry on, and got him in debt, on purpose to make him willing to sell me. That he got him in love with another woman; and that I might know, after all that, that he should not give up for a few airs and tears, and things of that sort.

"I gave up, for my hands were tied. He had my children;—whenever I resisted his will anywhere, he would talk about selling them, and he made me as submissive as he desired. O, what a life it was! to live with my heart breaking, every day,—to keep on, on, on, loving, when it was only misery; and to be bound, body and soul, to one I hated. I used to love to read to Henry, to play to him, to waltz with him, and sing to him; but everything I did for this one was a perfect drag,—yet I was afraid to refuse anything. He was very imperious, and harsh to the children. Elise was a timid little thing; but Henry was bold and high-spirited, like his father, and he had never been brought under, in the least, by any one. He was always finding fault, and quarrelling with him; and I used to live in daily fear and dread. I tried to make the child respectful,—I tried to keep them apart, for I held on to those children like death; but it did no good. *He sold both those children.* He took me to ride, one day, and when I came home, they were nowhere to be found! He told me he had sold them; he showed me the money, the price of their blood. Then it seemed as if all good forsook me. I raved and cursed,—cursed God and man; and, for a while, I believe, he really was afraid of me. But he didn't give up so. He told me that my children were sold, but whether I ever saw their faces again, depended on him; and that, if I wasn't quiet, they should smart for it. Well, you can do anything with a woman, when you've got her children. He made me submit; he made me be peaceable; he flattered me with hopes that, perhaps, he would buy them back; and so things went on, a week or two. One day, I was out walking, and passed by the calaboose; I saw a crowd about the gate, and heard a child's voice,—and suddenly my Henry broke away from two or three men who were holding him, and ran, screaming, and caught my dress. They came up to him, swearing dreadfully; and one man, whose face I shall never forget, told him that he wouldn't get away so; that he was going with him into the calaboose, and he'd get a lesson there he'd never forget. I tried to beg and plead,—they only laughed; the poor boy screamed and looked into my face, and held on to me, until, in tearing him off, they tore the skirt of my dress half away; and they carried him in, screaming 'Mother! mother! mother!' There was one man stood there seemed to pity me. I offered him all the money I had, if he'd only interfere. He shook his head, and said that the man said the boy had been impudent and disobedient, ever since he bought him; that he was going to break him in, once for all. I turned and ran; and every step of the way, I thought that I heard him scream. I got into the house; ran, all out of breath, to the parlor, where I found Butler. I told him, and begged him to go and interfere. He only laughed, and told me the boy had got his deserts. He'd got to be broken in,—the sooner the better; 'what did I expect?' he asked.

"It seemed to me something in my head snapped, at that moment. I felt dizzy and furious. I remember seeing a great sharp bowie-knife on the table; I remember something about catching it, and flying upon him; and then all grew dark, and I didn't know any more—not for days and days.

"When I came to myself, I was in a nice room,—but not mine. An old black woman tended me; and a doctor came to see me, and there was a great deal of care taken of me. After a while, I found that he had gone away, and left me at this house to be sold; and that's why they took such pains with me.

"I didn't mean to get well, and hoped I shouldn't; but, in spite of me, the fever went off, and I grew healthy, and finally got up. Then, they made me dress up, every day; and gentlemen used to come in and stand and smoke their cigars, and look at me, and ask questions, and debate my price. I was so gloomy and silent, that none of them wanted me. They threatened to whip me, if I wasn't gayer, and didn't take some pains to make myself agreeable. At length, one day, came a gentleman named Stuart. He seemed to have some feeling for me; he saw that something dreadful was on my heart, and he came to see me alone, a great many times, and finally persuaded me to tell him. He bought me, at last, and promised to do all he could to find and buy back my children. He went to the hotel where my Henry was; they told him he had been sold to a planter up on Pearl river;[4] that was the last that I ever heard. Then he found where my daughter was; an old woman was keeping her. He offered an immense sum for her, but they would not sell her. Butler found out that it was for me he wanted her; and he sent me word that I should never have her. Captain Stuart was very kind to me; he had a splendid plantation, and took me to it. In the course of a year, I had a son born. O, that child!—how I loved it! How just like my poor Henry the little thing looked! But I had made up my mind,—yes, I had. I would never again let a child live to grow up! I took the little fellow in my arms, when he was two weeks old, and kissed him, and cried over him; and then I gave him laudanum, and held him close to my bosom, while he slept to death. How I mourned and cried over it! and who ever dreamed

4. River in central Mississippi, flowing into Lake Borgne.

that it was anything but a mistake, that had made me give it the laudanum? but it's one of the few things that I'm glad of, now. I am not sorry, to this day; he, at least, is out of pain. What better than death could I give him, poor child! After a while, the cholera came, and Captain Stuart died; everybody died that wanted to live,—and I,—I, though I went down to death's door,—I *lived!* Then I was sold, and passed from hand to hand, till I grew faded and wrinkled, and I had a fever; and then this wretch bought me, and brought me here,—and here I am!"

The woman stopped. She had hurried on through her story, with a wild, passionate utterance; sometimes seeming to address it to Tom, and sometimes speaking as in a soliloquy. So vehement and overpowering was the force with which she spoke, that, for a season, Tom was beguiled even from the pain of his wounds, and, raising himself on one elbow, watched her as she paced restlessly up and down, her long black hair swaying heavily about her, as she moved.

"You tell me," she said, after a pause, "that there is a God,—a God that looks down and sees all these things. May be it's so. The sisters in the convent used to tell me of a day of judgment, when everything is coming to light;—won't there be vengeance, then!

"They think it's nothing, what we suffer,—nothing, what our children suffer! It's all a small matter; yet I've walked the streets when it seemed as if I had misery enough in my one heart to sink the city. I've wished the houses would fall on me, or the stones sink under me. Yes! and, in the judgment day, I will stand up before God, a witness against those that have ruined me and my children, body and soul!

"When I was a girl, I thought I was religious; I used to love God and prayer. Now, I'm a lost soul, pursued by devils that torment me day and night; they keep pushing me on and on—and I'll do it, too, some of these days!" she said, clenching her hand, while an insane light glanced in her heavy black eyes. "I'll send him where he belongs,—a short way, too,—one of these nights, if they burn me alive for it!" A wild, long laugh, rang through the deserted room, and ended in a hysteric sob; she threw herself on the floor, in convulsive sobbings and struggles.

In a few moments the frenzy fit seemed to pass off; she rose slowly, and seemed to collect herself.

"Can I do anything more for you, my poor fellow?" she said, approaching where Tom lay; "shall I give you some more water?"

There was a graceful and compassionate sweetness in her voice and manner, as she said this, that formed a strange contrast with the former wildness.

Tom drank the water, and looked earnestly and pitifully into her face.

"O, Missis, I wish you'd go to him that can give you living waters!"

"Go to him! Where is he? Who is he?" said Cassy.

"Him that you read of to me,—the Lord."

"I used to see the picture of him, over the altar, when I was a girl," said Cassy, her dark eyes fixing themselves in an expression of mournful reverie; "but, *he isn't here!* there's nothing here, but sin and long, long, long despair! O!" She laid her hand on her breast and drew in her breath, as if to lift a heavy weight.

Tom looked as if he would speak again; but she cut him short, with a decided gesture.

"Don't talk, my poor fellow. Try to sleep, if you can." And, placing water in his reach, and making whatever little arrangements for his comfort she could, Cassy left the shed.

## Chapter XXXV

### *The Tokens*

"And slight, withal, may be the things that bring
Back on the heart the weight which it would fling
Aside forever; it may be a sound,
A flower, the wind, the ocean, which shall wound,—
Striking the electric chain wherewith we're darkly bound."
—*Childe Harold's Pilgrimage, Can.* 4.[1]

The sitting-room of Legree's establishment was a large, long room, with a wide, ample fireplace. It had once been hung with a showy and expensive paper, which now hung mouldering, torn and discolored, from the damp walls. The place had that peculiar sickening, unwholesome smell, compounded of mingled damp, dirt and decay, which one often notices in close old houses. The wall-paper was defaced, in spots, by slops of beer and wine; or garnished with chalk memorandums, and long sums footed up,[2] as if somebody had been practising arithmetic there. In the fireplace stood a brazier full of burning charcoal; for, though the weather was not cold, the evenings always seemed damp and chilly in that great room; and Legree, moreover, wanted a place to light his cigars, and heat his water for punch. The ruddy glare of the charcoal displayed the confused and unpromising aspect of the room,—saddles, bridles, several sorts of harness, riding-whips, overcoats, and various articles of clothing, scattered up and down the room in confused variety; and the dogs, of whom we have before spoken,

1. From the long poem (1812–18) by Lord Byron; in this stanza Childe Harold meditates on the decline of Venice from glory and on the equivocal powers of memory.
2. Totaled, as a column of numbers.

had encamped themselves among them, to suit their own taste and convenience.

Legree was just mixing himself a tumbler of punch, pouring his hot water from a cracked and broken-nosed pitcher, grumbling, as he did so,

"Plague on that Sambo, to kick up this yer row between me and the new hands! The fellow won't be fit to work for a week, now,—right in the press of the season!"

"Yes, just like you," said a voice, behind his chair. It was the woman Cassy, who had stolen upon his soliloquy.

"Hah! you she-devil! you've come back, have you?"

"Yes, I have," she said, coolly; "come to have my own way, too!"

"You lie, you jade! I'll be up to my word. Either behave yourself, or stay down to the quarters, and fare and work with the rest."

"I'd rather, ten thousand times," said the woman, "live in the dirtiest hole at the quarters, than be under your hoof!"

"But you *are* under my hoof, for all that," said he, turning upon her, with a savage grin; "that's one comfort. So, sit down here on my knee, my dear, and hear to reason," said he, laying hold on her wrist.

"Simon Legree, take care!" said the woman, with a sharp flash of her eye, a glance so wild and insane in its light as to be almost appalling. "You're afraid of me, Simon," she said, deliberately; "and you've reason to be! But be careful, for I've got the devil in me!"

The last words she whispered in a hissing tone, close to his ear.

"Get out! I believe, to my soul, you have!" said Legree, pushing her from him, and looking uncomfortably at her. "After all, Cassy," he said, "why can't you be friends with me, as you used to?"

"Used to!" said she, bitterly. She stopped short,—a world of choking feelings, rising in her heart, kept her silent.

Cassy had always kept over Legree the kind of influence that a strong, impassioned woman can ever keep over the most brutal man; but, of late, she had grown more and more irritable and restless, under the hideous yoke of her servitude, and her irritability, at times, broke out into raving insanity; and this liability made her a sort of object of dread to Legree, who had that superstitious horror of insane persons which is common to coarse and uninstructed minds. When Legree brought Emmeline to the house, all the smouldering embers of womanly feeling flashed up in the worn heart of Cassy, and she took part with the girl; and a fierce quarrel ensued between her and Legree. Legree, in a fury, swore she should be put to field service, if she would not be peaceable. Cassy, with proud scorn, declared she *would* go to the field. And she worked there one day, as we have described, to show how perfectly she scorned the threat.

Legree was secretly uneasy, all day; for Cassy had an influence over him from which he could not free himself. When she presented her basket at the scales, he had hoped for some concession, and addressed her in a sort of half conciliatory, half scornful tone; and she had answered with the bitterest contempt.

The outrageous treatment of poor Tom had roused her still more; and she had followed Legree to the house, with no particular intention, but to upbraid him for his brutality.

"I wish, Cassy," said Legree, "you'd behave yourself decently."

"*You* talk about behaving decently! And what have you been doing?—you, who haven't even sense enough to keep from spoiling one of your best hands, right in the most pressing season, just for your devilish temper!"

"I was a fool, it's a fact, to let any such brangle[3] come up," said Legree; "but, when the boy set up his will, he had to be broke in."

"I reckon you won't break *him* in!"

"Won't I?" said Legree, rising, passionately. "I'd like to know if I won't? He'll be the first nigger that ever came it round me! I'll break every bone in his body, but he *shall* give up!"

Just then the door opened, and Sambo entered. He came forward, bowing, and holding out something in a paper.

"What's that, you dog?" said Legree.

"It's a witch thing, Mas'r!"

"A what?"

"Something that niggers gets from witches. Keeps 'em from feelin' when they's flogged. He had it tied round his neck, with a black string."

Legree, like most godless and cruel men, was superstitious. He took the paper, and opened it uneasily.

There dropped out of it a silver dollar, and a long, shining curl of fair hair,—hair which, like a living thing, twined itself round Legree's fingers.

"Damnation!" he screamed, in sudden passion, stamping on the floor, and pulling furiously at the hair, as if it burned him. "Where did this come from? Take it off!—burn it up!—burn it up!" he screamed, tearing it off, and throwing it into the charcoal. "What did you bring it to me for?"

Sambo stood, with his heavy mouth wide open, and aghast with wonder; and Cassy, who was preparing to leave the apartment, stopped, and looked at him in perfect amazement.

"Don't you bring me any more of your devilish things!" said he, shaking his fist at Sambo, who retreated hastily towards the door; and, picking up the silver dollar, he sent it smashing through the window-pane, out into the darkness.

3. A squabble or wrangle.

Sambo was glad to make his escape. When he was gone, Legree seemed a little ashamed of his fit of alarm. He sat doggedly down in his chair, and began sullenly sipping his tumbler of punch.

Cassy prepared herself for going out, unobserved by him; and slipped away to minister to poor Tom, as we have already related.

And what was the matter with Legree? and what was there in a simple curl of fair hair to appall that brutal man, familiar with every form of cruelty? To answer this, we must carry the reader backward in his history. Hard and reprobate as the godless man seemed now, there had been a time when he had been rocked on the bosom of a mother,—cradled with prayers and pious hymns,—his now seared brow bedewed with the waters of holy baptism. In early childhood, a fair-haired woman had led him, at the sound of Sabbath bell, to worship and to pray. Far in New England that mother had trained her only son, with long, unwearied love, and patient prayers. Born of a hard-tempered sire, on whom that gentle woman had wasted a world of unvalued love, Legree had followed in the steps of his father. Boisterous, unruly, and tyrannical, he despised all her counsel, and would none of her reproof; and, at an early age, broke from her, to seek his fortunes at sea. He never came home but once, after; and then, his mother, with the yearning of a heart that must love something, and has nothing else to love, clung to him, and sought, with passionate prayers and entreaties, to win him from a life of sin, to his soul's eternal good.

That was Legree's day of grace; then good angels called him; then he was almost persuaded, and mercy held him by the hand. His heart inly relented,—there was a conflict,—but sin got the victory, and he set all the force of his rough nature against the conviction of his conscience. He drank and swore,—was wilder and more brutal than ever. And, one night, when his mother, in the last agony of her despair, knelt at his feet, he spurned her from him,—threw her senseless on the floor, and, with brutal curses, fled to his ship. The next Legree heard of his mother was, when, one night, as he was carousing among drunken companions, a letter was put into his hand. He opened it, and a lock of long, curling hair fell from it, and twined about his fingers. The letter told him his mother was dead, and that, dying, she blest and forgave him.

There is a dread, unhallowed necromancy of evil, that turns things sweetest and holiest to phantoms of horror and affright. That pale, loving mother,—her dying prayers, her forgiving love,—wrought in that demoniac heart of sin only as a damning sentence, bringing with it a fearful looking for of judgment and fiery indignation. Legree burned the hair, and burned the letter; and when he saw them hissing and crackling in the flame, inly shuddered as he thought of everlasting fires. He tried to drink, and revel, and swear away the memory; but often, in the deep night, whose solemn stillness arraigns the bad soul in forced communion with herself, he had seen that pale mother rising by his bedside, and felt the soft twining of that hair around his fingers, till the cold sweat would roll down his face, and he would spring from his bed in horror. Ye who have wondered to hear, in the same evangel, that God is love, and that God is a consuming fire,[4] see ye not how, to the soul resolved in evil, perfect love is the most fearful torture, the seal and sentence of the direst despair?

"Blast it!" said Legree to himself, as he sipped his liquor; "where did he get that? If it didn't look just like—whoo! I thought I'd forgot that. Curse me, if I think there's any such thing as forgetting anything, any how,—hang it! I'm lonesome! I mean to call Em. She hates me—the monkey! I don't care,—I'll *make* her come!"

Legree stepped out into a large entry, which went up stairs, by what had formerly been a superb winding staircase; but the passageway was dirty and dreary, encumbered with boxes and unsightly litter. The stairs, uncarpeted, seemed winding up, in the gloom, to nobody knew where! The pale moonlight streamed through a shattered fanlight over the door; the air was unwholesome and chilly, like that of a vault.

Legree stopped at the foot of the stairs, and heard a voice singing. It seemed strange and ghostlike in that dreary old house, perhaps because of the already tremulous state of his nerves. Hark! what is it?

A wild, pathetic voice, chants a hymn common among the slaves:

"O there'll be mourning, mourning, mourning,
O there'll be mourning, at the judgment-seat of Christ!"[5]

"Blast the girl!" said Legree. "I'll choke her.—Em! Em!" he called, harshly; but only a mocking echo from the walls answered him. The sweet voice still sung on:

"Parents and children there shall part!
Parents and children there shall part!
Shall part to meet no more!"

4. In Deuteronomy 4.24, Moses instructs his people to obey God: "For the Lord thy God is a consuming fire, even a jealous God."
5. From the spiritual titled "Judgment Seat":

O, there will be mourning before the judgment-seat,
When this world is burning beneath Jehovah's feet!
Friends and kindred there will part,
Will part to meet no more!
Wrath will sink the rebel's heart
While saints on high adore.
O, there will be mourning before the judgment-seat.

And clear and loud swelled through the empty halls the refrain,

> "O there'll be mourning, mourning, mourning,
> O there'll be mourning, at the judgment-seat of Christ!"

Legree stopped. He would have been ashamed to tell of it, but large drops of sweat stood on his forehead, his heart beat heavy and thick with fear; he even thought he saw something white rising and glimmering in the gloom before him, and shuddered to think what if the form of his dead mother should suddenly appear to him.

"I know one thing," he said to himself, as he stumbled back in the sitting-room, and sat down; "I'll let that fellow alone, after this! What did I want of his cussed paper? I b'lieve I am bewitched, sure enough! I've been shivering and sweating, ever since! Where did he get that hair? It couldn't have been *that!* I burnt *that* up, I know I did! It would be a joke, if hair could rise from the dead!"

Ah, Legree! that golden tress *was* charmed; each hair had in it a spell of terror and remorse for thee, and was used by a mightier power to bind thy cruel hands from inflicting uttermost evil on the helpless!

"I say," said Legree, stamping and whistling to the dogs, "wake up, some of you, and keep me company!" but the dogs only opened one eye at him, sleepily, and closed it again.

"I'll have Sambo and Quimbo up here, to sing and dance one of their hell dances, and keep off these horrid notions," said Legree; and, putting on his hat, he went on to the verandah, and blew a horn, with which he commonly summoned his two sable drivers.

Legree was often wont, when in a gracious humor, to get these two worthies into his sitting-room, and, after warming them up with whiskey, amuse himself by setting them to singing, dancing or fighting, as the humor took him.

It was between one and two o'clock at night, as Cassy was returning from her ministrations to poor Tom, that she heard the sound of wild shrieking, whooping, halloing, and singing, from the sitting-room, mingled with the barking of dogs, and other symptoms of general uproar.

She came up on the verandah steps, and looked in. Legree and both the drivers, in a state of furious intoxication, were singing, whooping, upsetting chairs, and making all manner of ludicrous and horrid grimaces at each other.

She rested her small, slender hand on the window-blind, and looked fixedly at them;—there was a world of anguish, scorn, and fierce bitterness, in her black eyes, as she did so. "Would it be a sin to rid the world of such a wretch?" she said to herself.

She turned hurriedly away, and, passing round to a back door, glided up stairs, and tapped at Emmeline's door.

# Chapter XXXVI

## *Emmeline and Cassy*

Cassy entered the room, and found Emmeline sitting, pale with fear, in the furthest corner of it. As she came in, the girl started up nervously; but, on seeing who it was, rushed forward, and catching her arm, said, "O, Cassy, is it you? I'm so glad you've come! I was afraid it was—. O, you don't know what a horrid noise there has been, down stairs, all this evening!"

"I ought to know," said Cassy, dryly. "I've heard it often enough."

"O Cassy! do tell me,—couldn't we get away from this place? I don't care where,—into the swamp among the snakes,—anywhere! *Couldn't* we get *somewhere* away from here?"

"Nowhere, but into our graves," said Cassy.

"Did you ever try?"

"I've seen enough of trying, and what comes of it," said Cassy.

"I'd be willing to live in the swamps, and gnaw the bark from trees. I an't afraid of snakes! I'd rather have one near me than him," said Emmeline, eagerly.

"There have been a good many here of your opinion," said Cassy; "but you couldn't stay in the swamps,—you'd be tracked by the dogs, and brought back, and then—then—"

"What would he do?" said the girl, looking, with breathless interest, into her face.

"What *wouldn't* he do, you'd better ask," said Cassy. "He's learned his trade well, among the pirates in the West Indies. You wouldn't sleep much, if I should tell you things I've seen,—things that he tells of, sometimes, for good jokes. I've heard screams here that I haven't been able to get out of my head for weeks and weeks. There's a place way out down by the quarters, where you can see a black, blasted tree, and the ground all covered with black ashes. Ask any one what was done there, and see if they will dare to tell you."

"O! what do you mean?"

"I won't tell you. I hate to think of it. And I tell you, the Lord only knows what we may see to-morrow, if that poor fellow holds out as he's begun."

"Horrid!" said Emmeline, every drop of blood receding from her cheeks. "O, Cassy, do tell me what I shall do!"

"What I've done. Do the best you can,—do what you must,—and make it up in hating and cursing."

"He wanted to make me drink some of his hateful brandy," said Emmeline; "and I hate it so—"

"You'd better drink," said Cassy. "I hated it, too; and now I can't live without it. One must have something;—things don't look so dreadful, when you take that."

"Mother used to tell me never to touch any such thing," said Emmeline.

"*Mother* told you!" said Cassy, with a thrilling and bitter emphasis on the word mother. "What use is it for mothers to say anything? You are all to be bought and paid for, and your souls belong to whoever gets you. That's the way it goes. I say, *drink* brandy; drink all you can, and it'll make things come easier."

"O, Cassy! do pity me!"

"Pity you!—don't I? Haven't I a daughter,—Lord knows where she is, and whose she is, now,—going the way her mother went, before her, I suppose, and that her children must go, after her! There's no end to the curse—forever!"

"I wish I'd never been born!" said Emmeline, wringing her hands.

"That's an old wish with me," said Cassy. "I've got used to wishing that. I'd die, if I dared to," she said, looking out into the darkness, with that still, fixed despair which was the habitual expression of her face when at rest.

"It would be wicked to kill one's self," said Emmeline.

"I don't know why,—no wickeder than things we live and do, day after day. But the sisters told me things, when I was in the convent, that make me afraid to die. If it would only be the end of us, why, then—"

Emmeline turned away, and hid her face in her hands.

While this conversation was passing in the chamber, Legree, overcome with his carouse, had sank to sleep in the room below. Legree was not an habitual drunkard. His coarse, strong nature craved, and could endure, a continual stimulation, that would have utterly wrecked and crazed a finer one. But a deep, underlying spirit of cautiousness prevented his often yielding to appetite in such measure as to lose control of himself.

This night, however, in his feverish efforts to banish from his mind those fearful elements of woe and remorse which woke within him, he had indulged more than common; so that, when he had discharged his sable attendants, he fell heavily on a settle in the room, and was sound asleep.

O! how dares the bad soul to enter the shadowy world of sleep?—that land whose dim outlines lie so fearfully near to the mystic scene of retribution! Legree dreamed. In his heavy and feverish sleep, a veiled form stood beside him, and laid a cold, soft hand upon him. He thought he knew who it was; and shuddered, with creeping horror, though the face was veiled. Then he thought he felt *that hair* twining round his fingers; and then, that it slid smoothly round his neck, and tightened and tightened, and he could not draw his breath; and then he thought voices *whispered* to him,—whispers that chilled him with horror. Then it seemed to him he was on the edge of a frightful abyss, holding on and struggling in mortal fear, while dark hands stretched up, and were pulling him over; and Cassy came behind him laughing, and pushed him. And then rose up that solemn veiled figure, and drew aside the veil. It was his mother; and she turned away from him, and he fell down, down, down, amid a confused noise of shrieks, and groans, and shouts of demon laughter,—and Legree awoke.

Calmly the rosy hue of dawn was stealing into the room. The morning star stood, with its solemn, holy eye of light, looking down on the man of sin, from out the brightening sky. O, with what freshness, what solemnity and beauty, is each new day born; as if to say to insensate man, "Behold! thou hast one more chance! *Strive* for immortal glory!" There is no speech nor language where this voice is not heard; but the bold, bad man heard it not. He woke with an oath and a curse. What to him was the gold and purple, the daily miracle of morning! What to him the sanctity of that star which the Son of God has hallowed as his own emblem? Brute-like, he saw without perceiving; and, stumbling forward, poured out a tumbler of brandy, and drank half of it.

"I've had a h—l of a night!" he said to Cassy, who just then entered from an opposite door.

"You'll get plenty of the same sort, by and by," said she, dryly.

"What do you mean, you minx?"

"You'll find out, one of these days," returned Cassy, in the same tone. "Now, Simon, I've one piece of advice to give you."

"The devil, you have!"

"My advice is," said Cassy, steadily, as she began adjusting some things about the room, "that you let Tom alone."

"What business is't of yours?"

"What? To be sure, I don't know what it should be. If you want to pay twelve hundred for a fellow, and use him right up in the press of the season, just to serve your own spite, it's no business of mine. I've done what I could for him."

"You have? What business have you meddling in my matters?"

"None, to be sure. I've saved you some thousands of dollars, at different times, by taking care of your hands,—that's all the thanks I get. If your crop comes shorter into market than any of theirs, you won't lose your bet, I suppose? Tompkins won't lord it over you, I suppose,—and you'll pay down your money like a lady, won't you? I think I see you doing it!"

Legree, like many other planters, had but one form of ambition,—to have in the heaviest crop of the season,—and he had several bets on this very present season pending in the next town. Cassy, therefore, with woman's tact, touched the only string that could be made to vibrate.

"Well, I'll let him off at what he's got," said Legree; "but he shall beg my pardon, and promise better fashions."

"That he won't do," said Cassy.

"Won't,—eh?"

"No, he won't," said Cassy.

"I'd like to know *why*, Mistress," said Legree, in the extreme of scorn.

"Because he's done right, and he knows it, and won't say he's done wrong."

"Who a cuss cares what he knows? The nigger shall say what I please, or—"

"Or, you'll lose your bet on the cotton crop, by keeping him out of the field, just at this very press."

"But he *will* give up,—course, he will; don't I know what niggers is? He'll beg like a dog, this morning."

"He won't, Simon; you don't know this kind. You may kill him by inches,—you won't get the first word of confession out of him."

"We'll see;—where is he?" said Legree, going out.

"In the waste-room of the gin-house," said Cassy.

Legree, though he talked so stoutly to Cassy, still sallied forth from the house with a degree of misgiving which was not common with him. His dreams of the past night, mingled with Cassy's prudential suggestions, considerably affected his mind. He resolved that nobody should be witness of his encounter with Tom; and determined, if he could not subdue him by bullying, to defer his vengeance, to be wreaked in a more convenient season.

The solemn light of dawn—the angelic glory of the morning-star—had looked in through the rude window of the shed where Tom was lying; and, as if descending on that star-beam, came the solemn words, "I am the root and offspring of David, and the bright and morning star."[1] The mysterious warnings and intimations of Cassy, so far from discouraging his soul, in the end had roused it as with a heavenly call. He did not know but that the day of his death was dawning in the sky; and his heart throbbed with solemn throes of joy and desire, as he thought that the wondrous *all*, of which he had often pondered,—the great white throne, with its ever radiant rainbow; the white-robed multitude, with voices as many waters; the

1. In Revelation 22.16, Jesus sends his angel to make this announcement.

crowns, the palms, the harps,—might all break upon his vision before that sun should set again. And, therefore, without shuddering or trembling, he heard the voice of his persecutor, as he drew near.

"Well, my boy," said Legree, with a contemptuous kick, "how do you find yourself? Didn't I tell yer I could larn yer a thing or two? How do yer like it,—eh? How did yer whaling agree with yer, Tom? An't quite so crank[2] as ye was last night. Ye couldn't treat a poor sinner, now, to a bit of a sermon, could ye,—eh?"

Tom answered nothing.

"Get up, you beast!" said Legree, kicking him again.

This was a difficult matter for one so bruised and faint; and, as Tom made efforts to do so, Legree laughed brutally.

"What makes ye so spry, this morning, Tom? Cotched cold, may be, last night."

Tom by this time had gained his feet, and was confronting his master with a steady, unmoved front.

"The devil, you can!" said Legree, looking him over. "I believe you haven't got enough yet. Now, Tom, get right down on yer knees and beg my pardon, for yer shines last night."

Tom did not move.

"Down, you dog!" said Legree, striking him with his riding-whip.

"Mas'r Legree," said Tom, "I can't do it. I did only what I thought was right. I shall do just so again, if ever the time comes. I never will do a cruel thing, come what may."

"Yes, but ye don't know what may come, Master Tom. Ye think what you've got is something. I tell you 't an't anything,—nothing 't all. How would ye like to be tied to a tree, and have a slow fire lit up around ye;—wouldn't that be pleasant,—eh, Tom?"

"Mas'r," said Tom, "I know ye can do dreadful things, but,"—he stretched himself upward and clasped his hands,—"but, after ye've killed the body, there an't no more ye can do. And O, there's all ETERNITY to come, after that!"

ETERNITY,—the word thrilled through the black man's soul with light and power, as he spoke; it thrilled through the sinner's soul, too, like the bite of a scorpion. Legree gnashed on him with his teeth, but rage kept him silent; and Tom, like a man disenthralled, spoke, in a clear and cheerful voice,

"Mas'r Legree, as ye bought me, I'll be a true and faithful servant to ye. I'll give ye all the work of my hands, all my time, all my strength; but my soul I won't give up to mortal man. I will hold on to the Lord, and put his commands before all,—die or live; you may be sure on 't. Mas'r Legree, I an't a grain afeard to die. I'd as soon

2. Vigorous, high-spirited, or cocky.

die as not. Ye may whip me, starve me, burn me,—it'll only send me sooner where I want to go."

"I'll make ye give out, though, 'fore I've done!" said Legree, in a rage.

"I shall have *help*," said Tom; "you'll never do it."

"Who the devil's going to help you?" said Legree, scornfully.

"The Lord Almighty," said Tom.

"D—n you!" said Legree, as with one blow of his fist he felled Tom to the earth.

A cold soft hand fell on Legree's, at this moment. He turned,—it was Cassy's; but the cold soft touch recalled his dream of the night before, and, flashing through the chambers of his brain, came all the fearful images of the night-watches, with a portion of the horror that accompanied them.

"Will you be a fool?" said Cassy, in French. "Let him go! Let me alone to get him fit to be in the field again. Isn't it just as I told you?"

They say the alligator, the rhinoceros, though enclosed in bullet-proof mail, have each a spot where they are vulnerable; and fierce, reckless, unbelieving reprobates, have commonly this point in superstitious dread.

Legree turned away, determined to let the point go for the time.

"Well, have it your own way," he said, doggedly, to Cassy.

"Hark, ye!" he said to Tom; "I won't deal with ye now, because the business is pressing, and I want all my hands; but I *never* forget. I'll score it against ye, and sometime I'll have my pay out o' yer old black hide,—mind ye!"

Legree turned, and went out.

"There you go," said Cassy, looking darkly after him; "your reckoning's to come, yet!—My poor fellow, how are you?"

"The Lord God hath sent his angel, and shut the lion's mouth, for this time,"[3] said Tom.

"For this time, to be sure," said Cassy; "but now you've got his ill will upon you, to follow you day in, day out, hanging like a dog on your throat,—sucking your blood, bleeding away your life, drop by drop. I know the man."

3. Daniel 6.22.

# Chapter XXXVII

## *Liberty*

> "No matter with what solemnities he may have been devoted upon the altar of slavery, the moment he touches the sacred soil of Britain, the altar and the God sink together in the dust, and he stands redeemed, regenerated, and disenthralled, by the irresistible genius of universal emancipation."—*Curran.*[1]

A while we must leave Tom in the hands of his persecutors, while we turn to pursue the fortunes of George and his wife, whom we left in friendly hands, in a farm-house on the road-side.

Tom Loker we left groaning and touzling[2] in a most immaculately clean Quaker bed, under the motherly supervision of Aunt Dorcas, who found him to the full as tractable a patient as a sick bison.

Imagine a tall, dignified, spiritual woman, whose clear muslin cap shades waves of silvery hair, parted on a broad, clear forehead, which overarches thoughtful gray eyes. A snowy handkerchief of lisse crape is folded neatly across her bosom; her glossy brown silk dress rustles peacefully, as she glides up and down the chamber.

"The devil!" says Tom Loker, giving a great throw to the bed-clothes.

"I must request thee, Thomas, not to use such language," says Aunt Dorcas, as she quietly rearranged the bed.

"Well, I won't, granny, if I can help it," says Tom; "but it is enough to make a fellow swear,—so cursedly hot!"

Dorcas removed a comforter from the bed, straightened the clothes again, and tucked them in till Tom looked something like a chrysalis; remarking, as she did so,

"I wish, friend, thee would leave off cursing and swearing, and think upon thy ways."

"What the devil," said Tom, "should I think of *them* for? Last thing ever *I* want to think of—hang it all!" And Tom flounced over, untucking and disarranging everything, in a manner frightful to behold.

"That fellow and gal are here, I 'spose," said he, sullenly, after a pause.

"They are so," said Dorcas.

"They'd better be off up to the lake," said Tom; "the quicker the better."

1. John Philpot Curran (1750–1817), Irish orator and magistrate, on the famous case of James Somerset, a black slave from Jamaica who, after coming to England with his master, declared his freedom and was brought to court. The case was decided in 1772 in Somerset's favor (Curran, *Works*, bk. 1, chap. 5).
2. Tossing.

"Probably they will do so," said Aunt Dorcas, knitting peacefully.

"And hark ye," said Tom; "we've got correspondents in Sandusky, that watch the boats for us. I don't care if I tell, now. I hope they *will* get away, just to spite Marks,—the cursed puppy!—d—n him!"

"Thomas!" said Dorcas.

"I tell you, granny, if you bottle a fellow up too tight, I shall split," said Tom. "But about the gal,—tell 'em to dress her up some way, so's to alter her. Her description's out in Sandusky."

"We will attend to that matter," said Dorcas, with characteristic composure.

As we at this place take leave of Tom Loker, we may as well say, that, having lain three weeks at the Quaker dwelling, sick with a rheumatic fever, which set in, in company with his other afflictions, Tom arose from his bed a somewhat sadder and wiser man; and, in place of slave-catching, betook himself to life in one of the new settlements, where his talents developed themselves more happily in trapping bears, wolves, and other inhabitants of the forest, in which he made himself quite a name in the land. Tom always spoke reverently of the Quakers. "Nice people," he would say; "wanted to convert me, but could n't come it, exactly. But, tell ye what, stranger, they do fix up a sick fellow first rate,—no mistake. Make jist the tallest kind o' broth and knick-nacks."

As Tom had informed them that their party would be looked for in Sandusky, it was thought prudent to divide them. Jim, with his old mother, was forwarded separately; and a night or two after, George and Eliza, with their child, were driven privately into Sandusky, and lodged beneath a hospitable roof, preparatory to taking their last passage on the lake.

Their night was now far spent, and the morning star of liberty rose fair before them. Liberty!—electric word! What is it? Is there anything more in it than a name—a rhetorical flourish? Why, men and women of America, does your heart's blood thrill at that word, for which your fathers bled, and your braver mothers were willing that their noblest and best should die?

Is there anything in it glorious and dear for a nation, that is not also glorious and dear for a man? What is freedom to a nation, but freedom to the individuals in it? What is freedom to that young man, who sits there, with his arms folded over his broad chest, the tint of African blood in his cheek, its dark fires in his eye,—what is freedom to George Harris? To your fathers, freedom was the right of a nation to be a nation. To him, it is the right of a man to be a man, and not a brute; the right to call the wife of his bosom his wife, and to protect her from lawless violence; the right to protect and educate his child; the right to have a home of his own, a religion of his own, a character of his own, unsubject to the will of another. All these thoughts were rolling and seething in George's breast, as he was pensively leaning his head on his hand, watching his wife, as she was adapting to her slender and pretty form the articles of man's attire, in which it was deemed safest she should make her escape.

"Now for it," said she, as she stood before the glass, and shook down her silky abundance of black curly hair. "I say, George, it's almost a pity, isn't it," she said, as she held up some of it, playfully,—"pity it's all got to come off?"

George smiled sadly, and made no answer.

Eliza turned to the glass, and the scissors glittered as one long lock after another was detached from her head.

"There, now, that'll do," she said, taking up a hair-brush; "now for a few fancy touches."

"There, an't I a pretty young fellow?" she said, turning around to her husband, laughing and blushing at the same time.

"You always will be pretty, do what you will," said George.

"What does make you so sober?" said Eliza, kneeling on one knee, and laying her hand on his. "We are only within twenty-four hours of Canada, they say. Only a day and a night on the lake, and then—oh, then!—"

"O, Eliza!" said George, drawing her towards him; "that is it! Now my fate is all narrowing down to a point. To come so near, to be almost in sight, and then lose all. I should never live under it, Eliza."

"Don't fear," said his wife, hopefully. "The good Lord would not have brought us so far, if he didn't mean to carry us through. I seem to feel him with us, George."

"You are a blessed woman, Eliza!" said George, clasping her with a convulsive grasp. "But,—oh, tell me! can this great mercy be for us? Will these years and years of misery come to an end?—shall we be free?"

"I am sure of it, George," said Eliza, looking upward, while tears of hope and enthusiasm shone on her long, dark lashes. "I feel it in me, that God is going to bring us out of bondage, this very day."

"I will believe you, Eliza," said George, rising suddenly up. "I will believe,—come, let's be off. Well, indeed," said he, holding her off at arm's length, and looking admiringly at her, "you *are* a pretty little fellow. That crop of little, short curls, is quite becoming. Put on your cap. So—a little to one side. I never saw you look quite so pretty. But, it's almost time for the carriage;—I wonder if Mrs. Smyth has got Harry rigged?"

The door opened, and a respectable, middle-aged woman entered, leading little Harry, dressed in girl's clothes.

"What a pretty girl he makes," said Eliza, turning him round. "We call him Harriet, you see;—don't the name come nicely?"

The child stood gravely regarding his mother in her new and strange attire, observing a profound silence, and occasionally drawing deep sighs, and peeping at her from under his dark curls.

"Does Harry know mamma?" said Eliza, stretching her hands toward him.

The child clung shyly to the woman.

"Come, Eliza, why do you try to coax him, when you know that he has got to be kept away from you?"

"I know it's foolish," said Eliza; "yet, I can't bear to have him turn away from me. But come,—where's my cloak? Here,—how is it men put on cloaks, George?"

"You must wear it so," said her husband, throwing it over his shoulders.

"So, then," said Eliza, imitating the motion,—"and I must stamp, and take long steps, and try to look saucy."

"Don't exert yourself," said George. "There is, now and then, a modest young man; and I think it would be easier for you to act that character."

"And these gloves! mercy upon us!" said Eliza; "why, my hands are lost in them."

"I advise you to keep them on pretty strictly," said George. "Your little slender paw might bring us all out. Now, Mrs. Smyth, you are to go under our charge, and be our aunty,—you mind."

"I've heard," said Mrs. Smyth, "that there have been men down, warning all the packet[3] captains against a man and woman, with a little boy."

"They have!" said George. "Well, if we see any such people, we can tell them."

A hack now drove to the door, and the friendly family who had received the fugitives crowded around them with farewell greetings.

The disguises the party had assumed were in accordance with the hints of Tom Loker. Mrs. Smyth, a respectable woman from the settlement in Canada, whither they were fleeing, being fortunately about crossing the lake to return thither, had consented to appear as the aunt of little Harry; and, in order to attach him to her, he had been allowed to remain, the two last days, under her sole charge; and an extra amount of petting, joined to an indefinite amount of seedcake[4] and candy, had cemented a very close attachment on the part of the young gentleman.

The hack drove to the wharf. The two young men, as they appeared, walked up the plank into the boat, Eliza gallantly giving her arm to Mrs. Smyth, and George attending to their baggage.

3. Passenger boat carrying mail and cargo on a regular schedule.
4. Cakes or cookies made with sesame or caraway seeds.

George was standing at the captain's office, settling for his party, when he overheard two men talking by his side.

"I've watched every one that came on board," said one, "and I know they're not on this boat."

The voice was that of the clerk of the boat. The speaker whom he addressed was our sometimes friend Marks, who, with that valuable perseverance which characterized him, had come on to Sandusky, seeking whom he might devour.

"You would scarcely know the woman from a white one," said Marks. "The man is a very light mulatto; he has a brand in one of his hands."

The hand with which George was taking the tickets and change trembled a little; but he turned coolly around, fixed an unconcerned glance on the face of the speaker, and walked leisurely toward another part of the boat, where Eliza stood waiting for him.

Mrs. Smyth, with little Harry, sought the seclusion of the ladies' cabin, where the dark beauty of the supposed little girl drew many flattering comments from the passengers.

George had the satisfaction, as the bell rang out its farewell peal, to see Marks walk down the plank to the shore, and drew a long sigh of relief, when the boat had put a returnless distance between them.

It was a superb day. The blue waves of Lake Erie[5] danced, rippling and sparkling, in the sun-light. A fresh breeze blew from the shore, and the lordly boat ploughed her way right gallantly onward.

O, what an untold world there is in one human heart! Who thought, as George walked calmly up and down the deck of the steamer, with his shy companion at his side, of all that was burning in his bosom? The mighty good that seemed approaching seemed too good, too fair, even to be a reality; and he felt a jealous dread, every moment of the day, that something would rise to snatch it from him.

But the boat swept on. Hours fleeted, and, at last, clear and full rose the blessed English shores; shores charmed by a mighty spell,—with one touch to dissolve every incantation of slavery, no matter in what language pronounced, or by what national power confirmed.

George and his wife stood arm in arm, as the boat neared the small town of Amherstberg, in Canada. His breath grew thick and short; a mist gathered before his eyes; he silently pressed the little hand that lay trembling on his arm. The bell rang; the boat stopped. Scarcely seeing what he did, he looked out his baggage, and gathered his little party. The little company were landed on the shore. They stood still till the boat had cleared; and then, with tears and

5. One of the Great Lakes, between Lake Huron and Lake Ontario, bordered by Pennsylvania and Ohio on the south, New York on the east, and Canada on the north. Amherstberg (mentioned below) is a Canadian town on Lake Erie, just south of Detroit.

embracings, the husband and wife, with their wondering child in their arms, knelt down and lifted up their hearts to God!

"'Twas something like the burst from death to life
From the grave's cerements to the robes of heaven;
From sin's dominion, and from passion's strife,
To the pure freedom of a soul forgiven;
Where all the bonds of death and hell are riven,
And mortal puts on immortality,
When Mercy's hand hath turned the golden key,
And Mercy's voice hath said, *Rejoice, thy soul is free.*"[6]

The little party were soon guided, by Mrs. Smyth, to the hospitable abode of a good missionary, whom Christian charity has placed here as a shepherd to the out-cast and wandering, who are constantly finding an asylum on this shore.

Who can speak the blessedness of that first day of freedom? Is not the *sense* of liberty a higher and a finer one than any of the five? To move, speak and breathe,—go out and come in unwatched, and free from danger! Who can speak the blessings of that rest which comes down on the free man's pillow, under laws which insure to him the rights that God has given to man? How fair and precious to that mother was that sleeping child's face, endeared by the memory of a thousand dangers! How impossible was it to sleep, in the exuberant possession of such blessedness! And yet, these two had not one acre of ground,—not a roof that they could call their own,—they had spent their all, to the last dollar. They had nothing more than the birds of the air, or the flowers of the field,—yet they could not sleep for joy. "O, ye who take freedom from man, with what words shall ye answer it to God?"[7]

## Chapter XXXVIII

### *The Victory*

"Thanks be unto God, who giveth us the victory."[1]

Have not many of us, in the weary way of life, felt, in some hours, how far easier it were to die than to live?

The martyr, when faced even by a death of bodily anguish and horror, finds in the very terror of his doom a strong stimulant and

6. Reference unknown.
7. Reference unknown.
1. "O death, where is thy sting? O grave, where is thy victory? The sting of death is sin; and the strength of sin is the law. But thanks be to God, which giveth us the victory through our Lord Jesus Christ" (1 Corinthians 15.55–57).

tonic. There is a vivid excitement, a thrill and fervor, which may carry through any crisis of suffering that is the birth-hour of eternal glory and rest.

But to live,—to wear on, day after day, of mean, bitter, low, harassing servitude, every nerve dampened and depressed, every power of feeling gradually smothered,—this long and wasting heart-martyrdom, this slow, daily bleeding away of the inward life, drop by drop, hour after hour,—this is the true searching test of what there may be in man or woman.

When Tom stood face to face with his persecutor, and heard his threats, and thought in his very soul that his hour was come, his heart swelled bravely in him, and he thought he could bear torture and fire, bear anything, with the vision of Jesus and heaven but just a step beyond; but, when he was gone, and the present excitement passed off, came back the pain of his bruised and weary limbs,—came back the sense of his utterly degraded, hopeless, forlorn estate; and the day passed wearily enough.

Long before his wounds were healed, Legree insisted that he should be put to the regular field-work; and then came day after day of pain and weariness, aggravated by every kind of injustice and indignity that the ill-will of a mean and malicious mind could devise. Whoever, in *our* circumstances, has made trial of pain, even with all the alleviations which, for us, usually attend it, must know the irritation that comes with it. Tom no longer wondered at the habitual surliness of his associates; nay, he found the placid, sunny temper, which had been the habitude of his life, broken in on, and sorely strained, by the inroads of the same thing. He had flattered himself on leisure to read his Bible; but there was no such thing as leisure there. In the height of the season, Legree did not hesitate to press all his hands through, Sundays and week-days alike. Why shouldn't he?—he made more cotton by it, and gained his wager; and if it wore out a few more hands, he could buy better ones. At first, Tom used to read a verse or two of his Bible, by the flicker of the fire, after he had returned from his daily toil; but, after the cruel treatment he received, he used to come home so exhausted, that his head swam and his eyes failed when he tried to read; and he was fain to stretch himself down, with the others, in utter exhaustion.

Is it strange that the religious peace and trust, which had upborne him hitherto, should give way to tossings of soul and despondent darkness? The gloomiest problem of this mysterious life was constantly before his eyes,—souls crushed and ruined, evil triumphant, and God silent. It was weeks and months that Tom wrestled, in his own soul, in darkness and sorrow. He thought of Miss Ophelia's letter to his Kentucky friends, and would pray earnestly that God would send him deliverance. And then he would watch, day

The fugitives are safe in a free land.

after day, in the vague hope of seeing somebody sent to redeem him; and, when nobody came, he would crush back to his soul bitter thoughts,—that it was vain to serve God, that God had forgotten him. He sometimes saw Cassy; and sometimes, when summoned to the house, caught a glimpse of the dejected form of Emmeline, but held very little communion with either; in fact, there was no time for him to commune with anybody.

One evening, he was sitting, in utter dejection and prostration, by a few decaying brands, where his coarse supper was baking. He put a few bits of brushwood on the fire, and strove to raise the light, and then drew his worn Bible from his pocket. There were all the marked passages, which had thrilled his soul so often,—words of patriarchs and seers, poets and sages, who from early time had spoken courage to man,—voices from the great cloud of witnesses who ever surround us in the race of life. Had the word lost its power, or could the failing eye and weary sense no longer answer to the touch of that mighty inspiration? Heavily sighing, he put it in his pocket. A coarse laugh roused him; he looked up,—Legree was standing opposite to him.

"Well, old boy," he said, "you find your religion don't work, it seems! I thought I should get that through your wool, at last!"

The cruel taunt was more than hunger and cold and nakedness. Tom was silent.

"You were a fool," said Legree; "for I meant to do well by you, when I bought you. You might have been better off than Sambo, or Quimbo either, and had easy times; and, instead of getting cut up and thrashed, every day or two, ye might have had liberty to lord it round, and cut up the other niggers; and ye might have had, now and then, a good warming of whiskey punch. Come, Tom, don't you think you'd better be reasonable?—heave that ar old pack of trash in the fire, and join my church!"

"The Lord forbid!" said Tom, fervently.

"You see the Lord an't going to help you; if he had been, he wouldn't have let *me* get you! This yer religion is all a mess of lying trumpery, Tom. I know all about it. Ye'd better hold to me; I'm somebody, and can do something!"

"No, Mas'r," said Tom; "I'll hold on. The Lord may help me, or not help; but I'll hold to him, and believe him to the last!"

"The more fool you!" said Legree, spitting scornfully at him, and spurning him with his foot. "Never mind; I'll chase you down, yet, and bring you under,—you'll see!" and Legree turned away.

When a heavy weight presses the soul to the lowest level at which endurance is possible, there is an instant and desperate effort of every physical and moral nerve to throw off the weight; and hence the heaviest anguish often precedes a return tide of joy and courage. So was it now with Tom. The atheistic taunts of his cruel master sunk his before dejected soul to the lowest ebb; and, though the hand of faith still held to the eternal rock, it was with a numb, despairing grasp. Tom sat, like one stunned, at the fire. Suddenly everything around him seemed to fade, and a vision rose before him of one crowned with thorns, buffeted and bleeding. Tom gazed, in awe and wonder, at the majestic patience of the face; the deep, pathetic eyes thrilled him to his inmost heart; his soul woke, as, with floods of emotion, he stretched out his hands and fell upon his knees,—when, gradually, the vision changed: the sharp thorns became rays of glory; and, in splendor inconceivable, he saw that same face bending compassionately towards him, and a voice said, "He that overcometh shall sit down with me on my throne, even as I also overcame, and am set down with my Father on his throne."[2]

How long Tom lay there, he knew not. When he came to himself, the fire was gone out, his clothes were wet with the chill and drenching dews; but the dread soul-crisis was past, and, in the joy that filled him, he no longer felt hunger, cold, degradation, disappointment, wretchedness. From his deepest soul, he that hour loosed and parted from every hope in the life that now is, and offered his own will an unquestioning sacrifice to the Infinite. Tom looked up to the silent, everliving stars,—types of the angelic hosts who ever look down on man; and the solitude of the night rung with the triumphant words of a hymn, which he had sung often in happier days, but never with such feeling as now:

"The earth shall be dissolved like snow,
The sun shall cease to shine;
But God, who called me here below,
Shall be forever mine.

"And when this mortal life shall fail,
And flesh and sense shall cease,
I shall possess within the veil
A life of joy and peace.

"When we've been there ten thousand years,
Bright shining like the sun,
We've no less days to sing God's praise
Than when we first begun."[3]

Those who have been familiar with the religious histories of the slave population know that relations like what we have narrated are very common among them. We have heard some from their own

2. Revelation 3.21.
3. These verses come from the hymn "Amazing Grace."

lips, of a very touching and affecting character. The psychologist tells us of a state, in which the affections and images of the mind become so dominant and overpowering, that they press into their service the outward senses, and make them give tangible shape to the inward imagining. Who shall measure what an all-pervading Spirit may do with these capabilities of our mortality, or the ways in which He may encourage the desponding souls of the desolate? If the poor forgotten slave believes that Jesus hath appeared and spoken to him, who shall contradict him? Did He not say that his mission, in all ages, was to bind up the broken-hearted, and set at liberty them that are bruised?

When the dim gray of dawn woke the slumberers to go forth to the field, there was among those tattered and shivering wretches one who walked with an exultant tread; for firmer than the ground he trod on was his strong faith in Almighty, eternal love. Ah, Legree, try all your forces now! Utmost agony, woe, degradation, want, and loss of all things, shall only hasten on the process by which he shall be made a king and a priest unto God!

From this time, an inviolable sphere of peace encompassed the lowly heart of the oppressed one,—an ever-present Saviour hallowed it as a temple. Past now the bleeding of earthly regrets; past its fluctuations of hope, and fear, and desire; the human will, bent, and bleeding, and struggling long, was now entirely merged in the Divine. So short now seemed the remaining voyage of life,—so near, so vivid, seemed eternal blessedness,—that life's uttermost woes fell from him unharming.

All noticed the change in his appearance. Cheerfulness and alertness seemed to return to him, and a quietness which no insult or injury could ruffle seemed to possess him.

"What the devil's got into Tom?" Legree said to Sambo. "A while ago he was all down in the mouth, and now he's peart as a cricket."

"Dunno, Mas'r; gwine to run off, mebbe."

"Like to see him try that," said Legree, with a savage grin, "wouldn't we, Sambo?"

"Guess we would! Haw! haw! ho!" said the sooty gnome, laughing obsequiously. "Lord, de fun! To see him stickin' in de mud,—chasin' and tarin' through de bushes, dogs a holdin' on to him! Lord, I laughed fit to split, dat ar time we cotched Molly. I thought they'd a had her all stripped up afore I could get 'em off. She car's de marks o' dat ar spree yet."

"I reckon she will, to her grave," said Legree. "But now, Sambo, you look sharp. If the nigger's got anything of this sort going, trip him up."

"Mas'r, let me lone for dat," said Sambo. "I'll tree de coon. Ho, ho, ho!"

This was spoken as Legree was getting on to his horse, to go to the neighboring town. That night, as he was returning, he thought he would turn his horse and ride round the quarters, and see if all was safe.

It was a superb moonlight night, and the shadows of the graceful China trees lay minutely pencilled on the turf below, and there was that transparent stillness in the air which it seems almost unholy to disturb. Legree was at a little distance from the quarters, when he heard the voice of some one singing. It was not a usual sound there, and he paused to listen. A musical tenor voice sang,

"When I can read my title clear
To mansions in the skies,
I'll bid farewell to every fear,
And wipe my weeping eyes.

"Should earth against my soul engage,
And hellish darts be hurled,
Then I can smile at Satan's rage,
And face a frowning world.

"Let cares like a wild deluge come,
And storms of sorrow fall,
May I but safely reach my home,
My God, my Heaven, my All."[4]

"So ho!" said Legree to himself, "he thinks so, does he? How I hate these cursed, Methodist hymns! Here, you nigger," said he, coming suddenly out upon Tom, and raising his riding-whip, "how dare you be gettin' up this yer row, when you ought to be in bed? Shut yer old black gash, and get along in with you!"

"Yes, Mas'r," said Tom, with ready cheerfulness, as he rose to go in.

Legree was provoked beyond measure by Tom's evident happiness; and, riding up to him, belabored him over his head and shoulders.

"There, you dog," he said, "see if you'll feel so comfortable, after that!"

But the blows fell now only on the outer man, and not, as before, on the heart. Tom stood perfectly submissive; and yet Legree could not hide from himself that his power over his bond thrall was somehow gone. And, as Tom disappeared in his cabin, and he wheeled his horse suddenly round, there passed through his mind one of those vivid flashes that often send the lightning of conscience across the dark and wicked soul. He understood full well that it

4. Isaac Watts, *Hymns and Spiritual Songs* (bk. 2, hymn 65).

was GOD who was standing between him and his victim, and he blasphemed him. That submissive and silent man, whom taunts, nor threats, nor stripes, nor cruelties, could disturb, roused a voice within him, such as of old his Master roused in the demoniac soul, saying, "What have we to do with thee, thou Jesus of Nazareth?—art thou come to torment us before the time?"[5]

Tom's whole soul overflowed with compassion and sympathy for the poor wretches by whom he was surrounded. To him it seemed as if his life-sorrows were now over, and as if, out of that strange treasury of peace and joy, with which he had been endowed from above, he longed to pour out something for the relief of their woes. It is true, opportunities were scanty; but, on the way to the fields, and back again, and during the hours of labor, chances fell in his way of extending a helping-hand to the weary, the disheartened and discouraged. The poor, worn-down, brutalized creatures, at first, could scarce comprehend this; but, when it was continued week after week, and month after month, it began to awaken long-silent chords in their benumbed hearts. Gradually and imperceptibly the strange, silent, patient man, who was ready to bear every one's burden, and sought help from none,—who stood aside for all, and came last, and took least, yet was foremost to share his little all with any who needed,—the man who, in cold nights, would give up his tattered blanket to add to the comfort of some woman who shivered with sickness, and who filled the baskets of the weaker ones in the field, at the terrible risk of coming short in his own measure,—and who, though pursued with unrelenting cruelty by their common tyrant, never joined in uttering a word of reviling or cursing,—this man, at last, began to have a strange power over them; and, when the more pressing season was past, and they were allowed again their Sundays for their own use, many would gather together to hear from him of Jesus. They would gladly have met to hear, and pray, and sing, in some place, together; but Legree would not permit it, and more than once broke up such attempts, with oaths and brutal execrations,—so that the blessed news had to circulate from individual to individual. Yet who can speak the simple joy with which some of those poor outcasts, to whom life was a joyless journey to a dark unknown, heard of a compassionate Redeemer and a heavenly home? It is the statement of missionaries, that, of all races of the earth, none have received the Gospel with such eager docility as the African. The principle of reliance and unquestioning faith, which is its foundation, is more a native element in this race than any other; and it has often been found among them, that a stray seed of truth, borne on some breeze of accident into hearts the most ignorant, has sprung

5. The words of the demons to Christ in Matthew 8.29.

up into fruit, whose abundance has shamed that of higher and more skilful culture.

The poor mulatto woman, whose simple faith had been well-nigh crushed and overwhelmed, by the avalanche of cruelty and wrong which had fallen upon her, felt her soul raised up by the hymns and passages of Holy Writ, which this lowly missionary breathed into her ear in intervals, as they were going to and returning from work; and even the half-crazed and wandering mind of Cassy was soothed and calmed by his simple and unobtrusive influences.

Stung to madness and despair by the crushing agonies of a life, Cassy had often resolved in her soul an hour of retribution, when her hand should avenge on her oppressor all the injustice and cruelty to which she had been witness, or which *she* had in her own person suffered.

One night, after all in Tom's cabin were sunk in sleep, he was suddenly aroused by seeing her face at the hole between the logs, that served for a window. She made a silent gesture for him to come out.

Tom came out the door. It was between one and two o'clock at night,—broad, calm, still moonlight. Tom remarked, as the light of the moon fell upon Cassy's large, black eyes, that there was a wild and peculiar glare in them, unlike their wonted fixed despair.

"Come here, Father Tom," she said, laying her small hand on his wrist, and drawing him forward with a force as if the hand were of steel; "come here,—I've news for you."

"What, Misse Cassy?" said Tom, anxiously.

"Tom, wouldn't you like your liberty?"

"I shall have it, Misse, in God's time," said Tom.

"Ay, but you may have it to-night," said Cassy, with a flash of sudden energy. "Come on."

Tom hesitated.

"Come!" said she, in a whisper, fixing her black eyes on him. "Come along! He's asleep—sound. I put enough into his brandy to keep him so. I wish I'd had more,—I shouldn't have wanted you. But come, the back door is unlocked; there's an axe there, I put it there,—his room door is open; I'll show you the way. I'd a done it myself, only my arms are so weak. Come along!"

"Not for ten thousand worlds, Misse!" said Tom, firmly, stopping and holding her back, as she was pressing forward.

"But think of all these poor creatures," said Cassy. "We might set them all free, and go somewhere in the swamps, and find an island, and live by ourselves; I've heard of its being done. Any life is better than this."

"No!" said Tom, firmly. "No! good never comes of wickedness. I'd sooner chop my right hand off!"

"Then *I* shall do it," said Cassy, turning.

"O, Misse Cassy!" said Tom, throwing himself before her, "for the dear Lord's sake that died for ye, don't sell your precious soul to the devil, that way! Nothing but evil will come of it. The Lord hasn't called us to wrath. We must suffer, and wait his time."

"Wait!" said Cassy. "Haven't I waited?—waited till my head is dizzy and my heart sick? What has he made me suffer? What has he made hundreds of poor creatures suffer? Isn't he wringing the life-blood out of you? I'm called on; they call me! His time's come, and I'll have his heart's blood!"

"No, no, no!" said Tom, holding her small hands, which were clenched with spasmodic violence. "No, ye poor, lost soul, that ye mustn't do. The dear, blessed Lord never shed no blood but his own, and that he poured out for us when we was enemies. Lord, help us to follow his steps, and love our enemies."[6]

"Love!" said Cassy, with a fierce glare; "love *such* enemies! It isn't in flesh and blood."

"No, Misse, it isn't," said Tom, looking up; "but *He* gives it to us, and that's the *victory.* When we can love and pray over all and through all, the battle's past, and the victory's come,—glory be to God!" And, with streaming eyes and choking voice, the black man looked up to heaven.

And this, oh Africa! latest called of nations,—called to the crown of thorns, the scourge, the bloody sweat, the cross of agony,—this is to be *thy* victory; by this shalt thou reign with Christ when his kingdom shall come on earth.

The deep fervor of Tom's feelings, the softness of his voice, his tears, fell like dew on the wild, unsettled spirit of the poor woman. A softness gathered over the lurid fires of her eye; she looked down, and Tom could feel the relaxing muscles of her hands, as she said,

"Didn't I tell you that evil spirits followed me? O! Father Tom, I can't pray,—I wish I could. I never have prayed since my children were sold! What you say must be right, I know it must; but when I try to pray, I can only hate and curse. I can't pray!"

"Poor soul!" said Tom, compassionately. "Satan desires to have ye, and sift ye as wheat. I pray the Lord for ye. O! Misse Cassy, turn to the dear Lord Jesus. He came to bind up the broken-hearted, and comfort all that mourn."

Cassy stood silent, while large, heavy tears dropped from her downcast eyes.

"Misse Cassy," said Tom, in a hesitating tone, after surveying her a moment in silence, "if ye only could get away from here,—if the

6. From Christ's Sermon on the Mount: "Ye have heard that it hath been said, Thou shalt love thy neighbour, and hate thine enemy. But I say unto you, love your enemies, bless them that despitefully use you, and persecute you" (Matthew 5.43–44).

thing was possible,—I'd 'vise ye and Emmeline to do it; that is, if ye could go without blood-guiltiness,—not otherwise."

"Would you try it with us, Father Tom?"

"No," said Tom; "time was when I would; but the Lord's given me a work among these yer poor souls, and I'll stay with 'em and bear my cross with 'em till the end. It's different with you; it's a snare to you,—it's more 'n you can stand,—and you'd better go, if you can."

"I know no way but through the grave," said Cassy. "There's no beast or bird but can find a home somewhere; even the snakes and the alligators have their places to lie down and be quiet; but there's no place for us. Down in the darkest swamps, their dogs will hunt us out, and find us. Everybody and everything is against us; even the very beasts side against us,—and where shall we go?"

Tom stood silent; at length he said,

"Him that saved Daniel in the den of lions,—that saved the children in the fiery furnace,—Him that walked on the sea, and bade the winds be still,—He's alive yet; and I've faith to believe he can deliver you. Try it, and I'll pray, with all my might, for you."

By what strange law of mind is it that an idea long overlooked, and trodden under foot as a useless stone, suddenly sparkles out in new light, as a discovered diamond?

Cassy had often revolved, for hours, all possible or probable schemes of escape, and dismissed them all, as hopeless and impracticable; but at this moment there flashed through her mind a plan, so simple and feasible in all its details, as to awaken an instant hope.

"Father Tom, I'll try it!" she said, suddenly.

"Amen!" said Tom; "the Lord help ye!"

# Chapter XXXIX

## *The Stratagem*

"The way of the wicked is as darkness; he knoweth not at what he stumbleth."[1]

The garret of the house that Legree occupied, like most other garrets, was a great, desolate space, dusty, hung with cobwebs, and littered with cast-off lumber. The opulent family that had inhabited the house in the days of its splendor had imported a great deal of splendid furniture, some of which they had taken away with them, while some remained standing desolate in mouldering, unoccupied rooms, or stored away in this place. One or two immense packing-boxes, in which this furniture was brought, stood against the sides

1. Proverbs 4.19.

of the garret. There was a small window there, which let in, through its dingy, dusty panes, a scanty, uncertain light on the tall, high-backed chairs and dusty tables, that had once seen better days. Altogether, it was a weird and ghostly place; but, ghostly as it was, it wanted not in legends among the superstitious negroes, to increase its terrors. Some few years before, a negro woman, who had incurred Legree's displeasure, was confined there for several weeks. What passed there, we do not say; the negroes used to whisper darkly to each other; but it was known that the body of the unfortunate creature was one day taken down from there, and buried; and, after that, it was said that oaths and cursings and the sound of violent blows, used to ring through that old garret, and mingled with wailings and groans of despair. Once, when Legree chanced to overhear something of this kind, he flew into a violent passion, and swore that the next one that told stories about that garret should have an opportunity of knowing what was there, for he would chain them up there for a week. This hint was enough to repress talking, though, of course, it did not disturb the credit of the story in the least.

Gradually, the staircase that led to the garret, and even the passage-way to the staircase, were avoided by every one in the house, from every one fearing to speak of it, and the legend was gradually falling into desuetude. It had suddenly occurred to Cassy to make use of the superstitious excitability, which was so great in Legree, for the purpose of her liberation, and that of her fellow-sufferer.

The sleeping-room of Cassy was directly under the garret. One day, without consulting Legree, she suddenly took it upon her, with some considerable ostentation, to change all the furniture and appurtenances of the room to one at some considerable distance. The under-servants, who were called on to effect this movement, were running and bustling about with great zeal and confusion, when Legree returned from a ride.

"Hallo! you Cass!" said Legree, "what's in the wind now?"

"Nothing; only I choose to have another room," said Cassy, doggedly.

"And what for, pray?" said Legree.

"I choose to," said Cassy.

"The devil you do! and what for?"

"I'd like to get some sleep, now and then."

"Sleep! well, what hinders your sleeping?"

"I could tell, I suppose, if you want to hear," said Cassy, dryly.

"Speak out, you minx!" said Legree.

"O! nothing. I suppose it wouldn't disturb *you!* Only groans, and people scuffling, and rolling round on the garret floor, half the night, from twelve to morning!"

"People up garret!" said Legree, uneasily, but forcing a laugh; "who are they, Cassy?"

Cassy raised her sharp, black eyes, and looked in the face of Legree, with an expression that went through his bones, as she said, "To be sure, Simon, who are they? I'd like to have *you* tell me. You don't know, I suppose!"

With an oath, Legree struck at her with his riding-whip; but she glided to one side, and passed through the door, and looking back, said, "If you'll sleep in that room, you'll know all about it. Perhaps you'd better try it!" and then immediately she shut and locked the door.

Legree blustered and swore, and threatened to break down the door; but apparently thought better of it, and walked uneasily into the sitting-room. Cassy perceived that her shaft had struck home; and, from that hour, with the most exquisite address, she never ceased to continue the train of influences she had begun.

In a knot-hole in the garret she had inserted the neck of an old bottle, in such a manner that when there was the least wind, most doleful and lugubrious wailing sounds proceeded from it, which, in a high wind, increased to a perfect shriek, such as to credulous and superstitious ears might easily seem to be that of horror and despair.

These sounds were, from time to time, heard by the servants, and revived in full force the memory of the old ghost legend. A superstitious creeping horror seemed to fill the house; and though no one dared to breathe it to Legree, he found himself encompassed by it, as by an atmosphere.

No one is so thoroughly superstitious as the godless man. The Christian is composed by the belief of a wise, all-ruling Father, whose presence fills the void unknown with light and order; but to the man who has dethroned God, the spirit-land is, indeed, in the words of the Hebrew poet, "a land of darkness and the shadow of death,"[2] without any order, where the light is as darkness. Life and death to him are haunted grounds, filled with goblin forms of vague and shadowy dread.

Legree had had the slumbering moral element in him roused by his encounters with Tom,—roused, only to be resisted by the determinate force of evil; but still there was a thrill and commotion of the dark, inner world, produced by every word, or prayer, or hymn, that reacted in superstitious dread.

The influence of Cassy over him was of a strange and singular kind. He was her owner, her tyrant and tormentor. She was, as he knew, wholly, and without any possibility of help or redress, in his hands; and yet so it is, that the most brutal man cannot live in

2. Job 11.20–21.

constant association with a strong female influence, and not be greatly controlled by it. When he first bought her, she was, as she had said, a woman delicately bred; and then he crushed her, without scruple, beneath the foot of his brutality. But, as time, and debasing influences, and despair, hardened womanhood within her, and waked the fires of fiercer passions, she had become in a measure his mistress, and he alternately tyrannized over and dreaded her.

This influence had become more harassing and decided, since partial insanity had given a strange, weird, unsettled cast to all her words and language.

A night or two after this, Legree was sitting in the old sitting-room, by the side of a flickering wood fire, that threw uncertain glances round the room. It was a stormy, windy night, such as raises whole squadrons of nondescript noises in rickety old houses. Windows were rattling, shutters flapping, the wind carousing, rumbling, and tumbling down the chimney, and, every once in a while, puffing out smoke and ashes, as if a legion of spirits were coming after them. Legree had been casting up accounts and reading newspapers for some hours, while Cassy sat in the corner, sullenly looking into the fire. Legree laid down his paper, and seeing an old book lying on the table, which he had noticed Cassy reading, the first part of the evening, took it up, and began to turn it over. It was one of those collections of stories of bloody murders, ghostly legends, and supernatural visitations, which, coarsely got up and illustrated, have a strange fascination for one who once begins to read them.

Legree poohed and pished, but read, turning page after page, till, finally, after reading some way, he threw down the book, with an oath.

"You don't believe in ghosts, do you, Cass?" said he, taking the tongs and settling the fire. "I thought you'd more sense than to let noises scare *you*."

"No matter what I believe," said Cassy, sullenly.

"Fellows used to try to frighten me with their yarns at sea," said Legree. "Never come it round me that way. I'm too tough for any such trash, tell ye."

Cassy sat looking intensely at him in the shadow of the corner. There was that strange light in her eyes that always impressed Legree with uneasiness.

"Them noises was nothing but rats and the wind," said Legree. "Rats will make a devil of a noise. I used to hear 'em sometimes down in the hold of the ship; and wind,—Lord's sake! ye can make anything out o' wind."

Cassy knew Legree was uneasy under her eyes, and, therefore, she made no answer, but sat fixing them on him, with that strange, unearthly expression, as before.

"Come, speak out, woman,—don't you think so?" said Legree.

"Can rats walk down stairs, and come walking through the entry, and open a door when you've locked it and set a chair against it?" said Cassy; "and come walk, walk, walking right up to your bed, and put out their hand, so?"

Cassy kept her glittering eyes fixed on Legree, as she spoke, and he stared at her like a man in the nightmare, till, when she finished by laying her hand, icy cold, on his, he sprung back, with an oath.

"Woman! what do you mean? Nobody did?"—

"O, no,—of course not,—did I say they did?" said Cassy, with a smile of chilling derision.

"But—did—have you really seen?—Come, Cass, what is it, now,—speak out!"

"You may sleep there, yourself," said Cassy, "if you want to know."

"Did it come from the garret, Cassy?"

"*It*,—what?" said Cassy.

"Why, what you told of—"

"I didn't tell you anything," said Cassy, with dogged sullenness.

Legree walked up and down the room, uneasily.

"I'll have this yer thing examined. I'll look into it, this very night. I'll take my pistols—"

"Do," said Cassy; "sleep in that room. I'd like to see you doing it. Fire your pistols,—do!"

Legree stamped his foot, and swore violently.

"Don't swear," said Cassy; "nobody knows who may be hearing you. Hark! What was that?"

"What?" said Legree, starting.

A heavy old Dutch clock, that stood in the corner of the room, began, and slowly struck twelve.

For some reason or other, Legree neither spoke nor moved; a vague horror fell on him; while Cassy, with a keen, sneering glitter in her eyes, stood looking at him, counting the strokes.

"Twelve o'clock; well, *now* we'll see," said she, turning, and opening the door into the passage-way, and standing as if listening.

"Hark! What's that?" said she, raising her finger.

"It's only the wind," said Legree. "Don't you hear how cursedly it blows?"

"Simon, come here," said Cassy, in a whisper, laying her hand on his, and leading him to the foot of the stairs: "do you know what *that* is? Hark!"

A wild shriek came pealing down the stairway. It came from the garret. Legree's knees knocked together; his face grew white with fear.

"Hadn't you better get your pistols?" said Cassy, with a sneer that froze Legree's blood. "It's time this thing was looked into, you know. I'd like to have you go up now; *they're at it.*"

"I won't go!" said Legree, with an oath.

"Why not? There an't any such thing as ghosts, you know! Come!" and Cassy flitted up the winding stairway, laughing, and looking back after him. "Come on."

"I believe you *are* the devil!" said Legree. "Come back, you hag,—come back, Cass! You shan't go!"

But Cassy laughed wildly, and fled on. He heard her open the entry doors that led to the garret. A wild gust of wind swept down, extinguishing the candle he held in his hand, and with it the fearful, unearthly screams; they seemed to be shrieked in his very ear.

Legree fled frantically into the parlor, whither, in a few moments, he was followed by Cassy, pale, calm, cold as an avenging spirit, and with that same fearful light in her eye.

"I hope you are satisfied," said she.

"Blast you, Cass!" said Legree.

"What for?" said Cassy. "I only went up and shut the doors. *What's the matter with that garret*, Simon, do you suppose?" said she.

"None of your business!" said Legree.

"O, it an't? Well," said Cassy, "at any rate, I'm glad *I* don't sleep under it."

Anticipating the rising of the wind, that very evening, Cassy had been up and opened the garret window. Of course, the moment the doors were opened, the wind had drafted down, and extinguished the light.

This may serve as a specimen of the game that Cassy played with Legree, until he would sooner have put his head into a lion's mouth than to have explored that garret. Meanwhile, in the night, when every-body else was asleep, Cassy slowly and carefully accumulated there a stock of provisions sufficient to afford subsistence for some time; she transferred, article by article, a greater part of her own and Emmeline's wardrobe. All things being arranged, they only waited a fitting opportunity to put their plan in execution.

By cajoling Legree, and taking advantage of a good-natured interval, Cassy had got him to take her with him to the neighboring town, which was situated directly on the Red river. With a memory sharpened to almost preternatural clearness, she remarked every turn in the road, and formed a mental estimate of the time to be occupied in traversing it.

At the time when all was matured for action, our readers may, perhaps, like to look behind the scenes, and see the final *coup d'état*.[3]

3. A sudden violent change of government.

It was now near evening. Legree had been absent, on a ride to a neighboring farm. For many days Cassy had been unusually gracious and accommodating in her humors; and Legree and she had been, apparently, on the best of terms. At present, we may behold her and Emmeline in the room of the latter, busy in sorting and arranging two small bundles.

"There, these will be large enough," said Cassy. "Now put on your bonnet, and let's start: it's just about the right time."

"Why, they can see us yet," said Emmeline.

"I mean they shall," said Cassy, coolly. "Don't you know that they must have their chase after us, at any rate? The way of the thing is to be just this:—We will steal out of the back door, and run down by the quarters. Sambo or Quimbo will be sure to see us. They will give chase, and we will get into the swamp; then, they can't follow us any further till they go up and give the alarm, and turn out the dogs, and so on; and, while they are blundering round, and tumbling over each other, as they always do, you and I will just slip along to the creek, that runs back of the house, and wade along in it, till we get opposite the back door. That will put the dogs all at fault; for scent won't lie in the water. Every one will run out of the house to look after us, and then we'll whip in at the back door, and up into the garret, where I've got a nice bed made up in one of the great boxes. We must stay in that garret a good while; for, I tell you, he will raise heaven and earth after us. He'll muster some of those old overseers on the other plantations, and have a great hunt; and they'll go over every inch of ground in that swamp. He makes it his boast that nobody ever got away from him. So let him hunt at his leisure."

"Cassy, how well you have planned it!" said Emmeline. "Who ever would have thought of it, but you?"

There was neither pleasure nor exultation in Cassy's eyes,—only a despairing firmness.

"Come," she said, reaching her hand to Emmeline.

The two fugitives glided noiselessly from the house, and flitted, through the gathering shadows of evening, along by the quarters. The crescent moon, set like a silver signet in the western sky, delayed a little the approach of night. As Cassy expected, when quite near the verge of the swamps that encircled the plantation, they heard a voice calling to them to stop. It was not Sambo, however, but Legree, who was pursuing them with violent execrations. At the sound, the feebler spirit of Emmeline gave way; and, laying hold of Cassy's arm, she said, "O, Cassy, I'm going to faint!"

"If you do, I'll kill you!" said Cassy, drawing a small, glittering stiletto, and flashing it before the eyes of the girl.

The diversion accomplished the purpose. Emmeline did not faint, and succeeded in plunging, with Cassy, into a part of the labyrinth of swamp, so deep and dark that it was perfectly hopeless for Legree to think of following them, without assistance.

"Well," said he, chuckling brutally; "at any rate, they've got themselves into a trap now—the baggages! They're safe enough. They shall sweat for it!"

"Hulloa, there! Sambo! Quimbo! All hands!" called Legree, coming to the quarters, when the men and women were just returning from work. "There's two runaways in the swamps. I'll give five dollars to any nigger as catches 'em. Turn out the dogs! Turn out Tiger, and Fury, and the rest!"

The sensation produced by this news was immediate. Many of the men sprang forward, officiously, to offer their services, either from the hope of the reward, or from that cringing subserviency which is one of the most baleful effects of slavery. Some ran one way, and some another. Some were for getting flambeaux[4] of pine-knots. Some were uncoupling the dogs, whose hoarse, savage bay added not a little to the animation of the scene.

"Mas'r, shall we shoot 'em, if we can't cotch 'em?" said Sambo, to whom his master brought out a rifle.

"You may fire on Cass, if you like; it's time she was gone to the devil, where she belongs; but the gal, not," said Legree. "And now, boys, be spry and smart. Five dollars for him that gets 'em; and a glass of spirits to every one of you, anyhow."

The whole band, with the glare of blazing torches, and whoop, and shout, and savage yell, of man and beast, proceeded down to the swamp, followed, at some distance, by every servant in the house. The establishment was, of a consequence, wholly deserted, when Cassy and Emmeline glided into it the back way. The whooping and shouts of their pursuers were still filling the air; and, looking from the sitting-room windows, Cassy and Emmeline could see the troop, with their flambeaux, just dispersing themselves along the edge of the swamp.

"See there!" said Emmeline, pointing to Cassy; "the hunt is begun! Look how those lights dance about! Hark! the dogs! Don't you hear? If we were only *there*, our chance wouldn't be worth a picayune. O, for pity's sake, do let's hide ourselves. Quick!"

"There's no occasion for hurry," said Cassy, coolly; "they are all out after the hunt,—that's the amusement of the evening! We'll go up stairs, by and by. Meanwhile;" said she, deliberately taking a key from the pocket of a coat that Legree had thrown down in his hurry, "meanwhile I shall take something to pay our passage."

She unlocked the desk, took from it a roll of bills, which she counted over rapidly.

4. Flaming torches.

"O, don't let's do that!" said Emmeline.

"Don't!" said Cassy; "why not? Would you have us starve in the swamps, or have that that will pay our way to the free states? Money will do anything, girl." And, as she spoke, she put the money in her bosom.

"It would be stealing," said Emmeline, in a distressed whisper.

"Stealing!" said Cassy, with a scornful laugh. "They who steal body and soul needn't talk to us. Every one of these bills is stolen,—stolen from poor, starving, sweating creatures, who must go to the devil at last, for his profit. Let *him* talk about stealing! But come, we may as well go up garret; I've got a stock of candles there, and some books to pass away the time. You may be pretty sure they won't come *there* to inquire after us. If they do, I'll play ghost for them."

When Emmeline reached the garret, she found an immense box, in which some heavy pieces of furniture had once been brought, turned on its side, so that the opening faced the wall, or rather the eaves. Cassy lit a small lamp, and, creeping round under the eaves, they established themselves in it. It was spread with a couple of small mattresses and some pillows; a box near by was plentifully stored with candles, provisions, and all the clothing necessary to their journey, which Cassy had arranged into bundles of an astonishingly small compass.

"There," said Cassy, as she fixed the lamp into a small hook, which she had driven into the side of the box for that purpose; "this is to be our home for the present. How do you like it?"

"Are you sure they won't come and search the garret?"

"I'd like to see Simon Legree doing that," said Cassy. "No, indeed; he will be too glad to keep away. As to the servants, they would any of them stand and be shot, sooner than show their faces here."

Somewhat reassured, Emmeline settled herself back on her pillow.

"What did you mean, Cassy, by saying you would kill me?" she said, simply.

"I meant to stop your fainting," said Cassy, "and I did do it. And now I tell you, Emmeline, you must make up your mind *not* to faint, let what will come; there's no sort of need of it. If I had not stopped you, that wretch might have had his hands on you now."

Emmeline shuddered.

The two remained some time in silence. Cassy busied herself with a French book; Emmeline, overcome with the exhaustion, fell into a doze, and slept some time. She was awakened by loud shouts and outcries, the tramp of horses' feet, and the baying of dogs. She started up, with a faint shriek.

"Only the hunt coming back," said Cassy, coolly; "never fear. Look out of this knot-hole. Don't you see 'em all down there? Simon has to give it up, for this night. Look, how muddy his horse is, flouncing about in the swamp; the dogs, too, look rather crestfallen. Ah, my good sir, you'll have to try the race again and again,—the game isn't there."

"O, don't speak a word!" said Emmeline; "what if they should hear you?"

"If they do hear anything, it will make them very particular to keep away," said Cassy. "No danger; we may make any noise we please, and it will only add to the effect."

At length the stillness of midnight settled down over the house. Legree, cursing his ill luck, and vowing dire vengeance on the morrow, went to bed.

## Chapter XL

### *The Martyr*

"Deem not the just by Heaven forgot!
Though life its common gifts deny,—
Though, with a crushed and bleeding heart,
And spurned of man, he goes to die!
For God hath marked each sorrowing day,
And numbered every bitter tear;
And heaven's long years of bliss shall pay
For all his children suffer here."—BRYANT.[1]

The longest way must have its close,—the gloomiest night will wear on to a morning. An eternal, inexorable lapse of moments is ever hurrying the day of the evil to an eternal night, and the night of the just to an eternal day. We have walked with our humble friend thus far in the valley of slavery; first through flowery fields of ease and indulgence, then through heart-breaking separations from all that man holds dear. Again, we have waited with him in a sunny island, where generous hands concealed his chains with flowers; and, lastly, we have followed him when the last ray of earthly hope went out in night, and seen how, in the blackness of earthly darkness, the firmament of the unseen has blazed with stars of new and significant lustre.

The morning-star now stands over the tops of the mountains, and gales and breezes, not of earth, show that the gates of day are unclosing.

The escape of Cassy and Emmeline irritated the before surly temper of Legree to the last degree; and his fury, as was to be expected,

1. Adapted from "Blessed Are They That Mourn" by William Cullen Bryant (1794–1878); the first line should read, "Nor let the good man's trust depart."

fell upon the defenceless head of Tom. When he hurriedly announced the tidings among his hands, there was a sudden light in Tom's eye, a sudden upraising of his hands, that did not escape him. He saw that he did not join the muster of the pursuers. He thought of forcing him to do it; but, having had, of old, experience of his inflexibility when commanded to take part in any deed of inhumanity, he would not, in his hurry, stop to enter into any conflict with him.

Tom, therefore, remained behind, with a few who had learned of him to pray, and offered up prayers for the escape of the fugitives.

When Legree returned, baffled and disappointed, all the long-working hatred of his soul towards his slave began to gather in a deadly and desperate form. Had not this man braved him,—steadily, powerfully, resistlessly,—ever since he bought him? Was there not a spirit in him which, silent as it was, burned on him like the fires of perdition?

"I *hate* him!" said Legree, that night, as he sat up in his bed; "I *hate* him! And isn't he MINE? Can't I do what I like with him? Who's to hinder, I wonder?" And Legree clenched his fist, and shook it, as if he had something in his hands that he could rend in pieces.

But, then, Tom was a faithful, valuable servant; and, although Legree hated him the more for that, yet the consideration was still somewhat of a restraint to him.

The next morning, he determined to say nothing, as yet; to assemble a party, from some neighboring plantations, with dogs and guns; to surround the swamp, and go about the hunt systematically. If it succeeded, well and good; if not, he would summon Tom before him, and—his teeth clenched and his blood boiled—*then* he would break that fellow down, or——there was a dire inward whisper, to which his soul assented.

Ye say that the *interest* of the master is a sufficient safe-guard for the slave. In the fury of man's mad will, he will wittingly, and with open eye, sell his own soul to the devil to gain his ends; and will he be more careful of his neighbor's body?

"Well," said Cassy, the next day, from the garret, as she reconnoitred through the knot-hole, "the hunt's going to begin again, to-day!"

Three or four mounted horsemen were curvetting[2] about, on the space front of the house; and one or two leashes of strange dogs were struggling with the negroes who held them, baying and barking at each other.

The men are, two of them, overseers of plantations in the vicinity; and others were some of Legree's associates at the tavern-bar of

2. I.e., frolicking or bounding. A curvet is a horse's leap in which all four of its legs are in the air at the same time.

a neighboring city, who had come for the interest of the sport. A more hard-favored set, perhaps, could not be imagined. Legree was serving brandy, profusely, round among them, as also among the negroes, who had been detailed from the various plantations for this service; for it was an object to make every service of this kind, among the negroes, as much of a holiday as possible.

Cassy placed her ear at the knot-hole; and, as the morning air blew directly towards the house, she could overhear a good deal of the conversation. A grave sneer overcast the dark, severe gravity of her face, as she listened, and heard them divide out the ground, discuss the rival merits of the dogs, give orders about firing, and the treatment of each, in case of capture.

Cassy drew back; and, clasping her hands, looked upward, and said, "O, great Almighty God! we are *all* sinners; but what have *we* done, more than all the rest of the world, that we should be treated so?"

There was a terrible earnestness in her face and voice, as she spoke.

"If it wasn't for *you*, child," she said, looking at Emmeline, "I'd *go* out to them; and I'd thank any one of them that *would* shoot me down; for what use will freedom be to me? Can it give me back my children, or make me what I used to be?"

Emmeline, in her child-like simplicity, was half afraid of the dark moods of Cassy. She looked perplexed, but made no answer. She only took her hand, with a gentle, caressing movement.

"Don't!" said Cassy, trying to draw it away; "you'll get me to loving you; and I never mean to love anything, again!"

"Poor Cassy!" said Emmeline, "don't feel so! If the Lord gives us liberty, perhaps he'll give you back your daughter; at any rate, I'll be like a daughter to you. I know I'll never see my poor old mother again! I shall love you, Cassy, whether you love me or not!"

The gentle, child-like spirit conquered. Cassy sat down by her, put her arm round her neck, stroked her soft, brown hair; and Emmeline then wondered at the beauty of her magnificent eyes, now soft with tears.

"O, Em!" said Cassy, "I've hungered for my children, and thirsted for them, and my eyes fail with longing for them! Here! here!" she said, striking her breast, "it's all desolate, all empty! If God would give me back my children, then I could pray."

"You must trust him, Cassy," said Emmeline; "he is our Father!"

"His wrath is upon us," said Cassy; "he has turned away in anger."

"No, Cassy! He will be good to us! Let us hope in Him," said Emmeline,—"I always have had hope."

The hunt was long, animated, and thorough, but unsuccessful; and, with grave, ironic exultation, Cassy looked down on Legree, as, weary and dispirited, he alighted from his horse.

"Now, Quimbo," said Legree, as he stretched himself down in the sitting-room, "you jest go and walk that Tom up here, right away! The old cuss is at the bottom of this yer whole matter; and I'll have it out of his old black hide, or I'll know the reason why!"

Sambo and Quimbo, both, though hating each other, were joined in one mind by a no less cordial hatred of Tom. Legree had told them, at first, that he had bought him for a general overseer, in his absence; and this had begun an ill will, on their part, which had increased, in their debased and servile natures, as they saw him becoming obnoxious to their master's displeasure. Quimbo, therefore, departed, with a will, to execute his orders.

Tom heard the message with a forewarning heart; for he knew all the plan of the fugitives' escape, and the place of their present concealment;—he knew the deadly character of the man he had to deal with, and his despotic power. But he felt strong in God to meet death, rather than betray the helpless.

He sat his basket down by the row, and, looking up, said, "Into thy hands I commend my spirit! Thou hast redeemed me, oh Lord God of truth!"[3] and then quietly yielded himself to the rough, brutal grasp with which Quimbo seized him.

"Ay, ay!" said the giant, as he dragged him along; "ye'll cotch it, now! I'll boun' Mas'r's back's up *high!* No sneaking out, now! Tell ye, ye'll get it, and no mistake! See how ye'll look, now, helpin' Mas'r's niggers to run away! See what ye'll get!"

The savage words none of them reached that ear!—a higher voice there was saying, "Fear not them that kill the body, and, after that, have no more that they can do."[4] Nerve and bone of that poor man's body vibrated to those words, as if touched by the finger of God; and he felt the strength of a thousand souls in one. As he passed along, the trees and bushes, the huts of his servitude, the whole scene of his degradation, seemed to whirl by him as the landscape by the rushing car. His soul throbbed,—his home was in sight,—and the hour of release seemed at hand.

"Well, Tom!" said Legree, walking up, and seizing him grimly by the collar of his coat, and speaking through his teeth, in a paroxysm of determined rage, "do you know I've made up my mind to KILL you?"

"It's very likely, Mas'r," said Tom, calmly.

"I *have*," said Legree, with grim, terrible calmness, "*done—just—that—thing*, Tom, unless you'll tell me what you know about these yer gals!"

3. Christ's last words on the Cross were "Father, into thy hands I commend my spirit" (Luke 23.46).
4. Christ said to the apostles: "Fear not them which kill the body, but are not able to kill the soul: but rather fear him which is able to destroy both soul and body in hell" (Matthew 11.28).

Tom stood silent.

"D' ye hear?" said Legree, stamping, with a roar like that of an incensed lion. "Speak!"

"*I han't got nothing to tell, Mas'r,*" said Tom, with a slow, firm, deliberate utterance.

"Do you dare to tell me, ye old black Christian, ye don't *know?*" said Legree.

Tom was silent.

"Speak!" thundered Legree, striking him furiously. "Do you know anything?"

"I know, Mas'r; but I can't tell anything. *I can die!*"

Legree drew in a long breath; and, suppressing his rage, took Tom by the arm, and, approaching his face almost to his, said, in a terrible voice, "Hark'e, Tom!—ye think, 'cause I've let you off before, I don't mean what I say; but, this time, I've *made up my mind*, and counted the cost. You've always stood it out agin' me: now, I'll *conquer ye, or kill ye!*—one or t'other. I'll count every drop of blood there is in you, and take 'em, one by one, till ye give up!"

Tom looked up to his master, and answered, "Mas'r, if you was sick, or in trouble, or dying, and I could save ye, I'd *give* ye my heart's blood; and, if taking every drop of blood in this poor old body would save your precious soul, I'd give 'em freely, as the Lord gave his for me. O, Mas'r! don't bring this great sin on your soul! It will hurt you more than 't will me! Do the worst you can, my troubles'll be over soon; but, if ye don't repent, yours won't *never* end!"

Like a strange snatch of heavenly music, heard in the lull of a tempest, this burst of feeling made a moment's blank pause. Legree stood aghast, and looked at Tom; and there was such a silence, that the tick of the old clock could be heard, measuring, with silent touch, the last moments of mercy and probation to that hardened heart.

It was but a moment. There was one hesitating pause,—one irresolute, relenting thrill,—and the spirit of evil came back, with seven-fold vehemence; and Legree, foaming with rage, smote his victim to the ground.

Scenes of blood and cruelty are shocking to our ear and heart. What man has nerve to do, man has not nerve to hear. What brother-man and brother-Christian must suffer, cannot be told us, even in our secret chamber, it so harrows up the soul! And yet, oh my country! these things are done under the shadow of thy laws! O, Christ! thy church sees them, almost in silence!

But, of old, there was One whose suffering changed an instrument of torture, degradation and shame, into a symbol of glory, honor, and immortal life; and, where His spirit is, neither degrading stripes, nor blood, nor insults, can make the Christian's last struggle less than glorious.

Was he alone, that long night, whose brave, loving spirit was bearing up, in that old shed, against buffeting and brutal stripes?

Nay! There stood by him One,—seen by him alone,—"like unto the Son of God."[5]

The tempter stood by him, too,—blinded by furious, despotic will;—every moment pressing him to shun that agony by the betrayal of the innocent. But the brave, true heart was firm on the Eternal Rock. Like his Master, he knew that, if he saved others, himself he could not save; nor could utmost extremity wring from him words, save of prayer and holy trust.

"He's most gone, Mas'r," said Sambo, touched, in spite of himself, by the patience of his victim.

"Pay away, till he gives up! Give it to him!—give it to him!" shouted Legree. "I'll take every drop of blood he has, unless he confesses!"

Tom opened his eyes, and looked upon his master. "Ye poor miserable critter!" he said, "there an't no more ye can do! I forgive ye, with all my soul!" and he fainted entirely away.

"I b'lieve, my soul, he's done for, finally," said Legree, stepping forward, to look at him. "Yes, he is! Well, his mouth's shut up, at last,—that's one comfort!"

Yes, Legree; but who shall shut up that voice in thy soul? that soul, past repentance, past prayer, past hope, in whom the fire that never shall be quenched is already burning!

Yet Tom was not quite gone. His wondrous words and pious prayers had struck upon the hearts of the imbruted blacks, who had been the instruments of cruelty upon him; and, the instant Legree withdrew, they took him down, and, in their ignorance, sought to call him back to life,—as if *that* were any favor to him.

"Sartin, we's been doin' a drefful wicked thing!" said Sambo; "hopes Mas'r'll have to 'count for it, and not we."

They washed his wounds,—they provided a rude bed, of some refuse cotton, for him to lie down on; and one of them, stealing up to the house, begged a drink of brandy of Legree, pretending that he was tired, and wanted it for himself. He brought it back, and poured it down Tom's throat.

"O, Tom!" said Quimbo, "we's been awful wicked to ye!"

"I forgive ye, with all my heart!" said Tom, faintly.

"O, Tom! do tell us who is *Jesus*, anyhow?" said Sambo;—"Jesus, that's been a standin' by you so, all this night!—Who is he?"

5. See Hebrews 7.3.

The word roused the failing, fainting spirit. He poured forth a few energetic sentences of that wondrous One,—his life, his death, his ever-lasting presence, and power to save.

They wept,—both the two savage men.

"Why didn't I never hear this before?" said Sambo; "but I do believe!—I can't help it! Lord Jesus, have mercy on us!"

"Poor critters!" said Tom, "I'd be willing to bar' all I have, if it'll only bring ye to Christ! O, Lord! give me these two more souls, I pray!"

That prayer was answered!

# Chapter XLI

## *The Young Master*

Two days after, a young man drove a light wagon up through the avenue of china-trees, and, throwing the reins hastily on the horses' neck, sprang out and inquired for the owner of the place.

It was George Shelby; and, to show how he came to be there, we must go back in our story.

The letter of Miss Ophelia to Mrs. Shelby had, by some unfortunate accident, been detained, for a month or two, at some remote post-office, before it reached its destination; and, of course, before it was received, Tom was already lost to view among the distant swamps of the Red river.

Mrs. Shelby read the intelligence with the deepest concern; but any immediate action upon it was an impossibility. She was then in attendance on the sick-bed of her husband, who lay delirious in the crisis of a fever. Master George Shelby, who, in the interval, had changed from a boy to a tall young man, was her constant and faithful assistant, and her only reliance in superintending his father's affairs. Miss Ophelia had taken the precaution to send them the name of the lawyer who did business for the St. Clares; and the most that, in the emergency, could be done, was to address a letter of inquiry to him. The sudden death of Mr. Shelby, a few days after, brought, of course, an absorbing pressure of other interests, for a season.

Mr. Shelby showed his confidence in his wife's ability, by appointing her sole executrix upon his estates; and thus immediately a large and complicated amount of business was brought upon her hands.

Mrs. Shelby, with characteristic energy, applied herself to the work of straightening the entangled web of affairs; and she and George were for some time occupied with collecting and examining accounts, selling property and settling debts; for Mrs. Shelby was determined that everything should be brought into tangible and recognizable shape, let the consequences to her prove what they might. In the mean time, they received a letter from the lawyer to whom Miss Ophelia had referred them, saying that he knew nothing of the matter; that the man was sold at a public auction, and that, beyond receiving the money, he knew nothing of the affair.

Neither George nor Mrs. Shelby could be easy at this result; and, accordingly, some six months after, the latter, having business for his mother, down the river, resolved to visit New Orleans, in person, and push his inquiries, in hopes of discovering Tom's whereabouts, and restoring him.

After some months of unsuccessful search, by the merest accident, George fell in with a man, in New Orleans, who happened to be possessed of the desired information; and with his money in his pocket, our hero took steamboat for Red river, resolving to find out and re-purchase his old friend.

He was soon introduced into the house, where he found Legree in the sitting-room.

Legree received the stranger with a kind of surly hospitality.

"I understand," said the young man, "that you bought, in New Orleans, a boy, named Tom. He used to be on my father's place, and I came to see if I couldn't buy him back."

Legree's brow grew dark, and he broke out, passionately: "Yes, I did buy such a fellow,—and a h—l of a bargain I had of it, too! The most rebellious, saucy, impudent dog! Set up my niggers to run away; got off two gals, worth eight hundred or a thousand dollars apiece. He owned to that, and, when I bid him tell me where they was, he up and said he knew, but he wouldn't tell; and stood to it, though I gave him the cussedest flogging I ever gave nigger yet. I b'lieve he's trying to die; but I don't know as he'll make it out."

"Where is he?" said George, impetuously. "Let me see him." The cheeks of the young man were crimson, and his eyes flashed fire; but he prudently said nothing, as yet.

"He's in dat ar shed," said a little fellow, who stood holding George's horse.

Legree kicked the boy, and swore at him; but George, without saying another word, turned and strode to the spot.

Tom had been lying two days since the fatal night; not suffering, for every nerve of suffering was blunted and destroyed. He lay, for the most part, in a quiet stupor; for the laws of a powerful and well-knit frame would not at once release the imprisoned spirit. By stealth, there had been there, in the darkness of the night, poor desolated creatures, who stole from their scanty hours' rest, that they might repay to him some of those ministrations of love in which he had always been so abundant. Truly, those poor disciples had little to give,—only the cup of cold water; but it was given with full hearts.

Tears had fallen on that honest, insensible face,—tears of late repentance in the poor, ignorant heathen, whom his dying love and patience had awakened to repentance, and bitter prayers, breathed over him to a late-found Saviour, of whom they scarce knew more than the name, but whom the yearning ignorant heart of man never implores in vain.

Cassy, who had glided out of her place of concealment, and, by over-hearing, learned the sacrifice that had been made for her and Emmeline, had been there, the night before, defying the danger of detection; and, moved by the few last words which the affectionate soul had yet strength to breathe, the long winter of despair, the ice of years, had given way, and the dark, despairing woman had wept and prayed.

When George entered the shed, he felt his head giddy and his heart sick.

"Is it possible,—is it possible?" said he, kneeling down by him. "Uncle Tom, my poor, poor old friend!"

Something in the voice penetrated to the ear of the dying. He moved his head gently, smiled, and said,

> "Jesus can make a dying-bed
> Feel soft as downy pillows are."[1]

Tears which did honor to his manly heart fell from the young man's eyes, as he bent over his poor friend.

"O, dear Uncle Tom! do wake,—do speak once more! Look up! Here's Mas'r George,—your own little Mas'r George. Don't you know me?"

"Mas'r George!" said Tom, opening his eyes, and speaking in a feeble voice; "Mas'r George!" He looked bewildered.

Slowly the idea seemed to fill his soul; and the vacant eye became fixed and brightened, the whole face lighted up, the hard hands clasped, and tears ran down the cheeks.

"Bless the Lord! it is,—it is,—it's all I wanted! They haven't forgot me. It warms my soul; it does my old heart good! Now I shall die content! Bless the Lord, oh my soul!"

1. A similar theme is expressed in the black spiritual "Jesus Goin' to Make Up My Dyin' Bed":

> Oh, don't you worry 'bout me dyin'
> Oh, don't you worry 'bout me dyin'
> Oh, don't you worry 'bout me dyin'
> Jesus goin' to make up my dyin' bed.

"You shan't die! you *mustn't* die, nor think of it! I've come to buy you, and take you home," said George, with impetuous vehemence.

"O, Mas'r George, ye're too late. The Lord's bought me, and is going to take me home,—and I long to go. Heaven is better than Kintuck."

"O, don't die! It'll kill me!—it'll break my heart to think what you've suffered,—and lying in this old shed, here! Poor, poor fellow!"

"Don't call me poor fellow!" said Tom, solemnly. "I *have* been poor fellow; but that's all past and gone, now. I'm right in the door, going into glory! O, Mas'r George! *Heaven has come!* I've got the victory!—the Lord Jesus has given it to me! Glory be to His name!"

George was awe-struck at the force, the vehemence, the power, with which these broken sentences were uttered. He sat gazing in silence.

Tom grasped his hand, and continued,—"Ye mustn't, now, tell Chloe, poor soul! how ye found me;—'t would be so drefful to her. Only tell her ye found me going into glory; and that I couldn't stay for no one. And tell her the Lord's stood by me everywhere and al'ays, and made everything light and easy. And oh, the poor chil'en, and the baby!—my old heart's been most broke for 'em, time and agin! Tell 'em all to follow me—follow me! Give my love to Mas'r, and dear good Missis, and everybody in the place! Ye don't know! 'Pears like I loves 'em all! I loves every creatur' everywhar!—it's nothing *but* love! O, Mas'r George! what a thing 't is to be a Christian!"

At this moment, Legree sauntered up to the door of the shed, looked in, with a dogged air of affected carelessness, and turned away.

"The old satan!" said George, in his indignation. "It's a comfort to think the devil will pay *him* for this, some of these days!"

"O, don't!—oh, ye mustn't!" said Tom, grasping his hand; "he's a poor mis'able critter! it's awful to think on't! O, if he only could repent, the Lord would forgive him now; but I'm 'feared he never will!"

"I hope he won't!" said George; "I never want to see *him* in heaven!"

"Hush, Mas'r George!—it worries me! Don't feel so! He an't done me no real harm,—only opened the gate of the kingdom for me; that's all!"

At this moment, the sudden flush of strength which the joy of meeting his young master had infused into the dying man gave way. A sudden sinking fell upon him; he closed his eyes; and that mysterious and sublime change passed over his face, that told the approach of other worlds.

He began to draw his breath with long, deep inspirations; and his broad chest rose and fell, heavily. The expression of his face was that of a conqueror.

"Who,—who,—who shall separate us from the love of Christ?"[2] he said, in a voice that contended with mortal weakness; and, with a smile, he fell asleep.

George sat fixed with solemn awe. It seemed to him that the place was holy; and, as he closed the lifeless eyes, and rose up from the dead, only one thought possessed him,—that expressed by his simple old friend,—"What a thing it is to be a Christian!"

He turned: Legree was standing, sullenly, behind him.

Something in that dying scene had checked the natural fierceness of youthful passion. The presence of the man was simply loathsome to George; and he felt only an impulse to get away from him, with as few words as possible.

Fixing his keen dark eyes on Legree, he simply said, pointing to the dead, "You have got all you ever can of him. What shall I pay you for the body? I will take it away, and bury it decently."

"I don't sell dead niggers," said Legree, doggedly. "You are welcome to bury him where and when you like."

"Boys," said George, in an authoritative tone, to two or three negroes, who were looking at the body, "help me lift him up, and carry him to my wagon; and get me a spade."

One of them ran for a spade; the other two assisted George to carry the body to the wagon.

George neither spoke to nor looked at Legree, who did not countermand his orders, but stood, whistling, with an air of forced unconcern. He sulkily followed them to where the wagon stood at the door.

George spread his cloak in the wagon, and had the body carefully disposed of in it,—moving the seat, so as to give it room. Then he turned, fixed his eyes on Legree, and said, with forced composure,

"I have not, as yet, said to you what I think of this most atrocious affair;—this is not the time and place. But, sir, this innocent blood shall have justice. I will proclaim this murder. I will go to the very first magistrate, and expose you."

"Do!" said Legree, snapping his fingers, scornfully. "I'd like to see you doing it. Where you going to get witnesses?—how you going to prove it?—Come, now!"

George saw, at once, the force of this defiance. There was not a white person on the place; and, in all southern courts, the testimony of colored blood is nothing. He felt, at that moment, as if he could

2. "Who shall separate us from the love of Christ? shall tribulation, or distress, or persecution, or famine, or nakedness, or peril, or sword?" (Romans 8.35).

have rent the heavens with his heart's indignant cry for justice; but in vain.

"After all, what a fuss, for a dead nigger!" said Legree.

The word was as a spark to a powder magazine. Prudence was never a cardinal virtue of the Kentucky boy. George turned, and, with one indignant blow, knocked Legree flat upon his face; and, as he stood over him, blazing with wrath and defiance, he would have formed no bad personification of his great namesake triumphing over the dragon.

Some men, however, are decidedly bettered by being knocked down. If a man lays them fairly flat in the dust, they seem immediately to conceive a respect for him; and Legree was one of this sort. As he rose, therefore, and brushed the dust from his clothes, he eyed the slowly-retreating wagon with some evident consideration; nor did he open his mouth till it was out of sight.

Beyond the boundaries of the plantation, George had noticed a dry, sandy knoll, shaded by a few trees: there they made the grave.

"Shall we take off the cloak, Mas'r?" said the negroes, when the grave was ready.

"No, no,—bury it with him! It's all I can give you, now, poor Tom, and you shall have it."

They laid him in; and the men shovelled away, silently. They banked it up, and laid green turf over it.

"You may go, boys," said George, slipping a quarter into the hand of each. They lingered about, however.

"If young Mas'r would please buy us—" said one.

"We'd serve him so faithful!" said the other.

"Hard times here, Mas'r!" said the first. "Do, Mas'r, buy us, please!"

"I can't!—I can't!" said George, with difficulty, motioning them off; "it's impossible!"

The poor fellows looked dejected, and walked off in silence.

"Witness, eternal God!" said George, kneeling on the grave of his poor friend; "oh, witness, that, from this hour, I will do *what one man can* to drive out this curse of slavery from my land!"

There is no monument to mark the last resting-place of our friend. He needs none! His Lord knows where he lies, and will raise him up, immortal, to appear with him when he shall appear in his glory.

Pity him not! Such a life and death is not for pity! Not in the riches of omnipotence is the chief glory of God; but in self-denying, suffering love! And blessed are the men whom he calls to fellowship with him, bearing their cross after him with patience. Of such it is written, "Blessed are they that mourn, for they shall be comforted."[3]

3. From Christ's Sermon on the Mount (Matthew 5.3–5).

## Chapter XLII

### *An Authentic Ghost Story*

For some remarkable reason, ghostly legends were uncommonly rife, about this time, among the servants on Legree's place.

It was whisperingly asserted that footsteps, in the dead of night, had been heard descending the garret stairs, and patrolling the house. In vain the doors of the upper entry had been locked; the ghost either carried a duplicate key in its pocket, or availed itself of a ghost's immemorial privilege of coming through the keyhole, and promenaded as before, with a freedom that was alarming.

Authorities were somewhat divided, as to the outward form of the spirit, owing to a custom quite prevalent among negroes,—and, for aught we know, among whites, too,—of invariably shutting the eyes, and covering up heads under blankets, petticoats, or whatever else might come in use for a shelter, on these occasions. Of course, as everybody knows, when the bodily eyes are thus out of the lists, the spiritual eyes are uncommonly vivacious and perspicuous; and, therefore, there were abundance of full-length portraits of the ghost, abundantly sworn and testified to, which, as is often the case with portraits, agreed with each other in no particular, except the common family peculiarity of the ghost tribe,—the wearing of a *white sheet.* The poor souls were not versed in ancient history and did not know that Shakspeare had authenticated this costume, by telling how

> "The *sheeted* dead
> Did squeak and gibber in the streets of Rome."[1]

And, therefore, their all hitting upon this is a striking fact in pneumatology,[2] which we recommend to the attention of spiritual media generally.

Be it as it may, we have private reasons for knowing that a tall figure in a white sheet did walk, at the most approved ghostly hours, around the Legree premises,—pass out the doors, glide about the house,—disappear at intervals, and, reappearing, pass up the silent stair-way, into that fatal garret; and that, in the morning, the entry doors were all found shut and locked as firm as ever.

Legree could not help overhearing this whispering; and it was all the more exciting to him, from the pains that were taken to conceal it from him. He drank more brandy than usual; held up his head briskly, and swore louder than ever in the day-time; but he had bad

1. *Hamlet* 1.1.113.
2. The theory of spiritual beings; magical lore.

dreams, and the visions of his head on his bed were anything but agreeable. The night after Tom's body had been carried away, he rode to the next town for a carouse, and had a high one. Got home late and tired; locked his door, took out the key, and went to bed.

After all, let a man take what pains he may to hush it down, a human soul is an awful ghostly, unquiet possession for a bad man to have. Who knows the metes and bounds of it? Who knows all its awful perhapses,—those shudderings and tremblings, which it can no more live down than it can outlive its own eternity! What a fool is he who locks his door to keep out spirits, who has in his own bosom a spirit he dares not meet alone,—whose voice, smothered far down, and piled over with mountains of earthliness, is yet like the forewarning trumpet of doom!

But Legree locked his door and set a chair against it; he set a night-lamp at the head of his bed; and he put his pistols there. He examined the catches and fastenings of the windows, and then swore he "didn't care for the devil and all his angels," and went to sleep.

Well, he slept, for he was tired,—slept soundly. But, finally, there came over his sleep a shadow, a horror, an apprehension of something dreadful hanging over him. It was his mother's shroud, he thought; but Cassy had it, holding it up, and showing it to him. He heard a confused noise of screams and groanings; and, with it all, he knew he was asleep, and he struggled to wake himself. He was half awake. He was sure something was coming into his room. He knew the door was opening, but he could not stir hand or foot. At last he turned, with a start; the door *was* open, and he saw a hand putting out his light.

It was a cloudy, misty moonlight, and there he saw it!—something white, gliding in! He heard the still rustle of its ghostly garments. It stood still by his bed;—a cold hand touched his; a voice said, three times, in a low, fearful whisper, "Come! come! come!" And, while he lay sweating with terror, he knew not when or how, the thing was gone. He sprang out of bed, and pulled at the door. It was shut and locked, and the man fell down in a swoon.

After this, Legree became a harder drinker than ever before. He no longer drank cautiously, prudently, but imprudently and recklessly.

There were reports around the country, soon after, that he was sick and dying. Excess had brought on that frightful disease that seems to throw the lurid shadows of a coming retribution back into the present life. None could bear the horrors of that sick room, when he raved and screamed, and spoke of sights which almost stopped the blood of those who heard him; and, at his dying bed, stood a stern, white, inexorable figure, saying, "Come! come! come!"

By a singular coincidence, on the very night that this vision appeared to Legree, the house-door was found open in the morning, and some of the negroes had seen two white figures gliding down the avenue towards the high-road.

It was near sunrise when Cassy and Emmeline paused, for a moment, in a little knot of trees near the town.

Cassy was dressed after the manner of the Creole Spanish ladies,—wholly in black. A small black bonnet on her head, covered by a veil thick with embroidery, concealed her face. It had been agreed that, in their escape, she was to personate the character of a Creole[3] lady, and Emmeline that of her servant.

Brought up, from early life, in connection with the highest society, the language, movements and air of Cassy, were all in agreement with this idea; and she had still enough remaining with her, of a once splendid wardrobe, and sets of jewels, to enable her to personate the thing to advantage.

She stopped in the outskirts of the town, where she had noticed trunks for sale, and purchased a handsome one. This she requested the man to send along with her. And, accordingly, thus escorted by a boy wheeling her trunk, and Emmeline behind her, carrying her carpet-bag and sundry bundles, she made her appearance at the small tavern, like a lady of consideration.

The first person that struck her, after her arrival, was George Shelby, who was staying there, awaiting the next boat.

Cassy had remarked the young man from her loop-hole in the garret, and seen him bear away the body of Tom, and observed, with secret exultation, his rencontre[4] with Legree. Subsequently, she had gathered, from the conversations she had overheard among the negroes, as she glided about in her ghostly disguise, after nightfall, who he was, and in what relation he stood to Tom. She, therefore, felt an immediate accession of confidence, when she found that he was, like herself, awaiting the next boat.

Cassy's air and manner, address, and evident command of money, prevented any rising disposition to suspicion in the hotel. People never inquire too closely into those who are fair on the main point, of paying well,—a thing which Cassy had foreseen when she provided herself with money.

In the edge of the evening, a boat was heard coming along, and George Shelby handed Cassy aboard, with the politeness which comes naturally to every Kentuckian, and exerted himself to provide her with a good state-room.

3. Descended from the original Spanish settlers of the Gulf states.
4. Casual meeting.

Cassy kept her room and bed, on pretext of illness, during the whole time they were on Red river; and was waited on, with obsequious devotion, by her attendant.

When they arrived at the Mississippi river, George, having learned that the course of the strange lady was upward, like his own, proposed to take a state-room for her on the same boat with himself,—good-naturedly compassionating her feeble health, and desirous to do what he could to assist her.

Behold, therefore, the whole party safely transferred to the good steamer Cincinnati, and sweeping up the river under a powerful head of steam.

Cassy's health was much better. She sat upon the guards, came to the table, and was remarked upon in the boat as a lady that must have been very handsome.

From the moment that George got the first glimpse of her face, he was troubled with one of those fleeting and indefinite likenesses, which almost everybody can remember, and has been, at times, perplexed with. He could not keep himself from looking at her, and watching her perpetually. At table, or sitting at her state-room door, still she would encounter the young man's eyes fixed on her, and politely withdrawn, when she showed, by her countenance, that she was sensible of the observation.

Cassy became uneasy. She began to think that he suspected something; and finally resolved to throw herself entirely on his generosity, and intrusted him with her whole history.

George was heartily disposed to sympathize with any one who had escaped from Legree's plantation,—a place that he could not remember or speak of with patience,—and, with the courageous disregard of consequences which is characteristic of his age and state, he assured her that he would do all in his power to protect and bring them through.

The next state-room to Cassy's was occupied by a French lady, named de Thoux, who was accompanied by a fine little daughter, a child of some twelve summers.

This lady, having gathered, from George's conversation, that he was from Kentucky, seemed evidently disposed to cultivate his acquaintance; in which design she was seconded by the graces of her little girl, who was about as pretty a plaything as ever diverted the weariness of a fort-night's trip on a steamboat.

George's chair was often placed at her state-room door; and Cassy, as she sat upon the guards, could hear their conversation.

Madame de Thoux was very minute in her inquiries as to Kentucky, where she said she had resided in a former period of her life. George discovered, to his surprise, that her former residence must have been in his own vicinity; and her inquiries showed a knowledge of people and things in his region, that was perfectly surprising to him.

"Do you know," said Madame de Thoux to him, one day, "of any man, in your neighborhood, of the name of Harris?"

"There is an old fellow, of that name, lives not far from my father's place," said George. "We never have had much intercourse with him, though."

"He is a large slave-owner, I believe," said Madame de Thoux, with a manner which seemed to betray more interest than she was exactly willing to show.

"He is," said George, looking rather surprised at her manner.

"Did you ever know of his having—perhaps, you may have heard of his having a mulatto boy, named George?"

"O, certainly,—George Harris,—I know him well; he married a servant of my mother's, but has escaped, now, to Canada."

"He has?" said Madame de Thoux, quickly. "Thank God!"

George looked a surprised inquiry, but said nothing.

Madame de Thoux leaned her head on her hand, and burst into tears.

"He is my brother," she said.

"Madame!" said George, with a strong accent of surprise.

"Yes," said Madame de Thoux, lifting her head, proudly, and wiping her tears; "Mr. Shelby, George Harris is my brother!"

"I am perfectly astonished," said George, pushing back his chair a pace or two, and looking at Madame de Thoux.

"I was sold to the South when he was a boy," said she. "I was bought by a good and generous man. He took me with him to the West Indies, set me free, and married me. It is but lately that he died; and I was coming up to Kentucky, to see if I could find and redeem my brother."

"I have heard him speak of a sister Emily, that was sold South," said George.

"Yes, indeed! I am the one," said Madame de Thoux;—"tell me what sort of a—"

"A very fine young man," said George, "notwithstanding the curse of slavery that lay on him. He sustained a first rate character, both for intelligence and principle. I know, you see," he said; "because he married in our family."

"What sort of a girl?" said Madame de Thoux, eagerly.

"A treasure," said George; "a beautiful, intelligent, amiable girl. Very pious. My mother had brought her up, and trained her as carefully, almost, as a daughter. She could read and write, embroider and sew, beautifully; and was a beautiful singer."

"Was she born in your house?" said Madame de Thoux.

"No. Father bought her once, in one of his trips to New Orleans, and brought her up as a present to mother. She was about eight or nine years old, then. Father would never tell mother what he gave for her; but, the other day, in looking over his old papers, we came across the bill of sale. He paid an extravagant sum for her, to be sure. I suppose, on account of her extraordinary beauty."

George sat with his back to Cassy, and did not see the absorbed expression of her countenance, as he was giving these details.

At this point in the story, she touched his arm, and, with a face perfectly white with interest, said, "Do you know the names of the people he bought her of?"

"A man of the name of Simmons, I think, was the principal in the transaction. At least, I think that was the name on the bill of sale."

"O, my God!" said Cassy, and fell insensible on the floor of the cabin.

George was wide awake now, and so was Madame de Thoux. Though neither of them could conjecture what was the cause of Cassy's fainting, still they made all the tumult which is proper in such cases;—George upsetting a wash-pitcher, and breaking two tumblers, in the warmth of his humanity; and various ladies in the cabin, hearing that somebody had fainted, crowded the state-room door, and kept out all the air they possibly could, so that, on the whole, everything was done that could be expected.

Poor Cassy! when she recovered, turned her face to the wall, and wept and sobbed like a child,—perhaps, mother, you can tell what she was thinking of! Perhaps you cannot,—but she felt as sure, in that hour, that God had had mercy on her, and that she should see her daughter,—as she did, months afterwards,—when—but we anticipate.

## Chapter XLIII

### *Results*

The rest of our story is soon told. George Shelby, interested, as any other young man might be, by the romance of the incident, no less than by feelings of humanity, was at the pains to send to Cassy the bill of sale of Eliza; whose date and name all corresponded with her own knowledge of facts, and left no doubt upon her mind as to the identity of her child. It remained now only for her to trace out the path of the fugitives.

Madame de Thoux and she, thus drawn together by the singular coincidence of their fortunes, proceeded immediately to Canada, and began a tour of inquiry among the stations, where the numerous fugitives from slavery are located. At Amherstberg they found the missionary with whom George and Eliza had taken shelter, on their first arrival in Canada; and through him were enabled to trace the family to Montreal.

George and Eliza had now been five years free. George had found constant occupation in the shop of a worthy machinist, where he had been earning a competent support for his family, which, in the mean time, had been increased by the addition of another daughter.

Little Harry—a fine bright boy—had been put to a good school, and was making rapid proficiency in knowledge.

The worthy pastor of the station, in Amherstberg, where George had first landed, was so much interested in the statements of Madame de Thoux and Cassy, that he yielded to the solicitations of the former, to accompany them to Montreal, in their search,—she bearing all the expense of the expedition.

The scene now changes to a small, neat tenement, in the outskirts of Montreal; the time, evening. A cheerful fire blazes on the hearth; a tea-table, covered with a snowy cloth, stands prepared for the evening meal. In one corner of the room was a table covered with a green cloth, where was an open writing-desk, pens, paper, and over it a shelf of well-selected books.

This was George's study. The same zeal for self-improvement, which led him to steal the much coveted arts of reading and writing, amid all the toils and discouragements of his early life, still led him to devote all his leisure time to self-cultivation.

At this present time, he is seated at the table, making notes from a volume of the family library he has been reading.

"Come, George," says Eliza, "you've been gone all day. Do put down that book, and let's talk, while I'm getting tea,—do."

And little Eliza seconds the effort, by toddling up to her father, and trying to pull the book out of his hand, and install herself on his knee as a substitute.

"O, you little witch!" says George, yielding, as, in such circumstances, man always must.

"That's right," says Eliza, as she begins to cut a loaf of bread. A little older she looks; her form a little fuller; her air more matronly than of yore; but evidently contented and happy as woman need be.

"Harry, my boy, how did you come on in that sum, to-day?" says George, as he laid his hand on his son's head.

Harry has lost his long curls; but he can never lose those eyes and eyelashes, and that fine, bold brow, that flushes with triumph, as he answers, "I did it, every bit of it, *myself*, father; and *nobody* helped me!"

"That's right," says his father; "depend on yourself, my son. You have a better chance than ever your poor father had."

At this moment, there is a rap at the door; and Eliza goes and opens it. The delighted—"Why!—this you?"—calls up her husband; and the good pastor of Amherstberg is welcomed. There are two more women with him, and Eliza asks them to sit down.

Now, if the truth must be told, the honest pastor had arranged a little programme, according to which this affair was to develop itself; and, on the way up, all had very cautiously and prudently exhorted each other not to let things out, except according to previous arrangement.

What was the good man's consternation, therefore, just as he had motioned to the ladies to be seated, and was taking out his pocket-handkerchief to wipe his mouth, so as to proceed to his introductory speech in good order, when Madame de Thoux upset the whole plan, by throwing her arms around George's neck, and letting all out at once, by saying, "O, George! don't you know me? I'm your sister Emily."

Cassy had seated herself more composedly, and would have carried on her part very well, had not little Eliza suddenly appeared before her in exact shape and form, every outline and curl, just as her daughter was when she saw her last. The little thing peered up in her face; and Cassy caught her up in her arms, pressed her to her bosom, saying, what at the moment she really believed, "Darling, I'm your mother!"

In fact, it was a troublesome matter to do up exactly in proper order; but the good pastor, at last, succeeded in getting everybody quiet, and delivering the speech with which he had intended to open the exercises; and in which, at last, he succeeded so well, that his whole audience were sobbing about him in a manner that ought to satisfy any orator, ancient or modern.

They knelt together, and the good man prayed,—for there are some feelings so agitated and tumultuous, that they can find rest only by being poured into the bosom of Almighty love,—and then, rising up, the newfound family embraced each other, with a holy trust in Him, who from such peril and dangers, and by such unknown ways, had brought them together.

The note-book of a missionary, among the Canadian fugitives, contains truth stranger than fiction. How can it be otherwise, when a system prevails which whirls families and scatters their members, as the wind whirls and scatters the leaves of autumn? These shores of refuge, like the eternal shore, often unite again, in glad communion, hearts that for long years have mourned each other as lost. And affecting beyond expression is the earnestness with which every new arrival among them is met, if, perchance, it may bring tidings of mother, sister, child or wife, still lost to view in the shadows of slavery.

Deeds of heroism are wrought here more than those of romance, when, defying torture, and braving death itself, the fugitive voluntarily threads his way back to the terrors and perils of that dark land, that he may bring out his sister, or mother, or wife.

One young man, of whom a missionary has told us, twice recaptured, and suffering shameful stripes for his heroism, had escaped again; and, in a letter which we heard read, tells his friends that he is going back a third time, that he may, at last, bring away his sister. My good sir, is this man a hero, or a criminal? Would not you do as much for your sister? And can you blame him?

But, to return to our friends, whom we left wiping their eyes, and recovering themselves from too great and sudden a joy. They are now seated around the social board, and are getting decidedly companionable; only that Cassy, who keeps little Eliza on her lap, occasionally squeezes the little thing, in a manner that rather astonishes her, and obstinately refuses to have her mouth stuffed with cake to the extent the little one desires,—alleging, what the child rather wonders at, that she has got something better than cake, and doesn't want it.

And, indeed, in two or three days, such a change has passed over Cassy, that our readers would scarcely know her. The despairing, haggard expression of her face had given way to one of gentle trust. She seemed to sink, at once, into the bosom of the family, and take the little ones into her heart, as something for which it long had waited. Indeed, her love seemed to flow more naturally to the little Eliza than to her own daughter; for she was the exact image and body of the child whom she had lost. The little one was a flowery bond between mother and daughter, through whom grew up acquaintanceship and affection. Eliza's steady, consistent piety, regulated by the constant reading of the sacred word, made her a proper guide for the shattered and wearied mind of her mother. Cassy yielded at once, and with her whole soul, to every good influence, and became a devout and tender Christian.

After a day or two, Madame de Thoux told her brother more particularly of her affairs. The death of her husband had left her an ample fortune, which she generously offered to share with the family. When she asked George what way she could best apply it for him, he answered, "Give me an education, Emily; that has always been my heart's desire. Then, I can do all the rest."

On mature deliberation, it was decided that the whole family should go, for some years, to France; whither they sailed, carrying Emmeline with them.

The good looks of the latter won the affection of the first mate of the vessel; and, shortly after entering the port, she became his wife.

George remained four years at a French university, and, applying himself with an unintermitted zeal, obtained a very thorough education.

Political troubles in France, at last, led the family again to seek an asylum in this country.[1]

George's feelings and views, as an educated man may be best expressed in a letter to one of his friends.

"I feel somewhat at a loss, as to my future course. True, as you have said to me, I might mingle in the circles of the whites, in this country, my shade of color is so slight, and that of my wife and family scarce perceptible. Well, perhaps, on sufferance, I might. But, to tell you the truth, I have no wish to.

"My sympathies are not for my father's race, but for my mother's. To him I was no more than a fine dog or horse: to my poor heart-broken mother I was a *child*; and, though I never saw her, after the cruel sale that separated us, till she died, yet I *know* she always loved me dearly. I know it by my own heart. When I think of all she suffered, of my own early sufferings, of the distresses and struggles of my heroic wife, of my sister, sold in the New Orleans slave-market,—though I hope to have no unchristian sentiments, yet I may be excused for saying, I have no wish to pass for an American, or to identify myself with them.

"It is with the oppressed, enslaved African race that I cast in my lot; and, if I wished anything, I would wish myself two shades darker, rather than one lighter.

"The desire and yearning of my soul is for an African *nationality*. I want a people that shall have a tangible, separate existence of its own; and where am I to look for it? Not in Hayti; for in Hayti they had nothing to start with. A stream cannot rise above its fountain. The race that formed the character of the Haytiens was a worn-out, effeminate one; and, of course, the subject race will be centuries in rising to anything.

"Where, then, shall I look? On the shores of Africa I see a republic,[2]—a republic formed of picked men, who, by energy and self-educating force, have, in many cases, individually, raised themselves above a condition of slavery. Having gone through a preparatory stage

1. Stowe probably means Canada, although Frederick Douglass, for example, did return to the United States and buy his freedom after traveling and speaking on abolition in Europe.
2. The "republic" is Liberia, a nation on the coast of West Africa founded in 1821 by the American Colonization Society as a home for free African Americans. Before the end of the Civil War, fifteen thousand immigrants from America settled in Liberia. As Stowe's text goes on to acknowledge, many people believed that black emigration to Africa accommodated slavery by draining energy from abolitionism.

of feebleness, this republic has, at last, become an acknowledged nation on the face of the earth,—acknowledged by both France and England. There it is my wish to go, and find myself a people.

"I am aware, now, that I shall have you all against me; but, before you strike, hear me. During my stay in France, I have followed up, with intense interest, the history of my people in America. I have noted the struggle between abolitionist and colonizationist, and have received some impressions, as a distant spectator, which could never have occurred to me as a participator.

"I grant that this Liberia may have subserved all sorts of purposes, by being played off, in the hands of our oppressors, against us. Doubtless the scheme may have been used, in unjustifiable ways, as a means of retarding our emancipation. But the question to me is, Is there not a God above all man's schemes? May He not have overruled their designs, and founded for us a nation by them?

"In these days, a nation is born in a day. A nation starts, now, with all the great problems of republican life and civilization wrought out to its hand;—it has not to discover, but only to apply. Let us, then, all take hold together, with all our might, and see what we can do with this new enterprise, and the whole splendid continent of Africa opens before us and our children. *Our nation* shall roll the tide of civilization and Christianity along its shores, and plant there mighty republics, that, growing with the rapidity of tropical vegetation, shall be for all coming ages.

"Do you say that I am deserting my enslaved brethren? I think not. If I forget them one hour, one moment of my life, so may God forget me! But, what can I do for them, here? Can I break their chains? No, not as an individual; but, let me go and form part of a nation, which shall have a voice in the councils of nations, and then we can speak. A nation has a right to argue, remonstrate, implore, and present the cause of its race,—which an individual has not.

"If Europe ever becomes a grand council of free nations,—as I trust in God it will,—if, there, serfdom, and all unjust and oppressive social inequalities, are done away; and if they, as France and England have done, acknowledge our position,—then, in the great congress of nations, we will make our appeal, and present the cause of our enslaved and suffering race; and it cannot be that free, enlightened America will not then desire to wipe from her escutcheon[3] that bar sinister which disgraces her among nations, and is as truly a curse to her as to the enslaved.

"But, you will tell me, our race have equal rights to mingle in the American republic as the Irishman, the German, the Swede.

3. A shield or coat of arms, on which a bat sinister would indicate illegitimacy or some other stigma.

Granted, they have. We *ought* to be free to meet and mingle,—to rise by our individual worth, without any consideration of caste or color; and they who deny us this right are false to their own professed principles of human equality. We ought, in particular, to be allowed *here.* We have *more* than the rights of common men;—we have the claim of an injured race for reparation. But, then, *I do not want it;* I want a country, a nation, of my own. I think that the African race has peculiarities, yet to be unfolded in the light of civilization and Christianity, which, if not the same with those of the Anglo-Saxon, may prove to be, morally, of even a higher type.

"To the Anglo-Saxon race has been intrusted the destinies of the world, during its pioneer period of struggle and conflict. To that mission its stern, inflexible, energetic elements, were well adapted; but, as a Christian, I look for another era to arise. On its borders I trust we stand; and the throes that now convulse the nations are, to my hope, but the birth-pangs of an hour of universal peace and brotherhood.

"I trust that the development of Africa is to be essentially a Christian one. If not a dominant and commanding race, they are, at least, an affectionate, magnanimous and forgiving one. Having been called in the furnace of injustice and oppression, they have need to bind closer to their hearts that sublime doctrine of love and forgiveness, through which alone they are to conquer, which it is to be their mission to spread over the continent of Africa.

"In myself, I confess, I am feeble for this,—full half the blood in my veins is the hot and hasty Saxon; but I have an eloquent preacher of the Gospel ever by my side, in the person of my beautiful wife. When I wander, her gentler spirit ever restores me, and keeps before my eyes the Christian calling and mission of our race. As a Christian patriot, as a teacher of Christianity, I go to *my country,*—my chosen, my glorious Africa!—and to her, in my heart, I sometimes apply those splendid words of prophecy: 'Whereas thou hast been forsaken and hated, so that no man went through thee; *I* will make thee an eternal excellence, a joy of many generations!'[4]

"You will call me an enthusiast: you will tell me that I have not well considered what I am undertaking. But I have considered, and counted the cost. I go to *Liberia*, not as to an Elysium[5] of romance, but as to *a field of work*. I expect to work with both hands,—to work *hard*; to work against all sorts of difficulties and discouragements; and to work till I die. This is what I go for; and in this I am quite sure I shall not be disappointed.

4. Isaiah 60.15.
5. In Greek and Roman myth, the place of happy souls after death; any place of ideal happiness.

"Whatever you may think of my determination, do not divorce me from your confidence; and think that, in whatever I do, I act with a heart wholly given to my people.

"GEORGE HARRIS."

George, with his wife, children, sister and mother, embarked for Africa, some few weeks after. If we are not mistaken, the world will yet hear from him there.

Of our other characters we have nothing very particular to write, except a word relating to Miss Ophelia and Topsy, and a farewell chapter, which we shall dedicate to George Shelby.

Miss Ophelia took Topsy home to Vermont with her, much to the surprise of that grave deliberative body whom a New Englander recognizes under the term. "*Our folks.*" "Our folks," at first, thought it an odd and unnecessary addition to their well-trained domestic establishment; but, so thoroughly efficient was Miss Ophelia in her conscientious endeavor to do her duty by her elève,[6] that the child rapidly grew in grace and in favor with the family and neighborhood. At the age of womanhood, she was, by her own request, baptized, and became a member of the Christian church in the place; and showed so much intelligence, activity and zeal, and desire to do good in the world, that she was at last recommended, and approved, as a missionary to one of the stations in Africa; and we have heard that the same activity and ingenuity which, when a child, made her so multiform and restless in her developments, is now employed, in a safer and wholesomer manner, in teaching the children of her own country.

P.S.—It will be a satisfaction to some mother, also, to state, that some inquiries, which were set on foot by Madame de Thoux, have resulted recently in the discovery of Cassy's son. Being a young man of energy, he had escaped, some years before his mother, and been received and educated by friends of the oppressed in the north. He will soon follow his family to Africa.

## Chapter XLIV

### *The Liberator*

George Shelby had written to his mother merely a line, stating the day that she might expect him home. Of the death scene of his old friend he had not the heart to write. He had tried several times, and only succeeded in half choking himself; and invariably finished

6. Scholar or student (French).

by tearing up the paper, wiping his eyes, and rushing somewhere to get quiet.

There was a pleased bustle all through the Shelby mansion, that day, in expectation of the arrival of young Mas'r George.

Mrs. Shelby was seated in her comfortable parlor, where a cheerful hickory fire was dispelling the chill of the late autumn evening. A supper-table, glittering with plate and cut glass, was set out, on whose arrangements our former friend, old Chloe, was presiding.

Arrayed in a new calico dress, with clean, white apron, and high, well-starched turban, her black polished face glowing with satisfaction, she lingered, with needless punctiliousness, around the arrangements of the table, merely as an excuse for talking a little to her mistress.

"Laws, now! won't it look natural to him?" she said "Thar,—I set his plate just whar he likes it,—round by the fire. Mas'r George allers wants de warm seat. O, go way!—why, didn't Sally get out de *best* tea-pot,—de little new one, Mas'r George got for Missis, Christmas? I'll have it out! And Missis has heard from Mas'r George?" she said, inquiringly.

"Yes, Chloe; but only a line, just to say he would be home to-night, if he could,—that's all."

"Didn't say nothin' 'bout my old man, s'pose?" said Chloe, still fidgeting with the tea-cups.

"No, he didn't. He did not speak of anything, Chloe. He said he would tell all, when he got home."

"Jes like Mas'r George,—he's allers so ferce for tellin' everything hisself. I allers minded dat ar in Mas'r George. Don't see, for my part, how white people gen'lly can bar to hev to write things much as they do, writin' 's such slow, oneasy kind o' work."

Mrs. Shelby smiled.

"I'm a thinkin' my old man won't know de boys and de baby. Lor'! she's de biggest gal, now,—good she is, too, and peart, Polly is. She's out to the house, now, watchin' de hoe-cake. I's got jist de very pattern my old man liked so much, a bakin'. Jist sich as I gin him the mornin' he was took off. Lord bless us! how I felt, dat ar morning!"

Mrs. Shelby sighed, and felt a heavy weight on her heart, at this allusion. She had felt uneasy, ever since she received her son's letter, lest something should prove to be hidden behind the veil of silence which he had drawn.

"Missis has got dem bills?" said Chloe, anxiously.

"Yes, Chloe."

"'Cause I wants to show my old man dem very bills de *perfectioner* gave me. 'And,' says he, 'Chloe, I wish you'd stay longer.' 'Thank you, Mas'r,' says I, 'I would, only my old man's coming home, and

Missis,—she can't do without me no longer.' There's jist what I telled him. Berry nice man, dat Mas'r Jones was."

Chloe had pertinaciously insisted that the very bills in which her wages had been paid should be preserved, to show to her husband, in memorial of her capability. And Mrs. Shelby had readily consented to humor her in the request.

"He won't know Polly,—my old man won't. Laws, it's five year since they tuck him! She was a baby den,—couldn't but jist stand. Remember how tickled he used to be, cause she would keep a fallin' over, when she sot out to walk. Laws a me!"

The rattling of wheels now was heard.

"Mas'r George!" said Aunt Chloe, starting to the window.

Mrs. Shelby ran to the entry door, and was folded in the arms of her son. Aunt Chloe stood anxiously straining her eyes out into the darkness.

"O, *poor* Aunt Chloe!" said George, stopping compassionately, and taking her hard, black hand between both his; "I'd have given all my fortune to have brought him with me, but he's gone to a better country."

There was a passionate exclamation from Mrs. Shelby, but Aunt Chloe said nothing.

The party entered the supper-room. The money, of which Chloe was so proud, was still lying on the table.

"Thar," said she, gathering it up, and holding it, with a trembling hand, to her mistress, "don't never want to see nor hear on't again. Jist as I knew 'twould be,—sold, and murdered on dem ar' old plantations!"

Chloe turned, and was walking proudly out of the room. Mrs. Shelby followed her softly, and took one of her hands, drew her down into a chair, and sat down by her.

"My poor, good Chloe!" said she.

Chloe leaned her head on her mistress' shoulder, and sobbed out, "O Missis! 'scuse me, my heart's broke,—dat's all!"

"I know it is," said Mrs. Shelby, as her tears fell fast; "and *I* cannot heal it, but Jesus can. He healeth the broken hearted, and bindeth up their wounds."

There was a silence for some time, and all wept together. At last, George, sitting down beside the mourner, took her hand, and, with simple pathos, repeated the triumphant scene of her husband's death, and his last messages of love.

About a month after this, one morning, all the servants of the Shelby estate were convened together in the great hall that ran through the house, to hear a few words from their young master.

To the surprise of all, he appeared among them with a bundle of papers in his hand, containing a certificate of freedom to every one on the place, which he read successively, and presented, amid the sobs and tears and shouts of all present.

Many, however, pressed around him, earnestly begging him not to send them away; and, with anxious faces, tendering back their free papers.

"We don't want to be no freer than we are. We's allers had all we wanted. We don't want to leave de ole place, and Mas'r and Missis, and de rest!"

"My good friends," said George, as soon as he could get a silence, "there'll be no need for you to leave me. The place wants as many hands to work it as it did before. We need the same about the house that we did before. But, you are now free men and free women. I shall pay you wages for your work, such as we shall agree on. The advantage is, that in case of my getting in debt, or dying,—things that might happen,—you cannot now be taken up and sold. I expect to carry on the estate, and to teach you what, perhaps, it will take you some time to learn,—how to use the rights I give you as free men and women. I expect you to be good, and willing to learn; and I trust in God that I shall be faithful, and willing to teach. And now, my friends, look up, and thank God for the blessing of freedom."

An aged, patriarchal negro, who had grown gray and blind on the estate, now rose, and, lifting his trembling hand said, "Let us give thanks unto the Lord!" As all kneeled by one consent, a more touching and hearty Te Deum[1] never ascended to heaven, though borne on the peal of organ, bell and cannon, than came from that honest old heart.

On rising, another struck up a Methodist hymn, of which the burden was,

"The year of Jubilee is come,—
Return, ye ransomed sinners, home."[2]

"One thing more," said George, as he stopped the congratulations of the throng; "you all remember our good old Uncle Tom?"

George here gave a short narration of the scene of his death, and of his loving farewell to all on the place, and added,

1. "*Te deum laudamus*" (Thee, God, we praise)—the opening words of a hymn of thanksgiving and praise.
2. From the Methodist hymn "Blow Ye the Trumpet," with text by Charles Wesley (1707–88):

Blow ye the trumpet, blow!
The gladly solemn sound
Let all the nations know,
To earth's remotest bound,
The year of the jubilee is come!
The year of the jubilee is come!
Return, ye ransomed sinners, home.

"It was on his grave, my friends, that I resolved, before God, that I would never own another slave, while it was possible to free him; that nobody, through me, should ever run the risk of being parted from home and friends, and dying on a lonely plantation, as he died. So, when you rejoice in your freedom, think that you owe it to that good old soul, and pay it back in kindness to his wife and children. Think of your freedom, every time you see UNCLE TOM'S CABIN; and let it be a memorial to put you all in mind to follow in his steps, and be as honest and faithful and Christian as he was."

## Chapter XLV

### *Concluding Remarks*

The writer has often been inquired of, by correspondents from different parts of the country, whether this narrative is a true one; and to these inquiries she will give one general answer.[1]

The separate incidents that compose the narrative are, to a very great extent, authentic, occurring, many of them, either under her own observation, or that of her personal friends. She or her friends have observed characters the counterpart of almost all that are here introduced; and many of the sayings are word for word as heard herself, or reported to her.

The personal appearance of Eliza, the character ascribed to her, are sketches drawn from life. The incorruptible fidelity, piety and honesty, of Uncle Tom, had more than one development, to her personal knowledge. Some of the most deeply tragic and romantic, some of the most terrible incidents, have also their parallel in reality. The incident of the mother's crossing the Ohio river on the ice is a well-known fact.[2] The story of "old Prue," in the second volume, was an incident that fell under the personal observation of a brother of the writer, then collecting-clerk to a large mercantile house, in New Orleans. From the same source was derived the character of the planter Legree. Of him her brother thus wrote, speaking of visiting his plantation, on a collecting tour: "He actually made me feel of his fist, which was like a blacksmith's hammer, or a nodule of iron, telling me that it was 'calloused with knocking down niggers.' When I left the plantation, I drew a long breath, and felt as if I had escaped from an ogre's den."

1. Because the novel was first published in serial form, from June 1851 to April 1852, Stowe had the opportunity to respond in the text to comments from readers.
2. In *A Key to "Uncle Tom's Cabin,"* Stowe recounts a similar incident (34–36). Another model for Eliza may have been Cassy, heroine of Richard Hildreth's antislavery novel *The Slave, or Memoirs of Archy Moore* (1836).

That the tragical fate of Tom, also, has too many times had its parallel, there are living witnesses, all over our land, to testify. Let it be remembered that in all southern states it is a principle of jurisprudence that no person of colored lineage can testify in a suit against a white, and it will be easy to see that such a case may occur, wherever there is a man whose passions outweigh his interests, and a slave who has manhood or principle enough to resist his will. There is, actually, nothing to protect the slave's life, but the *character* of the master. Facts too shocking to be contemplated occasionally force their way to the public ear, and the comment that one often hears made on them is more shocking than the thing itself. It is said, "Very likely such cases may now and then occur, but they are no sample of general practice." If the laws of New England were so arranged that a master could *now and then* torture an apprentice to death, without a possibility of being brought to justice, would it be received with equal composure? Would it be said, "These cases are rare, and no samples of general practice"? This injustice is an *inherent* one in the slave system,—it cannot exist without it.

The public and shameless sale of beautiful mulatto and quadroon girls has acquired a notoriety, from the incidents following the capture of the Pearl. We extract the following from the speech of Hon. Horace Mann, one of the legal counsel for the defendants in that case.[3] He says: "In that company of seventy-six persons, who attempted, in 1848, to escape from the District of Columbia in the schooner Pearl, and whose officers I assisted in defending, there were several young and healthy girls, who had those peculiar attractions of form and feature which connoisseurs prize so highly. Elizabeth Russel was one of them. She immediately fell into the slave-trader's fangs, and was doomed for the New Orleans market. The hearts of those that saw her were touched with pity for her fate. They offered eighteen hundred dollars to redeem her; and some there were who offered to give, that would not have much left after the gift; but the fiend of a slave-trader was inexorable. She was despatched to New Orleans; but, when about half way there, God had mercy on her, and smote her with death. There were two girls named Edmundson in the same company. When about to be sent to the same market, an older sister went to the shambles,[4] to plead with the wretch who owned them, for the love of God, to spare his victims. He bantered her, telling what fine dresses and fine furniture they would have. 'Yes,' she said, 'that may do very well in this

3. The following is from Mann's remarks at the April 1848 trial of Daniel Drayton, who attempted to transport seventy-six slaves to freedom. Mann was an American educator (1796–1859).
4. A slaughterhouse or scene of great carnage.

life, but what will become of them in the next?' They too were sent to New Orleans; but were afterwards redeemed, at an enormous ransom, and brought back." Is it not plain, from this, that the histories of Emmeline and Cassy may have many counterparts?

Justice, too, obliges the author to state that the fairness of mind and generosity attributed to St. Clare are not without a parallel, as the following anecdote will show. A few years since, a young southern gentleman was in Cincinnati, with a favorite servant, who had been his personal attendant from a boy. The young man took advantage of this opportunity to secure his own freedom, and fled to the protection of a Quaker, who was quite noted in affairs of this kind. The owner was exceedingly indignant. He had always treated the slave with such indulgence, and his confidence in his affection was such, that he believed he must have been practised upon to induce him to revolt from him. He visited the Quaker, in high anger; but, being possessed of uncommon candor and fairness, was soon quieted by his arguments and representations. It was a side of the subject which he never had heard,—never had thought on; and he immediately told the Quaker that, if his slave would, to his own face, say that it was his desire to be free, he would liberate him. An interview was forthwith procured, and Nathan was asked by his young master whether he had ever had any reason to complain of his treatment, in any respect.

"No, Mas'r," said Nathan; "you've always been good to me."

"Well, then, why do you want to leave me?"

"Mas'r may die, and then who get me?—I'd rather be a free man."

After some deliberation, the young master replied, "Nathan, in your place, I think I should feel very much so, myself. You are free."

He immediately made him out free papers; deposited a sum of money in the hands of the Quaker, to be judiciously used in assisting him to start in life, and left a very sensible and kind letter of advice to the young man. That letter was for some time in the writer's hands.

The author hopes she has done justice to that nobility, generosity, and humanity, which in many cases characterize individuals at the South. Such instances save us from utter despair of our kind. But, she asks any person, who knows the world, are such characters *common*, anywhere?

For many years of her life, the author avoided all reading upon or allusion to the subject of slavery, considering it as too painful to be inquired into, and one which advancing light and civilization would certainly live down. But, since the legislative act of 1850, when she heard, with perfect surprise and consternation, Christian and humane people actually recommending the remanding escaped fugitives into slavery, as a duty binding on good citizens,—when she heard, on all hands, from kind, compassionate and estimable people, in the free states of the North, deliberations and discussions as to what Christian duty could be on this head,—she could only think, These men and Christians cannot know what slavery is; if they did, such a question could never be open for discussion. And from this arose a desire to exhibit it in a *living dramatic reality.* She has endeavored to show it fairly, in its best and its worst phases. In its *best* aspect, she has, perhaps, been successful; but, oh! who shall say what yet remains untold in that valley and shadow of death, that lies the other side?

To you, generous, noble-minded men and women, of the South,—you, whose virtue, and magnanimity, and purity of character, are the greater for the severer trial it has encountered,—to you is her appeal. Have you not, in your own secret souls, in your own private conversings, felt that there are woes and evils, in this accursed system, far beyond what are here shadowed, or can be shadowed? Can it be otherwise? Is *man* ever a creature to be trusted with wholly irresponsible power? And does not the slave system, by denying the slave all legal right of testimony, make every individual owner an irresponsible despot? Can anybody fail to make the inference what the practical result will be? If there is, as we admit, a public sentiment among you, men of honor, justice and humanity, is there not also another kind of public sentiment among the ruffian, the brutal and debased? And cannot the ruffian, the brutal, the debased, by slave law, own just as many slaves as the best and purest? Are the honorable, the just, the high-minded and compassionate, the majority anywhere in this world?

The slave-trade is now, by American law, considered as piracy.[5] But a slave-trade, as systematic as ever was carried on on the coast of Africa, is an inevitable attendant and result of American slavery. And its heart-break and its horrors, *can* they be told?

The writer has given only a faint shadow, a dim picture, of the anguish and despair that are, at this very moment, riving thousands of hearts, shattering thousands of families, and driving a helpless and sensitive race to frenzy and despair. There are those living who know the mothers whom this accursed traffic has driven to the murder of their children; and themselves seeking in death a shelter from woes more dreaded than death. Nothing of tragedy can be written, can be spoken, can be conceived, that equals the frightful reality of scenes daily and hourly acting on our shores, beneath the shadow of American law, and the shadow of the cross of Christ.

And now, men and women of America, is this a thing to be trifled with, apologized for, and passed over in silence? Farmers of

5. See above, p. 121, n. 2.

Massachusetts, of New Hampshire, of Vermont, of Connecticut, who read this book by the blaze of your winter-evening fire,—strong-hearted, generous sailors and ship-owners of Maine,—is this a thing for you to countenance and encourage? Brave and generous men of New York, farmers of rich and joyous Ohio, and ye of the wide prairie states,—answer, is this a thing for you to protect and countenance? And you, mothers of America,—you, who have learned, by the cradles of your own children, to love and feel for all mankind,—by the sacred love you bear your child; by your joy in his beautiful, spotless infancy; by the motherly pity and tenderness with which you guide his growing years; by the anxieties of his education; by the prayers you breathe for his soul's eternal good;—I beseech you, pity the mother who has all your affections, and not one legal right to protect, guide, or educate, the child of her bosom! By the sick hour of your child; by those dying eyes, which you can never forget; by those last cries, that wrung your heart when you could neither help nor save; by the desolation of that empty cradle, that silent nursery,—I beseech you, pity those mothers that are constantly made childless by the American slave-trade! And say, mothers of America, is this a thing to be defended, sympathized with, passed over in silence?

Do you say that the people of the free states have nothing to do with it, and can do nothing? Would to God this were true! But it is not true. The people of the free states have defended, encouraged, and participated; and are more guilty for it, before God, than the South, in that they have *not* the apology of education or custom.

If the mothers of the free states had all felt as they should, in times past, the sons of the free states would not have been the holders, and, proverbially, the hardest masters of slaves; the sons of the free states would not have connived at the extension of slavery, in our national body; the sons of the free states would not, as they do, trade the souls and bodies of men as an equivalent to money, in their mercantile dealings. There are multitudes of slaves temporarily owned, and sold again, by merchants in northern cities; and shall the whole guilt or obloquy of slavery fall only on the South?

Northern men, northern mothers, northern Christians, have something more to do than denounce their brethren at the South; they have to look to the evil among themselves.

But, what can any individual do? Of that, every individual can judge. There is one thing that every individual can do,—they can see to it that *they feel right.* An atmosphere of sympathetic influence encircles every human being; and the man or woman who *feels* strongly, healthily and justly, on the great interests of humanity, is a constant benefactor to the human race. See, then, to your sympathies in this matter! Are they in harmony with the sympathies of

Christ? or are they swayed and perverted by the sophistries of worldly policy?

Christian men and women of the North! still further,—you have another power; you can *pray!* Do you believe in prayer? or has it become an indistinct apostolic tradition? You pray for the heathen abroad; pray also for the heathen at home. And pray for those distressed Christians whose whole chance of religious improvement is an accident of trade and sale; from whom any adherence to the morals of Christianity is, in many cases, an impossibility, unless they have given them, from above, the courage and grace of martyrdom.

But, still more. On the shores of our free states are emerging the poor, shattered, broken remnants of families,—men and women, escaped, by miraculous providences, from the surges of slavery,—feeble in knowledge, and, in many cases, infirm in moral constitution, from a system which confounds and confuses every principle of Christianity and morality. They come to seek a refuge among you; they come to seek education, knowledge, Christianity.

What do you owe to these poor unfortunates, oh Christians? Does not every American Christian owe to the African race some effort at reparation for the wrongs that the American nation has brought upon them? Shall the doors of churches and school-houses be shut upon them? Shall states arise and shake them out? Shall the church of Christ hear in silence the taunt that is thrown at them, and shrink away from the helpless hand that they stretch out; and, by her silence, encourage the cruelty that would chase them from our borders? If it must be so, it will be a mournful spectacle. If it must be so, the country will have reason to tremble, when it remembers that the fate of nations is in the hands of One who is very pitiful, and of tender compassion.

Do you say, "We don't want them here; let them go to Africa"?

That the providence of God has provided a refuge in Africa, is, indeed, a great and noticeable fact; but that is no reason why the church of Christ should throw off that responsibility to this outcast race which her profession demands of her.

To fill up Liberia with an ignorant, inexperienced, half-barbarized race, just escaped from the chains of slavery, would be only to prolong, for ages, the period of struggle and conflict which attends the inception of new enterprises. Let the church of the north receive these poor sufferers in the spirit of Christ; receive them to the educating advantages of Christian republican society and schools, until they have attained to somewhat of a moral and intellectual maturity, and then assist them in their passage to those shores, where they may put in practice the lessons they have learned in America.

There is a body of men at the north, comparatively small, who have been doing this; and, as the result, this country has already seen examples of men, formerly slaves, who have rapidly acquired property, reputation, and education. Talent has been developed, which, considering the circumstances, is certainly remarkable; and, for moral traits of honesty, kindness, tenderness of feeling,—for heroic efforts and self-denials, endured for the ransom of brethren and friends yet in slavery,—they have been remarkable to a degree that, considering the influence under which they were born, is surprising.

The writer has lived, for many years, on the frontier-line of slave states, and has had great opportunities of observation among those who formerly were slaves. They have been in her family as servants; and, in default of any other school to receive them, she has, in many cases, had them instructed in a family school, with her own children. She has also the testimony of missionaries, among the fugitives in Canada, in coincidence with her own experience; and her deductions, with regard to the capabilities of the race, are encouraging in the highest degree.

The first desire of the emancipated slave, generally, is for *education*. There is nothing that they are not willing to give or do to have their children instructed; and, so far as the writer has observed herself, or taken the testimony of teachers among them, they are remarkably intelligent and quick to learn. The results of schools, founded for them by benevolent individuals in Cincinnati, fully establish this.[6]

The author gives the following statement of facts, on the authority of Professor C. E. Stowe,[7] then of Lane Seminary, Ohio, with regard to emancipated slaves, now resident in Cincinnati; given to show the capability of the race, even without any very particular assistance or encouragement.

The initial letters alone are given. They are all residents of Cincinnati.

"B——. Furniture maker; twenty years in the city; worth ten thousand dollars, all his own earnings; a Baptist.

"C——. Full black; stolen from Africa; sold in New Orleans; been free fifteen years; paid for himself six hundred dollars; a farmer; owns several farms in Indiana; Presbyterian; probably worth fifteen or twenty thousand dollars, all earned by himself.

"K——. Full black; dealer in real estate; worth thirty thousand dollars; about forty years old; free six years; paid eighteen hundred

6. A permanent school was organized through Lane Seminary in 1834 to educate the many freed slaves and fugitives who had settled in Cincinnati from the beginning of the nineteenth century. In 1844 the Reverend Hiram Gilmore opened a high school as well.

7. Calvin Ellis Stowe (1802–1886), husband of Harriet Beecher Stowe, was a preacher and educator who in 1833 moved to Cincinnati to be professor of biblical literature at Lane Theological Seminary, the institution of which Lyman Beecher was president.

dollars for his family; member of the Baptist church; received a legacy from his master, which he has taken good care of, and increased.

"G——. Full black; coal dealer; about thirty years old; worth eighteen thousand dollars; paid for himself twice, being once defrauded to the amount of sixteen hundred dollars; made all his money by his own efforts—much of it while a slave, hiring his time of his master, and doing business for himself; a fine, gentlemanly fellow.

"W——. Three-fourths black; barber and waiter; from Kentucky; nineteen years free; paid for self and family over three thousand dollars; worth twenty thousand dollars, all his own earnings; deacon in the Baptist church.

"G. D——. Three-fourths black; white-washer; from Kentucky; nine years free; paid fifteen hundred dollars for self and family; recently died, aged sixty; worth six thousand dollars."

Professor Stowe says, "With all these, except G——, I have been, for some years, personally acquainted, and make my statements from my own knowledge."

The writer well remembers an aged colored woman, who was employed as a washerwoman in her father's family. The daughter of this woman married a slave. She was a remarkably active and capable young woman, and, by her industry and thrift, and the most persevering self-denial, raised nine hundred dollars for her husband's freedom, which she paid, as she raised it, into the hands of his master. She yet wanted a hundred dollars of the price, when he died. She never recovered any of the money.

These are but few facts, among multitudes which might be adduced, to show the self-denial, energy, patience, and honesty, which the slave has exhibited in a state of freedom.

And let it be remembered that these individuals have thus bravely succeeded in conquering for themselves comparative wealth and social position, in the face of every disadvantage and discouragement. The colored man, by the law of Ohio, cannot be a voter, and, till within a few years, was even denied the right of testimony in legal suits with the white.[8] Nor are these instances confined to the State of Ohio. In all states of the Union we see men, but yesterday burst from the shackles of slavery, who, by a self-educating force, which cannot be too much admired, have risen to highly respectable stations in society. Pennington, among clergymen, Douglas and Ward, among editors, are well known instances.[9]

8. Citizenship was granted to ex-slaves by the Fourteenth Amendment to the Constitution (1868); voting rights for all men were provided in the Fifteenth Amendment (1870).
9. J. W. C. Pennington, the pastor of a Hartford church, was born a slave in Maryland. After his release, he became a Presbyterian preacher and spoke widely in the United

If this persecuted race, with every discouragement and disadvantage, have done thus much, how much more they might do, if the Christian church would act towards them in the spirit of her Lord!

This is an age of the world when nations are trembling and convulsed. A mighty influence is abroad, surging and heaving the world, as with an earthquake. And is America safe? Every nation that carries in its bosom great and unredressed injustice has in it the elements of this last convulsion.

For what is this mighty influence thus rousing in all nations and languages those groanings that cannot be uttered, for man's freedom and equality?

O, Church of Christ, read the signs of the times! Is not this power the spirit of HIM whose kingdom is yet to come, and whose will to be done on earth as it is in heaven?

But who may abide the day of his appearing? "for that day shall burn as an oven: and he shall appear as a swift witness against those that oppress the hireling in his wages, the widow and the fatherless, and that *turn aside the stranger in his right:* and he shall break in pieces the oppressor."[1]

Are not these dread words for a nation bearing in her bosom so mighty an injustice? Christians! every time that you pray that the kingdom of Christ may come, can you forget that prophecy associates, in dread fellowship, the *day of vengeance* with the year of his redeemed?

A day of grace is yet held out to us. Both North and South have been guilty before God; and the *Christian church* has a heavy account to answer. Not by combining together, to protect injustice and cruelty, and making a common capital of sin, is this Union to be saved,—but by repentance, justice and mercy; for, not surer is the eternal law by which the millstone sinks in the ocean, than that stronger law, by which injustice and cruelty shall bring on nations the wrath of Almighty God!

---

States and Europe. Frederick Douglass (c. 1817–1895) was a black American abolitionist, orator, and journalist. Born a slave, he escaped to the North in 1838, published an autobiographical *Narrative* (1845), and founded the abolitionist weekly *North Star* (1847). Samuel Ringgold Ward (1817–c. 1866), a black American abolitionist and orator, was born a slave, escaped with his parents to New York State in 1820, and later became a teacher. In 1839 he joined the American Anti-Slavery Society, and in the 1840s traveled widely in the northern states speaking for abolition.

1. Adapted from Malachi 4.1.

# BACKGROUNDS AND CONTEXTS

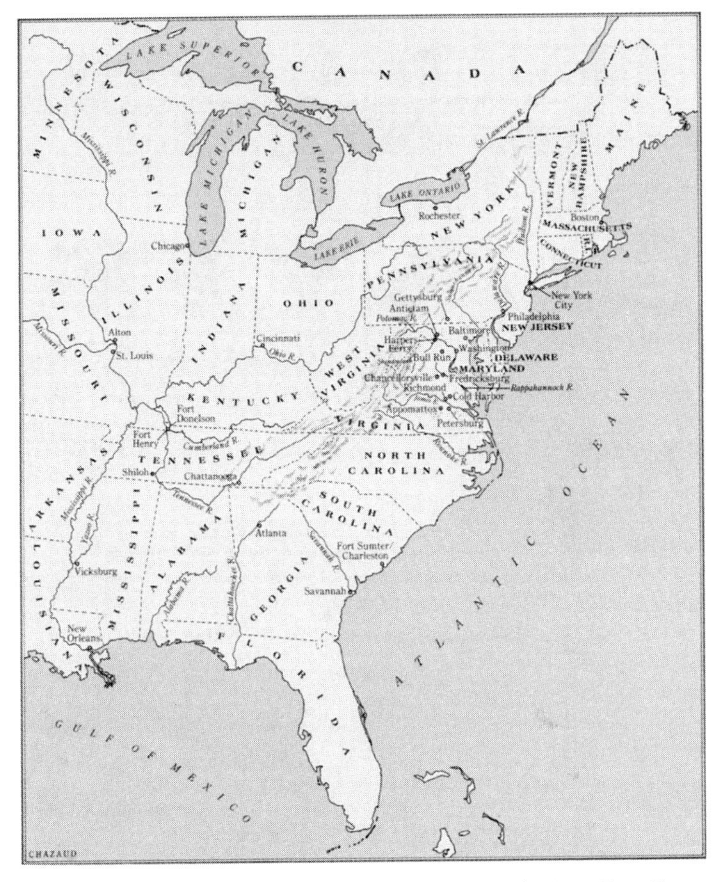


*The Eastern United States in the Antebellum Period.* From Eric Foner and Olivia Mahoney, *A House Divided: America in the Age of Lincoln* (New York: Norton, 1990).

BY

# HEWLETT & BRIGHT.

## SALE OF

## VALUABLE

# SLAVES,

## *(On account of departure)*

The Owner of the following named and valuable Slaves, being on the eve of departure for Europe, will cause the same to be offered for sale, at the NEW EXCHANGE, corner of St. Louis and Chartres streets, on *Saturday*, May 16, at Twelve o'Clock, *viz.*

1. SARAH, a mulatress, aged 45 years, a good cook and accustomed to house work in general, is an excellent and faithful nurse for sick persons, and in every respect a first rate character.

2. DENNIS, her son, a mulatto, aged 24 years, a first rate cook and steward for a vessel, having been in that capacity for many years on board one of the Mobile packets; is strictly honest, temperate, and a first rate subject.

3. CHOLE, a mulatress, aged 36 years, she is, without exception, one of the most competent servants in the country, a first rate washer and ironer, does up lace, a good cook, and for a bachelor who wishes a house-keeper she would be invaluable; she is also a good ladies' maid, having travelled to the North in that capacity.

4. FANNY, her daughter, a mulatress, aged 16 years, speaks French and English, is a superior hair-dresser, (pupil of Guilliac,) a good seamstress and ladies' maid, is smart, intelligent, and a first rate character.

5. DANDRIDGE, a mulatoo, aged 26 years, a first rate dining-room servant, a good painter and rough carpenter, and has but few equals for honesty and sobriety.

6. NANCY, his wife, aged about 24 years, a confidential house servant, good seamstress, mantuamaker and tailoress, a good cook, washer and ironer, etc.

7. MARY ANN, her child, a creole, aged 7 years, speaks French and English, is smart, active and intelligent.

8. FANNY or FRANCES, a mulatress, aged 22 years, is a first rate washer and ironer, good cook and house servant, and has an excellent character.

9. EMMA, an orphan, aged 10 or 11 years, speaks French and English, has been in the country 7 years, has been accustomed to waiting on table, sewing etc.; is intelligent and active.

10. FRANK, a mulatto, aged about 32 years speaks French and English, is a first rate hostler and coachman, understands perfectly well the management of horses, and is, in every respect, a first rate character, with the exception that he will occasionally drink, though not an habitual drunkard.

☞ All the above named Slaves are acclimated and excellent subjects; they were purchased by their present vendor many years ago, and will, therefore, be severally warranted against all vices and maladies prescribed by law, save and except FRANK, who is fully guaranteed in every other respect but the one above mentioned.

TERMS:—One-half Cash, and the other half in notes at Six months, drawn and endorsed to the satisfaction of the Vendor, with special mortgage on the Slaves until final payment. The Acts of Sale to be passed before WILLIAM BOSWELL, *Notary Public*, at the expense of the Purchaser.

***New-Orleans, May*** **13, 1835.**

PRINTED BY BENJAMIN LEVY.

*Announcement of slave sale, New Orleans, 1835.* Courtesy of the New York Historical Society.

# GREAT SALE

# of

# SLAVES

## JANUARY 10, 1855

THERE Will Be Offered For Sale at Public Auction at the SLAVE MARKET, CHEAPSIDE, LEXINGTON, All The SLAVES of JOHN CARTER, Esquire, of LEWIS COUNTY, KY., On Account of His Removal to Indiana, a Free State. The Slaves Listed Below Were All Raised on the CARTER PLANTATION at QUICK'S RUN, Lewis County, Kentucky.

**3 Bucks** Aged from 20 to 26, Strong, Ablebodied
**1 Wench,** Sallie, Aged 42, Excellent Cook
**1 Wench,** Lize, Aged 23 with 6 mo. old Picinniny
**One Buck** Aged 52, good Kennel Man
**17 Bucks** Aged from twelve to twenty, Excellent

TERMS: Strictly CASH at Sale, as owner must realize cash, owing to his removal to West. Offers for the entire lot will be entertained previous to sale by addressing the undersigned.

**JOHN CARTER, Esq.**

**Po. Clarksburg** **Lewis County, Kentucky**

*Announcement of slave sale, Lexington, Kentucky, 1855.* From J. Winston Coleman, Jr., *Slavery Times in Kentucky* (Chapel Hill: UNC Press, 1940). 

L. C. ROBARDS,

# DEALER IN NEGROES,

**LEXINGTON, KY.**

PERSONS wishing to Buy or Sell Negroes, will, at all times, find a market for them by calling at my *NEW JAIL* a few doors below the "Bruen House" on Short street.

N. B. The highest cash price will be paid for Young and Likely Negroes.

july 2-81-y

# Negroes Wanted.

THE undersigned wish to purchased a large number of **NEGROES**, of both sexes, for which they will

**Pay the Highest Prices in Cash.**

**Office on Main-street, opposite the Phœnix Hotel, and 2d door above the Statesman Office, Lexington.**

**SILAS MARSHALL & BRO.**

March 15, 1859–50–tf

*Announcement of slave sale, Lexington, Kentucky, 1859.* From J. Winston Coleman, Jr., *Slavery Times in Kentucky* (Chapel Hill: UNC Press, 1940). 

**Administrator's Sale, by Order of the Ordinary.**

**A PRIME AND ORDERLY GANG OF**

# 68 Long Cotton Field Negroes,

Belonging to the Estate of the late Christopher J. Whaley.

## WILBUR & SON

Will sell at PUBLIC AUCTION in Charleston,

## At the Mart in Chalmers Street,

**On Thursday, Feb. 2d, 1860,**

COMMENCING AT ELEVEN O'CLOCK,

**THE FOLLOWING GANG OF LONG COTTON NEGROES,**

**Who are said to be remarkably prime, and will be sold as per Catalogue.**

| NAMES. | | AGES. | NAMES. | | AGES. |
|---|---|---|---|---|---|
| Jimmy, | driver, | 30 | Carter, | | 36 |
| Flora, | seamstress, | 24 | Taffy, | | 13 |
| James, | | 5 | Rachel, | ($ 720,) | 8 |
| Charles, | ($ 125,) | 1 | Jannett, | | 18 |
| August, | | 52 | Phebe, | ($ 860,) | 40 |
| Mathias, | ($ 1,220,) | 18 | Judy, | | 8 |
| Sandy, | | 16 | Major, | | 40 |
| John, | | 13 | Lavinia, | | 30 |
| Tom, | | 70 | Billy, | ($ 550,) | 10 |
| Jack, | | 38 | Tamor, | | 6 |
| James, | | 6 | Jimmy, | | 52 |
| Leah, | | 5 | Kate, | | 46 |
| Flora, | | 2 | Susan, | | 25 |
| Andrew, | | 42 | Thomas, | ($ 380,) | 6 |
| Binah, | | 40 | Kate, | | 1 |
| Phillis, | | 20 | Edward, | coachman, | 49 |
| Mary, | | 15 | Amey, | | 22 |
| Lymus, | | 10 | Teneb, | washer, | 30 |
| Abram, | ($ 275,) | 2 | Josephine, | | 9 |
| Binah, | | 2 mos. | Sam, | | 11 |
| Andrew, | | 29 | Isaac, | | 5 |
| Hagar, | | 25 | William, | | 1 |
| Dayman, | | 4 | Amey, | | 27 |
| Cuffy, | | 21 | Louisa, | ($ 750,) | 8 |
| Hagar, | ($ 1,320,) | 20 | Joe, | | 3 |
| Margaret, | | 85 | Sam, | ruptured, | 65 |
| Lucy, | cripple, | 60 | Andrew, | dropsical, | 61 |
| John, | | 22 | Daniel, | | 70 |
| Ellick, | ($ 1,160,) | 18 | Lymus, | | 30 |
| Libby, | | 19 | Lucy, | nurse, | 58 |

**TERMS.**

One-third Cash; balance in one and two years, secured by bond, and mortgage of the negroes, with approved personal security. Purchasers to pay us for papers.

29

*Announcement of slave sale, Charleston, South Carolina, 1860.* From *Five Slave Narratives* in *The American Negro: His History and Literature*, gen. ed. William Loren Katz (New York: Arno, 1968). Reprinted by permission of Ayer Company Publications, Salem, N.H.

# 100 DOLLARS REWARD!

Ranaway from the subscriber on the 27th of July, my Black Woman, named

# EMILY,

Seventeen years of age, well grown, black color, has a whining voice. She took with her one dark calico and one blue and white dress, a red corded gingham bonnet; a white striped shawl and slippers. I will pay the above reward if taken near the Ohio river on the Kentucky side, or THREE HUNDRED DOLLARS, if taken in the State of Ohio, and delivered to me near Lewisburg, Mason County, Ky. THO'S. H. WILLIAMS.

August 4, 1853.

*Advertisement for runaway slave, Kentucky, 1853.* From J. Winston Coleman, Jr., *Slavery Times in Kentucky* (Chapel Hill: UNC Press, 1940). 

## $150 REWARD.

RANAWAY from the subscriber, on the night of Monday the 11th July, a negro man named

# TOM,

about 30 years of age, 5 feet 6 or 7 inches high; of dark color; heavy in the chest; several of his jaw teeth out; and upon his body are several old marks of the whip, one of them straight down the back. He took with him a quantity of clothing, and several hats.

A reward of $150 will be paid for his apprehension and security, if taken out of the State of Kentucky; $100 if taken in any county bordering on the Ohio river; $50 if taken in any of the interior counties except Fayette; or $20 if taken in the latter county.

july 12-84-tf B. L. BOSTON.

*Advertisement for runaway slave, Kentucky, n.d.* From J. Winston Coleman, Jr., *Slavery Times in Kentucky* (Chapel Hill: UNC Press, 1940). 

*Union with Freemen--No Union with Slaveholders.*

# ANTI-SLAVERY MEETINGS!

**Anti-Slavery Meetings will be held in this place, to commence on at in the**

## To be Addressed by

**Agents of the Western ANTI-SLAVERY SOCIETY.**

**Three millions of your fellow beings are in chains--the Church and Government sustains the horrible system of oppression.**

# Turn Out!

**AND LEARN YOUR DUTY TO YOURSELVES, THE SLAVE AND GOD.**

**EMANCIPATION or DISSOLUTION, and a FREE NORTHERN REPUBLIC!**

HOMESTEAD PRINT, SALEM, OHIO.

*Announcement of antislavery meeting, Salem, 1850.* Courtesy of The Library of Congress Printed Ephemera Collection, Portfolio 137, Folder 4.

# CAUTION!!

# COLORED PEOPLE

## OF BOSTON, ONE & ALL,

You are hereby respectfully CAUTIONED and advised, to avoid conversing with the

## Watchmen and Police Officers of Boston,

For since the recent ORDER OF THE MAYOR & ALDERMEN, they are empowered to act as

# KIDNAPPERS

AND

# Slave Catchers,

And they have already been actually employed in KIDNAPPING, CATCHING, AND KEEPING SLAVES. Therefore, if you value your LIBERTY, and the *Welfare of the Fugitives* among you, *Shun* them in every possible manner, as so many *HOUNDS* on the track of the most unfortunate of your race.

## Keep a Sharp Look Out for KIDNAPPERS, and have TOP EYE open.

*APRIL* 24, 1851.

*Broadside warning against kidnappers and slave catchers, Boston, 1851.* Courtesy of The Library of Congress Printed Ephemera Collection, Portfolio 60, Folder 22.

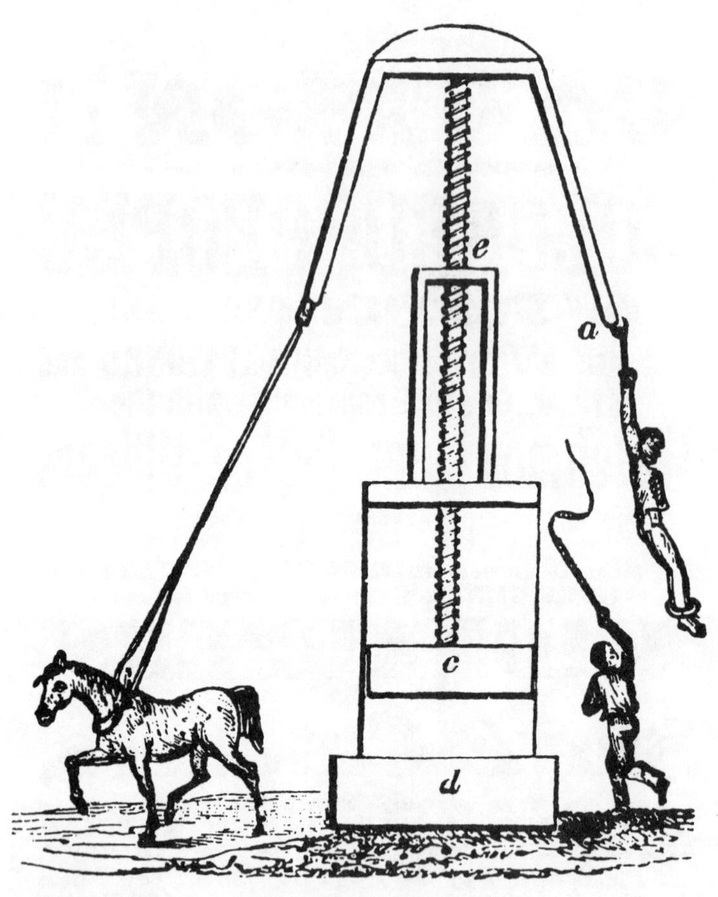


*Illustration of cotton screw torture instrument employed on former slave Moses Roper.* From Moses Roper, *Narrative of the Adventures and Escape of MOSES ROPER, from American Slavery* (Philadelphia: Merrihew and Gunn, 1838).

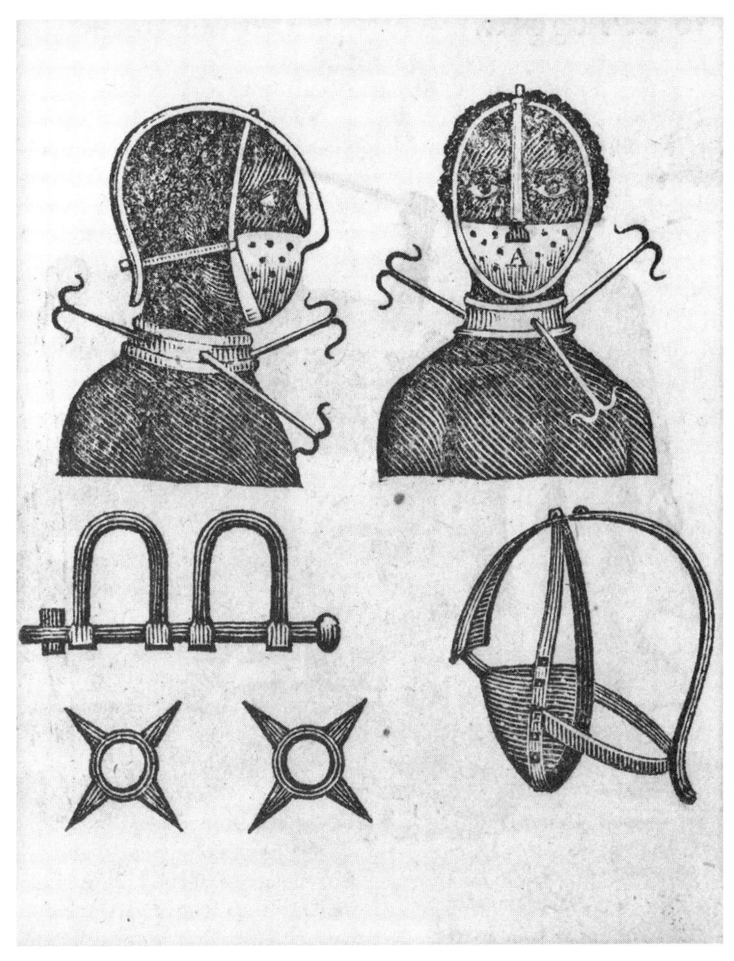

*Iron mask, collar, leg shackles and spurs used to restrict slaves.* Illus. in Thomas Branagan, *The Penitential Tyrant,* 1807. Woodcut printed by Samuel Wood, no. 362, New York, 1807. Courtesy of The Library of Congress Rare Book and Special Collections Division.

# J. HECTOR ST. JOHN DE CRÈVECOEUR

## [A Visitor's Description of Slavery's Atrocity]†

The following scene will, I hope, account for these melancholy reflections and apologize for the gloomy thoughts with which I have filled this letter: my mind is, and always has been, oppressed since I became a witness to it. I was not long since invited to dine with a planter who lived three miles from—, where he then resided. In order to avoid the heat of the sun, I resolved to go on foot, sheltered in a small path leading through a pleasant wood. I was leisurely travelling along, attentively examining some peculiar plants which I had collected, when all at once I felt the air strongly agitated, though the day was perfectly calm and sultry. I immediately cast my eyes toward the cleared ground, from which I was but a small distance, in order to see whether it was not occasioned, by a sudden shower, when at that instant a sound resembling a deep rough voice, uttered, as I thought, a few inarticulate monosyllables. Alarmed and surprised, I precipitately looked all round, when I perceived at about six rods distance something resembling a cage, suspended to the limbs of a tree, all the branches of which appeared covered with large birds of prey, fluttering about and anxiously endeavouring to perch on the cage. Actuated by an involuntary motion of my hands more than by any design of my mind, I fired at them; they all flew to a short distance, with a most hideous noise, when, horrid to think and painful to repeat, I perceived a Negro, suspended in the cage and left there to expire! I shudder when I recollect that the birds had already picked out his eyes; his cheek-bones were bare; his arms had been attacked in several places; and his body seemed covered with a multitude of wounds. From the edges of the hollow sockets and from the lacerations with which he was disfigured, the blood slowly dropped and tinged the ground beneath. No sooner were the birds flown than swarms of insects covered the whole body of this unfortunate wretch, eager to feed on his mangled flesh and to drink his blood. I found myself suddenly arrested by the power of affright and terror; my nerves were convulsed; I trembled; I stood motionless, involuntarily contemplating the fate of this Negro in all its dismal latitude. The living spectre, though deprived of his eyes, could still distinctly hear, and in his uncouth dialect begged me to give him some water to allay his thirst. Humanity herself would have recoiled back with horror; she would have balanced whether to lessen such reliefless distress or mercifully with one blow to end this dreadful scene of agonizing torture! Had I had a ball in my

† From "Letter XI" in *Letters from an American Farmer*, 1782.

gun, I certainly should have dispatched him, but finding myself unable to perform so kind an office, I sought, though trembling, to relieve him as well as I could. A shell ready fixed to a pole, which had been used by some Negroes, presented itself to me; filled it with water, and with trembling hands I guided it to the quivering lips of the wretched sufferer. Urged by the irresistible power of thirst, he endeavoured to meet it, as he instinctively guessed its approach by the noise it made in passing through the bars of the cage: "Tanky you, white man; tanky you; puta some poison and give me." "How long have you been hanging there?" I asked him. "Two days, and me no die; the birds, the birds; aaah me!" Oppressed with the reflections which this shocking spectacle afforded me, I mustered strength enough to walk away and soon reached the house at which I intended to dine. There I heard that the reason for this slave's being thus punished was on account of his having killed the overseer of the plantation. They told me that the laws of self-preservation rendered such executions necessary, and supported the doctrine of slavery with the arguments generally made use of to justify the practice, with the repetition of which I shall not trouble you at present. Adieu.

## DAVID WALKER

### *From* Appeal, in Four Articles†

But to prove farther that the condition of the Israelites was better under the Egyptians than ours is under the whites. I call upon the professing Christians, I call upon the philanthropist, I call upon the very tyrant himself, to show me a page of history, either sacred or profane, on which a verse can be found, which maintains, that the Egyptians heaped the *insupportable insult* upon the children of Israel, by telling them that they were not of the *human family*. Can the whites deny this charge? Have they not, after having reduced us to the deplorable condition of slaves under their feet, held us up as descending originally from the tribes of *Monkeys* or *Orang-Outangs?* O! my God! I appeal to every man of feeling—is not this insupportable? Is it not heaping the most gross insult upon our miseries, because they have got us under their feet and we cannot help ourselves? Oh! pity us we pray thee, Lord Jesus, Master.—Has Mr. Jefferson declared to the world, that we are inferior to the whites, both

† From *Walker's Appeal, in Four Articles; Together with a Preamble, to the Coloured Citizens of the World, but in Particular, and Very Expressly, to Those of the United States of America, Written in Boston, State of Massachusetts, September 28, 1829.* (Boston: published by the author, 1830).

in the endowments of our bodies and our minds? It is indeed surprising, that a man of such great learning, combined with such excellent natural parts, should speak so of a set of men in chains. I do not know what to compare it to, unless, like putting one wild deer in an iron cage, where it will be secured, and hold another by the side of the same, then let it go, and expect the one in the cage to run as fast as the one at liberty. So far, my brethren, were the Egyptians from heaping these insults upon their slaves, that Pharaoh's daughter took Moses, a son of Israel for her own. * * *

* * *

Are we MEN! !—I ask you, O my brethren! are we MEN? Did our Creator make us to be slaves to dust and ashes like ourselves? Are they not dying worms as well as we? Have they not to make their appearance before the tribunal of Heaven, to answer for the deeds done in the body, as well as we? Have we any other Master but Jesus Christ alone? Is he not their Master as well as ours?—What right then, have we to obey and call any other Master, but Himself? How we could be so *submissive* to a gang of men, whom we cannot tell whether they are *as good* as ourselves or not, I never could conceive. However, this is shut up with the Lord, and we cannot precisely tell—but I declare, we judge men by their works.

The whites have always been an unjust, jealous, unmerciful, avaricious and blood-thirsty set of beings, always seeking after power and authority.—We view them all over the confederacy of Greece, where they were first known to be any thing, (in consequence of education) we see them there, cutting each other's throats—trying to subject each other to wretchedness and misery—to effect which, they used all kinds of deceitful, unfair, and unmerciful means. We view them next in Rome, where the spirit of tyranny and deceit raged still higher. We view them in Gaul, Spain, and in Britain.—In fine, we view them all over Europe, together with what were scattered about in Asia and Africa, as heathens, and we see them acting more like devils than accountable men. But some may ask, did not the blacks of Africa, and the mulattoes of Asia, go on in the same way as did the whites of Europe. I answer, no—they never were half so avaricious, deceitful and unmerciful as the whites, according to their knowledge.

But we will leave the whites or Europeans as heathens, and take a view of them as Christians, in which capacity we see them as cruel, if not more so than ever. In fact, take them as a body, they are ten times more cruel, avaricious and unmerciful than ever they were; for while they were heathens, they were bad enough it is true, but it is positively a fact that they were not quite so audacious as to go and take vessel loads of men, women and children, and in cold blood, and through devilishness, throw them into the sea, and murder them in all kind of ways. While they were heathens, they were too ignorant for such barbarity. But being Christians, enlightened and sensible, they are completely prepared for such hellish cruelties.

* * *

* * * I will give here a very imperfect list of the cruelties inflicted on us by the enlightened Christians of America.—First, no trifling portion of them will beat us nearly to death, if they find us on our knees praying to God,—They hinder us from going to hear the word of God—they keep us sunk in ignorance, and will not let us learn to read the word of God, nor write—If they find us with a book of any description in our hand, they will beat us nearly to death—they are so afraid we will learn to read, and enlighten our dark and benighted minds—They will not suffer us to meet together to worship the God who made us—they brand us with hot iron—they cram bolts of fire down our throats—they cut us as they do horses, bulls, or hogs—they crop our ears and sometimes cut off bits of our tongues—they chain and hand-cuff us, and while in that miserable and wretched condition, beat us with cow-hides and clubs—they keep us half naked and starve us sometimes nearly to death under their infernal whips or lashes (which some of them shall have enough of yet)—They put on us fifty-sixes and chains, and make us work in that cruel situation, and in sickness, under lashes to support them and their families.—They keep us three or four hundred feet under ground working in their mines, night and day to dig up gold and silver to enrich them and their children.—They keep us in the most death-like ignorance by keeping us from all source of information, and call us, who are free men and next to the Angels of God, their property! ! ! ! ! ! They make us fight and murder each other, many of us being ignorant, not knowing any better.—They take us, (being ignorant,) and put us as drivers one over the other, and make us afflict each other as bad as they themselves afflict us—and to crown the whole of this catalogue of cruelties, they tell us that we the (blacks) are an inferior race of beings! incapable of self government! !—We would be injurious to society and ourselves, if tyrants should loose their unjust hold on us! ! ! That if we were free we would not work, but would live on plunder or theft! ! ! ! that we are the meanest and laziest set of beings in the world! ! ! ! ! That they are obliged to keep us in bondage to do us good! ! ! ! ! !—That we are satisfied to rest in slavery to them and their children! ! ! ! ! ! —That we ought not to be set free in America, but ought to be sent away to Africa! ! ! ! ! ! ! !—That if we were set free in America, we would involve the country in a civil war, which assertion is altogether

at variance with our feeling or design, for we ask them for nothing but the rights of man, viz. for them to set us free, and treat us like men, and there will be no danger, for we will love and respect them, and protect our country—but cannot conscientiously do these things until they treat us like men.

* * *

* * * Whether you believe it or not, I tell you that God will dash tyrants, in combination with devils, into atoms, and will bring you out from your wretchedness and miseries under these *Christian People!!!!!!*

Those philanthropists and lovers of the human family, who have volunteered their services for our redemption from wretchedness, have a high claim on our gratitude, and we should always view them as our greatest earthly benefactors.

If any are anxious to ascertain who I am, know the world, that I am one of the oppressed, degraded and wretched sons of Africa, rendered so by the avaricious and unmerciful, among the whites.—If any wish to plunge me into the wretched incapacity of a slave, or murder me for the truth, know ye, that I am in the hand of God, and at your disposal. I count my life not dear unto me, but I am ready to be offered at any moment. For what is the use of living, when in fact I am dead. But remember, Americans, that as miserable, wretched, degraded and abject as you have made us in preceding, and in this generation, to support you and your families, that some of you, (whites) on the continent of America, will yet curse the day that you ever were born. You want slaves, and want us for your slaves! ! ! My colour will yet, root some of you out of the very face of the earth! ! ! ! ! !

# JOSIAH HENSON

## Life of Josiah Henson†

I was born, June 15, 1789, in Charles County, Maryland, on a farm belonging to Mr. Francis N., about a mile from Port Tobacco. My mother was the property of Dr. Josiah McP., but was hired by Mr. N., to whom my father belonged. The only incident I can remember, which occurred while my mother continued on N.'s farm, was the appearance of my father one day, with his head bloody and his

† From *The Life of Josiah Henson, Formerly a Slave, Now an Inhabitant of Canada, As Narrated by Himself* (Boston: Arthur D. Phelps, 1849). Stowe named Henson's narrative as one of her sources; see the excerpt from her *Key to "Uncle Tom's Cabin,"* below, pp. 446–58. Also Henson, in later editions of his book, emphasized the connection between *Uncle Tom's Cabin* and his account of his own life.

back lacerated. He was in a state of great excitement, and though it was all a mystery to me at the age of three or four years, it was explained at a later period, and I understood that he had been suffering the cruel penalty of the Maryland law for beating a white man. His right ear had been cut off close to his head, and he had received a hundred lashes on his back. He had beaten the overseer for a brutal assault on my mother, and this was his punishment. Furious at such treatment, my father became a different man, and was so morose, disobedient, and intractable, that Mr. N. determined to sell him. He accordingly parted with him, not long after, to his son, who lived in Alabama; and neither my mother nor I, ever heard of him again. He was naturally, as I understood afterwards from my mother and other persons, a man of amiable temper, and of considerable energy of character; but it is not strange that he should be essentially changed by such cruelty and injustice under the sanction of law.

After the sale of my father by N., and his leaving Maryland for Alabama, Dr. McP. would no longer hire out my mother to N. She returned, therefore, to the estate of the doctor, who was very much kinder to his slaves than the generality of planters, never suffering them to be struck by any one. He was, indeed, a man of good natural impulses, kind-hearted, liberal, and jovial. The latter quality was so much developed as to be his great failing; and though his convivial excesses were not thought of as a fault by the community in which he lived, and did not even prevent his having a high reputation for goodness of heart, and an almost saint-like benevolence, yet they were, nevertheless, his ruin. My mother, and her young family of three girls and three boys, of which I was the youngest, resided on this estate for two or three years, during which my only recollections are of being rather a pet of the doctor's, who thought I was a bright child, and of being much impressed with what I afterwards recognized as the deep piety and devotional feeling and habits of my mother. I do not know how, or where she acquired her knowledge of God, or her acquaintance with the Lord's prayer, which she so frequently repeated and taught me to repeat. I remember seeing her often on her knees, endeavoring to arrange her thoughts in prayers appropriate to her situation, but which amounted to little more than constant ejaculation, and the repetition of short phrases, which were within my infant comprehension, and have remained in my memory to this hour.

After this brief period of comparative comfort, however, the death of Dr. McP. brought about a revolution in our condition, which, common as such things are in slave countries, can never be imagined by those not subject to them, nor recollected by those who have been, without emotions of grief and indignation deep and ineffaceable.

The doctor was riding from one of his scenes of riotous excess, when, falling from his horse, in crossing a little run, not a foot deep, he was unable to save himself from drowning.

In consequence of his decease, it became necessary to sell the estate and the slaves, in order to divide the property among the heirs; and we were all put up at auction and sold to the highest bidder, and scattered over various parts of the country. My brothers and sisters were bid off one by one, while my mother, holding my hand, looked on in an agony of grief, the cause of which I but ill understood at first, but which dawned on my mind, with dreadful clearness, as the sale proceeded. My mother was then separated from me, and put up in her turn. She was bought by a man named Isaac R., residing in Montgomery county, and then I was offered to the assembled purchasers. My mother, half distracted with the parting forever from all her children, pushed through the crowd, while the bidding for me was going on, to the spot where R. was standing. She fell at his feet, and clung to his knees, entreating him in tones that a mother only could command, to buy her *baby* as well as herself, and spare to her one of her little ones at least. Will it, can it be believed that this man, thus appealed to, was capable not merely of turning a deaf ear to her supplication, but of disengaging himself from her with such violent blows and kicks, as to reduce her to the necessity of creeping out of his reach, and mingling the groan of bodily suffering with the sob of a breaking heart? Yet this was one of my earliest observations of men; an experience which has been common to me with thousands of my race, the bitterness of which its frequency cannot diminish to any individual who suffers it, while it is dark enough to overshadow the whole after-life with something blacker than a funeral pall.—I was bought by a stranger.—Almost immediately, however, whether my childish strength, at five or six years of age, was overmastered by such scenes and experiences, or from some accidental cause, I fell sick, and seemed to my new master so little likely to recover, that he proposed to R., the purchaser of my mother, to take me too at such a trifling rate that it could not be refused. I was thus providentially restored to my mother; and under her care, destitute as she was of the proper means of nursing me, I recovered my health, and grew up to be an uncommonly vigorous and healthy boy and man.

The character of R., the master whom I faithfully served for many years, is by no means an uncommon one in any part of the world; but it is to be regretted that a domestic institution should anywhere put it in the power of such a one to tyrannize over his fellow beings, and inflict so much needless misery as is sure to be produced by such a man in such a position. Coarse and vulgar in his habits, unprincipled and cruel in his general deportment, and especially addicted to the vice of licentiousness, his slaves had little opportunity for relaxation from wearying labor, were supplied with the scantiest means of sustaining their toil by necessary food, and had no security for personal rights. The natural tendency of slavery is, to convert the master into a tyrant, and the slave into the cringing, treacherous, false, and thieving victim of tyranny. R. and his slaves were no exception to the general rule, but might be cited as apt illustrations of the nature of the case.

* * *

I obtained great influence with my companions, as well by the superiority I showed in labor and in sport, as by the assistance I yielded them, and the favors I conferred upon them, from impulses which I cannot consider as wrong, though it was necessary for me to conceal sometimes the act as well as its motive. I have toiled, and induced others to toil, many an extra hour, in order to show my master what an excellent day's work had been accomplished, and to win a kind word, or a benevolent deed from his callous heart. In general, indifference, or a cool calculation of my value to him, were my reward, chilling those hopes of an improvement in my condition, which was the ultimate object of my efforts. I was much more easily moved to compassion and sympathy than he was; and one of the means I took to gain the good-will of my fellow sufferers, was by taking from him some things that he did not give, in part payment of my extra labor. The condition of the male slave is bad enough, Heaven knows; but that of the female, compelled to perform unfit labor, sick, suffering, and bearing the burdens of her own sex unpitied and unaided, as well as the toils which belong to the other, has often oppressed me with a load of sympathy. And sometimes, when I have seen them starved, and miserable, and unable to help themselves, I have helped them to some of the comforts which they were denied by him who owned them, and which my companions had not the wit or the daring to procure. Meat was not a part of our regular food; but my master had plenty of sheep and pigs, and sometimes I have picked out the best one I could find in the flock, or the drove, carried it a mile or two into the woods, slaughtered it, cut it up, and distributed it among the poor creatures, to whom it was at once food, luxury, and medicine. Was this wrong? I can only say that, at this distance of time, my conscience does not reproach me for it, and that then I esteemed it among the best of my deeds.

* * *

My master fell into difficulty, and from difficulty into a lawsuit with a brother-in-law, who charged him with dishonest mismanagement of property confided to him in trust. * * * Before he would explain himself, however, he begged me to promise to do what he should propose, well knowing, from his past experience of my character, that I should hold myself bound by such promise to do all that it implied, if it were within the limits of possibility. Solicited in this way, with urgency and tears, by the man whom I had so zealously served for twenty years, and who now seemed absolutely dependent upon his slave,—impelled, too, by the fear which he skilfully awakened, that the sheriff would seize every one who belonged to him, and that all would be separated, or perhaps sold to go to Georgia, or Louisiana—an object of perpetual dread to the slave of the more northern States—I consented, and promised faithfully to do all I could to save him from the fate impending over him. He then told me I must take his slaves to his brother, in Kentucky. In vain I represented to him that I had never travelled a day's journey from his plantation, and knew nothing of the way, or the means of getting to Kentucky. He insisted that such a smart fellow as I could travel anywhere, he promised to give me all necessary instructions, and urged that this was the only course by which he could be saved. The result was, that I agreed to undertake the enterprise—certainly no light one for me, as it could scarcely be considered for even an experienced manager. There were eighteen negroes, besides my wife, two children, and myself, to transport nearly a thousand miles, through a country I knew nothing about, and in winter time, for we started in the month of February, 1825. My master proposed to follow me in a few months, and establish himself in Kentucky. He furnished me with a small sum of money, and some provisions; and I bought a one-horse wagon, to carry them, and to give the women and children a lift now and then, and the rest of us were to trudge on foot. Fortunately for the success of the undertaking, these people had been long under my direction, and were devotedly attached to me for the many alleviations I had afforded to their miserable condition, the comforts I had procured them, and the consideration which I had always manifested for them.

Under these circumstances no difficulty arose from want of submission to my authority, and none of any sort, except that which I necessarily encountered from my ignorance of the country, and my inexperience in such business. On arriving at Wheeling, I sold the horse and wagon, and purchased a boat of sufficient size, and floated down the river without further trouble or fatigue, stopping every night to encamp.

I said I had no further trouble, but there was one source of anxiety which I was compelled to encounter, and a temptation I had to resist, the strength of which others can appreciate as well as myself. In passing along the State of Ohio, we were frequently told that we were free, if we chose to be so. At Cincinnati, especially, the colored people gathered round us, and urged us with much importunity to remain with them; told us it was folly to go on; and in short used all the arguments now so familiar to induce slaves to quit their masters. My companions probably had little perception of the nature of the boon that was offered to them, and were willing to do just as I told them, without a wish to judge for themselves. Not so with me. From my earliest recollection, freedom had been the object of my ambition, a constant motive to exertion, an ever-present stimulus to gain and to save. No other means of obtaining it, however, had occurred to me, but purchasing myself of my master. The idea of running away was not one that I had ever indulged. I had a sentiment of honor on the subject, or what I thought such, which I would not have violated even for freedom; and every cent which I had ever felt entitled to call my own, had been treasured up for this great purpose, till I had accumulated between thirty and forty dollars. Now was offered to me an opportunity I had not anticipated. I might liberate my family, my companions, and myself, without the smallest risk, and without injustice to any individual, except one whom we had none of us any reason to love, who had been guilty of cruelty and oppression to us all for many years, and who had never shown the smallest symptom of sympathy with us, or with any one in our condition. But I need not make the exception. There would have been no injustice to R. himself—it would have been a retribution which might be called righteous—if I had availed myself of the opportunity thus thrust suddenly upon me.

But it was a punishment which it was not for me to inflict. I had promised that man to take his property to Kentucky, and deposit it with his brother; and this, and this only, I resolved to do. I left Cincinnati before night, though I had intended to remain there, and encamped with my entire party a few miles below the city. What advantages I may have lost, by thus throwing away an opportunity of obtaining freedom, I know not; but the perception of my own strength of character, the feeling of integrity, the sentiment of high honor, I have experienced,—these advantages I do know, and prize; and would not lose them, nor the recollection of having attained them, for all that I can imagine to have resulted from an earlier release from bondage. I have often had painful doubts as to the propriety of my carrying so many other individuals into slavery again, and my consoling reflection has been, that I acted as I thought at the time was best.

* * *

[After offering to let him buy his freedom, Henson's master cheats him out of his money and his free papers, then sends Henson down the

Mississippi River to be sold in New Orleans. En route, the captain of the boat suffers a severe "disease of the eyes."]

After the captain became blind, we were obliged to lie by at night, as none of the rest of us had been down the river before; and it was necessary to keep watch all night, to prevent depredations by the negroes on shore, who used frequently to attack such boats as ours, for the sake of the provisions on board. As I paced backwards and forwards on the deck, during my watch, it may well be believed I revolved many a painful and passionate thought. After all that I had done for Isaac and Amos R., after all the regard they professed for me, and the value they could not but put upon me, such a return as this for my services, such an evidence of their utter inattention to my claims upon them, and the intense selfishness with which they were ready to sacrifice me, at any moment, to their supposed interest, turned my blood to gall and wormwood, and changed me from a lively, and I will say, a pleasant-tempered fellow, into a savage, morose, dangerous slave. I was going not at all as a lamb to the slaughter, but I felt myself becoming more ferocious every day; and as we approached the place where this iniquity was to be consummated, I became more and more agitated with an almost uncontrollable fury. I had met, on the passage, with some of my Maryland acquaintance who had been sold off to this region; and their haggard and wasted appearance told a piteous story of excessive labor and insufficient food. I said to myself, "If this is to be my lot, I cannot survive it long. I am not so young as these men, and if it has brought them to such a condition, it will soon kill me. I am to be taken by my masters and owners, who ought to be my grateful friends, to a place and a condition where my life is to be shortened, as well as made more wretched. Why should I not prevent this wrong, if I can, by shortening their lives, or those of their agents in accomplishing such detestable injustice? I can do the last easily enough. They have no suspicion of me, and they are at this moment under my control, and in my power. There are many ways in which I can despatch them and escape, and I feel that I should be justified in availing myself of the first good opportunity." These were not thoughts which just flitted across my mind's eye, and then disappeared. They fashioned themselves into shapes which grew larger, and seemed firmer, every time they presented themselves; and at length my mind was made up to convert the phantom shadow into a positive reality. I resolved to kill my four companions, take what money there was in the boat, then to scuttle the craft, and escape to the north. It was a poor plan, may-be, and would very likely have failed; but it was as well contrived, under the circumstances, as the plans of murderers usually are; and blinded by passion, and stung to madness as I was, I could not see any difficulty about it. One dark, rainy night, within a few days of New Orleans, my hour seemed to have come. I was alone on the deck; Mr. Amos and the hands were all asleep below, and I crept down noiselessly, got hold of an axe, entered the cabin, and looking by the aid of the dim light there for my victims, my eye fell upon Master Amos, who was nearest to me; my hand slid along the axe-handle, I raised it to strike the fatal blow,—when suddenly the thought came to me, "What! commit *murder!* and you a Christian?" I had not called it murder before. It was self-defence,—it was preventing others from murdering me,—it was justifiable, it was even praiseworthy. But now, all at once, the truth burst upon me that it was a crime. I was going to kill a young man, who had done nothing to injure me, but obey commands which he could not resist; I was about to lose the fruit of all my efforts at self-improvement, the character I had acquired, and the peace of mind which had never deserted me. All this came upon me instantly, and with a distinctness which made me almost think I heard it whispered in my ear; and I believe I even turned my head to listen. I shrunk back, laid down the axe, crept up on deck again, and thanked God, as I have done every day since, that I had not committed murder.

My feelings were still agitated, but they were changed. I was filled with shame and remorse for the design I had entertained, and with the fear that my companions would detect it in my face, or that a careless word would betray my guilty thoughts. I remained on deck all night, instead of rousing one of the men to relieve me, and nothing brought composure to my mind, but the solemn resolution I then made to resign myself to the will of God, and take with thankfulness, if I could, but with submission, at all events, whatever he might decide should be my lot. I reflected that if my life were reduced to a brief term, I should have less to suffer, and that it was better to die with a Christian's hope, and a quiet conscience, than to live with the incessant recollection of a crime that would destroy the value of life, and under the weight of a secret that would crush out the satisfaction that might be expected from freedom and every other blessing.

* * *

[Henson avoids being sold when his master becomes ill; on returning to Kentucky, he decides to flee to Canada.]

It was not without long thought on the subject that I devised a plan of escape. * * * Some time previously I had got my wife to make me a large knapsack, big enough to hold the two smallest children; and I had arranged it that she should lead the second boy, while the oldest was stout enough to go by himself, and to help me carry the necessary food. I used to pack the little ones on my back, of an evening, after I had got through my day's work, and trot round the cabin with them, and go some little distance from it, in order to accustom both them and myself to the task before us.

At length the eventful night came. I went up to the house to ask leave to take Tom home with me, that he might have his clothes mended. No objection was made, and I bade Master Amos "good night" for the last time. It was about the middle of September, and by nine o'clock in the evening all was ready. It was a dark, moonless night, and we got into the little skiff in which I had induced a fellow-slave to take us across the river. It was an agitating and solemn moment. The good fellow who was rowing us over, said this affair might end in his death; "but," said he, "you will not be brought back alive, will you?" "Not if I can help it," I answered. "And if you are overpowered and return," he asked, "will you conceal my part of the business?" "That I will, so help me God," I replied. "Then I am easy," he answered, "and wish you success." We landed on the Indiana shore, and I began to feel that I was my own master. But in what circumstances of fear and misery still! We were to travel by night, and rest by day, in the woods and bushes. We were thrown absolutely upon our own poor and small resources, and were to rely on our own strength alone. The population was not so numerous as now, nor so well disposed to the slave. We dared look to no one for help. But my courage was equal to the occasion, and we trudged on cautiously and steadily, and as fast as the darkness, and the feebleness of my wife and boys would allow.

It was nearly a fortnight before we reached Cincinnati; and a day or two previous to getting there, our provisions were used up, and I had the misery to hear the cry of hunger and exhaustion from those I loved so dearly. It was necessary to run the risk of exposure by day-light upon the road; so I sprung upon it boldly from our hiding place one morning, and turned towards the south, to prevent the suspicion of my going the other way. I approached the first house I saw, and asked if they would sell me a little bread and meat. No, they had nothing for black fellows. At the next I succeeded better, but had to make as good a bargain as I could, and that was not very successful, with a man who wanted to see how little he could give me for my quarter of a dollar. As soon as I had succeeded in making a purchase, I followed the road, still towards the south, till I got out of sight of the house, and then darted into the woods again, and returned northward, just out of sight of the road. The food which I bought, such as it was, put new life and strength into my wife and children when I got back to them again, and we at length arrived safe at Cincinnati. There we were kindly received and entertained for several days, my wife and little ones were refreshed, and then we were carried on our way thirty miles in a wagon.

* * *

# SOLOMON NORTHUP

## A Slave Auction Described by a Slave, 1841†

* * *

In the first place we were required to wash thoroughly, and those with beards to shave. We were then furnished with a new suit each, cheap, but clean. The men had hat, coat, shirt, pants and shoes; the women frocks of calico, and handkerchief to bind about their heads. We were now conducted into a large room in the front part of the building to which the yard was attached, in order to be properly trained, before the admission of customers. The men were arranged on one side of the room, the women at the other. The tallest was placed at the head of the row, then the next tallest, and so on in the order of their respective heights. Emily was at the foot of the line of women. Freeman [Theophilus Freeman, owner of the slave-pen] charged us to remember our places; exhorted us to appear smart and lively,—sometimes threatening, and again, holding out various inducements. During the day he exercised us in the art of "looking smart," and of moving to our places with exact precision.

After being fed, in the afternoon, we were again paraded and made to dance. Bob, a colored boy, who had some time belonged to Freeman, played on the violin. Standing near him, I made bold to inquire if he could play the "Virginia Reel." He answered he could not, and asked me if I could play. Replying in the affirmative, he handed me the violin. I struck up a tune, and finished it. Freeman ordered me to continue playing, and seemed well pleased, telling Bob that I far excelled him—a remark that seemed to grieve my musical companion very much.

Next day many customers called to examine Freeman's "new lot." The latter gentleman was very loquacious, dwelling at much length upon our several good points and qualities. He would make us hold up our heads, walk briskly back and forth, while customers would

† From *Twelve Years a Slave* (Auburn, Buffalo, London, 1853) 78ff; qtd. in Herbert Aptheker, ed., *A Documentary History of the Negro People in the United States* (New York: Citadel, 1969) 206–8. 

feel of our hands and arms and bodies, turn us about, ask us what we could do, make us open our mouths and show our teeth, precisely as a jockey examines a horse which he is about to barter for or purchase. Sometimes a man or woman was taken back to the small house in the yard, stripped, and inspected more minutely. Scars upon a slave's back were considered evidence of a rebellious or unruly spirit, and hurt his sale.

An old gentleman, who said he wanted a coachman, appeared to take a fancy to me. From his conversation with Burch [Freeman's business associate], I learned he was a resident in the city. I very much desired that he would buy me, because I conceived it would not be difficult to make my escape from New Orleans on some northern vessel. Freeman asked him fifteen hundred dollars for me. The old gentleman insisted it was too much as times were very hard. Freeman, however, declared that I was sound of health, of a good constitution, and intelligent. He made it a point to enlarge upon my musical attainments. The old gentleman argued quite adroitly that there was nothing extraordinary about the Negro, and finally, to my regret, went out, saying he would call again. During the day, however, a number of sales were made. David and Caroline were purchased together by a Natchez planter. They left us, grinning broadly, and in a most happy state of mind, caused by the fact of their not being separated. Sethe was sold to a planter of Baton Rouge, her eyes flashing with anger as she was led away.

The same man also purchased Randall. The little fellow was made to jump, and run across the floor, and perform many other feats, exhibiting his activity and condition. All the time the trade was going on, Eliza was crying aloud, and wringing her hands. She besought the man not to buy him, unless he also bought herself and Emily. She promised, in that case, to be the most faithful slave that ever lived. The man answered that he could not afford it, and then Eliza burst into a paroxysm of grief, weeping plaintively. Freeman turned round to her, savagely, with his whip in his up-lifted hand, ordering her to stop her noise, or he would flog her. He would not have such work—such snivelling; and unless she ceased that minute, he would take her to the yard and give her a hundred lashes. Yes, he would take the nonsense out of her pretty quick—if he didn't, might he be d—d. Eliza shrunk before him, and tried to wipe away her tears, but it was all in vain. She wanted to be with her children, she said, the little time she had to live. All the frowns and threats of Freeman, could not wholly silence the afflicted mother. She kept on begging and beseeching them, most piteously, not to separate the three. Over and over again she told them how she loved her boy. A great many times she repeated her former promises—how very faithful and obedient she would be; how hard she would labor day and night, to the last moment of her life, if he would only buy them all together. But it was of no avail; the man could not afford it. The bargain was agreed upon, and Randall must go alone. Then Eliza ran to him; embraced him passionately; kissed him again and again; told him to remember her—all the while her tears falling in the boy's face like rain.

Freeman damned her, calling her a blubbering, bawling wench, and ordered her to go to her place, and behave herself, and be somebody. He swore he wouldn't stand such stuff but a little longer. He would soon give her something to cry about, if she was not mighty careful, and *that* she might depend upon.

The planter from Baton Rouge, with his new purchase, was ready to depart.

"Don't cry, mama. I will be a good boy. Don't cry," said Randall looking back, as they passed out of the door.

What has become of the lad, God knows. It was a mournful scene indeed. I would have cried myself if I had dared.

* * *

## HENRIETTA KING

## [A Freeperson's Memory of Slavery's Horror]†

* * *

* * * I seed dat peppermint stick layin' dere, an' I ain't dared go near it 'cause I knew ole Missus jus' waitin' for me to take it. Den one mornin' I so hungry dat I cain't resist. I went straight in dere an' grab dat stick of candy an' stuffed it in my mouf an' chew it down quick so ole Missus never fin' me wid it.

Nex' mornin' ole Missus say:

"Henrietta, you take dat piece o' candy out my room?" "No mam, ain't seed no candy." "Chile, you lyin' to me. You took dat candy." "Deed, Missus, I tel de truf. Ain't seed no candy." "You lyin' an' I'm gonna whup you. Come here." "Please, Missus, please don't whup me. I ain't seed no candy. I ain't took it." Well, she got her rawhide down from de nail by de fire place, an' she grabbed me by de arm an' she try to turn me 'cross her knees whilst she set in de rocker so's she could hol' me. I twisted an' turned till finally she called her daughter. De gal come an' took dat strap like her mother tole

† From *Remembering Slavery: African Americans Talk About Their Personal Experiences of Slavery and Emancipation*, ed. Ira Berlin, Marc Favreau, and Steven F. Miller (New York: The New Press, 1998) 19–21.

her and commence to lay it on real hard whilst Missus holt me. I twisted 'way so dere warn't no chance o' her gittin' in no solid lick. Den ole Missus lif' me up by de legs, an' she stuck my haid under de bottom of her rocker, an' she rock forward so's to hol' my haid an' whup me some mo'. I guess dey must of whupped me near a hour wid dat rocker leg a-pressin' down on my haid.

Nex' thing I knew de ole Doctor was dere, an' I was lyin' on my pallet in de hall, an' he was a-pushin' an' diggin' at my face, but he couldn't do nothin' at all wid it. Seem like dat rocker pressin' on my young bones had crushed 'em all into soft pulp. De nex' day I couldn' open my mouf an' I feel it an dey warn't no bone in de lef' side at all. An' my mouf kep' a-slippin' over to de right side an' I couldn't chaw nothin'—only drink milk. Well, ole Missus musta got kinda sorry 'cause she gits de doctor to come regular an' pry at my mouf. He git it arterwhile so's it open an' I could move my lips, but it kep' movin' over to de right, an' he couldn't stop dat. Arter a while it was over jes' whar it is now. An' I ain't never growed no mo' teef on dat side. Ain't never been able to chaw nothin' good since. Don't even 'member what it is to chaw. Been eatin' liquid, stews, an' soup ever since dat day, an' dat was eighty-six years ago.

Here, put yo' han' on my face—right here on dis lef' cheek—dat's what slave days was like. It made me so I been goin' roun' lookin' like a false face all my life. What chilluns laugh at an' babies gits to cryin' when dey see me. Course, I don't min' it no mo'. I been like dis so long now dat I don' never think on it, 'ceptin' when I see someone starin' hard an' wonderin' what debbil got in an' made me born dis way. An' it was a debbil dat done it—a she-debbil what's burnin' and twistin' in hell. She never would bother me much arter dat. Maybe it was 'cause Marsa raised such a rumpus 'cause of what she done. Never did beat me again. Used to see her sometime lookin' at me whilst I was dustin' or sweepin'. Never did say nothin', jus' set there lookin' widdout knowin' I knew it. Guess she got tired of havin' me round. When I got 'bout thirteen years ole she an Marsa give me to Marsa's cousin. Dey was good: all I had to do was mind de chillun. Was wid dem when freedom come an' dey let me stay on dere same as befo', 'ceptin' dey give me money each month. Stayed wid dem till I got married. Soon arter I got married, I heard dat ole Missus had died. Didn't make me drap no tears.

* * *

# HARRIET JACOBS

## The Trials of Girlhood†

During the first years of my service in Dr. Flint's family, I was accustomed to share some indulgences with the children of my mistress. Though this seemed to me no more than right, I was grateful for it, and tried to merit the kindness by the faithful discharge of my duties. But I now entered on my fifteenth year—a sad epoch in the life of a slave girl. My master began to whisper foul words in my ear. Young as I was, I could not remain ignorant of their import. I tried to treat them with indifference or contempt. The master's age, my extreme youth, and the fear that his conduct would be reported to my grandmother, made him bear this treatment for many months. He was a crafty man, and resorted to many means to accomplish his purposes. Sometimes he had stormy, terrific ways, that made his victims tremble; sometimes he assumed a gentleness that he thought must surely subdue. Of the two, I preferred his stormy moods, although they left me trembling. He tried his utmost to corrupt the pure principles my grandmother had instilled. He peopled my young mind with unclean images, such as only a vile monster could think of. I turned from him with disgust and hatred. But he was my master. I was compelled to live under the same roof with him—where I saw a man forty years my senior daily violating the most sacred commandments of nature. He told me I was his property; that I must be subject to his will in all things. My soul revolted against the mean tyranny. But where could I turn for protection? No matter whether the slave girl be as black as ebony or as fair as her mistress. In either case, there is no shadow of law to protect her from insult, from violence, or even from death; all these are inflicted by fiends who bear the shape of men. The mistress, who ought to protect the helpless victim, has no other feelings towards her but those of jealousy and rage. The degradation, the wrongs, the vices, that grow out of slavery, are more than I can describe. They are greater than you would willingly believe. Surely, if you credited one half the truths that are told you concerning the helpless millions suffering in this cruel bondage, you at the north would not help to tighten the yoke. You surely would refuse to do for the master, on your own soil, the mean and cruel work which trained bloodhounds and the lowest class of whites do for him at the south.

† From *Incidents in the Life of a Slave Girl*, ed. L. Maria Child (Boston: published for the author, 1861).

Every where the years bring to all enough of sin and sorrow; but in slavery the very dawn of life is darkened by these shadows. Even the little child, who is accustomed to wait on her mistress and her children, will learn, before she is twelve years old, why it is that her mistress hates such and such a one among the slaves. Perhaps the child's own mother is among those hated ones. She listens to violent outbreaks of jealous passion, and cannot help understanding what is the cause. She will become prematurely knowing in evil things. Soon she will learn to tremble when she hears her master's footfall. She will be compelled to realize that she is no longer a child. If God has bestowed beauty upon her, it will prove her greatest curse. That which commands admiration in the white woman only hastens the degradation of the female slave. I know that some are too much brutalized by slavery to feel the humiliation of their position; but many slaves feel it most acutely, and shrink from the memory of it. I cannot tell how much I suffered in the presence of these wrongs, nor how I am still pained by the retrospect. My master met me at every turn, reminding me that I belonged to him, and swearing by heaven and earth that he would compel me to submit to him. If I went out for a breath of fresh air, after a day of unwearied toil, his footsteps dogged me. If I knelt by my mother's grave, his dark shadow fell on me even there. The light heart which nature had given me became heavy with sad forebodings. The other slaves in my master's house noticed the change. Many of them pitied me; but none dared to ask the cause. They had no need to inquire. They knew too well the guilty practices under that roof; and they were aware that to speak of them was an offence that never went unpunished.

I longed for some one to confide in. I would have given the world to have laid my head on my grandmother's faithful bosom, and told her all my troubles. But Dr. Flint swore he would kill me, if I was not as silent as the grave. Then, although my grandmother was all in all to me, I feared her as well as loved her. I had been accustomed to look up to her with a respect bordering upon awe. I was very young, and felt shame-faced about telling her such impure things, especially as I knew her to be very strict on such subjects. Moreover, she was a woman of a high spirit. She was usually very quiet in her demeanor; but if her indignation was once roused, it was not very easily quelled. I had been told that she once chased a white gentleman with a loaded pistol, because he insulted one of her daughters. I dreaded the consequences of a violent outbreak; and both pride and fear kept me silent. But though I did not confide in my grandmother, and even evaded her vigilant watchfulness and inquiry, her presence in the neighborhood was some protection to me. Though she had been a slave, Dr. Flint was afraid of her. He dreaded her scorching rebukes. Moreover, she was known and patronized by many people; and he did not wish to have his villainy made public. It was lucky for me that I did not live on a distant plantation, but in a town not so large that the inhabitants were ignorant of each other's affairs. Bad as are the laws and customs in a slaveholding community, the doctor, as a professional man, deemed it prudent to keep up some outward show of decency.

O, what days and nights of fear and sorrow that man caused me! Reader, it is not to awaken sympathy for myself that I am telling you truthfully what I suffered in slavery. I do it to kindle a flame of compassion in your hearts for my sisters who are still in bondage, suffering as I once suffered.

I once saw two beautiful children playing together. One was a fair white child; the other was her slave, and also her sister. When I saw them embracing each other, and heard their joyous laughter, I turned sadly away from the lovely sight. I foresaw the inevitable blight that would fall on the little slave's heart. I knew how soon her laughter would be changed to sighs. The fair child grew up to be a still fairer woman. From childhood to womanhood her pathway was blooming with flowers, and overarched by a sunny sky. Scarcely one day of her life had been clouded when the sun rose on her happy bridal morning.

How had those years dealt with her slave sister, the little playmate of her childhood? She, also, was very beautiful; but the flowers and sunshine of love were not for her. She drank the cup of sin, and shame, and misery, whereof her persecuted race are compelled to drink.

In view of these things, why are ye silent, ye free men and women of the north? Why do your tongues falter in maintenance of the right? Would that I had more ability! But my heart is so full, and my pen is so weak! There are noble men and women who plead for us, striving to help those who cannot help themselves. God bless them! God give them strength and courage to go on! God bless those, every where, who are laboring to advance the cause of humanity!

# WILLIAM WELLS BROWN

## Another Kidnapping, 1844†

* * *

I left Cadiz this morning at four o'clock, on my way for Mount Pleasant [Ohio]. Passing through Georgetown at about five o'clock, I found the citizens standing upon the corners of the streets, talking as though something had occurred during the night. Upon inquiry, I learned that about ten o'clock at night, five or six men went to the house of a colored man by the name of John Wilkinson, broke open the door, knocked down the man and his wife, and beat them severely, and seized their boy, aged fourteen years, and carried him off into Slavery. After the father of the boy had recovered himself, he raised the alarm, and with the aid of some of the neighbors, put out in pursuit of the kidnappers, and followed them to the river; but they were too late. The villains crossed the river, and passed into Virginia. I visited the afflicted family this morning. When I entered the house, I found the mother seated with her face buried in her hands, weeping for the loss of her child. The mother was much bruised, and the floor was covered in several places with blood. I had been in the house but a short time, when the father returned from the chase of the kidnappers. When he entered the house, and told the wife that their child was lost forever, the mother wrung her hands and screamed out, "Oh, my boy! oh, my boy! I want to see my child!" and raved as though she was a maniac. I was compelled to turn aside and weep for the first time since I came into the State. I would that every Northern apologist for Slavery, could have been present to have beheld that scene. I hope to God that it may never be my lot to behold another such. One of the villains was recognized, but it was by a colored man, and the colored people have not the right of their oath in this State. This villain will go unwhipped of Justice. What have the North to do with Slavery? Ever yours, for the slave.

† From a letter written by the ex-slave, abolitionist, and author William Wells Brown, dated September 27, 1844, to Sydney H. Gay, editor of the *National Anti-Slavery Standard*, where it appeared on November 7, 1844; rep. in Herbert Aptheker, ed., *A Documentary History of the Negro People in the United States* (New York: Citadel, 1969) 245–46. 

# WILLIAM WELLS BROWN

## The Flight of Ellen and William Craft, 1849†

* * *

One of the most interesting cases of the escape of fugitives from American slavery that have ever come before the American people, has just occurred, under the following circumstances:— William and Ellen Craft, man and wife, lived with different masters in the State of Georgia. Ellen is so near white, that she can pass without suspicion for a white woman. Her husband is much darker. He is a mechanic, and by working nights and Sundays, he laid up money enough to bring himself and his wife out of slavery. Their plan was without precedent; and though novel, was the means of getting them their freedom. Ellen dressed in man's clothing, and passed as the *master*, while her husband passed as the *servant*. In this way they travelled from Georgia to Philadelphia. They are now out of the reach of the blood-hounds of the South. On their journey, they put up at the best hotels where they stopped. Neither of them can read or write. And Ellen, knowing that she would be called upon to write her name at the hotels, &c, tied her right hand up as though it was lame, which proved of some service to her, as she was called upon several times at hotels to "register" her name. In Charleston, S.C., they put up at the hotel which Gov. M'Duffie and John C. Calhoun generally make their home, yet these distinguished advocates of the "peculiar institution" say that the slaves cannot take care of themselves. They arrived in Philadelphia, in four days from the time they started. Their history, especially that of their escape, is replete with interest. They will be at the meeting of the Massachusetts Anti-Slavery Society, in Boston, in the latter part of this month, where I know the history of their escape will be listened to with great interest. They are very intelligent. They are young, Ellen 22, and William 24 years of age. Ellen is truly a heroine.

Yours, truly, William W. Brown

*P.S.* They are now hid away within 25 miles of Philadelphia, where they will remain until the 6th, when they will leave with me for New England. Will you please say in the *Liberator* that I will lecture, in connexion with them, as follows:—

† From a letter to the abolitionist William Lloyd Garrison, published in *The Liberator*, January 12, 1849; rep. in Herbert Aptheker, ed., *A Documentary History of the Negro People in the United States* (New York: Citadel, 1969) 277–78. 

At Norwich, Conn., Thursday evening, January 18
At Worcester, Mass., Friday evening, January 19
At Pawtucket, Mass., Saturday evening, January 20
At New Bedford, Mass., Sunday afternoon and evening, January 28.

## HARRIET BEECHER STOWE

### Letter to the Abolitionist Eliza Cabot Follen†

December 16, 1852

My Dear Madam,

I hasten to reply to your letter, the more interesting that I have long been acquainted with you, and during all the nursery part of my life made daily use of your poems for my children.

So you want to know what sort of woman I am! Well, if this is any object, you shall have statistics free of charge. To begin, then, I am a little bit of a woman,—somewhat more than forty, about as thin and dry as a pinch of snuff—never very much to look at in my best days and looking like a used up article now.

I was married when I was twenty-five years old to a man rich in Greek and Hebrew and Latin and Arabic, and alas, rich in nothing else. . . . But then I was abundantly furnished with wealth of another sort. I had two little curly headed twin daughters to begin with and my stock in this line has gradually increased, till I have been the mother of seven children, the most beautiful and the most loved of whom lies buried near my Cincinnati residence. It was at his dying bed and at his grave that I learned what a poor slave mother may feel when her child is torn away from her. In those depths of sorrow which seemed to me immeasurable, it was my only prayer to God that such anguish might not be suffered in vain. There were circumstances about his death of such peculiar bitterness, of what seemed almost cruel suffering that I felt that I could never be consoled for it unless this crushing of my own heart might enable me to work out some great good to others.

I allude to this here because I have often felt that much that is in that book had its root in the awful scenes and bitter sorrow of that summer. It has left now, I trust, no trace on my mind except a deep

† From *The Limits of Sisterhood: The Beecher Sisters on Women's Rights and Women's Sphere* by Jeanne Boydston, Mary Kelley, and Anne Margolis, pp. 178–80. 

compassion for the sorrowful, especially for mothers who are separated from their children.

During these long years of struggling with poverty and sickness and a hot debilitating climate my children grew up around me. The nursery and the kitchen were my principal fields of labor. Then one of my friends pitying my toils copied and sent a number of little sketches from my pen to certain liberally paying "Annuals" with my name. With the first money that I earned in this way I bought a *feather bed!* for as I had married into poverty and without a dowry, and as my husband had only a large library of books, and a great deal of learning—the bed and pillows was thought on the whole the most profitable investment. After that I thought that I had discovered the "Philosopher's Stone," and when a new carpet, or a new mattress, was going to be needed, or when at the close of the year, it began to be clear that my family accounts, like poor Dora's, "wouldn't add up"—then I used to say to my faithful friend and factotum Anna who shared all my joys and sorrows "Now if you will keep the babies and attend to the things in the house for one day I'll write a piece, and then we shall be out of the scrape." And so I became an authoress,—very modest at first, I do assure you, and remonstrating very seriously with the friends who had thought it best to put my name to the pieces by way of getting a reputation. . . .

You ask with regard to the remuneration which I have received for my work here in America. Having been poor all my life, and expecting to be poor to the end of it, the idea of making anything by a book, which I wrote just because I could not help it never occurred to me. It was therefore an agreeable surprise to receive ten thousand dollars as the first fruits of three months sale and presume as much more is now due.

I am now writing a work which will contain, perhaps, an equal amount of matter with "Uncle Tom's Cabin." It will contain all the facts and documents on which that story was founded, and an immense body of facts, reports of trials, legal documents, and testimony of people now living South, which will more than confirm every statement in "Uncle Tom's Cabin." . . .

I suffer exquisitely in writing these things. It may truly be said that I write with my heart's blood. Many times in writing "Uncle Tom's Cabin" I thought my health would fail utterly; but I prayed earnestly that God would help me till I got through, and still I am pressed beyond measure and above strength.

This horror, this nightmare abomination! can it be in my country! It lies like lead on my heart, it shadows my life with sorrow; the more so that I feel, as for my own brothers, for the South, and am pained by every horror I am obliged to write, as one who is forced by some awful oath to disclose in court some family disgrace. Many times I have thought that I must die, and yet I pray God that I may live to see something.

It seems to me so odd and dream-like that so many persons desire to see me, and now I cannot help thinking that they will think, when they do, that God hath chosen "the weak things of this world."

If I live till spring I shall hope to see Shakespeare's grave, and Milton's mulberry tree, and the good land of my fathers—old, old England! May that day come!

Yours affectionately,
H. B. Stowe

# HARRIET BEECHER STOWE

## *From* A Key to "Uncle Tom's Cabin"†

### *Uncle Tom*

The character of Uncle Tom has been objected to as improbable; and yet the writer has received more confirmations of that character, and from a great variety of sources, than of any other in the book.

Many people have said to her, "I knew an Uncle Tom in such-and-such a Southern State." All the histories of this kind which have thus been related to her would of themselves, if collected, make a small volume. The author will relate a few of them.

While visiting in an obscure town in Maine, in the family of a friend, the conversation happened to turn upon this subject, and the gentleman with whose family she was staying related the following. He said, that when on a visit to his brother in New Orleans, some years before, he found in his possession a most valuable negro man, of such remarkable probity and honesty that his brother literally trusted him with all he had. He had frequently seen him take out a handful of bills, without looking at them, and hand them to this servant, bidding him go and provide what was necessary for the family, and bring him the change. He remonstrated with his brother on this imprudence; but the latter replied that he had had such proofs of this servant's impregnable conscientiousness that he felt it safe to trust him to any extent.

The history of the servant was this. He had belonged to a man in Baltimore, who, having a general prejudice against all the religious exercises of slaves, did all that he could to prevent his having any

† From *A Key to "Uncle Tom's Cabin"* (Boston: John P. Jewett, 1853) 37–39, 40–41, 42–43, 44–46; and 177–79, 187–88.

time for devotional duties, and strictly forbade him to read the Bible and pray, either by himself or with the other servants; and because, like a certain man of old, named Daniel, he constantly disobeyed this unchristian edict, his master inflicted upon him that punishment which a master always has in his power to inflict—he sold him into perpetual exile from his wife and children, down to New Orleans.

The gentleman who gave the writer this information says that, although not a religious man at the time, he was so struck with the man's piety, that he said to his brother, "I hope you will never do anything to deprive this man of his religious privileges, for I think a judgment will come upon you if you do." To this his brother replied that he should be very foolish to do it, since he had made up his mind that the man's religion was the root of his extraordinary excellences.

Some time since there was sent to the writer from the South, through the mail, a little book, entitled "Sketches of Old Virginia Family Servants," with a preface by Bishop Meade. The book contains an account of the following servants: African Bella, Old Milly, Blind Lucy, Aunt Betty, Springsfield Bob, Mammy Chris, Diana Washington, Aunt Margaret, Rachel Parker, Nelly Jackson, My Own Mammy, Aunt Beck.

The following extract from Bishop Meade's preface may not be uninteresting:—[1]

> The following sketches were placed in my hands with a request that I would examine them with a view to publication.
>
> After reading them, I could not but think that they would be both pleasing and edifying.
>
> Very many such examples of fidelity and piety might be added from the old Virginia families. These will suffice as specimens, and will serve to show how interesting the relation between master and servant often is.
>
> Many will doubtless be surprised to find that there was so much intelligence as well as piety in some of the old servants of Virginia, and that they had learned to read the Sacred Scriptures, so as to be useful in this way among their fellow-servants. It is, and always has been true, in regard to the servants of the Southern States, that although public schools may have been prohibited, yet no interference has been attempted, where the owners have chosen to teach their servants, or permit them to learn in a private way how to read God's word. Accordingly, there always have been some who were thus taught. In the

1. The Right Reverend William Meade, Episcopal bishop of Virginia and author of *Sermons Addressed to Masters and Servants*, was one of a number of white preachers who attempted to use religion to defend slavery and pacify slaves [*Editor*].

more Southern States the number of these has most abounded. Of this fact I became well assured about thirty years since, when visiting the Atlantic States, with a view to the formation of auxiliary colonization societies, and the selection of the first colonists for Africa. In the city of Charleston, South Carolina, I found more intelligence and character among the free coloured population than anywhere else. The same was true of some of those in bondage. A respectable number might be seen in certain parts of the Episcopal churches which I attended, using their prayer-books, and joining in the responses of the church.

Many purposes of convenience and hospitality were subserved by this encouragement of cultivation in some of the servants, on the part of the owners.

When travelling many years since with a sick wife, and two female relatives, from Charleston to Virginia, at a period of the year when many of the families from the country resort to the town for health, we were kindly urged to call at the seat of one of the first families in South Carolina; and a letter from the mistress, then in the city, was given us, to her servant, who had charge of the house in the absence of the family. On reaching there, and delivering the letter to a most respectable-looking female servant, who immediately read it, we were kindly welcomed and entertained, during a part of two days, as sumptuously as though the owner had been present. We understood that it was no uncommon thing in South Carolina for travellers to be thus entertained by the servants in the absence of the owners, on receiving letters from the same.

Instances of confidential and affectionate relationship between servants and their masters and mistresses, such as are set forth in the following sketches, are still to be found in all the slave-holding States. I mention one, which has come under my own observation. The late Judge Upshur, of Virginia, had a faithful house-servant (by his will now set free), with whom he used to correspond on matters of business when he was absent on his circuit. I was dining at his house, some years since, with a number of persons, himself being absent, when the conversation turned on the subject of the presidential election, then going on through the United States, and about which there was an intense interest; when his servant informed us that he had that day received a letter from his master, then on the western shore, in which he stated that the friends of General Harrison might be relieved from all uneasiness, as the returns already received made his election quite certain.

Of course it is not to be supposed that we design to convey the impression that such instances are numerous, the nature of the relationship forbidding it; but we do mean emphatically

> to affirm that there is far more of kindly and Christian intercourse than many at a distance are apt to believe. That there is a great and sad want of Christian instruction, notwithstanding the more recent efforts put forth to impart it, we most sorrowfully acknowledge.

Bishop Meade adds that these sketches are published with the hope that they might have the effect of turning the attention of ministers and heads of families more seriously to the duty of caring for the souls of their servants.

* * *

In the free States there have been a few instances of such extraordinary piety among negroes, that their biography and sayings have been collected in religious tracts, and published for the instruction of the community.

One of these was, before his conversion, a convict in a State-prison in New York, and there received what was, perhaps, the first religious instruction that had ever been imparted to him. He became so eminent an example of humility, faith, and, above all, fervent love, that his presence in the neighbourhood was esteemed a blessing to the church. A lady has described to the writer the manner in which he would stand up and exhort in the church-meetings for prayer, when, with streaming eyes and the deepest abasement, humbly addressing them as his masters and misses, he would nevertheless pour forth religious exhortations which were edifying to the most cultivated and refined.

In the town of Brunswick, Maine, where the writer lived when writing "Uncle Tom's Cabin," may now be seen the grave of an aged coloured woman, named Phebe, who was so eminent for her piety and loveliness of character, that the writer has never heard her name mentioned except with that degree of awe and respect which one would imagine due to a saint. The small cottage where she resided is still visited and looked upon as a sort of shrine, as the spot where old Phebe lived and prayed. Her prayers and pious exhortations were supposed to have been the cause of the conversion of many young people in the place. Notwithstanding that the unchristian feeling of caste prevails as strongly in Maine as anywhere else in New England, and the negro, commonly speaking, is an object of aversion and contempt, yet so great was the influence of her piety and loveliness of character, that she was uniformly treated with the utmost respect and attention by all classes of people. The most cultivated and intelligent ladies of the place esteemed it a privilege to visit her cottage; and when she was old and helpless, her wants were most tenderly provided for. When the news of her death was spread abroad in the place, it excited a general and very tender sensation of regret. "We have lost Phebe's prayers," was the remark frequently made afterwards by members of the church, as they met one another. At her funeral, the ex-governor of the State and the professors of the college officiated as pallbearers, and a sermon was preached, in which the many excellences of her Christian character were held up as an example to the community. A small religious tract, containing an account of her life, was published by the American Tract Society, prepared by a lady of Brunswick. The writer recollects that on reading the tract, when she first went to Brunswick, a doubt arose in her mind whether it was not somewhat exaggerated. Some time afterwards she overheard some young persons conversing together about the tract, and saying that they did not think it gave exactly the right idea of Phebe. "Why, is it too highly coloured?" was the inquiry of the author. "Oh, no, no, indeed!" was the earnest response; "it doesn't begin to give an idea of how good she was."

Such instances as these serve to illustrate the words of the Apostle, "God hath chosen the foolish things of the world to confound the wise; and God hath chosen the weak things of the world to confound the things which are mighty."

* * *

A last instance parallel with that of Uncle Tom is to be found in the published memoirs of the venerable Josiah Henson, now, as we have said, a clergyman in Canada. He was "raised" in the State of Maryland. His first recollections were of seeing his father mutilated and covered with blood, suffering the penalty of the law for the crime of raising his hand against a white man—that white man being the overseer, who had attempted a brutal assault upon his mother. This punishment made his father surly and dangerous, and he was subsequently sold South, and thus parted for ever from his wife and children. Henson grew up in a state of heathenism, without any religious instruction, till, in a camp-meeting, he first heard of Jesus Christ, and was electrified by the great and thrilling news that He had tasted death for every man, the bond as well as the free. This story produced an immediate conversion, such as we read of in the Acts of the Apostles, where the Ethiopian eunuch, from one interview, hearing the story of the cross, at once believes and is baptized. Henson forthwith not only became a Christian, but began to declare the news to those about him; and, being a man of great natural force of mind and strength of character, his earnest endeavours to enlighten his fellow-heathen were so successful, that he was gradually led to assume the station of a negro preacher; and though he could not read a word of the Bible or hymn-book, his labours in this line were much prospered. He became immediately a very valuable slave to his master, and was intrusted by the latter with the oversight of his whole estate, which he managed with great judgment and prudence. His master appears to have been a very ordinary man in every respect,—to have been entirely incapable of estimating him in any other light than as exceedingly valuable property, and to have had no other feeling excited by his extraordinary faithfulness than the desire to make the most of him. When his affairs became embarrassed, he formed the design of removing all his negroes into Kentucky, and intrusted the operation entirely to his overseer. Henson was to take them alone, without any other attendant, from Maryland to Kentucky, a distance of some thousands of miles, giving only his promise as a Christian that he would faithfully perform this undertaking. On the way thither they passed through a portion of Ohio, and there Henson was informed that he could now secure his own freedom and that of all his fellows, and he was strongly urged to do it. He was exceedingly tempted and tried, but his Christian principle was invulnerable. No inducements could lead him to feel that it was right for a Christian to violate a pledge solemnly given, and his influence over the whole band was so great that he took them all with him into Kentucky. Those casuists among us who lately seem to think and teach that it is right for us to violate the plain commands of God, whenever some great national good can be secured by it, would do well to contemplate the inflexible principle of this poor slave, who, without being able to read a letter of the Bible, was yet enabled to perform this most sublime act of self-renunciation in obedience to its commands.

* * *

It would be well for the most cultivated of us to ask, whether our ten talents in the way of religious knowledge have enabled us to bring forth as much fruit to the glory of God, to withstand temptation as patiently, to return good for evil as disinterestedly, as this poor ignorant slave [Josiah Henson]. A writer in England has sneeringly remarked that such a man as Uncle Tom might be imported as a missionary to teach the most cultivated in England or America the true nature of religion. These instances show that what has been said with a sneer is in truth a sober verity; and it should never be forgotten that out of this race whom man despiseth have often been chosen of God true messengers of his grace, and temples for the indwelling of his Spirit.

*"For thus saith the high and lofty One that inhabiteth eternity, whose name is holy, I dwell in the high and holy place, with him also that is of a contrite and humble spirit, to revive the spirit of the humble, and to revive the heart of the contrite ones."*

The vision attributed to Uncle Tom introduces quite a curious chapter of psychology with regard to the negro race, and indicates a peculiarity which goes far to show how very different they are from the white race. They are possessed of a nervous organisation peculiarly susceptible and impressible. Their sensations and impressions are very vivid, and their fancy and imagination lively. In this respect the race has an Oriental character, and betrays its tropical origin. Like the Hebrews of old and the Oriental nations of the present, they give vent to their emotions with the utmost vivacity of expression, and their whole bodily system sympathises with the movements of their minds. When in distress, they actually lift up their voices to weep, and "cry with an exceeding bitter cry." When alarmed, they are often paralysed, and rendered entirely helpless. Their religious exercises are all coloured by this sensitive and exceedingly vivacious temperament. Like Oriental nations, they incline much to outward expressions, violent gesticulations, and agitating movements of the body. Sometimes in their religious meetings they will spring from the floor many times in succession, with a violence and rapidity which is perfectly astonishing. They will laugh, weep, and embrace each other convulsively, and sometimes become entirely paralysed and cataleptic. A clergyman from the North once remonstrated with a Southern clergyman for permitting such extravagances among his flock. The reply of the Southern minister was, in effect, this: "Sir, I am satisfied that the races are so essentially different that they cannot be regulated by the same rules. I at first felt as you do; and though I saw that genuine conversions did take place, with all this outward manifestation, I was still so much annoyed by it as to forbid it among my negroes, till I was satisfied that the repression of it was a serious hindrance to real religious feeling, and then I became certain that all men cannot be regulated in their religious exercises by one model. I am assured that conversions produced with these accessories are quite as apt to be genuine, and to be as influential over the heart and life, as those produced in any other way." The fact is, that the Anglo-Saxon race—cool, logical, and practical—have yet to learn the doctrine of toleration for the peculiarities of other races; and perhaps it was with a foresight of their peculiar character and dominant position in the earth, that God gave the Bible to them in the fervent language and with the glowing imagery of the more susceptible and passionate Oriental races.

Mesmerists have found that the negroes are singularly susceptible to all that class of influences which produce catalepsy, mesmeric sleep, and partial clairvoyant phenomena.

The African race, in their own climate, are believers in spells, in "fetish and obi," in "the evil eye," and other singular influences, for which probably there is an origin in this peculiarity of constitution. The magicians in scriptural history were Africans; and the so-called magical arts are still practised in Egypt, and other parts of Africa, with a degree of skill and success which can only be accounted for by supposing peculiarities of nervous constitution quite different from those of the whites. Considering those distinctive traits of the race, it is no matter of surprise to find in their religious histories, when acted upon by the powerful stimulant of the Christian religion, very peculiar features. We are not surprised to find almost constantly, in the narrations of their religious histories, accounts of visions, of heavenly voices, of mysterious sympathies and transmissions of knowledge from heart to heart without the intervention of the senses, or what the Quakers call being "baptized into the spirit" of those who are distant.

Cases of this kind are constantly recurring in their histories. The young man whose story was related to the Boston lady, and introduced above in the chapter on George Harris, stated this incident concerning the recovery of his liberty: That after the departure of his wife and sister, he for a long time, and very earnestly, sought some opportunity of escape, but that every avenue appeared to be closed to him. At length, in despair, he retreated to his room, and threw himself upon his bed, resolving to give up the undertaking, when just as he was sinking to sleep, he was roused by a voice saying in his ear, "Why do you sleep now? Rise up, if you ever mean to be free!" He sprang up, went immediately out, and in the course of two hours discovered the means of escape which he used.

* * *

## *The Execution of Justice*

State *v.* Eliza Rowand.—The "Ægis of Protection" to the Slave's Life.

> "We cannot but regard the fact of this trial as a salutary occurrence."
> —*Charleston Courier.*

Having given some account of what sort of statutes are to be found on the law-books of slavery, the reader will hardly be satisfied without knowing what sort of trials are held under them. We will quote one specimen of a trial, reported in the *Charleston Courier* of May 6th, 1847. The *Charleston Courier* is one of the leading papers of South Carolina, and the case is reported with the utmost apparent innocence that there was anything about the trial that could reflect in the least on the character of the State for the utmost legal impartiality. In fact, the *Charleston Courier* ushers it into public view with the following flourish of trumpets, as something which is for ever to confound those who say that South Carolina does not protect the life of the slave:—

THE TRIAL FOR MURDER.

Our community was deeply interested and excited yesterday, by a case of great importance and also of entire novelty in our jurisprudence. It was the trial of a lady of respectable family and the mother of a large family, charged with the murder of her own or her husband's slave. The court-house was thronged with spectators of the exciting drama, who remained, with unabated interest and undiminished numbers, until the verdict was rendered acquitting the prisoner. We cannot but regard the fact of this trial as a salutary, although in itself lamentable occurrence, as it will show to the world that, however panoplied in station and wealth, and although challenging those sympathies which are the right and inheritance of the female sex, no one will be suffered, in this community, to escape the most sifting scrutiny, at the risk of even an ignominious death, who stands charged with the suspicion of murdering a slave—to whose life our law now extends the ægis of protection, in the same manner as it does to that of the white man, save only in the character of the evidence necessary for conviction or defence. While evil-disposed persons at home are thus taught that they may expect rigorous trial and condign punishment, when, actuated by malignant passions, they invade the life of the humble slave, the enemies of our domestic institution abroad will find, their calumnies to the contrary notwithstanding, that we are resolved in this particular to do the full measure of our duty to the laws of humanity. We subjoin a report of the case.

The proceedings of the trial are thus given:—

TRIAL FOR THE MURDER OF A SLAVE.

*State v. Eliza Rowand.—Spring Term, May* 5, 1847
Tried before his Honour Judge O'Neall.

The prisoner was brought to the bar and arraigned, attended by her husband and mother, and humanely supported, during the trying scene, by the sheriff, J. B. Irving, Esq. On her arraignment she pleaded "Not Guilty," and for her trial, placed herself upon "God and her country." After challenging John M. Deas, James Bancroft, H. F. Harbers, C. J. Beckman, E. R. Cowperthwaite, Parker J. Holland, Moses D. Hyams, Thomas Glaze, John Lawrence, B. Archer, J. S. Addison, B. P. Colburn, B. M.

Jenkins, Carl Houseman, George Jackson, and Joseph Coppenberg, the prisoner accepted the subjoined panel, who were duly sworn, and charged with the case: 1. John L. Nowell, foreman; 2. Elias Whilden; 3. Jesse Coward; 4. Effington Wagner; 5. William Whaley; 6. James Culbert; 7. R. L. Baker; 8. S. Wiley; 9. W. S. Chisholm; 10. T. M. Howard; 11. John Bickley; 12. John Y. Stock.

The following is the indictment on which the prisoner was arraigned for trial:—

*The State* v. *Eliza Rowand.—Indictment for Murder of a Slave.*

State of South Carolina, }
*Charleston District,* } *to wit:*

At a Court of General Sessions, begun and holden in and for the district of Charleston, in the State of South Carolina, at Charleston, in the district and State aforesaid, on Monday, the third day of May, in the year of our Lord one thousand eight hundred and forty-seven:

The jurors of and for the district of Charleston aforesaid, in the State of South Carolina aforesaid, upon their oath present, that Eliza Rowand, the wife of Robert Rowand Esq., not having the fear of God before her eyes, but being moved and seduced by the instigation of the devil, on the sixth day of January, in the year of our Lord one thousand eight hundred and forty-seven, with force and arms, at Charleston, in the district of Charleston, and State aforesaid, in and upon a certain female slave of the said Robert Rowand, named Maria, in the peace of God, and of the said State, then and there being feloniously, maliciously, wilfully, deliberately, and of her malice aforethought, did make an assault; and that a certain other slave of the said Robert Rowand, named Richard, then and there, being then and there in the presence and by the command of the said Eliza Rowand, with a certain piece of wood, which he the said Richard in both his hands then and there had and held, the said Maria did beat and strike in and upon the head of her the said Maria, then and there giving to her the said Maria, by such striking and beating as aforesaid, with the piece of wood aforesaid, divers mortal bruises on the top, back, and sides of the head of her the said Maria, of which several mortal bruises she, the said Maria, then and there instantly died; and that the said Eliza Rowand was then and there present, and then and there feloniously, maliciously, wilfully, deliberately, and of her malice aforethought, did order, command, and require the said slave named Richard the murder and felony aforesaid, in manner and form aforesaid, to do and commit.

And as the jurors aforesaid, upon their oaths aforesaid, do say, that the said Eliza Rowand, her the said slave named Maria, in the manner and by the means aforesaid, feloniously, maliciously, wilfully, deliberately, and of her malice aforethought, did kill and murder, against the form of the Act of the General Assembly of the said State in such case made and provided, and against the peace and dignity of the same State aforesaid.

And the jurors aforesaid, upon their oaths aforesaid, do further present, that the said Eliza Rowand, not having the fear of God before her eyes, but being moved and seduced by the instigation of the devil, on the sixth day of January, in the year of our Lord one thousand eight hundred and forty-seven, with force and arms, at Charleston, in the district of Charleston, and State aforesaid, in and upon a certain other female slave of Robert Rowand, named Maria, in the peace of God, and of the said State, then and there being, feloniously, maliciously, wilfully, deliberately, and of her malice aforethought, did make an assault; and that the said Eliza Rowand, with a certain piece of wood, which she, the said Eliza Rowand, in both her hands then and there had and held, her the said last-mentioned slave named Maria did then and there strike, and beat, in and upon the head of her the said Maria, then and there giving to her the said Maria, by such striking and beating aforesaid, with the piece of wood aforesaid, divers mortal bruises, on the top, back, and side of the head, of her the said Maria, of which said several mortal bruises she the said Maria then and there instantly died. And so the jurors aforesaid, upon their oaths aforesaid, do say, that the said Eliza Rowand her the said last-mentioned slave named Maria, in the manner and by the means last mentioned, feloniously, maliciously, wilfully, deliberately, and of her malice aforethought, did kill and murder, against the form of the Act of the General Assembly of the said State in such case made and provided, and against the peace and dignity of the same State aforesaid.

H. BAILEY, Attorney-General.

As some of our readers may not have been in the habit of endeavouring to extract anything like common sense or information from documents so very concisely and luminously worded, the author will just state her own opinion that the above document is intended to charge Mrs. Eliza Rowand with having killed her slave Maria, in one of two ways: either with beating her on the head with her own hands, or having the same deed performed by proxy, by her slave-man Richard. The whole case is now presented. In order to make the reader clearly understand the arguments, it is necessary that he bear in mind that the law of 1740, as we have before shown, punished the murder of the slave only with fine and disfranchisement, while the law of 1821 punishes it with death.

* * *

There are some points which appear in this statement of the trial, especially in the plea for the defence. Particular attention is called to the following passage:—

> Fortunately (said the lawyer), the jury were of the country; acquainted with our policy and practice; composed of men too honourable to be led astray by the noise and clamour out of doors. All was now as it should be; at least, a court of justice had assembled to which his client had fled for refuge and safety; its threshold was sacred; no profane clamours entered there; but legal investigation was had of facts.

From this it plainly appears that the case was a notorious one; so notorious and atrocious as to break through all the apathy which slaveholding institutions tend to produce, and to surround the court-house with noise and clamour.

From another intimation in the same speech, it would appear that there was abundant testimony of slaves to the direct fact—testimony which left no kind of doubt on the popular mind. Why else does he thus earnestly warn the jury?

> He warned the jury that they were to listen to no evidence but that of free white persons, given on oath in open Court; they were to imagine none that came not from them. It was for this that they were selected; their intelligence putting them beyond the influence of unfounded accusations, unsustained by legal proof; of legends of aggravated cruelty, founded on the evidence of negroes, and arising from weak and wicked falsehoods.

See also this remarkable admission: "Truth had been distorted in this case, and murder manufactured out of what was nothing more than ORDINARY DOMESTIC DISCIPLINE." If the reader refers to the testimony, he will find it testified that the woman appeared to be about sixty years old; that she was much emaciated; that there had been a succession of blows on the top of her head, and one violent one over the ear; and that, in the opinion of a surgeon, these blows were sufficient to cause death. Yet the lawyer for the defence coolly remarks that "murder had been *manufactured* out of what was *ordinary domestic discipline*." Are we to understand that beating feeble old women on the head, in this manner, is a specimen of *ordinary domestic discipline* in Charleston? What would have been said if any anti-slavery newspaper at the North had made such an assertion as this? Yet the *Charleston Courier* reports this statement without comment or denial. But let us hear the lady's lawyer go still further in vindication of this ordinary domestic discipline: "Chastisement must be inflicted until subordination is produced; and the extent of the punishment is not to be judged by one's neighbours, but by himself. The event, IN THIS CASE, has been unfortunate and sad." The lawyer admits that the result of thumping a feeble old woman on the head has, *in this case*, been "unfortunate and sad." The old thing had not strength to bear it, and had no greater regard for the convenience of the family and the reputation of "the institution" than to die, and so get the family and the community generally into trouble. It will appear from this that in most cases where old women are thumped on the head, they have stronger constitutions—or more consideration.

Again he says, "When punishment is due to the slave, the master must not be held to strict account *for going an inch beyond the mark*." And finally, and most astounding of all, comes this: "*He bade the jury remember the words of Him who spake as never man spake*—'LET HIM THAT HATH NEVER SINNED THROW THE FIRST STONE.' They, as masters, might regret excesses to which they themselves might have carried punishment."

What sort of an insinuation is this? Did he mean to say that almost all the jurymen had probably done things of the same sort, and therefore could have nothing to say in this case? and did no member of the jury get up and resent such a charge? From all that appears, the jury acquiesced in it as quite a matter of course; and the *Charleston Courier* quotes it without comment, in the record of a trial which it says "will show to the world HOW the law extends the ægis of her protection alike over the white man and the humblest slave."

Lastly, notice the decision of the judge, which has become law in South Carolina. What point does it establish? That the simple oath of the master, in face of all circumstantial evidence to the contrary, may clear him, when the murder of a slave is the question. And this trial is paraded as a triumphant specimen of legal impartiality and equity! "If the *light* that is in thee be darkness, how great is that darkness!"

# HARRIET BEECHER STOWE

## Appeal to the Women of the Free States†

The Providence of God has brought our nation to a crisis of most solemn interest.

A question be now pending in our national legislature, which is most vitally to affect the temporal and eternal interests, not only of ourselves, but of our children, and our children's children for ages yet unborn. Through our nation, it is to affect the interests of liberty and Christianity throughout the whole world.

Of the woes, the injustice, and the misery of slavery, it is not needful to speak. There is but one feeling and one opinion on this among us all. I do not think there is a mother among us all, who clasps her child to her breast, who could ever be made to feel it right that that child should be a slave; not a mother among us all who would not rather lay that child in its grave.

Nor can I believe that there is a woman so unchristian as to think it right to inflict on her neighbor's child what she would think worse than death were it inflicted on her own. I do not think there is a wife who would think it right *her* husband should be sold to a trader, and worked all his life without rights and without wages. I do not believe there is a husband who would think it right that *his* wife should be considered, by law, the property of another man, and not his own. I do not think there is a father or mother who would believe it right, were they forbidden by law to teach their children to read. I do not believe there is a brother who would think it right to have his sister held as property, with no legal defense for her personal honor, by any man living.

All this is inherent in slavery. It is not the abuse of slavery, but the legal nature of it. And there is not a woman in the United States, when the question is fairly put before her, who thinks these things are right.

However ambition and the love of political power may blind the stronger sex, God has given to woman a deeper and more immovable knowledge, in those holier feelings, which are peculiar to womanhood, and which guard the sacredness of the family state.

But though our hearts have bled over this wrong there have been many things tending to fetter our hands, to perplex our efforts, and to silence our voice. We have been told that to speak of it, was an

† From *Independent* 6 (23 Feb. 1854) from *The Limits of Sisterhood: The Beecher Sisters on Women's Rights and Women's Sphere* by Jeanne Boydston, Mary Kelley, and Anne Margolis. 

invasion of the rights of other States. We have been told of promises and of compacts, and the natural expression of feeling has in many cases been restrained by an appeal to those honorable sentiments which respect the keeping of engagements.

The warm beatings of many hearts have been hushed; our yearnings and sympathies have been repressed because we have not known what to do; and many have come to turn a deaf ear to the whole tale of sorrow, because unwilling to harrow up the soul with feeling, where action was supposed to be impossible.

But a time has now come, when the subject is arising under quite another aspect.[1]

The question is not now, shall the wrongs of slavery exist, as they have, on their own territories? But shall we permit them to be extended over all the free territories of the United States? Shall the woes and miseries of slavery be extended over a region of fair, free, unoccupied territory, nearly equal, in extent, to the whole of the free States?

Nor is this all; this is not the last thing that is expected or intended. Should this movement be submitted to in silence, should the North consent to this breach of solemn contract on the part of the South, there yet remains one more step to be apprehended, vis: the legalizing of slavery throughout the free States. By a decision of the Supreme Court in the Lemmon case, it may be declared lawful for slave property to be held in the northern free States. Should this come to pass, it is no more improbable that there may be, four years hence, slave depots in New York city, than it was four years ago, that the South would propose a repeal of the "Missouri Compromise."

Women of the free States! the question is not, shall we remonstrate with slavery on its own soil? but are we willing to receive slavery into the free States and territories of the Union?

Shall the whole power of these United States go into the hands of slavery?

Shall every State in it be thrown open as a slave State? This will be the final result and issue of the question which is now pending. This is the fearful crisis at which we stand. And now, is there anything which the women of a country can do? Oh women of the free States! what did your grave mothers do in the time of our revolutionary struggle? Did not *liberty* in these days feel the strong impulse of woman's heart? . . .

1. Stowe refers to the 1854 congressional debate on the Kansas-Nebraska Act, whose doctrine of "popular sovereignty" would enable residents of territories to decide whether they would enter the Union as slave states or free states. The act was eventually passed by Congress in May 1854, repealing the Missouri Compromise and increasing sectional division and controversy over slavery.

What, then, is the duty of American women at this time? The first duty is for each woman, *for herself* thoroughly to understand the subject, and to feel that as mother, wife, sister, or member of society, she is bound to give her influence on the right side.

In the second place, women can make exertions to get up petitions, in their particular districts, to our national legislature. They can take measures to communicate information in their vicinity. They can employ lecturers to spread the subject before the people of their town or village. They can circulate the speeches of our members in Congress, and in many other ways secure a full understanding of the present position of our country.

Above all, it seems to be necessary and desirable that we should make this subject a matter of earnest prayer. The recent crisis in the history of the world, is one which calls upon all who believe in an Almighty Guardian and Ruler of nations, to betake themselves to his throne. . . .

Let us pray that in the agitation of this question between the North and the South, the war of principle may not become a mere sectional conflict, degenerating into the encounter of physical force. Let us raise our hearts to Him who has the power to restrain the wrath of man, that He will avert these consequences, which our sins as a nation have so justly deserved.

And as far as our social influence extends, let us guard against indiscriminate bitterness and vituperation.

Doubtless, there are noble minds at the South, who do not participate in the machinations of their political leaders, whose sense of honor and justice is outraged by this proposition, equally with our own.

While, then, we seek to sustain the cause of free principle unwaveringly, let us hold it also to be our true office, as women, to moderate the acrimony of political contest, remembering that the slaveholder and the slave are alike our brethren, whom the law of God commands us to love as ourselves.

For the sake of both, for the sake of our dear children, for the sake of our common country, for the sake of outraged and struggling liberty throughout the world, let every woman of America now do her duty.

# MARTIN DELANY

## *From* Blake; or, The Huts of America†

* * *

* * * [T]he Colonel ventured to declare that henceforth towards his servants, instead of leniency, he intended severity. They were becoming every day more and more troublesome, and less reliable. He intended, in the language of his friend the Judge, to "lay upon them a heavy hand" in future.

"I know your sentiments on this point," he said in reply to an admonition from Armsted, "and I used to entertain the same views, but experience has taught me better."

"I shall not argue the point Colonel, but let you have your own way!" replied Armsted.

"Well, Judge, as you wish to become a Southerner, you must first 'see the sights,' as children say, and learn to get used to them. I wish you to ride out with me to Captain Grason's, and you'll see some rare sport; the most amusing thing I ever witnessed," suggested Franks.

"What is it?" enquired the Major.

"The effect is lost by previous knowledge of the thing," replied he. "This will suit you, Armsted, as you're fond of Negro jokes."

"Then, Colonel, let's be off," urged the Major.

"Off it is!" replied Franks, as he invited the gentlemen to take a seat in the carriage already at the door.

"Halloo, halloo, here you are, Colonel! Why Major Armsted, old fellow, 'pon my word!" saluted Grason, grasping Armsted by the hand as they entered the porch.

"Judge Ballard, sir," said Armsted.

"Just in time for dinner, gentlemen! Be seated," invited he, holding the Judge by the hand. "Welcome to Mississippi, Sir! What's up, gentlemen?"

"We've come out to witness some rare sport the Colonel has been telling us about," replied the Major.

"Blamed if I don't think the Colonel will have me advertised as a showman presently! I've got a queer animal here; I'll show him to you after dinner," rejoined Grason. "Gentlemen, help yourself to brandy and water."

Dinner over, the gentlemen walked into the pleasure grounds, in the rear of the mansion.

† From *Blake; or, The Huts of America* from *The Weekly Anglo-African*, (1861–62); rep. in Floyd J. Miller, ed, *Blake; or, The Huts of America* (Boston: Beacon Press, 1970) 66–68. 

"Nelse, where is Rube? Call him!" said Grason to a slave lad, brother to the boy he sent for.

Shortly there came forward, a small black boy about eleven years of age, thin visage, projecting upper teeth, rather ghastly consumptive look, and emaciated condition. The child trembled with fear as he approached the group.

"Now gentlemen," said Grason, "I'm going to show you a sight!" having in his hand a long whip, the cracking of which he commenced, as a ringmaster in the circus.

The child gave him a look never to be forgotten; a look beseeching mercy and compassion. But the decree was made, and though humanity quailed in dejected supplication before him, the command was imperative, with no living hand to stay the pending consequences. He must submit to his fate, and pass through the ordeal of training.

"Wat maus gwine do wid me now? I know wat maus gwine do," said this miserable child, "he gwine make me see sights!" when going down on his hands and feet, he commenced trotting around like an animal.

"Now gentlemen, look!" said Grason. "He'll whistle, sing songs, hymns, pray, swear like a trooper, laugh, and cry, all under the same state of feelings."

With a peculiar swing of the whip, bringing the lash down upon a certain spot on the exposed skin, the whole person being prepared for the purpose, the boy commenced to whistle almost like a thrush; another cut changed it to a song, another to a hymn, then a pitiful prayer, when he gave utterance to oaths which would make a Christian shudder, after which he laughed outright; then from the fullness of his soul he cried:

"O maussa, I's sick! Please stop little!" casting up gobs of hemorrhage.[1]

Franks stood looking on with unmoved muscles. Armsted stood aside whittling a stick; but when Ballard saw, at every cut the flesh turn open in gashes streaming down with gore, till at last in agony he appealed for mercy, he involuntarily found his hand with a grasp on the whip, arresting its further application.

"Not quite a Southerner yet Judge, if you can't stand that!" said Franks on seeing him wiping away the tears.

"Gentlemen, help yourself to brandy and water. The little Negro don't stand it nigh so well as formerly. He used to be a trump!"

"Well, Colonel," said the Judge, "as I have to leave for Jackson this evening, I suggest that we return to the city."

1. This is a true Mississippi scene.

The company now left Grason's, Franks for the enjoyment of home, Ballard and Armsted for Jackson, and the poor boy Reuben, from hemorrhage of the lungs, that evening left time for eternity.

# GEORGE M. FREDRICKSON

## Uncle Tom and the Anglo-Saxons: Romantic Racialism in the North†

In literature and historical writing, as in science, there was a new stress in mid-nineteenth-century American thought on the peculiarities of diverse peoples and national "stocks," which approached, if it did not actually proclaim, a racialist explanation of society and culture. In Europe, intellectuals associated with the romantic movement in thought and literature were turning away from the universalism of the Enlightenment and embracing, at least implicitly, concepts of inbred national character and genius that could readily be transmuted into concepts of "racial" superiority. Initially, however, the romantic contemplation of how human psychology and behavior varied by nation or latitude did not always lead to ethnic chauvinism; there was in fact some tendency to celebrate diversity, as showing the richness and plenitude of the human spirit. The original exponent of an apparently cosmopolitan approach to the varieties of national genius was Johann Gottfried von Herder, a late-eighteenth-century German philosopher who was an important source of nineteenth-century cultural nationalism. Denying the rigid hierarchical division of mankind into four or five biological races, Herder attempted to deal impartially with a variety of cultural or national groups, each allegedly with special gifts manifested in the course of its historical development. In fulfilling its unique cultural or spiritual heritage, each *Volk* was bringing to fruition a single and laudable aspect of human character which no other people could express as well. The philosopher could contemplate these differences without making invidious comparisons, much as he appreciated diverse beauties of nature. Although nineteenth-century historians of the romantic nationalist school tended to emphasize the innate virtues of their own nation at the expense of others, Herder's willingness to see the good qualities of other peoples provided an example for those Europeans and Americans who sensed some spiritual inadequacies in their own heritage and looked to peoples "differently constituted" for the flowering of neglected human virtues.[1]

In the United States, the romantic fascination with differences in the character of nations and peoples was manifested around mid-century in the writings of William H. Prescott, Francis Parkman, and John Lothrop Motley—three great American practitioners of romantic historiography. In his histories of the Spanish conquest of Mexico and Peru, Prescott generalized about the Spanish character in comparison with that of both the Indians they conquered and the "Anglo-Saxon races" who settled to the North; Parkman compared the natural characteristics of the Anglo-Saxons and the "Celtic" French in the course of describing the struggle between the French and the English for the control of North America; and Motley in *The Rise of the Dutch Republic* invoked a Germanic-Celtic contrast in differentiating the two stocks that comprised the Dutch nation. From such descriptions of contacts between peoples of supposedly contrasting innate characteristics emerged a celebration of the Anglo-Saxon, or Germanic, stock at the expense of the Celtic or Iberian. The Anglo-Saxon was represented as carrying in his blood a love of liberty, a spirit of individual enterprise and resourcefulness, and a capacity for practical and reasonable behavior, none of which his rivals possessed.[2]

Such were the beginnings of a nationalistic glorification of the dominant stock, a tendency to make America's virtues racial rather than historical or environmental in origin. But antebellum "Anglo-Saxonism" can be distinguished from the late-nineteenth-century variety by its lack of exclusiveness, as reflected in a general unwillingness to acknowledge significant and enduring ethnic divisions among white Americans. The Know-Nothing movement of the 1850s, the principal prewar manifestation of anti-immigrant feeling, placed very little reliance on a quasi-racial contrast between Celts and Anglo-Saxons, despite the fact that the Irish were its principal targets. Its central theme was anti-Catholicism. It was clearly implied, as a rule, that all whites in the United States could readily be assimilated by the dominant stock without altering basic national characteristics, though Democratic politicians with their large Irish and

1. See Théophile Simar, *Étude Critique sur la Doctrine des Races au XVII^e Siècle et Son Expansion au XIX^e Siècle* (Brussels, 1922), pp. 91–94 and Chapter III, *passim;* and Johann Gottfried von Herder, *Reflections on the Philosophy of the History of Mankind*, ed. Frank E. Manuel (Chicago and London, 1968), *passim.* Professor Manuel's introduction contains an excellent analysis of Herder's romantic variety of cultural relativism.
2. Thomas F. Gossett discusses the "Anglo-Saxonism" of Prescott, Parkman, and Motley in *Race: The History of an Idea in America* (Dallas, 1963), pp. 89–96. On Parkman's racial comparisons see also Edward N. Saveth, *American Historians and European Immigrants, 1875–1925* (New York, 1948), pp. 103–104.

Scotch-Irish followings had to be wary in discussing this subject. To make this perspective absolutely clear, Senator Thomas Hart Benton of Missouri said in 1846 that the mission of the composite "Celtic-Anglo-Saxon" vanguard of the Caucasian race was to dominate both North and South America.[3]

Notions of white or Anglo-Saxon superiority were common even among critics of the slave system. Francis Lieber, a German-born political theorist who remained unsympathetic to slaveholding despite a long residence in the South, wrote in the 1850s of "Anglican liberty," that marvelous combination of individual freedom with the capacity for national unity and cooperative action which was "common to the whole Anglican race" and which had been "evolved first and chiefly by this race." It was on this ethnic and historical basis that the United States, according to Lieber, had developed its Republican institutions.[4]

Theodore Parker, liberal Unitarian minister and militant abolitionist, went even further. The early settlers of Massachusetts Bay, he announced in 1854, "had in them the ethnologic idiosyncrasy of the Anglo-Saxon—his restless disposition to invade and conquer other lands; his haughty contempt of humbler tribes which leads him to subvert, enslave, kill, and exterminate; his fondness for material things, preferring these to beauty; his love of personal liberty, yet coupled with most profound respect for peaceful and established law; his inborn skill to organize things to a mill, men to a company, a community, tribes to a federated state; and his slow, solemn, inflexible, industrious, and unconquerable will." Only in America, he continued, did "the peculiar characteristics of the Anglo-Saxon" come to full development.[5] As a humanitarian and an antislavery radical, Parker was not entirely happy with the harshly exploitative and genocidal side of the Anglo-Saxon character, but he concluded in another address of the same year that "the Anglo-Saxon," as "the Caucasian's best," was "a good hardy stock for national welfare to grow on,"[6] and in a letter to an English friend in 1857 he wrote: "I look with great pride on this

3. Cited in Edward McNall Burns, *The American Idea of Mission: Concepts of National Purpose and Destiny* (New Brunswick, N.J., 1957), pp. 199–200. See also Gossett, *Race*, p. 97; and Ray Allen Billington, *The Protestant Crusade: 1800–1860* (New York, 1938). For a typical expression of antebellum Anglo-Saxonism, with its emphasis on the ability of Anglo-Saxons to assimilate other Caucasian groups without losing their innate characteristics, see "The Anglo-Saxon Race," *North American Review*, LXXII (July, 1851), 34–71.
4. Francis Lieber, *On Civil Liberty and Self-Government*, Enlarged Edition (Philadelphia, 1859), pp. 53–57.
5. Theodore Parker, "The Nebraska Question," sermon of Feb. 12, 1854, *Collected Works*, ed. Francis P. Cobbe (London, 1863–1870), V, 250.
6. Theodore Parker, "Dangers Which Threaten the Rights of Man in America," sermon of July 2, 1854, *ibid.*, VI, 117.

Anglo-Saxon people. It has many faults, but I think it is the best specimen of mankind which has ever attained great power in the world."[7]

The American "ethnologic" self-image, whether described as Anglican, Anglo-Saxon, Celtic-Anglo-Saxon, or simply Caucasian, was being formulated and popularized at the very time when the slavery controversy focused interest on the Negro character. No longer were Americans in general being characterized primarily by their adherence to a set of political and social ideals allegedly representing the universal aspirations of all humanity, but democracy itself was beginning to be defined as racial in origin and thus realizable perhaps only by people with certain hereditary traits. The heightened consciousness of what were supposed to be white racial characteristics undoubtedly helped make it easy for many, on both sides of the sectional debate over slavery, to accept a stereotype of the Negro which made him a kind of anti-Caucasian.

In fact, the growing popularity of racialist thinking, with its emphasis on contrasting stereotypes, seems to have led to a change in the character of the debate over Negro personality and prospects. The discussion of the 1830s had been largely a dialogue between environmentalist defenders of a single human nature and proponents of deep-seated racial differences; the dialogue of the 1840s and 1850s tended increasingly to start from a common assumption that the races differed fundamentally. The biological school saw the Negro as a pathetically inept creature who was a slave to his emotions, incapable of progressive development and self-government because he lacked the white man's enterprise and intellect. But those who ascribed to the priority of feeling over intellect sanctioned both by romanticism and evangelical religion could come up with a strikingly different concept of Negro "differences." Whereas scientists and other "practical" men saw only weakness, others discovered redeeming virtues and even evidences of black superiority.

This comparatively benign view of black "peculiarities" has been neglected by historians, who have had difficulty distinguishing it from the mainstream of racist thought, but it is impossible to understand the antebellum discussion of Negro character and prospects without acknowledging its existence as a separate tradition, a body of thought and imagery about black-white differences that meshed at some points with scientific racial determinism, but which had, in the minds of its adherents at least, very different implications. This doctrine—which we shall call romantic racialism—resembled

7. Letter to Miss Cobbe, Dec. 4, 1857, in John Weiss, *Life and Correspondence of Theodore Parker* (New York, 1864), I, 463.

Herder's relativism more than Gobineau's hierarchical racism,[8] and was widely espoused by Northern humanitarians who were more or less antislavery. Although romantic racialists acknowledged that blacks were different from whites and probably always would be, they projected an image of the Negro that could be construed as flattering or laudatory in the context of some currently accepted ideals of human behavior and sensibility. At its most tentative, the romantic racialist view simply endorsed the "child" stereotype of the most sentimental school of proslavery paternalist and plantation romancers and then rejected slavery itself because it took unfair advantage of the Negro's innocence and good nature. The Reverend Orville Dewey, pastor of the Unitarian Church of the Messiah in New York City, hinted at the antislavery potentialities of racial romanticism when he contended in 1844 that the "inferiority" of the Negro meant simply "that he has not brought within the pale of civilization the rough, fierce Northern energies to rend and tear to pieces; that his nature is singularly childlike, affectionate, docile, and patient. . . ." Such "inferiority," Dewey argued, was "but an increased appeal to pity and generosity." "Is it," he asked, "the part of a chivalrous and Christian people to oppress the weak, to crush the helpless?"[9] A further development of the romantic racialist position was to deny unequivocally that these traits constituted inferiority, and its logical extreme was to argue, as Methodist Bishop Gilbert Haven did during the Civil War, that the Negro was the superior race—"the choice blood of America"—because his docility constituted the ultimate in Christian virtue.[1]

As previously suggested, one of the sources of this romantic conception of the Negro was the stereotype slave depicted in the proslavery plantation romances of the 1820s and 1830s. Along with more grotesque specimens of black humanity, the novels of George Tucker, William Gilmore Simms, James Kirke Paulding, John Pendleton Kennedy, and Nathaniel Beverley Tucker presented slaves who were, in the words of William R. Taylor, "responsive to kindness, loyal, affectionate, and cooperative." And, as Taylor has pointed out, proslavery novelists thus unwittingly opened the door to an antislavery use of the same stereotype: "To attribute to someone the simplicity of a child . . . especially in the middle of the nineteenth century, was a compliment of the first order, and dangerous,

8. That is, the racism expounded by Joseph Gobineau (1816–1882), a French diplomat and writer who was an antidemocratic and anti-Semitic proponent of Nordic supremacy [*Editor*].

9. Orville Dewey, *A Discourse on Slavery and the Annexation of Texas* (New York, 1844), p. 10.

1. Gilbert Haven, *National Sermons* (Boston, 1869), p. 358.

too, if the child were to be mistreated and sympathy was not the response sought for."[2]

One of the earliest uses of the stereotype by a moderate antislavery writer occurred in William Ellery Channing's 1835 essay *Slavery*. After asking how some slaves had escaped the moral degradation that seemed an inevitable consequence of their condition, Channing suggested a racial explanation: "The African is so affectionate, imitative, and docile that in favorable circumstances he catches much that is good; and accordingly the influence of a wise and kind master will be seen in the very countenance of his slaves."[3] In 1836 Charles Stuart, a British-born abolitionist, wrote an article for the *Quarterly Anti-Slavery Magazine*, in which he praised the black slaves for being so "eminently gentle, submissive, affectionate and grateful." "It is," he added, "almost impossible to excite them to revenge." "In making the best of their miserable lot," the blacks were "exhibiting better qualities, than probably any other people on earth would exhibit under similar provocation." Stuart concluded that the "virtuous" behavior of the slaves, far from showing how well adapted they were to their condition, showed how ready they were for emancipation and how criminal it was to take advantage of their naturally amiable qualities by keeping them in servitude.[4]

Although Channing and Stuart conveyed the rudiments of the romantic racialist image, there was an important step that remained to be taken—the obvious one of identifying the alleged Negro virtues with Christianity. The idea that the Negro was a natural Christian was set forth in detail, with many of the implications inherent in such a notion, in a series of lectures given in Cincinnati in 1837 and 1838 by Alexander Kinmont, a leading Midwestern exponent of Swedenborgianism. Kinmont, who conducted a school where scientific education was harmonized with classical literature and divine revelation, sought in his *Twelve Lectures on Man* to combine ethnology and religion in a new system. His efforts, it appears, excited great interest in Cincinnati, then the center of Western intellectual life. In response to the widespread praise for his ideas, Kinmont prepared his lectures for publication but died before they appeared in print in 1839.[5]

2. William R. Taylor, *Cavalier and Yankee: The Old South and American National Character* (New York, 1961), pp. 304–305, and Chapter IX, *passim*.
3. William Ellery Channing, *Works* (Boston, 1849), II, 95.
4. Charles Stuart, "On the Colored People of the United States," *Quarterly Anti-Slavery Magazine*, II (October, 1836), 12–14.
5. Alexander Kinmont, *Twelve Lectures on the Natural History of Man* (Cincinnati, 1839). Kinmont was born in 1799 in Scotland and attended the University of Edinburgh. After emigrating to America in 1823, he served for a time as the principal of an academy in Bedford, Pennsylvania, and became a convert to Swedenborgianism, a complex and mystical faith whose impact on nineteenth-century American intellectual history was greater than the number of its adherents would suggest. Going to Cincinnati in

Kinmont began from premises not unlike those of the scientific racists, contending that Negroes, in both "their physical and mental condition, . . . are naturally and originally distinct" from whites. He maintained further that it was "the effect of a particular providence, or, to speak in the dialect of science, an express law of nature, that each peculiar race of men should occupy those limits, which have been assigned and none other." Thus the enslavement and forced migration of the blacks was not only a violation of Christian morality but also a "sad error" that went in the teeth of natural law. But unlike the scientific proponents of polygenesis,[6] Kinmont did not accept the notion that blacks constituted a lower order of beings. Although the "original" differences between the races were not caused by "any combination of causes, natural or artificial, with which we are acquainted," and were in fact "*obscure*," they were nevertheless compatible with the religious doctrine of the unity and fraternity of the human race. Whites and blacks manifested different traits because this was part of what Kinmont saw as God's plan for the gradual fulfillment of man's intellectual, moral, and spiritual potentialities. The present epoch, he indicated, was obviously that of the Caucasians, a race which excelled all others in "intellectual expansion"; and it was the divinely appointed mission of the whites to develop the arts and sciences. But such intellectual advancement was not the last word in human aspiration. Negroes, even in their present unfulfilled state, possessed some very desirable traits sadly lacking in Caucasians—"light-heartedness," a "natural talent for music" and, above all, "willingness to *serve*, the most beautiful trait of humanity, which we, from our innate love of dominion, and in defiance of the Christian religion, brand with the name of *servility*, and abuse not less to our own dishonor than to their injury." The fact was that the Caucasian, with all his gifts, was almost constitutionally unable to be a true Christian: "All the sweeter graces of the Christian religion appear almost too tropical and tender plants to grow in the Caucasian mind; they require a character of human nature which you can see in the rude lineaments of the Ethiopian."[7]

It followed that the African race had a glorious future. Kinmont foresaw the eventual emergence in "the Peninsula of Africa" of a great civilization which would reflect the peculiarities of the Negro character. "Who can doubt," he asked, "that here, also, humanity in its more advanced and millennial state will reflect, under a sweet

1839, he opened a school which emphasized scientific education within a Swedenborgian religious framework. A man of broad scholarly interests, he gave his first set of public lectures in 1833–1834, taking as his subject "The Physical and Intellectual History of Man." (See *Twelve Lectures*, pp. 1–16.)

6. The derivation of a species from more than one ancestor [*Editor*].

7. Kinmont, *Twelve Lectures*, pp. 188–193, 198, 218.

and mellow light, the softer attributes of the Divine beneficence?" If the Caucasians were destined to reflect "the Divine science," was it not probable that the Negro would develop "a later but far nobler civilization," which would "return the splendor of the Divine attributes of mercy and benevolence in the practice and exhibition of the milder and gentler virtues?" In Kinmont's scheme, therefore, it was the blacks and not the whites who would first achieve millennial perfection.[8]

* * *

By the early 1840s the antislavery movement itself provided fertile soil for romantic racialism, a doctrine which acknowledged permanent racial differences but rejected the notion of a clearly defined racial hierarchy. In the Unitarian clergyman James Freeman Clarke's characteristic formulation of 1842 it meant that "in some faculties [the Negro] probably *is* inferior—in others superior," and that his superiority was found largely in "a strong religious tendency, and that strength of attachment which is capable of any kind of self-denial and self-sacrifice."[9] In 1845 James Russell Lowell, then a Garrisonian abolitionist[1] as well as an emerging literary figure, advocated an immediate and radical application of Kinmont's concepts. "We have never had any doubt," he wrote, "that the African race was intended to introduce a new element of civilization, and that the Caucasian would be benefited greatly by an infusion of its gentler and less selfish qualities. The Caucasian mind, which seeks always to govern at whatever cost, can never come to so beautiful or Christian a height of civilization, as with a mixture of those seemingly humbler but truly more noble qualities which teach it to obey." Lowell did not spell out exactly how this mixture would take place, but he made it clear that if Kinmont and others were right about the Negro character, it would not do to wait for a distant African millennium; Caucasians who genuinely believed in encouraging "the gentler and less selfish qualities" were duty bound to allow the Negro the fullest scope for exercising a corrective, mollifying influence on white civilization, and this meant not only emancipation but the elimination of "every barrier of invidious distinction" between the races.[2]

The growth of romantic racialism in antislavery circles can be accounted for in several ways. It was, first of all, a reflection of the

8. *Ibid.*, p. 91.
9. James Freeman Clarke, *Slavery in the United States: A Sermon Delivered on Thanksgiving Day, 1842* (Boston, 1843), p. 24.
1. A radical, uncompromising abolitionist; Garrison called for an immediate end to slavery and advocated Northern secession. See above, p. 31, n. 1 [*Editor*].
2. James Russell Lowell, *Anti-Slavery Papers* (Boston and New York, 1902), I, 21–22.

general trend of thought away from racial environmentalism and toward an acceptance of inherent diversity; more precisely, it was a way of adjusting to this compelling idea that was apparently compatible with Christian humanitarianism and opposition to slavery. It seemed to add strength to the antislavery argument to contend that slavery constituted the oppression of "one of the best races of the human family." But there was more to it than this. For romantic racialists, the Negro was a symbol of something that seemed tragically lacking in white American civilization. For those who resolutely adhered to Christian morality and idealized standards of gentility, the national spectacle during this period was far from edifying. With the "log cabin and hard cider" campaign of 1840,[3] politics had seemingly degenerated into an unprincipled and demagogic scramble for office. The economic growth of the country appeared to bring nothing but a gross materialism, a willingness to sacrifice anything for personal wealth. Worst of all, in the eyes of peaceable humanitarians, was the crude national expansionism, justified as "manifest destiny," that led to the annexation of Texas as a vast new slave territory and finally to an unjust war with Mexico. Some who were disturbed by such tendencies were attracted to the prevailing racial stereotypes as symbols of their discontent. If this was the way Caucasians behaved—and the proponents of slavery and expansionism were openly celebrating the aggressive, war-like, and domineering character of the Caucasian or Anglo-Saxon—then it was possible that something was wrong with the race. The idealized Negro was a convenient symbol to point up the deficiencies, not so much perhaps of the white race itself as of the racial self-image it seemed in danger of accepting.

In an age when traditional religious and moral values seemed to be losing their hold on whites, many could be consoled by contemplating a people supposedly free of a lust for wealth and power and therefore immune to desires that led Anglo-Saxons to expand their domain by enslaving or exterminating other peoples. Similarly, in an age of bad manners and vulgar materialism, there was something attractive about the idea that the black race possessed, in the words of James Freeman Clarke, "a native courtesy, a civility like that from which the word 'gentleman' has its etymological meaning, and a capacity for the highest refinement of character."[4] Hence benevolent reformers tended to see the Negro more as a symbol than as a person, more as a vehicle for romantic social criticism than as a human being with

3. The presidential campaign of 1840, in which the Whig party won its first national victory by promoting General William Henry Harrison as the "log cabin and hard cider" candidate, turning to Whig advantage a phrase meant as an insult by the Democrats [*Editor*].
4. Clarke, *Slavery*, p. 24.

the normal range of virtues and vices. A critical observer might also wonder how deeply and unequivocally white humanitarians really identified themselves with the stereotype of the submissive black. Meekness might be a virtue, but was it in fact the only virtue or even the cardinal one for those who celebrated its presence in the Negro?

Of course the whole conception would have been impossible if the slaves had risen up in large numbers and rebelled against their masters. Romantic racialism was facilitated by the fact that no massive insurrections took place in the South after the Nat Turner rebellion of 1831.[5] This apparent quiescence was widely interpreted in the North as reflecting a natural black docility. Senator Charles Sumner of Massachusetts confidently asserted in 1862 that a Northern act of emancipation, which he was then advocating, would not lead, as some critics of the measure had charged, to a bloody slave rebellion in the unconquered areas of the South. "This whole objection," he told a Faneuil Hall audience, "proceeds on a mistaken idea of the African slave. . . . The African is not cruel, vindictive, or harsh, but gentle, forgiving, and kind."[6]

The image of the Negro as natural Christian received its fullest treatment and most influential expression in Harriet Beecher Stowe's *Uncle Tom's Cabin*. This immensely popular novel, which more than any other published work served to crystallize antislavery feeling in the North in the 1850s, was also the classic expression of romantic racialism. Little is known of the precise sources of Mrs. Stowe's racial views, which were, in any case, commonplace by 1851, when *Uncle Tom's Cabin* began to appear serially in a moderate antislavery journal, the *National Era*. But there is a strong possibility that she was drawn initially to the romantic-religious concept of racial differences by the lectures of Alexander Kinmont. She was living in Cincinnati at the time Kinmont was lecturing; and little of a religious or cultural nature which could be provided by "the Athens of the West" escaped her attention as the member of a family that was at the center of Cincinnati's intellectual and spiritual life. If she failed to hear Kinmont, she almost certainly read him in the beautifully bound memorial edition which was a major publishing event in Cincinnati in 1839. Whatever the circumstances of her first encounter with Kinmont's ideas and whatever influence they may have had at the time, their presence in *Uncle Tom's Cabin* seems indisputable.[7]

5. In 1831, the slave Nat Turner led about sixty others in rebellion in Southampton County, Virginia; the uprising failed and led to more stringent slave laws in the South [*Editor*].
6. Charles Sumner, *Works* (Boston, 1874), VII, 226.
7. Mrs. Stowe's Cincinnati years (1832–1850) are described in detail in Forrest Wilson, *Crusader in Crinoline: The Life of Harriet Beecher Stowe* (Philadelphia, 1941), pp. 99–234. Unfortunately, we learn little from this source about what she read or what lectures she heard during this period.

## GEORGE CRUIKSHANK

### Illustrations for *Uncle Tom's Cabin*

*Tom reading his Bible.* By George Cruikshank. From the first British edition of *Uncle Tom's Cabin*, 1852.

*The poor bleeding heart.* By George Cruikshank. From the first British edition of *Uncle Tom's Cabin*, 1852. This engraving shows Lucy killing herself when her baby is sold away.

*Emmeline about to be sold to the highest bidder.* By George Cruikshank. From the first British edition of *Uncle Tom's Cabin*, 1852.

# THOMAS F. GOSSETT

## Anti–Uncle Tom Literature[†1]

* * *

In nearly all anti–Uncle Tom literature, the major figure is the benign and patriarchal slavemaster. Always he is a plantation owner. Nearly always he is financially well off, if not wealthy, though sometimes he suffers reverses apparently in order to allow the slaves an opportunity to demonstrate their loyalty to him. Colonel Montrose in Maria J. McIntosh's *The Lofty and the Lowly* returns early in the novel to his plantation in Virginia after a trip to town. He assembles his slaves together before a pitchpine bonfire. "Each had a kind clasp of the hand, a word of pleasant greeting, and a testimonial of remembrance—a bright bandana handkerchief, and calico dress to the women—a jacket and muffler to the men," the narrator says. To Old Cato, his slave and right-hand man, Montrose brings a special gift of a coat with "cloth of a finer quality than that usually worn by the negroes," a muffler, and a fur cap. Cato thanks his master, saying, "I 'fraid you make me proud, sir, when I get all dese on." A kindly white neighbor of Colonel Montrose gives the slaves their cue. "We have a great deal to be thankful for to-night, my friends—have we not?" And the meeting ends with the singing of a hymn, "Come Thou Fount of Every Blessing." In Caroline Lee Hentz's novel, *Marcus Warland*, the narrator says of some of the slave characters, "It is true, they were *slaves*, but their chains never clanked. Each separate link was kept moist and bright with the oil of kindness."[2]

The slaveowners in most of the novels are so benign that one can hardly help wondering how they handle the discipline problems which at times must inevitably come up. In Mary H. Eastman's *Aunt Phillis's Cabin*, the master mildly rebukes the slave Aunt Phillis because she has allowed a runaway slave to hide in her cabin. He tells her it would never do for him to get the reputation of allowing his "servants" to abet the crimes of those of his neighbors. Instantly contrite, Aunt Phillis promises never to repeat her offense.

† From *Uncle Tom's Cabin and American Culture*. Copyright © 1985 by Southern Methodist University Press. Complete citations in following notes can be found here.

1. Most of the anti–*Uncle Tom's Cabin* novels mentioned in this essay were written by white southerners. The exceptions are as follows. Robert Criswell, Baynard R. Hall, J. Thorton Randolph [pseudonym of Charles Jacobs Peterson], and Caroline E. Rush were white northerners. Caroline Lee Hentz was a white northerner transplanted to the South. The novel, *Mr. Frank: the Underground Mail-Agent*, was written under the pseudonym "Vidi," and the region he or she came from is unknown.
2. McIntosh, *The Lofty and the Lowly*, 1:198–99; Caroline Lee Hentz, *Marcus Warland; or, The Long Moss Spring: A Tale of the South* (Philadelphia: T. B. Peterson & Bros., 1852), p. 59.

Sometimes the proslavery writers profess themselves to be bewildered by accounts in the North that slaves are cruelly punished. In McIntosh's *The Lofty and the Lowly*, the daughter of a slaveowner is puzzled and saddened to read in northern newspapers of the supposed mistreatment of slaves. She "searched in vain the tablets of her memory for the sounds of rattling chain or the lash; or the sight of scar or brand, or mutilation, or any of those thousand acts of tyrannical power which it sickens the very soul to recall, and of which every northern paper she perused was full." When punishments do take place in these proslavery literary works, they are not often examples of physical chastisement. In W. L. G. Smith's *Life at the South*, a slave named Tom is mildly punished for failing to do his work. Another slave has bested him in a cotton chopping contest and he sullenly refuses to work at all. His master, after several gentle reprimands, imprisons Tom in a cabin for twenty-four hours without food. As a result, Tom changes his attitude. When asked whether the punishment has been sufficient, he replies, "Massa, I have now no oder than good thoughts; the bad ones I have parted with."[3]

Whippings are rare for the slaves in anti–Uncle Tom literature, but they do take place sometimes. In Caroline E. Rush's *The North and South* a slave boy named Jim steals a silver dollar from the pocketbook of his mistress. Jim is "a bright mulatto boy, about fourteen years old." The evidence of his guilt is not wholly conclusive; he has been seen coming out of the room in which the purse had been left. Under questioning, he steadfastly denies that he took the money. He "stood before his master and mistress, very pale, even beneath his brown skin," says the narrator, "but anyone could plainly see that he was guilty." His master calls him a "black dog" and orders the overseer to give him ten lashes every hour until he confesses. After the first whipping, Jim confesses to having stolen the dollar but says that he has lost it. Another whipping is administered and he admits that he has hidden the dollar in the woodpile. The narrator explains that Jim was, "like the most of his race, a great thief; and he added to this crime its usual attendant disregard for truth."[4]

Most slavemasters in anti–Uncle Tom literature are more kindly than this man. When they are obliged to whip their slaves, they do so reluctantly and only when other methods of reformation have failed. Mr. Wardloe, the benevolent slaveowner of Baynard R. Hall's *Frank Freeman's Barber Shop*, serves as a member of a patrol of white men organized to catch slaves away from their quarters without a pass. They catch Sambo, one of Wardloe's slaves, who says he

3. Eastman, *Aunt Phillis's Cabin*, pp. 115–16; McIntosh, *The Lofty and the Lowly*, 2:162; Smith, *Life at the South*, p. 66.
4. [Rush], *The North and South*, pp. 224–25.

has only "bin down to meetin'" and begs for mercy. The other members of the patrol think Sambo should be given two dozen lashes in order to "teach him to pray a little faster" next time. Mr. Wardloe asks to be allowed to take Sambo aside and to administer the punishment himself. He whispers to Sambo to yell loudly as he flogs a near-by gatepost, and Sam naturally complies. Wardloe gives his last two blows to Sambo himself as an indication that he is not wholly to be trifled with. "Reader! I well know that there are many Uncle Wardloes in the South," says the narrator of the novel. The benevolent slaveholder described in Smith's *Life at the South* is a man with "a kind heart and a scrupulously honest disposition. If he ever plied the lash to the stubbornly disobedient slave, he used it, as nearly as we can recollect, precisely as a father does in the wholesome correction of his children. He did not punish with wantonness." Sometimes the anti–Uncle Tom novelists used the device of having a faithful slave reply to critics of slavery. In the anonymous *Yankee Slave-Dealer; or, an Abolitionist Down South*, a skulking abolitionist tries to get Uncle Moses, a slave, to admit that he is often flogged. Uncle Moses denies the charge and adds, "I don't b'leve any servant who does right's ever whipped like a brute as you say."[5]

Other anti–Uncle Tom novelists leave vague the matter of how frequently and how severely slaves are whipped, but they emphasize the point that such punishments are necessary. "Africans hate civilization," explains the narrator of Mrs. Henry B. Schoolcraft's *The Black Gauntlet*, "and are never happier . . . than when allowed to live in the abandonment, nakedness, and filth, their instincts crave." There is no reason to worry that they will be permanently injured by mistreatment. "[A]ll the calumnies about the planters knocking the slaves senseless to the earth is [*sic*] the purest fiction," says the narrator; "for their skulls are so thick that it is doubtful whether any white man's strength could consummate such a feat, even if he was indiscreet enough to make the attempt." Billy Buck, a slave character in Ebenezer Starnes's *The Slaveholder Abroad*, argues that slaves are necessary in the South because only they can work in the fields in a hot climate. Supposedly, because of their inherent character traits, the masters will have to punish them. He replies to Englishmen skeptical of the virtues of slavery as follows: "Wa da been gwin git [where are they going to get] anybody able to work in cottonfield in brilin hot sun, but black nigger? I want know dat! An wa de debbil da gwine find nigger wid head to work widout buckra [white] man to show um? or dat gwine be willin, cepin he druv?"

5. Hall, *Frank Freeman's Barber Shop*, pp. 97–100; Smith, *Life at the South*, p. 261; anon., *The Yankee Slave-Dealer*, p. 30.

Billy Buck does not go on to explain how a slave is "druv," but he probably means by whippings.[6]

A number of the anti–Uncle Tom novels express the familiar proslavery argument that slaveholders are not likely to mistreat their slaves because of their value as property. The narrator of James M. Smythe's *Ethel Somers; or, the Fate of the Union* says that property itself is almost enough to insure the kindly treatment of slaves. He knows of "slaveholders who are kind to their slaves when they are kind to nobody else." Hall's *Frank Freeman's Barber Shop* expresses a similar idea. He admits that an occasional slaveowner is cruel to his slaves, but he says that other slaveowners in the community will refuse to sell to such a man. Yet the speaker also seems to think that a few cruel slaveowners in a community have a useful function. Sometimes, he says, a "wicked negro would be turned over to severe and cruel owners that served the community as a public whipping post." Even so, he adds, these cruel owners were "never esteemed" by respectable people. He does not speculate on the question of whether a mistreated slave was likely to derive much benefit from the fact that his owner was not esteemed by his white neighbors. When cruelties to slaves are shown in anti–Uncle Tom literature, they are the result of the personal defects of particular masters or, in rare instances, of mistresses. They are obviously not meant to be an indictment of the institution of slavery itself. In Eastman's *Aunt Phillis's Cabin*, there is a cruel slaveowner character, Mr. Lee, who sells seven of the children of one of his women slaves away from her, one after another. The narrator explains Lee's evil as the result of "money, drink, and the devil."[7]

In Robert Criswell's anti–Uncle Tom novel, *"Uncle Tom's Cabin" Contrasted with Buckingham Hall*, a kindly slaveowner gently disputes the charge of an idealistic young northern man that slaves are frequently mistreated. When the young man asks skeptically whether all the masters are kindly, the southern slaveowner replies that of course they are not. He himself could point to some masters who are "hard and cruel," but he adds that "as a general thing, the slaves have reason to be, and are, contented with their condition." Mr. Harding, one of the cruel slaveowners described in Criswell's novel, was an abolitionist when he lived in Ohio, but because a southern plantation was left to him by one of his wife's relatives, he had come to the South "in spite of his prejudices." After nine years of operating the plantation, Harding "abuses his slaves worse than any Southerner I ever heard of." It is true that he is "naturally despotic,"

6. Schoolcraft, *The Black Gauntlet*, pp. 218–19, 61; [Starnes], *The Slaveholder Abroad*, p. 67.

7. [Smythe], *Ethel Somers*, p. 199; Hall, *Frank Freeman's Barber Shop*, p. 78; Eastman, *Aunt Phillis's Cabin*, pp. 42–44.

but his chief fault is that as a northerner he does not understand the inherent nature of the blacks in the way that southern slave-owners do. He expects his slaves "to do as much in a day as white men; and because they do not he beats and half starves them." The wife is "as barbarous as her husband." When her riding horse is brought to her in the morning, she takes a white handkerchief and rubs it over him. If it is in the least "soiled or dusty," she immediately orders her groom to be whipped.[8]

Though they generally describe southern characters as kindly, the anti–Uncle Tom writers sometimes argue that violence is justifiable, or at least excusable, against abolitionists. A slaveowner in Eastman's *Aunt Phillis's Cabin* says,

> Mobs of any kind are rare in the Southern country. We are not (in spite of the bad qualities ascribed to us by the Abolitionists) a fussy people. Sometimes when an Abolitionist comes along, we have a little fun with him, the negroes enjoying it exceedingly. Slaveholders, as a general thing, desire to live a peaceful, quiet life; yet they are not willing to have their rights wrested from them.

Uncle Bacchus, a slave, tells his white masters that he wishes the Lord would see fit to bring all the abolitionists to Virginia so that they could be tarred and feathered. He himself would be willing, he says, "to spread de tar on neat, and to stick de feathers close and thick." In Hall's *Frank Freeman's Barber Shop*, the narrator describes the destruction of an abolitionist editor's printing press. Lynch law is sometimes justifiable, he argues, because "the most atrocious of all crimes may be committed under cover of law, when the law itself instead of preventing is compelled to aid them." Nobody would argue, he said, that a mailman should be compelled to deliver packages with dangerous explosives in them. He would be justified in throwing them in the water. "Of course, the powder packers and massacre-mongers would be very angry, and give pages of constitutional law and other legal flummydiddle," he said, "but such would never convince an unsophisticated citizen that he ought to sit still and be killed."[9]

In anti–Uncle Tom literature, the wives of the slaveowners are even more kindly than their husbands, as we might expect. In Schoolcraft's *The Black Gauntlet*, the narrator contrasts the beautiful southern belle with the mature matron she will become after she has married and has had years of experience as mistress of a plantation. As a young girl she has had no responsibilities "except in her

8. Criswell, *"Uncle Tom's Cabin" Contrasted with Buckingham Hall*, pp. 131–32.
9. Eastman, *Aunt Phillis's Cabin*, pp. 135, 218; Hall, *Frank Freeman's Barber Shop*, pp. 395–96.

flower-garden, in reading, or perfecting her education, and doing amateur fine needlework." Her life changes dramatically when "she becomes a planter's wife." No longer is she "a laughing, thoughtless flirt, seeking only to make herself beautiful and admired." Instead she develops into "a responsible, conscientious 'sister of charity' to her husband's numerous dependants [*sic*]. Northern ladies never saw a day in all their lives that could comprise all the responsibilities of a Southern planter's wife." Anthony Trollope visited the United States in 1861 and noted that this particular argument was still often heard in defense of slavery. He mentioned the complaint of a slavemistress who said that Stowe had no idea how much trouble it was to look after "our people." Trollope remarked that politeness forbade him to answer this argument with "the plain truth." Nonetheless, he admitted that he had an almost uncontrollable urge to reply, "Madam—dear madam, your sorrow is great; but that sorrow is the necessary result of your position."[1]

* * *

The greatest failures in anti–Uncle Tom literature are the slave characters, who are all too obviously patterned to fit the proslavery argument. The slaves are either contented in their condition and loyal to their masters or they are foolish rebels who do not understand their own best interests. Stephen A. Hirsch, a modern critic, has perceptively pointed out that in virtually all the anti–Uncle Tom novels, the slaves themselves play only a minor role. "Despite the uncles, aunts, and cabins populating the titles," he says, "only one novel, Smith's *Life at the South*, has a black as its main character." In one respect, however, nearly all the black characters are unlike those in the nostalgic fiction of the old plantation, written by white southern writers in the 1880s and 1890s. The slaves in the anti–Uncle Tom literature of the 1850s seldom exhibit a profound and mystical attachment to their white masters and mistresses. Their loyalty has a strongly matter-of-fact character. Friendly familial associations are mentioned, but the major point is that the blacks in these novels see slavery as a system which prevents them from falling into want and deprivation. The slaves may praise "massa" or "missis," but freedom from worry over their material needs is their usual reason for speaking favorably of slavery. Old Rufus, a slave in Martha Haines Butt's *Antifanaticism: A Tale of the South*, serves as a representative of many other slave characters of this sort. "Dis nigger never leab his massa to go wid nobody," he says, "'caze he

1. Schoolcraft, *The Black Gauntlet*, pp. 113–15; Anthony Trollope, *North America* (New York: Harper & Bros., 1862), p. 343.

know dat nobody ain't gwine to treat him good no how like massa does."[2]

One of the anti–Uncle Tom novels does, it is true, attempt to portray an exalted relationship between master and slave. In *Old Toney and His Master* by Theodore Dehone Mathews, Colonel Shelton is portrayed as an aristocrat of truly grand proportions. As host to the guests at his plantation mansion, he is shown "bowing as a courtier at the palace of the Tuilleries [*sic*] in the days of Louis XV." Old Toney, Colonel Shelton's slave, is scarcely less magnificent. Though the hair on his "venerable head" is as white as "freshly ginned cotton," there is nothing else old and feeble about him. One of his differences from Stowe's Uncle Tom is that he is his master's overseer of the slaves and that he "flogged the boys [slaves] by way of exercise, if they neglected their duties."[3]

Colonel Shelton and Old Toney have a sublime attachment for each other, which fully matches anything that the white southern romancers of the late nineteenth century would be able to imagine between master and slave. When his son is killed, Colonel Shelton falls "weeping like a child on the breast of his slave." Yet Old Toney is quite unlike the faithful slaves of post–Civil War white southern fiction. The principal difference is that he is not meek and gentle. Slave characters in later fiction sometimes accompany their masters as servants when they go to war, but they take no part in the fighting. Old Toney, on the other hand, is a formidable soldier. Many years before he had fought alongside his master against the Indians of Florida. Old Toney had "scalped many a Seminole." Their "scalps he still retained and exhibited with pride to the 'rest of the niggers,' as trophies of his . . . prowess." It is probably the fact that Old Toney is so dashing a warrior and so flamboyant a character that explains why other proslavery novelists did not attempt to create characters like him in their fiction. He is so aggressive a hero that one cannot imagine him as a slave.[4]

Slaves in anti–Uncle Tom literature are usually shown as happy, often singing at their work. In J. Thornton Randolph's *The Cabin and Parlor*, however, the narrator of the novel is momentarily puzzled when he notices that the minor key of many of the songs of the slaves is "almost mournful." He soon thinks of an explanation which will preclude the possibility that they might be unhappy. The music of native Africans is also seemingly sad, he says, but the

2. Stephen A. Hirsch, "Uncle Tom's Companions: The Literary and Popular Reaction to *Uncle Tom's Cabin*" (Ph.D. diss., State University of New York at Albany, 1975), p. 21; Butt, *Antifanaticism*, p. 16.
3. [Mathews], *Old Toney and His Master*, pp. 27, 52.
4. Ibid., pp. 94, 48.

likelihood is that this is merely the impression white listeners receive. The reader can easily determine for himself, he observes, that the music of American blacks does not indicate they are unhappy as slaves. On the contrary, they think of their music as an occasion for "mirthful enjoyment." In only one of the anti–Uncle Tom novels is there a suggestion that blacks might have great talent in music. In Mathews's *Uncle Toney and His Master*, the narrator praises the singing of a black church choir on a South Carolina plantation. He speaks of "the deep bass tones, like the swell of an organ, in perfect unison with the flute-like tones of the women—the tenor, the alto, the treble, and the bass often heard upon different octaves, but all in perfect accord." The narrator says that he has often heard trained singers in Charleston, but none of them was equal to the black singers in this choir. The comment stands alone in the proslavery fiction of this period in its willingness to concede that blacks might have a higher talent of any kind.[5]

* * *

A succession of black characters in the anti–Uncle Tom novels proclaim their devotion to old massa and missis and pay tribute to the benefits of slavery. Many of these are aged and infirm, and the reader may wonder what the young and healthy slaves think of the institution. Aunt Peggy, in Eastman's *Aunt Phillis's Cabin*, is one of a number of dying slaves who expire blessing the kindness of their owners. Old Bacchus, a slave, explains to his master that Aunt Peggy is obviously near the end of her life. "She's failin', sir," says Bacchus, "you can see by de way she sets in de sun all day, wid a long switch in her hand, trying to hit de little niggers as dey go by. Sure sign she's gwine home. . . . She sarved her time cookin and bakin, and she's gwin to a country what there's no 'casion to cook any more." A standard device in the novels is to have a northern woman, opposed to slavery, marry a southern man and gradually learn the beneficence of the institution. Sometimes the change in the northern woman's attitude takes place at the bedside of a dying slave or at a slave funeral. In John W. Page's *Uncle Robin in his Cabin in Virginia*, the Pennsylvania-born wife of the southern master visits the cabin of the dying Aunt Juno, an aged black woman who was born in Africa. "My dear husband," says the wife, "what a beautiful thought it is that a poor African, once condemned to be eaten by cannibals, should now be on her death-bed in a Christian country, surrounded by Christian friends, and rejoicing in the assurance of eternal salvation, procured by the death of her Savior."

5. Randolph, *The Cabin and Parlor*, pp. 78–79; [Mathews], *Old Toney and His Master*, p. 54.

"Yes, my dear," her husband replies, "it might carry consolation to the bosom of a Wilberforce,[6] mourning over the horrors of the African slave-trade." Caroline Lee Hentz and W. L. G. Smith also included death-bed scenes of slaves in their novels. In Butt's *Antifanaticism: A Tale of the South*, the formula is slightly varied. Her dying slave is a little girl. The death of this child suggests, at least to some degree, a black version of the death of little Eva. To her white mistress, the little black slave girl says, "Don't grieve for Hannah, Miss Dora. I am going home to heaven. I dreamed last night that I saw a little angel beckoning to me. I love you, Miss Dora, but must leave you soon. I hope to meet you in heaven."[7]

Sometimes, the anti–Uncle Tom writers apparently felt the need to have slaves who would philosophize on the subject of slavery, justifying it in principle. Since wholly black slaves are generally intellectually unequal to this sort of endeavor in these novels, the task is usually left to slaves who are partly white. One such character is Aunt Phillis in Eastman's *Aunt Phillis's Cabin*. "The blood of the freeman [a white freeman] and the slave mingled in her veins," and thus she has "a well regulated mind." She does not argue that she is content to be a slave. The narrator tells us that she "would have been truly happy to have obtained her own freedom, and that of her children, but she scorned the idea of . . . obtaining it otherwise than as a gift from her owner." Her ideas about slavery are a mixture of a pious belief in scripture and in the sanctity of laws regarding property. In reading the Bible, she "often pondered on the words of the angel [to Hagar], 'Return and submit thyself to thy mistress.'" Aunt Phillis accompanies her owners on a visit to the North, and, while there, some wicked abolitionists endeavor to persuade her to attempt to escape. "I want none of your help," says Aunt Phillis. "My husband and children are at home [down South]; but if they wasn't I am an honest woman, and am not in the habit of *taking* anything. . . . I am not going to begin stealing, and I fifty years of age." Having said this, Aunt Phillis straightens her tall figure and her eyes flash. The abolitionists, discomfited, slink away. In James M. Smythe's *Ethel Somers; or, The Fate of the Union*, a slave character philosophizes that principles of freedom are not applicable to blacks. "The Declaration of 'Dependence may do . . . for white folks, an not all of them," he says, "but it isn't worth a chaw of backer to a nigger. . . . I don't b'leeve it was ever 'tended for them."[8]

6. See above, p. 5, n. 9 [*Editor*].
7. Eastman, *Aunt Phillis's Cabin*, pp. 33–34; Page, *Uncle Robin in his Cabin in Virginia*, p. 136; Butt, *Antifanaticism*, p. 85.
8. Eastman, *Aunt Phillis's Cabin*, pp. 102–3; Gen. 16:1–6; [Smythe], *Ethel Somers*, p. 118.

The opposite of the loyal black slave in anti–Uncle Tom literature is the rebellious slave who runs away. It is never cruel treatment which causes him to flee. Either he is sullen or unruly by nature or he is too foolish to know when he is well off and is thus vulnerable to the wiles of abolitionists who whisper the delights of freedom in his ear. The slave Charles in Randolph's *The Cabin and Parlor* is portrayed as one of these foolish persons. "His light and graceful figure, as he walked, had that swaying motion, which seems peculiar to races of tropical blood," says the narrator of the novel. "His eyes were large and bright and intelligent. Yet his face, expressive as it was, gave the idea of weakness. His attire was somewhat dandyfied. Having always lived at the mansion, where he heard only the most refined conversation, he had a vocabulary almost as correct as that of his late master." When he runs away to Philadelphia with his wife Cora, also a slave, he loses his self-confidence immediately. "Not every one of the harder and sterner race to which we belong," says the narrator, "can realize, to its full extent at least, the prostration of spirits which overcame both Charles and Cora. Self-reliance is the peculiar characteristic of the Anglo-Saxon."[9]

* * *

In anti–Uncle Tom literature there are generally two quite different kinds of abolitionists. In a few instances, they are well intentioned but foolish and misguided. Usually, however, they are mean, narrow, and hypocritical. Their meanness to the people with whom they associate contrasts with the philanthropy they frequently feel for slaves who are a long way off. Nearly all the abolitionists are men. In Hall's *Frank Freeman's Barber Shop*, the president of the abolition society in Boston is the Reverend Ananias Sharpington, D.D. He has an "ultra-bilious complexion," a nose like the bill of a hawk, and two "gray-green" eyes which are crossed. His theological creed is unorthodox. He believes in the "higher law," and if it should lead to "theft, murder, anarchy, all was *fiat justia!*" Black is his "all absorbing color." His clothes are black, including his stockings. He loves funerals because of their black crepe. He has a black horse, keeps a "black boy" to "black" his boots, drinks a "black tea," and "in short, was black inside as well as out." The level of hatred of abolitionists by some of the anti–Uncle Tom writers is suggested by the fact that in Mathews's *Old Toney and His Master* there is an abolitionist who dies and goes to hell. Abolition is not specifically mentioned as the reason for his damnation, but it is probably meant to figure as part of the indictment against him. Alfred Orton, the abolitionist, confronts after his death "an infinite ocean of fire,

9. Randolph, *The Cabin and Parlor*, pp. 27, 110.

whose waves, hot and burning, would ever roll, and surge, and hiss and roar, above his guilty head and his damned-forever spirit."[1]

Sometimes the abolitionists in anti–Uncle Tom literature are the victims of their own duplicity. In Hall's *Frank Freeman's Barber Shop*, an abolitionist is fairly caught when he attends a black wedding and is asked to kiss the bride. He shows his hypocrisy by refusing and slinking off. In Criswell's *"Uncle Tom's Cabin" Contrasted with Buckingham Hall*, there is a foolish abolitionist who comes to the South. He is unable to distinguish pure whites from those mulattoes who have a small amount of black intermixture. When southern white men introduce him to a woman who is partly black, he woos and marries her, ignorant of the trick which has been played upon him. Criswell has another abolitionist in the novel, a man with the revealing name of S. S. Doubleface. He leaves his home in Boston to visit for several months in the South. He buys a woman slave who can pass as a white and takes her to stay with him at a fashionable hotel in New Orleans. He writes to his wife back in Boston, telling her that he is "daily instilling *moral precepts* into the minds of all." Unluckily for him, one of his Boston acquaintances who is also visiting in New Orleans sees him in the hotel with his paramour, and threatens to expose Doubleface unless he leaves her. Doubleface is obliged to sell her at a "half price" discount.[2]

The sexual motive as an explanation for abolitionism is prominent in anti–Uncle Tom literature. In her *Ellen; or the Fanatic's Daughter*, Mrs. V. G. Cowdin has a profligate abolitionist character. He "professed to be a minister of the Gospel, but in reality, used religion as a mere cloak beneath which, for a time, his vices were effectively hid." Sometimes abolitionist characters come to the South in disguise. They foment rebellion among the slaves and seduce the slave women. Cassie, one of the slave women in W. L. G. Smith's *Life at the South*, tells her master that Mr. Bates, the northern tutor of the white children on the plantation, has "been gallant" with her and has coaxed her "to go ober de hill" with him. The abolitionist is thus discovered and is obliged to flee to the North. In the anonymous *Mr. Frank, the Underground Mail Agent*, a novel written under the pseudonym *Vidi*, the narrator describes an abolition convention. Several "rakish-looking old Quakers" are careful to seat themselves beside "buxom-looking negro-wenches." They engage in "sly ogling, and secret pressure of the waist," and are rewarded with "a corresponding rolling of the eye, with an unlimited display of ivory." Also at the convention are "huge, amorous-looking negro gallants"

1. Hall, *Frank Freeman's Barber Shop*, pp. 174–81; [Mathews], *Old Toney and His Master*, p. 383.
2. Hall, *Frank Freeman's Barber Shop*, pp. 281–82; Criswell, *"Uncle Tom's Cabin" Contrasted with Buckingham Hall*, pp. 60–62, 143–45.

who have come to flirt with white "country girls." They begin with "sly and sheepish glances." As they grow bolder, they cause "some very deep blushes to mantle over fair faces, except in those cases in which all traces of female modesty . . . [have] disappeared." A different kind of evil afflicts other abolitionists at the convention. Wealthy people, they grieve over the wrongs done to slaves in the South, but not to their own servants. Not far away their white coachmen are patiently awaiting them atop their carriages in freezing weather.[3]

* * *

Anti–Uncle Tom writers discuss colonization as a possible answer to the problem of slavery. The narrator of Hall's *Frank Freeman's Barber Shop* advises free blacks to go to Africa, where they can hold up their heads. The narrator of Page's *Uncle Robin in his Cabin in Virginia* says that if slaves could by some extraordinary means be freed, they should be returned to Africa. The narrator of Randolph's *The Cabin and Parlor* says that colonization of blacks in Africa may be "God's will." The narrator of *Mr. Frank, the Underground Mail-Agent*, thinks colonization would be a blessing for the United States but that it would be too expensive to reimburse the slaveholders for their property and to transport the former slaves to Africa.[4]

With the exception of Thomas Bangs Thorpe in *The Master's House*, the authors of anti–Uncle Tom literature have few suggestions to make concerning possible reforms of slavery. Maria J. McIntosh in *The Lofty and the Lowly* has her narrator say that southerners need to consider some changes in their treatment of slaves. "[W]e have sinned against them not by cruelty, but by neglect," the narrator observes. "To acknowledge the truth, we Southerners have a great deal of 'Laissez faire' about us in all things. . . . But we are waking up, and if we can only shut our ears to the crude speculations of those who seek to teach where they ought to be contented to learn—we may yet make amends to our people and the world for our long sleep." The narrator does not go on to list what changes in slavery should be made. In a backhanded way, other anti–Uncle Tom writers sometimes admit that slavery may have serious faults as an institution. "I have no wish to uphold slavery," says the narrator of Eastman's *Aunt Phillis's Cabin*. "I would that every human being that God has made were free, were it in accordance with His

3. Cowdin, *Ellen*, p. 5; Smith, *Life at the South*, p. 270; Vidi [pseud.], *Mr. Frank, the Underground Mail-Agent*, p. 28.
4. Hall, *Frank Freeman's Barber Shop*, p. 236; Page, *Uncle Robin in His Cabin in Virginia*, p. 217; Randolph, *The Cabin and Parlor*, pp. 259–60; Vidi [pseud.], *Mr. Frank, the Underground Mail-Agent*, pp. 234–35.

will. . . . Neither do I desire to deny the evils of slavery. . . . I only assert the necessity of the existence of slavery at present in our Southern states, and that, as a general thing, the slaves are comfortable and contented, and their owners humane and kind." Sometimes the defenders of slavery came near throwing up their hands in despair at the stubbornness of abolitionists. "[S]how us any fair, open, practical system for universal emancipation," says the narrator of Hall's *Frank Freeman's Barber Shop*, "and the South will erect you a monument, and call you *Pater Patriae*." The narrator of Rush's *The North and South* says she would "rejoice to see the bondsman go free, and every slave walk forth in the light of liberty." Whether and when the slaves should be free, she adds, should be left wholly to the discretion of white southerners, and abolitionists were only making things worse. The narrator of Mr. *Frank, the Underground Mail-Agent* tells of a slaveowner who is at the point of emancipating his slaves. Irritated past endurance by the fanaticism of abolitionists, he changes his mind at the last moment and keeps them in slavery.[5]

It is not the South which should change its ways, the anti–Uncle Tom writers generally say. The North is the region which needs most to examine its conscience and pursue a new course. The narrator of Hentz's *The Planter's Northern Bride* sorrowfully contemplates the evils which lie ahead. "[T]he stars of the Union may be quenched in the smoking, and the American eagle flap its wings in blood," she says. She bitterly reflects that the children of abolitionists of the North may emigrate to the South only to be killed in a slave insurrection. "[Y]our daughter, clasping her innocent babes to her bosom," she says, "may lift her dying eyes to heaven, feeling the conviction, keener than her last death pang, that a father's hand guided the blow of which she is the victim." Even worse is the possibility of civil war. "Can you sever the interests of the North and the South," she asks the people of the North, "without lifting a fratricidal hand?" Most of the other anti–Uncle Tom writers were not as pessimistic as Caroline Lee Hentz on this point. On the other hand, they express the conviction that if serious trouble were to come, it would be the fault of the North. The South, in their view, was almost wholly blameless in the disaster which seemed to be approaching.[6]

5. McIntosh, *The Lofty and the Lowly*, 2:318; Eastman, *Aunt Phillis's Cabin*, p. 277; Hall, *Frank Freeman's Barber Shop*, p. 76; [Rush], *The North and South*, p. 24; Vidi [pseud.], *Mr. Frank, the Underground Mail-Agent*, pp. 162–63.
6. Hentz, *The Planter's Northern Bride*, 1:237–39.

# MARY C. HENDERSON

## [Tom-Shows]†

* * *

Recognizing [*Uncle Tom's Cabin's*] dramatic possibilities, several playwrights soon turned the book, or parts of it, into melodrama. The most successful theatrical adaptation was made by a member of a company housed in the Troy Museum, an imitation of P. T. Barnum's famous American Museum in New York City. George C. Howard, leading man and manager of the upstate New York troupe, had a precocious four-year-old daughter, Cordelia, who had captivated Troy Museum audiences as an "infant prodigy" (in that age Americans doted on child actors). Howard was looking for a theater piece that would enable him to capitalize on his daughter's popularity. Mrs. Stowe's novel was on everyone's lips, and someone suggested that it might be dramatized so that Cordelia could play Little Eva. Howard approached his cousin George L. Aiken, an actor in the company and a would-be playwright. For forty dollars and a gold watch, Aiken made a four-act play out of the part of the novel in which Little Eva figured prominently. A short time later, he wrote a four-act sequel, which carried Uncle Tom to his death on Simon Legree's plantation. Eventually the two plays were combined in a six-act drama with thirty scenes and eight tableaux. Beginning in the fall of 1852, it ran at the Troy Museum for one hundred performances which, to use Howard's comparison, was like a seven-year run in New York.

Howard took Aiken's play to New York and to instant success, and he and his family continued to troupe with it for the next thirty-five years. Though its initial attraction was little Cordelia as Eva, its triumphant character was Uncle Tom. Never before had there been a stage Negro like him. For many years, the black man had been portrayed onstage as a lazy, shifty, ungrammatical servant and was exploited for his comic possibilities. During the evolution of the minstrel show, musical and dancing talents were added to his comic portrait, but no one had ever attempted a serious treatment, on the supposition that it would not be accepted by audiences. The early dramatizations of *Uncle Tom's Cabin* changed all that, and the impact of the play was incalculable. Not only did it travel like wildfire throughout the United States (with, of course, the exception of the South), it jumped the ocean and became, if imag-

† From *Theater in America* by Mary C. Henderson (New York: Abrams, 1986). 

inable, even more popular in England and Europe. The number of productions fell off somewhat during the Civil War, but *Uncle Tom's Cabin* played on and was revived in the postwar years to become a national institution and a theatrical industry called "Tomming." In 1900 there were five hundred troupes performing it on the road, and in 1931, after *Theatre Arts Monthly* published an article entitled "Uncle Tom Is Dead," letters poured in to report that the show was alive, well, and playing in cities and towns throughout the country.

Since 1852 the play has undergone a multitude of transformations. It has been musicalized, minstrelized, filmed, broadcast, telecast, excerpted, and choreographed. Little Eva has been played by a host of actresses, including Shirley Temple. In the hands of Mrs. Howard,[1] Judy Garland, and many others, Topsy, the black elf, has elicited both tears and laughter from audiences for nearly a century and a half. Uncle Tom's original character was almost totally obliterated in the worst and cheapest dramatizations. Somewhere in tents set among the cornfields he lost his dignity and his persona and became the servile, obedient, sycophantic black man who gave the term "Uncle Tom" its terrible taint. The play continued to represent both the best and worst of American society long after the novel had disappeared from the family library. There is no adequate explanation for its durability. Perhaps in the absence of an American mythology it has slipped in to fill the gap. Whatever the reasons, no other play before or since has had such a special life on the American stage, and its reverberations have continued to be felt in the work of such twentieth-century playwrights as Tennessee Williams.

* * *

1. In the 1850s, Mrs. George C. Howard was famous for her portrayal of Topsy in productions of *Uncle Tom's Cabin* by her husband's theater company [*Editor*].

*Tom-Show Poster.* From J. C. Furnas, *Goodbye to Uncle Tom* (New York: William Sloane, 1956).

# CRITICISM

# Nineteenth-Century Reviews and Reception

## GEORGE SAND

### Review of *Uncle Tom's Cabin*†

To review a book, the very morrow after its appearance, in the very journal where it has just been published, is doubtless contrary to usage, but in this case it is the most disinterested homage that can be rendered, since the immense success attained by this work at its publication does not need to be set forth.

This book is in all hands and in all journals. It has, and will have, editions in every form; people devour it, they cover it with tears. It is no longer permissible to those who can read not to have read it, and one mourns that there are so many souls condemned never to read it,—helots of poverty, slaves through ignorance, for whom society has been unable as yet to solve the double problem of uniting the food of the body with the food of the soul.

It is not, then, it cannot be, an officious and needless task to review this book of Mrs. Stowe. We repeat, it is a homage, and never did a generous and pure work merit one more tender and spontaneous. She is far from us; we do not know her who has penetrated our hearts with emotions so sad and yet so sweet. Let us thank her the more. Let the gentle voice of woman, the generous voice of man, with the voices of little children, so adorably glorified in this book, and those of the oppressed of this old world, let them cross the seas and hasten to say to her that she is esteemed and beloved!

If the best eulogy which one can make of the author is to love her, the truest that one can make of the book is to love its very faults. It has faults,—we need not pass them in silence, we need not

† From Annie Fields, ed., *Life and Letters of Harriet Beecher Stowe* (Boston: Houghton Mifflin, 1898); originally published in *La Presse* (17 Dec. 1852). In autumn 1852, three French periodicals were simultaneously serializing unauthorized translations of the enormously popular *Uncle Tom's Cabin*; for one of these publications, *La Presse*, the French writer George Sand (1804–1876) wrote two columns celebrating the novel.

evade the discussion of them,—but you need not be disturbed about them, you who are rallied on the tears you have shed over the fortunes of the poor victims in a narrative so simple and true.

These defects exist only in relation to the conventional rules of art, which never have been and never will be absolute. If its judges, possessed with the love of what they call "artistic work," find unskillful treatment in the book, look well at them to see if their eyes are dry when they are reading this or that chapter.

They will recall to your mind that Ohio senator, who, having sagely demonstrated to his little wife that it is a political duty to refuse asylum and help to the fugitive slave, ends by taking two in his own carriage, in a dark night, over fearful roads, where he must from time to time plunge into mud to his waist to push on the vehicle. This charming episode in "Uncle Tom" (a digression, if you will) paints well the situation of most men placed between their prejudices and established modes of thought and the spontaneous and generous intuitions of their hearts.

It is the history, at the same time affecting and pleasing, of many independent critics. Whatever they may be in the matter of social or literary questions, those who pretend always to judge by strict rules are often vanquished by their own feelings, and sometimes vanquished when unwilling to avow it.

I have always been charmed by the anecdote of Voltaire, ridiculing and despising the fables of La Fontaine,[1] seizing the book and saying, "Look here, now, you will see in the very first one"—he reads one. "Well, that is passable, but see how stupid this is!"—he reads a second, and finds after all that it is quite pretty; a third disarms him again, and at last he throws down the volume, saying, with ingenuous spite, "It's nothing but a collection of masterpieces." Great souls may be bilious and vindictive, but it is impossible for them to remain unjust and insensible.

It, however, should be said to people of culture, who profess to be able to give correct judgments, that if their culture is of the truest kind it will never resist a just and right emotion. Therefore it is that this book, defective according to the rules of the modem French romance, intensely interests everybody and triumphs over all criticisms in the discussions it causes in domestic circles.

For this book is essentially domestic and of the family,—this book, with its long discussions, its minute details, its portraits carefully studied. Mothers of families, young girls, little children, servants even, can read and understand them, and men themselves, even the most superior, cannot disdain them. We do not say that the suc-

1. Jean de La Fontaine (1621–1695), French poet. François Voltaire (1694–1778), French author of the Enlightenment [*Editor*].

cess of the book is because its great merits redeem its faults; we say its success is because of these very alleged faults.

For a long time we have striven in France against the prolix explanations of Walter Scott. We have cried out against those of Balzac,[2] but on consideration have perceived that the painter of manners and character has never done too much, that every stroke of the pencil was needed for the general effect. Let us learn then to appreciate all kinds of treatment, when the effect is good, and when they bear the seal of a master hand.

Mrs. Stowe is all instinct; it is the very reason that she appears to some not to have talent. Has she not talent? What is talent? Nothing, doubtless, compared to genius; but has she genius? I cannot say that she has talent as one understands it in the world of letters, but she has genius, as humanity feels the need of genius,—the genius of goodness, not that of the man of letters, but of the saint. Yes,—a saint! Thrice holy the soul which thus loves, blesses, and consoles the martyrs. Pure, penetrating, and profound the spirit which thus fathoms the recesses of the human soul. Noble, generous, and great the heart which embraces in her pity, in her love, an entire race, trodden down in blood and mire under the whip of ruffians and the maledictions of the impious.

Thus should it be, thus should we value things ourselves. We should feel that genius is heart, that power is *faith*, that talent is *sincerity*, and, finally, *success is sympathy*, since this book overcomes us, since it penetrates the breast, pervades the spirit, and fills us with a strange sentiment of mingled tenderness and admiration for a poor negro lacerated by blows, prostrate in the dust, there gasping on a miserable pallet, his last sigh exhaled towards God.

In matters of art there is but one rule, to paint and to move. And where shall we find creations more complete, types more vivid, situations more touching, more original, than in "Uncle Tom,"—those beautiful relations of the slave with the child of his master, indicating a state of things unknown among us; the protest of the master himself against slavery during that innocent part of life when his soul belongs to God alone? Afterwards, when society takes him, the law chases away God, and interest deposes conscience. In coming to mature years the infant ceases to be *man* and becomes master. God dies in his soul.

What hand has ever drawn a type more fascinating and admirable than St. Clair,—this exceptional nature, noble, generous, and loving, but too soft and too nonchalant to be really great? Is it not man himself, human nature itself, with its innate virtues, its good

2. Honoré de Balzac (1799–1850), French novelist. Sir Walter Scott (1771–1832), Scottish novelist and poet [*Editor*].

aspirations, and its deplorable failures?—this charming master who loves and is beloved, who thinks and reasons, but concludes nothing and does nothing? He spends in his day treasures of indulgence, of consideration, of goodness; he dies without having accomplished anything. The story of his precious life is all told in a word,—"to aspire and to regret." He has never learned to *will.* Alas! is there not something of this even among the bravest and best of men?

The life and death of a little child and of a negro slave!—that is the whole book! This negro and this child are two saints of heaven! The affection that unites them, the respect of these two perfect ones for each other, is the only love-story, the only passion of the drama. I know not what other genius but that of sanctity itself could shed over this affection and this situation a charm so powerful and so sustained. The child reading the Bible on the knees of the slave, dreaming over its mysteries and enjoying them in her exceptional maturity; now covering him with flowers like a doll, and now looking to him as something sacred, passing from tender playfulness to tender veneration, and then fading away through a mysterious malady which seems to be nothing but the wearing of pity in a nature too pure, too divine, to accept earthly law; dying finally in the arms of the slave, and calling him after her to the bosom of God,—all this is so new, so beautiful, that one asks one's self in thinking of it whether the success which has attended the work is after all equal to the height of the conception.

Children are the true heroes of Mrs. Stowe's works. Her soul, the most motherly that could be, has conceived of these little creatures in a halo of grace. George Shelby, the little Harry, the cousin of Eva, the regretted babe of the little wife of the Senator, and Topsy, the poor, diabolic, excellent Topsy,—all the children that one sees, and even those that one does not see in this romance, but of whom one has only a few words from their desolate mothers, seem to us a world of little angels, white and black, where any mother may recognize some darling of her own, source of her joys and tears. In taking form in the spirit of Mrs. Stowe, these children, without ceasing to be children, assume ideal graces, and come at last to interest us more than the personages of an ordinary love-story.

Women, too, are here judged and painted with a master hand; not merely mothers who are sublime, but women who are not mothers either in heart or in fact, and whose infirmities are treated with indulgence or with rigor. By the side of the methodical Miss Ophelia, who ends by learning that duty is good for nothing without love, Marie St. Clair is a frightfully truthful portrait. One shudders in thinking that she exists, that she is everywhere, that each of us has met her and seen her, perhaps, not far from us, for it is only necessary that this charming creature should have slaves to torture, and we should see her revealed complete through her vapors and her nervous complaints.

The saints also have their claw! it is that of the lion. She buries it deep in the conscience, and a little of burning indignation and of terrible sarcasm does not, after all, misbecome this Harriet Stowe, this woman so gentle, so humane, so religious, and full of evangelical unction. Ah! yes, she is a very good woman, but not what we derisively call "goody good." Hers is a heart strong and courageous, which in blessing the unhappy and applauding the faithful, tending the feeble and succoring the irresolute, does not hesitate to bind to the pillory the hardened tyrant, to show to the world his deformity.

She is, in the true spirit of the word, consecrated. Her fervent Christianity sings the praise of the martyr, but permits no man the right to perpetuate the wrong. She denounces that strange perversion of Scripture which tolerates the iniquity of the oppressor because it gives opportunity for the virtues of the victims. She calls on God himself, and threatens in his name; she shows us human law on one side, and God on the other!

Let no one say that, because she exhorts to patient endurance of wrong, she justifies those who do the wrong. Read the beautiful page where George Harris, the white slave, embraces for the first time the shores of a free territory, and presses to his heart wife and child, who at last are *his own*. What a beautiful picture, that! What a large heart-throb! what a triumphant protest of the eternal and inalienable right of man to liberty!

Honor and respect to you, Mrs. Stowe! Some day your recompense, which is already recorded in heaven, will come also in this world.

# WILLIAM G. ALLEN

## [About *Uncle Tom's Cabin*]†

* * *

I have recently read "Uncle Tom." What a book! It is, in its line, the wonder of wonders. How its descriptions stir the blood, indeed almost make it leap out of the heart! What delineations of character—St. Clare and Legree, extremes of slaveholders. While the latter is a fit representative of the system of the pit, the former shows that not even slaveholding itself can blot out every whit of whatsoever is good

† Originally a letter to the editor, this piece is from *Frederick Douglass' Paper* 20 May 1852: 3. All notes are by the editor of this Norton Critical Edition.

in the human heart. Thank God for this little space wherein one vivifying ray may enter!

Uncle Tom was a good soul, thoroughly and perfectly pious. Indeed, if any man had too much piety, Uncle Tom was that man. I confess to more of "total depravity." More shame to me, possibly, but nevertheless, such is the fact. My non-resistance is that of the Douglass, Parker, and Phillips[1] school. I believe, as you do, that it is not light the slaveholder wants, but *fire*, and he ought to have it. I do not advocate revenge, but simply, resistance to tyrants; if it need be, to the death.

The religious conversation between the slave-traders, on the 102nd and 3rd pages,[2] is a capital thing. Why do you not copy it?—How it tells upon the miserable spittle-licking religionists of the present day; who, as Tom Loker has it, are running up a bill all their lives with the devil, calculating to sneak out when pay time comes. Such religion is "p'ison mean,"—it is "dog meanness."

The story of the Quadroon girl, second book, thirty-fourth chapter, exceeds anything that I have ever read, in all that is soul-searching and thrilling. Indeed, the book is marvellous for its dramatic power, and I do not wonder that cheap editions are now being called for throughout the Northern States.

I have one regret, with regard to the book, and that is that the chapter favoring colonization was ever written. I do not, however, apprehend so much harm from it, as some others seem to anticipate. Many of the bad features of that chapter, are somewhat modified by the admission, on the 302nd page,[3] of the right of the colored people to meet and mingle in this country—to rise by their individual worth, and without distinction of caste or color; and that they have not only the rights of the common men here, but more than these, the rights of an injured race for reparation; and still further, that those who deny this right to rise without distinction of caste or color, and in particular to rise *here*, are false to their own professed principles of human equality.

I have no objection to the christianization of Africa. God speed the missionaries who go thither for so high and holy purpose—Those also, be they white or colored, who go to build republics upon her shores, go to perform a work, great, grand, and glorious—God speed them also. Liberia is a pigmy, and cannot be more. Great men could as soon grow up and flourish in Greenland, as

1. For Douglass, see above, p. 407, n. 9. Theodore Parker (1810–1860) was a Boston theologian, Transcendentalist, and social reformer active in the abolitionist movement. Wendell Phillips (1811–1884), a reformer and orator, was an associate of William Lloyd Garrison and a contributor to the *Liberator*.
2. See above, pp. 60–61.
3. See above, p. 397.

on that part of the Guinea Coast, where these colonists have settled.

As to the talk about African nationality, this is sheer nonsense, if by African nationality is meant, a nation composed entirely of pure Africans. Nations worthy of the name, are only produced by a fusion of races. If Americans had less prejudice, they could read history more clearly. Whence the Romans! The Magyars! The English! The Americans! The latter, at least, notwithstanding they roll up their eyes, and go into pretended fits, at the mere mention of amalgamation, are, of all the races, the most amalgamated under the sun; and, as a matter of course—the most energetic and powerful. Indeed, fusion of races seems to be a trait distinctive of Americans. The shades of night scarce gather round them, ere they (the Americans) seek amalgamation with even the very race which they affect most to despise. Talk of the "instincts of nature"—the hypocrites!

That the bona fide African race has peculiarities, I admit; and I admit, farther, that if these peculiarities are drawn out without intermixture, they will develop a civilization very good indeed; indeed, so good as to be almost good for nothing. The Saxons unmixed with the Romans, the Normans and the Danes were a clever people—no more—The feeble Asiatics unmixed with the Persians and the Hunns, are not Magyars. And the Jews, who are Jews still, excite next to no interest in the great world of science, literature, and art. The plain truth is, God has made us of one blood, and thereby, to intermingle. We progress by adhering to this rule, we go backward by its violation. Nations, there must be, but merely as conveniences, not to abrogate the great law of equal brotherhood.

One word more, with regard to the book. It contains some happy hits at prejudice against color. These are timely. Abolitionists, by the hundreds, are not yet rid of this soul-harrowing and heart-belittling feeling, this "blasphemy against God," and "quarrel with Jehovah." It is so easy to talk, and so comparatively easy to practice within circles not exceedingly obnoxious to the community, that many delude themselves with the belief that they are at one with the doctrine of an equal brotherhood, and are even christian, when their hearts are polluted, with a prejudice which is, beyond all question, a sin meaner than which none ever rankled in the freeman's heart. Oh, for more good, great men, and more great good men. A friend wrote me, not long since, and in his letter, wished that the Lord would let Gerrit Smith[4] live to be as old as Methuselah. Did I believe that slavery and prejudice could exist in this land nine hundred years longer, I would second the wish, and not only that Gerrit Smith should live thus

4. A reformer and abolitionist (1797–1874) who organized the Liberty party and served in Congress in 1853.

long, but Lyndon King, Beriah Green, Garrison,[5] and such as these, who have bedwarfed themselves in their age, as Milton did in his, by keeping ahead so far. These are earth's noble spirits. Thank God, the time will come if not speedily, still surely, when men shall acknowledge, by word as in their inmost soul, that righteousness is true greatness, and that there is no glory but in living in accordance with principles which are just and holy, and true.

I do not despair.

> "Still achieving, still pursuing,
> Learn to labor and to wait."[6]

Let us take this to our hearts, at least, that slavery is a national sin, and nations are not fixed facts, but are continually, though may be slowly, passing away.

Faithfully yours,
WILLIAM G. ALLEN
MCGRAWVILLE, N.Y., May 6, 1852.

# ETHIOP

## Review of *Uncle Tom's Cabin*†

### *From Our Brooklyn Correspondent*

* * * "*Uncle Tom's Cabin*!" "*Uncle Tom's Cabin*" is all the topic here, aside from the vulgar theme of politics; which, (though surface broad penetrates no deeper) is at present well nigh being eclipsed by its greater rival, my "*Uncle Tom's Cabin,*" since its entry into Gotham.[1]

*Mrs. Beecher Stowe* has deserved well of her country, in thus bringing *Uncle Tom's Cabin*, and all its associations, from the sunny *South*, into these *Northern regions*, and placing it upon the *Northern track*, and sending it thence round the land. This species of abolitionism finds its way into quarters here, hitherto so faced over with the adamant of pro-slavery politics, unionism, churchism, and every other shade of "*ism*" hammered out, and welded on by his *satanic majesty* and faithful subjects, for the last half century, that it completely staggers belief and puts credulity wholly at fault. Shopkeepers that heretofore exposed for sale, but fancy articles for South-

5. All three were prominent abolitionists.
6. From "A Psalm of Life" (1839) by Henry Wadsworth Longfellow (1807–82).
† From *Frederick Douglass' Paper* 17 June 1852: 3. Ethiop is the pen name of William J. Wilson.
1. I.e., New York City [*Editor*].

ern gentry, ponderous volumes for the benefit of Southern slavery, Webster speeches and other dough-faced articles for Southern benefits; or, exhibited in their windows Zip Coon, or JIM CROW,[2] with his naked toes kicking out the panes, for general amusement, profit and loyalty to the Southern God; I say that these very shopkeepers are now proud to illume those very windows through the windows of my *Uncle Tom's Cabin*; while good *Old Aunt Chloe* peeps out just to see what the matter is. May she continue to look out until every Uncle Tom is restored to his *God-given rights*—his full manhood—. till every vestige of justice is done him.

The truth is, this species of literature will soon assume its wanted place here, which is one of high eminence, and it may yet be regretted should its march be in an invented [*sic*][3] order; the blacks (who by position ought to be the more faithful delineators of oppression, and the keenest searchers after justice, that she fully does her office-work) being found in the REAR instead of being found, not merely in the FRONT RANK, but in the very LEAD. Of one thing, however, be assured, there is something in the heart of this community deeper rooted than the teachings of *politicians, demagogues*, and *robed priests*, and it is growing, and will, if they do not mend their ways, and change their teaching, in its giant-strength, eject them from society, and consign them to their proper place—*Oblivion*.

One thing more; prosaic writers—*white* or *black*, may ere long lay down their pens, that are not whetted to wield in behalf of the rights, and the equality of man; for "to this complexion we must all come at last:" and high on the willows may poets hang their harps, if not attuned to sing of this noble theme:

> For who that hath a soul, can no longer wake their muse,
> E'en now, to sing of tyrants baser deeds in praise;
> Or who can longer string their harps in praise of wrong!
> Base, black, unmittigated wrong, and feel he's not a thing!!
> A dog whose steps are hurrying from the road where tread
> the truly good.

When, my dear sir, I take a perspective look up the path of the bright future, the reflection it induces, "brings the light of other days around me."

* * *

Yours truly,
ETHIOP

Brooklyn Heights, June 5th, 1852.

2. Both are derogatory caricatures of African Americans [*Editor*].
3. See below, p. 570, n. 5 [*Editor*].

# GEORGE F. HOLMES

## Review of *Uncle Tom's Cabin*†

Macaulay,[1] in the opening paragraph of his *Essay on the Life of Addison*, discusses the question whether lady authors should or should not be dealt with according to strict critical justice. The gallant reviewer gives as his opinion, that while lady writers should not be permitted to teach "inaccurate history or unsound philosophy" with impunity, it were well that critics should so far recognize the immunities of the sex as to blunt the edge of their severity towards the offenders. And he instances, as pertinent to the critic's position, the case of the Knight, who being compelled by duty to keep the lists against Bradamante, was fain, before the combat commenced, to exchange Balisarda for a lighter and less fatal weapon, with which, however, he fought well and successfully.[2]

For ourselves, we are free to say that we quite coincide with Mr. Macaulay, in the exact terms of his proposition. But we beg to make a distinction between *lady* writers and *female* writers. We could not find it in our hearts to visit the dulness or ignorance of a well-meaning lady with the rigorous discipline which it is necessary to inflict upon male dunces and blockheads. But where a writer of the softer sex manifests, in her productions, a shameless disregard of truth and of those amenities which so peculiarly belong to her sphere of life, we hold that she has forfeited the claim to be considered a lady, and with that claim all exemption from the utmost stringency of critical punishment. It will not indeed suffice, to work this forfeiture, that she merely step beyond the limits of female delicacy. A Joan of Arc, unsexed though she be, in complete armour, mounted *en chevalier*, and battling for the defence of her native land, might, perhaps come within the rule of knightly courtesy. But the Thalestris of Billingsgate,[3] coarse of speech and strong of arm, hurling unwomanly oaths and unwomanly blows at whom she chooses to assail, would probably be met by a male opponent, (if he could not run away from her,) in a very different manner.

Mrs. Stowe—to whose work of "Uncle Tom's Cabin" we now propose to devote ourselves—is neither one nor the other of the characters we have described. She is not a Joan of Arc. She is not a fishwoman. She is something less noble than the Gallic heroine: she

† From *The Southern Literary Messenger* 18 (October 1852). Except where otherwise indicated, all notes are by the editor of this Norton Critical Edition.

1. Thomas Babington Macaulay (1800–1859), English historian and author.
2. Bradamante is a female adventurer in *Orlando Furioso*, by Ludovico Ariosto (1474–1533).
3. In Greek myth, Thalestris was queen of the Amazons, a tribe of women warriors; here the name refers ironically to a fishwife of a London market famous for foul language.

is certainly a much more refined person than the virago of the Thames. Yet with all her cultivation she has placed herself without the pale of kindly treatment at the hands of Southern criticism. Possessed of a happy faculty of description, an easy and natural style, an uncommon command of pathos and considerable dramatic skill, she might, in the legitimate exercise of such talents, have done much to enrich the literature of America, and to gladden and elevate her fellow beings. But she has chosen to employ her pen for purposes of a less worthy nature. She has volunteered officiously to intermeddle with things which concern her not—to libel and vilify people from among whom have gone forth some of the noblest men that have adorned the race—to foment heartburnings and unappeasable hatred between brethren of a common country, the joint heirs of that country's glory—to sow, in this blooming garden of freedom, the seeds of strife and violence and all direful contentions. Perhaps, indeed, she might declare that such was not her design—and she wished, by the work now under consideration, to *persuade* us of the horrible guilt of Slavery, and with the kindest feelings for us as brethren, to teach us that our constitution and laws are repugnant to every sentiment of humanity. We know that among other novel doctrines in vogue in the land of Mrs. Stowe's nativity—the pleasant land of New England—which we are old-fashioned enough to condemn, is one which would place woman on a footing of political equality with man, and causing her to look beyond the office for which she was created—the high and holy office of maternity—would engage her in the administration of public affairs; thus handing over the State to the perilous protection of diaper diplomatists and wet-nurse politicians. Mrs. Stowe, we believe, belongs to this school of Woman's Rights, and on this ground she may assert her prerogative to teach us how wicked are we ourselves and the Constitution under which we live. But such a claim is in direct conflict with the letter of scripture, as we find it recorded in the second chapter of the First Epistle to Timothy—

> "Let the woman learn in silence with all subjection."
> *"But I suffer not a woman to teach, nor to usurp authority over the man, but to be in silence."*

But whatever her designs may have been, it is very certain that she has shockingly traduced the slaveholding society of the United States, and we desire to be understood as acting entirely on the defensive, when we proceed to expose the miserable misrepresentations of her story. We shall be strongly tempted, in the prosecution of this task, to make use, now and then, of that terse, expressive, little Saxon monosyllable which conventionalism has properly judged inadmissible in debate, yet we trust we shall be able to overcome the temptation, and in the very torrent and tempest of our wrath, (while declining to "carry the war into *Africa*,") to "acquire and beget a temperance which may give it smoothness."

While we deem it quite necessary, in this place, to lay before our readers in detail the plot of "Uncle Tom's Cabin," still we shall best accomplish our purpose by running over the leading incidents of the novel. But even this will not be the easiest thing in the world. We have given Mrs. Stowe credit for dramatic skill. Yet it will be seen that as a dramatist she is, by no means, without some glaring faults. It is a rule of art, (judged by which Fielding's *Tom Jones*[4] has been pronounced by the best critics to be almost perfect,) that a work of fiction should be so joined together, that every passage and incident should contribute to bring about an inevitable though unexpected catastrophe. Mrs. Stowe's events have many of them no connection with each other whatever. She has two principal characters, for whom the reader's sympathy is enlisted, whose paths never lie within a thousand miles of each other. Whenever she brings Uncle Tom forward, George Harris is moved backward, whenever she entertains us with George Harris, Uncle Tom's rights as a hero are in abeyance, wherein Mrs. Stowe reminds us of the ventriloquial vaudevilles of the facetious Mr. Love, who, individually representing the entire *dramatis personae*, is compelled to withdraw as Captain Cutandthrust, before he can fascinate his audience with Miss Matilda Die-away. Perhaps, indeed, Mrs. Stowe has proceeded upon the principle laid down by Peif in the *Critic*—

> "O Lord, yes; ever while you live have two plots to your tragedy. The grand point in managing them is only to let your under-plot have as little connection with your main plot as possible."

* * *

* * * We must pause to notice two points in the narrative. The first is the conduct which the authoress ascribes to Mrs. Shelby in conniving at Eliza's escape—conduct which is held up to us as, in the highest degree, commendable. Now, the reader must know that Mr. Shelby has acquainted his wife with the fact that Haley has become the purchaser of the slaves. The good faith of Mr. Shelby, therefore, was pledged, and his wife knew it, to the fulfilment of this portion of the contract by putting Haley in possession of them. And however painful to the feelings of that kind and excellent lady might have been the separation, the obedience due to her husband, and the regard she was bound to cherish for his word, should have restrained

4. Henry Fielding (1707–1754), English novelist, published *Tom Jones* in 1749.

her from throwing any obstacle in the way of the performance of his engagements, much more from assisting in the escape of a valuable servant. But at this place the authoress brings the "Higher Law" to bear upon Mrs. Shelby's line of duty, and as obedience to one's husband is not recognised by the new school of Woman's Rights, perhaps there is no departure herein from ethical consistency. The second point to which we wish to refer, is the utter indifference to fact and probability displayed in a conversation which the authoress details between the men who become engaged in the pursuit of Eliza. Haley, having given chase, after some delay at the Shelby mansion, comes up with Eliza just in time to see her, with the child in her arms, brave the dangers of the ice-bound Ohio and gain the opposite bank in safety * * * The matter is debated at length and a bargain is struck. The parties agree that in case of a recapture, the child is to be surrendered to Haley, who shall thereupon interpose no objection to the kidnapping of Eliza by his comrades—the said Haley paying down the just and full sum of Fifty Dollars in advance, as an indemnity against loss in the event of a failure. * * *

The reader will observe that two charges against the South are involved in this precious discourse—one, that it is the habit of Southern masters to offer a reward with the alternative of "dead or alive," for their fugitive slaves,[5] and the other, that it is usual for pursuers to shoot them. Indeed, we are led to infer that as the shooting is the easier mode of obtaining the reward, it is the more frequently employed in such cases. Now, when a Southern master offers a reward for his runaway slave, it is because he has lost a certain amount of property, represented by the negro, which he wishes to recover. To allege then that the owner, so deprived of his property, would be willing to pay an extravagant sum of money to the man who should place that property forever beyond the possibility of recovery, is so manifestly absurd and preposterous, that Mrs. Stowe will not find many readers weak enough to believe it, even in New England. What man of Vermont, having an ox or an ass that had gone astray, would forthwith offer half the full value of the animal, not for the carcass which might be turned to some useful purpose, but for the unavailing satisfaction of its head? Yet are the two cases exactly parallel. With regard to the assumption that men are permitted to go about, at the South, with double-barrelled guns, shooting down runaway negroes in preference to apprehending them, we can only say that it is as wicked and wilful as it is ridiculous. Such Thugs there may have been as Marks and Loker, who have killed negroes in this unprovoked manner, but if they have

5. Notices offering rewards for fugitive slaves captured "dead or alive" are documented in Theodore Dwight Weld's *American Slavery as It Is* (1839) 156–57.

escaped the gallows, they are probably to be found within the walls of our State Penitentiaries where they are comfortably provided for at public expense. The laws of the Southern States, which are designed, as in all good governments, for the protection of persons and property, have not been so loosely framed as to fail of their object where person and property are one.[6]

* * *

We think it well here to advert to a prominent fault of Mrs. Stowe's production, because it is exhibited as conspicuously, perhaps, in the earlier chapters as any where else. It lies in the cruel disparity, both intellectual and physical, which our authoress makes between the white and black races, to the prejudice of the former. The negro under her brush invariably becomes handsome in person or character, or in both, and not one figures in *Uncle Tom's Cabin*, no matter how benighted or besotted his condition, who does not ultimately get to heaven. But while Mrs. Stowe can thus "see Helen's beauty in a brow of Egypt," she is unable to look upon a white face without tracing in it something sinister and repulsive. The fairest of her Southern ladies retain some ugly marks of their descent from the erring mother of our race—

> Some flowers of Eden they still inherit,
> But the trail of the serpent is over them all.[7]

The white villains she describes are villains indeed. Dante[8] fell into some rather bad company when he descended with Virgil to the realms of the lost, but the demons of the Inferno are amiable and well-behaved gentlemen in comparison with Marks and Loker. On the other hand, Beatrice, soaring to the loftiest circles of the glorified, is but a commonplace damsel by the side of Eliza. See with what Titianesque[9] touches she is represented to us. The "rich, full, dark

6. It is scarcely worth our while to say more on this subject, yet the law with regard to the killing of runaways is laid down with so much clearness and precision by a South Carolina judge that we cannot forbear quoting his dictum as directly in point. In the case of *Witsell v. Earnest and Parker*, Colcock, J. delivered the opinion of the Court—

> By the statute of 1740, any white man may apprehend, and moderately correct, any slave who may be found out of the plantation at which he is employed; and if the slave assaults the white person, he may be killed; but a slave who is merely flying away cannot be killed. Nor can the defendants be justified by the common law, if we consider the negro as a person; for they were not clothed with the authority of the law to apprehend him as a felon, and without such authority he could not be killed. January term, 1818. 1 Nott & McCord's S.C. Reports. 182.

[*Holmes's note*]

7. From *Lalla Rookh* (1871), pt. 4, by the poet Thomas Moore.
8. Dante Alighieri (1265–1321), Italian poet, author of the *Divine Comedy*, a long poem describing the poet's journey through Heaven, Purgatory, and Hell.
9. I.e., in the manner of Titian, a Venetian painter (c. 1490–1576), known for his use of color.

eye with its long lashes;" the "ripples of silky black hair;" the "delicately formed hand" and "trim foot and ankle;" "the dress of the neatest possible fit," setting off to advantage "her finely moulded shape"—all these make up a picture the effect of which is heightened by the assurance that the original possesses "that peculiar air of refinement, that softness of voice and manner, which seems in many cases *to be a particular gift to the quadroon and mulatto woman.*" As for Uncle Tom, he is an epitome of the cardinal virtues, a sort of ebony St. Paul undergoing the perils, the stripes, the watchings and ultimately the martyrdom of the Apostle, with all of the Apostle's meekness and fortitude, carrying a stainless soul in an unoffending body, and walking through much tribulation, without a single turn from the straight course, to the portals of the Heavenly Kingdom. In person he is finely and powerfully made, and as manager of Mr. Shelby's estate his judgment and discretion are unparalleled in Southern agriculture. Trusted with untold gold, he never yields to the temptation of appropriating a piece of it to his own use. Resentment for injury was what Uncle Tom had never experienced. Whisky, the "peculiar wanity" of his race, has never passed his lips. Finally, whatsoever things are true, whatsoever things are honest, whatsoever things are just, whatsoever things are pure, whatsoever things are lovely, whatsoever things are of good report; if there be any virtue, and if there be any praise, all these things were blended in Uncle Tom.

In attributing this perfection to the negro character, Mrs. Stowe not only "o'ersteps the modesty of nature," but she places in a strong light the absurdity of the whole story of Mr. Shelby's sacrifice. An Irish soldier in our army was once rebuked by his commanding officer for getting drunk. "Arrah! yer honor," said Pat, "yer wouldn't be after expectin' all the Christian virtues in a man, for eight dollars a month!" In like manner we would ask if a sensible man like Mr. Shelby could be expected to sell so much of prudence, honesty, foresight, sobriety and affection as were found in Uncle Tom, for any sum that Haley would be willing to allow him? We are not told what this sum was, but judging from Haley's grinding disposition, and the fact that he afterwards sold Uncle Tom for thirteen hundred dollars, it is fair to fix his original price at One Thousand Dollars. Now, admitting Mr. Shelby's embarrassments and conceiving it possible that he could set aside all his long-standing attachment for Uncle Tom at the bidding of an insolent trader, is it likely that so valuable, or rather so invaluable, a piece of property would have been relinquished for so small a "consideration?" But a high-toned and chivalrous Kentuckian can not so easily divest himself of his humanity, and it is a slander upon that gallant State to represent the scene within her borders. The dialogue with which Mrs. Stowe's novel opens, if carried to its legitimate conclusion, would have been a short one. Mr. Shelby would have "participated matters," as Mrs. Malaprop[1] says, by knocking Haley down stairs.

* * *

St. Clare says—

> "'For pity's sake, for shame's sake, because we are men born of women, and not savage beasts, many of us do not, and dare not,—we would *scorn* to use the full power which our savage laws put into our hands. *And he who goes furthest, and does the worst, only uses within limits the power that the law gives him.*'"

We have italicised a sentence or two of this conversation to direct attention to the reckless manner in which our authoress puts loose statements into the mouths of her characters. We are told in the appendix[2] that this incident of the killing of Prue occurred "under the personal observation" of a brother of the authoress who was a clerk to a large mercantile house in New Orleans at the time. If we understand the force of language, it is here meant that this gentleman was an actual eyewitness of the murder. If so, then was he, before God and man, an accessory to the crime. For he had only, in the event that his own interposition would not have sufficed to prevent it, to call in the police to have saved Prue's life. And failing to do this—standing by, in cold blood, while a fellow-being was brutally scourged to death without an effort to rescue her—not even volunteering his evidence subsequently to ensure the punishment of the murderers, in what light can we regard his conduct other than as making him *particeps criminis*[3] of Prue's death! But Mrs. Stowe tells us, through St. Clare, that "there is no law that amounts to anything" in such cases, and that he who goes furthest in severity towards his slave, i.e. to the deprivation of an eye or a limb or even the destruction of life, "only uses within limits the power that the law gives him." This is an awful and tremendous charge, which lightly and unwarrantably made, must subject the maker to a fearful accountability. Let us see how the matter stands upon the statute-book of Louisiana. By referring to the Civil Code of that State, Chapter 3rd, Article 173, the reader will find this general declaration—

> The slave is entirely subject to the will of his master, who may correct and chastise him, *though not with unusual rigor,*

1. A character in the comedy *The Rivals* (1775) by Richard Brinsley Sheridan (1751–1816), noted for her misuse of words.
2. Stowe describes this incident in *A Key to "Uncle Tom's Cabin"* (87–88).
3. Partner in crime (Latin).

> *nor so as to maim or mutilate him, or to expose him to the danger of loss of life, or to cause his death.*

On a subsequent page of the same Volume and Chapter, Article 192, we find provision made for the slave's protection against his master's cruelty, in the statement that one of two cases, in which a master can be compelled to sell his slave, is

> When the master shall be convicted of cruel treatment of his slave, and the judge shall deem proper to pronounce, *besides the penalty established for such cases*, that the slave shall be sold at public auction, *in order to place him out of the reach of the power which the master has abused.*

A code, thus watchful of the negro's safety in life and limb, confines not its guardianship to inhibitory clauses, but proscribes extreme penalties in case of their infraction. In the Code Noir (Black Code) of Louisiana, under the head of Crimes and Offences, No. 55, § xvi, it is laid down that

> If any person whatsoever shall wilfully kill his slave or the slave of another person, the said person being convicted thereof shall be tried and condemned agreeably to the laws.

And because negro testimony is inadmissible in the courts of the State, and therefore the evidence of such crimes might be with difficulty supplied, it is further provided that

> If any slave be mutilated, beaten or ill treated contrary to the true intent and meaning of this act, when no one shall be present, in such case, the owner or other person having the management of said slave thus mutilated, shall be prosecuted without further evidence, unless the said owner or other person so as aforesaid can prove the contrary by means of good and sufficient evidence, or can clear himself by his own oath, which said oath every court under the cognizance of which such offence shall have been examined and tried, is by this act authorized to administer.
>
> Code Noir. Crimes and Offences, 56. xvii

Enough has been quoted to establish the utter falsity of the statement, made by our authoress through St. Clare, that brutal masters are "irresponsible despots"—at least in Louisiana. It would extend our review to a most unreasonable length, should we undertake to give the law, with regard to the murder of slaves, as it stands in each of the Southern States. The crime is a rare one, and therefore the Reporters have had few cases to record.

* * *

We have devoted a much larger space to the plot of "Uncle Tom's Cabin" than we designed, when we commenced this review; it only remains for us to consider briefly those points upon which the authoress rests her abuse of the Southern States, in the book as a whole. These may be reduced to three—the cruel treatment of the slaves, their lack of religious instruction, and a wanton disregard of the sacred ties of consanguinity in selling members of the same family apart from each other.

We have already shown, by a reference to the laws regulating slavery in the Southern States, that many of the allegations of cruelty towards the slaves, brought forward by Mrs. Stowe, are absolutely and unqualifiedly false. As for the comfort of their daily lives and the almost parental care taken of them on well-regulated plantations, we may say that the picture of the Shelby estate, drawn by Mrs. Stowe herself, is no bad representation. The world may safely be challenged to produce a laboring class, whose regular toil is rewarded with more of the substantial comforts of life than the negroes of the South. The "property interest" at which the authoress sneers so frequently in "Uncle Tom's Cabin," is quite sufficient to ensure for the negro a kindness and attention, which the day-laborer in New England might in vain endeavor to win from his employer. But we surely need not elaborate a point which has been settled so well by Southern writers before us.

The lack of religious instruction for slaves is a charge against the South, in great favor with Northern fanatics, many of whom are deplorably in want of "religious instruction" themselves, and vastly beneath the pious slave in that love for their neighbour which is the keystone of the Christian arch. Yet never was there a charge more extravagant. We can tell these worthies that throughout the Southern States a portion of every house of worship is set apart for the accommodation of slaves; that upon very many plantations, may be seen rude but comfortable buildings, dedicated to God, where stated preaching of His Holy Word is ordained; that Sabbath schools for negroes are established in several of the Southern cities; and that in every Southern family, almost without an exception, where morning and evening prayers are held, the domestics of the household are called together to unite in them. Instances of fervent and unaffected piety among the negroes, where they have not been tampered with by Abolitionists, are by no means rare. The entire absence of anxiety of mind, with the negro, arising from the perplexities of business and the lack of employment, and the practice, habitual to him from his birth, of resigning all care for the morrow to his master, are favorable to the reception of religious truth, and we believe that statistics would show a larger proportion of professing Christians among the negroes than among the whites. Writers like Mrs. Stowe, in treating of this subject, assume that there can be no acquaintance with gospel truth among a class who are not permitted to learn to read. But how many of the early Christians were ignorant and illiterate persons? The fishermen of Galilee were men without instruction when they first followed the fortunes of the lowly Nazarene. As for Mrs. Stowe, she is answered upon this point in her own pages. Uncle Tom was no scholar, and after many years of diligent application could at last read his bible with difficulty. Yet where shall we find a nobler and purer exemplification of the "beauty of holiness" than in him? It is, indeed, a triumphant vindication of the institution of slavery against Mrs. Stowe's assaults, that in a slaveholding community, a character so perfect as "Uncle Tom" could be produced. We have, it is true, intimated that "Uncle Tom" is somewhat overdrawn, not one dash of human frailty entering into his composition. Yet making due allowance for this, and relying solely upon his biblical lore, we may take "Uncle Tom" and deny, in the face of New England that there can be any serious lack of religious instruction in a society of which he was a member. Mrs. Stowe is, we believe, peculiarly favored in the way of spiritual advantages. Daughter of one clergyman, wife of another and sister to a third, she is redolent of the "odor of sanctity." Yet for ourselves we would not exchange Uncle Tom's unlettered, but trustful and unpretending piety for the erudite godliness of the Rev. Henry Ward Beecher, who can read his *ευ αρχη ηυ ξ λογοζ*[4] in the original Greek, or the intellectual devotion of his worthy sister, who can "make a storybook," as the children say, "all out of her own head."

The sundering of family ties among the negroes is undoubtedly a dreadful thing as represented by Abolition pamphleteers. Nor have we any desire to close our eyes to the fact that occasionally there do occur instances of compulsory separation involving peculiar hardship. But we have shown that in the very State which Mrs. Stowe has chosen for her most painful incident of this character, there are statutory regulations mitigating very much the severity of this condition of affairs, and we may add that every where the salutary influence of an enlightened public opinion enforces the sale of near relatives in such manner as that they may be kept as much as possible together. We are of opinion too that heart-rending separations are much less frequent under the institution of slavery than in countries where poverty rules the working classes with despotic sway. But admit the hardship to its full extent, and what does it prove? Evils are inseparable from all forms of society and this giant evil (if you will call it so) is more than counterbalanced by the advantages the negro

4. In the beginning was the Word (John 1.1).

enjoys. Ever since the day that St. Paul bade adieu to the little flock at Miletum,[5] who followed him down to the ship, "sorrowing most of all for the words which he spake, that they should see his face no more"—there have been mournful partings and sobbing farewells. The English soldier ordered to the distant coast of India, with a high probability that he will die there of a fever, weeps above his wife and children before he marches off to the tap of the drum; and yet is no argument for the disbanding of the English army that family ties are rent by its stern and undiscriminating discipline.

There are some who will think we have taken upon ourselves an unnecessary trouble in exposing the inconsistencies and false assertions of "Uncle Tom's Cabin." It is urged by such persons that in devoting so much attention to Abolition attacks we give them an importance to which they are not entitled. This may be true in general. But let it be borne in mind that this slanderous work has found its way to every section of our country, and has crossed the water to Great Britain, filling the minds of all who know nothing of slavery with hatred for that institution and those who uphold it. Justice to ourselves would seem to demand that it should not be suffered to circulate longer without the brand of falsehood upon it. Let it be recollected, too, that the importance Mrs. Stowe will derive from Southern criticism will be one of infamy. Indeed she is only entitled to criticism at all, as the mouthpiece of a large and dangerous faction which if we do not put down with the pen, we may be compelled one day (God grant that day may never come!) to repel with the bayonet. There are questions that underlie the story of "Uncle Tom's Cabin" of far deeper significance than any mere false coloring of Southern society, and our readers will probably see the work discussed, in other points of view, in the next number of the Messenger, by a far abler and more scholar-like hand than our own. Our editorial task is now ended and in dismissing the disagreeable subject, we beg to make a single suggestion to Mrs. Stowe—that, as she is fond of referring to the bible, she will turn over, before writing her next work of fiction, to the twentieth chapter of Exodus and there read these words—"THOU SHALT NOT BEAR FALSE WITNESS AGAINST THY NEIGHBOR."

5. Also Miletus, a Mediterranean seaport visited by St. Paul. See Acts 20.15–17.

# ANONYMOUS

## Review of *Uncle Tom's Cabin*†

Twenty thousand copies of this book, according to its title-page, are circulating among the American people, but three times as many thousands more have probably issued from the American press since the title-page was written. According to the *Boston Traveller*, the authoress has already received from her publishers the sum of "$10,300 as her copyright premium on three months' sales of the work,—we believe the largest sum of money ever received by any author, either American or European, from the sales of a single work in so short a period of time." *Uncle Tom's Cabin* is at every railway book-stall in England, and in every third traveller's hand. The book is a decided hit. It takes its place with "Pickwick," with Louis Napoleon, with the mendicant who suddenly discovers himself heir to 20,000 a-year, and, in fact, with every man whose good fortune it has been to fall asleep Nobody, and to awake in the morning an institution in the land. It is impossible not to feel respect for *Uncle Tom's Cabin*.

The object of the work is revealed in the pictorial frontispiece. Mrs. Harriet Beecher Stowe is an abolitionist, and her book is a vehement and unrestrained argument in favour of her creed. She does not preach a sermon, for men are accustomed to nap and nod under the pulpit: she does not indite a philosophical discourse, for philosophy is exacting, is solicitous for truth, and scorns exaggeration. Nor does the lady condescend to survey her intricate subject in the capacity of a judge, for the judicial seat is fixed high above human passion, and she is in no temper to mount it. With the instinct of her sex, the clever authoress takes the shortest road to her purpose, and strikes at the convictions of her readers by assailing their hearts. She cannot hold the scales of justice with a steady hand, but she has learnt to perfection the craft of the advocate. *Euclid*, she well knows, is no child for effecting social revolutions, but an impassioned song may set a world in conflagration. Who shall deny to a true woman the use of her true weapons? We are content to warn the unsuspecting reader of their actual presence!

Perhaps there is, after all, but one method of carrying on a crusade, and that unscrupulous fighting is the rightful warfare of the crusader. Mrs. Stowe, having made up her mind that slavery is an abomination in the sight of God and man, thinks of nothing but the annihilation of the pernicious system. From the first page of her narrative to the last this idea is paramount in her mind, and colours

† From *The Times* (London) 3 Sept. 1852.

all her drawing. That she will secure proselytes we take for granted; for it is in the nature of enthusiasm to inoculate with passionate zeal the strong-hearted as well as the feeble-minded. That she will convince the world of the purity of her own motives and of the hatefulness of the sin she denounces is equally clear; but that she will help in the slightest degree towards the removal of the gigantic evil that afflicts her soul is a point upon which we may express the greatest doubt; nay, is a matter upon which, unfortunately, we have very little doubt at all, inasmuch as we are certain that the very readiest way to rivet the fetters of slavery in these critical times is to direct against all slave-holders in America the opprobrium and indignation which such works as *Uncle Tom's Cabin* are sure to excite.

* * *

Uncle Tom is a paragon of virtue. He is more than mortal in his powers of endurance, in his devotion, in his self-denial, in his Christian profession and practice, and in his abhorrence of spirituous liquors. When Mr. Haley in his turn sold Tom to a new master, the good-natured owner informed his new acquisition that he would make him "coachy" on condition that he would not get drunk more than once a-week, unless in cases of emergency, whereupon "Tom looked surprised and rather hurt, and said, 'I never drink, Mas'r.'" This may be taken as a keynote to the tune Tom is eternally playing for our edification and moral improvement. He always "looks surprised and rather hurt" on such occasions. He is described as a fine powerful negro, walking through the world with a Bible in his hands, and virtuous indignation on his lips, both ready to be called into requisition on the slightest provocation, in season and out of season, at work or at play, by your leave or without it, in sorrow or in joy, for the benefit of his superiors or for the castigation of his equals. A prominent fault of this production is indicated in these facts. In her very eagerness to accomplish her amiable intention, Mrs. Stowe ludicrously stumbles and falls very far short of her object. She should surely have contented herself with proving the infamy of the slave system, and not been tempted to establish the superiority of the African nature over that of the Anglo-Saxon and of every other known race. We have read some novels in our time, and occupied not a few precious hours in the proceedings of their heroines and heroes; but we can scarcely remember ever to have encountered either gentle knight or gentler dame to whom we could not easily have brought home the imputation of human frailty. The mark of the first fall has been there, though the hues might be of the faintest. Now, if Adam, before his decline, had been a black, as some ethnologists still insist, he could not possibly have been more thoroughly without flaw than Uncle Tom. In him the said mark is eradicated once and for ever. He represents in his person the only well-authenticated instance we know, in modern times, of that laudable principle, in virtue of which a man presents his left cheek to be smitten after his first has been slapped. The more you "larrup" Uncle Tom the more he blesses you; the greater his bodily agony the more intense becomes his spiritual delight. The more he ought to complain, the more he doesn't; the less he has cause for taking a pleasant view of life and human dealings, the less he finds reason to repine; and his particular sentiments are all to match. Tom has reason to believe that Mr. Shelby will not wish him "good by" before he starts off for the south with Mr. Haley. "That ar hurt me more than sellin, it did." Tom's wife is heartbroken at his departure, and naturally reproaches Mr. Shelby for turning him into money. Tom, always superior to human nature, tenderly rebukes her. "I'll tell ye, Chloe, it goes agin me to hear one word agin Mas'r. Wasn't he put in my arms a baby? It's natur I should think a heap of him." Tom "had every facility and temptation to dishonesty," but his "simplicity of nature was impregnable," and he was never known to make a mistake in his life, although "trusted to an unlimited extent by a careless master, who handed him a bill without looking at it, and pocketed the change without counting it." What have we been doing all these years, during which, at great cost of time, labour, and money, we have despatched missionary after missionary to the heathen, but neglected needful labours at home in order to effect works of supererogation abroad? Before we export another white enthusiast from Exeter-hall, let us import a dozen or two blacks to teach Exeter-hall[1] its most obvious Christian duties. If Mrs. Stowe's portraiture is correct, and if Uncle Tom is a type of a class, we deliberately assert that we have nothing more to communicate to the negro, but everything to learn from his profession and practice. No wonder that Tom works miracles by his example. Such sudden conversions from brutality to humility, from glaring infidelity to the most childlike belief, as are presented to our admiration in these volumes, have never been wrought on earth since the days of the Apostles. One of the best sketches in the book is that of a little black imp, by name Topsy, who loves lying for the sake of lying, who is more mischievous than a monkey, and in all respects as ignorant; yet she has hardly had time to remove from her soul the rubbish accumulated there from her birth, and to prepare her mind for the reception of the most practical truths, before—without any sufficient reason—"a ray of real belief, a ray of heavenly love, penetrates the darkness of her heathen

1. The London headquarters of most of the philanthropic and reform societies in England [*Editor*].

soul," and enables her in due time to accept the responsible appointment of missionary to a station in Africa. Uncle Tom not only converts by his arguments Mr. St. Clare, his master in New Orleans, who is a gentleman, a scholar, a philosopher, and as shrewd a hand in a discussion as you are ever likely to encounter, but positively redeems in a moment from utter savageness and the lowest degradation wretches in whom the sense of feeling is extinct, and from whom we have been taught, until Tom took them in hand, to recoil in horror. It is no respect for religion that we feel when Tom, beaten almost to death by his owner, is visited by a poor woman, who offers him water to relieve his mortal pains, but who is quietly informed by the sufferer that a chapter from the Bible is better than drink. Well-fed and comfortably-housed hypocrisy is apt to deliver itself of such utterances, but certainly not true piety in its hours of anguish and physical extremity. A quadroon slave called Cassy is introduced to the reader under the most painful circumstances. Her career has been one of compelled vice until her spirit has finally acquired a wild and positively fiendish character. You read the authoress's vivid descriptions, you note the creature's conduct, and you are convinced that it will take years to restore human tenderness to that bruised soul, to say nothing of belief in Heaven and its solemn and mysterious promises. But you err! In an instant, and most miraculously, "the long winter of despair, the ice of years gives way, and the dark despairing woman weeps and prays." She, too, "yields at once, and with her whole soul, to every good influence, and becomes a devout and tender Christian." This monstrous instance is out-done by another. Sambo and Quimbo are two black rascals, who have been trained "in savageness and brutality as systematically as bulldogs, and, by long practice in hardness and cruelty, have brought their whole nature to about the same range of capacities." When we first behold them we are told to mark "their coarse, dark, heavy features; their great eyes, rolling enviously on each other; their barbarous, guttural, half-brute intonation; their dilapidated garments fluttering in the wind," and to remember the apt illustration before us "of the fact that brutal men are lower even than animals." So long as these worthies are on the scene, their actions correspond exactly with their appearance, and with the account given of their canine bringing up; they go on from bad to worse, and at the worst, when their restitution to humanity seems utterly and for ever hopeless, then it is that Tom "pours a few energetic sentences of that wondrous One,—his life, his death, his everlasting presence and power to save,"—that "they weep—both the two savage men,"—that Tom cries to Heaven to give him two more souls, and that the prayer is immediately and satisfactorily answered by their happy and most astounding conversion. Surely there is something more real and substantial in Mrs. Stowe's volumes to account for their extraordinary popularity than such absolute and audacious trash. It would be blasphemy to believe in such revelations, and common sense and a feeling of what is due to our better nature will assuredly prevent all but the veriest fanatics from accepting as truth such exaggerated and unholy fables.

* * *

The gravest fault of the book has, however, to be mentioned. Its object is to abolish slavery. Its effect will be to render slavery more difficult than ever of abolishment. Its very popularity constitutes its greatest difficulty. It will keep ill-blood at boiling point, and irritate instead of pacifying those whose proceedings Mrs. Stowe is anxious to influence on behalf of humanity. *Uncle Tom's Cabin* was not required to convince the haters of slavery of the abomination of the "institution;" of all books, it is the least calculated to weigh with those whose prejudices in favour of slavery have yet to be overcome, and whose interests are involved in the perpetuation of the system. If slavery is to cease in America, and if the people of the United States, who fought and bled for their liberty and nobly won it, are to remove the disgrace that attaches to them for forging chains for others which they will not tolerate on their own limbs, the work of enfranchisement must be a movement, not forced upon slaveowners, but voluntarily undertaken, accepted and carried out by the whole community. There is no federal law which can compel the slave States to resign the "property" which they hold. The States of the south are as free to maintain slavery as are the States of the north to rid themselves of the scandal. Let the attempt be made imperiously and violently to dictate to the south, and from that hour the Union is at an end. We are aware that to the mind of the "philanthropist" the alternative brings no alarm, but to the rational thinkers, to the statesman, and to all men interested in the world's progress, the disruption of the bond that holds the American States together is fraught with calamity, with which the present evil of slavery—a system destined sooner or later to fall to pieces under the weight of public opinion and its own infamy—bears no sensible comparison. The writer of *Uncle Tom's Cabin* and similar well-disposed authors have yet to learn that to excite the passions of their readers in favour of their philanthropic schemes is the very worst mode of getting rid of a difficulty, which, whoever may be to blame for its existence, is part and parcel of the whole social organization of a large proportion of the States, and cannot be forcibly removed without instant anarchy, and all its accompanying mischief.

* * *

* * * The world is working its way towards liberty, and the blacks will not be left behind in the onward march. Since the adoption of the American constitution seven States have voluntarily abolished slavery. When that constitution was proclaimed there was scarcely a free black in the country. According to the last census, the free blacks amount to 418,173, and of these 233,691 are blacks of the South, liberated by their owners, and not by the force of law. We cannot shut our eyes to these facts. Neither can we deny that, desirable as negro emancipation may be in the United States, abolition must be the result of growth, not of revolution, must be patiently wrought out by means of the American constitution, and not in bitter spite of it. America cannot for any time resist the enlightened spirit of our age, and it is manifestly her interest to adapt her institutions to its temper. That she will eventually do so if she be not a divided household—if the South be not goaded to illiberality by the North—if public writers deal with the matter in the spirit of conciliation, justice, charity, and truth, we will not permit ourselves to doubt. * * * We have said that the process of liberation is going on, and that we are convinced the South in its own interests will not be laggard in the labour. Liberia and similar spots on the earth's surface proffer aid to the South, which cannot be rejected with safety. That the aid may be accepted with alacrity and good heart let us have no more *Uncle Tom's Cabins* engendering illwill, keeping up bad blood, and rendering well-disposed, humane, but critically placed men their own enemies and the stumbling blocks to civilisation and to the spread of glad tidings from Heaven.

## CHARLES DUDLEY WARNER

### [*Uncle Tom's Cabin* a Half Century Later]†

* * *

[*Uncle Tom's Cabin*] is still read, and read the world over, with tears and with laughter; it is still played to excited audiences. Is it a great novel, or was it only an event of an era of agitation and passion? Has it the real dramatic quality—the poet's visualizing of human life—that makes works of fiction, of imagination, live? Till recently, I had not read the book since 1852. I feared to renew acquaintance with it lest I should find only the shell of an exploded cartridge. I took it up at the beginning of a three-hours'-railway journey. To my surprise the journey did not seem to last half an hour,

† From the *Atlantic Monthly* 78 (July 1896). All notes are by the editor of this Norton Critical Edition.

and half the time I could not keep back the tears from my eyes. A London critic, full of sympathy with Mrs. Stowe and her work, recently said, "Yet she was not an artist, she was not a great woman." What is greatness? What is art? In 1862 probably no one who knew General Grant[1] would have called him a great man. But he took Vicksburg. This woman did something with her pen,—on the whole, the most remarkable and effective book in her generation. How did she do it? Without art? George Sand[2] said, "In matters of art there is but one rule, to paint and to move. And where shall we find conditions more complete, types more vivid, situations more touching, more original, than in *Uncle Tom?*" If there is not room in our art for such a book, I think we shall have to stretch our art a little. "Women, too, are here judged, and painted with a master hand." This subtle critic, in her overpoweringly tender and enthusiastic review, had already inquired about the capacity of this writer. "Mrs. Stowe is all instinct; it is the very reason that she appears to some not to have talent. Has she not talent? What is talent? Nothing, doubtless, compared to genius; but has she genius? I cannot say that she has talent as one understands it in the world of letters, but she has genius as humanity feels the need of genius,—the genius of goodness, not that of the man of letters, but of the saint." It is admitted that Mrs. Stowe was not a woman of letters in the common acceptation of that term, and it is plain that in the French tribunal, where form is of the substance of the achievement, and which reluctantly overlooked the crudeness of Walter Scott, in France where the best English novel seems a violation of established canons, *Uncle Tom* would seem to belong where some modern critics place it, with works of the heart, and not of the head. The reviewer is, however, candid: "For a long time we have striven in France against the prolix explanations of Walter Scott. We have cried out against those of Balzac, but on consideration have perceived that the painter of manners and character has never done too much, that every stroke of the pencil was needed for the general effect. Let us learn then to appreciate all kinds of treatment, where the effect is good, and where they bear the seal of a master hand."

It must be admitted to the art critic that the book is defective according to the rules of the modern French romance; that Mrs. Stowe was possessed by her subject, and let her fervid interest in it be felt; that she had a definite purpose. That purpose was to quicken the sense of responsibility of the North by showing the real character of slavery, and to touch the South by showing that the

1. Ulysses S. Grant (1822–1885), commander in chief of the Union army during the Civil War and eighteenth president of the United States (1869–77).
2. See above, p. 495–99.

inevitable wrong of it lay in the system rather than in those involved in it. Abundant material was in her hands, and the author burned to make it serviceable. What should she do? She might have done what she did afterwards in *The Key*, presented to the public a mass of statistics, of legal documents. The evidence would have been unanswerable, but the jury might not have been moved by it; they would have balanced it by considerations of political and commercial expediency. I presume that Mrs. Stowe made no calculation of this kind. She felt her course, and went on in it. What would an artist have done, animated by her purpose and with her material? He would have done what Cervantes did, what Tourgenieff[3] did, what Mrs. Stowe did. He would have dramatized his facts in living personalities, in effective scenes, in vivid pictures of life. Mrs. Stowe exhibited the system of slavery by a succession of dramatized pictures, not always artistically welded together, but always effective as an exhibition of the system. Cervantes also showed a fading feudal romantic condition by a series of amusing and pathetic adventures, grouped rather loosely about a singularly fascinating figure.

Tourgenieff, a more consummate artist, in his hunting scenes exhibited the effect of serfdom upon society, in a series of scenes with no necessary central figure, without comment, and with absolute concealment of any motive. I believe the three writers followed their instincts, without an analytic argument as to the method, as the great painter follows his when he puts an idea upon canvas. He may invent a theory about it afterwards; if he does not, some one else will invent it for him. There are degrees of art. One painter will put in unnecessary accessories, another will exhibit his sympathy too openly, the technique or the composition of another can be criticised. But the question is, is the picture great and effective?

Mrs. Stowe had not Tourgenieff's artistic calmness. Her mind was fused into a white heat with her message. Yet, how did she begin her story? Like an artist, by a highly dramatized scene, in which the actors, by a few strokes of the pen, appear as distinct and unmistakable personalities, marked by individual peculiarities of manner, speech, motive, character, living persons in natural attitudes. The reader becomes interested in a shrewd study of human nature, of a section of life, with its various refinement, coarseness, fastidiousness and vulgarity, its humor and pathos. As he goes on he discovers that every character has been perfectly visualized, accurately limned from the first; that a type has been created which

3. Ivan Turgenev (1818–1883), Russian novelist, dramatist, and short-story writer. "Miguel de Cervantes" (1547–1616), Spanish novelist, dramatist, and poet, author of *Don Quixote de la Mancha* (1605–15).

remains consistent, which is never deflected from its integrity by any exigencies of plot. This clear conception of character (not of earmarks and peculiarities adopted as labels), and faithful adhesion to it in all vicissitudes, is one of the rarest and highest attributes of genius. All the chief characters in the book follow this line of absolutely consistent development, from Uncle Tom and Legree down to the most aggravating and contemptible of all, Marie St. Clare. The selfish and hysterical woman has never been so faithfully depicted by any other author.

Distinguished as the novel is by its character-drawing and its pathos, I doubt if it would have captivated the world without its humor. This is of the old-fashioned kind, the large humor of Scott, and again of Cervantes, not verbal pleasantry, not the felicities of Lamb,[4] but the humor of character in action, of situations elaborated with great freedom, and with what may be called a hilarious conception. This quality is never wanting in the book, either for the reader's entertainment by the way, or to heighten the pathos of the narrative by contrast. The introduction of Topsy into the New Orleans household saves us in the dangerous approach to melodrama in the religious passages between Tom and St. Clare. Considering the opportunities of the subject, the book has very little melodrama; one is apt to hear low music on the entrance of little Eva, but we are convinced of the wholesome sanity of the sweet child. And it is to be remarked that some of the most exciting episodes, such as that of Eliza crossing the Ohio River on the floating ice (of which Mr. Ruskin[5] did not approve), are based upon authentic occurrences. The want of unity in construction of which the critics complain is partially explained by the necessity of exhibiting the effect of slavery in its entirety. The parallel plots, one running to Louisiana and the other to Canada, are tied together by this consideration, and not by any real necessity to each other.

There is no doubt that Mrs. Stowe was wholly possessed by her theme, rapt away like a prophet in a vision, and that, in her feeling at the time, it was written through her quite as much as by her. This idea grew upon her mind in the retrospective light of the tremendous stir the story made in the world, so that in her later years she came to regard herself as a providential instrument, and frankly to declare that she did not write the book; "God wrote it." In her own account, when she reached the death of Uncle Tom, "the whole vital force left her." The inspiration there left her, and the end of the story, the weaving together of all the loose ends of the plot, in the joining together almost by miracle the long separated, and the

4. Charles Lamb (1775–1834), English essayist.
5. John Ruskin (1819–1900) English art critic and social theorist.

discovery of the relationships, is the conscious invention of the novelist.

It would be perhaps going beyond the province of the critic to remark upon what the author considered the central power of the story, and its power to move the world, the faith of Uncle Tom in the Bible. This appeal to the emotion of millions of readers cannot, however, be overlooked. Many regard the book as effective in regions remote from our perplexities by reason of this grace. When the work was translated into Siamese, the perusal of it by one of the ladies of the court induced her to liberate all her slaves, men, women, and children, one hundred and thirty in all. "Hidden Perfume," for that was the English equivalent of her name, said she was wishful to be good like Harriet Beecher Stowe. And as to the standpoint of Uncle Tom and the Bible, nothing more significant can be cited than this passage from one of the latest writings of Heinrich Heine:[6]—

"The reawakening of my religious feelings I owe to that holy book the Bible. Astonishing that after I have whirled about all my life over all the dance-floors of philosophy, and yielded myself to all the orgies of the intellect, and paid my addresses to all possible systems, without satisfaction like Messalina[7] after a licentious night, I now find myself on the same standpoint where poor Uncle Tom stands,—on that of the Bible! I kneel down by my black brother in the same prayer! What a humiliation! With all my science I have come no further than the poor ignorant negro who has scarce learned to spell. Poor Tom, indeed, seems to have seen deeper things in the holy book than I. . . . Tom, perhaps, understands them better than I, because more flogging occurs in them; that is to say, those ceaseless blows of the whip which have aesthetically disgusted me in reading the Gospels and the Acts. But a poor negro slave reads with his back, and understands better than we do. But I, who used to make citations from Homer,[8] now begin to quote the Bible as Uncle Tom does."

The one indispensable requisite of a great work of imaginative fiction is its universality, its conception and construction so that it will appeal to universal human nature in all races and situations and climates. *Uncle Tom's Cabin* does that. Considering certain artistic deficiencies, which the French writers perceived, we might say that it was the timeliness of its theme that gave it currency in England and America. But that argument falls before the world-

6. German lyric poet (1797–1856).
7. The Roman empress Messalina (d. 48 C.E.), wife of Claudius I, was known for her greed and lust.
8. First Greek poet (fl. 9th–8th? century B.C.E.), composer of the epic poems *The Iliad* and *The Odyssey*.

wide interest in it as a mere story, in so many languages, by races unaffected by our own relation to slavery.

It was the opinion of James Russell Lowell[9] that the anti-slavery element in *Uncle Tom* and *Dred* stood in the way of a full appreciation, at least in her own country, of the remarkable genius of Mrs. Stowe. Writing in 1859, he said, "From my habits and the tendency of my studies I cannot help looking at things purely from an aesthetic point of view, and what I valued in *Uncle Tom* was the genius, and not the moral." This had been his impression when he read the book in Paris, long after the whirl of excitement produced by its publication had subsided, and far removed by distance from local influences. Subsequently, in a review, he wrote, "We felt then, and we believe now, that the secret of Mrs. Stowe's power lay in that same genius by which the great successes in creative literature have always been achieved,—the genius that instinctively goes to the organic elements of human nature, whether under a white skin or a black, and which disregards as trivial the conventions and fictitious notions which make so large a part both of our thinking and feeling. . . . The creative faculty of Mrs. Stowe, like that of Cervantes in *Don Quixote* and of Fielding in *Joseph Andrews*,[1] overpowered the narrow specialty of her design, and expanded a local and temporary theme with the cosmopolitanism of genius."

A half-century is not much in the life of a people; it is in time an inadequate test of the staying power of a book. Nothing is more futile than prophecy on contemporary literary work. It is safe, however, to say that *Uncle Tom's Cabin* has the fundamental qualities, the sure insight into human nature, and the fidelity to the facts of its own time which have from age to age preserved works of genius.

# FRANCES ELLEN WATKINS [HARPER]

## Eliza Harris[†]

Like a fawn from the arrow, startled and wild,
A woman swept by us, bearing a child;
In her eyes was the night of a settled despair,
And her brow was o'ershaded with anguish and care.

9. American poet, critic, and educator (1819–1891).
1. See above, p. 506, n. 4.
† From *Poems on Miscellaneous Subjects* (Philadelphia: Merrihew and Thompson, 1857). Frances Ellen Watkins Harper (1825–1911) was an African American writer, orator, and activist. Born to free parents in Baltimore, she spoke widely against slavery and was involved in the Underground Railroad before Emancipation. She published both poetry and fiction—including a novel, *Iola Leroy*, in 1892—and was active in anti-lynching campaigns, the temperance movement, and the fight for women's suffrage.

She was nearing the river—in reaching the brink,
She heeded no danger, she paused not to think;
For she is a mother—her child is a slave—
And she'll give him his freedom, or find him a grave!

It was a vision to haunt us, that innocent face—
So pale in its aspect, so fair in its grace;
As the tramp of the horse and the bay of the hound,
With the fetters that gall, were trailing the ground!

She was nerv'd by despair, and strengthened by woe,
As she leap'd o'er the chasms that yawn'd from below;
Death howl'd in the tempest, and rav'd in the blast,
But she heard not the sound till the danger was past.

Oh! how shall I speak of my proud country's shame
Of the stains on her glory, how give them their name?
How say that her banner in mockery waves—
Her star-spangled banner—o'er millions of slaves?

How say that the lawless may torture and chase
A woman whose crime is the hue of her face?
How the depths of the forest may echo around
With the shrieks of despair, and the bay of the hound?

With her step on the ice, and her arm on her child,
The danger was fearful, the pathway was wild;
But, aided by Heaven, she gained a free shore,
Where the friends of humanity open'd their door.

So fragile and lovely, so fearfully pale,
Like a lily that bends to the breath of the gale,
Save the heave of her breast, and the sway of her hair,
You'd have thought her a statue of fear and despair.

In agony close to her bosom she press'd
The life of her heart, the child of her breast—
Oh! love from its tenderness gathering might,
Had strengthen'd her soul for the dangers of light.

But she's free:—yes, free from the land where the slave
From the hound of oppression must rest in the grave;
Where bondage and torture, where scourges and drains
Have plac'd on our banner indelible stains.

The bloodhounds have miss'd the scent of her way;
The hunter is rifled and foil'd of his prey;

Fierce jargon and cursing, with clanking of chains,
Make sounds of strange discord on Liberty's plains.

With the rapture of love and fulness of bliss,
She plac'd on his brow a mother's fond kiss:—
Oh! poverty, danger and death she can brave,
For the child of her love is no longer a slave!

# HELEN GRAY CONE

## [Harriet Beecher Stowe and American Women Writers]†

* * *

* * * The woman who was destined to bring the novel of New England to a fuller development reached fame at a bound with "Uncle Tom's Cabin." At last the artist's instinct and the purpose of the reformer were fused, as far as they are capable of fusion, in a story that still holds its reader, whether passive or protesting, with the grip of the master-hand. * * * Whatever blemishes or extravagances may appear to a critical eye in the great antislavery novel, it still beats with that intense life which nearly forty years ago awoke a deep responsive thrill in the repressed heart of the North. We are at present chiefly concerned with its immense practical success. It was a "shot heard round the world." Ten thousand copies were sold in a few days; over three hundred thousand in a year; eight power-presses were kept running day and night to supply the continual demand. The British Museum now contains thirty-five complete editions in English; and translations exist in at least twenty different languages. "Never did any American work have such success!" exclaims Mrs. Child,[1] in one of her enthusiastic letters. . . . "It has done much to command respect for the faculties of woman." The influences are, indeed, broad and general, which have since that day removed all restrictions tending to impress inferiority on the woman writer, so that the distinction of sex is lost in the distinction of schools. Yet a special influence may be attributed to this single marked manifestation of force, to this imposing popular triumph. In the face of the fact that the one American book which had stormed Europe was the work of a woman, the old tone of patronage became ridiculous,

† From "Woman in Literature," in *Woman's Work in America*, ed. Annie Nathan Meyer (New York, 1891). Book available from Ayer Company Publishers, Box 958, Salem, N.H. 03079.

1. Lydia Maria Child (1802–1880), American author and abolitionist [*Editor*].

the old sense of ordained and inevitable weakness on the part of "the female writer" became obsolete. Women henceforth, whatever their personal feelings in regard to the much-discussed book, were enabled, consciously or unconsciously, to hold the pen more firmly, to move it more freely.

* * *

# PAUL LAURENCE DUNBAR

## Harriet Beecher Stowe†

She told the story, and the whole world wept
    At wrongs and cruelties it had not known
    But for this fearless woman's voice alone.
    She spoke to consciences that long had slept:
Her message, Freedom's clear reveille, swept
    From heedless hovel to complacent throne.
    Command and prophecy were in the tone,
    And from its sheath the sword of justice leapt.
Around two peoples swelled a fiery wave,
    But both came forth transfigured from the flame.
    Blest be the hand that dared be strong to save,
And blest be she who in our weakness came—
    Prophet and priestess! At one stroke she gave
    A race to freedom, and herself to fame.

# G. GRANT WILLIAMS

## Reminiscences of the Life of Harriet Beecher Stowe and Her Family‡

No family is more highly or justly honored by the American people of a past generation, especially Afro-Americans, than the Beecher family, which has so effectually assisted in enriching the intellectual field of achievement in this New World by its contribution of able writers, public speakers, eloquent preachers and noted philanthropists.

† From the *Century Magazine* 57 (Nov. 1898).
‡ From the *Colored American Magazine* (Dec. 1902). All notes are by the editor of this Norton Critical Edition. The *Colored American Magazine*, published in Boston from 1900 to 1904 and then in New York until 1910, was an African American-owned and -run monthly publication.

Everybody now is anti-slavery. It is honorable now to be a child of the man who "cast the first anti-slavery vote in our town"; or "called our first anti-slavery meeting"; or first entertained Garrison as guest, or Abbey Kelley, or Frederick Douglass; or rescued Stephen Foster or Lucy Stone[1] from the hands of a ferocious mob; or raised, or commanded the first company of colored troops in the war of Rebellion, at the time when not a musical band could be found in the whole city of New York to play for a colored regiment, as it marched from the New Haven railway station to the steamer at the foot of Canal street to embark for the seat of war! says Parker Pillsbury. But Garrison, Birney, Dr. Bailey, Lovejoy, Henry Ward Beecher[2] and their associates found the world loving the trespasses and sins of intemperance, slavery, war, capital punishment and woman's enslavement, and refusing to part with them, especially slavery which had enriched even Rhode Island; it was the sin and crime of the whole nation. It was sustained by the government, it was sanctified by the religion of the nation, even the Quakers gravely considered the question, not whether it was right to hold slaves, but whether it was right to brand them with red-hot branding irons.

Today the old battle of the abolitionists must be fought over again on the question of disfranchisement; happily, we hope, without the horrors of war if only the American people will be persuaded to be just toward a weaker race; but if not, then, indeed, we may tremble for this country when we reflect that God is just.

Under the baleful influence of slavery, Harriet Beecher Stowe, the author of "Uncle Tom's Cabin," was born in Litchfield, Conn., June 14, 1811. Her father, Lyman Beecher, was a Congregational minister of remarkable ability, both as an orator and a thinker.

Harriet attended the village school with her brother, Henry Ward Beecher—afterwards world-famous as a preacher and a lecturer—who was two years younger than herself. When twelve years of age she wrote a composition of such merit that it was selected to be read with two others at the annual exhibition—the subject: "Can the immortality of the soul be proved by the light of nature?"—and her father, being one of the judges, after listening with deep interest,

1. Abby Kelley (1811–1887), an abolitionist and suffragist, was the first woman to lecture to mixed audiences on the subject of slavery. Stephen Foster (1809–1881), her husband, was also active in the abolitionist cause. Lucy Stone (1818–1893) organized the American Woman Suffrage Association in 1869 and also spoke on abolition. For Garrison and Douglass, see above, p. 31, n. 1, and p. 407, n. 9.
2. Parker Pillsbury (1809–1898) edited several antislavery papers as well as a woman's suffrage paper. James Gillespie Birney (1792–1857), founder of the antislavery *Philanthropist* in Cincinnati, ran for president as an antislavery candidate in 1840 and 1844. Dr. Gamaliel Bailey (1807–1859), a journalist and physician, edited the *Philanthropist* and later the *National Era*. Elijah Parish Lovejoy (1802–1837), editor of the St. Louis *Observer*, was killed by a proslavery mob. Henry Ward Beecher (1813–1887), Stowe's brother, was a Presbyterian clergyman and abolitionist editor and orator.

turned to the master and asked, "Who wrote that?" "Your daughter, sir," was the reply, and she was so overjoyed that in later years she declared that it was the proudest moment of her life.

It was from her father also that in these young days she learned the true nature of slavery and the slave trade. This is her own story as written to a friend in 1851: "I was a child in 1820, when the Missouri Compromise[3] was agitated, and one of the strongest and deepest impressions on my mind was that made by my father's sermons and prayers, and the anguish of his soul for the poor slave at that time. I remember his preaching drawing tears down the hardest faces of the old farmers in his congregation. I well remember his prayers morning and evening in the family, for poor, oppressed, bleeding Africa, that the time of her deliverance might come; prayers offered with strong crying and tears, and which indelibly impressed my heart and made me what I am from my very soul, the enemy of all slavery."

* * *

The anti-slavery movement in Cincinnati began at this time [the 1830s, the decade of the Beecher family's arrival]. James G. Birney, of Huntersville, Alabama, at one time a slave-holder, judge in the courts, and a ruling elder in the Presbyterian church, emancipated his slaves, provided for their future support, and took them over into the free State of Ohio, by the advice of Theodore D. Weld.[4] Thus washing his own hands of the guilt of slave-holding, Judge Birney set himself to the work of abolishing the foul system. He came to Cincinnati, and in connection with Dr. Gamaliel Bailey, founded an anti-slavery paper called "The Philanthropist." He suffered every possible indignity and outrage at the hands of infuriated mobs, and the vengeance of church and state. In the darkness of midnight the mob entered and carried press, types and all other paraphernalia of the office and sunk them in the Ohio river.

In 1836, Mrs. Stowe's domestic life began with the birth of her twin daughters, and in 1838 her son Henry was born. For fourteen years life was a struggle with ill health and poverty, until in 1850 Mr. Stowe became a Professor in Bowdoin College, Brunswick, Me., and in 1852 "Uncle Tom's Cabin" was published, and brought her $10,000 at once, and a yearly income which made her comfortable for life. A few years after the Birney incident, Dr. Bailey published an anti-slavery paper at Washington. He was a man of remarkable ability as an editor, greatly respected by his brother journalists, and

3. An 1820 agreement passed by Congress allowing Maine to enter the United States as a free state and Missouri to be admitted as a slave state, as well as making other northwestern territories free; declared unconstitutional by the Dred Scott decision of 1857.
4. A well-known abolitionist orator and pamphlet writer (1803–1895).

it was in this paper that "Uncle Tom's Cabin" was first published as a serial.

It was during her life in Ohio that Mrs. Stowe became familiar with the cruelties of slavery, through the fugitives of Kentucky who were continually crossing the Ohio river and being helped on their way by the "Underground Railroad," the house and barn of the Beechers being one of the first stations. Talking with these fugitives nearly broke her heart, and thus it was she was able, in after years, to draw tears of sympathy from thousands all over the world, arousing that irresistible force of public opinion which put an end to the whole system and caused President Lincoln to greet her, upon the occasion of their first meeting, at Washington, D.C., "So this is the little woman who brought on the war."

In 1853 the family removed to Andover, Mass., and Mrs. Stowe visited England with her husband and her brother Charles, and was royally entertained by some of the most distinguished families because of her "wonderful book"; twice again she traveled in Europe, writing "Sunny Memories of Foreign Lands," and "Agnes of Sorrento." While abroad she rendered Miss Elizabeth Greenfield—"The Black Swan"[5]—signal service in getting concerts and patronage from the influential nobles of London.

In 1863, by reason of Mr. Stowe's failing health, the family moved to Hartford, the home of Mrs. Stowe's early days, where she resided until her death, July 1, 1896. She lies buried in the village churchyard at Andover, beside her husband and her son Henry.

Mrs. Stowe was a woman of great genius who lived as seeing the invisible inhabitants beyond the Veil. Patient under severe trials, of great courage and executive ability, hating the sin but tender toward the sinner, she was the personification of gentle womanhood. What greater tribute can we give her?

"It lies around us like a cloud.
A world we do not see;
Yet the sweet closing of an eye
May bring us there to be."[6]
—*From a poem by Mrs. Stowe.*

5. African American concert singer (1809–1876), popular both in the United States and in Europe.
6. This poem, titled "The Other World," can be found in Stowe's *Religious Poems*, published in 1867.

# Modern Critical Views

## JAMES BALDWIN

### Everybody's Protest Novel†

In *Uncle Tom's Cabin*, that cornerstone of American social protest fiction, St. Clare, the kindly master, remarks to his coldly disapproving Yankee cousin, Miss Ophelia, that, so far as he is able to tell, the blacks have been turned over to the devil for the benefit of the whites in this world—however, he adds thoughtfully, it may turn out in the next. Miss Ophelia's reaction is, at least, vehemently right-minded: "This is perfectly horrible!" she exclaims. "You ought to be ashamed of yourselves!"

Miss Ophelia, as we may suppose, was speaking for the author; her exclamation is the moral, neatly framed, and incontestable like those improving mottoes sometimes found hanging on the walls of furnished rooms. And, like these mottoes, before which one invariably flinches, recognizing an insupportable, almost an indecent glibness, she and St. Clare are terribly in earnest. Neither of them questions the medieval morality from which their dialogue springs: black, white, the devil, the next world—posing its alternatives between heaven and the flames—were realities for them as, of course, they were for their creator. They spurned and were terrified of the darkness, striving mightily for the light; and considered from this aspect, Miss Ophelia's exclamation, like Mrs. Stowe's novel, achieves a bright, almost a lurid significance, like the light from a fire which consumes a witch. This is the more striking as one considers the novels of Negro oppression written in our own, more enlightened day, all of which say only: "This is perfectly horrible! You ought to be ashamed of yourselves!" (Let us ignore, for the moment, those novels of oppression written by Negroes, which add only a raging near-paranoiac postscript to this statement and actually reinforce, as I

† From *Notes of a Native Son* by James Baldwin (Boston: Beacon Press, 1955). Copyright © 1955, 1983 by James Baldwin. Reprinted by permission of Beacon Press and the Estate of James Baldwin. All notes are by the editor of this Norton Critical Edition.

hope to make clear later, the principles which activate the oppression they decry.)

*Uncle Tom's Cabin* is a very bad novel, having, in its self-righteous, virtuous sentimentality, much in common with *Little Women*.[1] Sentimentality, the ostentatious parading of excessive and spurious emotion, is the mark of dishonesty, the inability to feel; the wet eyes of the sentimentalist betray his aversion to experience, his fear of life, his arid heart; and it is always, therefore, the signal of secret and violent inhumanity, the mask of cruelty. *Uncle Tom's Cabin*—like its multitudinous, hard-boiled descendants—is a catalogue of violence. This is explained by the nature of Mrs. Stowe's subject matter, her laudable determination to flinch from nothing in presenting the complete picture; an explanation which falters only if we pause to ask whether or not her picture is indeed complete; and what constriction or failure of perception forced her to so depend on the description of brutality—unmotivated, senseless—and to leave unanswered and unnoticed the only important question: what it was, after all, that moved her people to such deeds.

But this, let us say, was beyond Mrs. Stowe's powers; she was not so much a novelist as an impassioned pamphleteer; her book was not intended to do anything more than prove that slavery was wrong; was, in fact, perfectly horrible. This makes material for a pamphlet but it is hardly enough for a novel; and the only question left to ask is why we are bound still within the same constriction. How is it that we are so loath to make a further journey than that made by Mrs. Stowe, to discover and reveal something a little closer to the truth?

But that battered word, truth, having made its appearance here, confronts one immediately with a series of riddles and has, moreover, since so many gospels are preached, the unfortunate tendency to make one belligerent. Let us say, then, that truth, as used here, is meant to imply a devotion to the human being, his freedom and fulfillment; freedom which cannot be legislated, fulfillment which cannot be charted. This is the prime concern, the frame of reference; it is not to be confused with a devotion to Humanity which is too easily equated with a devotion to a Cause; and Causes, as we know, are notoriously bloodthirsty. We have, as it seems to me, in this most mechanical and interlocking of civilizations, attempted to lop this creature down to the status of a time-saving invention. He is not, after all, merely a member of a Society or a Group or a deplorable conundrum to be explained by Science. He is—and how old-fashioned the words sound!—something more than that, something resolutely indefinable, unpredictable. In overlooking, denying,

1. An 1868 novel by Louisa May Alcott (1832–1888).

evading his complexity—which is nothing more than the disquieting complexity of ourselves—we are diminished and we perish; only within this web of ambiguity, paradox, this hunger, danger, darkness, can we find at once ourselves and the power that will free us from ourselves. It is this power of revelation which is the business of the novelist, this journey toward a more vast reality which must take precedence over all other claims. What is today parroted as his Responsibility—which seems to mean that he must make formal declaration that he is involved in, and affected by, the lives of other people and to say something improving about this somewhat self-evident fact—is, when he believes it, his corruption and our loss; moreover, it is rooted in, inter-locked with and intensifies this same mechanization. Both *Gentlemen's Agreement* and *The Postman Always Rings Twice*[2] exemplify this terror of the human being, the determination to cut him down to size. And in *Uncle Tom's Cabin* we may find foreshadowing of both: the formula created by the necessity to find a lie more palatable than the truth has been handed down and memorized and persists yet with a terrible power.

It is interesting to consider one more aspect of Mrs. Stowe's novel, the method she used to solve the problem of writing about a black man at all. Apart from her lively procession of field-hands, house-niggers, Chloe, Topsy, etc.—who are the stock, lovable figures presenting no problem—she has only three other Negroes in the book. These are the important ones and two of them may be dismissed immediately, since we have only the author's word that they are Negro and they are, in all other respects, as white as she can make them. The two are George and Eliza, a married couple with a wholly adorable child—whose quaintness, incidentally, and whose charm, rather puts one in mind of a darky boot-black doing a buck and wing to the clatter of condescending coins. Eliza is a beautiful, pious hybrid, light enough to pass—the heroine of *Quality*[3] might, indeed, be her reincarnation—differing from the genteel mistress who has overseered her education only in the respect that she is a servant. George is darker, but makes up for it by being a mechanical genius, and is, moreover, sufficiently un-Negroid to pass through town, a fugitive from his master, disguised as a Spanish gentleman, attracting no attention whatever beyond admiration. They are a race apart from Topsy. It transpires by the end of the novel, through one of those energetic, last-minute convolutions of the plot, that Eliza has some connection with French gentility. The figure from whom the novel takes its name, Uncle Tom, who is a figure of con-

2. *Gentleman's Agreement* (1947), a novel by Laura Z. Hobson, and *The Postman Always Rings Twice* (1934) by James M. Cain; both were made into films in the 1940s.
3. A 1946 novel by Cid Ricketts Sumner.

troversy yet, is jet-black, wooly-haired, illiterate; and he is phenomenally forbearing. He has to be; he is black; only through this forbearance can he survive or triumph. (Cf. Faulkner's preface to *The Sound and the Fury*:[4] These others were not Compsons. They were black:—They endured.) His triumph is metaphysical, unearthly; since he is black, born without the light, it is only through humility, the incessant mortification of the flesh, that he can enter into communion with God or man. The virtuous rage of Mrs. Stowe is motivated by nothing so temporal as a concern for the relationship of men to one another—or, even, as she would have claimed, by a concern for their relationship to God—but merely by a panic of being hinted into the flames, of being caught in traffic with the devil. She embraced this merciless doctrine with all her heart, bargaining shamelessly before the throne of grace: God and salvation becoming her personal property, purchased with the coin of her virtue. Here, black equates with evil and white with grace; if, being mindful of the necessity of good works, she could not cast out the blacks—a wretched, huddled mass, apparently, claiming, like an obsession, her inner eye—she could not embrace them either without purifying them of sin. She must cover their intimidating nakedness, robe them in white, the garments of salvation; only thus could she herself be delivered from ever-present sin, only thus could she bury, as St. Paul demanded, "the carnal man, the man of the flesh."[5] Tom, therefore, her only black man, has been robbed of his humanity and divested of his sex. It is the price for that darkness with which he has been branded.

*Uncle Tom's Cabin*, then, is activated by what might be called a theological terror, the terror of damnation; and the spirit that breathes in this book, hot, self-righteous, fearful, is not different from that spirit of medieval times which sought to exorcize evil by burning witches; and is not different from that terror which activates a lynch mob. One need not, indeed, search for examples so historic or so gaudy; this is a warfare waged daily in the heart, a warfare so vast, so relentless and so powerful that the interracial handshake or the interracial marriage can be as crucifying as the public hanging or the secret rape. This panic motivates our cruelty, this fear of the dark makes it impossible that our lives shall be other than superficial; this, interlocked with and feeding our glittering, mechanical, inescapable civilization which has put to death our freedom.

4. Novel (1929) by William Faulkner, in which the Compsons are a white family.
5. Probably a reference to Romans 8.7–8: ". . . the carnal mind is enmity against God: for it is not subject to the law of God, neither indeed can be. So then they that are in the flesh cannot please God."

This, notwithstanding that the avowed aim of the American protest novel is to bring greater freedom to the oppressed. They are forgiven, on the strength of these good intentions, whatever violence they do to language, whatever excessive demands they make of credibility. It is, indeed, considered the sign of a frivolity so intense as to approach decadence to suggest that these books are both badly written and wildly improbable. One is told to put first things first, the good of society coming before niceties of style or characterization. Even if this were incontestable—for what exactly is the "good" of society?—it argues an insuperable confusion, since literature and sociology are not one and the same; it is impossible to discuss them as if they were. Our passion for categorization, life neatly fitted into pegs, has led to an unforeseen, paradoxical distress; confusion, a break-down of meaning. Those categories which were meant to define and control the world for us have boomeranged us into chaos; in which limbo we whirl, clutching the straws of our definitions. The "protest" novel, so far from being disturbing, is an accepted and comforting aspect of the American scene, ramifying that framework we believe to be so necessary. Whatever unsettling questions are raised are evanescent, titillating; remote, for this has nothing to do with us, it is safely ensconced in the social arena, where, indeed, it has nothing to do with anyone, so that finally we receive a very definite thrill of virtue from the fact that we are reading such a book at all. This report from the pit reassures us of its reality and its darkness and of our own salvation; and "As long as such books are being published," an American liberal once said to me, "everything will be all right."

But unless one's ideal of society is a race of neatly analyzed, hard-working ciphers, one can hardly claim for the protest novel the lofty purpose it claims for itself or share the present optimism concerning them. They emerge for what they are: a mirror of our confusion, dishonesty, panic, trapped and immobilized in the sunlit prison of the American dream. They are fantasies, connecting nowhere with reality, sentimental; in exactly the same sense that such movies as *The Best Years of Our Lives* or the works of Mr. James M. Cain[6] are fantasies. Beneath the dazzling pyrotechnics of these current operas one may still discern, as the controlling force, the intense theological preoccupations of Mrs. Stowe, the sick vacuities of *The Rover Boys*.[7] Finally, the aim of the protest novel becomes something very

6. *The Best Years of Our Lives* is a 1946 film directed by William Wyler concerning three servicemen's return home after World War II; James M. Cain (1892–1977) was an American novelist whose novels *Double Indemnity, Mildred Pierce,* and *The Postman Always Rings Twice* were made into Hollywood movies.

7. A popular series of books for boys, over thirty in all, first published in 1899 by Edward Stratemeyer under the pen name Arthur M. Winfield.

closely resembling the zeal of those alabaster missionaries to Africa to cover the nakedness of the natives, to hurry them into the pallid arms of Jesus and thence into slavery. The aim has now become to reduce all Americans to the compulsive, bloodless dimensions of a guy named Joe.

It is the peculiar triumph of society—and its loss—that it is able to convince those people to whom it has given inferior status of the reality of this decree; it has the force and the weapons to translate its dictum into fact, so that the allegedly inferior are actually made so, insofar as the societal realities are concerned. This is a more hidden phenomenon now than it was in the days of serfdom, but it is no less implacable. Now, as then, we find ourselves bound, first without, then within, by the nature of our categorization. And escape is not effected through a bitter railing against this trap; it is as though this very striving were the only motion needed to spring the trap upon us. We take our shape, it is true, within and against that cage of reality bequeathed us at our birth; and yet it is precisely through our dependence on this reality that we are most endlessly betrayed. Society is held together by our need; we bind it together with legend, myth, coercion, fearing that without it we will be hurled into that void, within which, like the earth before the Word was spoken, the foundations of society are hidden. From this void—ourselves—it is the function of society to protect us; but it is only this void, our unknown selves, demanding, forever, a new act of creation, which can save us—"from the evil that is in the world." With the same motion, at the same time, it is this toward which we endlessly struggle and from which, endlessly, we struggle to escape.

It must be remembered that the oppressed and the oppressor are bound together within the same society; they accept the same criteria, they share the same beliefs, they both alike depend on the same reality. Within this cage it is romantic, more, meaningless, to speak of a "new" society as the desire of the oppressed, for that shivering dependence on the props of reality which he shares with the *Herrenvolk*[8] makes a truly "new" society impossible to conceive. What is meant by a new society is one in which inequalities will disappear, in which vengeance will be exacted; either there will be no oppressed at all or the oppressed and the oppressor will change places. But, finally, as it seems to me, what the rejected desire is, is an elevation of status, acceptance within the present community. Thus, the African, exile, pagan, hurried off the auction block and into the fields, fell on his knees before that God in Whom he must now believe; who had made him, but not in His image. This tableau, this impossibility, is the heritage of the Negro in America: *Wash me*, cried the

8. Master race (German); the Nazi idea of the German people as destined for mastery.

slave to his Maker, *and I shall be whiter, whiter than snow!* For black is the color of evil; only the robes of the saved are white. It is this cry, implacable on the air and in the skull, that he must live with. Beneath the widely published catalogue of brutality—bringing to mind, somehow, an image, a memory of church-bells burdening the air—is this reality which in the same nightmare notion, he both flees and rushes to embrace. In America, now, this country devoted to the death of the paradox—which may, therefore, be put to death by one—his lot is as ambiguous as a tableau by Kafka.[9] To flee or not, to move or not, it is all the same, his doom is written on his forehead, it is carried in his heart. In *Native Son*,[1] Bigger Thomas stands on a Chicago street corner watching air-planes flown by white men racing against the sun and "Goddamn" he says, the bitterness bubbling up like blood, remembering a million indignities, the terrible, rat-infested house, the humiliation of home-relief, the intense, aimless, ugly bickering, hating it; hatred smoulders through these pages like sulphur fire. All of Bigger's life is controlled, defined by his hatred and his fear. And later, his fear drives him to murder and his hatred to rape; he dies, having come, through this violence, we are told, for the first time, to a kind of life, having for the first time redeemed his manhood. Below the surface of this novel there lies, as it seems to me, a continuation, a complement of that monstrous legend it was written to destroy. Bigger is Uncle Tom's descendant, flesh of his flesh, so exactly opposite a portrait that, when the books are placed together, it seems that the contemporary Negro novelist and the dead New England woman are locked together in a deadly, timeless battle; the one uttering merciless exhortations, the other shouting curses. And, indeed, within this web of lust and fury, black and white can only thrust and counter-thrust, long for each other's slow, exquisite death; death by torture, acid, knives and burning; the thrust, the counter-thrust, the longing making the heavier that cloud which blinds and suffocates them both, so that they go down into the pit together. Thus has the cage betrayed us all, this moment, our life, turned to nothing through our terrible attempts to insure it. For Bigger's tragedy is not that he is cold or black or hungry, not even that he is American, black; but that he has accepted a theology that denies him life, that he admits the possibility of his being sub-human and feels constrained, therefore, to battle for his humanity according to those brutal criteria bequeathed him at his birth. But our humanity is our burden, our life, we need not battle for it; we need only do what is infinitely more difficult, that is,

9. Franz Kafka (1883–1924), German novelist and short-story writer born in Prague.
1. Novel by Richard Wright (1940).

accept it. The failure of the protest novel lies in its rejection of life, the human being, the denial of his beauty, dread, power, in its insistence that it is his categorization alone which is real and which cannot be transcended.

## JANE P. TOMPKINS

### Sentimental Power: *Uncle Tom's Cabin* and the Politics of Literary History†

Once, during a difficult period of my life, I lived in the basement of a house on Forest Street in Hartford, Connecticut, which had belonged to Isabella Beecher Hooker—Harriet Beecher Stowe's half-sister. This woman at one time in her life had believed that the millennium was at hand and that she was destined to be the leader of a new matriarchy.[1] When I lived in that basement, however, I knew nothing of Stowe, or of the Beechers, or of the Utopian visions of nineteenth-century American women. I made a reverential visit to the Mark Twain house a few blocks away, took photographs of his study, and completely ignored Stowe's own house—also open to the public—which stood across the lawn. Why should I go? Neither I nor anyone I knew regarded Stowe as a serious writer. At the time I was giving my first lecture course in the American Renaissance—concentrated exclusively on Hawthorne, Melville, Poe, Emerson, Thoreau, and Whitman—and although *Uncle Tom's Cabin* was written in exactly the same period, and although it is probably the most influential book ever written by an American, I would never have dreamed of including it on my reading list. To begin with, its very popularity would have militated against it; as everybody knew, the classics of American fiction were, with a few exceptions, all *succès d'estime*.

In 1969, when I lived on Forest Street, the women's movement was just getting under way. It was several years before Kate Chopin's *The Awakening* and Charlotte Perkins Gilman's "The Yellow Wallpaper" would make it onto college reading lists, sandwiched in between Theodore Dreiser and Frank Norris. These women, like some of their male counterparts, had been unpopular in their own time and owed their reputations to the discernment of latter-day critics. Because of their work, it is now respectable to read these writers, who, unlike Nathaniel Hawthorne, had to wait several generations for their champions to appear in the literary establishment.

† From *Glyph* 2 (1978). Reprinted by permission.
1. Johanna Johnston, *Runaway to Heaven* (Garden City, N.Y.: Doubleday, 1963).

But despite the influence of the women's movement, and despite the explosion of work in nineteenth-century American social history, and despite the new historicism that is infiltrating literary studies, the women, like Harriet Beecher Stowe, whose names were household words in the nineteenth century—women such as Susan Warner, Sarah J. Hale, Augusta Evans, Elizabeth Stuart Phelps, her daughter Mary, who took the same name, and Frances Hodgson Burnett—these women remain excluded from the literary canon. And while it has recently become fashionable to study their works as examples of cultural deformation, even critics who have invested their professional careers in that study and who declare themselves feminists still refer to their novels as trash.[2]

My principal target of concern, however, is not feminists who have written on popular women novelists of the nineteenth century but the male-dominated scholarly tradition that controls both the canon of American literature (from which these novelists are excluded) and the critical perspective that interprets the canon for society. For the tradition of Perry Miller, F. O. Matthiessen, Harry Levin, Richard Chase, R. W. B. Lewis, Yvor Winters, and Henry Nash Smith has prevented even committed feminists from recognizing and asserting the *value* of a powerful and specifically female novelistic tradition. The very grounds on which sentimental fiction has been dismissed by its detractors, grounds that have come to seem universal standards of aesthetic judgment, were established in a struggle to supplant the tradition of evangelical piety and moral commitment these novelists represent. In reaction against their world view, and perhaps even more against their success, twentieth-century critics have taught generations of students to equate popularity with debasement, emotionality with ineffectiveness, religiosity with fakery, domesticity with triviality, and all of these, implicitly, with womanly inferiority.

In this view, sentimental novels written by women in the nineteenth century were responsible for a series of cultural evils whose effects still plague us: the degeneration of American religion from theological rigor to anti-intellectual consumerism, the rationaliza-

2. Edward Halsey Foster, for example, prefaces his book-length study of the work of Susan and Anna Warner by saying: "If one searches nineteenth century popular fiction for something that has literary value, one searches, by and large, in vain" (*Susan and Anna Warner* [Boston: G. K. Hall, 1978]). At the other end of the spectrum stands a critic like Sally Mitchell, whose excellent studies of Victorian women's fiction contain statements that, intentionally or not, condescend to the subject matter: e.g., "Thus, we should see popular novels as emotional analyses, rather than intellectual analyses, of a particular society" ("Sentiment and Suffering: Women's Recreational Reading in the 1860's," *Victorian Studies* 21 [Fall 1977]: 34). The most typical move, however, is to apologize for the poor literary quality of the novels in a concessive clause—melodramatic and simplistic though the plots may be, wooden and stereotyped as the characters may appear"—and then to assert that these texts are valuable on historical grounds.

tion of an unjust economic order, the propagation of the debased images of modern mass culture, and the encouragement of self-indulgence and narcissism in literature's most avid readers—women.[3] To the extent that they protested the evils of society, their protest is seen as duplicitous, the product and expression of the very values they pretended to condemn. Unwittingly or not, so the story goes, they were apologists for an oppressive social order. In contrast to male authors like Thoreau, Whitman, and Melville, who are celebrated as models of intellectual daring and honesty, these women are generally thought to have traded in false stereotypes, dishing out weak-minded pap to nourish the prejudices of an ill-educated and underemployed female readership. Self-deluded and unable to face the harsh facts of a competitive society, they are portrayed as manipulators of a gullible public who kept their readers imprisoned in a dream world of self-justifying clichés. Their fight against the evils of their society was a fixed match from the start.[4]

The thesis I will argue in this essay is diametrically opposed to these. It holds that the popular domestic novel of the nineteenth century represents a monumental effort to reorganize culture from the woman's point of view; that this body of work is remarkable for its intellectual complexity, ambition, and resourcefulness; and that, in certain cases, it offers a critique of American society far more devastating than any delivered by better-known critics such as Hawthorne and Melville. Finally, it suggests that the enormous popularity of these novels, which has been cause for suspicion bordering on disgust, is a reason for paying close attention to them. *Uncle Tom's Cabin* was, in almost any terms one can think of, the most important book of the century. It was the first American novel ever to sell over a million copies, and its impact is generally thought to have been incalculable. Expressive of and responsible for the values of its time, it also belongs to a genre, the sentimental novel, whose chief characteristic is that it is written by, for, and about women. In this respect, *Uncle Tom's Cabin* is not exceptional

3. Ann Douglas is the foremost of the feminist critics who have accepted this characterization of the sentimental writers, and it is to her formulation of the antisentimentalist position that my arguments throughout are principally addressed (*The Feminization of American Culture* [New York: Alfred A. Knopf, 1977]). Although her attitude toward the vast quantity of literature written by women between 1820 and 1870 is the one that the male-dominated tradition has always expressed—contempt—Douglas's book is nevertheless extremely important because of its powerful and sustained consideration of this long-neglected body of work. Because Douglas successfully focused critical attention on the cultural centrality of sentimental fiction, forcing the realization that it can no longer be ignored, it is now possible for other critics to put forward a new characterization of these novels and not be dismissed. For these reasons, it seems to me, her work is invaluable.

4. These attitudes are forcefully articulated by Douglas, ibid., p. 9.

but representative. It is the *summa theologica* of nineteenth-century America's religion of domesticity, a brilliant redaction of the culture's favorite story about itself: the story of salvation through motherly love. Out of the ideological materials they had at their disposal, the sentimental novelists elaborated a myth that gave women the central position of power and authority in the culture; and of these efforts *Uncle Tom's Cabin* is the most dazzling exemplar.

I have used words like "monumental" and "dazzling" to describe Stowe's novel and the tradition of which it is a part because they have for too long been the casualties of a set of critical attitudes that equate intellectual merit with certain kinds of argumentative discourse and certain kinds of subject matter. A long tradition of academic parochialism has enforced this sort of discourse through a series of cultural contrasts: light "feminine" novels versus tough-minded intellectual treatises; domestic "chattiness" versus serious thinking; and summarily, the "damned mob of scribbling women" versus a few giant intellects, unappreciated and misunderstood in their time, struggling manfully against a flood of sentimental rubbish.[5]

The inability of twentieth-century critics either to appreciate the complexity and scope of a novel like Stowe's or to account for its enormous popular success stems from their assumptions about the nature and function of literature. In modernist thinking, literature is by definition a form of discourse that has no designs on the world. It does not attempt to change things, but merely to represent them, and it does so in a specifically literary language whose claim to value lies in its uniqueness. Consequently, works whose stated purpose is to influence the course of history, and which therefore employ a language that is not only not unique but common and accessible to everyone, do not qualify as works of art. Literary texts such as the sentimental novel, which make continual and obvious appeals to the reader's emotions and use technical devices that are distinguished by their utter conventionality, epitomize the opposite of everything that good literature is supposed to be. "For the literary critic," writes J. W. Ward, summing up the dilemma posed by *Uncle Tom's Cabin*, "the problem is how a book so seemingly artless,

5. The phrase "a damned mob of scribbling women," coined by Nathaniel Hawthorne in a letter he wrote to his publisher in 1855 and clearly the product of Hawthorne's own feelings of frustration and envy, comes embedded in a much-quoted passage that has set the tone for criticism of sentimental fiction ever since: "America is now wholly given over to a d * * * * d mob of scribbling women, and I should have no chance of success while the public taste is occupied with their trash—and should be ashamed of myself if I did succeed. What is the mystery of these innumerable editions of *The Lamplighter*, and other books neither better nor worse? Worse they could not be, and better they need not be, when they sell by the hundred thousand." As quoted by Fred Lewis Pattee, *The Feminine Fifties* (New York: D. Appleton-Century, 1940), p. 110.

so lacking in apparent literary talent, was not only an immediate success but has endured."[6]

How deep the problem goes is illustrated dramatically by George F. Whicher's discussion of Stowe's novel in *The Literary History of the United States.* Reflecting the consensus view on what good novels are made of, Whicher writes: "Nothing attributable to Mrs. Stowe or her handiwork can account for the novel's enormous vogue; its author's resources as a purveyor of Sunday-school fiction were not remarkable. She had at most a ready command of broadly conceived melodrama, humor, and pathos, and of these popular elements she compounded her book."[7] At a loss to understand how a book so compounded was able to "convulse a mighty nation," Whicher concludes—incredibly—that Stowe's own explanation, that "God wrote it," "solved the paradox." Rather than give up his bias against "melodrama," "pathos," and "Sunday-school fiction," Whicher takes refuge in a solution which, even according to his lights, is patently absurd.[8] And no wonder. The modernist literary aesthetic cannot account for the unprecedented and persistent popularity of a book like *Uncle Tom's Cabin,* for this novel operates according to principles quite other than those which have been responsible for determining the currently sanctified American literary classics.

It is not my purpose, however, to drag Hawthorne and Melville from their pedestals, nor to claim that the novels of Harriet Beecher Stowe, Fanny Fern, and Elizabeth Stuart Phelps are good in the same way that *Moby Dick* and *The Scarlet Letter* are; rather, I will argue that the work of the sentimental writers is complex and significant in ways *other than* those which characterize the established

6. J. W. Ward, *Red, White, and Blue: Men, Books, and Ideas in American Culture* (New York: Oxford University Press, 1961), p. 75.
7. George F. Whicher, "Literature and Conflict," in *The Literary History of the United States*, ed. Robert E. Spiller et al., 3rd ed., rev. (New York: Macmillan, 1963), p. 583.
8. Ibid., p. 586. Edmund Wilson, despite his somewhat sympathetic treatment of Stowe in *Patriotic Gore*, seems to concur in this opinion, reflecting a characteristic tendency of commentators on the most popular works of sentimental fiction to regard the success of these women as some sort of mysterious eruption, inexplicable by natural causes (*Patriotic Gore: Studies in the Literature of the American Civil War* [New York: Oxford University Press, 1966], pp. 5, 32). Henry James gives this attitude its most articulate, though perhaps least defensible, expression in a remarkable passage from *A Small Boy and Others* (New York: Charles Scribner's Sons, 1913) where he describes Stowe's book as really not a book at all but "a fish, a wonderful 'leaping' fish"—the point being to deny Stowe any role in the process that produced such a wonder:

> Appreciation and judgment, the whole impression, were thus an effect for which there had been no process—any process so related having in other cases *had* to be at some point or other critical; nothing in the guise of a written book, therefore, a book printed, published, sold, bought and "noticed," probably ever reached its mark, the mark of exciting interest, without having at least groped for that goal *as* a book or by the exposure of some literary side. Letters, here, languished unconscious, and Uncle Tom, instead of making even one of the cheap short cuts through the medium in which books breathe, even as fishes in water, went gaily roundabout it altogether, as if a fish, a wonderful "leaping" fish, had simply flown in through the air. (Pp. 159–60)

masterpieces. I will ask the reader to set aside some familiar categories for evaluating fiction—stylistic intricacy, psychological subtlety, epistemological complexity—and to see the sentimental novel, not as an artifice of eternity answerable to certain formal criteria and to certain psychological and philosophical concerns, but as a political enterprise, halfway between sermon and social theory, that both codifies and attempts to mold the values of its time.

The power of a sentimental novel to move its audience depends upon the audience's being in possession of the conceptual categories that constitute character and event. That storehouse of assumptions includes attitudes towards the family and towards social institutions, a definition of power and its relation to individual human feeling, notions of political and social equality, and above all, a set of religious beliefs that organize and sustain the rest. Once in possession of the system of beliefs that undergirds the patterns of sentimental fiction, it is possible for modern readers to see how its tearful episodes and frequent violations of probability were invested with a structure of meanings that fixed these works, for nineteenth-century readers, not in the realm of fairy tale or escapist fantasy, but in the very bedrock of reality. I do not say that we can read sentimental fiction exactly as Stowe's audience did—that would be impossible—but that we can and should set aside the modernist prejudices that consign this fiction to oblivion, in order to see how and why it worked for its readers, in its time, with such unexampled effect.

Let us consider the episode in *Uncle Tom's Cabin* most often cited as the epitome of Victorian sentimentalism—the death of little Eva—because it is the kind of incident most offensive to the sensibilities of twentieth-century academic critics. It is on the belief that this incident is nothing more than a sob story that the whole case against sentimentalism rests. Little Eva's death, so the argument goes, like every other sentimental tale, is awash with emotion but does nothing to remedy the evils it deplores. Essentially, it leaves the slave system and the other characters unchanged. This trivializing view of the episode is grounded in assumptions about power and reality so common that we are not even aware they have been invoked. Thus generations of critics have commented with condescending irony on little Eva's death. But in the system of belief that undergirds Stowe's enterprise, dying is the supreme form of heroism. In *Uncle Tom's Cabin*, death is the equivalent not of defeat but of victory; it brings an access of power, not a loss of it; it is not only the crowning achievement of life, it *is* life, and Stowe's entire presentation of little Eva is designed to dramatize this fact.

Stories like the death of little Eva are compelling for the same reason that the story of Christ's death is compelling: they enact a philosophy, as much political as religious, in which the pure and powerless die to save the powerful and corrupt, and thereby show themselves more powerful than those they save. They enact, in short, a *theory* of power in which the ordinary or "commonsense" view of what is efficacious and what is not (a view to which most modern critics are committed) is simply reversed, as the very possibility of social action is made dependent on the action taking place in individual hearts. Little Eva's death enacts the drama of which all the major episodes of the novel are transformations: the idea, central to Christian soteriology,[9] that the highest human calling is to give one's life for another. It presents one version of the ethic of sacrifice on which the entire novel is based and contains in some form all of the motifs that, by their frequent recurrence, constitute the novel's ideological framework.

Little Eva's death, moreover, is also a transformation of stories circulating in the culture at large. It may be found, for example, in a dozen or more versions in the evangelical sermons of the Reverend Dwight Lyman Moody when he preached in Great Britain and Ireland in 1875. In one version it is called "The Child Angel," and it concerns a beautiful golden-haired girl of seven, her father's pride and joy, who dies and, by appearing to him in a dream in which she calls to him from heaven, brings him salvation.[1] The tale shows that by dying even a child can be the instrument of redemption for others, since in death she acquires over those who loved her a spiritual power beyond what she possessed in life.

The power of the dead or the dying to redeem the unregenerate is a major theme of nineteenth-century popular fiction and religious literature. Mothers and children are thought to be uniquely capable of this work. In a sketch entitled "Children," published the year after *Uncle Tom* came out, Stowe writes: "Wouldst thou know, O parent, what is that faith which unlocks heaven? Go not to wrangling polemics, or creeds and forms of theology, but draw to thy bosom thy little one, and read in that clear trusting eye the lesson of eternal life."[2] If children through their purity and innocence can lead adults to God while living, their spiritual power when they are dead is greater still. Death, Stowe argues in a pamphlet entitled *Ministration of Departed Spirits*, enables the Christian to begin his "real work." God takes people from us sometimes so that their "ministry can act upon us more powerfully from the unseen world."[3]

9. A branch of theology that deals with salvation as the effect of divine agency [*Editor*].
1. Reverend Dwight Lyman Moody, *Sermons and Addresses*, in *Narrative of Messrs. Moody and Sankey's Labors in Great Britain and Ireland with Eleven Addresses and Lectures in Full* (New York: Anson D. F. Randolph, 1875).
2. Harriet Beecher Stowe, "Children," in *Uncle Sam's Emancipation; Earthly Care, a Heavenly Discipline; and other sketches* (Philadelphia: W. P. Hazard, 1853), p. 83.
3. Harriet Beecher Stowe, *Ministration of Departed Spirits* (Boston: American Tract Society, n.d.), pp. 4, 3.

> The mother would fain electrify the heart of her child. She yearns and burns in vain to make her soul effective on its soul, and to inspire it with a spiritual and holy life; but all her own weaknesses, faults and mortal cares, cramp and confine her till death breaks all fetters; and then, first truly alive, risen, purified, and at rest, she may do calmly, sweetly, and certainly, what, amid the tempest and tossings of her life, she labored for painfully and fitfully.[4]

When the spiritual power of death is combined with the natural sanctity of childhood, the child becomes an angel endowed with salvific force.

Most often, it is the moment of death that saves, when the dying child, glimpsing for a moment the glory of heaven, testifies to the reality of the life to come. Uncle Tom knows that this will happen when little Eva dies, and explains it to Miss Ophelia as follows:

> "You know it says in Scripture, 'At midnight there was a great cry made. Behold the bridegroom cometh.' That's what I'm specting' now, every night, Miss Feely,—and I couldn't sleep out o' hearin' no ways."
>
> "Uncle Tom, what makes you think so?"
>
> "Miss Eva, she talks to me. The lord, he sends his messenger in the soul. I must be thar, Miss Feely; for when that ar blessed child goes into the kingdom, they'll open the door so wide, we'll all get a look in at the glory, Miss Feely."[5]

Little Eva does not disappoint them. At the moment when she passes "from death into life," she exclaims, "O, love!—joy!—peace!" And her exclamation echoes those of scores of children who die in Victorian fiction and sermon literature with heaven in their eyes. Dickens's Paul Dombey, seeing the face of his dead mother, dies with the words "The light about the head is shining on me as I go!" The fair, blue-eyed young girl in Lydia Sigourney's *Letters to Mothers*, "death's purple tinge upon her brow," when implored by her mother to utter one last word, whispers "Praise!"[6]

Of course, it could be argued by critics of sentimentalism that the prominence of stories about the deaths of children is precisely what is wrong with the literature of the period; rather than being cited as a source of strength, the presence of such stories in *Uncle Tom's*

4. Ibid., p. 3.
5. Harriet Beecher Stowe, *Uncle Tom's Cabin; or, Life Among the Lowly* (New York: Harper & Row, 1965), pp. 295–96 [268]. This Harper Classic gives the text of the first edition originally published by John P. Jewett & Company of Boston and Cleveland in 1852. All future references to *Uncle Tom's Cabin* will be to this edition; page numbers are given in parentheses in the text. [Norton Critical Edition page numbers appear in brackets—*Editor.*]
6. Charles Dickens, *Dombey and Son* (Boston: Estes & Lauriat, 1882), p. 278; Lydia H. Sigourney, *Letters to Mothers* (Hartford, Conn.: Hudson & Skinner, 1838).

*Cabin* should be regarded as an unfortunate concession to the age's fondness for lachrymose scenes. But to dismiss such scenes as "all tears and flapdoodle" is to leave unexplained the popularity of the novels and sermons that are filled with them, unless we choose to believe that a generation of readers was unaccountably moved to tears by matters that are intrinsically silly and trivial. That popularity is better explained, I believe, by the relationship of these scenes to a pervasive cultural myth which invests the suffering and death of an innocent victim with just the kind of power that critics deny to Stowe's novel: the power to work in, and change, the world.

This is the kind of action that little Eva's death in fact performs. It proves its efficacy, not through the sudden collapse of the slave system, but through the conversion of Topsy, a motherless, godless black child who has up until that point successfully resisted all attempts to make her "good." Topsy will not be "good" because, never having had a mother's love, she believes that no one can love her. When Eva suggests that Miss Ophelia would love her if only she were good, Topsy cries out, "No, she can't bar me, cause I'm a nigger!—she'd as soon have a toad touch her! Ther can't nobody love niggers, and niggers can't do nothin'! *I* don't care."

> "O, Topsy, poor child, *I* love you!" said Eva with a sudden burst of feeling and laying her little thin, white hand on Topsy's shoulder; "I love you, because you haven't had any father, or mother, or friends;—because you've been a poor, abused child! I love you, and I want you to be good. I am very unwell, Topsy, and I think I shan't live a great while; and it really grieves me, to have you be so naughty. I wish you would try to be good, for my sake;—it's only a little while I shall be with you."
>
> The round, keen eyes of the black child were overcast with tears:—large, bright drops rolled heavily down one by one, and fell on the little white hand. Yes, in that moment, a ray of real belief, a ray of heavenly love, had penetrated the darkness of her heathen soul! She laid her head down between her knees, and wept and sobbed,—while the beautiful child, bending over her, looked like the picture of some bright angel stooping to reclaim a sinner. (P. 283) [258]

The rhetoric and imagery of this passage, its little white hand, its ray from heaven, bending angel, and plentiful tears, suggest a literary version of the kind of polychrome religious picture that hangs on Sunday school walls. Words like "kitsch," "camp," and "corny" come to mind. But what is being dramatized here bears no relation to these designations. By giving Topsy her love, Eva initiates a process of redemption whose power, transmitted from heart to heart, can change the entire world. And indeed, the process has begun.

From that time on, Topsy is "different from what she used to be" (eventually she will go to Africa and become a missionary to her entire race), and Miss Ophelia, who overhears the conversation, is different too. When little Eva is dead and Topsy cries out, "Ther an't *nobody* left now," Miss Ophelia answers her in Eva's place:

> "Topsy, you poor child," she said, as she led her into her room, "don't give up! *I* can love you, though I am not like that dear little child. I hope I've learnt something of the love of Christ from her. I can love you; I do, and I'll try to help you to grow up a good Christian girl."
>
> Miss Ophelia's voice was more than her words, and more than that were the honest tears that fell down her face. From that hour, she acquired an influence over the mind of the destitute child that she never lost. (P. 300) [273]

The tears of Topsy and of Miss Ophelia, which we find easy to ridicule, are the sign of redemption in *Uncle Tom's Cabin;* not words but the emotions of the heart bespeak a state of grace, and these are known by the sound of a voice, the touch of a hand, but chiefly, in moments of greatest importance, by tears. When Tom lies dying on the plantation on the Red River, the disciples to whom he has preached testify to their conversion by weeping.

> Tears had fallen on that honest, insensible face,—tears of late repentance in the poor, ignorant heathen, whom his dying love and patience had awakened to repentance. . . . (P. 420) [380]

Even the bitter and unregenerate Cassy, "moved by the sacrifice that had been made for her," breaks down; "moved by the few last words which the affectionate soul had yet strength to breathe, . . . the dark, despairing woman had wept and prayed" (p. 420) [380]. When George Shelby, the son of Tom's old master, arrives too late to free him, "tears which did honor to his manly heart fell from the young man's eyes as he bent over his poor friend." And when Tom realizes who is there, "the whole face lighted up, the hard hands clasped, and tears ran down the cheeks" (p. 420) [380]. The vocabulary of clasping hands and falling tears is one we associate with emotional exhibitionism, with the over-acting that kills true feeling off through exaggeration. But the tears and gestures of Stowe's characters are not in excess of what they feel; if anything, they fall short of expressing the experiences they point to—salvation, communion, reconciliation.

If the language of tears seems maudlin and little Eva's death ineffectual, it is because both the tears and the redemption they signify belong to a conception of the world that is now generally regarded as naïve and unrealistic. Topsy's salvation and Miss Ophelia's do not alter the anti-abolitionist majority in the Senate or prevent Southern plantation owners and Northern investment bankers from doing business to their mutual advantage. Because most modern readers regard such political and economic facts as final, it is difficult for them to take seriously a novel that insists on religious conversion as the necessary precondition for sweeping social change. But in Stowe's understanding of what such change requires it is the *modern* view that is naïve. The political and economic measures that constitute effective action for us, she regards as superficial, mere extensions of the worldly policies that produced the slave system in the first place. Therefore, when Stowe asks the question that is in every reader's mind at the end of the novel, namely, "What can any individual do?" she recommends, not specific alterations in the current political and economic arrangements, but rather a change of heart.

> There is one thing that every individual can do—they can see to it that *they feel right.* An atmosphere of sympathetic influence encircles every human being; and the man or woman who *feels* strongly, healthily and justly, on the great interests of humanity, is a constant benefactor to the human race. See, then, to your sympathies in this matter! Are they in harmony with the sympathies of Christ? or are they swayed and perverted by the sophistries of worldly policy? (P. 448) [404]

Stowe is not opposed to concrete measures such as the passage of laws or the formation of political pressure groups; it is just that by themselves, such actions would be useless. For if slavery *were* to be abolished by these means, the moral conditions that produced slavery in the first place would continue in force. The choice is not between action and inaction, programs and feelings; the choice is between actions that spring from "the sophistries of worldly policy" and those inspired by "the sympathies of Christ." Reality, in Stowe's view, cannot be changed by manipulating the physical environment; it can only be changed by conversion in the spirit because it is the spirit alone that is finally real.

The notion that historical change takes place only through religious conversion, which is a theory of power as old as Christianity itself, is dramatized and vindicated in *Uncle Tom's Cabin* by the novel's insistence that all human events are organized, clarified, and made meaningful by the existence of spiritual realities.[7] The

7. Religious conversion as the basis for a new social order was the mainspring of the Christian evangelical movement of the mid-nineteenth century. The emphasis on "feeling," which seems to modern readers to provide no basis whatever for the organization of society, was the key factor in the evangelical theory of reform. See Sandra Sizer's discussions of this phenomenon in *Gospel Hymns and Social Religion: The Rhetoric of Nineteenth-Century Revivalism* (Philadelphia: Temple University Press, 1979): "It is clear from the available literature that prayer, testimony, and exhortation were employed to create a *community* of intense *feeling*, in which individuals underwent similar experiences (centering on conversion) and would thenceforth unite with

novel is packed with references to the four last things—Heaven, Hell, Death, and Judgment—references which remind the reader constantly that historical events can only be seen for what they are in the light of eternal truths. When St. Clare stands over the grave of little Eva, unable to realize "that it was his Eva that they were hiding from his sight," Stowe interjects, "Nor was it!—not Eva, but only the frail seed of that bright immortal form in which she shall yet come forth, in the day of the Lord Jesus!" (p. 300) [273]. And when Legree expresses satisfaction that Tom is dead, she turns to him and says, "Yes, Legree; but who shall shut up that voice in thy soul? that soul, past repentance, past prayer, past hope, in whom the fire that never shall be quenched is already burning?" (p. 416) [377]. These reminders come thick and fast; they are present in Stowe's countless quotations from Scripture, introduced at every possible opportunity—in the narrative, in dialogue, in epigraphs, in quotations from other authors; they are present in the Protestant hymns that thread their way through scene after scene, in asides to the reader, in apostrophes to the characters, in quotations from religious poetry, sermons, and prayers, and in long stretches of dialogue and narrative devoted to the discussion of religious matters. Stowe's narrative stipulates a world in which the facts of Christ's death and resurrection and coming day of judgment are never far from our minds because it is only within this frame of reference that she can legitimately have Tom claim, as he dies, "I've got the victory."

The eschatological vision, by putting all individual events in relation to an order that is unchanging, collapses the distinctions between them so that they become interchangeable representations of a single timeless reality. Groups of characters blend into the same character, while the plot abounds in incidents that mirror one another. These features are the features, not of classical nineteenth-century fiction, but of typological narrative. It is this tradition rather than that of the English novel which *Uncle Tom's Cabin* reproduces and extends; for this novel does not simply quote the Bible, it rewrites the Bible as the story of a Negro slave. Formally and philosophically, it stands opposed to works like *Middlemarch* and *The Portrait of a Lady* in which everything depends on human action and decision unfolding in a temporal sequence that withholds revelation

others in matters of moral decision and social behavior" (p. 52). "People in similar states of feeling, in short, would 'walk together,' would be agreed" (p. 59). "Conversion established individuals in a particular kind of relationship with God, by virtue of which they were automatically members of a social company, alike in interests and feelings" (pp. 70–71). Good order would be preserved by "relying on the spiritual and moral discipline provided by conversion, and on the company of fellow Christians, operating without the coercive force of government" (p. 72).

until the final moment. The truths that Stowe's narrative conveys can only be reembodied, never discovered, because they are already revealed from the beginning. Therefore, what seem from a modernist point of view to be gross stereotypes in characterization and a needless proliferation of incident are essential properties of a narrative aimed at demonstrating that human history is a continual reenactment of the sacred drama of redemption. It is the novel's reenactment of this drama that made it irresistible in its day.

*Uncle Tom's Cabin* retells the culture's central religious myth, the story of the crucifixion, in terms of the nation's greatest political conflict—slavery—and of its most cherished social beliefs—the sanctity of motherhood and the family. It is because Stowe is able to combine so many of the culture's central concerns in a narrative that is immediately accessible to the general population that she is able to move so many people so deeply. The novel's typological organization allows her to present political and social situations both as themselves and as transformations of a religious paradigm which interprets them in a way that readers can both understand and respond to emotionally. For the novel functions both as a means of describing the social world and as a means of changing it. It not only offers an interpretative framework for understanding the culture and, through the reinforcement of a particular code of values, recommends a strategy for dealing with cultural conflict, but it is itself an agent of that strategy, putting into practice the measures it prescribes. As the religious stereotypes of "Sunday school fiction" define and organize the elements of social and political life, so the "melodrama" and "pathos" associated with the underlying myth of crucifixion put the reader's heart in the right place with respect to the problems the narrative defines. Hence, rather than making the enduring success of *Uncle Tom's Cabin* inexplicable, these popular elements that puzzled Whicher and have puzzled so many modern scholars—melodrama, pathos, Sunday school fiction—are the *only* terms in which the book's success can be explained.

The nature of these popular elements also dictates the terms in which any full-scale analysis of *Uncle Tom's Cabin* must be carried out. As I have suggested, its distinguishing features, generically speaking, are not those of the realistic novel but of typological narrative. Its characters, like the figures in an allegory, do not change or develop but reveal themselves in response to the demands of a situation. They are not defined primarily by their mental and emotional characteristics—that is to say, psychologically—but soteriologically, according to whether they are saved or damned. The plot, likewise, does not unfold according to Aristotelian standards of probability but in keeping with the logic of a preordained design, a design that every incident is intended, in one way or another, to enforce.[8] The setting does not so much describe the features of a particular time and place as point to positions on a spiritual map. In *Uncle Tom's Cabin* the presence of realistic detail tends to obscure its highly programmatic nature and to lull readers into thinking that they are in an everyday world of material cause and effect. But what pass for realistic details—the use of dialect, the minute descriptions of domestic activity—are in fact performing a rhetorical function dictated by the novel's ruling paradigm; once that paradigm is perceived, even the homeliest details show up not as the empirically observed facts of human existence but as the expressions of a highly schematic intent.[9]

This schematization has what one might call a totalizing effect on the particulars of the narrative, so that every character in the novel, every scene, and every incident comes to be apprehended in terms of every *other* character, scene, and incident: all are caught up in a system of endless cross-reference in which it is impossible to refer to one without referring to all the rest. To demonstrate what I mean by this kind of narrative organization—a demonstration that will have to stand in lieu of a full-scale reading of the novel—let me show how it works in relation to a single scene. Eva and Tom are seated in the garden of St. Clare's house on the shores of Lake Pontchartrain.

> It was Sunday evening, and Eva's Bible lay open on her knee. She read,—"And I saw a sea of glass, mingled with fire."
>
> "Tom," said Eva, suddenly stopping, and pointing to the lake, "there 't is."
>
> "What, Miss Eva?"
>
> "Don't you see,—there?" said the child, pointing to the glassy water, which, as it rose and fell, reflected the golden glow of the sky. "There's a 'sea of glass, mingled with fire.'"
>
> "True enough, Miss Eva," said Tom: and Tom sang—

8. Angus Fletcher's *Allegory: The Theory of a Symbolic Mode* (Ithaca, N.Y.: Cornell University Press, 1964) discusses the characteristic features of allegory in such a way as to make clear the family resemblance between sentimental fiction and the allegorical mode. See, particularly, his analysis of character (pp. 35, 60), symbolic action (pp. 150 ff., 178, 180, 182), and imagery (p. 171).
9. Fletcher's comment on the presence of naturalistic detail in allegory is pertinent here:

> The apparent surface realism of an allegorical agent will recede in importance, as soon as he is felt to take part in a magical plot, as soon as his causal relations to others in that plot are seen to be magically based. This is an important point because there has often been confusion as to the function of the naturalist detail of so much allegory. In terms I have been outlining, this detail now appears not to have a journalistic function; it is more than a mere record of observed facts. It serves instead the purposes of magical containment, since the more the allegorist can circumscribe the attributes, metonymic and synecdochic, of his personae, the better he can shape their fictional destiny. Naturalist detail is "cosmic," universalizing, not accidental as it would be in straight journalism. (Pp. 198–99)

> *"O, had I the wings of the morning,*
> *I'd fly away to Canaan's shore;*
> *Bright angels should convey me home,*
> *To the new Jerusalem."*

"Where do you suppose new Jerusalem is, Uncle Tom?" said Eva.

"O, up in the clouds, Miss Eva."

"Then I think I see it," said Eva. "Look in those clouds!—they look like great gates of pearl; and you can see beyond them—far, far off—it's all gold. Tom, sing about 'spirits bright.'"

Tom sang the words of a well-known Methodist hymn,

> *"I see a band of spirits bright,*
> *That taste the glories there;*
> *They are all robed in spotless white,*
> *And conquering palms they bear."*

"Uncle Tom, I've seen them." said Eva. . . . "They come to me sometimes in my sleep, those spirits;" and Eva's eyes grew dreamy, and she hummed, in a low voice,

> *"They are all robed in spotless white,*
> *And conquering palms they bear."*

"Uncle Tom," said Eva, "I'm going there."

"Where, Miss Eva?"

The child rose, and pointed her little hand to the sky; the glow of evening lit her golden hair and flushed cheek with a kind of unearthly radiance, and her eyes were bent earnestly on the skies.

"I'm going *there*," she said, "to the spirits bright, Tom; *I'm going, before long.*" (Pp. 261–62) [238–39]

The iterative nature of this scene presents in miniature the structure of the whole novel. Eva reads from her Bible about a "sea of glass, mingled with fire," then looks up to find one before her. She reads the words aloud a second time. They remind Tom of a hymn that describes the same vision in a slightly different form (Lake Pontchartrain and the sea of glass become "Canaan's shore" and the "new Jerusalem"), and Eva sees what he has sung, this time in the clouds, and offers her own description. Eva asks Tom to sing again, and his hymn presents yet another form of the same vision, which Eva again says she has seen: the spirits bright come to her in her sleep. Finally, Eva repeats the last two lines of the hymn and declares that she is going "there"—to the place that has now been referred to a dozen times in this passage. Stowe follows with another description of the golden skies and then with a description of Eva as a spirit bright, and closes the passage with Eva's double reiteration that she is going "there."

The entire scene itself is a re-presentation of others that come before and after. When Eva looks out over Lake Pontchartrain, she sees the "Canaan of liberty" which Eliza saw on the other side of the Ohio River, and the "eternal shores" Eliza and George Harris will reach when they cross Lake Erie in the end. Bodies of water mediate between worlds: the Ohio runs between the slave states and the free; Lake Erie divides the United States from Canada, where runaway slaves cannot be returned to their masters; the Atlantic Ocean divides the North American continent from Africa, where Negroes will have a nation of their own; Lake Pontchartrain shows Eva the heavenly home to which she is going soon; the Mississippi River carries slaves from the relative ease of the Middle States to the grinding toil of the Southern plantations; the Red River carries Tom to the infernal regions ruled over by Simon Legree. The correspondences between the episodes I have mentioned are themselves based on correspondences between earth and heaven (or hell). Ohio, Canada, and Liberia are related to one another by virtue of their relationship to the one "bright Canaan" for which they stand; the Mississippi River and the Ohio are linked by the Jordan. (Ultimately, there are only three places to be in this story: heaven, hell, or Kentucky, which represents the earthly middle ground in Stowe's geography.)

Characters in the novel are linked to each other in exactly the same way that places are: with reference to a third term that is the source of their identity. The figure of Christ is the common term that unites all of the novel's good characters, who are good precisely in proportion as they are imitations of him. Eva and Tom head the list (she reenacts the Last Supper and he the crucifixion) but they are also linked to most of the slaves, women, and children in the novel by the characteristics they all share: piety, impressionability, spontaneous affection—and victimization.[1] In this scene, Eva is linked with the "spirits bright" (she later becomes a "bright immortal form") both because she can see them and is soon to join them and because she, too, always wears white and is else-

1. The associations that link slaves, women, and children are ubiquitous and operate on several levels. Besides being described in the same set of terms, these characters occupy parallel structural positions in the plot. They function chiefly as mediators between God and the unredeemed, so that, e.g., Mrs. Shelby intercedes for Mr. Shelby, Mrs. Bird for Senator Bird, Simon Legree's mother (unsuccessfully) for Simon Legree, little Eva and St. Clare's mother for St. Clare, Tom Loker's mother for Tom Loker, Eliza for George Harris (spiritually, she is the agent of his conversion) and for Harry Harris (physically, she saves him from being sold down the river), and Tom for all the slaves on the Legree plantation (spiritually, he converts them) and for all the slaves of the Shelby plantation (physically, he is the cause of their being set free).

where several times referred to as an "angel." When Eva dies, she will join her father's mother, who was also named Evangeline and who herself always wore white, and who, like Eva, is said to be "the direct and living embodiment of the New Testament." And this identification, in its turn, refers back to Uncle Tom, who is "all the moral and Christian virtues bound in black morocco complete." The circularity of this train of association is typical of the way the narrative doubles back on itself: later on, Cassy, impersonating the ghost of Legree's saintly mother, will wrap herself in a white sheet.[2]

The scene I have been describing is a node with a network of allusion in which every character and event in the novel has a place. The narrative's rhetorical strength derives in part from the impression it gives of taking every kind of detail in the world into account, from the preparation of breakfast to the orders of the angels, and investing those details with a purpose and a meaning that are both immediately apprehensible and finally significant. The novel reaches out into the reader's world and colonizes it for its own eschatology: that is, it not only incorporates the homely particulars of "Life Among the Lowly" into its universal scheme, but it gives them a power and a centrality in that scheme which turns the sociopolitical order upside down. The totalizing effect of the novel's iterative organization and its doctrine of spiritual redemption are inseparably bound to its political purpose, which is to bring in the day when the meek—that is to say, women—will inherit the earth.

The specifically political intent of the novel is apparent in its forms of address. Stowe addresses her readers not simply as individuals but as citizens of the United States: "to you, generous, noble-minded men and women of the South," "farmers of Massachusetts, of New Hampshire, of Vermont," "brave and generous men of New York," "and you, mothers of America." She speaks to her audience directly in the way the Old Testament prophets spoke to Israel, exhorting, praising, blaming, warning of the wrath to come. "This is an age of the world when nations are trembling and convulsed. Almighty influence is abroad, surging and heaving the world, as with an earthquake. And is America safe? . . . O, Church of Christ, read the signs of the times!" (p. 451) [408]. Passages like these, descended from the revivalist rhetoric of *Sinners in the Hands of an Angry God*, are intended, in the words of a noted scholar, "to direct an imperiled people toward the fulfillment of their destiny, to

2. For a parallel example, see Alice Crozier's analysis of the way the lock of hair that little Eva gives Tom becomes transformed into the lock of hair that Simon Legree's mother sent to Simon Legree. *The Novels of Harriet Beecher Stowe* (New York: Oxford University Press, 1969), pp. 29–31.

guide them individually towards salvation, and collectively toward the American city of God."[3]

These sentences are from Sacvan Bercovitch's *The American Jeremiad*, an influential work of modern scholarship which, although it completely ignores Stowe's novel, makes us aware that *Uncle Tom's Cabin* is a jeremiad in the fullest and truest sense. A jeremiad, in Bercovitch's definition, is "a mode of public exhortation . . . designed to join social criticism to spiritual renewal, public to private identity, the shifting 'signs of the times' to certain traditional metaphors, themes, and symbols."[4] Stowe's novel provides the most obvious and compelling instance of the jeremiad since the Great Awakening, and its exclusion from Bercovitch's book is a striking instance of how totally academic criticism has foreclosed on sentimental fiction; for, because *Uncle Tom's Cabin* is absent from the canon, it is not "there" to be referred to even when it fulfills a man's theory to perfection; hence its exclusion from critical discourse is perpetuated automatically, and absence begets itself in a self-confirming cycle of neglect. Nonetheless, Bercovitch's characterization of the jeremiad provides an excellent account of how *Uncle Tom's Cabin* actually worked: among its characters, settings, situations, symbols, and doctrines, the novel establishes a set of correspondences that unite the disparate realms of experience Bercovitch names—social and spiritual, public and private, theological and political—and, through the vigor of its representations, attempts to move the nation as a whole toward the vision it proclaims.

The tradition of the jeremiad throws light on *Uncle Tom's Cabin* because Stowe's novel was political in exactly the same way the jeremiad was: both were forms of discourse in which "theology was wedded to politics and politics to the progress of the kingdom of God."[5] The jeremiad strives to persuade its listeners to a providential view of human history which serves, among other things, to maintain the Puritan theocracy in power. Its fusion of theology and politics is not only doctrinal, in that it ties the salvation of the individual to the community's historical enterprise; it is practical as well, for it reflects the interests of Puritan ministers in their bid to retain spiritual and secular authority. The sentimental novel, too, is an act of persuasion aimed at defining social reality; the difference is that the jeremiad represents the interests of Puritan ministers, while the sentimental novel represents the interests of middle-class women. But the relationship between rhetoric and history in both cases is the same. In both cases it is not as if rhetoric and history

3. Sacvan Bercovitch, *The American Jeremiad* (Madison: University of Wisconsin Press, 1978), p. 9.
4. Ibid., p. xi.
5. Ibid., p. xiv.

stand opposed, with rhetoric made up of wish fulfillment and history made up of recalcitrant facts that resist rhetoric's onslaught. Rhetoric *makes* history by shaping reality to the dictates of its political design; it makes history by convincing the people of the world that its description of the world is the true one. The sentimental novelists make their bid for power by positing the kingdom of heaven on earth as a world over which women exercise ultimate control. If history did not take the course these writers recommended, it is not because they were not political, but because they were insufficiently persuasive.

*Uncle Tom's Cabin*, however, unlike its counterparts in the sentimental tradition, was spectacularly persuasive in conventional political terms: it induced a nation to go to war and to free its slaves. But in terms of its own conception of power, a conception it shares with other sentimental fiction, the novel was a political failure. Stowe conceived her book as an instrument for bringing about the day when the world would be ruled not by force but by Christian love. The novel's deepest political aspirations are expressed only secondarily in its devastating attack on the slave system; the true goal of Stowe's rhetorical undertaking is nothing less than the institution of the kingdom of heaven on earth. Embedded in the world of *Uncle Tom's Cabin*, which is the fallen world of slavery, there appears an idyllic picture, both Utopian and Arcadian, of the form human life would assume if Stowe's readers were to heed her moral lesson. In this vision, described in the chapter entitled "The Quaker Settlement," Christian love fulfills itself not in war but in daily living, and the principle of sacrifice is revealed not in crucifixion but in motherhood. The form that society takes bears no resemblance to the current social order. Man-made institutions—the church, the courts of law, the legislatures, the economic system—are nowhere in sight. The home is the center of all meaningful activity, women perform the most important tasks, work is carried on in a spirit of mutual cooperation, and the whole is guided by a Christian woman who, through the influence of her "loving words," "gentle moralities," and "motherly loving kindness," rules the world.

> For why? for twenty years or more, nothing but loving words and gentle moralities, and motherly loving kindness, had come from that chair;—head-aches and heart-aches innumerable had been cured there,—difficulties spiritual and temporal solved there,—all by one good, loving woman, God bless her! (P. 136) [122]

The woman in question *is* God in human form. Seated in her kitchen at the head of her table, passing out coffee and cake for breakfast, Rachel Halliday, the millenarian counterpart of little

Eva, enacts the redeemed form of the Last Supper. This is Holy Communion as it will be under the new dispensation: instead of the breaking of bones, the breaking of bread. The preparation of breakfast exemplifies the way people will work in the ideal society; there will be no competition, no exploitation, no commands. Motivated by self-sacrificing love, and joined to one another by its cohesive power, people will perform their duties willingly and with pleasure: moral suasion will take the place of force.

> All moved obediently to Rachel's gentle "Thee had better," or more gentle "Hadn't thee better?" in the work of getting breakfast. . . . Everything went on sociably, so quietly, so harmoniously, in the great kitchen,—it seemed so pleasant to everyone to do just what they were doing, there was an atmosphere of mutual confidence and good fellowship everywhere. (Pp. 141–42) [127]

The new matriarchy that Isabella Beecher Hooker[6] had dreamed of leading, pictured here in the Indiana kitchen ("for a breakfast in the luxurious valleys of Indiana is . . . like picking up the rose-leaves and trimming the bushes in Paradise"), constitutes the most politically subversive dimension of Stowe's novel, more disruptive and far-reaching in its potential consequences than even the starting of a war or the freeing of slaves. Nor is the ideal of matriarchy simply a daydream; Catharine Beecher, Stowe's elder sister, had offered a ground plan for the realization of such a vision in her *Treatise on Domestic Economy* (1841), which the two sisters republished in 1869 in an enlarged version entitled *The American Woman's Home.*[7] Dedicated "To the Women of América, in whose hands rest the real destinies of the republic," this is an instructional book on homemaking in which a wealth of scientific information and practical advice is pointed toward a millenarian goal. Centering on the home, for these women, is not a way of indulging in narcissistic fantasy, as critics have argued, or a turning away from the world into self-absorption and idle reverie; it is the prerequisite of world conquest, defined as the reformation of the human race through proper care and nurtur-

6. Younger sister of Harriet Beecher Stowe. Hooker (1822–1907) was a radical feminist who was active in campaigns for women's rights and suffrage. She believed that a new millennium was coming in which the world would be ruled by a matriarchy and she would serve as one of the leaders [*Editor*].

7. For an excellent discussion of Beecher's *Treatise* and of the entire cult of domesticity, see Kathryn Kish Sklar, *Catharine Beecher: A Study in American Domesticity* (New York: W. W. Norton, 1976; Copyright © 1973 by Yale University). For other helpful discussions of the topic, see Barbara G. Berg, *The Remembered Gate: Origins of American Feminism, The Woman and the City, 1800–1860* (New York: Oxford University Press, 1978); Sizer, *Gospel Hymns and Social Religion;* Ronald G. Walters, *The Antislavery Appeal: American Abolitionism after 1830* (Baltimore: Johns Hopkins University Press, 1976); and Barbara Welter, "The Cult of True Womanhood, 1820–1860," *American Quarterly* 18 (Summer 1966): 151–74.

ing of its young. Like *Uncle Tom's Cabin, The American Woman's Home* situates the minutiae of domestic life in relation to their soteriological function: "What, then, is the end designed by the family state which Jesus Christ came into this world to secure? It is to provide for the training of our race . . . by means of the self-sacrificing labors of the wise and good . . . with chief reference to a future immortal existence."[8] "The family state," the authors announce at the beginning, "is the aptest earthly illustration of the heavenly kingdom, and . . . woman is its chief minister."[9] In the body of the text the authors provide women with everything they need to know for the proper establishment and maintenance of home and family, from the construction of furniture ("The bed frame is to be fourteen inches wide, and three inches in thickness. At the head, and at the foot, is to be screwed a notched two-inch board, three inches wide, as in Fig. 8"), to architectural plans, to chapters of instruction on heating, ventilation, lighting, healthful diet and preparation of food, cleanliness, the making and mending of clothes, the care of the sick, the organization of routines, financial management, psychological health, the care of infants, the managing of young children, home amusement, the care of furniture, the planting of gardens, the care of domestic animals, the disposal of waste, the cultivation of fruit, and providing for "the helpless, the homeless, and the vicious." After each of these activities has been treated in detail, they conclude by describing the ultimate aim of the domestic enterprise: the founding of a "truly 'Christian family'" will lead to the gathering of a "Christian neighborhood." This "cheering example," they continue,

> would soon spread, and ere long colonies from these prosperous and Christian communities would go forth to shine as "lights of the world" in all the now darkened nations. Thus the "Christian family" and "Christian neighborhood" would become the grand ministry, as they were designed to be, in training our whole race for heaven.[1]

The imperialistic drive behind the encyclopedism and determined practicality of this household manual flatly contradicts the traditional derogations of the American cult of domesticity as a "mirror-phenomenon," "self-immersed" and "self-congratulatory."[2]

*The American Woman's Home* is a blueprint for colonizing the world in the name of the "family state" under the leadership of

8. Catharine Beecher and Harriet Beecher Stowe, *The American Woman's Home: or Principles of Domestic Science; Being a Guide to the Formation and Maintenance of Economical, Healthful, Beautiful, and Christian Homes* (New York: J. B. Ford, 1869), p. 18.
9. Ibid., p. 19.
1. Ibid., pp. 458–59.
2. These are Douglas's epithets; see *Feminization of American Culture*, p. 307.

Christian women. What is more, people like Stowe and Catharine Beecher were speaking not simply for a set of moral and religious values. In speaking for the home, they spoke for an economy—household economy—which had supported New England life since its inception. The home, rather than representing a retreat or a refuge from a crass industrial-commercial world, offers an economic *alternative* to that world, one which calls into question the whole structure of American society that was growing up in response to the increase in trade and manufacturing.[3] Stowe's image of a utopian community as presented in Rachel Halliday's kitchen is not simply a Christian dream of communitarian cooperation and harmony; it is a reflection of the real communitarian practices of village life, practices that had depended upon cooperation, trust, and a spirit of mutual supportiveness such as characterize the Quaker community of Stowe's novel.

One could argue, then, that for all its revolutionary fervor *Uncle Tom's Cabin* is a conservative book, because it advocates a return to an older way of life—household economy—in the name of the nation's most cherished social and religious beliefs. Even the woman's centrality might be seen as harking back to the "age of homespun" when the essential goods were manufactured in the home and their production was carried out and guided by women. But Stowe's very conservatism—her reliance on established patterns of living and traditional beliefs—is precisely what gives her novel its revolutionary potential. By pushing those beliefs to an extreme and by insisting that they be applied universally, not just to one segregated corner of civil life but to the conduct of all human affairs, Stowe means to effect a radical transformation of her society. The brilliance of the strategy is that it puts the central affirmations of a culture into the service of a vision that would destroy the present economic and social institutions; by resting her case, absolutely, on the saving power of Christian love and on the sanctity of motherhood and the family, Stowe relocates the center of power in American life, placing it not in the government, nor in the courts of law, nor in the factories, not in the marketplace, but in the kitchen. And that means that the new society will not be controlled by men but by women. The image of the home created by Stowe and Catharine Beecher in their treatise on domestic science is in no sense a shelter from the stormy blast of economic and political life, a haven from reality divorced from fact which allows the machinery of

3. For a detailed discussion of the changes referred to here, see Christopher Clark, "Household Economy, Market Exchange, and the Rise of Capitalism in the Connecticut Valley, 1800–1860," *Journal of Social History* 13 (Winter 1979): 169–89, and Nancy F. Cott, *The Bonds of Womanhood: "Woman's Sphere" in New England, 1780–1835* (New Haven, Conn.: Yale University Press, 1977).

industrial capitalism to grind on; it is conceived as a dynamic center of activity, physical and spiritual, economic and moral, whose influence spreads out in ever-widening circles. To this activity—and this is the crucial innovation—men are incidental. Although the Beecher sisters pay lip service on occasion to male supremacy, women's roles occupy virtually the whole of their attention and dominate the scene. Male provender is deemphasized in favor of female processing. Men provide the seed, but women bear and raise the children. Men provide the flour, but women bake the bread and get the breakfast. The removal of the male from the center to the periphery of the human sphere is the most radical component of this millenarian scheme, which is rooted so solidly in the most traditional values: religion, motherhood, home, and family. Exactly what position men will occupy in the millennium is specified by a detail inserted casually into Stowe's description of the Indiana kitchen. While the women and children are busy preparing breakfast, Simeon Halliday, the husband and father, stands "in his shirt-sleeves before a little looking-glass in the corner, engaged in the anti-patriarchal activity of shaving" (pp. 141–42) [128].

With this detail, so innocently placed, Stowe reconceives the role of men in human history: while Negroes, children, mothers, and grandmothers do the world's primary work, men groom themselves contentedly in a corner. The scene, as critics have noted is often the case in sentimental fiction, is "intimate," the backdrop is "domestic," the tone at times is even "chatty"; but the import, as critics have failed to recognize, is world-shaking. The enterprise of sentimental fiction, as Stowe's novel attests, is anything but domestic, in the sense of being limited to purely personal concerns; its mission, on the contrary, is global and its interests identical with the interests of the race. If the fiction written in the nineteenth century by women whose works sold in the hundreds of thousands has seemed narrow and parochial to the critics of the twentieth century, that narrowness and parochialism belong not to these works nor to the women who wrote them; they are the beholders' share.[4]

4. In a recent article in *Signs*, Mary Kelley characterizes the main positions in the debate over the significance of sentimental fiction as follows: (1) the Cowie-Welter thesis, which holds that women's fiction expresses an "ethics of conformity" and accepts the stereotype of the woman as pious, pure, submissive, and dedicated to the home, and (2) the Papashvily-Garrison thesis, which sees sentimental fiction as profoundly subversive of traditional ideas of male authority and female subservience. Kelley locates herself somewhere in between, holding that sentimental novels convey a "contradictory message": "they tried to project an Edenic image," but their own tales "subverted their intentions" by showing how often women were frustrated and defeated in the performance of their heroic roles. My own position is that the sentimental novelists are both conformist and subversive, but not, as Kelley believes, in a self-contradictory way. They used the central myth of their culture, the story of Christ's death for the sins of mankind, as the basis for a new myth that reflected their own interests. They regarded their vision of the Christian home as God's kingdom on earth as the fulfillment of the Gospel, "the

# ROBERT S. LEVINE

## *Uncle Tom's Cabin* in *Frederick Douglass' Paper*: An Analysis of Reception†

More than any other American novel, *Uncle Tom's Cabin* (1852) presses its critical commentators to take account of its popular reception and cultural influence. Considerations of reception and influence have been especially pronounced among critics addressing Stowe's representations of race. In perhaps the most scathing indictment extant of *Uncle Tom's Cabin*, J. C. Furnas, a white critic, blames Stowe for "the wrongheadness, distortions and wishful thinkings about Negroes in general and American Negroes in particular that still plague us today."[1] Although some of the more spirited defenses of Stowe's racial politics, black characterizations, and overall influence on the culture have come from African American critics,[2] the fact remains that numerous other African Americans have been troubled by the cultural consequences of Stowe's sentimentalism and racialism. Donald Chaput is one of many who lament the "irreparable harm" done by Stowe's portrayal of Tom's Christian resignation; and Addison Gayle Jr. argues that the stereotypical portrayal of Tom and other slaves simply reinforced Southern views of black inferiority and submissiveness.[3] More recently,

---

end . . . which Jesus Christ came into this world to secure," in exactly the same way that the Puritans believed their mission was to found the "American city of God," and that Christians believe the New Testament to be a fulfillment of the old. Revolutionary ideologies typically announce themselves as the fulfillment of old promises or as a return to a golden age. What I am suggesting here, in short, is that the argument over whether the sentimental novelists were radical or conservative is a false issue. The real problem is how we, in the light of everything that has happened since they wrote, can understand and appreciate their work. Mary Kelley, "The Sentimentalists: Promise and Betrayal in the Home," *Signs* 4 (Spring 1979): 434–46; Alexander Cowie, "The Vogue of the Domestic Novel, 1850–1870," *South Atlantic Quarterly* 41 (October 1942): 420; Welter, "Cult of True Womanhood," pp. 151–74; Helen Waite Papashvily, *All the Happy Endings: A Study of the Domestic Novel in America, the Women Who Wrote It, the Women Who Read It, in the Nineteenth Century* (New York: Harper & Bros., 1956); Dee Garrison. "Immoral Fiction in the Late Victorian Library," *American Quarterly* 28 (Spring 1976): 71–80.

† From *American Literature* 64. 

1. J. C. Furnas, *Goodbye to Uncle Tom* (New York: William Sloane Associates, 1956), 8.
2. See, for example, Benjamin Hudson, "Another View of 'Uncle Tom,'" *Phylon* 24 (1963): 79–87; and Ernest Cassara, "The Rehabilitation of Uncle Tom: Significant Themes in Mrs. Stowe's Antislavery Novel," *CLA Journal* 17 (1973): 230–40. For a defense of Stowe's racial politics, see also Thomas Graham, "Harriet Beecher Stowe and the Question of Race," *New England Quarterly* 46 (1973): 614–22.
3. Donald Chaput, "Uncle Tom and Predestination," *Negro History Bulletin* 27 (1964): 143; Addison Gayle Jr., *The Way of the New World: The Black Novel in America* (Garden City, N.Y.: Anchor Press, 1975), 6. Surely the most influential attack on the novel by an African American writer is James Baldwin's "Everybody's Protest Novel" (1949),

Richard Yarborough criticizes Stowe for her use of racial stereotypes, for her unwillingness to grant to Uncle Tom a "sense of racial solidarity," and for her "tragic failure of imagination [which] prevented her from envisioning blacks (free or slave, mulatto or full-blood) as viable members of American society." The "failure" is "tragic" because so influential: "*Uncle Tom's Cabin* was the epicenter of a massive cultural phenomenon, the tremors of which still affect the relationship of blacks and whites in the United States."[4]

I call attention to the ways in which evaluations of *Uncle Tom's Cabin* are tied to the critic's sense of the novel's cultural reception and influence in order to suggest that an important index of the novel's relative success or failure, particularly when it is viewed (as we inevitably view it) in a social-historical context, should be its reception by those who had the most at stake in its reformatory social program: the free and enslaved blacks of the 1850s. For this reason, I think we need to take more seriously than we usually do the published record of the responses of literate free Northern blacks, who, outraged and despairing over the adoption of the Compromise of 1850's Fugitive Slave Law, regarded *Uncle Tom's Cabin*, as Yarborough puts it, "as a godsend destined to mobilize white sentiment against slavery just when resistance to the southern forces was urgently needed."[5] My focus in this essay will be on the reception of Stowe's novel in the pages of *Frederick Douglass' Paper*, principally between 1852 and 1854, a reception that paid particular attention to the question of the novel's influence on the culture, and a reception that in its complexities and debates should help critics of the 1990s to historicize their own reception of the novel in a larger and longer perspective.

A few prefatory words about *Frederick Douglass' Paper* and Douglass's cultural situation in the 1850s: As is well known, following the publication of his *Narrative* (1845) Douglass emerged as the most visible and respected black abolitionist of the time. Confident of his intellectual abilities as an opponent of slavery, he became increasingly troubled by the efforts of Garrison and others of the American Anti-Slavery Society—for whom he was a paid agent—to

---

which excoriates Stowe for her "self-righteous, virtuous sentimentality" (rpt. in *Critical Essays on Harriet Beecher Stowe*, ed. Elizabeth Ammons [Boston: G. K. Hall, 1980], 92) [see above, pp. 532–39—*Editor*]. Interestingly, Langston Hughes wrote a praising Introduction to a 1952 edition of *Uncle Tom's Cabin*, rpt. in *Critical Essays on Harriet Beecher Stowe*, 102–04.

4. Richard Yarborough, "Strategies of Black Characterization in *Uncle Tom's Cabin* and the Early Afro-American Novel," in *New Essays on Uncle Tom's Cabin*, ed. Eric J. Sundquist (Cambridge: Cambridge Univ. Press, 1986), 54, 65, 46. On the post-1941 reception of *Uncle Tom's Cabin* by African American critics, see Thomas F. Gossett, *Uncle Tom's Cabin and American Culture* (Dallas: Southern Methodist Univ. Press, 1985), 388–96.
5. "Strategies of Black Characterization," 68.

limit his lectures to just the facts of slavery, and not analysis. A symbolic break with Garrison occurred in 1847 when following Douglass's British tour of 1845–47, he used funds from English supporters to found the *North Star*, an antislavery newspaper perceived by Garrison as in direct competition with his own *The Liberator*. Published in Rochester, New York, on a weekly basis, with Martin Delany working as co-editor for most of its first year, Douglass's paper quickly became "the most important black abolitionist newspaper in the country."[6] In 1851, the year *Uncle Tom's Cabin* began to appear in the *National Era*, Douglass broke openly with Garrison, as he came to believe, contra Garrison, that the most effective way to combat the Fugitive Slave Law and slavery generally was to champion political activism over moral suasion, an antislavery reading of the Constitution over a proslavery reading, and Unionism over dissolution. Attracted to Gerrit Smith's Liberty Party politics and his considerable financial resources, Douglass merged the *North Star* with Smith's *Liberty Party Paper* and changed its name to *Frederick Douglass' Paper*, which he continued to publish up to 1860. Despite the fact that much of the four-page newspaper was devoted to reprinting antislavery speeches from Congress, the proceedings of numerous black, abolitionist, and women's conventions, and antislavery news from a wide range of newspapers and journals, the paper, as Benjamin Quarles notes (and as its name unambiguously indicates), "was to an unusual degree the product of one man's thinking."[7] The strong personal stamp that Douglass put on the paper should be kept in mind when we turn to the various articles on *Uncle Tom's Cabin* that he began to publish. These articles, I will be arguing, reveal Douglass as a creatively appropriative reader of Stowe's novel. Though many of the articles were reprinted from other sources, Douglass had an enormous amount of material to choose from; his selection process needs to be considered as a central part of his efforts to shape a particular way of reading the novel.[8]

The first mention of *Uncle Tom's Cabin*, however, was an in-house review of 8 April 1852, which may have been written by Douglass

6. Eric J. Sundquist, "Introduction," *Frederick Douglass: New Literary and Historical Essays*, ed. Sundquist (Cambridge: Cambridge Univ. Press, 1990), 10.
7. Benjamin Quarles, *Frederick Douglass* (Washington, D.C.: Associated Publishers, Inc., 1948), 83. On Douglass's newspapers, see pp. 80–98. Also useful is Shelly Fisher Fishkin and Carla L. Peterson, " 'We Hold These Truths to Be Self-Evident': The Rhetoric of Frederick Douglass's Journalism," in *Frederick Douglass: New Literary and Historical Essays*, 166–88. On Douglass and Smith, see John R. McKivigan, "The Frederick Douglass-Gerrit Smith Friendship and Political Abolitionism in the 1850s," in *Frederick Douglass: New Literary and Historical Essays*, 205–32. The most reliable biography is William S. McFeely, *Frederick Douglass* (New York: W. W. Norton, 1991), though McFeely has little to say about Douglass's interactions with black writers and intellectuals—such as Martin Delany—during the 1850s.
8. See the two articles reprinted above, p. 499, and p. 502 [*Editor*].

but more likely was the work of his English comrade, financial supporter, and managing editor, Julia Griffiths, who wrote most of the reviews appearing in the weekly "Literary Notices" section. Because the review is an important one and not widely available, I quote it in its entirety:

> This work has not yet reached us, from the publishers, but when we hear that the first edition of five thousand copies (issued on the 20th of March,) was sold in four days, we are not surprised at the delay.
>
> This thrilling Story, from the accomplished pen of Mrs. Stowe, has appeared week after week, by installments, in the *National Era*, and has been perused with intense interest by thousands of people. The friends of freedom owe the Authoress a large debt of gratitude for this essential service rendered by her to the cause they love.
>
> We are well sure that the touching portraiture she has given of *"poor Uncle Tom,"* will, of itself, enlist the kindly sympathies, of numbers, in behalf of the oppressed African race, and will raise up a host of enemies against the fearful system of slavery.
>
> Mrs. Stowe has, in this work, won for herself a chief place among American writers.—She has evinced great keenness of insight into the workings of slavery and a depth of knowledge of all its various parts, such as few writers have equalled, and none, we are sure, have exceeded. She has wonderful powers of description, and invests her characters with a reality perfectly life-like. Fine as she is in description, she is not less so in argumentation. We doubt if abler arguments have ever been presented, in favor of the *"Higher Law"* theory, than may be found here. Mrs. Stowe's truly great work, is destined to occupy a niche in every American Library, north of "Mason and Dixon's Line."[9]

This initial review, of course, is not a review of the book proper, but of the serialized novel, which, despite the reviewer's assertion of the book's social impact, had a relatively limited audience in the *National Era*. The rapid sale of five thousand copies of the published book would hardly have indicated the full extent of its eventual popularity and influence. Still, the moral and aesthetic evaluation of the "truly great work" is very much tied to the reviewer's sense of its social function: Stowe's descriptive powers, realism, fine characterizations, and "argumentation," we are told, cannot but "enlist the kindly sympathies, of numbers" to the antislavery cause. Sympathy is a key concept here—Stowe in her Preface announced that she

9. *Frederick Douglass' Paper*, 8 April 1852, 2, hereafter abbreviated as *FDP*.

wanted "to awaken sympathy and feeling"[1] for the slave—and it should be emphasized that Douglass, as his *Narrative* and subsequent remarks on *Uncle Tom's Cabin* reveal, thought that the ability of the writer to create in the (white) reader a sympathetic identification with the plight of the slave was central to a text's potential to bring about social change. Perceiving the impact of *Uncle Tom's Cabin* to be potentially decisive to the antislavery cause, Douglass, by the printing and/or authoring of this review, conveys his belief that Stowe deserves "a large debt of gratitude" from the "friends of freedom," be those readers (so it is implied) white or black. "Cultural work," to use Jane Tompkins's helpful term,[2] is what the reviewer perceives Stowe's novel to be performing, a subversive and revolutionary sort of work in that it encourages readers to honor a *"Higher Law"* than that of the Federal Government.

Whether or not Douglass authored the review, the values celebrated therein—sympathy, realism, social influence—will continue to be celebrated in *Frederick Douglass' Paper.* In part, the willingness of Douglass to embrace the novel uncritically owes much to his commitment to Enlightenment ideals of egalitarianism and universalism. As Waldo E. Martin Jr. remarks, for Douglass "the liberating spirit of humanism ideally subsumed and eventually overrode the stifling spirit of race."[3] Despite that commitment, the next two mentions of *Uncle Tom's Cabin* in *Frederick Douglass' Paper* addressed matters of racial politics and difference. In a letter printed six weeks after the initial review, William G. Allen, who identifies himself as "a free black teacher," praises Stowe's "wonder of wonders" of a novel, but then challenges the idealization of Tom's Christic heroism. "[I]f any man had too much piety," he remarks, "Uncle Tom was that man." Failing to note that Tom in fact did resist Legree by refusing his order to flog the slave Lucy, Allen, perhaps with Douglass's own account of his resistance to Covey in the back of his mind, declares that "there should be resistance to tyrants, if it need be, to the death."[4]

Approximately one month after the appearance of Allen's letter, Douglass printed a column on the reception of *Uncle Tom's Cabin* in New York City. The piece, signed "Ethiop" and authored by William J. Wilson, one of Douglass's regular contributing editors,

1. Harriet Beecher Stowe, *Uncle Tom's Cabin; or, Life Among the Lowly*, ed. Kenneth S. Lynn (Cambridge: Harvard Univ. Press, 1962), 1.
2. See Jane Tompkins, *Sensational Designs: The Cultural Work of American Fiction, 1790–1860* (New York: Oxford Univ. Press, 1985), xi–xix. [See above, pp. 539–61 —*Editor.*]
3. Waldo E. Martin Jr., *The Mind of Frederick Douglass* (Chapel Hill: Univ. of North Carolina Press, 1984), 96.
4. *FDP*, 20 May 1852, 3. Similar hesitations about Tom's passivity would be voiced two more times in *FDP*; see the issues of 17 June 1853, 1; and 22 December 1854, 3.

expresses amazement at the extraordinary impact of *Uncle Tom's Cabin* on a city "hitherto so faced over with the adamant of pro-slavery politics, unionism, churchism, and every other shade of '*ism*' hammered out, and welded on by his *satanic majesty* and faithful subjects, for the last half century, that it completely staggers belief and puts credulity at fault." But that impact, Wilson warns, threatens to become less transformative than narrowly commercial. Where once were "exhibited in their windows Zip Coon, or Jim Crow . . . shopkeepers are now proud to illume these very windows through the windows of my *Uncle Tom's Cabin*." In short, stocking Stowe's novel makes for good business, which Wilson can only hope speaks to "something in the heart of this community deeper rooted than the teachings of *politicians, demagogues*, and *robed priests*." Wilson's cynical sense of the *Uncle Tom's Cabin* phenomenon as a white phenomenon—a white author appropriated by white businessmen for white consumers—leads him to wish that it had been a black who had written the first acclaimed antislavery novel, for he fears that black antislavery novelists inevitably will be subsumed by the (marketplace) tradition headed by Stowe. He explains in his concluding cautionary paragraph on the literature of antislavery: "it may yet be regretted should its march be in an invented [*sic*] order; the blacks (who by position ought to be the more faithful delineators of oppression, and the keenest searchers after justice, that she fully does her office-work) being found in the *REAR* instead of being found not merely in the FRONT RANK, but in the VERY LEAD."[5]

Ultimately, Wilson begs a very important question: Can a white writer do "faithful" justice to the black experience of slavery? The question would not be raised explicitly in the pages of *Frederick Douglass' Paper* for nearly a year, and then with a vengeance in an epistolary debate between Frederick Douglass and Martin Delany. Instead, there emerge two large motifs in the articles on *Uncle Tom's Cabin* printed by Douglass: the unprecedented impact of the novel, not only on readers "north of 'Mason and Dixon's Line,'" but in the South and across the Atlantic as well; and a concomitant near-hagiographic celebration and defense of Stowe's moral and literary virtues.

A front-page article in an issue of August 1852, reprinted from the New York *Evening Post*, is the first of many testimonials to the moral influence and representational authority of *Uncle Tom's Cabin*. "I am a slaveholder myself," writes a New Orleans citizen who was

5. "From Our Brooklyn Correspondent," *FDP*, 17 June 1852, 3. Though "inverted order" was probably meant over "invented order," the typo speaks in interesting ways to the constructedness of an antislavery canon.

given Stowe's novel by a family friend. "I now wish to bear my testimony to its just delineation of the position the slave occupies." A like-minded letter, reprinted from the New York *Independent*, appeared in an issue of October 1852. Again, the correspondent is a New Orleans citizen, who, unlike the first correspondent, questions Stowe's realism. "My own view is," he declares, "that Mrs. Stowe has presented the institution of slavery in too favorable a light." This tongue-in-cheek criticism aside, the writer, perhaps picking up on Stowe's own ideals of influence as expressed in the novel's final chapter, places special emphasis on the transformative power of the novel: "No book can be made to take the place of *Uncle Tom's Cabin*. People will read it, and as its keys are touched, conscience and the heart will give forth sweetly responsive notes."[6]

Though Douglass would have distrusted such rosy language, he no doubt wanted to believe that the novel could mobilize enough people, North and South, to influence Americans to abolish slavery. As Douglass assessed the situation, influence would come from within and without; thus he printed numerous articles on the marshaling power of *Uncle Tom's Cabin* overseas. The issue of 8 October 1852, for example, reprinted as its lead article the review in *Frazer's Magazine*, which spoke of how the novel's realistic portrayal of slavery "horrifies and haunts."[7] Two months later Douglass reprinted the Earl of Carlisle's Introduction to the English edition of *Uncle Tom's Cabin*, a novel which, so the Earl claims, marks "a kind of epoch in the literary, as well as, I trust, in themoral history of the time."[8] With an article printed in that same December issue, on a meeting of the Glasgow Emancipation Society to "testify to our gratitude and approbation under providence to Harriet Beecher Stowe, the authoress of 'Uncle Tom's Cabin,'"[9] Douglass initiated his practice of reprinting formal testimonials from British antislavery groups. Two articles on the front page of a March 1853 issue, discussing the popularity of *Uncle Tom's Cabin* in Paris and Moscow, enlarged the sphere of Stowe's influence. As Douglass would

6. *FDP*, 13 August 1852, 1; and 22 October 1852, 4.
7. *FDP*, 8 October 1852, 1. The following week Douglass reprinted the London *Examiner's* glittering review; see *FDP*, 15 October 1852, 1.
8. *FDP*, 24 December 1852, 2. Both the reviewer for *Frazer's* and the Earl of Carlisle broached one relatively minor criticism of *Uncle Tom's Cabin*: that it appeared to endorse the view that chattel slavery and "wage slavery" were moral equivalents. For English readers of the upper classes, such a suggestion was an affront to their sense of the organic coherence of English society.
9. *FDP*, 24 December 1852, 1. The novelist William Wells Brown was reported as having attended that meeting. For similar testimonials from British antislavery groups, see, for example, the "Address to Mrs. Stowe" from an antislavery group based in Belfast, Ireland, in *FDP*, 21 January 1853, 2; and "Testimonial to Mrs. Stowe," in *FDP*, 12 August 1853, 1. On the influence of *Uncle Tom's Cabin* in England, see also "'Uncle Tom's Cabin' in England," *FDP*, 17 December 1852, 1; Douglass's speech, "A Nation in the Midst of a Nation," in *FDP*, 27 May 1853, 1; and William Wells Brown's report in *FDP*, 26 August 1853, 2.

remark editorially after reprinting yet another such article: "Uncle Tom has his mission in Europe, and most conscientiously is he fulfilling it."[1]

Convinced both of the social uses of the novel and of Stowe's humanitarianism, Douglass, in addition to printing articles on the novel's cultural influence, also sprinkled the pages of his paper with treacly *Uncle Tom's Cabin* poems and worshipful profiles of Stowe.[2] Additionally, as flameholder for the cause, Douglass took it upon himself to defend Stowe from all who might challenge or smear her reputation. Thus he found the space to print two reviews of W. L. G. Smith's *Life at the South; or, Uncle Tom's Cabin as It Is* (1852), among other novelistic proslavery "responses" to *Uncle Tom's Cabin*. As he (or Julia Griffiths) comments on Smith's effort: "To enter the lists in competition with Mrs. Stowe and be defeated, is no disgrace; but . . . we really feel it is a disparagement of the genius of the accomplished authoress before named, to connect, in any way, the mention of her almost perfect work with the trash before us."[3]

Douglass's most significant effort to counter criticism of Stowe's novel from a "respectable" source, prior to his debate with Martin Delany, occurred over two issues in early 1853. In response to an attack on Stowe by George R. Graham in the February 1853 *Graham's Magazine*, Douglass remarks in his "Literary Notices" section that he has "perused" the piece, entitled "Black Letters; or Uncle Tom-Foolery in Literature," "with attention, regret, and (we would add) disgust. It is the most unjust, the most ungenerous and the least refined review of the world-renowned book we have ever read." And it is a review, Douglass makes clear, that is thoroughly informed by racism: "'*[W]e hate this niggerism*,'" Douglass asserts, is Graham's

1. *FDP*, 11 March 1853, 1; and 13 May 1853, 3. The following year Douglass reprinted an article from the New York *Tribune*, which declared: "Our most prominent and extraordinary representative abroad is really Uncle Tom.—His influence is in permanent evidence at Paris" (*FDP*, 17 November 1854, 3).
2. Here is a sample stanza from Mary H. Collier's "Eva's Parting":

> And father, when I'm sleeping,
> In my quiet grave so green,
> And my soul the Lord is keeping
> In the world of bliss unseen;
> You will give the boon of Freedom
> To the old and faithful friend,
> Who has borne me on his bosom,
> Where the white magnolias bend.

See *FDP*, 13 August 1852, 4. For another example, see A. N. Cole's "Lines to the Lowly, Written upon Reading *Uncle Tom's Cabin*," *FDP*, 10 September 1852, 4. The most hagiographic of the profiles, "Some Account of Mrs. Beecher Stowe's Family, By an Alabama Man," from *Frazer's Magazine*, proclaims that "*Uncle Tom's Cabin* is the agonizing cry of feelings pent up for years in the heart of a true woman" (*FDP*, 17 December 1852, 1).

3. *FDP*, 13 August 1852, 2. For examples of other reviews of similar such novels, see *FDP*, 15 October 1852, 1; and 21 January 1853, 4.

"solution of the whole matter."[4] Evidently content that Graham damns himself with his own words, that his vituperations "will be greeted as THEY DESERVE TO BE," Douglass, in a front page article of March 1853, reprints the entirety of Graham's angry rejoinder to several of his critics, which has this to say about Douglass:

> Mr. Fred. Douglass has read our article 'with disgust,' and says it may be accounted for thus: *'we hate niggerism!'* He is mistaken. We have taught blacks in a Sunday-school for years, as a duty. We rather like Fred. himself—and so far as by study, industry, and an honest life he sets an example moral and intellectual to his race—we respect him; but we hate the present negro literature—especially that of Fred.'s, which by abusing the white, is intended to elevate the black man.[5]

Patronizing as they are, Graham's comments on Douglass touch upon a crucial issue of the time, particularly for Northern black abolitionists: how to "elevate the black man." For it was believed by many blacks that as long as the free blacks were poor, intemperate, and lawless, whites would fail to mobilize around the abolitionist cause. Thus a large aim of the black convention movement and newspapers of the period was to build self-confidence and a sense of community among the free blacks, not only for the sake of the free blacks but also of the slaves. As Douglass declared in a January 1854 issue of his paper, *"the free colored man's elevation is essential to the* slave *colored man's emancipation."*[6] Though he occasionally argued for black elevation as if white racism were an unrelated issue—that individual will alone could help blacks to succeed—it was much more often the case that he presented black self-help programs in the North as part of an antiracist struggle intimately related to, if not a necessary condition of, the struggle against racism and slavery in the South.

Given Stowe's emphasis in *Uncle Tom's Cabin* on the need to educate America's blacks, Douglass could not help regarding her as a fellow believer in the importance of black elevation. His conviction of their shared vision was only underscored when in March

4. *FDP*, 21 January 1853, 3.
5. "Graham vs. Uncle Tom," *FDP*, 4 March 1853, 1.
6. *FDP*, 2 January 1854, 1. On Douglass and black self-help, see August Meier, "Frederick Douglass' Vision for America: A Case Study in Nineteenth-Century Negro Protest" (1967), rpt. in *Frederick Douglass*, ed. Benjamin Quarles (Englewood Cliffs, N.J.: Prentice-Hall, Inc., 1968), 143–64. See also Douglass's Franklinian lecture, "Self-Help" (1849), in *The Frederick Douglass Papers: Series One: Speeches, Debates, and Interviews*, ed. John Blassingame (New Haven: Yale Univ. Press, 1982), 2:167–70; and Rafia Zafir, "Franklinian Douglass: The Afro-American as Representative Man," in *Frederick Douglass: New Literary and Historical Essays*, 141–65. The seminal study of black self-elevation is Frederick Cooper, "Elevating the Race: The Social Thought of Black Leaders, 1827–50," *American Quarterly* 24 (1972): 604–25.

1853 she invited him to her home in Andover, Massachusetts, in order to sound him out on how best she could help America's free blacks. This was not the first time Stowe had requested information from Douglass. Two years earlier, as she was planning the Legree sections of the novel, she had written him in the hope that he or an acquaintance could supply her with first-hand information on the workings of a cotton plantation. In the same letter, after praising his newspaper, she declares her intention to "modify" his views on "two subjects,—the church and African colonization,"[7] though she focuses mainly on defending the church (and hence her family) from the charge of being proslavery. There is no evidence that Douglass responded to or even received the letter, but his decision in late 1852 to reprint three articles on Stowe's controversy with the Presbyterian clergyman Dr. Joel Parker—wherein Henry Ward Beecher, Calvin Stowe, and Harriet Stowe herself challenged Parker's public accusation that a reference in *Uncle Tom's Cabin* to his putative proslavery views was libelous—may well have been an ironic rejoinder to her defense of the church and churchmen.[8] More pertinently, the reprintings would have spoken to his camaraderie with Stowe the novelist on the issue of church complicity in slavery, an author-reader camaraderie that would develop into a tentative friendship following his March visit.

Douglass's articles in *Frederick Douglass' Paper* on the visit to Stowe and its aftermath can be taken as a further effort to set forth a social-transformative reading of *Uncle Tom's Cabin*. In an article of March 1853 titled "A Day and a Night in 'Uncle Tom's Cabin,'" Douglass assures his readers that his visit to Stowe will eventually benefit the free blacks. He discloses the specifics one month later in an article on Stowe's departure for England: "The chief good which we anticipate from Mrs. Stowe's mission, is the founding of an INSTITUTION, in which our oppressed and proscribed youth, MALE and FEMALE, may obtain a plain English education, and a practical knowledge of various useful TRADES." Douglass believed that such an institution, by teaching free blacks the industrial and mechanical skills currently denied them by racist apprenticing practices, would allow blacks to lessen their dependency on merely servile occupations. Confident that Stowe shared his goals on this project—that she would in fact turn over funds to Douglass so that he could establish just such an institution in his hometown of Rochester—Douglass devoted numerous columns to her six-month's

7. Letter of 9 June 1851, in *Life and Letters of Harriet Beecher Stowe*, ed. Annie Fields (Boston and New York: Houghton, Mifflin and Co., 1897), 134.
8. On Stowe and Parker, see the following issues of *FDP*: 29 October 1852, 3; 5 November 1852, l; and 12 November 1852, 1. Parker objected to the remarks on his preaching in chapter twelve of *Uncle Tom's Cabin*.

visit to Great Britain, repeatedly reminding his readers of its principal purpose: "the establishment of some institution, which shall be of *efficient* and *permanent* benefit to the colored people of the United States."[9]

Seeking to gain additional support for the institution, Douglass in July of 1853 presented to participants of the Colored National Convention at Rochester, a number of whom were opposed to such an expensive and segregated school, a March 1853 letter he had written to Stowe detailing the benefits of his industrial college plan; he printed the letter in a December issue of his newspaper. The December publication would suggest that Douglass was beginning to despair of obtaining funds from Stowe, who had returned to America several months earlier and had not yet offered him a major contribution. In the letter he asserts that Stowe's authorship of *Uncle Tom's Cabin* "alone, involves us in a debt of gratitude which cannot be measured." But he calls on her to go one step further, to do what the novel urges its white readers to do: educate the blacks. Stowe herself, he asserts, can now help Douglass to eradicate the "disease" afflicting his people—"POVERTY, IGNORANCE AND DEGRADATION"—by contributing to the construction of an industrial college, which should help them both to achieve their mutual desire: the end of slavery. As Douglass explains, "The most telling, the most killing refutation of slavery, is the presentation of an industrious, enterprising, thrifty, and intelligent free black population. Such a population I believe would rise in the Northern States under the fostering care of such a college as that proposed."[1]

But should blacks place themselves under the "fostering care" of a white philanthropist, particularly one who in her novel appears to be advocating not black elevation but rather emigration under the aegis of a colonization society? That was one of the large concerns troubling Martin Delany, whose resentment of Douglass for failing to review *The Condition, Elevation, Emigration and Destiny of the Colored People of the United States* (1852)—perhaps the most significant black nationalist text of the nineteenth century—underlies a series of angry letters to Douglass, which Douglass printed, along with his rejoinders, in *Frederick Douglass' Paper* during April and May 1853. Of course Douglass could have chosen to ignore Delany's letters, just as he had chosen to ignore his book. The fact that Douglass published them suggests he was aware that Delany raised issues of fundamental importance.[2] And as Douglass waited for Stowe to provide the funding he so desired, he may well have shared

9. *FDP*, 4 March 1853, 1; 15 April 1853, 2; and 6 May 1853, 2.
1. *FDP*, 2 December 1853, 2.
2. On the importance of Douglass's debate with Delany, see also Yarborough, "Strategies of Black Characterization," 71–72.

some of the suspicions voiced so vociferously by Delany. Printing Delany's letters allowed Douglass to convey through Delany any doubts he might have had about his response to *Uncle Tom's Cabin* and its author, while at the same time putting those doubts, at least on the pages of *Frederick Douglass' Paper*, to rest.

Delany's first letter appeared approximately one month after Douglass's meeting with Stowe. In it, Delany addresses the crucial question of how the free blacks should go about the task of improving their lot in America. In *The Condition . . . of the Colored People of the United States*, Delany stated unequivocally: "Our elevation must be the result of *self-efforts*, and the work of our *own hands*."[3] His letter to Douglass reasserts this dictum, as he worries over blacks' (especially Douglass's) tendencies to depend on whites for their elevation: "Now I simply wish to say, that we have always fallen into great errors in efforts of this kind, giving to others than the *intelligent* and *experienced* among *ourselves;* and in all due respect and difference [*sic*] to Mrs. Stowe, I beg leave to say that she *knows nothing about us*, 'the Free Colored people of the United States,' neither does any other white person—and, consequently, can contrive no successful scheme for our elevation; it must be done for ourselves."[4]

In his prior and subsequent writings, Douglass came close to agreeing with Delany on this point. "We must rise or fall, succeed or fail, by our own merits," he had declared in 1848. In the first published version of his famous "Self-Help" lecture (1849), he again had allowed whites only a limited role in blacks' efforts at self-improvement, asserting that though "[o]ur white friends may do much for us," a large fact remains: "Equality and respectability can only be attained by our own exertions." And in an 1855 article in *Frederick Douglass' Paper* calling on expatriated blacks to return to the United States, Douglass would proclaim as a central truth: "THAT OUR ELEVATION AS A RACE, IS ALMOST WHOLLY DEPENDENT UPON OUR OWN EXERTIONS."[5] That "ALMOST," of course, signals the key difference between Douglass and Delany, since Douglass, especially during the 1850s when political developments seemed so grim, was willing to take help wherever he could find it. Moreover, unlike Delany, he was not so sanguine about the existence of a cohesive black community that could elevate itself on its own. Thus he writes in response to Delany: "To scornfully reject

3. Martin Delany, *The Condition, Elevation, Emigration and Destiny of the Colored People of the United States* (1852; rpt., New York: Arno Press, 1968), 45.
4. *FDP*, 1 April 1853, 2. Is Delany punning on "deference"? Or did Douglass perhaps allow this typo in order to underscore Delany's *difference* from Stowe?
5. Frederick Douglass, "WHAT ARE THE COLORED PEOPLE DOING FOR THEMSELVES?" *The North Star*, 14 July 1848, 1; *The Frederick Douglass Papers*, 2:169; "Self-Elevation—Rev. S. R. Ward," *FDP*, 13 April 1855, 1.

all aid from our white friends, and to denounce them as unworthy of our confidence, looks high and mighty enough on paper; but unless the background is filled up with facts demonstrating our independence and self-sustaining power, of what use is such display of self-consequence?" As for Delany's doubts on Stowe's sympathies for black people, Douglass testily remarks: "The assertion that Mrs. Stowe 'knows nothing about us,' shows that Bro. DELANY knows nothing about Mrs. Stowe."[6]

Four weeks later Douglass printed three Stowe-related items in his paper: an article from *Lloyd's Weekly Newspaper* on Stowe's visit to the Duchess of Sutherland, a glowing review (most likely by Douglass or Griffiths) of Stowe's *A Key to Uncle Tom's Cabin*, and a cantankerous, actually rather humorous, letter from Delany insisting that if Josiah Henson is "the real *Uncle Tom*," then he should be granted a "portion of the profits." Perhaps even Douglass himself, Delany adds, should be granted profits, for "I am of the opinion, that Mrs. Stowe has draughted largely on all the best fugitive slave narratives . . . but of this I am not competent to judge, not having as yet *read* 'Uncle Tom's Cabin,' my *wife* having *told* me the most I know about it."[7]

Delany's joking mood goes into retreat, however, in his next letter, printed the following week, which raises perhaps the most troubling issue of all for black readers of the time (and beyond): Stowe's apparent advocacy, in the final chapters of *Uncle Tom's Cabin*, of colonizationism. In fact, Delany's letter marks only the third time the colonization issue is broached in *Frederick Douglass' Paper*,[8] which is surprising given that Douglass was an outspoken opponent of colonization projects, whether they be white racist attempts to ship blacks to Liberia or black nationalist calls for African or Haitian emigration. (His hostility to colonizationism may help to explain his unwillingness to review Delany's *The Condition . . . of the Colored People*, which had called for black emigration to Central and South America and the West Indies.) Delany, in his letter on Stowe's colonizationist stance, somewhat coyly begins by stating that in his earlier letter he was being "ironical" when he claimed that whites know nothing of blacks. What he meant was "that they know nothing, comparatively, about us." Having settled that score, he moves

6. *FDP*, 1 April 1853, 2.
7. *FDP*, 29 April 1853, 3. The reviewer of *A Key to Uncle Tom's Cabin* declares: "'Key' not only proves the correctness of every essential part of 'Uncle Tom's Cabin,' but proves more and worse things against the murderous system than are alleged in that great book" (2).
8. William G. Allen noted, in his aforementioned letter printed in the 20 May 1852 issue of *FDP*: "I have one regret, with regard to the book, and that is, that the chapter favoring colonization was ever written. I do not, however, apprehend so much harm from it, as some others seem to anticipate" (3). See also the letter of C. C. Foote, in *FDP*, 22 April 1853, 2.

to his central charge, which he makes with an ironic praising of *Uncle Tom's Cabin:* "is not Mrs. Stowe a *Colonizationist?* having so avowed, or at least subscribed to, and recommended their principles in her great work of Uncle Tom." Equally worthy of questioning and censure, from Delany's perspective, are Stowe's "sneers at Hayti—the only truly free and independent civilized black nation as such, or colored if you please, on the face of the earth."[9]

In his rebuttal to Delany's letter, Douglass points to contradictions in Delany's own colonizationist stance while purporting not to care about Stowe's: "He says *she* is a colonizationist; and we ask, what if she is?—names do not frighten us. A little while ago, brother Delany was a colonizationist. . . . Yet, we never suspected his friendliness to the colored people."[1] For Douglass the larger issue is precisely that of "friendliness," particularly as it translates into usefulness, and so he wants to keep faith with Stowe despite his disappointment with her sentiments on African colonization in the final chapters of *Uncle Tom's Cabin.* In fact, he had broached the issue with her in his letter of 8 March 1853 (published, as mentioned earlier, in *Frederick Douglass' Paper* in December of 1853) when he linked his plan for an industrial college to his abhorrence for colonizationism: "The truth is, dear madam, we are *here*, and we are likely to remain. Individuals emigrate—nations never. We have grown up with this republic, and I see nothing in her character, or even in the character of the American people as yet, which compels the belief that we must leave the United States."[2] What is appealing about Douglass's interactions with Stowe is his working assumption that he could influence a writer who herself is so influential—that he could play a shaping role in her thought and actions, and ultimately in the cultural reception and influence of her novel. In contrast, with Delany he remains censorious and dismissive. Terming Delany's letter "unfair, uncalled for," he announces. "We shall not . . . allow the sentiments put in the brief letter of GEORGE HARRIS, at the close of Uncle Tom's Cabin, to vitiate forever Mrs. Stowe's power to do us good. Who doubts that Mrs. Stowe is more of an abolitionist than when she wrote that chapter?"[3] And perhaps she *was* "more of an abolitionist," for that same month, stung by criticism from Douglass and other black readers, she sent a note to the New York meeting of the American and Foreign Anti-Slavery Society declaring, in

9. *FDP*, 6 May 1853, 3.
1. Ibid., 2. (Note that Douglass, aware of the incendiary nature of Delany's charges, places his response on the page before Delany's letter.) On the conservative nature of some black colonization projects, and in particular on the contradictions informing Delany's various colonization ventures, see Wilson Jeremiah Moses, *The Golden Age of Black Nationalism* (Hamden, Conn.: Archon Books, 1978), esp. 27–45.
2. *FDP*, 2 December 1853, 2.
3. *FDP*, 6 May 1853, 2.

the paraphrased words of the proceedings, "that if she were to write 'Uncle Tom' again, she would not send George Harris to Liberia."[4]

The belief that whites have the power "to do us good"—a power, as Douglass understands it, very much dependent on the ability of blacks to put that "good" to use—centrally informs at least one other response to *Uncle Tom's Cabin* in *Frederick Douglass' Paper:* Douglass's novella "The Heroic Slave." Despite the fact that it was serialized in the paper several weeks prior to the Douglass-Delany debate, the novella can be read as a proleptic response to Delany as well. An account of the slave Madison Washington from 1835 until he led a successful revolt on the slave ship *Creole* in 1841, the historical novella revises *Uncle Tom's Cabin* by presenting the reader with a revolutionary slave who is "black, but comely."[5] Unlike Stowe, who bifurcates her blacks into "white-blooded" rebels and "black-blooded" docilities, Douglass merges the two character types in the person of Madison Washington. "A child might play in his arms, or dance on his shoulders. . . . His broad mouth and nose spoke only of good nature and kindness," Douglass writes of Washington's Tom-like attributes. And yet, like George Harris, "He had the head to conceive, and the hand to execute. In a word, he was one to be sought as a friend, but to be dreaded as an enemy" (103). But though Douglass's novella revises elements of *Uncle Tom's Cabin*'s characterizations, there are significant parallels between the two works: both make use of temperance themes, particularly in delineating the moral degeneracy of slave owners; both idealize the family; and both temper their portrayals of black violence.[6] Douglass tones down the violence of the slave rebellion by having the revolt on the *Creole* narrated by a white sailor, who not only remains passed out during most of it but also twice has his life saved from vengeful slaves by Washington's intervention. Unlike the revengeful Babo of Melville's "Benito Cereno" (1855), Washington simply desires the liberty of his people. Presenting him in this way, as several critics have pointed out, Douglass hopes to find a receptive

4. Cited in Gossett, *Uncle Tom's Cabin and American Culture*, 294.
5. "The Heroic Slave," rpt. in *Frederick Douglass: The Narrative and Selected Writings*, ed. Michael Meyer (New York: Modern Library, 1984), 303. The novella appeared in the 4, 11, 18, and 25 March issues of *FDP*; I use the more widely available reprinting. Subsequent parenthetical page references are to the Modern Library edition. On American Revolutionary ideology in the novella, see Eric J. Sundquist, "Frederick Douglass: Literacy and Paternalism," *Raritan* 6 (1986): 112. For background to the historical slave rebellion, see Howard Jones, "The Peculiar Institution and National Honor: The Case of the *Creole* Slave Revolt," *Civil War History* 21 (1975): 28–50.
6. See Robert B. Stepto, "Sharing the Thunder: The Literary Exchanges of Harriet Beecher Stowe, Henry Bibb, and Frederick Douglass," in *New Essays on Uncle Tom's Cabin*, 135–53. The best close reading of Douglass's novella is Stepto, "Storytelling in Early Afro-American Fiction: Frederick Douglass' 'The Heroic Slave,'" *Georgia Review* 36 (1982): 355–68.

audience among those white readers who might otherwise be alienated by representations of black rage.[7]

These same contemporary white readers would probably also admire the portrayal of Listwell, the white Ohioan who, under the sway of Washington's opening soliloquy, embraces abolitionism and comes to play a key role in the novella. Five years after overhearing Washington speak in a Virginia forest of his desires for freedom, Listwell helps him board a steamer in Ohio bound for Canada. In a subsequent letter to Listwell, Washington addresses him thus: "My dear friend,—for such you truly are" (323). When Washington, after a failed effort to free his wife, is recaptured in Virginia and put on a slave ship headed for New Orleans, Listwell again seeks to offer his assistance. Washington exclaims to the slaves, who are startled by Listwell's friendly overtures: "We are all chained here together,—ours is a common lot; and that gentleman is not less *your* friend than *mine*" (332). Listwell's initial response to Washington's dire situation is to counsel him to become, in a sense, an Uncle Tom: "Put your trust in God, and bear your sad lot with the manly fortitude which becomes a man" (335). On second thought, however, Listwell decides to act: he purchases "three strong *files*" from a local hardware store and, as the slave ship departs, manages to slip them into Madison's pocket as he passes (337).

In a searching critique of the novella, Yarborough expresses his concerns about the prominent role played by Listwell. Compared to other accounts of the *Creole* revolt—by William Wells Brown, Lydia Maria Child, and Pauline Hopkins—Douglass places "the greatest emphasis upon the role played by whites in the protagonist's life." Perhaps, Yarborough suggests, the granting of near-heroic stature to Listwell "reflects [Douglass's] desire to reach and move white readers." But the end result is this: "he implies that even the most self-reliant and gifted black male slave needs white assistance."[8] The problem with Yarborough's reading is that it overgeneralizes and to some extent dehistoricizes. Douglass's point is surely not that in all moments of oppression—whether in the American 1840s or beyond and elsewhere—blacks need the assistance of whites, but rather that in Madison's particular situation—or in the blacks' particular situation in the American 1850s—there can exist a sympathetic response to suffering that crosses the lines of race. Additionally, and this seems to me the really crucial point, Douglass

7. See esp. William L. Andrews, "The Novelization of Voice in Early African American Narrative," *PMLA* 105 (1990): 27–28; and Richard Yarborough, "Race, Violence, and Manhood: The Masculine Ideal in Frederick Douglass's 'The Heroic Slave,'" in *Frederick Douglass: New Literary and Historical Essays*, 178–79. Yarborough is more critical of Douglass's rhetorical strategies than Andrews.
8. "Race, Violence, and Manhood," 178–79.

suggests that the white sympathy and assistance that help to produce the slaves' revolutionary action in no way compromises the self-reliance or heroism of such action, and in fact is the product of a black's influence on a white: it is Madison Washington's opening soliloquy, after all, that converts Listwell to the antislavery cause and makes him so useful to the slaves. Nevertheless, in his presentation of the slave revolt in the final section of the novella, Douglass stresses that the blacks act on their own. They are liberated not by Listwell, but as the result of "the triumphant leadership of their heroic chief and deliverer" (348).[9] Thus, although the novella revises Stowe's conception of black heroism by portraying an actively revolutionary hero with black skin, I would maintain that parallels between Douglass's and Stowe's discourse of sympathy and community outweigh the revisionary strain and that the large thrust of the novella is to counter the views of those, like Martin Delany, who were unwilling to grant that whites can genuinely sympathize with the plight of the slaves, those who would insist that white beneficence only further contributes to black docility and subordination.

For Douglass, the ability to sympathize was a key indication of one's humanity, and those whom he believed possessed capacities for sympathy—such as Stowe—were viewed as *nearly* transcending the limits of race (Douglass never closed his eyes to racial difference). Sympathy allows for the possibility of dialogue and influence; and I do not think it too farfetched to read "The Heroic Slave," in part, as an allegory of Douglass's relationship with Stowe, particularly if we take Listwell's overhearing of Washington's soliloquy and subsequent conversion to antislavery as analogous to Stowe's reading of Douglass's *Narrative* and eventual authoring of *Uncle Tom's Cabin*. In this model of influence, as I hypothesize it here between Douglass and Stowe, and as Douglass in "The Heroic Slave" presents it between Washington and Listwell, power is shared and mutually constitutive. From this perspective, Douglass, in his championing of *Uncle Tom's Cabin*, cannot be regarded (pace Delany) as a dupe or a lackey, for he himself had a role in the production of the novel and continued to play a significant role in its cultural reproduction.

Yet Douglass's specific plan to beget a black industrial college from *Uncle Tom's Cabin* failed to transpire. While Stowe, in a letter of December 1853 to William Garrison, could declare that Douglass's "plans for the elevation of his own race are manly, sensible,

9. I would agree with Yarborough that Douglass's emphasis on Washington's manly individualism is troubling. The other slaves seem to play but a small role in the rebellion, and women slaves, such as Washington's wife, disappear from the novella; see "Race, Violence, and Manhood," 176–77.

comprehensive,"[1] one month later Douglass announced in the pages of *Frederick Douglass' Paper*, in an article on his proposed industrial college, that "Mrs. Stowe, for reasons which she deems quite satisfactory, does not, at present, see fit to stand forth as the patron of the proposed institution."[2] For various reasons, Stowe lost interest in the project while in England, perhaps because she thought blacks could not successfully run their own school, or perhaps because she was aware of criticisms of the project from other blacks. "Thus cold-watered," Benjamin Quarles reports, "Mrs. Stowe's money-raising efforts realized the meagre sum of $535. This she turned over to Douglass for his personal use."[3] It would be tempting to assert that Douglass therefore became disillusioned with Stowe, but the evidence suggests that Douglass's relationship with her remained a cordial one, and that his admiration for *Uncle Tom's Cabin* remained undiminished. Between 27 January and 22 December of 1854, Douglass reprinted from the New York *Independent* a series of ten articles by Stowe, "Shadows on the Hebrew Mountains." That same year Stowe contributed, as she had in 1853, a piece for Julia Griffith's *Autographs for Freedom*, a fundraising volume for *Frederick Douglass' Paper*. The following year saw the publication of *My Bondage and My Freedom*, a text which elicited from Anna Adams, who reviewed it in Douglass's newspaper, the highest form of praise: she had "read nothing since *Uncle Tom's Cabin* which so thrilled every fibre of the soul and awoke such intense sympathy for the slave."[4] As Douglass proclaimed in an 1857 speech reprinted in his paper: "the name of Harriet Beecher Stowe can never die while the love of freedom lives in the world."[5]

No doubt Douglass was distressed, after the Civil War, by Stowe's initial opposition to black suffrage, but that did not stop him from attending a party celebrating her seventy-first birthday in 1882. Nor did he seem to harbor any undue resentment in his retrospective remarks on Stowe and *Uncle Tom's Cabin* in *Life and Times of Frederick Douglass* (1892). His belief in the importance of the novel to the antislavery cause is consistent with his position of the 1850s: "In the midst of these fugitive slave troubles came the book known as *Uncle Tom's Cabin*, a work of marvelous depth and power. Nothing could have better suited the moral and humane requirements of the hour. Its effect was amazing, instantaneous, and universal." In his

1. Letter of 19 December 1853, rpt. in *Life and Letters of Harriet Beecher Stowe*, 214. Stowe wrote the letter to defend Douglass against Garrison's charge that he was an "apostate" from the cause. She demanded of Garrison: "Is there but one true anti-slavery church and all others infidels? Who shall declare what it is?" (214–15).
2. "The Industrial College," *FDP*, 20 January 1854, 3.
3. *Frederick Douglass* (1948), 131.
4. *FDP*, 21 September 1855, 4.
5. "The Significance of Emancipation in the West Indies," *FDP*, 7 August 1857, 1.

account of his meeting with Stowe in Andover, he remains convinced of her sympathies for the free and enslaved blacks: "There was no contradiction between the author and her book." Thus he defends her from proslavery smears that her British travels were meant only to make her rich: "I denounced their accusations as groundless and through the columns of my paper, assured the public that the testimonial then being raised in England by Mrs. Stowe would be sacredly devoted to the establishment of an industrial school for colored youth." As a result of his efforts, he maintains, "the attacks ceased," yet her financial support, he learns upon her return, will not be forthcoming. His disappointment, even after nearly forty years, is palpable: "I have never been able to see any force in the reasons for this change. It is enough, however, to say that they were sufficient for her, and that she no doubt acted conscientiously, though her change of purpose . . . placed me in an awkward position before the colored people of this country, as well as to friends abroad."[6]

Though restrained, a sense of betrayal informs these final observations on Stowe, as her change of mind would have made Douglass appear foolish in the eyes, say, of Martin Delany. Arguably, it would also make him appear foolish in the eyes of his future readers, who, armed with their knowledge of Stowe's failure to support the institution and her unattractive response to the debate on African American suffrage, could criticize Douglass for being so naive as to put his faith in a white woman who, at bottom, perhaps did lack full sympathy for America's blacks, as Delany claimed. This very essay on the reception of *Uncle Tom's Cabin* in *Frederick Douglass' Paper* may, for some readers, only further put Douglass in an "awkward position," because it reveals him, rather unfashionably, as clinging to Enlightenment universalist values, transracial claims of sympathy, and an optimistic faith in black elevation at a time when the institutions of antebellum culture were working to thwart that elevation. Though it is hardly my intention to do so, this overview of Douglass's response to *Uncle Tom's Cabin*—a text that, despite the claims of Tompkins and others for its feminism, has increasingly been implicated in dominant modes of antebellum social power[7]—may only provide further evidence for those convinced that Douglass himself was complicitous in upholding or reinforcing dominant modes of power. For we have been instructed of late on Douglass's naivete in evoking the

6. *Life and Times of Frederick Douglass* (1892; rpt., New York: Collier Books, 1962), 282, 290, 291.
7. The most persuasive recent examples are Richard H. Brodhead, "Sparing the Rod: Discipline and Fiction in Antebellum America," *Representations* 2 (1988): 67–96; Lora Romero, "Bio-Political Resistance in Domestic Ideology and *Uncle Tom's Cabin*," *American Literary History* 1 (1989): 715–34; and Myra Jehlen, "The Family Militant: Domesticity versus Slavery in *Uncle Tom's Cabin*," *Criticism* 31 (1989): 383–400.

principles of 1776 in support of slave liberation, as to do so was to "appeal to the authorizing mythology of an oppressive culture"; we have learned of his misguided efforts to speak to white readers, in that he "succeeded only in reproducing the cliches of his oppressors"; and we have been told that Douglass's affirmations of conventional antebellum notions of individualism and manhood inevitably led to the marginalization of women in his writings and gave "credence to the patriarchal structure largely responsible for his oppression."[8]

Whether these critiques of Douglass tell us more about Douglass or the imprisoning ideological imperatives of our newly dominant New Historical critical practice is something that critics will no doubt be debating for some time. In an excellent rejoinder to the New Historicist emphasis on Douglass's complicity in antebellum modes of power, Gregory S. Jay views Douglass as a rhetorician who makes tactical use of dominant languages; thus Jay warns against viewing "Douglass's invocation of humanistic discourse as only ideology in the negative sense—that is, as a maneuver in the name of the hegemonic forces of control." According to Jay, because a black speaker or writer has an "alienated relation to white language, one can argue that the black subject makes a space for opposition within ideology just by opening his or her mouth."[9] It has been my contention that in voicing his praise for Stowe's novel Douglass appropriated the novel, insisting that it do the work it announced itself as doing. In addition, by attempting to enlist Stowe to the cause of his industrial college in the name of her novel, Douglass sought to make *Uncle Tom's Cabin* do the cultural work that he wanted it to do. That a figure such as Douglass truly believed Stowe's novel could counteract the effects of the Compromise of 1850 should temper our skepticism about Stowe's large intentions and achievements and about her complicity in the power structure. Douglass's pragmatic refusal to give up on Stowe for her racialist and colonizationist ideas speaks well for his historicist perception of the cultural forces that could impinge upon the mind and rheto-

8. Yarborough, "Race, Violence, and Manhood," 180; Joseph Fichtelberg, *Faith and Method in American Autobiography* (Philadelphia: Univ. of Pennsylvania Press, 1989), 120; and Valerie Smith, *Self-Discovery and Authority in Afro-American Narrative* (Cambridge: Harvard Univ. Press, 1987), 27. On Douglass and gender, see also David Leverenz, *Manhood and the American Renaissance* (Ithaca: Cornell Univ. Press, 1989), 108–34; Jenny Franchot, "The Punishment of Esther: Frederick Douglass and the Construction of the Feminine," in *Frederick Douglass: New Literary and Historical Essays*, 141–65; and Yarborough, "Race, Violence, and Manhood." For a less censorious view of Douglass's appeal to American Revolutionary ideals, see Sundquist, "Frederick Douglass: Literacy and Paternalism."

9. "American Literature and the New Historicism: The Example of Frederick Douglass," *boundary 2* 17 (1990): 241. On Douglass's complex interactions with the discourse of the dominant white culture, see also Houston A. Baker Jr., *The Journey Back: Issues in Black Literature and Criticism* (Chicago: Univ. of Chicago Press, 1980), 32–47; and Wilson J. Moses, "Dark Forests and Barbarian Vigor: Paradox, Conflict, and Africanity in Black Writing Before 1914," *American Literary History* 1 (1989): esp. 638–43.

ric of even the most sympathetic of white Americans. His efforts to persuade Stowe to rethink her colonizationist stance and (through "The Heroic Slave") her racialism suggest that Douglass came to believe that the publication of a text—even one with so massive an authority as *Uncle Tom's Cabin*—does not foreclose the possibility of dialogue between authors and readers, blacks and whites, oppressed and oppressors, when glimmers of mutual sympathy can be discerned.

## SOPHIA CANTAVE

## Who Gets to Create the Lasting Images? The Problem of Black Representation in *Uncle Tom's Cabin*†

For late-twentieth-century teachers, the significance of Harriet Beecher Stowe as a white woman creating a national space for an "empathetic" discourse on the slave experience raises several questions. For instance, why didn't Mary Prince's exposé of slavery in the West Indies, *The History of Mary Prince* (1831), or Harriet Wilson's account of de facto slavery in the American North, *Our Nig* (1859), become the proverbial "shot heard around the world"? What enabled Stowe to write *Uncle Tom's Cabin* and begin a national and international literary exchange on slavery? The novel invented the modern idea of a "best-seller," and many of Stowe's characters became national stock types and icons. Even today, readers cry at the right places and express horror, relief, or disbelief where textually appropriate. Most important, Stowe's text allows whites to talk to other whites about the personal and national issues surrounding the slave experience and establishes the character types usually associated with African Americans. Indeed, throughout the second half of the nineteenth century and then the early twentieth century, Stowe's novel provided the nation with a shared cultural context for its discourse on slavery, offering reductive images, phrases, and symbols that quickly became the accepted norm.

For example, early in the twentieth century *Uncle Tom's Cabin* permitted the nameless narrator of James Weldon Johnson's *The Autobiography of an Ex-Colored Man* (1912) to talk finally to his mother about their racial identity. But what does it mean when two highly miscegenated characters use a white woman's novel as the

† From *Approaches to Teaching Stowe's* Uncle Tom's Cabin, eds., Elizabeth Ammons and Susan Belasco. 

basis for a discussion of their blackness in the United States? In contrast, *The History of Mary Prince*, though heavily edited, failed to galvanize the literate community or fill the racial imaginings of Americans. And the suppression of Harriet Wilson's *Our Nig* prevented it from shaping the national conceptions of the slave and nonslave experience.

When we use Stowe's novel in the classroom, I think it is important to ask who gets to make our national symbols and who gets to determine when a particular symbol or icon has outlived its usefulness. Although *Uncle Tom's Cabin* was essential in creating an earlier discourse on the slave experience, what is the usefulness of teaching the novel today? I reexamine that question. At the turn into the twenty-first century, I think modern readers want to bury the discourse Stowe began under the fiction that "we already know about slavery"—yet we do not know. To begin a broader discussion of American women's involvement in the "peculiar institution" as slaves, as slave owners, and as writers, readers need to go beyond the humiliating or embarrassing surface of the text and examine the issues that the existence of the novel raises. In this essay, I focus on Stowe's problematic status and symbols to ask where the United States slave experience, as Stowe writes it, should fit in a modern literary context—a question that should surely precede any teaching of the novel.

At first, a return to *Uncle Tom's Cabin* feels like a return to a crime scene with too many nagging questions left unanswered. Because of these questions, Stowe's novel should regain its place in contemporary classrooms and be taught for what it signifies about United States race relations 150 years after slavery. Few African Americans criticized Stowe's novel at the time of its initial publication. In the mid-nineteenth century, African American emancipation depended on acknowledging and supporting the national and international debate sparked by *Uncle Tom's Cabin*. Where all other writers "failed," Stowe succeeded. The significance of her success, and the instant commercialization of her subject, placed many of the African American abolitionists in an odd position. How does Frederick Douglass criticize a novel he feels beholden to? For the most part, Douglass praised the novel's efficacy and tirelessly referred to *Uncle Tom's Cabin* as the "master book of the nineteenth century" (Donovan 17). Of her text, Stowe said, "My vocation is simply that of a painter, and my object will be to hold up in the most lifelike and graphic manner possible Slavery, its reverses, changes, and the negro character, which I have had ample opportunities for studying. There is no arguing with *pictures*, and everybody is impressed by them, whether they mean to be or not" (Hedrick, *Stowe* 208). The power, efficacy, and timeliness of *Uncle Tom's Cabin* cannot be denied. But the unsettling issues surrounding Stowe's access and her relation to the "objects of her study" should not be denied either. At the turn into the twenty-first century, Stowe's novel continues to evoke uneasiness when readers consider blackness and, more important, slavery as the "canvas" that allowed her to write her most famous novel.

As is well known, Stowe's "sketches of slave life," as she popularly referred to her novel (Hedrick, *Stowe* 208), would eventually influence the development of the modern theater, the development of philanthropy as a business, and the marketing of "Uncle Tom" paraphernalia. Less well known is the fact that a viewing of *Uncle Tom's Cabin* served as the catalyst for Thomas Dixon's literary career. As part of his refutation of Stowe's version of Southern slavery, Dixon wrote *The Clansman* (1905), which later became the basis for D. W. Griffith's classic, racist movie, *The Birth of a Nation* (1915). In other words, the negative influence of Stowe's novel on the development of United States popular culture even in cases such as this, where Stowe's text is being attacked, must be considered. And the readily available "canvas of blackness" that allowed Stowe's sketches to come to life continues to enable the nation to solidify its power not only to relegate black people to the margins but also to regulate the discourses surrounding what constitutes human suffering and degradation. The slave experience, far from being understood, is trapped in multiple hegemonic constructions of power and nation as well as by self-imposed restrictions on language.

Many middle-class African Americans want to forget, or get past, the images of Topsy "just growing," of Sambo and Quimbo, of Sam and Andy, of Chloe and Uncle Tom himself. Members of the African American middle class shun what the black urban masses, largely the working poor, often vilify and reclaim with their popular usage of such terms as *niggers* and *hoes*, *players*, and *freaks* when referring to one another. Which national face should African Americans present as what they understand of their positionality and blackness in America? The slave experience, in the African American psyche, continues metaphorically to grope for the words to explain the silence, including the profusion of reactions to a white woman writing and creating a national discourse on slavery. These anxieties, in part, explain late-twentieth-century returns to the Middle Passage and its aftermath. Questions remain about black speaking subjects even as modern writers like Toni Morrison, Octavia Butler, Gloria Naylor, Charles Johnson, and others travel back in time in attempts to wrest control of black images from benevolent but racist white supporters and their detractors.

Josephine Donovan points out that Stowe, in explaining her construction of *Uncle Tom's Cabin*, said:

> "The writer acknowledges that the book is a very inadequate representation of slavery [because] slavery, in some of its workings, is too dreadful for the purposes of art. A work which should represent it strictly as it is would be a work which could not be read; and all works which ever mean to give pleasure must draw a veil somewhere, or they cannot succeed." In fiction, therefore, one can "find refuge from the hard and the terrible, by inventing scenes and characters of a more pleasing nature." (62)

In her successful attempt to make slavery readable, Stowe falls back on the comic interactions of blacks with other blacks and of blacks while in the presence of whites. By mixing the tragic and the laughable, *Uncle Tom's Cabin* gives white people and black people a way to read slavery together. This does not mean that African Americans did not then, and do not now, make use of comedy to explain parts of slavery. They had to and often did so for the benefit of their owners. Thus the joking relationship and the various uses of the comic exist as one of the earliest accepted signs of black subordination and one that slaves continuously manipulated. But the comic interactions as Stowe uses them do not so much subvert as reinforce the existing order.

This shared reading almost always insists that slavery, in its entirety, cannot be read and that slavery and the slave experience do not make for "good art." In some ways, this designation of slavery as unreadable and unfit for the purposes of high art continues, almost 150 years after the publication of *Uncle Tom's Cabin*. In assessing her novel, Stowe gives herself the power to decide on the purposes of art and when and where to draw the veil when writing on slavery. Thus, despite even her best intentions, *Uncle Tom's Cabin* betrays her overwhelming race and class privileges and the ways she herself helped to further limit African Americans' access to the dominant language and their own literary portrayal of the slave experience.

To do the necessary research for *Beloved* (1987), Toni Morrison went to Brazil to see various slave restraints like the iron collar and muzzle used to control and torture. The United States sterilized and reduced the slave narratives and slavery into formulaic stories that the nation as a whole felt more comfortable reading. Morrison confronts, in writing, what many of the early United States narratives could not when she writes about the devastating psychological trauma of slavery. She exposes the ease with which an exploding national discourse reduced the grossest human violations into instances of comic relief and shows how sentimental release acts as a potent signifier of white hegemonic control. For example, fearing competition where none existed before, Fuzzy Zoeller made a disparaging comment to an understanding white CNN newscaster about fried chicken littering a once exclusive golf tournament, a remark that immediately undercut the record-breaking achievement of Tiger Woods. Despite black excellence and achievement, such jokes, at key moments, perpetuate age-old images of nonwhite incompetence and buffoonery. In choosing to intersperse the comic alongside the tragic, Stowe inadvertently provided a way for white people, when threatened or challenged, to regulate black achievement, black national mobility, and black cultural expression. Even the relationships that black people form with one another are circumscribed by such strategies of the dominant culture and its definitions of blackness.

One way to illuminate these issues is by teaching *Uncle Tom's Cabin* side by side with Harriet Wilson's *Our Nig*, published just seven years after *Uncle Tom's Cabin*. Harriet Wilson, a severely marginalized black woman, began in her writing to make powerful connections with other black people about their shared economic and color oppression. Her disastrous marriage to a black man claiming to be a former slave goes beyond what Stowe imagines as the motivating force behind black female-male relationships. That is, Wilson's Frado leaves the best home she has ever known and her only moment of relative independence because she is drawn to a man who she believes shares her experiences. Aside from Frado's dead father and the man her mother runs off with, her husband makes the third black man to enter her life. Wilson makes a point of saying that Frado reacts to the bond created by their similar backgrounds. Ironically, however, Frado's husband lies about his slave experience and quickly abandons his new bride. Yet Wilson does not dwell on this lie. Instead, she hints that Frado's husband felt compelled to play the role of a former slave in order to get Northern abolitionists' sympathy and assistance. My point here has to do with the complexity of Wilson's perspective. Although Frado's marriage leads to her further physical deterioration, it shows Frado making choices that do not depend on white benevolence or white fictions of black desire. Yet because of her husband's dependence on white Northern sympathy, Frado indirectly suffers.

Wilson's multiple strategies of reappropriation and renaming help her subversively assert herself as a speaking subject. Even though heavily circumscribed and limited, she directs her appeals to her colored brethren, not the white masses. She asks her colored brethren to forgive her faulty prose and purchase her novel or, rather, her "sketches from the life of a free black, in a two-story white house,

North." She says in her preface, "I have purposefully omitted what would most provoke shame in our good anti-slavery friends at home"(4). Wilson echoes almost the same sentiments as Stowe—that the worst of slavery has been omitted—but for different reasons. After her abandonment first by her mother and then by her husband, Wilson had to depend on the "good anti-slavery friends at home," the class that Stowe belonged to. Wilson's disclaimer says that she leaves out what would show Northern white abolitionists to be very much like their Southern white slaveholding counterparts. Wilson assumes much more subjectivity than the nation, in 1859, was prepared to accept or believe in a black speaker. If Stowe's detractors vehemently refuted "her blacks" as thinking subjects, *Our Nig*, written by a black woman in the North, gave white readers even more reason to dismiss Wilson's text altogether. At least with *Uncle Tom's Cabin*, later dramatic adaptations could exclude the heavily abolitionist tracts and overplay the comic moments that comfortably disrupt sections assigning blame or showing black agency since the joke always has a derogatory black reference that serves as the punch line. Students need to know that Topsy, on the stage, became an instant hit with the audiences in part because her reformation into a serious-minded missionary was conveniently left out. In contrast, Frado, far from being the butt of the jokes, instigates them and possesses more self-awareness than Topsy, who is primarily constructed as the antithesis of Little Eva.

Wilson offers her readers Frado's body both in its linguistic negation and as the epitome of Northern conceptions of blackness despite her light skin and white mother. Mrs. Bellmont, her keeper, delights in her complete control of Frado's body. She keeps on hand special blocks that she forces into the child's mouth in order to beat her with even greater abandon. Mrs. Bellmont cripples Frado's body without ever losing her status as a respectable member of her community. These spaces in Wilson's text of possible catharsis through the sadistic pleasure of physically or mentally violating black bodies present an unexplored area for students to think about. In contrast, Stowe emphasizes the sadism and ruthlessness of slave violation at the hands of white men, making Marie St. Clare the monstrous exception to the rule, while Mary Prince and Harriet Wilson delve deep into the pleasure white women derive from the physical energy expended in beating bodies even more marginalized than their own.

Harriet Wilson, writing her fictionalized autobiography only a few years after *Uncle Tom's Cabin*, gave considerable thought to her audience. She appealed to a black readership while simultaneously considering how white readers might receive her text. Wilson says in her preface, "I do not pretend to divulge every transaction in my own life, which the unprejudiced would declare unfavorable in comparison with treatment of legal bondmen" (4). Because she lived in the North, Wilson left out the worst of what she experienced as a free black there, lest she alienate abolitionists. She wrote her autobiographical novel in an attempt to earn enough money to support herself and her son, who died before she sold one copy and her entire project slipped into obscurity. Conversely, Stowe as a writer committed to the abolitionist movement but also desiring a modicum of success in her endeavor, made the slave's experience readable, palatable for her expected audience. In Uncle Tom's Cabin: *Evil, Affliction, and Redemptive Love* Josephine Donovan says, "The slave narratives tended to focus on one person's unhappy experiences from that individual's point of view. Stowe realized that no one would read a novel that was relentlessly grim (indeed *Uncle Tom's Cabin* outsold all of the slave narratives and abolition novels put together)" (62). The fact that "*Uncle Tom's Cabin* outsold all of the slave narratives" underscores the significance of Stowe's literary and transgressive access to her potent subject matter that fueled the uninhibited imagination of the country. *Uncle Tom's Cabin* sold more copies than any American novel before or, for a long time, after it because Stowe's position as a white woman from a family of preachers enabled her to write not only with moral conviction but also with the necessary distance to calculate a specific textual effect. While being driven by a moral obligation to write against an institution she saw as diametrically opposed to Christianity, Stowe produced a text that surpassed even her wildest expectations.

But what has been the effect of this book on black people? An experiment lasting over fifteen years conducted by Albion Tourgee, a novelist, judge, and activist who spoke out against racial segregation, provides one answer. Tourgee had former slaves read or listen to readings of *Uncle Tom's Cabin* because he wanted "to determine to what extent [they] thought [*Uncle Tom's Cabin*] was an accurate portrayal of southern slavery" (Gossett, *American Culture* 361). "'Choosing the most intelligent colored people' available he 'found that most ex-slaves did not think Uncle Tom was too meek as later generations of black activists would. Instead they thought of him as unrealistically critical of his masters. Tom spoke out more frankly than a real slave might have dared to'" (Donovan 17). The few recordings of black responses to *Uncle Tom's Cabin* vacillate between evasive silences and complete acceptance of Stowe's words and reactions, suggesting that her depictions are better than what slaves could have produced. Donovan gives the example of a female former slave perfectly content with Stowe's words standing in for her own. "Sella Martin [ . . . ] in speaking of her difficulty in describing the horrors of being sold at the auction block, remarked, 'happily this [ . . . ] task is now unnecessary. Mrs. Stowe [has] thrown sufficient light upon the horrible and inhuman agency of slavery'"(17). Stowe also felt that it was *she* who should represent (and profit from) the telling of slave experiences, as her treatment of Harriet Jacobs's narrative illustrates. Instead of giving Jacobs the literary advice she sought, Stowe offered to include Jacobs's narrative in her *Key to* Uncle Tom's Cabin. The slave experience, with all its violations and humiliations, was the property of Harriet Beecher Stowe.

Yet according to one male former slave in Tourgee's study, Stowe "didn't know what slavery was so left out the worst of it" (Gossett, *American Culture* 361). To give even this cautious yet pointed critique was daring. He provides a reason completely different from the one Stowe gives for leaving out the worst of slavery. Attributing only this line to the speaker, Tourgee does not give any more space for the former slave to describe "the worst of it" beyond saying "the worst of it." Tourgee, though, provides his own analysis of speech and non-speech patterns in slave communities. He says, "Perhaps the most striking feature characteristic of slavery was the secretiveness it imposed upon slave nature. [ . . . ] To the slave, language became in very truth an instrument for the concealment of thought, rather than its expression" (Donovan 17). Little wonder that language "became an instrument of concealment" in the face of overwhelming racial inequality and racial violence. Tourgee himself says, "Men do not argue with those who have the power of life and death over them" (Gossett, *American Culture* 361). Language itself continues to place black bodies as speaking subjects, then and now, at risk. In Uncle Tom's Cabin *and American Culture*, Thomas F. Gossett also discusses the conflicted responses of black people to Stowe's novel. Stowe wrote her novel at a time when African humanity, intelligence, and subjectivity were still being debated. Gossett says that many white readers criticized Stowe's portrayals of black people as being too complimentary. This sentiment, in combination with little or no access to the text, made it difficult for African American readers of that period to challenge the novel's reductiveness. After the publication of *Uncle Tom's Cabin*, African Americans who wanted to speak about blackness in America and be heard had to do it through Stowe or not at all.

Consequently, James Weldon Johnson's protagonist can begin a serious and thoughtful discussion of race only in the context of *Uncle Tom's Cabin*. Ironically, a man who sees himself as white and eventually decides to pass as white reads Stowe's novel in much the same way that sympathetic white readers read *Uncle Tom's Cabin*. The "thingness" of blacks, despite the richness of a culture little understood and searching for its expression, leads the Ex-Colored Man to live the life of "an ordinarily successful white man who has made a little money" (510). The risk involved in expressing himself as a black person causes him to "[sell his] heritage for a mess of pottage" (511), and the unspeakable act of lynching another human being remains uncontested. Significantly, the lynching occurs at the moment the Ex-Colored Man finishes his documentation of black music and cultural expression in the South and begins contemplating the future publication of his findings. Confronted with such a display of power—the lynching of a black man by a group of respectable citizens—a miscegenated black man chooses whiteness and the suppression of any and all claims to black subjectivity and authorship.

In considering issues of authorship and vocality, the following question also needs to be raised in the classroom: When can black people speak and in what words that do not already replicate in some way the dialectic of past ownership and subordination? Even as modern writers anxiously go back to write and say the things that enslaved or freed blacks could not say, what are the words and images that will not leave them at risk and produce yet again another silencing in the present age? Too little has been done with the contemporary resurgence in pop culture of "niggers," "boys," "players," "freaks," and "hoes," all old images with old origins. The comic, the hypersexualized, and the desexualized remain as the most readily available symbols of African Americans in the United States. In place of words, Stowe and a minstrel tradition older than the one she helped formalize give black expression wholly over to hand gestures, mimicry, stoicism, and other non-speech acts.

Given this reduction of black expression to the guttural, the comical, and the lewd, the dominating theoretical framework for analyzing black literature and black culture, in the early twentieth century, focused on psychic doubling, veils, tricksterism, and masks. All these approaches centered on black performance and the stifling relation of black bodies to a power structure that did not see itself as oppressive or feel culpable in demanding these performances of race. The current discourse on race allows for too many gaps, too many silences, while whole discussions about race and racial equity continue to take place without the participation or presence of black people. Stowe's discarded subtitle, *The Man That Was a Thing*, accurately describes the role of black people when white people gather to discuss who they will and will not allow entry into their coveted circles. African American struggles to wrest control of our national images, icons, and symbols from the white power structure must continue as part of the fight against objectification and erasure.

African American discourse, even in urban slang, still manages to conceal, evade, and leave much, sometimes too much, unsaid.

The silent ironies of early African American discourses, though ensuring African American survival despite physical and psychic violation, need to "call Stowe out of her name." To do this "calling out" (and make Stowe's text useful in the classroom) students must question the novel's runaway success and influence not only in the United States but also around the world. Similarly, students must also question the complex social, cultural, and political context, at this fin de siècle, that keeps Stowe's text from being read by both black and white readers. The resistance to the kinds of remembrances that *Uncle Tom's Cabin* provokes about the nation's slave past provides other ways to discuss issues of African American textual silence, erasure, and the continuing appropriation of black images. In rethinking black people's reaction to this encroachment, what happens when irony is lost on its audience, when silence, double subversions, reversals get buried so deep they become undecipherable and completely disconnected from their original negation? African American literary discourse began with multiple capitulations to a white reading public that made discussing and writing about the worst of slavery unacceptable. In addition to the frayed and moldy bills of sale, the "owners" of the slave experience and its symbols also own and regulate the national discourses on slavery. *Uncle Tom's Cabin* may have wanted to show how slave owners could overcome the reification and reduction of human beings to the status of things but this reduction and reification are precisely what happen in the novel and particularly in the Tom shows it inspired. For teachers today, the novel exists as an uncomfortable but necessary place to begin critical discussions about the racial dynamics of literary access, power, and popular culture.

As the writer who helped shape the national discourse on slavery, Stowe provided the parameters of that discourse, establishing where slavery can and cannot go in the popular imagination and as high literature. These stifling limitations explain, in part, why two subversive black women's texts, Wilson's *Our Nig* and Prince's narrative, received little or no literary attention at the time of their original publication. In many ways, 150 years after Stowe published her novel, African Americans still do not have the words to say what the worst of slavery really was, or rather, African Americans did not create the terms that define the slave experience in the national consciousness. African Americans who step outside the accepted parameters of slavery's discourse risk shutting down discussions, arousing white defensive or apologetic barrages and black desires to acquiesce and make nice in the face of such responses. All these responses take away from speaking honestly and critically about power inequities even in some of the most common social interactions. In acquiescing, in giving up the national discursive space to white culture, unspeakable things remain unspoken, especially in the academy where one's vocality, erudition, and authorship matter. "Being nice," helping to keep one's colleagues comfortable, results in the loss of too much ground. All these issues in one way or another come into play in Stowe's novel. *Uncle Tom's Cabin*, precisely because of its literary success and its continuing, though unadmitted, influence on United States cultural history, needs to reenter current, critical discussions of race to shed light on some of the nagging issues that are still too difficult to name.

Historically, *Uncle Tom's Cabin* provided a framework for the United States and the European nations to discuss the "peculiar institution" and their positions within that institution. Stowe's novel in a late-twentieth-century classroom context should highlight issues of appropriation, privilege, national accountability, and the intricate workings of power in the United States. After the publication of *Uncle Tom's Cabin*, almost all slave narratives by black people became a part of Harriet Beecher Stowe's *Key to* Uncle Tom's Cabin. That is, the telling of the slave experience became a strangely white affair, being told in ways that let white audiences be moved to tears and still find the work enjoyable. Yet the former slaves' responses to the novel seem to tell a different story, one about the absence of their words and what it means to accept someone else's language. Stowe's own admission, that slavery as it existed did not make for good art, supports my belief that what the nation as a collective understands about race relations it does not write or readily discuss except, possibly, in the joking relationship. The national fiction of understanding and knowing slavery exists as a complex cultural production depending on black and white people to play their parts. The very idea of Stowe giving her words to a former slave woman disturbingly points to the issues at stake in questions of authority and ownership. The quote of the nameless male former slave who lamented the absence of "the worst of slavery" in literature represents what remains forever out of reach when black people fail to resist and question master/mistress narratives, even ones that are done with the best intentions.

Denying African Americans the opportunity to tell their story without comic interjections left whole things unsaid. Early on, African Americans, the majority of whom were unable to write freely in their own words about their experiences, did not create the lasting images of the slave experience. Simultaneously, Stowe refused to write the worst of slavery. African Americans, unable to tell the worst of slavery directly, packed multiple meanings in generic evasive responses that lessened the linguistic and physical risks involved in speaking in a repressive society. The unspoken, the unspeakable, became its own signifier. Arguing these points in the classroom does not mean that black people did not imagine themselves in relation to other blacks, other people of color, or that black people were not instrumental in advocating for changes that established legal precedents for other groups to follow. It does mean that African American cultural production and discourses need to move from the margins, where they are easily appropriated and reauthored, to the center.

Locating Stowe in her historical moment and outside it, a century and a half later, provides the setting for a discussion of the politics involved in her discursive access to her black subjects and the continuing use of black bodies as fodder for the nation's intellectual, cultural, economic, and political revisions and reassessments. To read the criticism on Stowe, even that which goes beyond questioning her literary status, is to confront over and over again the "thingness" of the African American slave body. Despite Stowe's own marginalization as a woman in her own period, the "thingness" of African American bodies and the pervasive acceptance of a culture based on human ownership made the figures of Uncle Tom, Topsy, Eliza, Cassy, Dinah, Sam, Andy, Sambo, and Quimbo available to her. These images of African Americans persist in their original and updated forms, as efforts to denounce the persistence of the mammy figure in the late 1980s illustrate. After threatened boycotts, the makers of Aunt Jemima pancakes responded to the criticism of their logo by unveiling a new version of the mammy figure. Since removing the logo was out of the question, the Quaker Oats Company decided to remove Aunt Jemima's head scarf and give her a perm. Thus the new "Aunt Jemima" cut short any and all efforts to denounce continued use of the mammy figure. Silence, shame, embarrassment, and powerless indignation filled the space where anger and continued activism belonged. African Americans, in Stowe's time and now, do not own the images and symbols of African American culture, long wedded to big business and commercial success. Only a perm separates a mammy of the slave era from one in the late twentieth century.

To have this myriad of black bodies at the nation's collective disposal bespeaks a power that white culture rarely admits to owning. In the late twentieth century, Uncle Tom/Sam is Clarence Thomas, Eliza/Chloe/Cassy is Anita Hill, and George Harris is potentially a young O. J. on the rise.[1] These black figures act as catalysts for national debates on racial parity, equity in the justice and law

1. O. J. Simpson (1947– ), a prominent African American athlete, was tried and acquitted in 1995 on charges of murdering his ex-wife and her friend. Anita Hill (1956– ) an African American who accused Clarence Thomas (1948– ), a conservative African American appointed to the Supreme Court in 1991, of sexual harassment at Thomas's confirmation hearing.

enforcement systems, sexual harassment, spousal abuse, and the responsibilities of government agencies to the working poor. Renewed attacks on affirmative action, white culture's only begrudging capitulation to the intricate and exclusive workings of white privilege, reassert white culture's power to decide what constitutes African American access and redress for past inequities. In these displays of power, white hegemony reasserts its control by limiting not only the extent of black people's access but also their creative and competitive potential.

Without any particular acknowledgment or any sense of appropriation, expression of the slave experience became Stowe's own. It is this ownership, this appropriation of African American images, phrases, and culture by white culture, that continues to threaten the legitimacy of African American literature in the academy and that needs to be interrogated in the classroom. Blackness remains, at the turn into the twenty-first century, one of the few subjects that does not go beyond genteel academic or social discussion. In discussing blackness and making it readable for a predominantly white power structure, Stowe says, the jokes, the moments of comic relief at the expense of black people, are indispensable. Thus, as Toni Morrison argues, unspeakable things do remain unspoken and the worst of the slave experience continues to search for its words ("Unspeakable Things").

## WORKS CITED

Dixon, Thomas, Jr. *The Clansman: An Historical Romance of the Ku Klux Klan.* New York: Doubleday, Page, 1905.

Donovan, Josephine. Uncle Tom's Cabin: *Evil, Affliction, and Redemptive Love.* Boston: Twayne, 1991.

Gossett, Thomas F. Uncle Tom's Cabin *and American Culture.* Dallas: Southern Methodist UP, 1985.

Griffith, D. W., dir. *The Birth of a Nation.* 1915. New York: Kino on Video, 1992.

Hedrick, Joan. *Harriet Beecher Stowe: A Life.* New York: Oxford UP, 1994.

Jacobs, Harriet A. *Incidents in the Life of a Slave Girl, Written by Herself.* Ed. Jean Fagan Yellin. Cambridge: Harvard UP, 1987.

Johnson, James Weldon. *The Autobiography of an Ex-Colored Man.* 1912. Ed. Henry Louis Gates Jr. New York: Avon, 1965.

Morrison, Toni. *Beloved.* New York: Plume, 1987.

Morrison, Toni. "Unspeakable Things Unspoken: The Afro-American Presence in American Literature." *Within the Circle: An Anthology of African American Literary Criticism from the Harlem Renaissance to the Present.* Ed. Angelyn Mitchell. Durham: Duke UP, 1994. 368–98.

Prince, Mary. *The History of Mary Prince*. Ed. Henry Louis Gates Jr. New York: Mentor, 1987.
Stowe, Harriet Beecher. *A Key to Uncle Tom's Cabin*. Boston: Jewett, 1853.
Stowe, Harriet Beecher. *Uncle Tom's Cabin; or, Life among the Lowly*. Boston: Jewett, 1852.
Wilson, Harriet E. *Our Nig: or, Sketches from the Life of a Free Black*. 1859. Ed. Henry Louis Gates Jr. New York: Vintage, 1983.

## SUSAN M. RYAN

## Charity Begins at Home: Stowe's Antislavery Novels and the Forms of Benevolent Citizenship†

Scholarly work on Harriet Beecher Stowe, at least since the recuperation of sentimentalism, has tended to foreground her cultural and racial politics. Much of her critical rehabilitation, in fact, has rested on assertions of her fiction's progressivism. Most notably, Jane Tompkins, in her landmark study *Sensational Designs* (1985), finds in *Uncle Tom's Cabin* a revolutionary agenda that calls for both the emancipation of slaves and the cultural empowerment of women.[1] But the late 1980s and 1990s saw a backlash, not against Stowe's sentimentalism per se but against certain of the ideological and racial projects in which she (and other sentimental authors) participated. In particular, the colonizationist ending of *Uncle Tom's Cabin* has fueled the charge that Stowe's representations are more damaging than liberating. Karen Sánchez-Eppler articulates many critics' dismay at the novel's segregationist resolution when she decries "Stowe's failure to imagine an America in which blacks could be recognized as persons."[2] By invoking this disagreement, I do not wish to suggest that a simple binary pits Stowe's advocates against her critics, in stark contrast and ongoing conflict; indeed, much of the scholarship highlighting Stowe's politics has attended closely to the ambivalence her antislavery fiction engenders. My point, rather, is that it continues to matter how "good" Stowe's politics were, and not only because her most famous novel is so explicitly and passionately

† From *American Literature* 72.4 (Dec. 2000).  [Notes are shortened from the original with the author's permission. *Editor*]

1. Jane Tompkins, *Sensational Designs: The Cultural Work of American Fiction*, 1790–1860 (New York: Oxford Univ. Press, 1985), 122–46, an excerpt from which appears in this volume, pp. 539–61.
2. Karen Sánchez-Eppler, "Bodily Bonds: The Intersecting Rhetorics of Feminism and Abolition," in *The Culture of Sentiment: Race, Gender, and Sentimentality in Nineteenth-Century America*, ed. Shirley Samuels (New York: Oxford Univ. Press, 1992), 113.

activist. Stowe has come to represent—perhaps most pointedly for Euro-American women in the academy—earnest, middle-class, white activism. In the process, she has proven to be a vexing icon—both an honored foremother and a specter of good intentions gone awry.[3]

To some extent, the current critical preoccupation with Stowe mirrors her "iterative" style, best exemplified by her figuring and refiguring of the suffering mother.[4] Scholars, that is, figure and refigure the activist author, struggling to devise a way of understanding her that escapes the opposing dangers of presentist recrimination and hagiography. The resolution of this dilemma, if such a resolution is possible, will not come through a retreat from politics; such a move would necessitate not only separating Stowe's early novels from the cultural matrix in which they were produced and whose terms they helped to shape but also ignoring vast segments of their content. I argue, instead, that Stowe's moral and racial politics should be historicized more thoroughly, along the lines of recent work by Robert Levine and others.[5] Specifically, I am claiming that neither Stowe's literary representations nor her politics can be well understood apart from the antebellum discourse of benevolence within which she wrote her antislavery novels and in whose construction she participated. Her articulations of racial and national identity in *Uncle Tom's Cabin* (1851–1852) and *Dred* (1856) must be contextualized within a broader debate over the terms of what we might call benevolent citizenship—a way of thinking about national membership and national character through the paradigm of doing good.

In the decades before the Civil War, Americans used the terms *benevolence* and *benevolent* with astonishing frequency, not only where one would expect, as in reports by charitable organizations and in sermons or religious tracts, but also in political pamphlets, newspaper articles, poetry, and fiction. Moreover, in much antebellum discourse, the nation was said to be legitimized through the benevolence of its policies. Echoing the Puritan John Winthrop's notion of a city upon a hill, Americans repeatedly asserted that this was a benevolent nation, or they foretold national destruction should a particular humanitarian course of action be shunned. Debates over the future composition and character of the United States—

3. See Robyn Wiegman's chapter "The Alchemy of Disloyalty" in *American Anatomies: Theorizing Race and Gender* (Durham, N.C.: Duke Univ. Press, 1995), 179–202; and June Howard's call for literary historians "[t]o resist positions 'for' and 'against' sentimentality" in "What Is Sentimentality?" *American Literary History* (Spring 1999): 65.
4. Tompkins, 137.
5. Robert S. Levine, *Martin Delany, Frederick Douglass, and the Politics of Representative Identity* (Chapel Hill: Univ. of North Carolina Press, 1997), 145.

most notably, over slavery, Indian removal, African colonization, and immigration—were suffused with benevolent rhetoric, a rhetoric that speakers on all sides, even those who seem to us patently malevolent, used frequently and artfully. Stowe, in the preface to *Dred*, invokes this widely disseminated idea that the United States is a proving ground for benevolence: "[N]ever has there been a crisis in the history of this nation so momentous as the present. If ever a nation was raised up by Divine Providence, and led forth upon a conspicuous stage, as if for the express purpose of solving a great moral problem in the sight of all mankind, it is this nation."[6] Defining the specific form that such a solution might take, however, proved more complicated than this confident assertion would suggest.

Crucial to this conversation was a series of contestations over how to prioritize benevolent responsibility and how to define affiliation. To whom does one owe benevolence? Should activist allegiance be organized by regional, racial, or national affiliation, to name a few of the many options? If charity begins at home, as Americans endlessly reminded one another, then how might the boundaries around home and family be drawn? As Amy Kaplan, Lora Romero, and others have argued, the family and the nation were concepts intimately linked for antebellum Americans; defining them—each in relation to the other—was among the principal ideological projects of the day.[7] In that sense, the configuration of the family within benevolent discourse bore a strong relationship, metaphorical and analogical, to the configuration of the United States.

When read against contributions to this discourse, Stowe's shifting representations of family, nation, and benevolent allegiance resonate differently. Both *Uncle Tom's Cabin* and *Dred* are meditations on benevolent citizenship and on the ideological construction of the homes where charity might begin. And both, to some degree, undermine proslavery belief structures—in particular, the tenets that loyalty to one's region should supersede other considerations and that people of African descent would always need white aid. But the novels diverge significantly in their resettlement of fugitive slaves and in the utopic visions they offer. *Uncle Tom's Cabin* ends with a movement toward racially separate Utopias, with the characters who survive slavery leaving North America to do the work of benevolence among their "own" people in Africa, while *Dred* ends with the establishment of permanent interracial communities in the

6. Harriet Beecher Stowe, preface to *Dred: A Tale of the Great Dismal Swamp*, 2 vols. (Boston: Phillips, Sampson, 1856), 1: iii–iv.
7. Amy Kaplan, "Manifest Domesticity," *American Literature* 70 (September 1998): 581–606; Lora Romero, *Home Fronts: Domesticity and Its Critics in the Antebellum United States* (Durham, N.C.: Duke Univ. Press, 1997), 86.

northern United States and Canada. Much colonizationist rhetoric asserted that African Americans' benevolent activity in Liberia—especially the work of christianizing the African natives—would be the catalyst that transformed them from slaves and outcasts into citizens of a new nation. Stowe implies a similar transformation at the end of *Uncle Tom's Cabin*, though her rhetoric has a somewhat different tone. But as her writings and statements after that novel's publication suggest, Stowe ultimately comes down on the side of an interracial affiliation that, played out in the context of maternal or pseudomaternal domesticity, prefigures—indeed makes possible—a harmoniously interracial United States. *Dred's* conclusion grants at least some former slaves access to U.S. citizenship, largely by means of their role in the repair and reproduction of the family-as-nation through selfless acts of foster parenthood. Thus benevolent agency becomes, for Stowe, both the mark of their inclusion and the price of the ticket.

Scholars have explained Stowe's shift in strategy from African colonization to domestic emancipation as deriving from her initiation in the mid-1850s into abolitionist orthodoxies, which included learning to "feel right," to use one of her key phrases, about a permanent black presence in North America.[8] Stowe's dialogues with black and white abolitionists, among whom Liberian emigration had long been discredited, surely played an important role in her rejection of colonization. But I argue for the salience of her engagement with a much broader discourse on benevolent affiliation that includes sermons, polemical tracts spanning the political spectrum, and, especially, the proslavery novels written in response to *Uncle Tom's Cabin*. By the time Stowe wrote *Dred* she was a veteran of these debates; she had weathered criticism from both abolitionists and proslavery ideologues and had experienced, along with great celebrity, great derision. Restoring elements of this discourse that have faded from view will not make Stowe's legacy any less complex or contradictory, but it may enable a more nuanced understanding of both her politics and her iconic status.

### *Families, Neighbors, and Nations*

At least since the mid-eighteenth century, Americans (and others, to be sure) have debated the question of how far benevolence could or should extend. Were human beings obliged to cultivate a

8. See Levine, 58–98 and 144–76; Robert Stepto, "Sharing the Thunder: The Literary Exchanges of Harriet Beecher Stowe, Henry Bibb, and Frederick Douglass," in *New Essays on Uncle Tom's Cabin*, ed. Eric Sundquist (New York: Cambridge Univ. Press, 1986), 135–53.

general benevolence toward all, as Jonathan Edwards claimed, or was a prioritizing model ever in effect, whereby proximity (geographical, cultural, racial) determined the disposition of activist energies?[9] By the antebellum period, a discourse of priority had largely won out. While some clung to the notion that one owed benevolence to anyone, anywhere in need, more often mid-nineteenth-century commentators resorted to variations on localizing themes, arguing that charity begins at home or that one was first obligated to love one's neighbor rather than a stranger. Most presumed that sympathetic identification, widely identified as foundational to benevolent action, could only extend so far. The abolitionist lawyer Lysander Spooner, for example, in an 1846 tract titled *Poverty*, voices the commonly held view that doing good to others "depends almost entirely upon sympathy—upon one's susceptibility of being affected by the feelings of others." "[T]his sympathy, or susceptibility," he continues, "is mostly . . . the result of having had, in some measure, a similar experience with others, or of . . . having had social relations with them. Thus those who have been sick, sympathize with the sick; the sorrowful sympathize with the sorrowful; the rich sympathize with the rich; . . . and all men more or less with their immediate personal acquaintances." A more just society, Spooner goes on (far less conventionally) to argue, would therefore necessitate minimizing the experiential differences among citizens, especially those that arose from economic disparities.[1] The antislavery play *The Kidnapped Clergyman* (1839) introduced a similar identity of experience as the key to benevolent acts. Its protagonist, a self-serving clergyman who preaches against abolition, is converted to the antislavery cause only after a long and vivid dream in which he and his family are enslaved.[2]

The play's attention to imperiled family members tapped into a broader discourse on familial love, loyalty, and responsibility. Not only did antebellum Americans often describe benevolent relations in familial terms (note, for example, proslavery ideologues' frequent insistence that caretaking masters and loyal slaves formed a family), but they also tended to describe benevolence toward one's blood relations as a primary and unavoidable responsibility. . . .

9. See, e.g., Evan Radcliffe, "Revolutionary Writing, Moral Philosophy, and Universal Benevolence in the Eighteenth Century," *Journal of the History of Ideas* 54 (April 1993): 222.
1. Lysander Spooner, *Poverty: Its Illegal Causes, and Legal Cure. Part 1* (Boston: Bela Marsh, 1846), 45, 46.
2. *The Kidnapped Clergyman: or, Experience the Best Teacher* (Boston: Dow and Jackson), 1839.

In the antebellum United States, concepts of familial bonds and racial bonds slid easily into each other. Racial mixing was figured as a threat to the purity and safety of the family, and both kinds of relationships were described in terms of blood. In fact, *family* was at times used as a metaphor for race, as when the New Jersey senator Frederick Frelinghuysen remarked that "colored" men's "swarthy complexion ever marks them as members of a family different from ours."[3] Oliver Wendell Holmes, in an 1855 discussion of slavery, linked race, family, and benevolent responsibility more directly. "[O]ur sympathies," he argued, "will go with our own color first. . . . [N]o abstract principle of benevolence can reverse the great family instinct that settles the question for us."[4] For Holmes, allegiance to one's own race was simply an expression of "family instinct," one that overrode abstract benevolence and installed in its place a situated and entirely racialized process of judgment. Perhaps the strongest articulation of these sentiments, though from a black nationalist perspective, appeared in the writings of Alexander Crummell, a U.S.-born Liberian. "Races," he wrote, "like families, are the organisms and the ordinance of God; and race feeling, like the family feeling, is of divine origin. . . . Indeed, a race *is* a family."[5]

Anglo-American proponents of African colonization invoked similar notions of racial allegiance. An 1851 article in the *Colonization Herald*, titled "Africa to Be Christianized by Africans," asserted that "God in his all-wise providence has reserved this great and important work (the civilizing and evangelizing of Africa,) for her own sons and daughters" and noted that white missionaries "have all either died, or been driven to their native homes" without effecting the conversion of Africans.[6] Many cited blacks' comparative resistance to what we now identify as malaria as proof that God had ordained a program of intraracial benevolence. Others used social rather than medical justifications for sending black missionaries to Africa, asserting that "permanent results" could only "come from men whose race is similar to the people among whom they dwell, and with whom it can mingle freely and advantageously."[7] While

3. Frederick T. Frelinghuysen, *Address of Hon. F. T. Frelinghuysen, Senator from New Jersey* (Washington, D.C.: American Colonization Society, 1868), 4.
4. Oliver Wendell Holmes, *Oration Delivered before the New England Society, in the City of New York, by Oliver Wendell Holmes, M.D., at Their Semi-Centennial Anniversary, December 22, 1855* (New York: William C. Bryant, 1856), 42–43.
5. Alexander Crummell, "The Race Problem in America," in *Negro Social and Political Thought, 1850–1920*, ed. Howard Brotz (New York: Basic Books, 1966), 184; italics in original.
6. "Africa to Be Christianized by Africans," *Colonization Herald* (Philadelphia, July 1851): 52.
7. William Aikman, *The Future of the Colored Race in America: Being an Article in the "Presbyterian Quarterly Review," of July 1862* (New York: Anson D. F. Randolph, 1862), 34; see also Frederick Freeman, *Africa's Redemption, the Salvation of Our Country* (New York: D. Fanshaw, 1852), 139.

free blacks deplored the white supremacism that underlay much colonizationist rhetoric, some expressed an analogous belief in a primary benevolent responsibility to one's own race. The constitution of a black-run charitable organization, for instance, related its commitment "to do good unto all men," but "especially those of *our* race."[8] This organization surely recognized that "mutual aid," as such intraracial efforts were termed, might prove less burdensome than the acceptance of white benevolence, but the remark also suggests a more general belief in racial allegiance.

Other free African Americans resisted this emphasis on racial or, as one *National Reformer* article put it, "complexional considerations" and argued instead for allegiance to, and benevolent action within, the nation of one's nativity: "We have been born and reared in America. . . . [H]ere are all our general and local interests implanted—here let us cherish and sustain them . . . until they bud, blossom, and bring forth fruit that will make our country renowned in the eyes of civilized nations."[9] Drawing on a similar sentiment, the prominent white abolitionist Gerrit Smith argued for national allegiance and interracial responsibility in an 1847 broadside that chastised his neighbors for sending food to "the starving Irish" while forgetting their "infinitely greater debt" to their "enslaved countrymen."[1] Others, usually anti-abolitionists, invoked region rather than nation as the relevant grounds of affiliation, arguing that benevolent slaveholders were best equipped to care for Southern blacks, while Northerners of conscience should devote their efforts to the poor within their own communities.

While assertions of benevolent priority usually employed a language of primacy rather than of explicit exclusion—insisting that Americans deal first (rather than only) with whatever need the speaker identified—the intransigence of most social problems and the limits on resources strongly suggested that one's first project would consume all one's energy into the foreseeable future. Moreover, the flexibility that this rhetoric of primacy suggested belied the vitriol many speakers reserved for those who violated their proposed priorities. These violations elicited the charges of hypocrisy that dominated much of the antebellum discourse on benevolence. Practitioners of such "misguided" benevolence were asked why they did not "remove the beam from [their] own eyes" before concerning themselves with "motes in the eyes of [their] neighbors."[2]

8. "The Address and Constitution of the Union Benevolent Association of the People of Color of the City of Washington" *National Reformer* (March 1839): 107; italics mine.
9. "The Influence of Early Education" *National Reformer* (January 1839): 82.
1. Gerrit Smith, *To the People of the County of Madison* (Peterboro, N.Y.: 16 March 1847), Broadsides Collection, American Antiquarian Society, Worcester, Massachusetts.
2. Theophilus Fiske, "Extracts from an Oration," in *The National Crisis. An Antidote to Abolition Fanaticism, Treason and Sham Philanthropy* (15 May 1860): 4.

One outraged citizen described thousands of homeless people in New York City and wondered why the "sham philanthropists" who supported abolition did not utter "a solitary 'shriek' in behalf of these perishing classes,"[3] while anti-abolitionist cartoons and lithographs opposed plump, happy, dancing slaves to cold, emaciated white seamstresses or overworked English factory workers.[4] The popular author Emerson Bennett, whose 1855 novel *Ellen Norbury* featured the sweetest and most hapless fictional orphan since Oliver Twist, asked in his preface why Northerners supported missionary and antislavery efforts when "hundreds of human beings, both white and black, were annually perishing of cold, starvation, and neglect" in their own cities.[5] This mode of recrimination was flexible enough to serve opposed political ends; the anonymous author of "Missionary Hymn, for the South," for example, used a similar argument against slaveholders, who concerned themselves with faraway "heathen" but barred slaves from reading the scripture:

> Send Bibles to the heathen,
> Their famish'd spirits feed!
> Oh! haste, and join your efforts,
> The priceless gift to speed!
> *Then flog the trembling bondman,*
> *If he shall learn to read!*[6]

Slaveholders, the poet argued, perverted benevolence by seeing to it that reading the Bible resulted in flogging and degradation rather than comfort and salvation.

As the nation moved toward disunion, disagreements over the questions of benevolent citizenship in general and racial allegiance in particular produced especially bitter accusations. An unsigned lithograph (see Fig. 1) critiques the commitment to interracial benevolence by portraying a well-dressed white man (who bears a striking resemblance to the abolitionist senator Charles Sumner) giving alms to a ragged, barefoot black girl while her equally ragged and far thinner white counterpart goes empty-handed. The white girl, with her outstretched arm pointing toward the coins dropping from white hand to black, protests her exclusion by asserting, "I'm not to blame for being white, sir!" While the man concedes her point, he adds that "charity ought to begin where it is most needed, and you,

3. "Lodging Places" *National Crisis* (15 May 1860): 13.
4. For such images, see "The Horrors of Slavery in Black and White," *Lantern* (7 February 1852): 46; and *Slavery As It Exists in America. Slavery As It Exists in England* (Boston: J. Haven, 1850).
5. Emerson Bennett, *Ellen Norbury: or, the Adventures of an Orphan* (Philadelphia: T. B. Peterson, 1855), 12.
6. "Missionary Hymn, for the South," in *Voices of the True-Hearted* (Philadelphia: Merrihew and Thompson, 1846), 160; italics in original.

Fig. 1 "I'm Not to Blame for Being White, Sir!" (n.d.) 32°—22.3 cm. Graphic Arts Collection. Courtesy, American Antiquarian Society.

certainly, are the better off, having more friends and less oppressors." The donor here serves as an emblem of selfishness and sophistry. In his right hand is a cane positioned for decoration rather than support, suggesting his relative prosperity and reinforcing his heartless refusal to aid more than one supplicant, however deserving. In this image the "unnatural" act of turning away a needy child blends with the supposed unnaturalness of helping a member of another race rather than a member of one's own. This donor's abstract hierarchy of need, which privileges African Americans at the expense of whites, is represented as a violation of good sense and human sympathy.

## *Segregating Benevolence*

As the conversation I have outlined demonstrates, no consensus emerged in the antebellum United States as to how benevolent responsibility—and, by extension, benevolent citizenship—ought to be defined and structured. While some of these volleys seem plainly calculated to justify the speaker's own exploitative practices, the debates taken as a whole betray deep conflicts within notions of social justice and social authority—conflicts that undergirded the era's most divisive political issues. In particular, such debates expose a disjunction within the larger discourse of benevolence: the notion that benevolence required some preexisting similarity or proximity would seem incongruent with the fact that much benevolent rhetoric and most actual benevolent practices instead foregrounded the social and spiritual distance between helper and helped. In other words, the "neighbor" that this prioritizing discourse championed existed in tension with the "degraded" and fearsome supplicant that so much charity literature conjured. So while gradations of responsibility were often articulated in terms of affiliation—helping members of one's own family, neighborhood, race, region, or nation—this language of benevolence also asserted the superiority (racial, regional, moral) of the helper and the otherness of the helped.

The complicated and shifting logic of benevolent responsibility in *Uncle Tom's Cabin* offers a way of exploring this paradox. In order to achieve its mission of generating antislavery sentiment and action, particularly in the North, the novel asks readers to identify with suffering people across racial and regional divides. Stowe uses the psychology of benevolent affiliation (a sense of immediacy, proximity, even empathy) to create a feeling of responsibility where actual proximity and similarity may not exist, asking readers to imagine or relive the loss of their own children, for example, with the slaves whose actual or threatened losses she represents. Mrs. Bird, the senator's wife who takes pity on the runaway slave Eliza and her son, enacts within the text the very process of benevolence via identification that Stowe encourages among readers: she weeps over her dead child's folded garments as she prepares a care package for the fugitives. As Philip Fisher has pointed out, *Uncle Tom's Cabin*, like other sentimental novels, creates an "extension of feeling . . . by means of equations between the deep common feelings of the reader and the exotic but analogous situations of the characters"; Elizabeth Barnes puts the matter more directly, claiming that, within Stowe's novel, "sympathy is made contingent upon similarity."[7]

The terms of that similarity shift, however, in the course of the novel. Initially, like her abolitionist peers, Stowe invokes a sense of national responsibility that supersedes regional or racial loyalty. Northern readers are invited to concern themselves with the condition of Southern slaves, while characters within the narrative are applauded for their willingness to rise above racial and regional affiliations. But Stowe's conclusion removes most of the novel's surviving black characters from the United States and thus fundamentally alters the construction of the nation whose cohesion she advocates elsewhere in the text. Despite the fact that the success of its overall argument depends on creating a sense of responsibility across racial lines, the novel ends with a resegregation of benevolent relations and a reinscription of racial allegiance. Stowe relies, then, on an imagined affiliation that renders itself superfluous, thus making possible a final appeal to an essential, "real" affiliation.

This position has made Stowe into a favorite target, in her own time and in ours. In an 1852 article that appeared in the *Pennsylvania Freeman*, the Philadelphian Robert Purvis encapsulated the responses of many Northern free blacks when he wrote, in reference to Stowe, "Alas! . . . save us from our friends."[8] Along similar lines, contemporary critics often cite the novel's conclusion as proof of Stowe's intractable racism. Such dismay is certainly comprehensible. It likely gave Stowe a kind of comfort, or even pleasure, to imagine the United States as a white utopia secure in the belief that former slaves were happily and successfully christianizing Africa. Nevertheless, I am suggesting that the colonizationism evident at the end of the novel is not simply Stowe's adherence to her own family's values (her father, Lyman Beecher, was a prominent colonizationist), nor should it be read exclusively as a retreat from the

7. Philip Fisher, *Hard Facts: Setting and Form in the American Novel* (New York: Oxford Univ. Press, 1987), 118; Elizabeth Barnes, *States of Sympathy: Seduction and Democracy in the American Novel* (New York: Columbia Univ. Press, 1997), 92.
8. Robert Purvis, "The Serpent of Colonization in 'Uncle Tom's Cabin,'" *Pennsylvania Freeman*, new series, (29 April 1852): 70. See also Marva Banks, "Uncle Tom's Cabin and Antebellum Black Response," in *Readers in History: Nineteenth-Century American Literature and the Contexts of Response*, ed. James L. Machor (Baltimore: Johns Hopkins Univ. Press, 1993), 209–27; and Levine, *Politics*, 58–98.

novel's progressive emancipatory politics. It is possible to read the Liberian ending of *Uncle Tom's Cabin* instead as Stowe's pointed, if troubling, attempt to undermine the logic of the proslavery "family" and its figuring of perpetual black dependency and white supervision. The accusations leveled at Stowe as a result of the novel's conclusion testify to the hazards of this project: her effort at interracial benevolence—authoring this book as a spur to end slavery—embroiled her in the very complications she was apparently trying to write her way past.

This Liberian solution, in which a regenerated Topsy teaches the children of what Stowe calls "her own country," while a self-sufficient and newly educated George Harris goes to Liberia as "a teacher of Christianity," constitutes one of Stowe's many literary interventions into the question of how to prioritize benevolent responsibility.[9] By choosing Africa as the site of their good works, Topsy and the Harris family assert the primacy of racial affiliation over both regional and national considerations. In the process, they defy the proslavery faction's claim that slaves were naturally dependent on their white masters and could never attain basic economic security, much less benevolent agency, on their own. Moreover, the former slaves' move to Liberia also allows them to distance themselves (at least geographically) from ties of gratitude and obligation toward whites, ties that benevolent rhetoric insisted should structure their relationships with their Northern benefactors. Their emigration serves as evidence that they have thrown off all dependence on white aid, a theme reinforced by the self-asserting rhetoric George Harris uses to justify his decision. Significantly, this rhetoric aligns him far more closely with the era's black nationalists and emigrationists than with white colonizationists, who tended to emphasize whites' roles in preparing and guiding the emigrants. Given that interracial responsibility as articulated in the antebellum United States often rested on reified structures of superiority and inferiority, it makes sense that Stowe, in the context of an antislavery project, might test out a theory that establishes interracial benevolence as a temporary means to its own elimination.

Still, this resolution is difficult to interpret. In one sense, Stowe minimizes the otherness of slaves and former slaves by remaking them into benevolent agents on a familiar, white-authored model. But at the same time, her plan reinforces racial separation, ultimately providing for the benevolent, both black and white, objects

9. Harriet Beecher Stowe, *Uncle Tom's Cabin: or, Life among the Lowly*, ed. Elizabeth Ammons (1852; reprint, New York: W. W. Norton and Company, 1994), 377, 376. Citations in my text appear as *UTC*.

of aid who belong to their own racial group and who thus seem more like themselves. That is, while black emigrants serve Africans, in a postemigration United States Anglo-Americans are left to serve the needy whites who remain within its borders. (Or so colonizationists typically theorized; they tended to ignore the nation's non-black and non-Anglo racial groups.) By eliminating or minimizing racial difference within benevolent relations—and, importantly, within nations—Stowe's plan works to reestablish the conventional notions of affiliation that so often initiated and compelled benevolent projects. But the alterity of those being helped remains intact here, insofar as African Americans' christianizing and civilizing mission in Liberia retains the hierarchical structure of American benevolence, with an enlightened emigrant elite reforming and reshaping Africans' belief systems and social structures. Those who are helped, in this schema, are definitionally "benighted," "degraded," and inferior to the helpers. So rather than truly departing from the structures of interracial benevolence, Stowe's intraracial model replicates its terms but grants African Americans access to positions of control and authority within it.

Such retrenchment notwithstanding, Stowe's interest in colonization's potential to promote racial solidarity or affinity should not be dismissed out of hand or reduced to its most conservative elements. In his boldly revisionist article "Racial Essentialism and Family Values in *Uncle Tom's Cabin*," Arthur Riss argues that Stowe's Liberian conclusion is less an example of white racist wish-fulfillment than a logical extension of an emancipatory politics based on a notion of essential racial identity. According to Riss, Stowe defines legitimate families exclusively by "the bond of biology" and, by extension, the bond of a common racial identity, which invalidates proslavery notions of the family as a group whose relations are based not on literal blood ties but on participation in a domestic economy structured around mutual obligations.[1] Stowe's much-maligned racial essentialism, Riss astutely argues, is thus integral to, rather than in conflict with, her progressive politics. And since, for Stowe, "[n]ational solidarity is simply the extension of loving one's family," the utopic nation must be racially homogeneous, and Topsy must leave those Ophelia calls "'our folks' for *her folks*."[2]

Riss's rethinking of Stowe's essentialism, however, elides the complications that certain characters' mixed racial identities introduce. Riss writes that George Harris's letter at the end of *Uncle Tom's*

1. Arthur Riss, "Racial Essentialism and Family Values in *Uncle Tom's Cabin*," *American Quarterly* 46 (December 1994): 532; on proslavery notions of the family, see 526–29.
2. Riss, 534; italics in original.

*Cabin* (in which he justifies his decision to emigrate) "makes clear that, according to Stowe, an individual's communal identity is not generated by culture or by choice but by race. Nature is nation, and a nation is just a large family."[3] This claim, though applicable to Topsy's emigration, does not account for George Harris's more ambiguous racial positioning. Riss's argument echoes the logic of the one-drop rule, designating as monolithically black any character with some African forebears, despite the fact that Stowe's novel dwells at length on the differences between mixed-race people and "pure" Africans, and particularly on the internal conflict George Harris experiences between disparate (though still essential) racial characteristics. The novel situates him somewhere between *black* and *white*; although U.S. law and custom define him as black, Stowe writes that he and his family are light enough to "mingle in the circles of the whites" (*UTC*, 374). As George's letter makes clear, he *chooses* to annul his blood ties to whites and to declare allegiance to his mother's race. Racial identification, for Stowe's biracial characters, is to some extent an act of volition, one that in George's case derives more from moral and affectional considerations than from some sense of his "true" African essence. He acknowledges, after all, that the "hot and hasty Saxon" will persist within him even after his emigration (*UTC*, 376).

Love and benevolence, rather than ancestry, determine George Harris's priorities: the love he has felt for and received from his mother translates into loyalty and benevolence toward others of her race, while his abhorrence of white Americans' moral choices, including his father's, forestalls the love that is a prerequisite for effective benevolence toward them.[4] George is not simply choosing racial allegiance over other possible allegiances, as Oliver Wendell Holmes or white colonizationists might expect or insist; instead, he is choosing his race and, ultimately, his nationality in part on the basis of love and moral responsibility. Within the world of *Uncle Tom's Cabin*, racial identity is certainly a factor in benevolent choice, as Topsy's move to Africa demonstrates. But the converse is also true, that is, benevolence is a factor in racial allegiance, at least for those who, like George Harris, could conceivably adopt one of two racial identities. These doubled choices dramatize what was true of the broader culture as well—that benevolent identities and racial identities, through the rhetorics that created and described them, were interdependent and in some sense mutually constitutive. Just as notions of race

3. Riss, 536.
4. While George Harris's discussion of Liberia focuses on the rights he will enjoy there and on the injustices that abound in the United States, his decision nevertheless entails an element of benevolent responsibility in his commitment to teach Christianity in Liberia.

informed how benevolent acts would be theorized and carried out, so did benevolence inform how a race was defined—in terms of its religiosity, its potential for self-reliance, or the weight of its guilt, to name only the most salient features.

## Dred *and the Proslavery Family*

Stowe's *Dred*, published just four years after *Uncle Tom's Cabin*, offers a substantially different outcome for its fugitive slaves, in terms of their ultimate destinations as well as their benevolent priorities. *Dred*'s conclusion marks a departure from the racial separatism that underlies the earlier novel's resolution: none of *Dred*'s surviving characters leaves North America, though several settle in Canada, and all retain close interracial ties. Instead of racially defined *blood* families, Stowe here champions (non-kin) interracial families and communities that, while radically unlike the plantation family of proslavery rhetoric, nevertheless involve ongoing benevolent relations across racial lines. Both novels engage with proslavery perspectives, depicting enlightened slaveholders and the mildest of servitude on picturesque upper-South plantations, but then demonstrate the instability of such scenes by depicting how financial and familial collapse can plunge the once protected slave into the institution's worst horrors: separation from family, overwork, sexual exploitation, and brutal violence. But while Stowe's earlier rejection of the perpetual black dependence figured in proslavery ideology involved segregating her surviving characters and thus insisting on blacks' capacity for self-reliance, her strategy in *Dred* is to retain a kind of interracial family but to reconfigure the logics of affiliation and responsibility that undergird it.

* * *

In our own time, the term *benevolence* has come to signify a misguided and paternalistic approach to social activism, one that reifies hierarchies and forestalls genuine change. Gayatri Spivak, for example, has used it as a synonym for a well-intentioned misapprehension, a blind spot that its possessor must be prodded to recognize.[5] But while the term has been discredited, many of the sentiments, conflicts, and practices it once represented have remained very much alive. Other terms—*humanitarianism*, for example—have been deployed in its place, and while their uses are not identical to antebellum uses of *benevolence*, there is a "discursive consistency," to use

5. Gayatri Spivak, "The New Historicism: Political Commitment and the Postmodern Critic," interview by Harold Veeser, in *The Postcolonial Critic: Interviews, Strategies, Dialogues*, ed. Sarah Harasym (New York: Routledge, 1990), 160.

Edward Said's phrase,[6] from the nineteenth-century context to our own. The articulations of tough love that accompanied welfare reform in the 1990s, for example, bear a strong similarity to the rhetoric of self-reliance that suffused nineteenth-century poverty relief efforts, and the language used to describe and justify the "humanitarian bombing" of Kosovo recalls antebellum concerns that inaction, or more often the wrong action, with respect to imperiled others would undermine the moral credibility of the United States. Current versions of benevolent nationality and benevolent citizenship have their analogue within literary studies in the search for authors who might serve as exemplars, figures we can identify as transcending the prejudices of their time and place, as advocating the forms of inclusion or tolerance that resemble and seem to prefigure currently held values. Scholars' counterbalancing gestures of critique operate within this matrix as well, excavating and analyzing these figures' shortcomings, their failure to live up to our ideals. Wanting to be good people—*a* good people—and wanting our canonized authors to espouse good politics (however vexatious the attendant processes of definition may be) are imbricated forms of benevolent citizenship, as national literatures and icons blend into and inform more broadly available articulations of national identity.

While I am ambivalent about the search for literary role models, particularly in the arena of U.S. race relations, I would not advocate a wholesale dismantling of the paradigm of benevolent citizenship. In fact, I am very much in favor of ongoing conversations about what it might mean to be a good nation or to be good citizens within a nation (or, for that matter, within a university). But the quality of the insights and the policies that emerge from those conversations depends in large part upon greater attentiveness to the history of our national rhetorics of social responsibility and, especially, to the bitter contests over humanitarian priorities. Stowe's rich and troubling antislavery novels are among the many sites where such investigations might take place.

6. Edward Said, *Orientalism* (New York: Pantheon, 1978), 273.

# Harriet Beecher Stowe: A Chronology

1811 Harriet Elizabeth Beecher, the seventh of nine children, born on June 14 to Lyman Beecher and Roxana Foote Beecher, Litchfield, Connecticut.

1816 Mother dies.

1817 Father remarries.

1823 Attends the Hartford Female Seminary, where she later teaches; academy founded and run by older sister, Catharine Beecher.

1832 Moves with family to Cincinnati, Ohio, where father becomes president of Lane Theological Seminary.

1834 Publishes first story in *Western Monthly Magazine.*

1836 Marries Calvin Stowe; twin daughters, Harriet and Eliza, born.

1838 Son, Henry, born.

1840 Son, Frederick, born.

1843 Publishes *The Mayflower; or, Sketches of Scenes and Characters Among the Descendants of the Puritans;* daughter, Georgiana, born.

1846–47 Spends fifteen months at a water cure in Vermont recovering from exhaustion, regaining mental as well as physical strength, and, it is clear to scholars, achieving a respite from pregnancy and childbearing.

1848 Son, Samuel Charles (Charley) born; Calvin spends a year at Vermont water cure.

1849 Charley dies in cholera epidemic.

1850 Moves to Brunswick, Maine, where Calvin joins the Bowdoin College faculty. Son, Charles, born.

1850 Fugitive Slave Law passed requiring everyone to turn in runaway slaves, North or South; a major catalyst in Stowe's antislavery writing.

1851 *Uncle Tom's Cabin* serialized in antislavery paper the *National Era.*

1852 *Uncle Tom's Cabin* published as a two-volume book.

1853 *A Key to "Uncle Tom's Cabin"* published to corroborate the novel's facts; triumphant trip to Europe as antislavery author.
1856 Publishes second antislavery novel, *Dred, A Tale of the Great Dismal Swamp;* again travels to Europe.
1859 Third successful trip to Europe; novel, *The Minister's Wooing*, published.
1862 Novel, *The Pearl of Orr's Island.*
1863 Moves to Hartford, Connecticut.
1869 Novel, *Oldtown Folks;* publishes with sister Catharine *The American Woman's Home.*
1871–75 Three society novels published.
1872 *Sam Lawson's Oldtown Fireside Stories* published.
1878 Last novel, *Poganuc People.*
1886 Calvin dies.
1896 Dies at home in Hartford.

# A Brief Time Line of Slavery in America

1619 First Africans brought to Britain's North American colonies.

1641 Slavery established as a legal institution in North American colonies.

1705 Virginia Slave Code Law. Enslaved Africans defined as real estate. Owners allowed to bequeath slaves and punish runaway slaves by death.

1739 Stono Rebellion. Africans in South Carolina revolt. Crushed by white armed forces.

1775 World's first abolitionist society founded by Anthony Benezet of Philadelphia.

1776 American Revolution.

1804 Haitian Revolution. Successful slave rebellion led by Toussaint Louverture establishes Haiti as a free republic.

1807 Britain abolishes the slave trade.

1808 United States abolishes the slave trade. Smuggling continues.

1816 The American Colonization Society formed. Promotes transportation of freed Africans in the United States to Liberia, a colony on the coast of West Africa.

1820 The Missouri Compromise. Missouri admitted to the Union as a slave state and Maine as a free state. Slavery outlawed north of latitude 36°30′ in U.S. western territories.

1822 Denmark Vesey's Revolt. Freed slave Denmark Vesey attempts to revolt in Charleston, South Carolina. Thirty-five blacks charged with conspiracy and hanged, including Vesey.

1831 Nat Turner's Rebellion. Enslaved African American Nat Turner leads slaves to revolt in Southampton, Virginia. Crushed after two days by white armed forces. Turner executed by hanging.

1833 Britain abolishes slavery.

1835 Censorship of abolitionists. Southern states prohibit the mailing of antislavery propaganda.

1845 Frederick Douglass publishes *Narrative of the Life of Frederick Douglass.*

1850 Fugitive Slave Act. Requires all citizens, North and South, to turn in fugitive slaves.

1850 The Underground Railroad continues to aid in the escape of thousands of slaves. A network of secret routes and safe houses organized by Harriet Tubman and other abolitionists.

1852 Harriet Beecher Stowe publishes *Uncle Tom's Cabin.*

1854 Kansas-Nebraska Act. Kansas and Nebraska granted choice whether or not to legalize slavery.

1857 Dred Scott Decision. U.S. Supreme Court rules people of African descent ineligible for citizenship.

1859 John Brown's Raid. White abolitionist John Brown plots slave rebellion at Harpers Ferry, West Virginia. Crushed within 36 hours by white armed forces. Brown executed by hanging.

1861–65 United States Civil War.

1863 Emancipation Proclamation. President Abraham Lincoln declares all slaves free on January 1.

1865 Thirteenth Amendment. U.S. Constitution officially abolishes slavery.

# Selected Bibliography

Recent biographies include *A Biographical Chronicle of Her Life, Drawn from Recollections, Interviews, and Memoirs by Family, Friends and Associates*, ed. Susan Belasco (Iowa City: U of Iowa Press, 2008/9); and *Harriet Beecher Stowe: A Life*, by Joan Hedrick (New York: Oxford UP, 1994). Also, a good, short account can be found in the biographical chapters in Thomas F. Gossett's *"Uncle Tom's Cabin" and American Culture* (1985).

For volumes of critical essays on Stowe see Elizabeth Ammons, ed., *Critical Essays on Harriet Beecher Stowe* (1980); Eric J. Sundquist, ed., *New Essays on "Uncle Tom's Cabin"* (1986); Elizabeth Ammons and Susan Belasco, eds., *Approaches to Teaching Uncle Tom's Cabin* (2000); Debra Rosenthal, ed., *A Routledge Literary Sourcebook on Harriet Beecher Stowe's "Uncle Tom's Cabin"* (2003); Cindy Weinstein, ed., *The Cambridge Companion to Harriet Beecher Stowe* (2004); and Elizabeth Ammons, ed., *Harriet Beecher Stowe's Uncle Tom's Cabin: A Casebook* (2007). For a history of the book's publication, see Michael Winship, *The Greatest Book of Its Kind: A Publishing History of "Uncle Tom's Cabin"* (American Antiquarian Society, 1999).

A large body of commentary exists on *Uncle Tom's Cabin.* Criticism before 1974 is listed in Jean W. Ashton's annotated bibliography, *Harriet Beecher Stowe: A Reference Guide* (1977). For more recent work see Josephine Donovan, *"Uncle Tom's Cabin": Evil, Affliction, and Redemptive Love* (1991); Sarah Robbins, *Managing Literacy, Mothering America: Women's Narratives of Reading and Writing in the Nineteenth Century* (2004); Sarah Meer, *Uncle Tom Mania: Slavery, Minstrelsy, and Transatlantic Culture in the 1850s* (2005); Jo-Ann Morgan, *Uncle Tom's Cabin as Visual Culture* (2007); and this copiously annotated edition of the novel: Henry Louis Gates, Jr., and Hollis Robbins, ed., *The Annotated Uncle Tom's Cabin* (2006).

Additional important individual studies not anthologized in the collections above include Hortense Spillers, "Changing the Letter: The Yokes, the Jokes of Discourse, or, Mrs. Stowe, Mr. Reed," in *Slavery and the Literary Imagination*, ed. Deborah McDowell and Arnold Rampersad (1989); Christina Zwarg, "Fathering and Blackface in *Uncle Tom's Cabin,*" *NOVEL: A Forum on Fiction* (1989); Lauren Berlant, "Poor Eliza," *American Literature* (1998); Carolyn Vellenga Berman, "Creole Family Politics in *Uncle Tom's Cabin* and *Incidents in the Life of a Slave Girl,*" *NOVEL: A Forum on Fiction* (2000); Michael Borgstrom, "Passing Over: Setting the Record Straight in *Uncle Tom's*

*Cabin*," *PMLA* (2003); and Jason Richards, "Imitation Nation: Blackface Minstrelsy and the Making of African American Selfhood in *Uncle Tom's Cabin*," *NOVEL: A Forum of Fiction* (2006).

An excellent online resource is Stephen Railton's UTC *and American Culture: A Multi-Media Archive* (University of Virginia, 2007) www.iath.virginia.edu/utc.